The SAGE Handbook of
Gender
and *Communication*

The SAGE Handbook of
Gender
and *Communication*

EDITORS

Bonnie J. Dow
The University of Georgia

Julia T. Wood
The University of North Carolina at Chapel Hill

SAGE Publications
Thousand Oaks ▪ London ▪ New Delhi

For information:

Sage Publications, Inc.
2455 Teller Road
Thousand Oaks, California 91320
E-mail: order@sagepub.com

Sage Publications Ltd.
1 Oliver's Yard
55 City Road
London EC1Y 1SP
United Kingdom

Sage Publications India Pvt. Ltd.
B-42, Panchsheel Enclave
Post Box 4109
New Delhi 110 017 India

Printed in the United States of America.

Library of Congress Cataloging-in-Publication Data

The SAGE handbook of gender and communication / edited by
Bonnie J. Dow, Julia T. Wood.
    p. cm.
Includes bibliographical references and indexes.
ISBN 1-4129-0423-4 (cloth)
  1. Communication—Sex differences. I. Dow, Bonnie J. II. Wood, Julia T.
P96.S48S34 2006
305.301′4—dc22   2006001824

This book is printed on acid-free paper.

06   07   08   09   10   10 9 8 7 6 5 4 3 2 1

Acquiring Editor:	Todd R. Armstrong
Editorial Assistant:	Camille Herrera
Project Editor:	Astrid Virding
Copyeditor:	Tom Lacey
Typesetter:	C&M Digitals (P) Ltd.
Indexer:	Paul Corrigton
Cover Designer:	Candice Harman

CONTENTS

THE EVOLUTION OF GENDER AND COMMUNICATION RESEARCH
Intersections of Theory, Politics, and Scholarship

◆ Bonnie J. Dow and Julia T. Wood

In 1975 one of us—Julia— took her first faculty position. As part of familiarizing herself with her new professional home, she visited the campus bookstore. There she found an impressive inventory of scholarly books, as would be expected at a research university. The newest category in the bookstore was women's studies. The entire section devoted to it was half a shelf in a bookcase of 6-foot shelves.

Until the 1970s there were no courses in and no textbooks about gender and communication. San Diego State University had founded the first women's studies program in 1969, but such programs were still sparse in the early 1970s (Boxer, 1998). Relevant academic publications were rare, although then as now popular psychology publications on the sexes proliferated. Gender was simply not recognized as a distinct concept three and a half decades ago.

The political and philosophical changes that were launched in the 1970s and the conceptual trajectory that leads to this *Handbook of Gender and Communication* have their origins in the second wave of U.S. feminism that began in the mid-1960s. This book is not a handbook of feminism and communication, and the study of gender is distinct from feminist studies, although there is significant overlap in much scholarship. Yet as we explain below, feminism gave birth to what we now term the study of gender, and it infuses our personal histories as gender scholars as well as the history of the study of gender and communication. We begin this essay with two narratives tracing our genesis and development as gender scholars and conclude with a discussion of the growth of research on gender and communication over the past three decades. While mapping the terrain of inquiry, we will suggest why interest in gender and communication emerged in the 1970s and why it has expanded and evolved at such a stunning pace in the decades since. We also want to note how cultural influences formed and informed intellectual frameworks for the study of gender.

Next we sketch the kinds of theories, questions, and issues that are ascending to define the next stage of work. We acknowledge that our ideas about provocative and productive directions for scholarship are speculative, although they are informed by our familiarity with a range of existing work and opinion. Finally, we explain our choices for organizing the *Handbook*.

◆ Gender and Communication Research: Two Personal Accounts

Julia's undergraduate education began in 1968. By 1970, many campuses, including hers, throbbed with protests against the war in Vietnam and for civil rights. Julia became so engaged with those issues that she was only peripherally aware of the ascension of the second wave of feminism in the United States. Her personal and intellectual interest in feminism did not take root until graduate school. When not being educated through participation in teach-ins, riots, and marches, Julia took course work in her two majors: communication (then called speech) and English. She never

considered studying gender and communication, or gender more broadly, because no courses focused on those topics. Nor did a women's studies department, program, or even curriculum exist at her school.

In 1972 when Julia started her M.A. program, she met Lucinda Mims, who became a close personal friend and a political mentor. Lucinda introduced her to feminism with *Woman in Sexist Society: Studies in Power and Powerlessness*, edited by Vivian Gornick and Barbara Moran and published in 1971. Click! ("Click!" is the term feminists use to describe a woman's unexpected and startling recognition of an aspect of sexism which affects all women but which she had not perceived or been able to name. Reading *Woman in Sexist Society* provoked such an experience for Julia.)

A few months later, Karlyn Kohrs Campbell intellectually complemented the personal introduction to feminism Julia received from Lucinda, though she and Karlyn did not meet for years. In the spring of 1973, Julia read Karlyn's article, "The Rhetoric of Women's Liberation: An Oxymoron" (1973). Click! Excited by the article and the intellectual questions it spurred, Julia looked for communication courses that included attention to feminism, sex, and gender. There were none. Click! Each realization she had about women and women's place—physically and intellectually—in society and in the academy jolted a worldview that until then she had not questioned. From then on, Julia complemented her graduate studies with consciousness-raising groups and other politically charged and politically charging feminist contexts.

When Julia received her Ph.D. in 1975, she took a faculty position as a specialist in small-group communication, a perfect fit with the focus of her doctoral studies. During the next 13 years, Julia did not teach gender and communication. There were no such classes to teach, nor were any contemplated for her or anyone else. In fact, Julia's school was like most universities in that very few courses anywhere on the campus dealt with gender at all. When Julia began her faculty career, no scholarly organization, not even a unit within a discipline, focused on gender and communication. Thus, it is not surprising that Julia was on the faculty for 13 years until, working with graduate student Lynn O'Brien Hallstein, she developed the first course at her campus on gender and communication.

Bonnie entered college in 1982, the year the Equal Rights Amendment (ERA) was finally defeated and which historians regard as the end of the second wave of feminism (Evans, 2003; Rosen, 2000). She was able to take a course in women's history in her last year of college, though her university did not have a women's studies program. Even so, when she began her graduate work at the University of Kansas she had no conscious intent to study women or gender or anything other than rhetoric. In her first year of graduate school in 1985, she was able to take The Rhetoric of Woman's Rights, which generated her Click! experience. By the time she arrived at the University of Minnesota in 1987, she entered a university with a thriving women's studies program and the home of *Signs: Journal of Women in Culture and Society*, the preeminent journal for women's studies. Still, only two courses in her department focused on gender, and they were taught by Karlyn Kohrs Campbell, editor of the section on gender and rhetoric in the *Handbook*. One of them concerned the first wave of feminist rhetoric; the other, the second wave. Neither had a formal textbook, although Campbell would soon produce one, the first of its kind, in 1989.

Unlike Julia, however, Bonnie could avail herself of a wide-ranging women's studies curriculum at both of her graduate institutions. It was the 1980s, a time of tremendous expansion in studies of women and gender when scores of women's studies programs were founded, including the one at the University of Georgia where she now works. The dearth of books on women and gender that confronted Julia 10 years earlier had been remedied, and she was

being mentored by a feminist scholar, an opportunity Julia didn't enjoy. Even so, like Julia, she had to undergo a period of tremendous self-education while working toward her doctorate and during the early years of her career because resources in gender and media, her specialty, were still in short supply. By 1990, the first position Bonnie received as an assistant professor was for a gender and communication specialist, and the department she joined had a course called Women and Communication. Since that time, Bonnie has taught at least one course on some aspect of gender and communication every year.

These usefully different stories illustrate how social and political forces in the late 1960s through the early 1970s gave rise to the study of gender and communication and how much that field evolved from 1968 when Julia began college to 1982 when Bonnie did. Julia's feminist awareness was nurtured informally throughout her graduate education because it took place during the height of the second wave of feminism, when attention to gender and its social and political implications proliferated in the public sphere, even though it was not yet institutionalized in higher education and so was not a sustained focus for scholarship. Julia was motivated primarily by what she experienced in the world beyond the academy, while Bonnie was much more a product of what she found within it. Julia contributed to forming gender and communication as an area of specialization, and Bonnie was a beneficiary of that development.

Our individual stories converge in 2006 when the section in Julia's bookstore, now labeled Gender Studies, includes 12 overflowing shelves and when gender and communication textbooks abound. Since that first course in gender and communication she taught in 1988, Julia and her colleagues have developed other gender courses, most of them on the graduate level. Currently, her department offers courses in gender, sex, feminism, as well as queer and "trans" studies. Bonnie's department includes faculty who study gender and a graduate program with gender and feminist studies as an emphasis complete with courses in feminist criticism, gender and queer theory, women's rhetoric, and gender and media. Since 1980 more than 110,000 studies of gender and sex have been published (Campbell, 2002). The National Communication Association has a feminist and women's studies division. *Women's Studies in Communication* and *Women and Language* and their respective sponsoring organizations, the Organization for Research on Women and Communication and the Organization for the Study of Communication, Language, and Gender have existed for decades. The last three decades of scholarship have, in effect, established a new area of study, which, in turn, has given birth to new curricula, professional organizations, journals, and faculty lines. In short, the moment has arrived when a gender and communication handbook seems not just possible but necessary.

◆ The Development of Gender and Communication as an Area of Study

Although our narratives are personal, they also reveal more general insights about the development of gender and communication as an area of study, as well as about the origins of the study of gender across the academy. The questions raised by second-wave feminist activists about women's status, women's rights, and the function of what were then called sex roles led to both the growth of women's studies as a field of academic inquiry and to the incorporation, albeit uneven, of attention to women in a number of disciplines. Thus, these origins demonstrate that what scholars study in any particular historical moment reflects not only the objective significance of the topics but also cultural events, ideologies, and disciplinary inclinations (Dow & Condit, 2005; Wood & Duck, 1995). Research is a social enterprise because it is

conceived and conducted by humans embedded in social worlds that shape their choices of topics, methods, interpretative inclinations, and so on.

The contingent nature of academic (and all) history is illustrated by the emergence of organizational units interested in women and gender within the National Communication Association (once called the Speech Communication Association). Long before the national association had the research venue it called the feminist and women's studies division, feminist activists were having an impact on American society. At the New Orleans conference in 1970, a number of women talked about the need for an activist, political group to identify and challenge sexist practices within the organization. Two years later, the women's caucus was formally chartered (Taylor, personal communication, 2005).

Scholarly study soon followed. The initial focus of scholarship, spurred as it was by feminist activism, was to bring the study of women into academic research and to correct the biases that had constructed women as deviant, as other, and as not meriting study. Social scientists were persuaded to interrogate and then challenge the so-called deficit model, which held that men's communication was *the* standard for effective speech and that women failed to meet that standard (Kramer, Thorne, & Henley, 1978; Shimanoff, 1977; Spender, 1980). Feminist rhetorical scholars challenged the assumption that only men had a venerable rhetorical history, arguing for the need to study women's public communication (Campbell, 1980), and media scholars turned their attention to the representation of women in commercial mass media (Busby, 1975; Tedesco, 1974).

The term *gender* was not widely used in the first stage of academic work on women or, to a lesser extent, on men. Indeed, at this time, gender was not recognized as an analytic category and was not theorized in useful ways. During the 1970s, most research focused on men and women, not masculinity and femininity. In attending only to sex, it reflected the prevalent assumption that behaviors were tied to—and often the result of—biology (Eakins & Eakins, 1978; Patton & Patton 1976; see also Bate, 1988; Stewart, Stewart, Friedley, & Cooper, 1987).

A key development was differentiating sex and gender, the former referring to biological characteristics and the latter to the culturally constructed meanings, expectations, constraints, and prerogatives. The distinction directed scholars' attention to practices that construct gender—how parents communicate expectations of femininity to daughters and masculinity to sons, how teachers reward different behaviors in male and female students. The sex/gender distinction took shape by the 1980s when the first textbook explicitly focused on gender and communication appeared (Pearson, 1985). Later in this introduction we return to the sex/gender distinction to question its value to current and future scholarship.

Despite the conceptual recognizing of the difference between sex and gender, much of what was and still is written about gender in scholarly works as well as textbooks was actually about sex. Linguistic progress preceded substantive progress. Even today, many scholars conflate gender and sex by identifying only the sex of research participants and then announcing findings about gender (Duck & Wood, in press).

Whether textbooks and scholarship focused on gender or sex, most academic work focused on femininity and women's differences from men, cultivating the unfortunate implication that only women are gendered and men remain the genderless norm. The notable exception was a flurry of articles in the 1970s that argued that men were socialized to repress feelings. Among them, Balswick and Peek (1976) published "The Inexpressive Male: A Tragedy of American Society." Response to that essay was sufficient to motivate its senior author to extend attention to men's repressed emotions in *The Inexpressive Male* (Balswick, 1988). Reflecting liberal ideology, these and other articles were written by self-identified male feminists who argued that men were as innately capable as women of emotional sensitivity and expressiveness. According to them, males became alienated from their feelings—and even from a recognition of them—during socialization. The authors argued that men should work to develop their feelings or to resuscitate those that had been repressed.

Despite this early burst of attention in the 1970s and 1980s to the possibilities for men in the second wave of the feminist critique of sex roles, research continued to focus on sex/gender differences or on women/femininity. In the 1990s, the first sustained wave of attention to men and masculinity initially focused on mass media (Hanke, 1990; Trujillo, 1991), but soon included attention to interpersonal, political, performative, and organizational contexts (Gingrich-Philbrook, 1994; Mumby, 1998; Parry-Giles & Parry-Giles, 1996; Wood & Inman, 1993). By the late 1990s, such work was increasingly visible in communication journals, and our authors address work on masculinity where appropriate within their chapters or discuss its absence. As editors of the *Handbook of Gender and Communication*, we are committed to a definition of gender that includes both men/masculinity and women/femininity, since specific attention to the former has been uneven. In fact, it has been little more than a decade since a serious study of masculinity surfaced in the discipline, and it has not yet achieved the sort of prominence that has been earned by other lines of inquiry related to gender and communication. Indeed, as several of the authors in the *Handbook* note, in much communication scholarship, *gender* continues to serve as a code word for feminine.

FEMINIST AND GENDER RESEARCH: DISCRETE, YET INTERRELATED

Although early research on gender and communication may be understood as an outgrowth of the social awareness spurred by the second wave of feminism, not all research on gender is feminist, although there is significant overlap between gender studies and feminist studies (Stephen, 2000). A desire to investigate gender does not necessarily reflect a commitment to a feminist ideology. This is particularly true for traditional social scientific research, which prizes objectivity and claims to be immune to political motivation. Most feminist epistemologies, in contrast, assume that objectivity is a fiction that serves political purposes (Dallimore, 2000). Generally, explicitly feminist research is "self-reflective about operating from an orientation that links its specific data or theoretical or methodological concerns to a perspective that seeks to ameliorate the systems of domination that operate through the axis of gender (although never exclusively so)" (Dow & Condit, 2005, p. 449). Self-reflexivity in feminist research promotes awareness of gendered perspectives in general and gendered epistemologies in particular. Thus, feminist scholarship "raises questions about prevailing practices that name what is and is not significant knowledge, what do and do not count as useful data, and what are and are not legitimate ways to generate knowledge" (Wood, 1995, pp. 109–110).

MULTIPLE IDEOLOGICAL FRAMEWORKS

Even so, feminist research on gender is not monolithic in ideology. Just as second-wave feminism, as a category, comprises (and, not infrequently, glosses over) a variety of groups with distinct and sometimes conflicting ideologies such as liberal, cultural, and radical, so does feminist academic research include studies based on a range of ontological, epistemological, and axiological frameworks. A liberal orientation, in both feminist politics and research, embraces the premise that men and women are equal as humans and should be treated as such. Cultural feminism, the goal of which is to celebrate a distinctive women's

culture that reflects essentialist views of femininity, has influenced research that argues for the superiority of feminine modes of communication distinguished by, for example, collaboration, relationality, and a lack of hierarchy. Radical feminism, the least-represented strain in the first stage of research, rejects both the reformism of liberal feminism and the essentialism of cultural feminism, believing that feminist goals cannot be realized without total social transformation. As we discuss below, and as Bell and Blaeuer, Stormer, and Sloop in their essays in this volume concur, contemporary gender theories also hold that traditional categories of gender and sexuality and their orientation toward binary opposition (male/female, heterosexual/homosexual) need to be undone or "troubled" if feminist goals are to be realized (Butler, 1990, 2004).

From the start, research on gender and communication was influenced by liberal ideology. Proceeding from the premise that men and women are alike in most important respects, researchers sought to expose and challenge the discriminatory treatment of women that contributed to their marginalization. This quest produced challenges to a rhetorical canon dominated by the discourse of white male political leaders (Campbell, 1985) and analyses of the underrepresentation and stereotypical representation of women in mass media (Tuchman, Daniels, & Benét, 1978), as well as studies of sexist evaluations of women's communication in professional (Bradley, 1981) and interpersonal settings. Lakoff, in her tellingly titled book, *Language and Woman's Place* (1975), asserted that women's speech was weak and powerless because it was tentative. Communication scholars pointed out that Lakoff's evaluation of women's speech exposed androcentric and therefore inappropriate standards for interpreting women's communication (Kramarae, 1981). They explained that what might be described as tentativeness from a masculine perspective could also be described as inclusiveness from a feminine one (Spender, 1980).

A surge of intense interest in cultural feminism in the early 1980s was aided by the popularity of psychologist Carol Gilligan's work, *In a Different Voice: Psychological Theory and Women's Moral Development* (1982). Cultural feminism continued to influence research on gender and communication through the 1980s and 1990s in books that attracted both popular and academic readers, and it is still present in certain lines of study today. Exemplifying the basic cultural feminist influence are two books, *Women's Ways of Knowing* (Belenky, Clinchy, Goldberger, & Tarule, 1986) and *The Female Advantage* (Helgesen, 1990). The first asserts that the contexts in which most girls are socialized cultivate ways of knowing that are distinct from those of most boys. The second claims that their socialization gives women a noteworthy advantage in exercising leadership. This line of research provided some findings of limited value, but its essentialist tendencies explain why it could not sustain prominence.

In contrast, research and theory about gendered speech communities reflect cultural feminist ideology yet are not essentialist. They have been and remain among the most heuristic lines of inquiry. Launched by Labov's (1972) naming of speech communities and Maltz and Borker's (1982) classic study of socialization in children's sex-segregated play groups, this line of study named gendered speech communities that foster both gender-differentiated ways of communicating and of interpreting others' communication. Research on such communities has been prominent and productive for more than three decades (Coates, 1986, 1997; Coates & Cameron, 1989; Johnson, 1989, 2000; Murphy & Zorn, 1996; Spender, 1980; Wood, 1993a, 1993b; Wood & Inman, 1993).

Building on the study of gendered speech communities, Bate and Taylor's (1988) edited book, *Women Communicating: Studies of Women's Talk*, focused exclusively on women's communication in its own right rather than in comparison to men's communication. The book included Hall and Langellier's (1988) study of storytelling between mothers and daughters. In rhetorical studies, the most visible example of a cultural feminist perspective was Foss and Griffin's (1995) proposal for an invitational rhetoric, which they described as feminist because of its emphasis on equality, immanent value, and self-determination. Foss and Griffin asserted a direct contrast between those characteristics and what they claimed inheres in traditional persuasion, which they described as patriarchal because of its emphasis on control, competition, and coercion. As Stormer discusses in "Gender and Contemporary Rhetorical Theory" in the *Handbook*, a number of feminist scholars have criticized Foss and Griffin's proposal. They argue, first of all, that the description of invitational rhetoric (and of feminists) is essentialist. Second, they point out that invitational rhetoric is premised on a narrow and arguable definition of feminist. Third, they argue that its professed distinctiveness depends upon a questionable conception of traditional persuasion (Bruner, 1996; Condit, 1997; Dow, 1995).

The status of research that reflects cultural feminism is mixed. Some lines informed by cultural feminist ideology, such as that on gendered speech communities, have been well received and remain vital. On the other hand, the more essentialist and unsophisticated uses of cultural feminist ideology have not secured a strong following. In fact, the excesses of this ideology, as in Gray's popular book, *Men Are From Mars, Women Are From Venus* (1992), and the entire line of products which followed have been roundly criticized (Goldsmith & Fulfs, 1999; Wood, 2001).

We also should note that although liberal and cultural feminist ideologies are distinct, even contradictory, they sometimes collaborate in surprising ways that echo how, in tandem, they were responsible for achieving women's enfranchisement during the first wave of feminism in the United States. Beginning in the 1970s, a number of academic and popular writers reflected cultural feminist ideology in claiming that feminine socialization handicapped women professionally. Socialized to be cooperative rather than competitive, to seek approval rather than make an impact, and to support others rather than put themselves forward, women are disadvantaged in a business world that rewards self-promotion, displays of power, and competitiveness. At the same time, these writers embraced liberal feminist ideology in asserting that women were not irreversibly constrained by socialization. They could learn to think and act in ways consistent with organizational logic and, not coincidentally, with men's socialization. Exemplifying the combination of liberal and cultural ideologies in popular literature are Harragan, 1981; Henning and Jardim's *The Managerial Woman* (1977); and Harragan's *Games Your Mother Never Taught You* (1981). In academic literature a similar merger occurs in Kanter's *Men and Women of the Corporation* (1977).

Feminist standpoint theory currently imbricates liberal and cultural feminist ideologies in provocative ways. It assumes that women and men, in general, occupy different social locations that profoundly affect what they know and how they know it. At the same time, the different knowledges generated by these distinct social locations are not essentialist or fixed and do not fit on a conventional better–worse compendium—they may be different and equal in value. Thus, feminist standpoint theory refines understandings of sex and gender equality by insisting that the terms for women's equality do not have to imitate or embody men's perspectives, behaviors, and so on (Wood, 1993c, in press).

◆ *Poststructuralist, Postmodernist, Performative Lenses on Gender and Communication*

Feminist research had matured by the early 1990s, when strains of thought derived from developing academic theory rather than from social movements began to emerge. Noteworthy among them are two lines of theorizing: poststructuralist/postmodernist theories and theories of gender performativity.[1]

Poststructuralist/postmodernist theories are especially amenable to communication scholars because of their emphasis on the materiality of discourse. While fully recognizing that discursive activities reflect understandings of the world and one another, these theories focus on the ways that language and communication practices *create* those understandings. Such a perspective holds that discourse, in its various forms, makes gender "real." Thomson (2003) explains this well when she writes that "gender identity—or any other kind of identity—is not something that you *have*, but something that you *do*—or, at least, something that you have 'only' by doing it again and again and again" (p. 132). Our material bodies become gendered (as well as raced, sexualized, classed, and so on) when—and only when—they are performed and responded to by others, who are either physically present or imagined in ways that affect performance.

A poststructuralist orientation, therefore, is resolutely antiessentialist because discourse shifts and reforms itself in response to time, context, and location. Consequently, all notions of what is real or true about gender become historically and contextually contingent. Fully appreciating the constructedness of gender radically revises conceptual understandings that inform gender and feminist research in ways that explain the ascendance of the performative theories of gender.

Recognizing that performance brings gender into existence throws into question the longstanding distinction between (biological) sex and (cultural) gender. Judith Butler is generally credited with the general idea of performativity and the particular notion that gender is performative. However, before Butler jarred us (productively) with *Gender Trouble* (1990/1999), Lana Rakow (1986) asserted that *gender* should be a verb because it encompasses activities that sustain cultural belief in masculinity and femininity. And just a year later, Candace West and Don Zimmerman (1987) introduced the idea of "doing gender." In their classic essay of that title, they advanced the at-the-time outrageous proposition that gender is something we *do*, not have. In 1990 Butler offered a robust and provocative theory that the character of gender is performative (see also Sedgwick, 1990).

Butler and others (Bordwell, 1998; Diamond, 1996; Pollock, 1995, 1998; Sedgwick, 1990, 2003; Strine, 1998; Thomson, 2003) argue that categories of sexual difference—maleness or femaleness—are given meaning only through discourses about gender. Not even biology has intrinsic meaning without discourse. According to Butler, gender is performed—and recognized by others—because of discourses already embedded in the life of a culture. In Western culture those discourses frame performances of gender as either masculine or feminine, place the masculine above the feminine, and use that hierarchical binary to justify inequalities in the social, political, and material conditions of people's lives. We think that attention to the performative character of gender is possibly the best heuristic and most important direction(s) for research and theorizing and that its central role in contemporary research on gender and communication is evident in each section of the *Handbook*.

◆ Organization of the Handbook

Choosing a rubric to describe how a field is organized is not innocent. No single way of organizing or classifying is natural since all reflect intellectual and political commitments and shape readers' understandings of content. In the early stages of conceiving and organizing this book we considered a number of options. One was to use methodologies of research, such as the historical, critical, and experimental. Another was to present the field chronologically.

In the end we chose to use the primary emphases in communication studies. Our organization is, in other words, functional and familiar for those in the discipline. The *Handbook* consists of five sections.

GENDER AND COMMUNICATION IN INTERPERSONAL CONTEXTS

This section comprises five chapters on particularly prominent lines of inquiry. Framing it is the opening chapter by Elizabeth Bell and Daniel Blaeuer about the critical importance of performative, embodied understandings of gender as they operate in interpersonal (and all other) contexts. Bell and Blaeuer's insistence on attending to the body as performed echoes themes from this introductory essay as well as from various chapters throughout the *Handbook*. In Chapter 2, "Gendered Communication in Dating Relationships," Sandra Metts provides an extended example of the productivity of performative views of gender. Her survey of research on romantic relationships allows us to see that dating proceeds largely through performances of socially constructed rituals.

In Chapter 3, "Gender and Family Interaction: Dress Rehearsal for an Improvisation?" Kathleen Galvin uses a kaleidoscope to metaphorically frame her survey of research on gender in families. Families are changing just as a kaleidoscope changes the arrangement of pieces of glass or plastic. Galvin emphasizes the multiplicity of family forms and how it makes for enormous variation in what gender means and how it is enacted. Michael Monsour's essay in Chapter 4, "Communication and Gender Among Adult Friends," surveys differences in performance among male friendships, female friendships, female-male friendships, and, to lesser extents, straight, gay and lesbian, and intercultural friendships. Monsour's attention to the transgender community offers particularly intriguing insights as to how gender performances define and transform identities.

Michael Johnson concludes with "Gendered Communication and Intimate Partner Violence." He identifies three distinct types of intimate-partner violence, which entail different motives, patterns, goals, and dangers. Johnson highlights the role of communication in each type and gives particular insight into the gender dynamics that both constitute and reflect violence in intimate relationships.

The five chapters in this section provide an informed and informative summary of research. Equally important, each chapter offers thoughtful suggestions for research to increase our insight into the complex ways in which gender and communication construct each other while also constructing and being constructed by relationships.

GENDER AND COMMUNICATION IN ORGANIZATIONAL CONTEXTS

Dennis Mumby's introduction to this section notes the tremendous growth in this area during the past decade. From an early focus on women as exotics, negotiating their assimilation into hostile, male-dominated contexts, a more nuanced theorizing of gendered organizational identities and practices now shows the influence of poststructuralism and theories of performativity. In Chapter 6, Karen Ashcraft provides a valuable overview of the changing understandings of gender difference in organizational literatures, from seeing it as being located in specific male and female skills and traits to being negotiated, contested, and relatively unstable. She explains, for example, a turn toward the notion of the "gendered organization" rather than gendered people, making clear that "gender difference functions as a pivotal organizing mechanism that is actively—even strategically—deployed by founders, managers, and coworkers." The three remaining chapters in this section pursue this insight as they take up the relation of globalism, career, or the body, among other issues, to the constitution, function, and politics of gender identity.

In Chapter 7, Angela Tretheway, Cliff Scott, and Marianne LeGreco argue that "how our bodies become meaningful in everyday work life is a partial product or effect of the discursive structures that comprise our social worlds." They posit the body as a site and subject of discourses that alter, regulate, and control it in the pursuit of professional and nonprofessional (e.g., blue-collar) gendered identities. They conclude that organizational studies have tended to embrace a mind/body dualism in which organizational practices are largely mental and call for greater attention to the discursive and material implications of embodied organizational identities.

In Chapter 8, Nikki Townsley looks at the new international division of labor produced by global economic shifts. She offers brief case studies of women who work as nannies, sex workers, and global call center operators in whom the "gendered discourses of care, desire, and communication" are inflected by local contexts, traditional notions of gendered work, and global political economies. Patrice Buzzanell and Kristen Lucas, writing in Chapter 9 on career discourses, maintain that "career is actualized through individuals' identity construction along the lines of key career dimensions" studied by gender and organization scholars, including time, space, and identity. This research indicates that men and women produce and are affected by communication about these dimensions in meaningful ways that often disadvantage women. The authors conclude that career discourses deserve additional theoretical and methodological attention from scholars.

These four chapters demonstrate particularly well the profound influence of poststructuralist and performative theories. From the shifting understandings of difference, to the influence of global economic change, to the role of the body, to understandings of the meaning of career, the concepts and issues explored in this section offer a rich understanding of the role of gendered practices and identities in organizational life.

GENDER AND COMMUNICATION IN RHETORICAL CONTEXTS

The discipline of communication can trace its academic origins to the ancient art of rhetoric, and the five chapters in Part III offer a portrait of the contexts, assumptions, and goals that have animated the study of gender and rhetoric for more than 50 years. In Chapter 10, Karlyn Kohrs Campbell and Zornitsa Keremidchieva trace the implicit gendered premises in the history of public address and examine the scholarly developments that prompted projects to recover the history of women's public activism. They identify disciplinary traditions that affect the study of gender, examine the problems created by definitions of public and private, and look at research on alternative rhetorical practices that interact with and affect what has traditionally been considered "public address." Vanessa Beasley in Chapter 11 details how academic research on political communication and gender developed during and after the second wave of American feminism. Elaborating on our claim that intellectual attention to gender followed activist work, Beasley shows that political communication from differing methodological and disciplinary traditions reflects differing views of what counts as gender, as activism, and even of what constitutes politics.

In Chapter 12, Jacqueline Bacon explores the intersection and interaction of race/ethnicity, gender, and rhetorical practices. As Bacon shows, work in this area has uncovered nonoratorical but important rhetorical practices of women and men of color. Bacon calls particular attention to scholars who have examined the dual oppression of women of color as well as the ways that concepts of masculinity can oppress men of color. Accordingly, an emphasis on the intersectionality of race/ethnicity, class, gender, and nationality becomes essential to analyzing the rhetorical praxis of women and men of color.

Cheryl Glenn and Rosalyn Collings Eves offer a critical integration in Chapter 13 of studies of rhetoric and gender in ancient Greece and Rome, a central issue for the study of gender and rhetoric, given the roots of rhetorical study in classical traditions. They give particular attention to how ancient rhetorics constructed gender and attempted to discipline Greek and Roman males as well as females into proper gender behaviors. Glenn and Eves detail scholarship that attempts to explain how gender norms were both enacted and challenged within Greek and Roman rhetorical practices. This chapter demonstrates especially well how contemporary scholarship can challenge and revise our knowledge of the roots of rhetorical practices in antiquity in ways that are relevant to the continued investigation of the gendered dynamics of rhetorical action. In this section's final chapter, Nathan Stormer places dominant notions of gender in rhetorical theory in conversation with contemporary gender theory, including theories of gender performativity. He names as a problem the repression of embodied rhetoric—corporeal, concrete bodies that perform and are rhetorical—in theorizing about rhetoric. Stormer ultimately challenges scholars to study and theorize from an understanding that being gendered and being rhetorical are reciprocal and interactive, and he challenges us to think differently, asking, "What if we take the body as a rhetorical situation?"

Taken together, these five chapters explicate the dynamic relationship between gender and rhetoric, from the rhetorical practices and theories of antiquity to women's emergence on public platforms in the United States of the 19th century and from the interaction of race and gender in rhetorical practice to current theories of gender performativity and rhetorical embodiment.

GENDER AND COMMUNICATION IN MEDIATED CONTEXTS

The five chapters of Part IV are concerned with a broad range of media genres, forms, and representational themes but more generally with how mass media both communicate and challenge dominant norms and expectations related to gender. The pervasive influence of mass media in cultural life, including the formation, reinforcement, and performance of gendered identities, makes such a focus especially salient. The authors address the interaction of gender with other identity markers, cultural dynamics, and technological possibilities.

In the first chapter (Chapter 15), Angharad Valdivia and Sarah Projansky note the engagement of media study with feminist activism, theories, and methods, making the case that the contemporary study of gender and media has always been intertwined with feminist politics. They do not limit their purview to work within and on the United States, and they provide a needed recognition of the importance of research on the intersections of feminism, media study, and global contexts.

Chapters 16 and 17 take up gender's intersections with other identity categories in media representation. Dwight Brooks and Lisa Hébert provide an extensive review of the scholarship on race, gender, and media in Chapter 16, integrating a discussion of the development of the theories and assumptions used to analyze representations with description of the diverse body of work that has resulted. Although noting that research is more plentiful in some areas than others, they include examples of scholarship examining representations of African Americans, Native Americans, Latinos/Latinas, and Asians. They also look at developing areas such as masculinity and whiteness studies. In Chapter 17, John Sloop examines recent developments in media, gender, and sexuality studies, observing that theories of gender performativity have been especially influential. Including scholarship on representations of gays, lesbians, and the transgendered in film, broadcast, and print media, Sloop argues that studies tend to occupy a continuum from those that "emphasize the way gender/sexuality are ideologically contained

to work emphasizing the way audiences can read some texts as both/either liberatory or constraining to those emphasizing progressive or fluid understandings of gender/sexuality." This chapter is especially useful in demonstrating that cultural tensions attached to media representations of controversial issues such as gender identity and sexuality make media texts especially rich for critical study.

In Chapter 18, Lisa Cuklanz treats another cultural dynamic with a longstanding presence in mass media—gendered violence. She argues that mass media play a central role in communicating gendered norms through their depiction of violence, generally done to women by men. The chapter offers a complex picture of the gendered dynamics of these representations, pointing out, for instance, that violence against women cements the connection between violence and masculinity and between victimization and femininity. At the same time, however, media representations of such violence also routinely offer a vision of heroic masculinity performed by the men who use violence against those who have victimized women.

In Chapter 19, Mia Consalvo discusses work on gender and new media. She offers a broad look at an area of study that is distinguished by its engagement with such varied issues as the social function/construction of technology, the creation and representation of gendered identities (and their intersections with race, class, sexuality, and nationality) in virtual environments, as well as the relationship between gender and technological skill, use, and access. In the only chapter in this section that focuses on a specific medium, Consalvo persuasively argues that, despite claims for the limitless possibilities of performativity offered by these new technologies, scholarship increasingly demonstrates that gender matters at every level of new media interaction.

These five chapters demonstrate the varied and productive ways in which scholars have approached the interactions of media and gender through attention to the tremendous variety of forms, genres, themes, identities, contexts, and technologies that constitute the contemporary mediascape in national and international environments.

GENDER AND COMMUNICATION IN INTERCULTURAL AND GLOBAL CONTEXTS

In her introduction to this section, Fern Johnson provides the key frame for understanding and appreciating scholarship that insists on a global approach. She asserts that "the central proposition of cultural analysis is that culture is *con*-text which must be read *against* any and every text—pushing against it, changing it, shaping it, making it more than may appear on the surface. Culture and cultural diversity categories are neither variables nor unified containers. Culture makes texts, and texts make culture." This overarching frame is elaborated and embodied in the four chapters that, in different ways, address issues central to scholarship on gender and communication in intercultural and global contexts: intersectionality, center-margin relations, language and power relations, the limitations of domestic (U.S. or "American") analysis, and the political and epistemological significance of particular situational contexts.

The first and last chapters serve as bookends. In Chapter 20, Lisa Flores describes and transcends two distinct orientations that have characterized research on culture, communication, gender and race: (a) work on gender and race as identities associated with cultural differences, and (b) work on gender, race, and culture as contested ideologies. Radha Hegde (Chapter 23) addresses one of the most significant newer advances in the study of cultural contextualization of gender and communication with her attention to the analytical stances and methodologies brought to bear on feminism's global reach. The goal of research in this area must, she asserts, be "ultimately about

building an innovative feminist intellectual space that is both vibrant and responsive to global and local forces and which . . . does not fetishize the transnational over the national and the popular over the everyday." Hegde considers the transnational transformation of feminism, assesses the limitations of the area studies approach, and discusses the productive possibilities of scholarship that conjoins feminist, cultural studies, and postcolonial approaches.

Between Flores's and Hegde's analyses are two chapters that provide rich insights into particular cultural groups and their communicative practices. In Chapter 21, Marsha Houston and Karla Scott explore whether the history of unequal social status still permeates Black women's intercultural encounters. Houston and Scott's attention to the oppositional and resistant character of much communicative practice by Black women is echoed in Chapter 22 by Fern Johnson's critical reading of research on women's resistance in non-Western cultures, third-wave feminist gender expressions, and gender refusal and refusers (lesbians, gays, bisexuals, transgenders). As Johnson notes, "every act against cultural normativity of gender—whatever the culture and its codes—is an act of transgression." Her overview covers theoretical frameworks that are useful in understanding such transgression, from theories of gender performativity to the concept of a "community of practice" with its emphasis on the discursive practices that constitute identity, to queer linguistics and the production of sexuality through language.

In closing we note that, as an area of study, gender and communication is very, very young. That is not as mundane an observation as it may, at first, appear. The youth of the area implies that scholarship on gender and communication has not reached full intellectual maturity and, by extension, that researchers have only begun to recognize and explore the subject matter that makes up this area of inquiry. We hope that the *Handbook* will serve as a useful resource as this vital area of scholarship continues to develop.

◆ Note

1. Theories of performativity have influenced feminist activism outside the academy as well, most notably through what has been termed third-wave feminism. Third-wave writers place a great deal of emphasis on the political implications of performing feminist identity and of resistance to gendered norms through personal appearance, behavior, and sexuality. Johnson's chapter on "Transgressing Gender" discusses third-wave discourse.

◆ References

Balswick, J. O. (1988). *The inexpressive* male. Lexington, MA: Lexington Books.

Balswick, J. O., & Peek, C. W. (1976). The inexpressive male: A tragedy of American society. In D. S. David & R. Brannon (Eds.), *The forty-nine percent majority: The male sex-role* (pp. 55–57). Reading, MA: Addison Wesley.

Bate, B. (1988). *Communication between the sexes*. New York: Harper & Row.

Bate, B., & Taylor, A. (Eds.). (1988). *Women communicating: Studies of women's talk*. Norwood, NJ: Ablex.

Belenky, M., Clinchy, B., Goldberger, N., & Tarule, J. (1986). *Women's ways of knowing: The development of self, voice, and mind*. New York: Basic Books.

Bordwell, M. (1998). Dancing with death: Performativity and "undiscussable" bodies in *Still/Here. Text and Performance Quarterly, 18*, 369–379.

Boxer, M. J. (1998). *When women ask the questions: Creating women's studies in America*. Baltimore: Johns Hopkins.

Bradley, P. H. (1981). The folk-linguistics of women's speech: An empirical examination. *Communication Monographs, 48*, 73–90.

Bruner, M. L. (1996). Producing identities: Gender problematization and feminist argumentation. *Argumentation and Advocacy, 32*, 185–198.

Busby, L. (1975). Sex role research in the mass media. *Journal of Communication, 25*, 107–131.

Butler, J. (1999). *Gender trouble: Feminism and the subversion of identity*. New York: Routledge. (Original work published 1990)

Butler, J. (2004). *Undoing gender*. New York: Routledge.

Campbell, A. (2002). *A mind of her own*. Oxford, UK: Oxford University Press.

Campbell, K. K. (1973). The rhetoric of women's liberation: An oxymoron. *Quarterly Journal of Speech, 59*, 74–86.

Campbell, K. K. (1980). Stanton's "Solitude of Self": A rationale for feminism, *Quarterly Journal of Speech, 66*, 304–312.

Campbell, K. K. (1985). The communication classroom: A chilly climate for women? *ACA Bulletin, 51*, 68–72.

Coates, J. (1986). *Women, men, and language: Studies in language and linguistics*. London: Longman.

Coates, J. (Ed.). (1997). *Language and gender: A reader*. London: Basil Blackwell.

Coates, J., & Cameron, D. (1989). *Women in their speech communities: New perspectives on language and sex*. London: Longman.

Condit, C. M. (1997). In praise of eloquent diversity: Gender and rhetoric as public persuasion. *Women's Studies in Communication, 20*, 91–116.

Dallimore, E. J. (2000). A feminist response to issues of validity in research. *Women's Studies in Communication, 23*(2), 157–181.

Diamond, E. (1996). Introduction. In E. Diamond (Ed.), *Performance and cultural politics* (pp. 1–15). New York: Routledge.

Dow, B. J. (1995). Feminism, difference(s), and rhetorical studies. *Communication Studies, 46*, 106–117.

Dow, B. J., & Condit, C. M. (2005). The state of the art in feminist scholarship in communication. *Journal of Communication, 55*, 448–478.

Duck, S. W., & Wood, J. T. (in press). What goes up may come down: Sex and gendered patterns in relational dissolution. In M. Fine & J. Harvey (Eds.), *Relational dissolution*. Mahwah, NJ: Erlbaum.

Eakins, B. W., & Eakins, R. G. (1978). *Sex differences in human communication*. Boston: Houghton Mifflin.

Evans, S. (2003). *Tidal wave: How women changed America at century's end*. New York: Free Press.

Foss, S. K., & Griffin, C. L. (1995). Beyond persuasion: A proposal for an invitational rhetoric. *Communication Monographs, 62*, 2–19.

Gilligan, C. (1982). *In a different voice: Psychological theory and women's moral development*. Cambridge, MA: Harvard University Press.

Gingrich-Philbrook, C. (1994). "Good vibration" or domination? Stylized repetition in mythopoetic performance of masculinity. *Text and Performance Quarterly, 14*, 21–46.

Goldsmith, D., & Fulfs, P. (1999). "You just don't have the evidence": An analysis of claims and evidence in Deborah Tannen's *You just don't understand*. In M. Roloff (Ed.), *Communication Yearbook, 22*, (pp. 1–49). Thousand Oaks, CA: Sage.

Gornick, V., & Moran, B. (Eds.). (1971). *Woman in sexist society: Studies in power and powerlessness*. New York: Basic/Signet.

Gray, J. (1992). *Men are from Mars, women are from Venus: A practical guide for improving communication and getting what you want in relationships*. New York: HarperCollins.

Hall, D., & Langellier, K. (1988). Storytelling strategies in mother-daughter communication. In B. Bate & A. Taylor (Eds.), *Women communicating: Studies of women's talk* (pp. 107–126). Norwood, NJ: Ablex.

Hanke, R. (1990). Hegemonic masculinity in *Thirtysomething*. *Critical Studies in Mass Communication, 7*, 231–249.

Harragan, B. (1981). *Games your mother never taught you*. New York: Warner Books.

Helgesen, S. (1990). *The female advantage: Women's ways of leadership*. New York: Doubleday Currency.

Henning, M., & Jardim, A. (1977). *The managerial woman*. New York: Anchor Press/ Doubleday.

Johnson, F. (1989). Women's culture and communication: An analytical perspective. In C. M. Lont & S. A. Friedley (Eds.), *Beyond boundaries: Sex and gender diversity in communication* (pp. 301–316). Fairfax, VA: George Mason University Press.

Johnson, F. (2000). *Speaking culturally: Language diversity in the United States*. Thousand Oaks, CA: Sage.

Kanter, R. M. (1977). *Men and women of the corporation*. New York: Basic.

Kramarae, C. (1981). *Women and men speaking: Frameworks for analysis*. Rowley, MA: Newbury House.

Kramer, C., Thorne, B., & Henley, N. (1978). Perspectives on language and communication. *Signs: Journal of Women in Culture and Society, 3*, 638–651.

Labov, W. (1972). *Sociolinguistic patterns*. Philadelphia: University of Pennsylvania Press.

Lakoff, R. (1975). *Language and woman's place*. New York: Harper & Row.

Maltz, D., & Borker, R. (1982). A cultural approach to male-female miscommunication. In J. J. Gumperz (Ed.), *Language and social identity* (pp. 196–216). Cambridge, UK: Cambridge University Press.

Mumby, D. K. (1998). Organizing men: Power, discourse and the social construction of masculinity(s) in the workplace. *Communication Theory, 8*, 164–183.

Murphy, B., & Zorn, T. (1996). Gendered interaction in professional relationships. In J. T. Wood (Ed.), *Gendered relationships: A reader* (pp. 213–232). Mountain View, CA: Mayfield.

Parry-Giles, S., & Parry-Giles, T. (1996). Gendered politics and presidential image construction: A reassessment of the "feminine style." *Communication Monographs, 63*, 337–374.

Patton, B. R., & Patton, B. R. (1976). *Living together. . . : Female/male communication*. Columbus, OH: Merrill.

Pearson, J. (1985). *Gender and communication*. Dubuque, IA: William C. Brown.

Pollock, D. (1995). Performativity. In C. N. Davidson & L. Wagner-Martin (Eds.), *The Oxford companion to women's writing in the United States* (pp. 657–658). New York: Oxford University Press.

Pollock, D. (1998). A response to Dwight Conquergood's essay "Beyond the Text: Towards a performative cultural politics. In S. J. Dailey (Ed.), *The future of performance studies: Visions and revisions* (pp. 37–46). Annandale, VA: National Communication Association.

Rakow, L. (1986). Rethinking gender research in communication. *Journal of Communication, 36*, 11–26.

Rosen, R. (2000). *The world split open: How the women's movement changed America.* New York: Penguin.

Sedgwick, E. K. (1990). *Epistemology of the closet.* Berkeley: University of California Press.

Sedgwick, E. K. (2003). *Touching feeling: Affect, pedagogy, performativity.* Durham, NC: Duke University Press.

Shimanoff, S. B. (1977). Sex as a variable in communication research 1970–1976: An annotated bibliography. *Women's Studies in Communication, 1*, 8–20.

Spender, D. (1980). *Man-made language.* London: Routledge & Kegan Paul.

Stephen, T. (2000). Concept analysis of gender, feminist, and women's studies research in the communication literature. *Communication Monographs, 67*, 193–214.

Stewart, L. P., Stewart A. D., Friedley, S. A., & Cooper, P. J. (1987). *Communication between the sexes: Sex differences, and sex role stereotypes.* Scottsdale, AZ: Gorsuch Scarisbrick.

Strine, M. S. (1998). Articulating performance/performativity: Disciplinary tasks and the contingencies of practice. In J. S. Trent (Ed.), *Communication: Views from the helm for the 21st century* (pp. 312–317). Boston, MA: Allyn & Bacon.

Tedesco, N. S. (1974). Patterns in prime time. *Journal of Communication, 24*, 119–124.

Thomson, D. (2003). "Is race a trope?" Anna Deavere Smith and the question of racial performativity. *African American Review, 37*, 127–138.

Trujillo, N. (1991). Hegemonic masculinity on the mound: Media representations of Nolan Ryan and American sports culture. *Critical Studies in Mass Communication, 8*, 290–309.

Tuchman, G., Daniels, A. K., & Benét, J. (Eds.). (1978). *Hearth and home: Images of women in the mass media.* New York: Oxford University Press.

West, C., & Zimmerman, D. (1987). "Doing gender." *Gender and Society, 1*, 125–151.

Wood, J. T. (1993a). Engendered relationships: Interaction, caring, power, and responsibility in close relationships. In S. Duck (Ed.), *Processes in close relationships: Contexts of close relationships* (Vol. 3, pp. 26–54). Newbury Park, CA: Sage.

Wood, J. T. (1993b). Engendered identities: Shaping voice and mind through gender. In D. Vocate (Ed.), *Intrapersonal communication: Different voices, different minds* (pp. 145–167). Hillsdale, NJ: Erlbaum.

Wood, J. T. (1993c). From "woman's nature" to standpoint epistemology: Gilligan and the debate over essentializing in feminist scholarship. *Women's Studies in Communication, 15*, 1–24.

Wood, J. T. (1995). Feminist scholarship and the study of relationships. *Journal of Social and Personal Relationships, 12*, 103–120.

Wood, J. T. (2001). A critical response to John Gray's Mars and Venus portrayals of men and women. *Southern Communication Journal, 67*, 201–210.

Wood, J. T. (in press). Feminist standpoint theory and muted group theory: Commonalities and divergences. *Women and Language, 28.*

Wood, J. T., & Duck, S. (1995). Off the beaten track: New shores for relationship research. In J. T. Wood & S. Duck (Eds.), *Understanding relationship processes series, 6: Under-studied relationships: Off the beaten track* (pp. 1–21). Thousand Oaks, CA: Sage.

Wood, J. T., & Inman, C. (1993). In a different mode: Recognizing male modes of closeness. *Journal of Applied Communication Research, 21*, 279–295.

PART I

GENDER AND COMMUNICATION IN INTERPERSONAL CONTEXTS

Introduction

◆ Julia T. Wood

G ender cannot be understood apart from interpersonal relationships and the communication that continuously constructs them as well as the identities of the participants in them. At least since Mead (1934) began lecturing on what later came to be called symbolic interactionism, virtually all scholars who study interpersonal behavior have assumed that, as Mead told his students, the self arises in communication with others. Selves come into existence as biological beings interact with others who reflect appraisals of them, respond to their actions, and otherwise bring them into the social world of meaning in a particular time and space. Through others' definitions and others' responses to her or his actions, the individual begins to develop a self.

And the self that arises in communication with others is deeply gendered. Like all aspects of identity, gender is learned, initially, from the outside. We develop our first notions of gender in general and ourselves as gendered beings in particular from others who teach us directly and indirectly what is feminine and masculine, what is and is not appropriate for girls and boys, and which behaviors are acceptable and not acceptable. Gender is inherently and inescapably interpersonal. Thus, it is not surprising that many scholars interested in gender find it valuable to learn about interpersonal communication and that many scholars interested in interpersonal communication find that understanding gender is essential to their work.

In introducing this section of the *Handbook*, I offer a narrative, perhaps one of many that could be written, of the emergence of research and teaching about gender and interpersonal communication. First, I sketch a history—admittedly selective and incomplete—of gender's emergence as a focus of inquiry in the discipline and the subfield of interpersonal communication. Second, I highlight what I view as particularly important and provocative lines of inquiry. In the process of describing the interest in gender among scholars of interpersonal communication and pointing to promising directions in research, I explain my choices for chapters in this section and offer brief comments about each chapter.

◆ Development of Scholarship on Gender and Interpersonal Communication

The emergence of gender and interpersonal communication as an area of study follows the emergence of interest among communication scholars in gender generally. I begin with the field's awareness of gender and then in greater detail describe the history of research on gender in the more specific area of interpersonal communication.

EMERGENCE OF RESEARCH ON GENDER AND COMMUNICATION

My academic career parallels the trajectory of research on gender and interpersonal communication in some interesting ways. I began my first faculty appointment in 1975. At about the same time, research trickled into publication in an area that was then called sex differences. I paid no attention because I had no academic interest in sex or gender and had never studied them. In fact, I could not have studied them in any formal sense since there were few, if any, women's studies departments and even fewer courses on gender.

In the mid-1970s when I was an assistant professor, a few scholars of communication began to show awareness of and even interest in gender. Landmark articles by Kramarae (then Kramer, 1974) and Campbell (1973), among others, were the harbingers of the far more robust interest in gender that would soon surface. It was also in the 1970s that the first textbook on gender and communication (Eakins & Eakins, 1978) appeared.

By the mid-1980s that trickle of interest had become a raging river that threatened to overflow its banks with research on what was increasingly known as gender studies. Paralleling that, the limited interest in gender scholarship that I had had in the 1970s welled up in the 1980s. As it turns out, I was in good company. A number of communication scholars claimed gender as an area of interest and virtually all began to acknowledge its importance. A special issue of one journal was devoted to gender and communication (Wood, 1983), and a conference was established and began holding annual meetings (Wood & Phillips, 1984, 1985; Wood, 1986). Two journals, *Women's Studies in Communication* and *Women and*

Language, were established. These continue to be devoted to research on gender and communication, and it has been years since a volume of any national or regional journal did not include articles on gender.

By the 1980s both the National Communication Association and the International Communication Association had strong programming in gender and communication. With growing faculty interest in the area, it is not surprising that courses began appearing in schools around the nation. Naturally a second generation of textbooks (Bate, 1988; Pearson, 1985; Stewart, Stewart, Friedley, & Cooper, 1987) accompanied the new curricula.

During the 1990s and into the present decade, work on gender by communication scholars has continued to expand and to deepen. Courses in gender and communication are now the rule, rather than the exception, in the United States and many other countries. In fact, an increasing number of communication departments offer multiple such courses at the undergraduate and graduate levels.

RESEARCH ON GENDER AND INTERPERSONAL COMMUNICATION

Roughly spanning the first half of the 1970s, the first phase of research on gender and interpersonal communication focused primarily on sex-based differences. Scholars asked what differences there were between women's and men's speech. This early research focused on sex—not gender—differences in communication, and sex was usually treated as a discrete variable, the independent one. Perhaps the influence of Lakoff's *Language and Woman's Place* (1975) explains why much of the early work tacitly assumed that communication patterns typical of men were superior to those typical of women. Lakoff reported that women were less assertive rather than that men were more aggressive; that women were less self-confident rather than that men were overconfident; and, of course,

that women's speech is more tentative rather than that men's is less inclusive. Not surprisingly, Lakoff's findings—and, more specifically, her interpretation of them—inspired classes and workshops that encouraged women to learn to be more assertive, strong communicators (i.e., to speak more like men).

By the 1980s a number of scholars were rethinking Lakoff's conclusions and their implication that women's speech is somehow deficient (Johnson, 1983). They named and critiqued the tacit male standard and called for other frameworks for describing and understanding sex-related patterns of communication. Particularly visible and influential was Dale Spender's (1980) critique of Lakoff's conclusions and her warning not to assume that differences must always be graded as better and worse, superior and inferior. Many of us rejected Lakoff's conclusion that women's speech was weak and powerless. We moved from what communication is (e.g., male-female differences) to how it is examined (i.e., from a perspective that does not assume male as the standard).

In turn, critical reflection on the male-as-standard assumption paved the way for the study of speech communities, including ones defined by sex and gender. Scholars began paying attention to how groups of girls and boys use and interpret communication—the rules by which they operate. Later, when I highlight particularly promising directions in research, I will point out an additional line of inquiry that had its genesis in the recognition that gender is socially constructed.

Also in the 1980s, the early focus on sex and sex differences was giving way to a more complex interest in gender and gender differences. Increasingly, gender was recognized as a basic analytic category that could not be reduced to a mere variable or set of variables. Scholars argued that gender is central to identity, that it is constitutive of who we are in ways that transcend the influence of a variable. As Bell and Blaeuer note in the first chapter in this section, distinguishing between sex and gender was pivotal to the emergence of serious research on gender. They write:

> With great satisfaction, we were able to assert, "sex is a biological designation" and that "gender is the set of socially constructed expectations for women and men." With that distinction, we could make claims about material conditions, historical moments, and cultural pressures. In short, the separation of sex and gender allowed us to point to social constructions, not biological destiny, as the source of women's oppression and men's privilege.

Scholars moved ahead to study how femininity and masculinity are constructed in the nuclear family, the playground, schools, organizations, institutions, and so on. Yet as Bell and Blaeuer note and as I discuss in the next section, distinguishing sex from gender was perhaps not as groundbreaking or even as useful as many of us thought at the time.

Provocative Lines of Inquiry

In just three decades, research on gender and communication has expanded greatly. Instead of attempting to catalog or categorize the whole of this body of work, here I want to call attention to two especially provocative lines of research on gender and interpersonal communication.

GENDER AS PERFORMED AND EMBODIED

Beginning in the 1980s, Butler began to question the independent reality of gender and, eventually, of sex as well (see Sloop's chapter, "Critical Studies in Gender/Sexuality and Media," in Part IV). Her decision to trouble conventional notions of gender, led her (1988, 1990/1999) to argue that gender is not natural, normal, or otherwise given. For Butler, gender is a cultural performance that arises and exists—and only can arise and exist—through ongoing embodiments that are performed over and over again to sustain belief in the reality of that which is not real at all, namely, gender. As Diamond (1996) explains, "Butler's point is not that gender is just an act, but that gender is materially performative: it 'is real only to the extent that it is performed'" (p. 4). Phrasing this idea another way, Thomson (2003) claims that "gender identity—or any other kind of identity—is not something that you *have*, but something that you *do*—or, at least, something that you have 'only' by doing it again and again and again" (p. 132). But for Butler and others who view gender as performative, the process of performing gender is neither wholly spontaneous nor without boundaries and history. Butler (1988) explains that performing gender is "an act that has been going on before one arrived on the scene. Hence, gender is an act which has been rehearsed, much as a script survives the particular actors who make use of it, but which requires individual actors in order to be actualized and reproduced as reality once again" (p. 526).

The relevance of Butler's work to interpersonal communication comes from her argument that performing gender is not solitary but is collaboratively, or socially, accomplished. She writes:

> One does not "do" one's gender alone. One is always "doing" with or for another, even if the other is only imaginary. What I call my "own" gender appears perhaps at times as something that I author or, indeed, own. But the terms that make up one's own gender are, from the start, outside oneself, beyond oneself in a sociality that has no single author. (2004, p. 1)

Interpersonal relationships are primary sites where embodiments of gender are practiced, embraced, rejected, and modified. They are also sites where gender performances are critiqued, edited, and disciplined. Accordingly, this section of the *Handbook* includes chapters on familial, friendship, and dating relationships, which are particularly important in teaching us how to craft and sustain credible gender performances. Kathleen Galvin shows that in family relationships we see our first models of gendered identities and communication, we have our first opportunities to practice embodying gender, and we get our first responses to our efforts to perform masculinity and femininity. Monsour and Metts summarize what is known about the interaction between gender and communication in friendships and dating. Bookending those three chapters are Bell and Blaeuer's essay, which sets the tone for thinking about gender as performed, and Johnson's analysis of the deeply gendered nature of communication in violent personal relationships.

The centrality of Butler's work to understandings of gender suggests why, as section editor, I made a choice that may—at least on first glance—seem odd. I not only made room for but I gave priority to a chapter that deals with the performativity of gender. In that chapter, Bell and Blaeuer bring into dialogue two areas of scholarship that have experienced little interaction: performance studies and interpersonal communication. They reveal that performativity offers scholars a means of interrogating and critiquing binary, hierarchical, and heteronormative categories that have been used too frequently to define gender. Embracing performativity may allow research to move from the no-longer-productive idea that gender is learned to a more generative and heuristic question, How do particular performances maintain or destabilize belief in gender?

Bell and Blaeuer's attention to the body does not lead to a biological determinism. Instead, they insist that the body should be attended to but not be a foundation for claims about identity, gender, and communication. Research should acknowledge the body but should not position it as causal, ahistorical, or reducible to discrete variables. The body should be accounted for as inescapably present but not overdetermined in interpersonal theories of relationship development, dynamics, and cognition. In short, bodies matter in research that investigates gender.

Bell and Blaeuer foreshadow themes developed in other chapters in this section of the *Handbook*. Sandra Metts's richly detailed discussion of research on nonverbal communication used to flirt shows the complex ways that sexual and romantic interest and availability is communicated. Here is a performance of gender that is concretely, bodily gendered. Likewise, in his chapter on intimate-partner violence, Johnson demonstrates how patriarchy and patriarchal control are instantiated in interaction between partners. Galvin's chapter calls attention to the ways in which communication constitutes familial relationships and gendered identities within families. Likewise, Monsour shows how interaction between friends enacts and brings into existence both gender and friendship.

◆ Feminist Science

Another provocative and influential line of research focuses on developing feminist versions of science and scientific inquiry. Just as gender is not given but socially constructed, so is science, and, according to some feminist philosophers of science, has traditionally been constructed from and for a masculine perspective. Landmark works (Haraway, 1988; Harding, 1991; Hartsock, 1983; Hill Collins, 1986; Rose, 1983; Smith, 1987) have ushered in a feminist critique of the androcentrism in traditional science. Including those in interpersonal communication, these feminist scholars have critiqued male-derived earmarks of traditional science, including the ideal of objectivity and the separation of knower (researcher) and known (object of study). Moving beyond critique, feminist scholars have generated alternative epistemologies that attend to the ways that social location shapes knowledge. To counter the ensconced privileging of men, feminist epistemologies construct knowledge from the insights that arise from women's experiences. Women's lives—the material, everyday routines that compose them—immediately raise questions about what counts as knowledge. Yet the dominant ideology claims that the only acceptable knowledge comes from science, which relies on objectivity and separation of scientist and object of knowledge. Standpoint theorists reject restricting knowledge in this manner and instead consider how admitting subjectivity and placing knower and known on the same plane generate knowledge.

Although other lines of inquiry in research on gender and interpersonal communication are interesting and important, I believe none is so central to the area's future as attending to gender as embodied and performed and rethinking how we do science and what we count as knowledge.

◆ Overview of Chapters

In describing the evolution of research on gender and interpersonal communication, I have already referred to the chapters composing this section of the *Handbook*. Here I wish to call readers' special attention to some of the most important contributions of each chapter in this section.

Metts frames her chapter with the observation that both gender and dating are social constructions enacted through communication. She then summarizes research on typical phases in the dating process: initiation (first meeting, signaling interest, and first date); intensification (expressions of love/commitment, increased sexual involvement); maintenance (managing intimacy); and, sometimes, disengagement.

Galvin opens her chapter on gendered communication in families with the observation that childhood was once a rehearsal for adult life but that now and in the future adult life will be more of an improvisation than a performance of a rehearsed script. Children today will form families that may have little resemblance to their imaginings

of family life. Galvin demonstrates why that is by summarizing research showing that what children learn about gender and families varies widely due to diverse family structures, cultures, religions, sexual orientations, family models, and the pragmatic concerns of negotiating with one or more partners, their families, and children.

In Chapter 4, Monsour provides a thoughtful review of research on adult same-sex friendships, adult cross-sex friendships, and friendships among transgendered individuals. Monsour moves toward disentangling the influence of gender—and the presence of gendered communication patterns—from those of other aspects of identity, such as sexual orientation.

In his chapter on intimate-partner violence, Johnson begins by making the case that it is not a unitary phenomenon. He draws clear distinctions between violent resistance, which is essentially a defensive response most often used by a woman against a man; situational couple violence, which is perpetrated by both women and men and which is usually not severe; and intimate terrorism, which is severe and usually committed by men against women. Johnson then describes the kind of communication patterns typical of each type. Based on existing research, he reasons that intimate terrorism is likely to involve a pattern of male demand and female withdrawal, endemic communication that involves the assertion of control, and reliance on psychological abuse, assertion of male privilege, and a rhetoric of romance to justify the violence.

The thorough and thoughtful reviews of research provided by Bell and Blaeuer, Galvin, Monsour, Metts, and Johnson give us compelling evidence that this area is one of ongoing, vigorous research and theorizing. They make it clear that research on gender and interpersonal communication is becoming more sophisticated as the area matures. Finally, they direct our thinking forward by suggesting priorities and an ambitious and exciting agenda for the next generation of research on gender and interpersonal communication.

◆ References

Bate, B. (1988). *Communication between the sexes*. New York: Harper & Row.

Butler, J. (1988). Performative acts and gender constitution: An essay in phenomenology and feminist thought. *Theatre Journal, 40,* 519–531.

Butler, J. (1990/1999). *Gender trouble: Feminism and the subversion of identity*. New York: Routledge.

Butler, J. (1993). *Bodies that matter: On the discursive limits of "sex."* New York: Routledge.

Butler, J. (1997). *Excitable speech: A politics of the performative*. New York: Routledge.

Butler, J. (2004). *Undoing gender*. New York: Routledge.

Campbell, K. K. (1973). The rhetoric of women's liberation: An oxymoron. *Quarterly Journal of Speech, 59,* 74–86.

Collins, P. H. (1986). Learning from the outsider within. *Social Problems, 23,* 514–532.

Diamond, E. (1996). Introduction. In E. Diamond (Ed.), *Performance and cultural politics* (pp. 1–15). New York: Routledge.

Eakins, B., & Eakins, G. (1978). *Sex differences in human communication*. Boston: Houghton Mifflin.

Haraway, D. (1988). Situated knowledges: The science question in feminism and the privilege of partial perspective. *Signs, 14,* 575–599.

Harding, S. (1991). *Whose science? Whose knowledge? Thinking from women's lives*. Ithaca, NY: Cornell University Press.

Hartsock, N. (1983). The feminist standpoint: Developing the ground for a specifically feminist historical materialism. In S. Harding & M. B. Hintikka (Eds.), *Discovering reality* (pp. 283–310). Boston: Ridel.

Johnson, F. (1983). Political and pedagogical implications of attitudes towards women's language. *Quarterly Journal of Speech, 31,* 133–138.

Kramer, C. (1974). Folklinguistics. *Psychology Today, 8,* 82–85.

Lakoff, R. (1973). Language and woman's place. *Language in Society, 2,* 45–80.

Lakoff, R. (1975). *Language and woman's place*. New York: Harper & Row.

Mead, G. H. (1934). *Mind, self, and society*. Chicago: University of Chicago Press.

Pearson, J. (1985). *Gender and communication*. Dubuque, IA: William C. Brown.

Rose, H. (1983). Hand, brain and heart: Towards a feminist epistemology for the sciences. *Signs, 9,* 73–98.

Smith, D. (1987). *The everyday world as problematic*. Toronto, Ontario, Canada: University of Toronto Press.

Spender, D. (1980). *Man-made language*. London: Routledge & Kegan Paul.

Stewart, L. P., Stewart A. D., Friedley, S. A., & Cooper, P. J. (1987). *Communication between the sexes: Sex differences, and sex role stereotypes*. Scottsdale, AZ: Gorsuch Scarisbrick.

Thomson, D. (2003). "Is race a trope?" Anna Deavere Smith and the question of racial performativity. *African American Review, 37,* 127–138.

Wood, J. T. (Ed.). (1983). Women and communication. *Communication Quarterly, 31,* 99–184.

Wood, J. T. (1986). Report on the 1986 conference on gender and communication research. *Women's Studies in Communication, 10,* 90–93.

Wood, J. T., & Phillips, G. M. (1984). Report on the 1984 conference on gender and communication research. *Communication Quarterly, 32,* 175–177.

Wood, J. T., & Phillips, G. M. (1985). Report on the 1985 conference on gender and communication research. *Women's Studies in Communication, 8,* 94–97.

1

PERFORMING GENDER AND INTERPERSONAL COMMUNICATION RESEARCH

◆ Elizabeth Bell and Daniel Blaeuer

Most of us can trace the terms *sex* and *gender* through feminist theory. And most of us can point to the moment when their separation became an important theoretical move in talking about women, men, femininity, and masculinity (Rubin, 1975). With great satisfaction we were then able to assert that "sex is a biological designation," and "gender is a set of socially constructed expectations for women and men." That distinction permitted us to make claims about material conditions, historical moments, and cultural pressures. In short, the separation of sex and gender allowed us to point to social constructions, not biological destiny as the source of women's oppression and men's privilege.

But in 1990 two books took the sex/gender distinction to task: Sedgwick's *Epistemology of the Closet* and Butler's *Gender Trouble*. For Sedgwick, the sex/gender system failed to account for sexuality and its multiplicity of expressions. Although sex/gender can offer purchase to a feminist critique of oppressive social systems based on biology, sexuality falls outside both categories unless it is anchored to masculine and feminine terms within a heterosexist ideology. Sedgwick also questioned the political efficacy of pitting biology against culture: "I remember the buoyant enthusiasm with which feminist scholars used to greet the finding that one or another brutal form of oppression was not biological but 'only' cultural! I have often wondered what the basis was for our optimism about the malleability of culture by any one group or program" (p. 41).

In *Gender Trouble*, Butler built (1990/ 1999) a case that radically upset the sex/gender system. Beginning with the feminist *we* and the universal category *woman,* Butler questioned the ontological ground of any subject of feminism within the sex/gender system. Moving away from the foundations for gender in biology, constructionism, psychology, and sexual difference, Butler argued that gender—across these foundational approaches—is always already framed as binary, hierarchical, and compulsorily heterosexual. This triptych is important: Gender is always named as either masculine or feminine (binary); the masculine is always placed above the feminine (hierarchy); and compulsory heterosexuality (proscribed by discourses of law, family, religion, and education) secures that hierarchical binary in material ways. With those three theoretical moves, Butler arrived at gender as a cultural performance and not natural—whatever one posits *natural* to be.

Out of the closet and in trouble, these revisions of gender theory require rethinking the usefulness of the sex/gender system, its questionable foundations in either biology or constructionism, and the traditional ways of studying gender in communication. Some research now claims that gender is performed (Wood, 2005, 2006; Wood & Duck, in press), and performativity—as a theory of gender constitution, as strategy for its critique, and as political praxis—is a rich construct for returning the body to the study of interpersonal communication. A quick glance at almost any textbook in communication finds models drawn as not only de-gendered but disembodied: real people are replaced with boxes, arrows, circles, and silhouettes. The messy, material body of any act of communication— its relationality, dynamics, historical and cultural embeddedness, and emergent quality—is refigured as absent.

Performativity questions this figuration and demands attention to the body and its materiality: not as a site of biologically determined conditions that cause certain effects and not as a surface onto which culture writes gender. Both site and surface constructions of the material body foreclose questions of individual agency and the possibilities for cultural transformation. Instead, gender is a complex matrix of normative boundaries, constituted in discourse, materially embodied and performed, and mobilized through culture to secure political and social ends. Nor is gender a singular constitution, but gender is always articulated in, on, and through sexuality, race, ethnicity, class, age, and abilities.

Research on interpersonal communication, so aware of the messy ebullience of relationships—their stages, processes, tensions, norms, and dialectics—is well positioned to embrace performativity as a way to return materiality to relationality, sociality, and power. Returning the body, however, demands rethinking the body as situated in interpersonal research questions, methods, and findings. First, the body should be attended to but not be the foundation for claims about identity, gender, or communication. It should be seen as the center of interpersonal communication but not be fixed as causal, ahistorical, or reducible to measured variables. It should be accounted for as inescapably present but not overdetermined in theories of relationship development, instrumentality, or cognition. In short, bodies matter in research that investigates gender.

This chapter seeks to guide and to challenge investigations of gender in four ways. It (a) offers tentative definitions of the performative; (b) explores theatrical performance as a metaphor for the materialization, history, and politics of performing gender and notes where the metaphor breaks down; (c) surveys previous research on performativity; and (d) finally, challenges to interpersonal research on gender are offered.

◆ *Philosophical Traditions of the Performative*

Performativity defies definition. Even Butler (1990/1999), writing on the 10th anniversary of the publication of *Gender Trouble*, says,

> It is difficult to say precisely what performativity is not only because my own views on what "performativity" might mean have changed over time, most often in response to excellent criticisms, but because so many others have taken it up and given it their own formulations. (p. xiv)

In 1988, she defined gender as constituted in performance:

> Gender is in no way a stable identity or locus of agency from which various acts proceede [sic]; rather, it is an identity tenuously constituted in time—an identity instituted through a *stylized repetition of acts*. Further, gender is instituted through the stylization of the body and, hence, must be understood as the mundane way in which bodily gestures, movements, and enactments of various kinds constitute the illusion of an abiding gendered self. (p. 519)

Elin Diamond (1996) explains Butler's radical departure from both biology and constructionism: "Butler's point is not that gender is just an act, but that gender is materially performative: it 'is real only to the extent that it is performed.'" Through repeated enactments, gender is "both a doing—a performance that puts conventional gender attributes into possibly disruptive play—and a thing done—a pre-existing oppressive category" (pp. 4–5). And Bordwell (1998) contends that the constitution of gender through repetitive corporeal acts in time "recognizes that we are born into and must operate within a network of power relations not of our own making" (p. 375). Butler (1990/1999) locates the genesis of performativity in these power relations:

> I originally took my clue on how to read the performativity of gender from Jacques Derrida's reading of Kafka's "Before the Law." There the one who waits for the law, sits before the door of the law, attributes a certain force to the law for which one waits. The anticipation of an authoritative disclosure of meaning is the means by which that authority is attributed and installed: the anticipation conjures its object. I wondered whether we do not labor under a similar expectation concerning gender, that it operates as an interior essence that might be disclosed, an expectation that ends up producing the very phenomenon that it anticipates. (pp. xiv–xv)

Most explanations of the performativity of gender begin, not with Derrida, but with Austin's (1962/1975) *How to Do Things With Words*. In Lecture I, Austin introduces the performative as a class of utterances that "do not 'describe' or 'report' or constate anything at all, are not 'true or false.'" Instead, "the uttering of the sentence is, or is a part of, the doing of an action." With four simple examples ("I do," "I name this ship," "I give and bequeath my watch to my brother," and "I bet you sixpence it will rain tomorrow"), Austin isolates the performative, in which "the issuing of the utterance is the performing of an action" (p. 5).

In Lecture II, however, Austin (1962/1975) offers examples that are excluded from the performative:

> A performative utterance will, for example, be *in a peculiar way* hollow or void if said by an actor on the stage, or if introduced in a poem, or spoken in soliloquy. . . . Language in such circumstances is in special ways—intelligibly—used not seriously, but in ways *parasitic* upon its normal use—ways which fall under the doctrine of the *etiolations* of language. (p. 22)

Derrida turned Austin's examples of parasitic speech into the centerpiece for his theory of citationality. All language is cited, all language is always and already quoted and quotable. Derrida (1988) argues: "Every sign, linguistic or nonlinguistic, spoken or written . . . , in a small or large unit, can be cited, put between quotation marks; in so doing, it can break with every given context, engendering an infinity of new contexts in a manner which is absolutely illimitable" (p. 12). Theatrical utterances, then, are not outside ordinary language use but their use testifies to the condition of language as always already severed from context. Words do not refer to anything naturally, but are already unanchored from context, instead confirming an iterable model, not an original signature, event, or context.

For Butler, not only is gender a citation, an iteration of "ideals," but the body is subjected to norms—laws in Derrida's vocabulary—that are produced in speech acts. The laws depend on their citation and naturalization in repetition. The possibility of failure in speech acts—Austin's (1962/1975) "infelicities"—creates the space and agency for subversion of laws, for repetition, and for acts that do gender differently. Indeed, the terms *gender trouble, gender blending, transgender,* and *cross-gender* are already suggestive of the possibility "that gender has a way of moving beyond that naturalized binary" of masculine and feminine and their citational norms (Butler, 2004, pp. 42–43).

◆ Theater as Entrée to Performativity

If Austin, Derrida, and Butler are steeped in philosophical traditions, assumptions, and debates that may make it difficult to relate their arguments to some interpersonal research, the theater can be a productive space to engage an understanding of gender as performance. On stage, foundational approaches to body (as natural, as

biological, as socially constructed) are not taken for granted. The theater constantly tests the audience's faith in any biological or socially constructed truth under the costumes and the greasepaint. On stage and in life, gender is a matrix of boundaries—constituted in discourse, materially embodied and performed, and mobilized through culture to secure political and social ends. Theatrical performances are a fruitful starting point for understanding three interrelated concepts of performativity: (a) the materialization of bodies in performance, (b) the embeddedness of bodies in histories of performance conventions, and (c) the potential for political efficacy in and through performance.

BODIES MATERIALIZE IN PERFORMANCE

Butler (1988) reminds readers that the dramatic is how performers "materialize" a set of historical possibilities in and through their bodies on stage: "To do, to dramatize, to reproduce" are "some of the elementary structures of embodiment" (p. 521). For Thompson (2003), "gender identity—or any other kind of identity—is not something that you *have,* but something that you *do*—or, at least, something that you have 'only' by doing it again and again and again" (p. 132). The materialization of the body on the stage depends on presence—physical and discursive. Characters in a play do not exist until they appear onstage or are spoken of by others. This process of materialization of bodies—raced, gendered, classed, abled, disabled, and sexualized—is central to performativity.

Bodies on stage are always produced by and change through history. So actors always perform within a set of proscribed historical conventions and directorial cues for how the body ought to move, gesture, and articulate itself on stage. Butler (1988) extends the theatrical metaphor to gender: "Just as a script may be enacted in various ways, and just as the play requires both text and interpretation, so the gendered body acts its part in a culturally restricted corporeal space and enacts interpretations within the confines of already existing directives" (p. 526). The production of gender—in time and space—is a repetitive enactment of stylized acts that are ongoing.

This materialization is not about self-display or self-creation but is a reconstitution of social reality. Following Bourdieu (1995), Butler (1997) argues that "the body is not a mere positive datum, but the repository or the site of an incorporated history" (p. 152). According to Sedgwick (2003), these repositories are produced, for gay and lesbian identities, as sites of shame—at once powerfully visceral, beyond willful control, but experienced through bodies and constitutive of social reality:

> Shame floods into being as a moment, a disruptive moment, in a circuit of identity-constituting identificatory communication. Indeed, like a stigma, shame is itself a form of communication. Blazons of shame, the "fallen face" with eyes down and head averted—and, to a lesser extent, the blush—are semaphores of trouble and at the same time of a desire to reconstitute the interpersonal bridge. (p. 36)

Gender identity—constituted both inside and outside normative boundaries—is "a performative accomplishment compelled by social sanction and taboo" (Butler, 1988, p. 520). The performative, then, is a theory of material constitution and a critical strategy for acknowledging and critiquing the weight of this materiality on bodies.

◆ Repetitive Sites of Incorporated History

Theatrical events are public, with times and places for the performance carefully demarked and observed. Traditional theater requires a script to be memorized, rehearsed, and enacted anew in each performance. But scripts are starting places for interpretation, not fixed repositories of meaning. Despite the temporal and spatial specificity of a performance, performers, directors, and scripts are always part of the ongoing history of the theater. Butler (1988) draws parallels to the performance of gender: "The act that one does, the act that one performs, is, in a sense, an act that has been going on before one arrived on the scene. Hence, gender is an act which has been rehearsed, much as a script survives the particular actors who make use of it, but which requires individual actors in order to be actualized and reproduced as reality once again" (p. 526). In *Undoing Gender,* Butler (2004) continues to use a theatrical metaphor: "(Gender) is a practice of improvisation within a scene of constraints. Moreover, one does not 'do' one's gender alone. One is always 'doing' with or for another, even if the other is only imaginary" (p. 1).

The repetition required to produce gender is a double bind: The iterated performance is always risky. Despite an intention to perform gender, race, or sexuality as parody, subversion, or transgression, that iteration can continue to produce the harmful, violent, reinscriptions of effects it names. Tulloch (1999) summarizes this doubleness of "performativity as not only being constitutive of power but at the same time being implicated in that which it opposes" (p. 66). In speech acts, "when and how does a term like 'queer' become subject to an affirmative resignification for some when a term like 'nigger,' despite some recent efforts at reclamation, appears capable of only reinscribing its pain?" (Butler, 1993, p. 222).

These questions are difficult to answer, for the limits of critical reappropriation and resignification, especially on the stage, are all too real. But the stage metaphor enables critical examination of the production and relationships of power that produce those artifacts. Diamond (1996) reminds us that "to study performance is not to focus on completed forms, but to become aware of performance as itself a contested space, where meanings and desires are generated, occluded, and of course multiply interpreted" (p. 4). How bodies come to "bear meanings" in their material and cultural production shifts the question from what is or is not constituted to how these "theories are acted out with consequences" (Alexander, 2004a, p. 648). Performativity, then, is a theory of the relationship between materiality and history and a critical strategy for intervening in the production of that relationship.

◆ *Political Efficacy in and Through Performance*

The theater has long been a place to enact changes in the body politic—from Brecht's learning plays and Boal's Theatre of the Oppressed to Grotowski's Poor Theater. The visibility of bodies in the theater is at the heart of much political activism. U.S. history is peppered with examples of political coalitions making claims for social justice through theatrical tactics: the 1970s Black Power and Black-is-beautiful marches and sit-ins (Elam & Krasner, 2001); *actos,* the one-act performances created and staged by organizers of migrant field workers in California (Sandoval-Sanchez, 1999); Take-Back-the-Night marches that began in the 1970s; Confront the Rapist at Work, the NOW protests staged by feminist organizations (Fraser, 1999; Hennessy, 1995); and the contemporary performance work of the Guerrilla Girls and Radical Cheerleaders. Queer activism makes tremendous use of the visible, with the kiss-ins of Queer Nation, die-ins by ACT UP, and gay pride parades across the country (Case, 1996). Nor is the left the only end of the political spectrum to make use of visibility tactics. Peggy Phelan's (1993) analysis of Operation Rescue, the anti-abortion group, takes seriously their "shrewd understanding . . . of making a spectacle *for* the sake of publicity" (p. 130).

This theatricality, rooted in political enactment, analysis, and change, is not performativity. It is a site for exploring performativity as "the process by which

cultural norms are cited and reproduced" (Bordwell, 1998, p. 375). For Diamond (1996), "as soon as performativity comes to rest on *a* performance, questions of embodiment, of social relations, of ideological interpellations, of emotional and political effects, all become discussable" (p. 5).

Although theatrical metaphors are valuable points for understanding performativity as material production, as historical sedimentation, and as political strategy, they break down in two important ways. Performativity leaves the theater in a) its radical critique of the subject and b) its attention to all-too-real effects that are not at all pretend.

◆ *There Is No Subject Behind the Curtain/Under the Mask*

Most modernist conceptions of identity assume a coherent, interior, stable, and whole center—a self that exists prior to that self's expression in body and words. Most contemporary U.S. acting theory assumes likewise, and the job of acting is to outwardly manifest another's interior identity (Thompson, 2003). The theater, then, becomes a place where we can safely assume the stability of the subject. Actors are just acting. Performativity, however, critiques the stability, production, and reality of the subject. For Case (1996), "it strips the mask from the masquerade that would still retain an actor/subject behind the show" (p. 13). There is no subject—on stage or off—behind the mask. Instead, the subject is an effect produced through discursive and material regimes.

Gender masks not a "true" self but its construction. The performance of gender continually hides its construction as performers and audience collude in its fiction. For Butler (1988), the theatrical convention of the willing suspension of disbelief takes on a radical kind of belief: "If gender is instituted through acts which are internally discontinuous, then the appearance of substance is precisely that, a constructed identity, a performative accomplishment which the mundane social audience, including the actors themselves, come to believe and to perform in the mode of belief" (p. 520).

Belief in gender as binary, natural, given, and readable is rooted in the fiction of an inner "truth" of a gendered self that is outwardly and visibly expressed. A transvestite on a bus—no longer safely ensconced on stage where illusion is understood—is Butler's (1988) teaching example of our faith in and collusion regarding a true gender identity under the clothes: "If the 'reality' of gender is constituted by the performance itself, then there is no recourse to an essential and unrealized 'sex' or 'gender' which gender performances ostensibly express. Indeed, the transvestite's gender is as fully real as anyone whose performance complies with social expectations" (p. 527). Moving from drag to transsexuality, this faith and collusion in discrete gender categories and in the bimorphism of male and female bodies is even more shaken. How are we to read a preoperative, transitional, or postoperative, transsexual body?

◆ Performing Under Duress and Danger/Disease/Death

The theater is also a place where audiences can safely assume, "This is *just* a play." On stage, the "trouble" of gender is often comedic. The metaphor of the theater breaks down with performativity's notion that some bodies more than others perform under duress and never to comic effect. Orientalist hegemonies write exotic, erotic, and "ineffable foreignness" on Asian bodies (Kondo, 1997, p. 9). African Americans are accused of acting white in a violent resignification that is very much about inclusions and exclusions, complicity and positionality (Alexander, 2004a; Lei, 2003). Acting straight is a performance where "passing" (for straight) is a complex social practice that relies on codes of intelligibility (Robinson,

1994). Each offstage performance under duress brings punishment, social sanctions, and taboos that are all too real. Gil-Gomez (2000) offers the poignant reminder that "the gender trouble that Butler advocates can easily become gender danger for lesbians of color; danger that affects them financially, emotionally, spiritually and physically" (p. xix). Real bodies, real risks, real effects offstage mark the performative as dangerous business.

For queer theorists Parker and Sedgwick (1995), the distinction between the safety of the theater and the reality of the bus has little purchase. Interested in the relationship between language that says and language that does, they explore the performative utterance "I am queer" for producing the effects it names, especially in the U.S. military's policy of Don't Ask, Don't Tell in the 1990s. The complex relationships among speech acts, identity, and the effects produced by naming are at the heart of queer theories of the performative. Nor are these effects limited to stages or buses. Sedgwick ("Gender Criticism") writes:

> I almost never put "gay and lesbian" in the title of undergraduate gay and lesbian studies courses. . . . To ask students to mark their transcripts permanently with so much as the name of this subject of study would have unpredictably disabling consequences for them in the future: the military, the churches, the CIA, and much of the psychoanalytic establishment . . . are still unblinking about wanting to exclude suspected lesbians and gay men. (¶ 1)

Boundaries of exclusion and the regulatory schemas that produce, in their citation, their subjects and effects take queer theory to the streets in a charged relationship between theory and praxis with consequential, material effects.

"Perhaps it is no accident that the term 'queer performativity' grew up around acts of dying," writes Sue-Ellen Case (1996, p. 148). ACT UP and AIDS activism returned the dying body to the medical and state institutions that denied them. Gender is a complex matrix of boundaries of inclusion and exclusion that deems some bodies worthy, legitimate, and intelligible. The political effects of these constituted bodies are all too real.

◆ Communication Research and Performativity

General discussions of performativity in communication studies are rare, except for essays by Strine (1998) and Pollock (1995, 1998a). Most research mobilizes performativity for its critical efficacy in the service of other projects. This research can be broadly placed into five domains: narrative, body, performance criticism, performative writing, and pedagogy. Interpersonal communication research, with its contemporary interests in qualitative, ethnographic, narrative, and critical approaches to relationships and their dynamism, is well-equipped to add to the study of gender and its performances in these five domains and in new ones as well.

NARRATIVE

For the many interpersonal scholars interested in narrative (Bochner & Ellis, 1992; Bochner, Ellis, & Tillmann-Healy, 1997; Orbuch, 1997; Shank-Krusciewitz & Wood, 2001; Vangelisti, Crumley, & Baker, 1999; Veroff, Sutherland, Chadiha, & Ortega, 1993; Wood, 2000, 2001, 2004), performativity can anchor their research in body, history, and power. Langellier (1999), for example, mobilizes performativity to account for personal narrative as "a site where the social is articulated, structured, and struggled over" (p. 128). She maintains that identities created in personal narratives are always "situated, embodied, and material—stories of the body told through the body, which make

cultural conflict concrete and accessible" (p. 129). Scholars who have taken up Langellier's (1998) call for performativity's political usefulness to personal narrative include Spry (2000), Alexander (2000), and Carver (2003).

Langellier and Peterson's *Storytelling in Daily Life* (2004) utilizes performativity as a theory and strategy to critique storytelling in families as material practices that constitute and produce effects—both normative and transgressive. Pollock's *Telling Bodies/ Performing Birth* (1999) engages birth stories for the "convergence of performativity and maternity . . . in making history subject to the maternal body performing itself" (p. 10). In being told and retold, birth narratives are performative in "the endless (re)iteration of competing maternal norms" to which many of us are compelled (Pollock, 1999, p. 40).

Written narratives explored through performativity include Bennett's (2003) analyses of ex-gays and lesbians in the so-called reparative therapy movement of Exodus International, a Christian-right organization dedicated to "curing" homosexuality. Masequesmay (2003) details the discursive-identity work of a support group for Vietnamese lesbians, bisexual women, and female-to-male transgendered people.

THE MATERIAL BODY

Much of the communication research that takes performativity as a model for identity focuses on the body and its materialization within discourse. Sloop (2000) explores how both essentialism and social construction are mobilized in the accounts in the mass media and the medical community of a case of infant gender "reassignment." Jordan (2003) explores identities of temporary workers in texts that enable resistant labor practices. Grindstaff's (2003) critical rhetoric project explores gay marriage debates and S/M gay culture as both scenes of heteronormative power and sites of potential resistance to it. Nor are communication discourses excused from performativity's critique. Lovaas (2003) writes a stinging assessment of textbooks on nonverbal communication for their rigid essentialism of gendered bodies, pervasive heterosexism, and absence of queer subjectivities. Owen (2003) and Gingrich-Philbrook (1998) critique the List-serv responses by scholars to Corey and Nakayama's "Sextext" (1997) for their heteronormative policing of the boundaries of communication studies.

Given performativity's emphasis on intelligibility of bodies—the codes and conventions that make certain bodies worthy and legitimate—it is not surprising that scholars in disability studies and health communication find performativity particularly valuable. Disabled bodies realized performatively are the subjects of Kuppers's *Disability and Contemporary Performance* (2004) and Ferris (1998) in "Uncovery to Recovery." Ill bodies constituted performatively are the subjects of Bordwell's (1998) critical engagement with a multimedia dance concert about living with terminal illness, Langellier's (2001) analysis of one breast cancer story (re)marked on the body; and Baglia's (2005) analysis of Pfizer's construction of erectile dysfunction and masculinity.

Communication scholars are at the forefront of demonstrating performativity's utility for understanding bodies of color. Performativity that masks whiteness as normative and as readable is explored in Warren's *Performing Purity* (2003). Performative practices in African American culture are explored for appropriation and divergent political agendas in Johnson's *Appropriating Blackness* (2003a).

PERFORMANCE CRITICISM

When performativity "lands on" a specific performance, exposing naturalized codes and conventions of gender, race/ethnicity, and sexuality, analysis and critique of specific performances provide entrée for understanding that performance and performativity. Performances that are always double-edged include gay identity on stage (Kuppers, 1998; Gingrich-Philbrook, 1997; Peterson, 2000a, 200b); policed hetero/homosexual black masculinity in performances by Eddie Murphy, Damon Wayans, and David Alan Grier (Johnson, 2003b); Shylock in *The Merchant of Venice* (Scheie, 1997); Pee-Wee Herman (Slagle, 2003); Eva Peron in *Evita* (Ellison & Lockford, 2004); staged whiteness (Jackson, 1998; Warren & Kilgard, 2001); women's and men's bodies in daily life and on stage (Lockford, 2004; Stucky & Daughton, 2003); Matthew Bourne's "queered" *Swan Lake* (Drummond, 2003); Mary Kay cosmetics representatives' feminine "aesthetics of excess" (Waggoner, 1997); and Dublin's James Joyce festival (Spangler, 2002). Performance criticism in these works asks whether resistance and parody are possible without reiterating harm and violence. What are the limits of performativity for reimagining bodies? Critical limits are especially intriguing in Sikes's (2002) analysis of humanness and subjectivity in the human genome project and in Chvasta's (2003) exploration of bodies in cyberspace.

PERFORMATIVE WRITING

Performative writing, like performativity, questions the links between coherent, stable signs and their referents to expose the naturalized fictions of unified writers, readers, histories, or meanings available in texts. Performative writing undoes and deconstructs itself—never assuming that language can capture or reflect a totality. Pollock (1998b) provides six tentative directions: evocation, metonymy, subjectivity, nervousness, citationality, and consequence. As method, performative writing explores how textual practices can embody performative practices (Miller & Pelias, 2001; Pelias, 1999) and how writing and research is located within contested spaces of cultural production (Pollock, 1998a). Lockford (2004) and Jones (2002) utilize performative writing as an ethnographic and autoethnographic strategy for analysis and critique.

Kennerly (2002) uses performative writing to explore roadside shrines as performances situated within multiple discourses. Corey and Nakayama's infamous "Sextext" (1997) and "Nextext" (Nakayama and Corey, 2003) enlist performative writing to write "between the language of academia and the language of sex" (1997, p. 58). Spry (1997, 2000) makes use of performative writing to evoke her experiences during her mother's struggle with cancer. Bowman (2000) explores the history of the outlaw John Dillinger to demonstrate how performative writing forces its readers and writers to rethink both law-and-order and disciplinary boundaries.

PEDAGOGY

Performativity is a valuable lens for research on pedagogy, for it accounts for the ways that body, history, and power are doubly articulated in classrooms, which risk marginalizing and entrenching subjectivities while offering space for alternative identities and identification. These researchers explore the crisis of teaching within institutional restraints (Alexander 2004b; Jackson 2004); how schools can discipline and create subjects as sexualized, racialized, and gendered (Alexander 2004b; Alexander & Warren, 2002; Cooks, 2003; Gingrich-Philbrook, 2002; Warren 2001a, 2001b); and how performance is a technique in the classroom for exposing naturalized categories (Stucky & Tomell-Preso, 2004; Warren, 2001a; Warren & Kilgard, 2001).

◆ Research Challenges for Interpersonal Research in/on/through Gender

Performativity refigures bodies: female and male are not sex attributes that arise naturally from essentialized cores of identity; femininity and masculinity are not social roles constructed by cultures on bodies. Male/female and femininity/masculinity are discursive and social constructions that reaffirm and reinstate the binary, hierarchical, and heteronormative categories that performativity seeks to expose and to critique. Gender is a complex matrix of normative boundaries—constituted in discourse, materially embodied and performed, and mobilized through culture to secure political and social ends—always articulated in/on/through desire, race, ethnicity, class, age, and abilities. These bounded matrices, navigated by individuals, are open to scrutiny by interpersonal researchers.

This scrutiny depends on refusing both causal links and assumed correspondences between demographic categories (male/female, sexual orientation, socioeconomic status, race/ethnicity, age, abilities and disabilities) and the communication interactions studied. With performativity as a foundation, no longer does the box "M" or "F" provide *a priori* evidence of gendered communication styles, strategies, or perceptions, nor do the boxes stand as blank slates for inscription. This scrutiny depends on shifting notions of interpersonal contexts, participants, and processes to account for bodies as always culturally invested, historically specific, and materially performed. With performativity as a foundation, no longer is "gender is learned" a satisfactory explanation for the weight of history on minority communities, expanding technologies of reproduction, or the institutions—church, state, education, medicine, or family—that enforce those histories. And, finally, this scrutiny depends on politics to move beyond the question, "What is a good relationship?" to ask, "How are gender boundaries inclusionary and exclusionary? What rewards are reaped and costs paid in the lives of people? With performativity as a foundation for research, political structures and commitments can be more thoroughly interrogated, and the material effects of the research enhanced.

All paradigmatic shifts in approaches to the study of gender (or any other phenomenon) are uncomfortable: biological determinism, social construction, and performativity represent sea changes in how scholars ground claims about gender. Many will no doubt be wary of shifting premises. As Condit (2000) claims, "Scholars in communication have often been seduced by the approaches and methods of other disciplines. . . . Interpersonal scholars have often been tempted to imitate psychologists. Rhetoricians have often sought to imitate philosophers, literary theorists, or historians" (p. 23). Performativity, because of its complex genesis in gender theory, philosophy, and queer theory, may risk these imitations. At the same time, the American Psychological Association took the risk of theorizing differently and engaging in political critique of their own entrenched practices: *Gender Trouble* was one of the prompts that instigated reassessment and removal of homosexuality from the *DSM-IV's* (*Diagnostic and Statistical Manual of Mental Disorders,* 4th ed.) categories of sexual disorders (Butler, 1990/1999, p. xvii).

Interpersonal communication researchers might benefit from taking a similar risk: departing from primarily or exclusively cognitive foundational claims to acknowledge the body as materially performed and to bring that to bear on questions, methods, and findings to better account for power structures that produce subjects. Interpersonal communication scholars can enrich their work on gender, relationships, intimacy, disclosure, dialectics, and conflict by recognizing and studying human communication as performances that range from the mundane to the monumental, that are always materially consequential, and that are productive of and challenging to relations of power. Such work requires research questions and methods that expand notions of what counts as gender, what constitutes research, and how the matrix of boundaries within communication creates knowledge.

Bell, in the introduction to *Performativity and Belonging* (1999), provides an important caveat and direction for interpersonal research:

An emphasis on performativity, however, does not mean an assumption of fluid, forever changing identities. Indeed, taking the temporal performative nature of identities as a theoretical premise means that more than ever, one needs to question how identities continue to be produced, embodied and performed, effectively, passionately and with social and political consequence. (p. 2)

◆ References

Alexander, B. K. (2000). Skin Flint (or, The Garbage Man's Kid): A generative autobiographical performance based on Tami Spry's *Tattoo Stories. Text and Performance Quarterly, 20,* 97–114.

Alexander, B. K. (2004a). *Black Skin/White Masks:* The performative sustainability of whiteness (with apologies to Frantz Fanon). *Qualitative Inquiry, 10,* 647–672.

Alexander, B. K. (2004b). Racializing identity: Performance, pedagogy, and regret. *Cultural Studies/Critical Methodologies, 4,* 12–27.

Alexander, B. K., & Warren, J. T. (2002). The materiality of bodies: Critical reflections on pedagogy, politics, and positionality. *Communication Quarterly, 50,* 328–43.

Austin, J. L. (1975). *How to do things with words* (2nd ed.). Cambridge, MA: Harvard University Press. (Originally published 1962)

Baglia, J. (2005). *The Viagra ad venture: Masculinity, media, and performance of sexual health.* New York: Peter Lang.

Bell, V. (1999). Performativity and belonging: An introduction. In V. Bell (Ed.), *Performativity and belonging* (pp. 1–10). London: Sage.

Bennett, J. A. (2003). Love me gender: Normative homosexuality and "ex-gay" performativity in reparative therapy narratives. *Text and Performance Quarterly, 23,* 331–352.

Bochner, A., & Ellis, C. (1992). Personal narrative as a social approach to interpersonal communication. *Communication Theory, 2,* 65–72.

Bochner, A., Ellis, C., & Tillmann-Healy, L. (1997). Relationships as stories. In S. W. Duck (Ed.), *Handbook of personal relationships: Theory, research, and interventions* (2nd ed., pp. 107–224). Chichester, UK: Wiley.

Bordwell, M. (1998). Dancing with death: Performativity and "undiscussable" bodies in *Still/Here. Text and Performance Quarterly, 18,* 369–379.

Bourdieu, P. (1995). *Free exchange* (R. Johnson & H. Haacke, Trans.). Stanford, CA: Stanford University Press.

Bowman, M. (2000). Killing Dillinger: A mystery. *Text and Performance Quarterly, 20,* 341–374.

Butler, J. (1988). Performative acts and gender constitution: An essay in phenomenology and feminist thought. *Theatre Journal, 40,* 519–531.

Butler, J. (1999). *Gender trouble: Feminism and the subversion of identity.* New York: Routledge. (Originally published 1990)

Butler, J. (1993). *Bodies that matter: On the discursive limits of "sex."* New York: Routledge.

Butler, J. (1997). *Excitable speech: A politics of the performative.* New York: Routledge.

Butler, J. (2004). *Undoing gender.* New York: Routledge.

Carver, M. H. (2003). Risky business: Exploring women's autobiography and performance. In L. C. Miller, J. Taylor, & M. H. Carver (Eds.), *Voices made flesh: Performing women's autobiography* (pp. 15–29). Madison: University of Wisconsin Press.

Case, S. E. (1996). *The domain-matrix: Performing lesbian at the end of print culture.* Bloomington, IN: Indiana University Press.

Chvasta, M. (2003). Screening bodies: Performance and technology. *performance/text/technology, 1.* Retrieved October 15, 2004, from www.cyberdiva.org/PTT/index.html

Condit, C. M. (2000). Culture and biology in human communication: Toward a multicausal model. *Communication Education, 49,* 7–24.

Cooks, L. (2003). Pedagogy, performance, and positionality: Teaching about whiteness in interracial communication. *Communication Education, 52,* 245–257.

Corey, F. C., & Nakayama, T. (1997). Sextext. *Text and Performance Quarterly, 17,* 58–68.

Derrida, J. (1988). *Limited Inc.* Evanston, IL: Northwestern University Press.

Diamond, E. (1996). Introduction. In E. Diamond (Ed.), *Performance and cultural politics* (pp. 1–15). New York: Routledge.

Drummond, K. G. (2003). The queering of *Swan Lake:* A new male gaze for the performance of sexual desire. In G. A. Yep, K. E. Lovaas, & J. P. Elia (Eds.), *Queer theory and communication: From disciplining queers to queering the discipline(s)* (pp. 235–255). New York: Harrington Park.

Elam, H. J. Jr., & Krasner, D. (Eds.). (2001). *African American performance and theater history: A critical reader.* Oxford, UK: Oxford University Press.

Ellison, M., & Lockford, L. (2004). Power and personality as commodity in *Evita. Theatre Annual, 57,* 69–94.

Ferris, J. (1998). Uncovery to recovery: Reclaiming one man's body on a nude photo shoot. *Michigan Quarterly Review, 37,* 502–518.

Fraser, M. (1999). Classing queer: Politics in competition. *Theory, culture, and society, 16,* 107–131.

Gil-Gomez, E. M. (2000). *Performing la mestiza: Textual representations of lesbians of color and the negotiation of identities.* New York: Garland.

Gingrich-Philbrook, C. (1997). *Refreshment. Text and Performance Quarterly, 17,* 352–360.

Gingrich-Philbrook, C. (1998). Disciplinary violation as gender violation. *Communication Theory, 7,* 203–220.

Gingrich-Philbrook, C. (2002). The queer performance that will have been. In N. Stucky & C. Wimmer (Eds.), *Teaching performance studies* (pp. 69–85). Carbondale: Southern Illinois University Press.

Grindstaff, D. (2003). Queering marriage: An ideographic interrogation of heteronormative subjectivity. In G. A. Yep, K. E. Lovaas, & J. P. Elia (Eds.), *Queer theory and communication: From disciplining queers to queering the discipline(s)* (pp. 257–275). New York: Harrington Park.

Hennessy, R. (1995). Queer visibility in commodity culture. In L. Nicholson & S. Seidman (Eds.), *Social postmodernism: Beyond identity politics* (pp. 142–183). Cambridge, UK: Cambridge University Press.

Jackson, S. (1998). *White Noises:* On performing white, on writing performance. *Drama Review, 42,* 49–55.

Jackson, S. (2004). *Professing performance: Theatre in the academy from philology to performativity.* Cambridge, UK: Cambridge University Press.

Johnson, E. P. (2003a). *Appropriating blackness: Performance and the politics of authenticity.* Durham, NC: Duke University Press.

Johnson, E. P. (2003b). The specter of the black fag: Parody, blackness, and hetero/homosexual b(r)others. In G. A. Yep, K. E. Lovaas, & J. P. Elia (Eds.), *Queer theory and communication: From disciplining queers to queering the discipline(s)* (pp. 217–234). New York: Harrington Park.

Jones, S. H. (2002). The way we were, are, and might be: Torch singing as autoethnography. In A. P. Bochner & C. Ellis (Eds.), *Ethnographically speaking* (pp. 44–56). Walnut Creek, CA: AltaMira.

Jordan, J. W. (2003). Sabotage or performed compliance: Rhetorics of resistance in temp worker discourse. *Quarterly Journal of Speech, 89,* 19–40.

Kennerly, R. (2002). Getting messy: In the field and at the crossroads with roadside shrines. *Text and Performance Quarterly, 22,* 229–360.

Kondo, D. (1997). *About face: Performing race in fashion and theater.* New York: Routledge.

Kuppers, P. (1998). Vanishing in your face: Embodiment and representation in lesbian dance performance. *Journal of Lesbian Studies, 2,* 47–63.

Kuppers, P. (2004). *Disability and contemporary performance: Bodies on edge.* New York: Routledge.

Langellier, K. M. (1998). Voiceless bodies, bodiless voices: The future of personal narrative performance. In S. J. Daily (Ed.), *The future of performance studies: Visions and revisions* (pp. 207–213). Annandale, VA: National Communication Association.

Langellier, K. M. (1999). Personal narrative, performance, and performativity: Two or three things I know for sure. *Text and Performance Quarterly, 19,* 125–144.

Langellier, K. M. (2001). You're marked: Breast cancer, tattoo, and the narrative performance of identity. In J. Brockmeier & D. Carbaugh (Eds.), *Narrative and identity: Studies in autobiography, self, and culture* (pp. 145–184). Philadelphia: John Benjamins.

Langellier, K. M., & Peterson, E. E. (2004). *Storytelling in daily life: Performing narrative.* Philadelphia: Temple University Press.

Lei, J. L. (2003). (Un)necessary toughness: Those "loud Black girls" and those "quiet Asian boys." *Anthropology and Education Quarterly, 32,* 158–181.

Lockford, L. (2004). *Performing femininity: Rewriting gender identity.* Walnut Creek, CA: AltaMira Press.

Lovaas, K. E. (2003). Speaking to silence: Toward queering nonverbal communication. In G. A. Yep, K. E. Lovaas, & J. P. Elia (Eds.), *Queer theory and communication: From disciplining queers to queering the discipline(s)* (pp. 87–107). New York: Harrington Park.

Masequesmay, G. (2003). Negotiating multiple identities in a queer Vietnamese support group. In G. A. Yep, K. E. Lovaas, & J. P. Elia (Eds.), *Queer theory and communication: From disciplining queers to queering the discipline(s)* (pp. 193–215). New York: Harrington Park.

Miller, L., & Pelias, R. (Eds.). (2001). *The green window: Proceedings of the Giant City conference on performative writing.* Carbondale: Southern Illinois University.

Nakayama, T., & Corey, F. C. (2003). Nextext. In G. A. Yep, K. E. Lovaas, & J. P. Elia (Eds.), *Queer theory and communication:*

From disciplining queers to queering the discipline(s) (pp. 319–334). New York: Harrington Park.

Orbuch, T. (1997). People's accounts count: The sociology of accounts. *Annual Review of Sociology, 23,* 455–478.

Owen, A. S. (2003). Disciplining "Sextext": Queers, fears, and communication studies. In G. A. Yep, K. E. Lovaas, & J. P. Elia (Eds.), *Queer theory and communication: From disciplining queers to queering the discipline(s)* (pp. 297–317). New York: Harrington Park.

Parker, A., & Sedgwick, E. K. (1995). Introduction. In A. Parker & E. K. Sedgwick (Eds.), *Performativity and performance* (pp. 1–18). New York: Routledge.

Pelias, R. J. (1999). *Writing performance: Poeticizing the researcher's body.* Carbondale: Southern Illinois University Press.

Peterson, E. E. (2000a). Narrative identity in a solo performance: Craig Gingrich Philbrook's "The First Time." *Narrative Inquiry, 10,* 229–251.

Peterson, E. E. (2000b). One more first time: A response to Katz and Shotter. *Narrative Inquiry, 10,* 475–481.

Phelan, P. (1993). *Unmarked: The politics of performance.* New York: Routledge.

Pollock, D. (1995). Performativity. In C. N. Davidson & L. Wagner-Martin (Eds.), *The Oxford companion to women's writing in the United States* (pp. 657–658). Oxford, UK: Oxford University Press.

Pollock, D. (1998a). A response to Dwight Conquergood's essay "Beyond the text: Towards a performative cultural politics." In S. J. Dailey (Ed.), *The future of performance studies: Visions and revisions* (pp. 37–46). Annandale, VA: National Communication Association.

Pollock, D. (1998b). Performing writing. In P. Phelan & J. Lane (Eds.), *The ends of performance* (pp. 73–103). New York: New York University Press.

Pollock, D. (1999). *Telling bodies/performing birth.* New York: Columbia University Press.

Robinson, A. (1994). It takes one to know one: Passing and communities of common interest. *Critical Inquiry, 20,* 715–736.

Rubin, G. (1975). The traffic in women: Notes on the "political economy" of sex. In R. R. Reiter (Ed.), *Toward an anthropology of women.* New York: Monthly Review Press.

Sandoval-Sanchez, A. (1999). *Jose, can you see? Latinos on and off Broadway.* Madison: University of Wisconsin Press.

Scheie, T. (1997). "Questionable terms": Shylock, Celine's *L'Eglise,* and the performative. *Text and Performance Quarterly, 17,* 153–169.

Sedgwick, E. K. (1990). *Epistemology of the closet.* Berkeley: University of California Press.

Sedgwick, E. K. (2003). *Touching feeling: Affect, pedagogy, performativity.* Durham, NC: Duke University Press.

Sedgwick, E. K. (n.d.). Gender criticism: What gender isn't. Retrieved September 24, 2004, from www.duke.edu/~sedgwic/WRITING/gender.htm

Shank-Krusciewitz, E., & Wood, J. T. (2001). "He was our child from the moment we walked in that room": Entrance stories of adoptive parents. *Journal of Social and Personal Relationships, 18,* 785–803.

Sikes, A. W. (2002). The performing genome: Genetics and the rearticulation of the human. *Text and Performance Quarterly, 22,* 163–180.

Slagle, R. A. (2003). Queer criticism and sexual normativity: The case of Pee-Wee Herman. In G. A. Yep, K. E. Lovaas, & J. P. Elia (Eds.), *Queer theory and communication: From disciplining queers to queering the discipline(s)* (pp. 129–146). New York: Harrington Park.

Sloop, J. M. (2000). "A van with a bar and a bed": Ritualized gender norms in the John/Joan case. *Text and Performance Quarterly, 20,* 130–149.

Spangler, M. (2002). A fadograph of a yestern scene: Performance promising authenticity in Dublin's Bloomsday. *Text and Performance Quarterly, 22,* 120–137.

Spry, T. (1997). *Skins:* A daughter's (re)construction of cancer: A performative autobiography. *Text and Performance Quarterly, 17,* 361–365.

Spry, T. (2000). *Tattoo Stories:* A postscript to *Skins. Text and Performance Quarterly, 20,* 84–96.

Strine, M. S. (1998). Articulating performance/performativity: Disciplinary tasks and the contingencies of practice. In J. S. Trent (Ed.), *Communication: Views from the helm for the 21st century* (pp. 312–317). Boston: Allyn & Bacon.

Stucky, N., & Daughton, S. (2003). The body present: Reporting everyday life performance. In P. Glenn, C. LeBaron, & J. Mandelbaum (Eds.), *Studies in language and social interaction* (pp. 479–491). Mahwah, NJ: Lawrence Erlbaum.

Stucky, N., & Tomell-Presto, J. (2004). Acting and movement training as a pedagogy of the body. In G. S. Medford & A. Fliotsos (Eds.), *Theatre pedagogy* (pp. 103–124). New York: Palgrave Macmillan.

Thompson, D. (2003). "Is race a trope?" Anna Deavere Smith and the question of racial performativity. *African American Review, 37*, 127–138.

Tulloch, J. (1999). *Performing culture: Stories of expertise and the everyday.* Thousand Oaks, CA: Sage.

Vangelisti, A., Crumley, L., & Baker, J. (1999). Family portraits: Stories as standards for family relationships. *Journal of Social and Personal Relationships, 16*, 335–368.

Veroff, J., Sutherland, L., Chadiha, L., & Ortega, R. (1993). Newlyweds tell their stories: A narrative method for assessing marital experience. *Journal of Social and Personal Relationships, 10*, 437–457.

Waggoner, C. (1997). The emancipatory potential of feminine masquerade in Mary Kay cosmetics. *Text and Performance Quarterly, 17*, 256–272.

Warren, J. T. (2001a). Doing whiteness: On the performative dimensions of race in the classroom. *Communication Education, 50*, 91–108.

Warren, J. T. (2001b). The social drama of a "rice burner:" A (re)constitution of whiteness. *Western Journal of Communication, 65*, 184–205.

Warren, J. T. (2003). *Performing purity: Whiteness, pedagogy, and the reconstitution of power.* New York: Peter Lang.

Warren, J. T., & Kilgard, A. K. (2001). Staging *Stain Upon the Snow:* Performance as a critical enfleshment of whiteness. *Text and Performance Quarterly, 21*, 261–276.

Wood, J. T. (2000). "That wasn't the real him": Women's dissociation of violence from the men who enact it. *Qualitative Research in Review, 1*, 1–7.

Wood, J. T. (2001). The normalization of violence in heterosexual romantic relationships: Women's narratives of love and violence. *Journal of Social and Personal Relationships, 18*, 239–261.

Wood, J. T. (2004). Monsters and victims: Male felons' accounts of intimate partner violence. *Journal of Social and Personal Research, 21*, 555–576.

Wood, J. T. (2005). *Gendered lives* (6th ed.). Belmont, CA: Wadsworth.

Wood, J. T. (2006). *Communication in our lives* (4th ed.). Belmont, CA: Wadsworth.

Wood, J. T., & Duck, S. W. (Eds.). (in press). *Composing relationships: Communication in everyday life.* Belmont, CA: Wadsworth.

2

GENDERED COMMUNICATION IN DATING RELATIONSHIPS

◆ Sandra Metts

A lthough dating relationships vary in levels of satisfaction, commitment, and duration, they share general patterns of development, intensification, and dissolution. These commonalities stem from the fact that both gender and dating are social constructions enacted through communication. The purpose of this chapter is to elaborate the role of communication in the interface between gender roles and dating schemata.

The chapter is organized into six sections. The first elaborates on the notion that gender and dating are social constructions. The next four trace gender differences in communication during typical dating phases: initiation (the first meeting, signaling interest, and the first date); intensification (expressions of love/commitment and increased sexual involvement); maintenance (managing intimacy); and, sometimes, disengagement. The chapter closes with suggestions for further research.

◆ Gender, Dating, and Communication: A Coordinated Intersection

To say that gender is socially constructed is to recognize the distinction between biological sex and gender roles. Biological sex is a genetic distinction determined by chromosomal patterns at birth. Gender is fluid and a socially embedded construction (Canary & Emmers-Sommer, 1997; Duck & Wood, in press; Reiss, 1986). It "consists of meanings and expectations of men and women that are created and upheld by social structures and practices" (Wood, 2000, p. 302). Men and women are expected to display culturally defined masculinity and femininity. Girls and women typically embrace and enact greater degrees of feminine attitudes and behaviors, and boys and men typically embrace and enact greater degrees of masculine attitudes and behaviors.

Biological sex, however, is not isomorphic with gender. Individuals internalize socially ascribed gender differently. Researchers who compare gender with biological sex argue that although men and women tend to score in the expected direction on dimensions of masculinity and femininity, some men and some women are high on both dimensions (androgynous) or low on both (undifferentiated) (Bem, 1981). In addition among homosexuals, gender distinctions are less pronounced. Kurdek (2003) found that masculinity and femininity among gay men and lesbians did not differ significantly.

The distinction between gender and sex is further complicated by "interaction scripts," which vary in the extent to which they prescribe role-appropriate behavior for men and women (e.g., a first date versus a classroom discussion). The constraining influence of interaction scripts may account for the apparent inconsistency in findings that gay men and lesbians hold less psychological identification as masculine or feminine and still display dating and mate selection behaviors that are similar to heterosexual men and women (Bailey, Gaulin, Agyei, & Gladue, 1994).

In sum, sex is an innate, biological dichotomy, whereas gender is a socially derived, complex system of values and behavioral expectations that becomes more constraining in certain types of interactional contexts. Individuals internalize gender roles to varying degrees and use them more or less consistently in formulating their social actions and evaluating those of others (Acitelli & Young, 1996).

Dating is a socially scripted relationship sequence that activates gender-relevant behaviors for most men and women. Gender role expectations are particularly salient because dating is defined in Western society as a testing ground for mate selection and eventual reproduction. Although interpretations of mating may differ among social groups, research on dating motivations in homosexual men and women (Bailey et al., 1994) and elderly heterosexual singles (mostly widowed) (Bulcroft & O'Connor, 1986) indicates that dating is viewed as a mate selection process. In cultures in which marriages are arranged, dating is not relevant to mate selection. In many Western societies, however, it is the normative transition period between being single and being married (or being in a committed, cohabiting relationship). Within dating relationships, gender influences relationship expectations, presentational modes, relational goals, and strategies to meet those goals (Holmberg & MacKenzie, 2002).

Furthermore, because mental structures such as expectations and goals are inert until they are instantiated in communication behaviors, gender, dating, and communication are inextricably linked and interactive. Mental schemata, particularly interaction scripts, guide the production and interpretation of messages and predict behavior (Holmberg & MacKenzie, 2002). At the same time, messages induce change in existing schemata (e.g., they can redefine a platonic relationship as a romantic one) and activate new scripts. The following sections illustrate the interface of communication and gender role expectations in the initiation, intensification, maintenance, and disengagement phases of dating. Although terminology differs, these phases are recognized in the research on relationship schemata (Baldwin, 1992; Ginsburg, 1988), turning points (Baxter & Bullis, 1986; Baxter & Erbert, 2000), stages of development

(Knapp & Vangelesti, 2005; Levinger, 1983), and the process of dissolution (Baxter, 1986; Duck, 1982; Duck & Wood, in press).

Many of these researchers use the term *gender* when referring to the biological sex of respondents (Canary & Emmers-Sommer, 1997; Duck & Wood, 2006). As a result, the profiles offered here are, for the most part, inferred from self-reported measures of attitudes and behaviors. However, since gender roles are learned at an early age and are reinforced socially (Bailey et al., 1994), we can assume that sex differences are a reasonable, if not perfect, indication of gender role expectations in the domain of mate selection commonly referred to as dating.

♦ Relationship Initiation

Not all single people go out for an evening intending to select a lifelong partner. Most simply want to have fun in some form. But inherent in the small talk and laughter is a dating script that allows prospective mates to reveal their desirable qualities and negotiate interest in future interactions. This initial stage of relationship development reflects nascent forms of gender role mating scripts. Both men and women seek others who have similar interests, are physically attractive, and seem likely to reciprocate their dating intentions. Gays and lesbians seeking partners report similar preferences (Peplau & Spalding, 2000).

Beyond these basic criteria, however, men and women prioritize the desirable qualities of a potential mate differently. Regardless of sexual orientation, men place greater importance on physical attractiveness in a potential partner; women emphasize personality characteristics (Bailey, Kim, Hills, & Linsenmeier, 1997; Peplau & Spaulding, 2000). More specifically heterosexual men look for signs of youth and fertility and use communication to assess a woman's sexual interest and/or receptivity. Heterosexual women look for signs of

physical strength, maturity, and economic stability and use communication to assess a man's emotional maturity and interest in commitment (Sedikides, Oliver, & Campbell, 1994; Stewart, Stinnett, & Rosenfeld, 2000). The consistency of these patterns across groups and cultures leads some theorists to argue that mate assessment patterns emerge from biological-evolutionary constraints, particularly the relatively greater relational investment required by women for successful reproduction (Bailey et al., 1994; Buss, 1994; Gangestad & Simpson, 2000).

When manifested in communication practices, the stereotypical masculine gender role in relationship initiation is characterized by control and proactive moves and the feminine counterpart by submission and reactive moves (Rose & Frieze, 1989). These patterns contribute to the common view that men initiate escalation and women serve as "gatekeepers," especially as the relationship moves toward sexual intimacy (Allgeier & Royster, 1991). This pattern is evident in both the coordinated moves of a first meeting and the more fully scripted sequence of the first date.

FIRST MEETING: SIGNALING INTEREST, FLIRTING, SEDUCTION

Early studies of verbal and nonverbal signals of interest during a first meeting identified sequences of co-orientation. Scheflen's (1965) classic work on quasi-courtship behavior proposes four steps: courtship readiness, preening behavior, positional cues, and resolution (actions of appeal or invitation). Lockhard and Adams (1980) describe similar moves (attention, recognition, interaction, sexual arousal, and resolution) which have been observed during first meetings in bars (Perper, 1985).

While it is generally assumed that the first overt move to initiate contact is a masculine prerogative (i.e., the opening line), observational data suggest that the invitation to approach is a carefully choreographed feminine performance. In a detailed investigation of how they signal interest and invite men to approach, Moore (1985) observed women in singles bars, restaurants, and at parties. She identified 52 nonverbal behaviors that resulted in male approach. Glancing behaviors were finely tuned for both direction and duration: a type I glance encompassed the room or group; a type II was directed at a particular man, repeated several times, but limited to about 3 seconds; a type III was prolonged (more than 3 seconds) and directed at a man who often returned the glance. These glances were often accompanied by primping, head tossing, hair flipping, lip licking, smiling, laughing, giggling, nodding, touching, and so on. When Moore observed women in noncourtship settings, such as a library or women's center, these solicitation cues were not displayed. Consistent with socioevolutionary theory, she concluded that women rely on indirect moves to assess a man's interest before committing time and attention to further pursuit. McCormick and Jones (1989) offered indirect support for Moore's position. They found that women de-escalate their flirtatious behavior once they decide that they are not interested in pursuing a romantic relationship, whereas men continue flirtatious behavior even after they have lost interest and de-escalate it only much later in the encounter.

Moore (1996) also found evidence for the early socialization of typical feminine nonverbal behaviors. She observed 13- to 16-year-old girls in shopping malls, an ice-skating rink, a swimming pool, and at school events where boys were present. They displayed 31 of the 52 behaviors identified in her study of adult women. She saw no overt signals such as kissing or caressing, but often observed exaggerated forms of primping, head tossing, hair flipping, laughing, and giggling. Moore interpreted these exaggerated displays as an indication that the early teen years are a time for adolescents to practice and refine courtship signals.

Interestingly, males also employ nonverbal behaviors to signal their appeal as a potentially attractive mate in ways consistent with the gender script prescribing strength and assertiveness. Anolli and Ciceri (2002) found that males who were successful in arranging a second meeting with a woman displayed a characteristic "seductive voice" more often than those who were not successful. This voice profile revealed patterned variations during the seductive sequence: higher pitch, elevated intensity, and a faster rate of articulation at first; a gradually lower, weaker, and warmer voice (the self-disclosure voice); a higher pitch, higher intensity, and accelerated rate of articulation when the man was asking his partner to meet him again. Anolli and Ciceri concluded that men use the initial resonant voice to raise the interest of the female and impress her with his "strength, vitality, enthusiasm, sociability, virility, and confidence" (p. 167). The lower pitch and softer volume suggest warmth, tenderness, and affability, thereby facilitating conversational openness, relaxation, and self-disclosure.

Although men and women share a common understanding of the functions of flirting behaviors (Abrahams, 1994), they differ in both their motivations and in their judgments about what constitutes sexual as opposed to friendly interest. In a study of self-reported motivations for flirting, Henningsen (2004) found that men and women were equally likely to use it to enhance their self-esteem, to explore the interests of a potential partner, and to accomplish instrumental goals. Men, however, reported that they flirt more for explicitly sexual reasons whereas women reported more relational and fun motivations.

Men also have a comparatively lower threshold for interpreting a range of affiliative behaviors as sexually suggestive (Abbey, 1982; Shotland & Craig, 1988). Koukounas and Letch (2001) videotaped interactions between male and female confederates during which eye contact, touch, physical proximity, and the female actor's clothes were manipulated to indicate increasing levels of sexual interest. Across all levels of manipulation, male viewers perceived more sexual intent from the female actor than did women viewers, even when she made little eye contact, used no touch, retained social rather than interpersonal distance, and dressed conservatively.

This differential interest in sexual cues is apparent also in the socially defined scripts for the more formal act of relationship initiation—the first date.

FIRST-DATE SCRIPTS

Although men and women approach first dates with many of the same goals and expectations, gender scripts do distinguish between male-appropriate and female-appropriate behaviors (Morr & Mongeau, 2004; Winstead, Derlega, & Rose, 1997). Men are expected to initiate events, display their resources, and test for female sexual availability. Women are expected to respond to the man's initiative, display their physical attractiveness, and respond with interest but restraint to tests of sexual availability.

Rose and Frieze (1989) asked heterosexual college students to describe a typical first date. They identified 27 actions associated with the man's script and 19 with the woman's. Of these, 14 overlapped, primarily those expected during the conversation (e.g., get to know, compliment, joke, laugh, try to impress, and say that the date was a good time). Of the 13 actions unique to men, most signaled the roles of initiator and provider (e.g., plan, provide the economic resources, and initiate physical and/or sexual contact). The five unique to women were primarily reactions to a male initiative (e.g., wait for date, introduce to parents or roommates). Rose and Frieze (1993) subsequently confirmed these hypothetical patterns in descriptions of actual dates, and Nakanishi (1998) confirmed them in a sample of Japanese college students.

Other research indicates that despite economic and occupational changes during the past 50 years and despite young adults' endorsement of egalitarian ideals, gender role expectations are still prominent in first-date scripts, especially for college males. Laner and Ventrone (2000) provided college students with lists of behaviors and asked them to rate whether they would occur on a heterosexual first date and, if so, who would more likely enact them: the male, the female, both, or neither of them. Results indicated that the man was expected to initiate and organize the date (e.g., ask out, decide on plans, prepare the car, pick the woman up, pay all the bills, and make the first affectionate or sexual moves). The woman was expected to respond to male initiative and display her physical and relational attractiveness (e.g., wait to be asked out, buy new clothes, eat lightly at dinner, primp in the bathroom during the evening, and take the lead in moving toward deeper conversation). However, although only 9% of men thought either partner could pay for the date, 22% of women thought either person could.

Several studies have more specifically tested the prescriptive nature of dating scripts and the sex role behaviors they specify. These findings offer convincing evidence that deviations from the traditional script are difficult for dating couples to enact. Gilbert, Walker, McKinney, and Snell (1999) instructed college student dyads to participate in one of two conditions. The first reflected the traditional script or "dominant discourse theme," with male participants instructed to initiate a first date and then greater sexual intimacy, to which their female partners were instructed to say they were not ready. The second was intended to disrupt the dominant discourse, with female participants instructed to initiate the date and greater sexual intimacy, to which their male partners were instructed to say they were not ready. Codings of the audiotaped interactions revealed that no woman initiated the date when her partner was assigned the initiator role but that 31% of the men initiated the date even when their female partner was assigned the role. Likewise, all the men assigned to the initiator role initiated greater intimacy but only about half of the women did.

Research on the dating practices of homosexual men and women indicates a notable consistency with these findings (Peplau & Spalding, 2000; Rose, Zand, & Cini, 1993). Klinkenberg and Rose (1994) tested the assumption that homosexual dating practices would differ from heterosexual practices in that they would not have a clearly defined script or contain similar gender role expectations. However, analysis of both hypothetical and actual first dates indicated that gay men and lesbian behaviors were similar to those scripted for heterosexuals. Moreover, gay men were more likely than lesbians to associate sex with the first date and lesbians were more likely than gay men to associate emotional sharing.

INTENSIFICATION

Unlike the scripted first date, intensification moves are less temporally sequenced and more ambiguous. Several factors contribute to the complexity in the transition from first date and early dating to relationship development and intensification. First, the moves that function as transition indicators are both strategic (goal intended) and inadvertent but cumulative in their effect. For example, asking a partner not to date others is a clear message signaling one partner's goal to intensify the relationship. Alternatively, not dating other people over a period of time and being treated as a committed couple by the social network is a cumulative relationship definition.

Second, the meaning of intensification is multifaceted: it can be experienced as greater intimacy (sexual, emotional, and informational), as greater psychological commitment to a partner or a relationship, or as a combination of these. For example, although first sexual intercourse in a dating relationship typically serves as a relationship intensification move, Sprecher and McKinney (1993) report that sexual behavior also functions as an act of affection, love, self-disclosure, intimacy, interdependence, maintenance, and exchange.

Finally, intensification moves are necessarily embedded within an emerging and dynamic relationship culture. They may, ironically, increase certainty in some aspects of the developing relationship while simultaneously increasing uncertainty in others. This is illustrated in Baxter and Erbert's (2000) interviews with dating couples about turning points in their relationships. When respondents described the passion turning point (particularly the first "I love you" and sexual involvement), they referred to changes in other aspects of the relationship that Baxter and Erbert characterized as dialectical tensions (i.e., openness/closedness, autonomy/connection, and novelty/predictability). Baxter and Erbert speculate that the passion turning point forced couples to grapple with the "uncertain implications of such an expression for relational development" (p. 561).

Although intensification is not as explicitly structured as initiation, as Baxter and Erbert's work indicates, the passion turning point is recognized by dating couples as signifying a move toward greater commitment. Because the normative expectation is that expressions of love precede and frame sexual involvement (Metts, 2004), I will review research related to the first "I love you" before looking at that concerning the first sexual involvement.

◆ Expression of Affection: "I Love You"

Although the expression of love is not necessarily a strategic move, when asked to identify strategies that dating partners use to intensify a relationship (i.e., increase the level of commitment), college students reported professions of love (Tolhuizen, 1989). In addition, and consistent with gender scripts, such statements are more likely to originate with men. Tolhuizen identified 15 strategies in students' written accounts of how they intensify dating relationships. Men were more likely to make direct definitional bids and use verbal expressions of affection. Women were more likely to accept the definitional bid and use relationship negotiation strategies.

The male initiator role was also evident in spontaneous expressions of love during ordinary conversations. Owen (1987) analyzed audio recordings of telephone conversations between dating couples collected over the course of a semester. Men were overwhelmingly the first to say "I love you." In providing possible explanations for this pattern, Owen speculated that (a) men are less able to withhold their expressions of love when they feel it, (b) women can better discriminate love from other emotions, and/or (c) initiating declarations of love reflects the male role as proactive and the female role as reactive.

Booth-Butterfield and Trotta (1994) analyzed dating couples' written descriptions of the circumstances surrounding the first expression of love. They found that 70% of the sample indicated that men said "I love you" first. Respondents' attributions for the declarations of love were generally consistent with and extended Owen's speculations. Approximately half attributed them to true feelings and about 20% to situational influences (e.g., a delightful evening or having made love for the first time). About 13% attributed the expression to ulterior motives such as gaining sexual compliance or testing how the other person would respond. In a few cases, love was expressed as a sign of comfort/support when a partner was experiencing distress (5.5%) or when a person was simply at a loss for words (5.5%). Female receivers were more likely than male receivers to attribute an ulterior motive to the expression, but male receivers were also less likely to take it as a true expression, perhaps because female initiation violates the normative pattern.

FIRST SEX

Perhaps no other aspect of dating escalation reflects gender scripts as fully as first sexual involvement, particularly sexual intercourse. Inevitably framed by the socially constructed double standard, women link sexual intimacy more closely to emotional intimacy than do men. This association is evident in their scripted refusal to engage in sexual activity even when intending to do so. Each of these issues is addressed separately here, although they overlap in actual practice.

Sexual Activity and Relationship Meaning. One of the most consistent findings in studies of sexual activity in dating couples is that women more closely link sexual behavior and emotional involvement (Christopher & Cate, 1984; O'Sullivan & Gaines, 1998). This difference appears even in same-sex romantic relationships (Bailey et al., 1994).

Cohen and Shotland (1996) explored the link between sexual involvement and emotional attachment using surveys completed by heterosexual college students. Men reported that they would expect sexual intercourse after significantly fewer dates than women (9–11 versus 15–18). Almost all of them indicated that they would have sex with women whom they rated highly on physical attraction but for whom they felt no emotional involvement; less than two thirds of the women would have sex with men they did not find attractive. Even in relationships lacking physical attraction and emotional involvement, approximately 60% of the men reported they would have sex, but only about 20% of the women would. Approximately 33% of the men reported that they had actually engaged in sex when feeling no attraction and no emotional involvement, but only 5% of women reported doing so.

Hill (2002) confirmed this pattern using eight hypothetical situations, five that contained expressions of emotional investment (e.g., providing comfort) and three that did not. Both men and women indicated a greater likelihood of sexual behavior in the relationships with emotional investment, and the likelihood indicated by women was equivalent to that of men. In the no-investment situations, however, men reported significantly greater likelihood of sexual behavior compared to women.

In an examination of whether gender scripts predicted relationship escalation, Metts (2004) surveyed heterosexual college students about the first sexual experience in their current or most recent dating relationship. Expressions of love and commitment prior to sexual involvement (heavy petting, oral sex, and sexual intercourse) predicted relationship escalation for both men and women, but contributed substantially more variance beyond the control variables for women (12% versus 4%). Moreover, women reported significantly higher levels of explicit expressions of love and commitment prior to sexual involvement. This may suggest that framing sexual involvement as a response to emotional commitment is more important in a woman's decision to escalate a relationship. Men and women might also reconstruct the escalation of the relationship in line with gendered scripts—men not recalling expressions of affection even if they were spoken and women recalling them even if they were not.

In sum, men consistently report fewer sexual restraints in both attitude and behavior than women. Several scholars have proposed that women use scripted refusal or token resistance to balance the desire for sex with their knowledge of cultural expectations that a "nice woman" refuses sexual invitations unless in a committed relationship.

Token Resistance. Actions can communicate reluctance or refusal to engage in sexual activity while intending to do so. This practice is typically attributed to women's strategic accommodation to the sexual double standard (Muehlenhard & McCoy, 1991) and is perceived by both men and women as an enjoyable way to be both expressive and playful (O'Sullivan & Allgeier, 1994).

Unfortunately, the scripted ambiguity inherent in token resistance "perpetuates the belief that women's refusals of sexual advances are often insincere and need not be taken seriously" (Muehlenhard & Rodgers, 1998, p. 444). Indirect support for this position is evident in male and female evaluations of refusal messages. For example, Motley and Reeder (1995) provided college students with scenarios describing the progression of physical intimacy on a second or third date when the woman uses one of six resistance messages. Direct messages were: Please don't do that; I don't want to do this; Let's stop this. Indirect ones were: I can't do this unless you're committed to me; I'm seeing someone else; I don't have any protection. Men and women were equally likely to interpret the direct refusals as indicating no, and women also interpreted the indirect messages as no. However, men were significantly more likely than women to rate the indirect messages as "willing to be persuaded."

An important finding that appears to contradict the double standard premise is worth noting here. Several studies find that men are more likely than women to report using token resistance (O'Sullivan & Allgeier, 1994; Sprecher & Hatfield, 1994). Social structures may have simply framed the phenomenon as a female strategy when it is a common practice for both sexes. However, it is more likely that questionnaire items asking respondents about a time when they said no to sex when they really wanted it evoke a far broader range of situations than the scripted refusal episode known as token resistance.

A compelling argument for this position is offered by Muehlenhard and Hollabaugh (1988). In an effort to be very specific in their instructions to college student respondents, the authors asked them to describe the following situation:

> You were with a guy (or girl) who wanted to engage in sexual intercourse and you wanted to also, but for some reason you indicated that you didn't want to,

although you had every intention to and were willing to engage in sexual intercourse. In other words, you indicated "no" and you meant "yes." (p. 874)

Initial findings indicated that more men than women had engaged in token resistance. However, when analyzing the narratives, Muehlenhard and Hollabaugh (1988) realized that many respondents had misunderstood the instructions. In particular, the narratives reflected confusion about (a) desires and intentions (respondents actually did not want to have sex although the situation seemed conducive); (b) confusion about communicating no and yes simultaneously (they said no and meant no, but then changed their mind, presenting a sequential rather than simultaneous intention); and (c) confusion about which sexual activity was refused and which was intended (e.g., they might have said no to intercourse but intended to engage in petting). In the final analysis only 20 of the original 177 responses fit the criteria of the token resistance episode. When these narratives were analyzed for themes, five motivations emerged with a distribution reflective of gender expectations: moral concerns and discomfort about sex (two women); adding interest to an ongoing relationship (five women, one man); not wanting to be taken for granted (three women, one man); testing a partner's response or intention about the relationship (one woman, one man); and asserting power/control over the other person (five men, one woman).

Until further research clarifies whether men and women are responding to surveys in ways consistent with the conceptual definition of token resistance, claims that more men than women engage in this type of sexual negotiation should be taken with a note of caution. It is more likely that the scripted refusal to have sex when it is desired is more frequently used by women and functions to meet gender-related goals of self-presentation.

◆ Maintenance: Assessing Long-Term Potential

The maintenance stage varies in length and level of involvement. During this stage, couples move from reliance on scripted interactions to more idiosyncratic patterns. When uncertainty about the nature of the relationship still lingers or conflict and unexpected events increase uncertainty, couples typically employ information-seeking strategies (Baxter & Wilmot, 1984; Bell & Buerkel-Rothfuss, 1990; Emmers & Canary, 1996; Stafford & Canary, 1991). Under ordinary circumstances, however, couples simply engage in routine maintenance behaviors such as showing affection, participating in joint activities, and engaging in small talk (Dindia, 2000). Partners in same-sex relationships report similar maintenance behaviors, although they also employ unique strategies to maintain the relationship, such as socializing in gay/lesbian supportive environments and "being out" as a couple to other members of their social network (Haas & Stafford, 1998).

Interestingly, it appears that once relationships reach a level of commitment known variously as serious or exclusive dating, the sex role imperative for men to be in control recedes. By choice or necessity, women tend to become the more active relationship managers—actualizing the feminine gender role as the "social-emotional specialists in relationships" (Morrow, Clark, & Brock, 1995, p. 378). Although this assumption is derived largely from studies using biological sex, research by Stafford, Dainton, and Haas (2000) using married couples indicates that feminine gender identity (measured on the Sexual Identity Scale) was a much stronger predictor of maintenance behavior than was biological sex.

Evidence of a gender role shift from initiation to maintenance is available in research on relational maintenance and satisfaction. Dainton and Stafford (1993) found that married and dating couples use almost identical strategies but that in both cases, women use expressions of positivity, emotional openness, and talk more frequently than men. Other research focused more specifically on what men and women want from a partner indicates that they desire many of the same qualities—companionship, happiness, feeling loved (Sedikides et al., 1994). Both report more satisfaction, love, and commitment when sexual satisfaction is high. This association is stronger, however, for men than women (Sprecher, 2002).

Not only is relationship satisfaction comparatively more salient to women than men, it is also closely linked to the disparity between the level of emotional openness and communicative responsiveness that women desire and the level men typically exhibit. This disparity may be due, in part, to gender socialization. The feminine speech community values talk for its own sake and emphasizes its role in building/ maintaining intimacy. The masculine speech community more typically values talk for its instrumental functions (Wood, 1996).

These sex role differences appear to influence women's regard for communication as central to romantic relationships. When Peretti and Abplanalp (2004) asked college students to describe the "chemistry" in their current relationship, both men and women mentioned physical attractiveness more than any other feature. However, four other elements emerged as important for women: *reciprocity* (mutual exchange of mental, emotional, or physical qualities of equal or similar value); *spontaneous communication* (able to reveal selves, express feelings and ideas with a sense of being accepted, self-disclosure accompanied by trust and intimacy); *warm personality* (warmth, friendliness, concern, empathy, and understanding); and *longing* (feelings of arousal or excitement, tenderness, mutual affection, enhanced social and sexual intimacy, yearning or desire for someone often facilitated by communication over the telephone or by e-mail). Communicative expressiveness and responsiveness

are reflected in all the categories derived from the women's descriptions.

Critelli, Myers, and Loos (1986) explored gender expectations by asking dating couples to respond to items taken from scholarly literature and from love letters written by students. Women were more likely to endorse statements about romance, friendship, and intimacy (e.g., Someone I can really communicate with, Someone I can confide in about virtually everything, Someone I would most likely go to if I had a problem).

Sex role expectations also seem to influence the relatively lower level of emotionally expressive communication that men are likely to exhibit. Certainly, men and women exhibit many of the same communicative behaviors (see Aries, 1996; Canary & Emmers-Sommer, 1997), but gender scripts curtail emotional expression for men (Metts & Planalp, 2003). As Dosser, Balswick, and Halverson (1986) point out in their discussion of the so-called inexpressive male, "expressiveness is communicative and therefore is influenced by the context which includes the person's goals, the target of the expression, the relationship between the two of them and the type of feeling expressed" (p. 251).

The importance of framing the differences in emotional expression between men and women as responsive to context and guided by gender role constraints is evidenced in investigations of conversations between dating partners. Vogel, Tucker, Wester, and Heesacker (1999) videotaped dating couples having conversations about an intimate topic (their satisfaction in their relationship) or about everyday things. Behaviors were coded to the extent to which they represented feminine behaviors (e.g., letting another person talk first, talking softly, acting submissive) or masculine behaviors (e.g., being assertive, talking loudly, and taking charge of the conversation). In the intimate conversation, women exhibited more feminine behavior than women in everyday conversation, but men exhibited less feminine behaviors in the ordinary conversation. The authors suggest that intimate situations activate the male gender script because they hold potential for vulnerability or rejection.

In a subsequent investigation, Vogel, Wester, Heesacker, and Madon (2003) randomly assigned dating couples to discussions of either high or low emotional vulnerability. Coders did global ratings of demanding, withdrawing, and of emotionally expressive and emotionally restricted behaviors. Overall, couples were less expressive in the emotional vulnerability conversations. However, an interaction effect emerged. Women were more expressive in conversations of high emotional difficulty, but men exhibited more restricted affect and more withdrawal in difficult situations.

Taken together, the research findings on communication preferences and practices during the maintenance stage suggest a gendered profile. It appears that the feminine gender role encourages women to both value and practice emotional expression as fundamental to satisfaction and maintenance. The masculine gender role, however, encourages men to value and perform primarily instrumental functions. Whether motivated by fear of appearing somehow not masculine or because differential socialization fails to provide them with certain communicative skills, men are generally less verbally expressive, and they are especially less so when dealing with emotionally difficult topics.

Although some scholars have tried to situate male and female differences carefully within contexts and within gender role expectations, the simple view of men as generically inexpressive continues in the popular and pedagogical literature. Wood and Inman (1993) argue that the value of performing instrumental tasks and doing activities together in creating and sustaining closeness is not recognized. And yet for many men these expressions function in much the same way that verbal expressions function for many women. Apparently, women (and a number of researchers) do not code them as intimacy signals, although they likely will interpret a significant decline in such demonstrations as a sign of relationship deterioration.

◆ *Dissolution and Breakup*

The transition from a state of satisfaction and commitment to one of decline and disengagement is often presented by scholars as a movement through stages (Duck, 1982) and often aligned as parallel to stages of relationship development (Knapp & Vangelisti, 2005). Others suggest a model that focuses on relationship decline as a set of processes. Duck and Wood (2006), for example, integrate the literature on individual, dyadic, and network variables from a variety of relationship types to illustrate the fluid nature of deterioration and gender influences during this process.

Gender patterns in dissolution are consistent with those that characterize the maintenance phase. Men and women are more similar than different, but the differences are important. Both tend to terminate relationships when costs exceed rewards, when satisfaction and commitment fall below acceptable levels (Rusbult & Van Lange, 2003), and/or when a serious transgression or rule violation cannot be forgiven (Metts, 1994). However, the relatively greater expectation for maintenance efforts that attends the feminine gender role also applies to accomplishing relationship dissolution.

For example, although early investment factors predict whether a relationship stays intact or is broken up, they are a stronger predictor for women (Sacher & Fine, 1996). Women also report more reasons and more specific reasons for relationship breakup compared with men (Baxter, 1986). Women attribute the breakup to autonomy, openness, and equity concerns; men, to simply losing the "magical quality" of the relationship (Baxter, 1986).

As might be expected as well, women are more likely to initiate the actual breakup (Sprecher, Felmlee, Metts, Fehr, & Vanni, 1998). Consistent with gender role expectations and practice, women more closely monitor relationship quality and as a result are better able and more willing to communicate the desire to redefine a romantic relationship in a face-preserving way (Cupach & Metts, 1986).

◆ Conclusion

This review has highlighted communication differences between men and women that reflect patterns consistent with gender role scripts across the stages of relationship development and decline. Certainly men and women enjoy dating relationships for many of the same reasons, look for similar qualities in a long-term partner, and communicate in similar ways. They also, however, tend to display gender-relevant patterns. As a mate selection ritual, dating appears to evoke interaction scripts that guide behavior for most men and most women.

Research would benefit from addressing two issues. First, much of what has been done employs retrospective reports or laboratory manipulations. This should be complemented by longitudinal studies. The full influence and evolution of gendered communication in dating relationships is more likely to map clearly when they are followed over time. For example, we know little about how relationships are initiated and developed or what the long-term consequences are when partners do not follow gendered scripts. Indeed, much of the research on initiation seems to ignore the fact that most dating relationships emerge from school, work, and network connections, with only about 15% originating in bars, through personal ads, or on vacation (Michael, Gagnon, Laumann, & Kolata, 1994). Those that evolve from social relationships may exhibit less reliance on gender role scripts both in initiation and maintenance. Longitudinal research is a useful

approach to discovering patterns in behavior that are not influenced by retrospective sense making—a process that might activate gendered dating scripts after the fact.

Second, researchers need to complement the research on 20-year-old, heterosexual, able-bodied, Caucasian college students with more diverse samples. Dating occurs in many cultures, some of which configure gender identity much differently than do Western and industrialized cultures. We know very little about such cultures. Indeed, we know very little about cocultural groups within the United States. Some existing literature addresses the need to understand the interface between sexual orientation and gender (Bailey et al., 1994; Bailey et al., 1997), but clearly more is needed. Recent investigations have begun to profile the dating motivations and behaviors of African American youth (Harper, Gannon, Watson, Catania, & Dolcini, 2004; Smith, 1996), but to date, little effort has been made to determine whether gender role patterns might be similar to those found among Caucasian youth.

Dating also occurs across the life span (Shotland & Craig, 1988). Divorce, widowhood, and increasing longevity thrust many older adults back into the dating cycle. Although older single adults, like their younger counterparts, seek physically attractive mates who provide companionship and romance, they also assess dates as potential caregivers, a criterion that is not generally salient for younger people (Bulcroft & O'Connor, 1986). The greater number of women in older age lends prestige to those who have a male partner (Bulcroft & O'Connor, 1986), and the grief experienced from the death of a spouse moderates the desire to begin dating again much more strongly than does a breakup for young people (Carr, 2004). Attention to the experiences of older adults would enhance our understanding of gendered communication patterns during dating for various cohort groups.

It is certainly easier to advocate more systematic research in gender and dating relationships than to specify how that is to be accomplished. The task is inherently difficult and challenging. As Kramarae (1996) illustrates, race, class, and gender intersect in complicated ways. When individual differences in needs and personality traits are added, the number of pieces in the puzzle increases significantly. However, the effort to construct a representative profile is both theoretically and pragmatically worth making.

◆ References

Abbey, A. (1982). Sex differences in attributions for friendly behavior: Do males misperceive females' friendliness? *Journal of Personality and Social Psychology, 42,* 830–838.

Abrahams, M. (1994). Perceiving flirtatious communication: An exploration of the perceptual dimensions underlying judgments of flirtatiousness. *Journal of Sex Research, 31,* 283–292.

Acitelli, L. K., & Young, A. M. (1996). Gender and thought in relationships. In G. J. O. Fletcher & J. Fitness (Eds.), *Knowledge structures in close relationships: A social psychological approach* (pp. 147–168). Mahwah, NJ: Erlbaum.

Allgeier, E. R., & Royster, B. J. T. (1991). New approaches to dating and sexuality. In E. Grauerholz & M. Koralewski (Eds.), *Sexual coercion* (pp. 133–147). Lexington, MA: Lexington Books.

Anolli, L., & Ciceri, R. (2002). Analysis of the vocal profiles of male seduction: From exhibition to self-disclosure. *Journal of General Psychology, 129,* 149–169.

Aries, E. (1996). Men and women in interaction: Reconsidering the differences. New York: Oxford University Press.

Bailey, J. M., Gaulin, S., Agyei, Y., & Gladue, B. A. (1994). Effects of gender and sexual orientation on evolutionarily relevant aspects of human mating psychology. *Journal of Personality and Social Psychology, 66,* 1081–1093.

Bailey, J. M., Kim, P. Y., Hills, A., & Linsenmeier, J. A. W. (1997). Butch, femme, or straight acting? Partner preferences of gay men and lesbians. *Journal of Personality and Social Psychology, 73,* 960–973.

Baldwin, M. W. (1992). Relational schemas and the processing of social information. *Psychological Bulletin, 112,* 461–484.

Baxter, L. A. (1986). Gender differences in the heterosexual relationship rules embedded in break-up encounters. *Journal of Social and Personal Relationships, 3,* 289–306.

Baxter, L. A., & Bullis, C. (1986). Turning points in developing romantic relationships. *Human Communication Research, 12,* 469–493.

Baxter, L. A., & Erbert, L. A. (2000). Perceptions of dialectical contradictions in turning points of development in heterosexual romantic relationships. *Journal of Social and Personal Relationships, 16,* 547–569.

Baxter, L. A., & Wilmot, W. W. (1984). "Secret tests": Social strategies for acquiring information about the state of the relationship. *Human Communication Research, 11,* 171–201.

Bell, R. A., & Buerkel-Rothfuss, N. L. (1990). S(he) loves me, S(he) loves me not: Predictors of relational information-seeking in courtship and beyond. *Communication Quarterly, 38,* 64–82.

Bem, S. L. (1981). Gender schema theory: A cognitive account of sex typing. *Psychological Review, 88,* 369–371.

Booth-Butterfield, M., & Trotta, M. R. (1994). Attributional patterns for expressions of love. *Communication Reports, 7,* 119–129.

Bulcroft, K., & O'Connor, M. (1986). The importance of dating relationships on quality of life for older persons. *Family Relations, 35,* 397–401.

Buss, D. M. (1994). *The evolution of desire: Strategies of human mating.* New York: Basic Books.

Canary, D. J., & Emmers-Sommer, T. M. (1997). *Sex and gender differences in personal relationships.* New York: Guilford.

Carr, D. (2004). The desire to date and remarry among older widows and widowers. *Journal of Marriage and Family, 66,* 1051–1057.

Christopher, F. S., & Cate, R. M. (1984). Factors involved in premarital sexual decision-making. *Journal of Sex Research, 20,* 363–376.

Cohen, L. L., & Shotland, R. L. (1996). Timing of first sexual intercourse in a relationship: Expectations, experiences, and perceptions of others. *Journal of Sex Research, 33,* 291–299.

Critelli, J. W., Myers, E. J., & Loos, V. E. (1986). The components of love: Romantic attraction and sex role orientation. *Journal of Personality, 54,* 354–370.

Cupach, W. R., & Metts, S. (1986). Accounts of relational dissolution: A comparison of marital and non-marital relationships. *Communication Monographs, 53,* 311–334.

Dainton, M., & Stafford, L. (1993). Routine maintenance behaviors: A comparison of relationship type, partner similarity, and sex differences. *Journal of Social and Personal Relationships, 10,* 255–272.

Dindia, K. (2000). Relational maintenance. In C. Hendrick & S. S. Hendrick (Eds.), *Close relationships: A sourcebook* (pp. 287–299). Thousand Oaks, CA: Sage.

Dosser, D. A., Jr., Balswick, J. O., & Halverson, C. F., Jr. (1986). Male inexpressiveness and relationships. *Journal of Social and Personal Relationships, 3,* 241–258.

Duck, S. (1982). A topography of relationship disengagement and dissolution. In S. Duck (Ed.), *Personal relationships: Vol. 4. Dissolving personal relationships* (pp. 1–30). New York: Academic Press.

Duck, S. W., & Wood, J. T (2006). Gendered patterns in relational dissolution. In M. Fine & J. Harvey (Eds.), *The handbook of divorce and dissolution of romantic relationships.* Mahwah, NJ: Erlbaum.

Emmers, T. M., & Canary, D. J. (1996). The effect of uncertainty reducing strategies on young couples' relational repair and intimacy. *Communication Quarterly, 44,* 166–182.

Gangestad, S. W., & Simpson, J. A. (2000). The evolution of human mating: Trade-offs and strategic pluralism. *Behavioral and Brain Sciences, 23,* 573–644.

Gilbert, L. A., Walker, S. J., McKinney, S., & Snell, J. L. (1999). Challenging discourse themes reproducing gender in heterosexual dating: An analog study. *Sex Roles, 41,* 753–774.

Ginsburg, G. P. (1988). Rules, scripts and prototypes in personal relationships. In S. W. Duck (Ed.), *Handbook of personal relationships* (pp. 23–39). Chichester, UK: Wiley.

Haas, S. M., & Stafford, L. (1998). An initial examination of maintenance behaviors in gay and lesbian relationships. *Journal of Social and Personal Relationships, 15,* 846–855.

Harper, G. W., Gannon, C., Watson, S. E., Catania, J. A., & Dolcini, M. M. (2004). The role of close friends in African American adolescents' dating and sexual behavior. *Journal of Sex Research, 41,* 351–362.

Henningsen, D. D. (2004). Flirting with meaning: An examination of miscommunication in flirting interactions. *Sex Roles, 50,* 481–489.

Hill, C. A. (2002). Gender, relationship stage, and sexual behavior: The importance of partner emotional investment within specific situations. *Journal of Sex Research, 39,* 228–240.

Holmberg, D., & MacKenzie, S. (2002). So far, so good: Scripts for romantic relationship development as predictors of relational well-being. *Journal of Social and Personal Relationships, 19,* 777–796.

Klinkenberg, D., & Rose, S. (1994). Dating scripts of gay men and lesbians. *Journal of Homosexuality, 26,* 23–35.

Knapp, M. L., & Vangelisti, A. L. (2005). *Interpersonal communication and human relationships* (5th ed.). Boston: Allyn & Bacon.

Koukounas, E., & Letch, N. M. (2001). Psychological correlates of perception of sexual intent in women. *Journal of Social Psychology, 141,* 443–456.

Kramarae, C. (1996). Classified information: Race, class, and (always) gender. In J. T. Wood (Ed.), *Gendered relationships* (pp. 20–38). Mountain View, CA: Mayfield.

Kurdek, L. A. (2003). Differences between gay and lesbian cohabiting couples. *Journal of Social and Personal Relationships, 20,* 411–436.

Laner, M. R., & Ventrone, N. A. (2000). Dating scripts revisited. *Journal of Family Issues, 21,* 488–500.

Levinger, G. (1983). Development and change. In H. H. Kelley, E. Berscheid, A. Christensen,

J. Harvey, T. Huston, G. Levinger, G., E. McClintock, et al. (Eds.), *Close relationships* (pp. 315–359). San Francisco: Freeman.

Lockhard, J. S., & Adams, R. M. (1980). Courtship behaviors in public: Different age/sex roles. *Ethology and Sociobiology, 1,* 245–253.

McCormick, N. B., & Jones, A. J. (1989). Gender differences in nonverbal flirtation. *Journal of Sex Education and Therapy, 15,* 271–282.

Metts, S. (1994). Relational transgressions. In W. R. Cupach & B. Spitzberg (Eds.), *The dark side of interpersonal communication* (pp. 217–240). Hillsdale, NJ: Erlbaum.

Metts, S. (2004). First sexual involvement in romantic relationships: An empirical investigation of communicative framing, romantic beliefs, and attachment orientation in the passion turning point. In J. H. Harvey, A. Wenzel, & S. Sprecher (Eds.), *Handbook of sexuality in close relationships* (pp. 135–158). Mahwah, NJ: Erlbaum.

Metts, S., & Planalp, S. (2002). Emotional communication. In M. L. Knapp & J. A. Daly (Eds.), *Handbook of interpersonal communication* (3rd ed., pp. 339–373). Thousand Oaks, CA: Sage.

Michael, R. T., Gagnon, J. H., Laumann, E. O., & Kolata, G. (1994). *Sex in America.* Boston: Little & Brown.

Moore, M. M. (1985). Nonverbal courtship patterns in women: Context and consequences. *Ethology and Sociobiology, 6,* 237–247.

Moore, M. M. (1996). Courtship signaling and adolescents: "Girls just wanna have fun?" *Journal of Sex Research, 32,* 319–328.

Morr, M. C., & Mongeau, P. A. (2004). First date expectations: The impact of sex of initiator, alcohol consumption, and relationship type. *Communication Research, 31,* 3–35.

Morrow, G., Clark, E., & Brock, K. (1995). Individual and partner love styles: Implications for the quality of romantic involvements. *Journal of Social and Personal Relationships, 12,* 363–387.

Motley, M., & Reeder, H. (1995). Unwanted escalation of sexual intimacy: Male and female perceptions of connotations and relational consequences of resistance messages. *Communication Monographs, 62,* 355–382.

Muehlenhard, C. L., & Hollabaugh, L. C. (1988). Do women sometimes say no when they mean yes? The prevalence and correlates of women's token resistance to sex. *Journal of Personality and Social Psychology, 54,* 872–879.

Muehlenhard, C. L., & McCoy, M. L. (1991). Double standard/double bind: The sexual double standard and women's communication about sex. *Psychology of Women Quarterly, 15,* 447–461.

Muehlenhard, C. L., & Rodgers, C. S. (1998). Token resistance to sex: New perspectives on an old stereotype. *Psychology of Women Quarterly, 22,* 443–463.

Nakanishi, M. (1998). Gender enactment on a first date: A Japanese sample. *Women and Language, 21,* 10–17.

O'Sullivan, L. F., & Allgeier, E. R. (1994). Dissembling a stereotype: Gender differences in the use of token resistance. *Journal of Applied Social Psychology, 24,* 1035–1055.

O'Sullivan, L. F., & Gaines, M. E. (1998). Decision-making in college students' heterosexual dating relationships: Ambivalence about engaging in sexual activity. *Journal of Social and Personal Relationships, 15,* 347–363.

Owen, W. F. (1987). The verbal expression of love by women and men as a critical communication event in personal relationships. *Women's Studies in Communication, 10,* 15–24.

Peplau, L. A., & Spalding, L. R. (2000). The close relationships of lesbians, gay men, and bisexuals. In C. Hendrick & S. S. Hendrick (Eds.), *Close relationships: A sourcebook* (pp. 111–123). Thousand Oaks, CA: Sage.

Peretti, P. O., & Abplanalp, R. R., Jr. (2004). Chemistry in the college dating process: Structure and function. *Social Behavior and Personality, 32,* 147–154.

Perper, T. (1985). *Sex signals: The biology of love.* Philadelphia: ISI Press.

Reiss, I. L. (1986). A sociological journey into sexuality. *Journal of Marriage and the Family, 48,* 233–242.

Rose, S., & Frieze, I. H. (1989). Young singles' scripts for a first date. *Gender & Society, 3,* 258–268.

Rose, S., & Frieze, I. H. (1993). Young singles' contemporary dating scripts. *Sex Roles, 28,* 499–509.

Rose, S., Zand, D., & Cini, M. A. (1993). Lesbian courtship scripts. In E. D. Rothblum & K. T. Brehony (Eds.), *Boston marriages: Romantic but asexual relationships among contemporary lesbians* (pp. 70–85). Amherst: University of Massachusetts Press.

Rusbult, C. E., & Van Lange, P. A. M. (2003). Interdependence, interaction, and relationships. *Annual Review of Psychology, 54,* 351–375.

Sacher, J. A., & Fine, M. A. (1996). Predicting relationship status and satisfaction after six months among dating couples. *Journal of Marriage and the Family, 58,* 21–32.

Scheflen, A. E. (1965). Quasi-courtship behavior in psychotherapy. *Psychiatry, 28,* 245–257.

Sedikides, C., Oliver, M. B., & Campbell, W. K. (1994). Perceived benefits and costs of romantic relationships for women and men: Implications for exchange theory. *Personal Relationships, 1,* 5–21.

Shotland, R. L., & Craig, J. M. (1988). Can men and women differentiate between friendly and sexually interested behavior? *Social Psychology Quarterly, 51,* 66–73.

Smith, S. P. (1996). Dating-partner preferences among a group of inner-city African-American high school students. *Adolescence, 31,* 79–91.

Sprecher, S. (2002). Sexual satisfaction in premarital relationships: Associations with satisfaction, love, commitment, and stability. *Journal of Sex Research, 39,* 190–196.

Sprecher, S., Felmlee, D., Metts, S., Fehr, B., & Vanni, D. (1998). Factors associated with distress following the breakup of a close relationship. *Journal of Social and Personal Relationships, 15,* 791–809.

Sprecher, S., & Hatfield, E. (1994). Token resistance to sexual intercourse and consent to unwanted sexual intercourse: College students' dating experiences in three countries. *Journal of Sex Research, 31,* 125–133.

Sprecher, S., & McKinney, K. (1993). *Sexuality.* Newbury Park, CA: Sage.

Stafford, L., & Canary, D. J. (1991). Maintenance strategies and romantic relationship type, gender and relational characteristics. *Journal of Social and Personal Relationships, 8,* 217–242.

Stafford, L., Dainton, L., & Haas, S. M. (2000). Measuring routine and strategic relational maintenance: Scale revision, sex versus gender roles, and the prediction of relational characteristics. *Communication Monographs, 67,* 306–323.

Stewart, S., Stinnett, H., & Rosenfeld, L. B. (2000). Sex differences in desired characteristics of short-term and long-term relationship partners. *Journal of Social and Personal Relationships, 17,* 843–853.

Tolhuizen, J. H. (1989). Communication strategies for intensifying dating relationships: Identification, use and structure. *Journal of Social and Personal Relationships, 6,* 413–434.

Vogel, D. L., Tucker, C. M., Wester, S. R., & Heesacker, M. (1999). The impact of sex and situational cues on the endorsement of traditional gender-role attitudes and behaviors in dating couples. *Journal of Social and Personal relationships, 16,* 459–473.

Vogel, D. L., Wester, S. R., Heesacker, M., & Madon, S. (2003). Confirming gender stereotypes: A social role perspective. *Sex Roles, 48,* 519–528.

Winstead, B. A., Derlega, V. J., & Rose, S. (1997). *Gender and close relationships.* Thousand Oaks, CA: Sage.

Wood, J. T. (1996). She says/he says: Communication, caring, and conflict in heterosexual relationships. In J. T. Wood (Ed.), *Gendered relationships* (pp. 149–162). Mountain View, CA: Mayfield.

Wood, J. T. (2000). Gender and personal relationships. In C. Hendrick & S. S. Hendrick (Eds.), *Close relationships: A sourcebook* (pp. 301–313). Thousand Oaks, CA: Sage.

Wood, J. T., & Inman, C. (1993). In a different mode: Recognizing masculine modes of communicating closeness. *Journal of Applied Communication Research, 21,* 279–295.

3

GENDER AND FAMILY INTERACTION

Dress Rehearsal for an Improvisation?

◆ Kathleen M. Galvin

The kaleidoscope revolves even faster, patterns are in flux, gendered images do not hold for long. In 1983, Cahill depicted childhood as a dress rehearsal in which children perform and clarify their impressions of what it takes to play the role of girl, boy, man, and woman based on adult expectations and a composite of adult models. After decades of incremental change in family members' enactment of gender, the kaleidoscope's current turning creates new visions and possibilities for family interaction. Thirty years after Cahill's depiction, the last century's scripts are becoming outdated, due in part to the extraordinary changes in gendered U.S. family life, which is emerging as an improvisation rather than a classical drama. Childhood rehearsals become increasingly meaningless by the time we enter adulthood. What children learn during their formative years varies greatly; gendered messages are situationally driven, varying across family structures, cultures, religions, members' sexual orientations, multiple models, and pragmatic concerns. Thus, the meaning of the gendered adult experience in the family will often diverge from previous practice and personal experience and be influenced by the way other family members negotiate and play their parts. Communication takes on a starring role as families become increasingly dependent on discourse to create and manage their gendered identities.

Two approaches dominate understanding of gendered family communication. Historically, scholars conceptualized gender as role bound, with women and men playing distinct parts in response to socialization and particular settings or circumstances in which their roles were embedded. From a role perspective, men and women "are seen as enacting roles that are separable, often complementary, and necessary elements to the integrity of the social settings or structures in which the roles are embedded" (Fox & Murry, 2000, p. 1163). This approach reifies difference between the sexes and suggests that the gender-specific socialization of boys and girls takes place in and reproduces different masculine and feminine speech communities. Such communities are purported to represent different cultures—"people who have different ways of speaking, acting, and interpreting, as well as different values, priorities, and agendas" (MacGeorge, Graves, Feng, Gillihan, & Burleson, 2004, p. 144). The role perspective obscures the difference between the sex of the person playing a role and the role's gendered nature (Fox & Murry, 2000), a critical omission if the goal is to understand how gender shapes perspective, structures social action, and expresses cultural values.

Currently, the preferred approach views gender as a social construct that embodies cultural meanings of masculinity and femininity; essentially, gender is conceived as "a constituent element of social structures, intricately interwoven with other elements of social structures such as class and race, and tied to the social distribution of societal resources" (Fox & Murry, 2000, p. 1164). This approach assumes that "gender is disengaged from norms based on heterosexuality and power differences between men and women, and relationships are thought of in terms of equality rather than gender differences" (Knudson-Martin & Laughlin, 2005, p. 110). Given the increasing diversity of

family life, the social construction lens is an increasingly valuable way to view gender in families. In other words, many children no longer experience a dress rehearsal that prepares them for family life. Rather, more adults-to-be will have to make it up as they go along because, as the possibilities expand, so does the character of gendered family experiences.

This chapter focuses on gender, not sex, in family interaction. It assumes that humans are not born with gender; we learn it. Men and women with masculine inclinations tend to value independence and prefer a degree of distance from others. Conversely, women and men with feminine orientations place a premium on relationship and interpersonal closeness. As individuals negotiate and construct their gender and sexual orientation, they make transitory identifications with multiple discourses (Knudson-Martin & Laughlin, 2005). Persons of both sexes may assume masculine- and feminine-gendered identities within family interactions, and these may shift with changes in individual goals, family structure, familial circumstances and experiences, and trends and conditions in the overall culture.

This chapter is divided into three sections. First, to contextualize contemporary family life, it summarizes demographic trends that affect families in general and gender in particular. The second section addresses gendered family dynamics: parent-child interactions, the management of work/family boundaries, and health-related interaction. This section emphasizes the impact of increasing family diversity on gendered messages exchanged in families. Finally, future directions for examining gendered family interaction will be noted.

◆ Demographics

U.S. family life in general and gendered family dynamics in particular will undergo dramatic transformations in the first decades of the 21st century, including changes in the social definitions of family, variation in lived familial experiences, increased longevity, and medical/technological advances. Families in the 21st century will:

1. Reflect an increasing diversity of self-conceptions, evidenced through structural as well as cultural variations, which will challenge society to rethink historical, nucleocentric biases, traditional views of gender, and economic assumptions.

2. Live increasingly within four and five generations of relational connections. Escalating longevity, changing birth rates, and technological advances will normalize long-term developmental patterns, ongoing multiple intergenerational contacts, and generational reversals.

3. Continually reconfigure family identity across members' life spans as choices of individuals or subgroups create new family configurations through legal, biological, technological, and discursive means (Coontz, 1999; Galvin, 2004a).

◆ Increasing Variability in Families

In the United States, adults continue to partner across their life spans. The 2000 census reveals that the majority of people over 24 were married. Many are in second or third marriages for at least one partner. In recent years marriages have shifted from an ideal of companionship and a sharp division of labor to "individualized marriages," which focus more on each partner's sense of self-expression and work outside the home and less on building a family and embodying spouse and parent roles (Cherlin, 2004). Marriage is becoming more a choice than a necessity for adults who wish intimacy, companionship, and, sometimes, children (Coontz, 2005).

The divorce rate's upward curve has leveled out. In 2000, about 9.7% of males and 10.8% of females reported that they were currently divorced, with those in the 45- to 54-year-old age group reporting the highest percentage of divorces (Kreider & Simmons, 2003). Their children are likely to live in one or more stepfamilies. Stepfamilies, formed through remarriage or cohabitation, generally reflect divorce and recommitment, although an increasing number are formed by single mothers marrying for the first time. Married or cohabiting adults parent 4.4 million stepchildren (Kreider, 2003), who will experience multiple parenting models.

Single-parent families are increasing. In 2000, 22% of children lived with only their mothers; 4% lived with only their fathers (Simmons & O'Neill, 2001). Women under 30, pregnant for the first time, are more likely to be single than married. Approximately 40% of births to unmarried women occur in the context of cohabiting couples (Bumpass & Lu, 2000). Single women and men who adopt children add to the number of single-parent families.

Gay and lesbian committed couples and families are becoming more visible. The 2000 census found that more than half a million households were headed by same-sex partners, representing 1% of all coupled households; 33% of women and 22% of men in same-sex partnerships lived with children (Simmons & O'Connell, 2003). Same-sex partners tended to parent older children from former heterosexual unions; today, many are parents of infants or adopted young children. Increasingly, intentional families, those formed without biological and legal ties, are maintained by members' self-definitional discourse and shared experiences.

◆ Intergenerational Connections

As life spans increase, family members are faced with renegotiating their identities over decades and across generations. Multigenerational bonds are becoming critical for well-being and support (Bengston, 2001). The average life expectancy for an individual born in the United States in 2000 is 76.9 years: 74.1 years for males and 79.5 year for females. These are averages for all race/ethnicities (Arias, 2004). Because of increases in longevity and decreases in fertility, the population age structure in most industrialized nations has changed from a pyramid to a rectangle, creating "a family structure in which the shape is long and thin, with more family generations alive but with fewer members in the generation" (Bengston, 2001, p. 5). Grandparenting and its great and great-great variations is becoming a more prominent familial role (Simmons & Dye, 2003).

Ethnicity intersects with changes in family form and intergenerational ties. Black men and women represent the lowest percentages of currently married individuals. In 2000, 42% of Black men were married, while just 31% of Black women were (Kreider & Simmons, 2003). A growing number of African American women are choosing to become single parents rather than remain childless (Hines & Boyd-Franklin, 1996). As immigration increases, more variation in U.S. family life will occur. Certain religious and cultural traditions support strong male-female distinctions, and recent immigrant populations embrace strong extended-family ties. Many of these changes will influence gender enactment and family interaction across a wide spectrum of familial structures. Improvisation will be a key to successful family functioning.

◆ *Gendered Dynamics Within Families*

PARENT-CHILD INTERACTION

Parent-child interaction patterns are changing due, in part, to increasing family diversity. Traditionally, children were expected to learn about gender by relying on their parents as models and instructors. Heterosexual parents tended to socialize children into socially accepted norms for gender (West & Turner, 1995). Parents tend to talk more about emotion, for example, with daughters than sons (Fivush, Brotman, Buckner, & Goodman, 2000). Fagot and Lienbach (1989) found that when parents provide positive and negative responses to sex-typed toys, children become early labelers of gender. Parents are more likely to talk to and interact more with their daughters and play more actively with their sons (Doyle & Paludi, 1991). Yet heterosexual fathers may withdraw from sons whom they sense to be different or gay (Holleran, 2002), modeling a distant parenting style. It is more acceptable for girls to act masculine than it is for boys to act feminine, leading to the claim that "overall, boys are more intensively and rigidly pushed to become masculine than girls are to become feminine" (Wood, 2005, p. 156).

Although this unidirectional pattern of parent-to-child traditionally gendered interaction continues in some families, in others it is beginning to give way to a more bidirectional approach that includes reciprocal, mutual influence, reflecting changes in the life circumstances of parents as well as children. This bidirectional influence "recognizes the dual role of child and parent on the emergence and maintenance of parenting beliefs and practices" (Parke, 2002, p. 70).

Because many children will live in more than one family before reaching adulthood, parental gender socialization will be accomplished by multiple adults. As more children grow up in or witness single-parent families, stepfamilies, same-sex-parent families or other configurations, and as more families raise children who openly self-identify as gay or lesbian, cohabit rather than marry, or adopt as single parents, understandings of gender and family will continue to diversify. In African American families headed by single women, daughters frequently exhibit greater self-reliance and self-esteem than their Caucasian counterparts (Diggs, 1999). Weston (1991) suggests that, although doing so involves risk, those who encountered positive responses to coming out "quietly imported choice into the notion of blood family" (p. 73).

Gay fathers report efforts to maintain open communication with their children and involve their children in decision making (West & Turner, 1995). Tasker and Golombok (1997) found that young people raised by lesbian couples reported more positive relationships with their mother's female partner than did same-age respondents who reported on their relationship to their heterosexual mother's male partner.

Although the number of single-father families is small and understudied, Hatfield and Abrams (1995) found that they were highly cohesive and that father-child discussions are more extended and less competitive than discussions between fathers and children in two-parent families. As children are exposed to different family forms, they encounter multiple models and messages regarding gendered family life.

Historically, the majority of communication-oriented parenting studies address mother-daughter interaction (Segrin & Flora, 2005). Talk permits mothers and daughters to exchange information, advice, and encouragement, and it is the primary way that mothers and daughters demonstrate mutual care and support (Trad, 1995). Female children disclose significantly more information to parents than male children (Pennington & Turner, 2004). Children's self-disclosures vary by age. Noller and Callan (1990) suggest that mothers' more frequent initiation of discussions with their younger adolescent children and their greater recognition of their children's opinions lead older adolescents to interact more with mothers than fathers. Papini, Farmer, Clark, Micka, and Barnett's (1990) examination of age and gender differences in adolescents' emotional self-disclosure to parents and friends found females disclosed significantly more information to both parents and best friends than did males They also found that 12-year-olds were more likely to share emotional disclosure with parents whereas 15-year-olds preferred to disclose to friends.

The growing literature on mother-daughter discussions of sex reflects the tendency of mothers to discuss this topic more frequently with their children, particularly daughters. Sons engage in far less parent-child talk about sex than daughters (Warren, 2003). Girls who talk to their mothers about sexual topics are more likely to have conservative sexual values and are less likely to have engaged in sexual activity than girls who mostly talked to their friends (Dilorio, Kelley, & Hockenberry-Eaton, 1999). Mother-daughter discussion about condoms was associated with consistent condom use (Hutchinson, 2002). Although mothers have consistently been found to be the primary communicators of sexual topics with children, fathers may play an important role with daughters through the discussion of sociosexual issues such as "understanding men" or resisting pressure for sex (Hutchinson, 2002). Yet even when both parents are involved, they are more likely to talk about sex with daughters rather than sons (Warren, 2003).

In her ethnographic study of three female generations in one family, Miller-Day (2004) identified two distinct patterns of dominant forces and discursive practices within the maternal relationships, suggesting relational identities and personal identity are intertwined. In highly interconnected relational cultures, "individuals were empowered to construct their own identities within the context of the relational culture" (p. 224).

Fathers tend to talk less with children. Buerkel-Rothfuss, Fink, and Buerkel (1995) suggest that differences between father-son and father-daughter dyads may be due to a tendency for fathers to talk more with daughters and engage more in activities with sons. At the same time, Morman and Floyd (2002) report that contemporary fathers indicate higher levels of closeness with their sons and greater affectionate verbal and nonverbal communication with sons than they experienced with their fathers. In part, fathers report experiencing more time strain between work and children than mothers do (Milkie, Mattingly, Nomaguchi, Bianchi, & Robinson, 2004).

Fathers are less likely than mothers to be involved in nurturing children with special needs. Fathers of children with mood disorders struggle more with accepting the illness and are less likely to participate in therapy efforts than mothers are (Schock, Gavazzi, Fristad, & Goldberg-Arnold, 2002). Yet father involvement is important. Webb, Walker, Bollis, and Hebbani (2004) found that, "mothers had no direct influence over males' and females' self-esteem, whereas fathers' communication affected self-esteem" (p. 214), leading the authors to speculate that the fathers' interaction may be highly valued because, typically, fathers are not as available as mothers. Leaper, Anderson, and Sanders (1998) suggest that when fathers communicate, it represents an added value. The lack of father talk may reflect the fact that many males are socialized to view talk as a means for accomplishing instrumental tasks, providing information, and maintaining status and autonomy (Wood & Inman, 1993). But this is likely to change as the increase in single and same-sex-partner fathers compels men to communicate with daughters and sons about critical topics. Research indicates that parent-child communication patterns reflect parental availability. Traditionally, mothers have spent more time with their children than fathers. La Rossa (1998) found that men spend one third the time that women do in one-on-one communication with children. Yet Silverstein (2002) reports that fathers are spending increasing amounts of time with their children, and fathers in dual-shift working-class families are also more involved with them.

Finally, ethnicity influences parent-child interactions. Pennington and Turner (2004) found that African American mothers were more likely than European American mothers to characterize adolescent daughters as best friends, set more rules, tell more blunt stories, and use more sarcasm. Survival was a theme of key conversations. In their study of parenting, Socha, Sanchez-Hucles, Bromley, and Kelly (1995) found African American parents were more likely to act as cultural advisers and to use more stringent discipline than European American parents.

Recent thinking about parenting and gender has shifted from previous binary assumptions. Today there is an increasing focus on co-parenting within two-parent, as well as divorced, families, stressing parental negotiation of roles, responsibilities, and contributions to children rather than a reliance on sex roles to establish expectations (Doherty & Beaton, 2004). Parke (2002) suggests, "It may be helpful to recast the issue to ask whether it is exposure to the interactive style typically associated with either mothers or fathers that matters" (p. 78). Silverstein reports that gay fathers who established a gay identity and lifestyle and then decided to parent "developed their own ideology of degendered parenting" (p. 48).

◆ Work/Family Interface

Managing work and family boundaries creates a critical tension faced by many heterosexual, same-sex partners, and single parents as the culture transforms traditional role-bound understandings of marriage, partnering, parenting, and employment. It appears that family boundaries are asymmetrically permeable, suggesting that work interferes with family life more than family life interferes with work (Frone & Russell, 1992), a finding that defines the site of greater tension as within the family. Under the traditional role-bound gender model, males were breadwinners/providers and females were homemakers/caretakers. As women's employment outside of the home increased, the concept of the second shift, or the housework and child care responsibilities that needed to be managed by dual-earner partners, gained prominence (Hochschild & Machung, 2003). Family life has become increasingly unpredictable as men and women take on new responsibilities or struggle with partners' expectations that they change their provider or caretaker behaviors. The National Survey of the

Changing Workforce reported that, in 2002, 78% of all married employees had spouses who worked outside of the home whereas only 66% did in 1977 (Bond, Thompson, Galinsky, & Prottas, 2002). Changes in earning power further fray the traditional breadwinner/homemaker roles. In just over 30% of married, two-worker households, the woman earns more than the man (Tyre & McGinn, 2003), although in the general population women's annual earnings are still significantly less than men's (Bond et al., 2002).

Time spent managing work and home remains a stress point for most dual-career and dual-earner couples and single parents. Employed men tend to work an hour longer a day in jobs outside the home than employed women, while women employed outside of the home tend to work longer hours at home. In many two-earner families, women spend an hour a day more caring for young children and, if older children are involved, women spend six hours a day in "secondary care," such as shopping with children, while men spend four hours (McNeil, 2004). In some two-earner families, women are opting for more overtime at work because it feels more nurturing and provides an escape from the pressures of children and housework (Hochschild, 1997).

Most heterosexual couples confront frustrations as they negotiate their shifts. Men who may be doing more housework or child care than they saw their fathers perform view themselves as contributing actively or equally, but their partners frequently disagree. Women claim they are expected to fulfill the "maternal gatekeeper" role in which they still manage all the planning and oversight of tasks while men help with tasks (Allen & Hawkins, 1999). Males frequently argue that their partners insist on the housework or child care being done according to their specifications. When women criticize or redo tasks, their male partners may become angry or deliberately complete tasks poorly (Allen & Hawkins, 1999). Studies of the division of labor indicate that "although dual earner wives perform two to three times more household labor than their husbands, less than one third of these women report the allocation of tasks to be unfair" (Perry-Jenkins, Pierce, & Goldberg, 2004, p. 544). This finding may reflect an unspoken collusion between partners whereby women maintain control of the psychological responsibility by setting work standards that only they can meet. Men do less work because this is acceptable to their partners.

Few dual-earner couples share family responsibilities equally. Dual-earner families with children under 13 experience more negative home moods, more marital tension, and less marital support (Hughes & Galinsky, 1994). The costs of the second shift may explain why some female high-achievers with financially successful partners depart the fast-paced career track to raise children. This "opt-out revolution" raises questions about the future work/life management and creates controversy among those who see this as stalling the women's revolution (Belkin, 2003).

This work/family research is conducted routinely with married or cohabiting partners. Much less is known about how same-sex partners manage these boundaries. Limited studies indicate that most gay and lesbian partnerships reject dividing labor based on gender and a norm of greater male status and power. Most same-sex couples are in dual-provider relationships, with the common division of labor at home reflecting ongoing negotiation regarding sharing tasks or dividing them according to preference or necessity (Peplau & Beals, 2004).

Single parents face additional challenges in managing their work and family life because there is no partner with whom to share tasks or concerns and frustrations. Many also face serious economic pressures (Heath & Orthner, 1999). Some single parents choose to live with other family members in order to gain support. Mothers with total child care responsibilities tend to work longer hours outside of the home and experience more stress and less emotional support than other single mothers (Gringlas &

Weintraub, 1995). Whereas many low-income single parents work long hours and may hold more than one job, many economically self-sufficient, professional, single mothers attempt to negotiate changes in their work lives, such as telecommuting or shifting to contract work in order to gain parenting time (Hertz, 1999). Male and female single parents in comparable work environments adapt similarly to managing work and family responsibilities, although women tended to vary coping patterns during their work lives while men use the same pattern until later in their careers, when they prioritize family (Heath & Orthner, 1999). When their work and family demands are in conflict, single fathers and mothers are equally likely to prioritize work over family demands.

Finally, much less is known about how race interfaces with the work/family balance. For example, historically African American women have worked outside the home, often as sole wage earners, especially in times of high unemployment (Hines & Boyd-Franklin, 1996). Children working in close proximity to their mothers receive distinct types of mothering. Asian American children working in urban family businesses report long days split between work and school, while migrant farm children have less access to educational opportunities (Collins, 1999).

The majority of communication-oriented studies focus on how family issues are discussed or negotiated in the workplace; far fewer focus on interaction within the household (Kirby, Golden, Medved, Jorgenson, & Buzzanell, 2003). It appears that there is less talk about work at home than vice versa (Nippert-Eng, 1996). Perceived unfairness in the division of labor tends to predict marital conflict. Yet little is known about how dual-worker couples talk about ideas of fairness, how conversations take place, and how partners react to the requests or demands of the other (Perry-Jenkins, Repetti, & Crouter, 2004, p. 544). In Golden's (2001) study of the communicative management of multiple roles,

partners were very actively engaged in role redefinitions that take place on an ongoing basis but which are more salient during life crises. Many couples reported that such work-family decision making was part of an ongoing pattern, although for couples who talk about the issues, it appears that women disproportionately initiate the conversations (Perry-Jenkins et al., 2004). Increasingly, women, and some men, parent and work within a home-based context. In her study of home-based female artists and mothers, Jorgenson (1995) found that their boundaries tended to be fluid as they adjusted work rhythms to children's schedules, created work space adjoining living space, and redefined their artistic production. Edley's (2004) study of home-based female entrepreneurs who co-construct their identities online indicates that online text construction provides control of personal presentation as well as a sense of agency and power.

Men and their perspectives on family life remain understudied. Levine (2000) suggests that "any discussion about family life, including the father's role, is for the most part shaped by women's vision" (p. 37). Those who take advantage of parental leave or flexible work benefits are seen as less invested in their careers (Kirby & Krone, 2002). Men who take family leaves when their children are young assume more involved parenting roles as children grow older (Hochschild, 1997). In their study of after-work debriefing conversations, Vangelisti and Banski (1993) found that husbands' expressiveness and ability to self-disclose affects both husbands' and wives' relational satisfaction more than wives' ability to be open and expressive.

Certain careers present unique parenting challenges. In her study of Silicon Valley professional fathers, Cooper (2000) investigated how someone can simultaneously be the go-to guy in a high-pressure nerd culture of long hours and fast-paced involvement and still be an active father. She identified three coping models: "superdads" who attempt to meet all work and family obligations without sacrificing in either sphere; traditionals who view domestic duties along traditional gendered lines while emphasizing income production as the male role; and transitionals who resolve the contradiction by reneging on their egalitarian ideology, allowing their wives to carry much of the family work. Today, most fathers continue to be expected to provide economic support (Kirby & Krone, 2002) and face restricted choices when attempting to balance work and partnering/parenting (Galvin, 2004b).

◆ *Gendered Health in Families*

A growing number of health studies report gender differences across various family structures. Most studies focus on married couples, suggesting that married individuals experience better mental and physical health than unmarried ones, although the unmarried tend to be happier than the unhappily married (Kiecolt-Glaser & Newton, 2001). Two primary explanations for this finding exist. The selection hypothesis proposes that healthier people are more likely to marry and remain married; the protection hypothesis suggests that married people receive protections, such as a less risky lifestyle, companionship, and instrumental and/or emotional support, all of which buffer against health problems (Segrin & Flora, 2005).

Although generally good for both partners, marriage appears to create gendered health impacts. Waite and Gallagher (2000) suggest that, "both men and women live longer, healthier, and wealthier lives when married, but husbands typically get greater health benefits from marriages than do wives" (p. 163). Concurring, Kiecolt-Glaser and Newton (2001) report that, "marriages' protective effects are notably stronger for men than women" (p. 472).

Distressed or unhappy marriages have particularly notable consequences, especially for women. Gottman and Notarius's (2002) literature review suggests that whereas marriage offers health-buffering effects for men, women are likely to experience health-related problems in distressed marriages. Women are likely to experience more negative physiological changes as a result of negative interactions (Jones, Beach & Jackson, 2004). Marital disagreements are associated with women's higher blood pressure and heart rates (Kiecolt-Glaser & Newton, 2001). Women whose early marriage experiences were distressed had double the level of ACTH, a stress hormone, 10 years later than did women whose early marriages were not distressed (Kiecolt-Glaser, Bane, Glaser, & Malarkey, 2003). Even long-term married couples have immune responses to negative marital interaction (Kiecolt-Glaser et al., 1997). After reviewing a wide range of studies, Kiecolt-Glaser and Newton (2001) reported that women's physiological changes following marital conflict show greater persistence.

Yet Levenson, Cartensen, and Gottman (1994) reported that men experience greater negative physiological arousal to marital conflict—responses so intense that men tend to shut down or withdraw as a way to manage it. They suggest that wives push to resolve conflicts, undeterred by emotional arousal, whereas husbands experience the emotional arousal as extremely aversive and act to disengage from the conflict. This stonewalling, or withdrawal from the interaction, is a behavior exhibited primarily by males that negatively affects females. Whereas most men do not tend to get physiologically aroused when their wives withdraw, wives' heart rates increase significantly when their husbands stonewall (Gottman, 1994); this disengagement creates relief for men and distress for women.

The psychological impact of marital interaction also affects wives and husbands differently. Waite and Gallagher (2000) report that marriage is more positive for mental health than other lifestyles, yet husbands benefit more than wives. The emotional climate of distressed marriages, including less positive affect, more negative affect, and more reciprocity of negative, but not positive, affect, creates greater psychological suffering for women (Noller & Fitzpatrick, 1990). Women are more negatively affected by overt expressions of hostility than their spouses (Gaelick, Bodenhausen, & Wyer, 1985). Although women tended to be better at encoding positive messages than their spouses (Larson & Almeida, 1999). Noller and Fitzpatrick (1990) suggest that wives may act negatively to convey to their husbands the seriousness of their relational dissatisfaction. In married couples, daily emotions tend to flow from husbands to wives more often, possibly because women attempt to be empathetic (Larson & Almeida, 1999).

Everyday health-related marital interaction also reflects gender. Nagging, frequently perceived to be a feminine behavior, may be reframed as a protective strategy increasingly used by both partners. Women tended to be better at encoding positive messages than their spouses (Larson & Almeida, 1999). Soule (2003) found that married partners who nagged appeared motivated by love and a concern for their spouses' well-being. Although wives tend to monitor their husbands' health habits, discourage drinking and smoking, encourage regular sleeping habits and physical activity, and prepare healthy meals, nagging is not uniquely gendered. Eight of 10 married men and 6 of 10 married women reported that their spouse reminded them to do something to protect their health (Waite & Gallagher, 2000). Geist-Martin, Ray, and Sharf (2003) suggest that, in situations of illness, support does not appear to differ based on gender. Effective health strategies for both partners include engaging in the health behavior together, engaging in facilitative behavior, and providing emotional support (Tucker & Mueller, 2000).

Spousal illness affects marital interaction (Segrin & Flora, 2005). Healthy spouses may self-monitor complaints to avoid adding to their partners' problems, the illness may become a major topic, and the healthy spouse may be overburdened with caretaking responsibilities. Changes in couples' functioning, due to major health problems such as cancer, stroke, or heart attack, may affect their sex life and their social life.

Other areas of family health communication appear gendered. Brown (2001) found that men do not see health as part of day-to-day discourse except when facing critical health issues, such as suffering a heart attack. Most men reported the expectation that women would take care of the health of the family. Health-related family communication is managed more frequently by females than males. A study of female genetic counseling clients found that they were willing to talk with family members about relatives' conditions, though there were particular difficulties in initiating conversations if the respondents were male. Communication increased with female relatives (Green, Richards, Murton, Statham, & Hallowell, 1997). Fathers and mothers tend to react in different ways to the news that their child has a disability. Fathers tend to respond less emotionally and focus on the long–term effects, while mothers respond more emotionally. Some fathers reject their child and withdraw, while mothers tend to carry the major load of caretaking (Seligman & Darling, 1997). In her study of diabetics' siblings, Pavlik (2004) found that female siblings received more caretaking messages than did males, regardless of birth order.

Although family health communication reflects strong gender patterns, more recent work also indicates that an increasing number of males engage in caretaking, social support, and monitoring. As more men are involved in single parenting, in same-sex partnerships and parenting, in cohabiting stepfamilies, and as longevity is coupled with long-term illness maintenance, sharp distinctions in gendered health behaviors will continue to diminish.

◆ New Directions

Emerging technologies will impact gendered family interaction; the effects of evolving digital media and reproductive technologies on gendered family interaction needs systematic scholarly attention. Jordan (2003) calls for an exploration in which family members set up guidelines about how, when, and where the Internet is used. Currently little is known about how gender interacts with new digital media across a range of family structures. As reproductive technologies become more sophisticated, increasing numbers of heterosexual as well as gay and lesbian individuals or couples will become parents. Decisions about using reproductive technology involve family conversations before and after birth. Lesbian couples considering donor insemination are faced with multiple decisions including deciding on a donor and on which partner will bear the child (Chabot & Ames, 2004). Parke (2002) calls for studies on how donor involvement with the family interacts with family structural variables.

Each passing decade of kaleidoscopic change will bring more challenges to heteronormative gendering, binary roles, and the privileging of only biological and legal ties as "genuine" family (Oswald, Blume, & Marks, 2005). Communication research must reflect this ongoing shift from classical drama to improvisation in gendered family life.

◆ References

Allen, S. M., & Hawkins, A. J. (1999). Maternal gatekeeping: Mother's beliefs and behaviors that inhibit greater father involvement in family work. *Journal of Marriage and the Family, 61,* 199–212.

Arias, E. (2004). United States life tables, 2001. *National Vital Statistics Reports, 52*(14). Hyattsville, MD: National Center for Health Statistics. Retrieved August 10, 2004, from www.cdc.gov/nchsfastats/lifexpec.htm

Belkin, L. (2003, October 26). The opt-out revolution. *New York Times Magazine,* pp. 42–47, 58, 85–86.

Bengston, V. L. (2001). Beyond the nuclear family: The increasing importance of multigenerational bonds. *Journal of Marriage and the Family, 63,* 1–16.

Bond, J. T., Thompson, C., Galinsky, E., & Prottas, D. (2002). Highlights of the national study of the changing workforce: Executive summary. *Families and Work Institute, 3,* 1–4.

Brown, S. (2001). What makes men talk about health? *Journal of Gender Studies, 10,* 187–195.

Buerkel-Rothfuss, N. L., Fink, D. S., & Buerkel, R. (1995). Communication in the father-child dyad: The intergenerational transmission process. In T. J. Socha & G. H. Stamp (Eds.), *Parents, children, and communication: Frontiers of theory and research* (pp. 63–85). Mahwah, NJ: Erlbaum.

Bumpass, L. L., & Lu, H. H. (2000). Trends in cohabitation and implications for children's family contexts in the United States. *Population Studies, 54,* 19–41.

Bumpus, M. F., Crouter, A. C., & McHale, S. M. (1999). Work demands of dual–earner couples: Implications for parents' knowledge about children's daily lives in middle childhood. *Journal of Marriage and the Family, 61,* 465–475.

Cahill, S. E. (1983). Reexamining the acquisition of sex roles: A social interactionist approach. *Sex Roles, 9,* 1–15.

Chabot, J. M., & Ames, B. D. (2004). It wasn't "let's get pregnant and go do it": Decision making in lesbian couples planning motherhood via donor insemination. *Family Relations, 53,* 348–356.

Cherlin, A. J. (2004). The deinstitutionalization of American marriage. *Journal of Marriage and the Family, 66,* 848–861.

Collins, P. H. (1999). Shifting the center: Race, class, and feminist theorizing about motherhood. In S. Coontz (Ed.), *American families: A multicultural reader* (pp. 197-217). New York: Routledge.

Coontz, S. (Ed.). (1999). *American families: A multicultural reader.* New York: Routledge.

Coontz, S. (2005). *Marriage, a history: From obedience to intimacy, or how love conquered marriage.* New York: Viking.

Cooper, M. (2000). Being the "go-to-guy": Fatherhood, masculinity, and the organization of work in Silicon Valley. *Qualitative Sociology, 23,* 379–405.

Diggs, R. C. (1999). African-American and European-American adolescents' perceptions of self-esteem as influenced by parent and peer communication and support environments. In T. J. Socha & R. C. Diggs (Eds.), *Communication, race, and family* (pp. 105–146). Mahwah, NJ: Erlbaum.

Dilorio, C., Kelley, M., & Hockenberry-Eaton, M. (1999). Communication about sexual issues: Mothers, fathers, and friends. *Journal of Adolescent Health, 24,* 181–189.

Doherty, W. J., & Beaton, J. M. (2004). Mothers and fathers parenting together. In A. Vangelisti (Ed.), *Handbook of family communication* (pp. 269–286). Mahwah, NJ: Erlbaum.

Doyle, J. A., & Paludi, M. A. (1991). *Sex and gender: The human experience.* Dubuque, IA: William C. Brown.

Edley, P. P. (2004). Entrepreneurial mothers' balance of work and family. In P. M. Buzzanell, H. Sterk, & L. H. Turner (Eds.), *Gender in applied contexts* (pp. 255–273). Thousand Oaks, CA: Sage.

Fagot, B., & Lienbach, M. (1989). The young child's gender schema: Environmental input, internal organization. *Child Development, 60,* 663–672.

Fivush, R., Brotman, M. A., Buckner, J. P., & Goodman, S. H. (2000). Gender differences in parent-child emotion narratives. *Sex Roles, 42,* 223–253.

Fox, G. L., & Murry, V. M. (2000). Gender and families: Feminist perspectives and family research. *Journal of Marriage and the Family, 62,* 1160–1172.

Frone, M. R., & Russell, M. (1992). Prevalence of work-family conflict: Are work and family boundaries asymmetrically permeable? *Journal of Organizational Behavior, 13,* 723–729.

Gaelick, L., Bodenhausen, G. V., & Wyer, R. S. J. (1985). Emotional communication in close relationships. *Journal of Personality and Social Psychology, 49,* 1246–1265.

Galvin, K. M. (2004a). The family of the future: What do we face? In A. Vangelisti (Ed.), *Handbook of family communication* (pp. 675–697). Mahwah, NJ: Erlbaum.

Galvin, K. M. (2004b). The pastiche of gender and family communication. In P. M. Buzzanell, H. Sterk, & L. H. Turner (Eds.), *Gender in applied communication contexts* (pp. 311–316). Thousand Oaks, CA: Sage.

Geist-Martin, P., Ray, E. B., & Sharf, B. F. (2003). *Communicating health: Personal, cultural and political complexities.* Belmont, CA: Wadsworth.

Golden, A. (2001). Modernity and the communicative management of multiple roles: The case of the worker-parent. *Journal of Family Communication, 1,* 233–264.

Gottman, J. M. (1994). *Why marriages succeed or fail.* New York: Simon & Schuster.

Gottman, J. M., & Notarius, C. I. (2002). Marital research in the 20th century and a research agenda for the 21st century. *Family Process, 41,* 159–197.

Green, J., Richards, M., Murton, F. Statham, H., & Hallowell, N. (1997). Family communication & genetic counseling: The cure of hereditary breast & ovarian cancer. *Journal of Genetic Counseling, 6,* 45–60.

Gringlas, M., & Weintraub, M. (1995). The more things change . . . single parenting revisited. *Journal of Family Issues, 16,* 29–52.

Hatfield, S. R., & Abrams, Lori J. (1995). Interaction between fathers and their children in traditional and single-father families. In T. J. Socha & G. H. Stamp (Eds.), *Parents, children and communication: Frontiers of theory and research* (pp. 103–112). Mahwah, NJ: Erlbaum.

Heath, D. T., & Orthner, D. K. (1999). Stress and adaptation among male and female single parents. *Journal of Family Issues, 20,* 557–587.

Hertz, R. (1999). Working to place family at the center of life: Dual earner and single-parent strategies. *Annals of the American Academy of Political & Social Science, 562,* 16–32.

Hines, P. M., & Boyd-Franklin, N. (1996). African American families. In M. McGoldrick, J. Giordano, & J. K. Pearce (Eds.), *Ethnicity and family therapy* (pp. 66–84). New York: Guilford Press.

Hochschild, A. R. (1997). *The time bind: When work becomes home and home becomes work.* New York: Metropolitan Books.

Hochschild, A. (with Machung, A.). (2003). *The second shift: Working parents and the revolution at home* (Rev. ed.). New York: Viking/Penguin Press.

Holleran, A. (2002). Foreword. In B. Shenitz (Ed.), *The man I might become* (pp. xi–xiv). New York: Marlowe.

Hughes, D., & Galinsky, E. (1994). Work experiences and marital interactions: Elaborating the complexity of work. *Journal of Organizational Behavior, 15*, 423–438.

Hutchinson, M. K. (2002). The influence of sexual risk communication between parents and daughters on sexual risk behaviors. *Family Relations, 51*, 238–247.

Jones, D. J., Beach, S. R. H., & Jackson, H. (2004). Family influences on health: A framework to organize research and guide intervention. In A. Vangelisti (Ed.), *Handbook of family communication* (pp. 647–672). Mahwah, NJ: Erlbaum.

Jordan, A. B. (2003). A family systems approach to examining the role of the Internet in the home. In J. Turow & A. L. Kavanaugh (Eds.), *The wired homestead* (pp. 141–160). Cambridge: MIT Press.

Jorgenson, J. (1995). Marking the work-family boundary: Mother-child interaction and home-based work. In T. J. Socha & G. H. Stamp (Eds.), *Parents, children and communication: Frontiers of theory and research* (pp. 203–217). Mahwah, NJ: Erlbaum.

Kiecolt-Glaser, J. K., Bane, C., Glaser, R., & Malarkey, W. B. (2003). Love, marriage and divorce: Newlyweds stress hormones foreshadow relationship changes. *Journal of Consulting and Clinical Psychology, 71*, 176–188.

Kiecolt-Glaser, J. K., Glaser, R., Cacioppo, J. T., MacCallum, R. C., Syndersmith, M., Kim, C., & Malarkey, W. B. (1997). Marital conflict in older adults: Endochronological and immunological correlates. *Psychosomatic Medicine, 59*, 339–349.

Kiecolt-Glaser, J. K., & Newton, T. L. (2001). Marriage and health: His and hers. *Psychological Bulletin, 127*, 472–503.

Kirby, E. L., Golden, A. G., Medved, C. E., Jorgenson, J., & Buzzanell, P. M. (2003). An organizational communication challenge to the discourse of work and family research: From problematics to empowerment. In P. Kalbfleisch (Ed.), *Communication yearbook* (Vol. 27, pp. 1–44). Mahwah, NJ: Erlbaum.

Kirby, E. L., & Krone, K. J. (2002). "The policy exists but you can't really use it": Communication and the structuration of work-family policies. *Journal of Applied Communication Research, 30*, 50–77.

Knudson-Martin, C., & Laughlin, M. J. (2005). Gender and sexual orientation in family therapy: Toward a postgender approach. *Family Relations, 54*, 101–115.

Kreider, R. M. (2003, October). Adopted children and stepchildren: 2000 (C2KBR-30). *Census 2000 Special Reports*. Washington, DC: U.S. Census Bureau, Department of Commerce.

Kreider, R. M., & Simmons, T. (2003, October). Marital status: 2000 (C2KBR-30). *Census 2000 Special Reports*. Washington, DC: U.S. Census Bureau, Department of Commerce.

La Rossa, R. (1998). The culture and conduct of fatherhood. In K. V. Hansen & A. I. Garey (Eds.), *Family in the U.S.: Kinship and domestic policies* (pp. 377–385). Philadelphia: Temple University Press.

Larson, R. W., & Almeida, D. M. (1999). Emotional transmission in the daily lives of families: A new paradigm for studying family process. *Journal of Marriage and the Family, 61*, 5–20.

Leaper, C., Anderson, K. J., & Sanders, P. (1998). Moderators of gender effects on parents' talk to their children: A meta-analysis. *Developmental Psychology, 34*, 3–27.

Levenson, R. W., Cartensen, L. L., & Gottman, J. M. (1994). The influence of age and gender on affect, physiology, and their interrelations: A study of long-term marriages. *Journal of Personality and Social Psychology, 67*, 56–68.

Levine, S. B. (2000). *Father courage: What happens when men put family first*. New York: Harcourt.

MacGeorge, E. L., Graves, A. R., Feng, B., Gillihan, S. J., & Burleson, B. R. (2004). The myth of gender cultures: Similarities outweigh differences in men's and women's provision of and responses to supportive communication. *Sex Roles, 50*, 143–175.

McNeil Jr., D. G. (2004, September 19). Culture or chromosomes? Real men don't clean bathrooms. *New York Times*. Sec. 4, p. 3.

Milkie, M. A., Mattingly, M. J., Nomaguchi, K. M., Bianchi, S. M., & Robinson, J. P. (2004). The time squeeze: Parental strategies and feelings about time with children. *Journal of Marriage and Family, 66,* 739–761.

Miller-Day, M. (2004). *Communication among grandmothers, mothers, and adult daughters: A qualitative study of maternal relationships.* Mahwah, NJ: Erlbaum.

Morman, M. T., & Floyd, K. (2002). A "changing culture of fatherhood": Effects on affectionate communication, closeness, and satisfaction in men's relationships with their fathers and their sons. *Western Journal of Communication, 66,* 395–411.

Nippert-Eng, C. E. (1996). *Home and work.* Chicago: University of Chicago Press.

Noller, P., & Callan, V. J. (1990). Adolescents' perceptions of the nature of their communication with parents. *Journal of Youth and Adolescence, 19,* 349–362.

Noller, P., & Fitzpatrick, M. A. (1990). Marital communication in the eighties. *Journal of Marriage and the Family, 52,* 832–843.

Oswald, R. F., Blume, L. B., & Marks, S. R. (2005). Decentering heteronormativity: A model for family studies. In V. L. Bengston, A. C. Acock, K. R. Allen, P. Dilworth-Anderson, & D. M. Klein (Eds.), *Sourcebook of family theory and research* (pp. 143–154). Thousand Oaks, CA: Sage.

Papini, D. R., Farmer, F. F., Clark, S. M., Micka, J. C., & Barnett, J. K. (1990). Early adolescent age and gender differences in patterns of emotional self-disclosure to parents and friends. *Adolescence, 25,* 959–975.

Parke, R. D. (2002). Parenting in the new millennium: Prospects, promises and pitfalls. In J. P. McHale & W. S. Grolnick (Eds.), *Retrospect and prospect in the psychological study of families* (pp. 65–93). Mahwah, NJ: Erlbaum.

Pavlik, L. (2004). *The effect of a sibling's diabetes on a non-diabetic sibling: A communicative approach.* Unpublished undergraduate honors thesis, Northwestern University.

Pennington, B. A., & Turner, L. H. (2004). Playground or training ground? The function of talk in African American and European American mother-adolescent daughter dyads. In P. M. Buzzanell, H. Sterk, & L. H. Turner (Eds.), *Gender in applied contexts* (pp. 275–294). Thousand Oaks, CA: Sage.

Peplau, L. A., & Beals, K. B. (2004). The family lives of lesbians and gay men. In A. Vangelisti (Ed.), *Handbook of family communication* (pp. 233–248). Mahwah, NJ: Erlbaum.

Perry-Jenkins, M., Pierce, C. P., & Goldberg, A. E. (2004). Discourses on diapers and dirty laundry: Family communication about childcare and housework. In A. Vangelisti (Ed.), *Handbook of family communication* (pp. 541–561). Mahwah, NJ: Erlbaum.

Perry-Jenkins, M., Repetti, R. L., & Crouter, A. C. (2000). Work and family in the 1990's. *Journal of the Marriage and the Family, 62,* 981–998.

Schock, A. M., Gavazzi, S. M., Fristad, M. A., & Goldberg-Arnold, J. S. (2002). The role of father participation in the treatment of childhood mood disorders. *Family Relations, 51,* 230–237.

Segrin, C., & Flora, F. J. (2005). *Family communication.* Mahwah, NJ: Erlbaum.

Seligman, M., & Darling, R. B. (1997). *Ordinary families, special children.* New York: Guilford Press.

Silverstein, L. B. (2002). Fathers and families. In J. P. McHale & W. S. Grolnick (Eds.), *Retrospect and prospect in the psychological study of families* (pp. 35–64). Mahwah, NJ: Erlbaum.

Simmons, T., & Dye, A. L. (2003, October). Grandparents living with grandchildren: 2000 (C2KBR-31). *Census 2000 brief.* Washington, DC: U.S. Census Bureau, Department of Commerce. Retrieved December 12, 2004, from www.census.gov/population/www/cen2000/briefs.html

Simmons, T., & O'Connell, M. (2003, February). Couple and unmarried partner households: 2000 (CENSR-5). *Census 2000 Brief.* Washington, DC: U.S. Census Bureau, Department of Commerce. Retrieved January 15, 2005, from www.census.gov/population/www/cen2000/briefs.html

Simmons, T., & O'Neill, G. (2001, September). Households and families: 2000 (C2KBR/01–8). *Census 2000 Brief.* Washington, DC: U.S. Census Bureau, Department of Commerce.

Socha, T. J., Sanchez-Hucles, J., Bromley, J., & Kelly, B. (1995). Invisible parents and children: Exploring African-American parent-child communication. In T. J. Socha & G. H. Stamp (Eds.), *Parents, children and communication: Frontiers of theory and research* (pp. 127–145). Mahwah, NJ: Erlbaum.

Soule, K. P. (2003). The what, when, who, and why of nagging in interpersonal relationships. In K. M. Galvin & P. J. Cooper (Eds.), *Making connections: Readings in relational communication* (3rd ed., pp. 215–221). Los Angeles: Roxbury.

Tasker, F. L., & Golombok, S. (1997). *Growing up in a lesbian family: Effects on child development.* New York: Guilford Press.

Trad, P. V. (1995). Adolescent girls and their mothers: Realigning the relationship. *American Journal of Family Therapy, 23,* 11–24.

Tucker, S. J., & Mueller, J. S. (2000). Spouses' social control of health behaviors: Use and effectiveness of specific strategies. *Personality and Social Psychology Bulletin, 26,* 1120–1130.

Tyre, P., & McGinn, D. (2003, May 12). She works, he doesn't. *Newsweek,* pp. 44–54.

Vangelisti, A. L., & Banski, M. A. (1993). Couples debriefing conversations: The impact of gender, occupation and demographic characteristics. *Family Relations, 42,* 149–157.

Waite, L. J., & Gallagher, M. (2000). *The case for marriage.* New York: Doubleday.

Warren, C. (2003). Communicating about sex with parents and partners. In K. M. Galvin & P. J. Cooper (Eds.), *Making connections: Readings in relational communication* (pp. 317–324). Los Angeles: Roxbury.

Webb, L. M., Walker, K. L., Bollis, T. S., & Hebbani, A. G. (2004). Perceived parental communication, gender, and young adults' self-esteem. In O. M. Backlund & M. R. Williams (Eds.), *Reading in gender communication* (pp. 197–224). Belmont, CA: Thomson/Wadsworth.

West, R., & Turner, L. H. (1995). Communication in lesbian and gay families: Building a descriptive base. In T. J. Socha & Glen H. Stamp (Eds.), *Parents, children, and communication: Frontiers of theory and research* (pp. 147–167). Mahwah, NJ: Erlbaum.

Weston, K. (1991). *Families we choose: Lesbians, gays and kinship.* New York: Columbia University Press.

Wood, J. T. (2005). *Gendered lives: Communication, gender & culture* (6th ed.). Belmont, CA: Wadsworth/Thomson Learning.

Wood, J. T., & Inman, C. (1993). In a different mode: Recognizing male modes of closeness. *Journal of Applied Communication Research, 21,* 279–295.

COMMUNICATION AND GENDER AMONG ADULT FRIENDS

◆ Michael Monsour

This chapter comprises five sections. I start by defining three pivotal terms: *friendship, gender,* and *interpersonal communication.* The second section identifies and critiques theoretical and methodological issues in the exploration of gender. The third surveys those same issues in the study of adult friendship. Section 4 is a selective review of the literature on interpersonal communication, intimacy, and gender in adult same-sex friendships, adult cross-sex friendships, and friendships among transgendered individuals. In the last section, I recommend directions in the study of friendship and gender and I locate my work within the theory and research covered in this chapter.

◆ *Definitions: Friendship, Gender, and Interpersonal Communication*

FRIENDSHIP

Defining *friendship* is not a simple task because the definition depends upon the stage of life in which it occurs (Monsour, 2002), the culture in which it exists (Gudykunst & Ting Toomey, 1988), demographic variables such as age, biological sex, and education level (Wright, 1988), the level of intimacy (Fehr, 1996), and contextual features (Adams & Allan, 1998). Yet scholars generally agree on what it means. I find myself in agreement with Fehr's (2004) contention that expert conceptualizations of friendship should reflect lay definitions (Monsour, 1992). Most investigators and laypersons define it as a reciprocal, nonfamilial, nonromantic, voluntary relationship characterized by mutual trust, support, and affection (see Fehr, 1996, for a review of the definitions).

GENDER

Gender and *biological sex* are distinct concepts (Reeder, 1996), although some writers use the terms interchangeably. I have adopted the definitions employed by Wood (2005). The latter is a designation based on the biological characteristics of females and males; gender is "a social, symbolic construction that varies across cultures, over time within a given society, and in relation to the other gender" (p. 22). Wood's definitions encompass a variety of viewpoints reviewed in the discussion below of theoretical and methodological issues in the study of gender.

INTERPERSONAL COMMUNICATION

I define interpersonal communication as the creation of meaning through verbal and nonverbal messages exchanged by individuals in a relationship. This process is dynamic, systemic, and takes place on content and relationship levels (Wood, 2004). This definition originates with theoretical perspectives such as symbolic interactionism (Mead, 1934) and social constructionism (Berger & Luckman, 1966; Gergen, 1985), which contend that meaning is created through interaction with others.

◆ Theoretical and Methodological Issues in the Study of Gender

THEORETICAL ISSUES

I begin this section with an observation that has attained almost axiomatic status in academic communities: theories of gender, like many other theories, are sometimes motivated by political, religious, social, ideological, and even personal agendas (Allen, 1998). Some of them exemplify the claim of second-wave feminists that the personal is political. Harding (1991), a feminist philosopher of science, notes that scholars are currently operating within conceptual frameworks that restrict creative theorizing about gender. Harding believes that alternatives need to be developed but, as Allen notes, "One problem that negatively affects the scientific study of gender is the existence of polemic attitudes toward the issues" (1998, p. 442). Allen cites the work of Eagly (1995), who observes division within feminist schools of thought concerning what would advance equity between women and men: focusing on gender differences as a way to justify equitable practices or emphasizing their lack (Sommer, 1994). That theories of gender are sometimes motivated by other than purely academic and scholarly agendas is related to another pressing theoretical issue: a lack of consensus in scholarly communities on how to define gender.

Wood (2005) contends that theories about gender development and behavior come from three broad orientations, each of which generates its own theoretical issues. From a focus on the interpersonal come psychodynamic (Freud, 1957), social learning (Mischel, 1966), and cognitive development theories (Gilligan, 1982). I discuss the biological approach to gender in the following pages. Wood also identifies cultural approaches, which emerge from anthropology and sociology, and specific theories such as symbolic interactionism (Mead, 1934) and standpoint theory (Harding, 1991). Critiques of these theories reveal strengths and weaknesses, which suggest theoretical issues that must be grappled with (see Mawkesworth's, 2002, critique of standpoint theory).

Controversy over the distinction between gender and biological sex represents another theoretical issue. Just how different from one another are these concepts? Although gender is normally thought of as a social, symbolic construction, biological sex can also be (Hood-Williams, 1996). According to Wiesner-Hanks (2001), biology, anthropology, psychology, and history have all contributed to the debate about whether a distinction between biological sex and socially constructed gender is justifiable. I can offer only a brief summary of Wiesner-Hanks's analysis as it is relevant to interpersonal communication.

Biologists have difficulty drawing an absolute dichotomy between female and male. Their attempts to do so center on anatomical, chromosomal, and hormonal differences, as well as on variations in the structure and functioning of the brain (Wiesner-Hanks, 2001; Wood, 2005). Although most women can be anatomically distinguished from men based on their internal and external genitalia and secondary sexual characteristics, sharp distinctions are not possible when the external genitalia are ambiguous or have been altered by surgery. Dichotomously separating the sexes based upon chromosomes is also fraught with difficulties. An XY pair results in a male and an XX pair results in a female, but other pairings, such as XO, XXX, XXY, and XYY, are possible (Dreger, 1998) and raise questions about the appropriateness of binary categories.

Hormonal differences are another marker used to separate females and males because estrogen and testosterone influence behavior and brain development (Wood, 2005). Men and women have both, although most men have considerably more testosterone than most women, and most women have considerably more estrogen than most men. Yet there is variability, with some women having a higher level of testosterone than some men, and some men having higher levels of estrogen than some women. Biological theorists also focus attention on differences between male and female brains and on how hormonal differences affect gender and gender-related behaviors (Mustafa & van Kyk, 2005; Wood, 2005). The most extreme biological approach to theories of gender development is taken by sociobiologists, who claim that women and men are "the inevitable result of genetic factors that aim to ensure survival of the fittest" (Wood, 2005, p. 39; see also Bleske & Buss, 2000; Wilson, 1975).

Cultural anthropologists have demonstrated that some cultures have a third or even a fourth gender. Current, mainstream theories of gender in the United States assume that there are only two genders and that they correspond, at least roughly, to biological categories of female and male. Some cultures, however, recognize a third gender based on clothing and activities (Denny, 1997). The Xanith of Oman have a third sex role which a man can enter or exit (Wikan, 1977). Denny refers to it as an intermediate role distinct from male and female, what Westerners call transgenderism. The controversy over biological sex and socially constructed gender is exacerbated by disagreement between cultural and biological anthropologists about the relative contribution of biology and culture to human diversity (Worthman, 1995).

Psychology regards the rigid dichotomization of sex and gender as tenuous because men and women can have most or all of the traditional biological markers of their sex and yet think of themselves quite differently than the markers indicate they should. Some women feel they are men trapped in women's bodies, and some men feel they are women trapped in men's bodies: a condition referred to as gender dysphoria (Israel & Tarver, 1997). Psychology can also be credited with developing the concept of *sex role orientation*. Wright and Scanlon (1991) and Reeder (2003) argue that it offers a more compelling explanation of differences between women and men.

Most of the work on sex role orientation is based on the pioneering work of Bem (1974) and her sex role inventory. However, Bem's inventory, especially in its original form, has possibly outlived its usefulness. The adjectives used in the original inventory and even the variations of it may no longer be valid because of changes in gender roles, new gender constructs such as transgenderism and cultural, ethnic, and racial variability (Choi & Fuqua, 2003; Holt & Ellis, 1998; Konrad & Harris, 2002; but see Oswald, 2004).

Interpersonal communication scholars have devoted considerable attention to investigating gender differences and helping to differentiate between biological sex and gender (Wood & Dindia, 1998). Canary and Dindia (1998) have stated that

> sex refers to the genetic, biological differences between boys and girls, between men and women; gender refers to the psychological and social manifestations of what one believes to be male and/or female, which might—or might not—reflect one's biological sex. (p. 4)

Despite its clear definitions of gender and biological sex, the field recognizes and is addressing controversial issues and knotty methodological and conceptual considerations (Canary & Dindia, 1998). Some of those issues are addressed later in this chapter.

Borrowing heavily from symbolic interactionism (Mead, 1934) and relational schema theory (Baldwin, 1992), interpersonal communication scholars have described the role of face-to-face communication in the social and dyadic construction of gender (Wood, 2005). Employing a cognitive approach, I (Monsour, 2002) noted that, while gender schemas are a lifelong work in progress and are affected by a host of factors, interpersonal communication impacts the content and structuring of those schemas. Likewise, gender schemas influence how friends communicate about gender issues. The process of communication cannot be divorced from the process of gender schema construction, and they produce a shared perceptual reality.

Communication scholars also build on the work of other disciplines through the *different cultures* approach. They contend that the communication styles of men and women are strikingly different (a debatable point) (Wood & Dindia, 1998), and therefore constitute different cultural styles of relating. Although the different cultures approach has its roots in sociology, anthropology, linguistics, relationships research, and feminist theory, these scholars have made substantial contributions to a critical analysis of that approach (Kunkel & Burleson, 1998).

METHODOLOGICAL ISSUES

An excellent and enlightening chapter written by Allen (1998), provides the foundation for this section. Allen notes, as have others in interpersonal communication (Poole & McPhee, 1985), that discussions about methods should involve theory, because choices about theory often influence choices about methods (Duck, 1990). Along these same lines, a central methodological issue is that current theories of gender are still in their infancy and are sometimes motivated by ideological, religious, and political agendas rather than by purely scholarly commitments.

Another pivotal issue is whether gender is primarily a reflection of nature (biological sex), nurture (gender and socialization issues), or some combination of the two. Allen devotes considerable attention to how researchers measure sex and/or gender differences and what those measurements mean. How gender and/or biological sex are measured depends to a large degree on the conceptual and theoretical choices already made about the meaning of gender. Even an apparently simple survey item requesting participants in research to indicate whether they are female or male is problematic. Respondents may not define the terms *female* and *male* the same way the investigator does. A respondent may use biological sex as the basis for answering the question, while the researcher might be operating from a conceptual framework that emphasizes gender and socialization. However, even when researchers are interested in such issues as possible explanations for variations in some dependent variable, they sometimes mistakenly operationalize gender exclusively through replies given to the question, Are you male or female? When respondents are using biological criteria to respond to that question, investigators may incorrectly conclude that they have discovered gender differences in some dependent variable such as self-disclosure (see Leaper, Carson, Baker, Holliday, & Myers, 1995).

When an investigation involves friendship *and* gender, methodological issues concerning gender are inextricably tied to methodological and theoretical issues associated with friendship. Inadequate theorizing about friendship and inappropriate or weak methods of measuring variables such as intimacy will affect conclusions about gender and friendship.

◆ Theoretical and Methodological Issues in the Study of Friendship

THEORETICAL ISSUES

The literature on adult friendship is theoretically impoverished. Researchers have been content to employ theories of relationships and of interpersonal attraction to see what friendship processes those frameworks can explain (Fehr, 1996). However, even a cursory review of the literature reveals that many scholars adopt specific theoretical orientations (Blieszner & Adams, 1992; Rawlins, 1992; Werking, 1997; Yingling, 1994) and that some even label their endeavors as theories of friendship (Wright, 1978). Although the theoretical views of some friendship scholars make room for a consideration of gender (Monsour, 2002), none of those theories integrate gender and

friendship. Theorizing about the influence of gender in friendships and making methodological choices about studying it become less effective when scholars are not operating from an integrated and clearly articulated theoretical framework.

The paucity of theories of friendship generates other issues. No single, agreed-upon definition of the word exists. Types of friendship such as casual, good, close, best, same-sex, cross-sex, interracial, intergenerational, childhood, and so on, may require separate theories because the dynamics are distinct in each. Other key constructs in the literature have yet to be adequately defined, the most important of which is intimacy. The problem of a correct conceptualization of the intimacy construct is examined next.

METHODOLOGICAL ISSUES

Scholars who study gender and communication in friendship face a number of methodological issues, only a few of which are addressed in this chapter. The first concerns the inherent complexities of relationships, because of which the proper study of friendship *should be* a methodological nightmare (S. Duck, personal communication, March, 2000; Monsour, 2002). Adams and Allan (1998) present a compelling case that researchers need to devote more attention to the broader contexts in which friendships are embedded. By *context* they mean "the conditions external to the development, maintenance, and dissolution of specific friendships" (p. 4). They contend that contextual factors are boundless, always changing, and take place on personal, network, community, and societal levels. Although their point is well taken and generally agreed upon among relationship scholars (Surra & Perlman, 2003), operationalizing boundless contextual variables is not viable.

A second methodological issue is a lack of consensus on how to measure key constructs such as gender, intimacy, and friendship. This disagreement is connected to the broader theoretical issue of what those constructs mean. For example, experts are almost unanimous in their endorsement of intimacy as a construct worthy of close scrutiny but not about the appropriate way to define and operationalize it (Acitelli & Duck, 1987; Reis, 1998). The same can be said about gender. Scholars agree that it must be considered when theorizing about friendships but not about appropriate ways to conceptualize and operationalize it.

A third methodological issue is the failure of many friendship scholars to get the perspectives of both individuals in a friendship (Monsour, Betty, & Kurzweil, 1993). Since a friendship is negotiated, with both partners verbally and nonverbally constructing and defining what it means (Monsour, 2002), the perspective of only one of them provides an incomplete analysis of the relationship (Ickes, 2000). Gaines and Ickes (1997) make note of a similar methodological issue when they observe the tendency of researchers to focus more attention on the outsider's view of relationships, typically that of the researcher, rather than the insider's view, typically that of the participants. Researchers studying intimacy might already know or think they know what it means. They then operationalize it in a way that makes sense to them, the outsiders, and impose their conceptual view of it on the respondents, the insiders, despite the distinct possibility that insiders may have a different definition (Monsour, 1992).

Another issue is the underutilization of qualitative methodologies. Quantitative methods certainly contribute to a knowledge of friendship, but qualitative methods are more suited to the kinds of problems currently facing scholars interested in developing theories of gender and friendship as integrated concepts. They should employ qualitative methods because of their emphasis on accumulating large amounts of the kind of rich descriptive data (Babbie, 1998) necessary for the development of theories about personal relationships (Kelley et al., 1983).

◆ Review of the Literature on Communication and Gender in Adult Friendships

In this section I examine representative research conducted on friendships between same-sex adult heterosexuals and cross-sex adults and in the transgender community. Space limitations preclude an analysis of other kinds in which gender issues are particularly relevant such as friendships that are computer mediated (Adams, 1998), in the workplace (Sias, Smith, & Avdeyeva, 2003), between gays, lesbians, and bisexuals (Nardi, 1994), in racial minority groups (Gaines & Ickes, 1997), in non-Western cultures (Gudyknust & Ting-Toomey, 1988), and between children and older Americans (Adams & Blieszner, 1989; Monsour, 2002).

GENDER AND COMMUNICATION IN HETEROSEXUAL SAME-SEX FRIENDSHIPS

Because intimacy is considered a central construct in the conduct and understanding of relationships (Fehr, 2004; Reis, 1998), researchers have devoted much of their attention to exploring what it means in male and female same-sex friendships and which type is more intimate.

Intimacy is a broad and slippery concept considered by some to be the proverbial elephant because its definition depends upon which part of the elephant a researcher is touching (Acitelli & Duck, 1987). Nevertheless, a few generalizations about friendship intimacy can be made with a fair degree of confidence and empirical support. One of them is that *self-disclosure,* conceptually similar to openness and emotional expressiveness (Monsour, 1992), is considered by laypersons and scholars to be the most common and prototypical manifestation of intimacy in friendship (Fehr, 2004). Self-disclosure is often the construct of choice when trying to differentiate female from male same-sex friendships (Dindia, 2002).

Activity sharing is also recognized as a common way of expressing intimacy in friendships, particularly male same-sex friendships (Swain, 1989; Wright, 1998). Sharing activities has been relegated to a position of less importance than self-disclosure (Fehr, 2004), and some scholars contend that research has been biased toward self-disclosure and other forms of verbal expressiveness that reflect a feminine form of communicating intimacy (Wood & Inman, 1993). Wright's (1982) often quoted statement that men's friendships are "side-by-side" (implying activity sharing) and the friendships of women are "face-to-face" (implying self-disclosure) captures in some people's minds the primary gender difference between male and female same-sex friendships. But Wright (1998) also notes that not all shared activities are the same, and the degree of intimacy embedded within those activities depends upon many variables.

Fehr (2004) provides a succinct summary, with all the appropriate supporting citations, of the three major schools of thought on whether male or female friendship is more intimate and whether intimacy is achieved in the same way in each. According to the first school, women and men agree that self-disclosure is the major avenue for expressing intimacy, but men simply choose not to use it, resulting in less intimacy. Other theorists argue that men and women display intimacy on equal levels, but men express it primarily through sharing activities rather than through extensive self-disclosure. The third school says that women achieve intimacy through self-disclosure whereas men use both self-disclosure and sharing. I agree with Fehr's contention that the main criterion for deciding which school of thought is more valid is which is closest to lay beliefs concerning intimacy and intimate friendships.

In Fehr's (2004) testing of a prototype interaction-pattern model of intimacy, the results of six studies indicate that, for laypersons,

activity sharing is a less prototypical way of expressing intimacy in a same-sex friendship than is self-disclosure. Fehr's findings also reveal that women are more likely to regard self-disclosure as more central than activity sharing. However, in their meta-analysis of 205 investigations involving 23,702 respondents, Dindia and Allen (1992) concluded that sex differences in self-disclosure were so small, with women disclosing more than men, that those differences were probably of little importance in the actual practice of relationships (Dindia, 2002). Wright (1998) also observed that sex differences in intimacy disappear when close friendships are examined.

The debate (Fehr, 2004) over which type of same-sex friendship is more intimate begs the more important question of why friendship scholars should concern themselves with trying to make such an assessment in the first place. After all, women and men are not in competition to decide which of their friendships is more intimate. What would be gained if the results of hundreds of studies allowed friendship researchers to proclaim, "Female (or male) same-sex friendships are more (or less, or equally) intimate than male (or female) same-sex friendships"? Such a broad proclamation would encourage stereotyping, exalt one type of friendship over another, and set the agenda for another decade's worth of research, as investigators tried to prove or disprove it.

GENDER AND COMMUNICATION IN HETEROSEXUAL CROSS-SEX FRIENDSHIPS

Cross-sex friendships are an ideal place to explore the intersection of intimacy, gender, and interpersonal communication. O'Meara's (1989; also see Rawlins, 1982) landmark investigation of the challenges confronting friendships between women and men provides a good point of departure. Of the four O'Meara identifies, the romantic and sexual challenges are most relevant. In the first, heterosexual cross-sex friends try to decide whether the feelings they have for one another are friendship, romantic love, or some combination. The sexual challenge refers to the sexual energy, tension, and desire in many cross-sex friendships, which can energize or drain them (Monsour, 2002).

There have been at least a dozen studies on the romantic and sexual challenges (see Monsour, 2002 for a review; also see Hughes, Morrison, & Asada, 2005). The main conclusion is that intimacy in heterosexual cross-sex friendships is more complicated than in the same-sex friendships of heterosexual adults. Not only do cross-sex friends have to contend with the generic intimacy issues that pertain to all friendships such as trust, reciprocity, and emotional investment, but they also have to negotiate intimacy issues surrounding sexuality and romance. Another complicating factor is that, from an evolutionary perspective, the motives for being in a cross-sex friendship are quite different from the motives for being in a same-sex friendship and are directly connected to procreation. In a testing of their contention that cross-sex friendships evolved to solve adaptive problems females and males have faced over time, Bleske and Buss (2000) discovered that, much more than females, males viewed cross-sex friendship as an opportunity to gain sexual access to members of the other sex, whereas females viewed them as protective. In recent years a number of studies have been published documenting the frequency of sexual contact among young adults who claim to be just friends (see Afifi & Faulkner, 2000).

Perceived differences in one's own biological sex and that of one's friend are at the center of many of the complexities of friendships between men and women, including intimacy and the romantic/sexual challenges. Those perceptions of differences and similarities are often arrived at by how friends verbally and nonverbally communicate to one another on content and relationship levels. Symbolic interactionism (Mead, 1934),

social constructionism (Gergen, 1985), and relationship schema theory (Baldwin, 1992) lead to a number of conclusions about the connections between gender, intimacy, and interpersonal communication in cross-sex friendships. Perhaps the most important of those conclusions is that interpersonal communication is guided by schemas of gender, self, and friendship and that it reciprocally affects the structuring and content of those schemas (see Monsour, 2002, for a detailed treatment of this argument; Planalp, 1985). Cross-sex friends construct a shared reality about intimacy, gender, and issues surrounding sexual and romantic challenges through the communication practices they enact (Monsour, Betty, & Kurzweil, 1993).

GENDER, COMMUNICATION, AND FRIENDSHIPS IN THE TRANSGENDER COMMUNITY

One of the more compelling, complicated, and controversial gender issues facing friendship scholars is whether transgendered individuals represent a third category, and if so, what intimacy and communication dynamics exist in a friendship in which one or both individuals are part of the transgender community. A necessary and difficult first step in addressing this issue is arriving at a working definition of *transgenderism* (Bullough, Bullough, & Elias, 1997). According to Israel and Tarver (1997), it encompasses preoperative and postoperative transsexuals, transvestites or cross-dressers, transgenderists, androgynes, and intersex individuals. Because of the diversity within the transgender community, experts involved in transgender care prefer to refer to "transgender populations" rather than the "transgender population" (Israel & Tarver, 1997). For example, although transsexuals are typically interested in genital reassignment surgery, transgenderists and transvestites typically are not.

The transgender community is arguably one of the most marginalized in American society. Although the community has received a fair and growing amount of scholarly attention (Sisson & Moser, 2004), it is frequently overlooked in high-profile places. In the recently published (and otherwise excellent) *The Handbook of Sexuality in Close Relationships* (Harvey, Wenzel, & Sprecher, 2004), transgendered individuals are given only scant attention, even though their sexuality in close relationships is extremely complex. Part of the reason it has been marginalized is that the transgender community is quickly becoming an area of focus that inspires writers with other than scholarly agendas to voice their opinions (Califia, 1997; Sisson & Moser, 2004). This is unfortunate because the investigation of intimacy issues in friendships in which one or both individuals are transgendered would almost certainly challenge research findings and theoretical speculations about friendships of same-sex and cross-sex individuals.

Of particular interest to researchers are members of the transgender community who have undergone genital reassignment surgery and have transitioned from one sex and/or gender to another. If a biological male undergoes sex reassignment surgery and hormone treatments and now considers herself/himself a woman, do her friendships with women follow the same modal pattern of intimacy as friendships between women who have not made such a transition? Are the friendships she forges with biological males beset by the same challenges (O'Meara, 1989) that males and females often encounter in their friendships? Can a postoperative transsexual woman who was once a man truly offer her male friends an insider's perspective on what it is like to be a member of the opposite sex? Even if she feels she can, will her male friends accept her assessment? Transitioning from female to male introduces similar kinds of questions. Do males who were once females emphasize activity sharing as a way of expressing intimacy or do they retain the preference for self-disclosure they might have had when they were biological females? Other gender issues that have been shown to be important in

same-sex and cross-sex friendships such as sex role orientation may not be relevant when at least one friend has transcended traditional masculine and feminine categories.

◆ Future Directions in the Study of Gender and Communication Among Friends

In this final section I locate my work within the theory and research covered in this chapter, identify what I see as weaknesses in the literature, and offer suggestions for the study of gender and communication among friends. I have been guilty of conducting research from a heterocentric (or heterosexist) worldview, which implicitly and/or explicitly privileges heterosexual friendships (Werking, 1997). Through my adoption of such a worldview, I have inadvertently contributed to the marginalization of friendships in which one or both individuals are gay, lesbian, bisexual, transgendered, or members of the queer community. Because postoperative transgenders might constitute a third gender or at least one that transcends the traditional masculine and feminine categories (Bolin, 1994), researchers and theoreticians should devote more time and energy investigating a community that could possibly serve as a catalyst for a paradigm shift in how gender is conceptualized.

Sexual minority groups are not the only ones marginalized by friendship and gender scholars. Far too little research attention has focused on friendships of racial and ethnic minorities (Gaines & Ickes, 1997), of older Americans (Adams & Blieszner, 1989), and in non-Western societies. Gender is a universal concept, but understandings of it are not (J. T. Wood, personal communication, November 22, 2004). The meanings given to gender depend on a wide array of contextual factors such as culture, race, ethnicity, age, class, spirituality, history, and the relationship in which it is expressed. Yet scholars of friendship and gender have barely begun to explore how these factors are related to the conduct and understanding of friendships.

They should concentrate on developing integrated theories of friendship and gender, rather than addressing each one as if it was independent of the other. Doing so would require more creative approaches than are currently being used in determining the meaning(s) of gender and friendship (Harding, 1991). I have attempted such an integrated approach in which I detail the relationship between schemas and how they act in concert to produce various communication dynamics. Another important part of the friendship/gender puzzle is the role of self and self-schemas as they influence and are influenced by friendship and gender schemas (Monsour, 2002).

Scholars of interpersonal communication have much to offer in elucidating the complicated intersection of gender and friendship. As a starting point, they might consider a more collaborative approach in which they work with rather than in addition to scholars from other disciplines. More interdisciplinary cooperation and less competition will permit scholars to integrate knowledge across fields (Frost & Jean, 2003) and in doing so arrive at more creative and holistic ways of theorizing about gender and friendship (Harding, 1991). Creativity and collaboration often go hand in hand (Kohn, 1992), and breaking down disciplinary boundaries and downplaying allegiances are important first steps.

◆ References

Acitelli, L., & Duck, S. W. (1987). Intimacy as the proverbial elephant. In D. Perlman & S. W. Duck (Eds.), *Intimate relationships: Development, dynamics, and deterioration.* Newbury Park, CA: Sage.

Adams, R. G. (1998). The demise of territorial determinism. In R. G. Adams & G. Allan (Eds.), *Placing friendship in context* (pp. 153–182). Cambridge, UK: Cambridge University Press.

Adams, R. G., & Allan, G. (Eds.). (1998). *Placing friendship in context.* Cambridge, UK: Cambridge University Press.

Adams, R. G., & Blieszner, R. (1989). *Older adult friendships: Structure and process.* Newbury Park, CA: Sage.

Adams, R. G., Blieszner, R., & De Vries, B. (2000). Definitions of friendship in the third age: Age, gender, and study location effects. *Journal of Aging Studies, 14*(1), 117–133.

Afifi, W. A., & Faulkner, S. L (2000). On being "just friends": The frequency and impact of sexual activity in cross-sex friendships. *Journal of Social and Personal Relationships, 17,* 205–222.

Allen, M. (1998). Methodological considerations when considering a gendered world. In D. J. Canary & K. Dindia (Eds.), *Sex differences and similarities in communication* (pp. 427–444). Mahwah, NJ: Lawrence Erlbaum.

Babbie, E. (1998). *The practice of social research.* Belmont, CA: Wadsworth.

Baldwin, M. W. (1992). Relational schemas and the processing of social information. *Psychological Bulletin, 112,* 461–484.

Bem, S. L. (1974). The measurement of psychological androgyny. *Journal of Consulting and Clinical Psychology, 42,* 155–162.

Berger, P., & Luckmann, T. (1966). *The social construction of reality.* New York: Doubleday.

Blieszner, R., & Adams, G. R. (1992). *Adult friendships.* Newbury Park, CA: Sage.

Bleske, A. L., & Buss, D. M. (2000). Can men and women be just friends? *Personal Relationships, 7,* 131–151.

Bolin, A. (1994). Transcending and transgendering: Male-to-female transsexuals, dichotomy, and diversity. In G. Herdt (Ed.), *Third sex, third gender* (pp. 447–485). New York, NY: Zone Books.

Bullough, B., Bullough, V. L., & Elias, J. (Eds). (1997). *Gender blending.* Amherst, NY: Prometheus Books.

Califia, P. (1997). *Sex changes: The politics of transgenderism.* San Francisco, CA: Cleis Press.

Canary, D. J., & Dindia, K. (Eds.). (1998). *Sex differences and similarities in communication*. Mahwah, NJ: Erlbaum.

Cappella, J. (1987). Interpersonal communication: Definitions and fundamental questions. In C. R. Berger & S. H. Chaffee (Eds.), *Handbook of communication science* (pp. 184–218). Newbury Park, CA: Sage.

Choi, N., & Fuqua, D. R. (2003). The structure of the Bem Sex Role Inventory: A summary of 23 validation studies. *Educational and Psychological Measurement, 63*, 872–887.

Denny, D. (1997). Transgender: Some historical, cross-cultural, and contemporary models and methods of coping and treatment. In B. Bullough, V. L. Bullough, & J. Elias (Eds.), *Gender blending* (pp. 33–47). Amherst, NY: Prometheus.

Dindia, K. (2002). Self-disclosure research: Knowledge through meta-analysis. In M. Allen, R. Preiss, B. M. Gayle, & N. Burrell (Eds.), *Interpersonal communication research: Advances through meta-analysis* (pp. 169–185). Mahwah, NJ: Erlbaum.

Dindia, K., & Allen, M. (1992). Sex differences in self-disclosure: A meta-analysis. *Psychological Bulletin, 112*, 106–124.

Dreger, D. (1998, May-June). "Ambiguous sex"—or ambivalent medicine? Ethical treatments in the treatment of intersexuality. *Hastings Center Report, 28*, 24–36.

Duck, S. (1990). Relationships as unfinished business: Out of the frying pan and into the 1990s. *Journal of Social and Personal Relationships, 7*, 5–29.

Duck, S. (Ed.). (1993). *Social context and relationships*. Newbury Park, CA: Sage.

Eagly, A. (1995). The sciences and politics of comparing women and men. *American Psychologist, 50*, 169–171.

Fehr, B. (1996). *Friendship processes*. Thousand Oaks, CA: Sage.

Fehr, B. (2004). Intimacy expectations in same-sex friendships: A prototype interaction-pattern model. *Journal of Personality and Social Psychology, 86*, 265–285.

Freud, S. (1957). *The ego and the id*. (J. Riviere, Trans.). London: Hogarth.

Frost, S. H., & Jean, P. M. (2003). Bridging the disciplines: Interdisciplinary discourse and faculty scholarship. *Journal of Higher Education, 74*, 119–150.

Gaines, S. O., & Ickes, W. (1997). Perspectives on interracial relationships. In S. Duck (Ed.), *Handbook of personal relationships* (pp. 197–220). New York: John Wiley.

Gayle, B. M., & Preiss, R. W. (2002). An overview of individual processes in interpersonal communication. In M. Allen, R. W. Preiss, B. M. Gayle, & N. Burrell (Eds.), *Interpersonal communication research: Advances through meta-analysis* (pp. 45–57). Mahwah, NJ: Erlbaum.

Gergen, K. (1985). The social constructionist movement in modern psychology. *American Psychologist, 40*, 266–275.

Gilligan, C. (1982). *In a different voice: Psychological theory and women's development*. Cambridge, MA: Harvard University Press.

Gudykunst, W. K., & Ting-Toomey, S. (1988). *Culture and interpersonal communication*. Newbury Park, CA: Sage.

Harding, S. (1991). *Whose science? Whose knowledge? Thinking from women's lives*. Ithaca, NY: Cornell University Press.

Harvey, J. H., Wenzel, A., & Sprecher, S. (Eds.). (2004). *The handbook of sexuality in close relationships*. Mahwah, NJ: Erlbaum.

Holt, C. L., & Ellis, J. B. (1998). Assessing the current validity of the Bem Sex-Role Inventory. *Sex Roles, 39*, 929–941.

Hood-Williams, J. (1996). Goodbye to sex and gender. *Sociological Review, 44*, 1–17.

Hughes, M., Morrison, K., & Asada, K. J. K. (2005). What's love got to do with it: Exploring the impact of maintenance rules, love attitudes, and network support on friends with benefits relationships. *Western Journal of Communication, 69*, 49–66.

Ickes, W. (2000). Methods of studying close relationships. In W. Ickes & S. W. Duck (Eds.), *The social psychology of personal relationships*. New York: Wiley.

Israel, G. E., & Tarver, D. E. (1997). *Transgender care: Recommended guidelines, practical information, and personal accounts*. Philadelphia: Temple University Press.

Kelley, H. H., Berscheid, E., Christensen, A., Harvey, J. H., Huston, T. L., Levinger, G., et al. (1983). *Close relationships*. New York: W. H. Freeman.

Kohn, A. (1992). *No contest: The case against competition*. New York: Houghton Mifflin.

Konrad, A. M., & Harris, C. (2002). Desirability of the Bem-Sex Role Inventory items for women and men: A comparison between African Americans and European Americans. *Sex Roles: A Journal of Research*, 259–271.

Kunkel, A. W., & Burleson, B. R. (1998). Social support and the emotional lives of men and women: An assessment of the different cultures perspective. In D. J. Canary & K. Dindia (Eds.), *Sex differences and similarities in communication* (pp. 101–126). Mahwah, NJ: Erlbaum.

Leaper, C., Carson, M., Baker, C., Holliday, H., & Myers, S. (1995). Self-disclosure and listener verbal support in same-gender and cross-gender friends' conversations. *Sex Roles: A Journal of Research*, 33, 387–405.

Mawkesworth, M. (2002). Analyzing backlash: Feminist standpoint theory as an analytical tool. *Women and Language*, 25, 61–62.

Mead, G. H. (1934). *Mind, self, and society*. Chicago: University of Chicago Press.

Mischel, W. (1966). A social learning view of sex differences in behavior. In E. E. Maccoby (Ed.), *The development of sex differences* (pp. 93–106). Stanford, CA: Stanford University Press.

Monsour, M. (1992). Meanings of intimacy in cross- and same-sex friendships. *Journal of Social and Personal Relationships*, 9, 277–295.

Monsour, M. (2002). *Women and men as friends: Relationships across the life span in the 21st century*. Mahwah, NJ: Erlbaum.

Monsour, M., Betty, S., & Kurzweil, N. (1993). Levels of perspectives and the perception of intimacy in cross-sex friendships: A balance theory explanation of shared perceptual reality. *Journal of Social and Personal Relationships*, 10, 529–550.

Mustafa, N., & van Kyk, D. (2005, March 7). Who says a woman can't be Einstein? *Time*, 165(10), 51–57.

Nardi, P. M. (1994). Friendships in the lives of gay men and lesbians. *Journal of Social and Personal Relationships*, 11, 185–199.

Olson, D. H. (1977). Insiders' and outsiders' views of relationships: Research studies. In G. Levinger & H. Raush (Eds.), *Close relationships: Perspectives on the meaning of intimacy* (pp. 115–135). Amherst: University of Massachusetts Press.

O'Meara, D. (1989). Cross-sex friendship: Four basic challenges of an ignored relationship. *Sex Roles*, 21, 525–543.

Oswald, P. A. (2004). An examination of the current usefulness of the Bem Sex-Role Inventory. *Psychological Reports*, 94(13).

Planalp, S. (1985). Relational schemata: A test of alternative forms of relational knowledge as guides to communication. *Human Communication Research*, 12, 1–29.

Poole, S. M., & McPhee, R. D. (1985). Methodology in interpersonal communication research. In M. L. Knapp & G. Miller (Eds.), *Handbook of interpersonal communication* (pp. 100–170). Beverly Hills, CA: Sage.

Rawlins, W. K. (1982). Cross-sex friends and the communicative management of sex-role expectations. *Communication Quarterly*, 30, 343–352.

Rawlins, W. K. (1992). *Friendship matters: Communication, dialectics, and the life course*. New York: Walter de Gruyter.

Reeder, H. M. (1996). A critical look at gender differences in communication research. *Communication Studies*, 47, 318–330.

Reeder, H. M. (2003). The effect of gender role orientation on same- and cross-sex friendship formation. *Sex Roles: A Journal of Research*, 49, 143–153.

Reis, H. T. (1988). Gender effects in social participation: Intimacy, loneliness, and the conduct of social interaction. In R. Gilmour & S. W. Duck (Eds.), *The emerging field of personal relationships* (pp. 91–105). Hillsdale, NJ: Erlbaum.

Reis, H. T. (1998). Gender differences in intimacy and related behaviors: Context and process. In D. J. Canary & K. Dindia (Eds.), *Sex differences and similarities in communication* (pp. 203–231). Mahwah, NJ: Erlbaum.

Sias, P. M., Smith, G., & Avdeyeva, T. (2003). Sex and sex-composition differences and similarities in peer workplace friendship development. *Communication Studies, 54,* 322–351.

Sisson, K., & Moser, C. (2004). Sex changes: The politics of trangenderism. *Archives of Sexual Behavior, 33,* 418–421.

Sommer, C. (1994). *Who stole feminism? How women have betrayed women.* New York: Simon & Schuster.

Surra, C. A., & Perlman, D. (2003). Introduction: The many faces of context. *Personal Relationships, 10*(3), 283–285.

Swain, S. (1989). Covert intimacy. Closeness in men's friendships. In B. J. Risman & P. Swartz (Eds.), *Gender in intimate relationships* (pp. 71–86). Belmont, CA: Wadsworth.

Werking, K. (1997). *We're just good friends: Women and men in nonromantic relationships.* New York: Guilford.

Wiesner-Hanks, E. M. (2001). *Gender in history.* Malden, MA: Blackwell.

Wikan, U. (1977). Man becomes woman: Transsexualism in Oman as a key to gender roles. *Man, 12,* 304–319.

Wilson, E. (1975). *Sociobiology: The new synthesis.* Cambridge: MA: Belknap.

Wood, T. J. (2005). *Gendered lives: Communication, gender, and culture* (6th ed.). Belmont, CA: Wadsworth.

Wood, J. T. (2004). *Interpersonal communication: Everyday encounters* (4th ed.). Belmont, CA: Wadsworth.

Wood, J. T., & Dindia, K. (1998). What's the difference? A dialogue about differences and similarities between women and men. In D. J. Canary & K. Dindia (Eds.), *Sex differences and similarities in communication* (pp. 19–39). Mahwah, NJ: Lawrence Erlbaum.

Wood, J. T., & Inman, C. C. (1993). In a different mode: Masculine styles of communicating closeness. *Journal of Applied Communication Research, 21,* 279–295.

Worthman, C. M. (1995). Hormones, sex, and gender. *Annual Review of Anthropology, 24,* 593–618.

Wright, P. H. (1978). Toward a theory of friendship based on the conception of self. *Human Communication Research, 4,* 196–207.

Wright, P. H. (1982). Men's friendships, women's friendships, and the alleged inferiority of the latter. *Sex Roles, 8,* 1–20.

Wright, P. H. (1988). Interpreting research on gender differences in friendship: A case for moderation and a plea for caution. *Journal of Social and Personal Relationships, 5,* 367–373.

Wright, P. H. (1998). Toward an expanded orientation toward the study of sex differences in friendship. In D. J. Canary & K. Dindia (Eds.), *Sex differences and similarities in communication* (pp. 41–63). Mahwah, NJ: Lawrence Erlbaum.

Wright, P. H., & Scanlon, M. B. (1991). Gender role orientations and friendship: Some attenuation, but gender differences abound. *Sex Roles: A Journal of Research, 24,* 551–567.

Yingling, J. (1994). Constituting friendship in talk and metatalk. *Journal of Social and Personal Relationships, 11,* 411–426.

5

GENDERED COMMUNICATION AND INTIMATE PARTNER VIOLENCE

◆ Michael P. Johnson

The point of this chapter is that one cannot understand the role of communication in intimate partner violence without making distinctions among the major types of violence. Unlike most other kinds of violence (such as a mugging), which are essentially situational and do not involve a continuing relationship between the parties involved, personal relationship violence arises out of and shapes the dynamics of an ongoing relationship, in some cases but not always being a central feature of it. Thus, the most important distinctions among types of intimate partner violence go beyond the single incident to focus on the role of the violence within the context of the whole relationship between the partners.

My discussion of the implications of such distinctions for the analysis of violence and communication in intimate relationships begins with a discussion of the typology I have developed that is rooted in relationship patterns of coercive control. This first section defines and describes the three major types, addresses some of the methodological issues involved in assessing them, and discusses their relationships to gender and gender issues. The second major section briefly reviews the literature on communication and intimate partner violence, taking into account the implications of the control typology for assessing that literature. The final part of this second section focuses more closely on gender and communication in violent relationships. The third major section deals with communication about violent relationships, addressing both private and public speech. The conclusion briefly addresses some of the more general implications of this typological approach to gender and communication in and about violent relationships.

◆ Types of Intimate Partner Violence

The typology I have developed (Johnson, in press) is organized around issues of relationship power and control. Intimate terrorism, the first of the three types of intimate partner violence, involves a violent attempt to take complete control of, or at least to generally dominate, a relationship. The second, violent resistance, involves the use of violence to resist such an attempt; the third, situational couple violence, is a product of particular conflicts or tensions within the relationship.[1]

Intimate terrorism, violent resistance, and situational couple violence have different origins, dynamics, and consequences. They require different theoretical frameworks to explain them and different strategies for prevention or intervention. I will briefly summarize some of the evidence about differences among them below, but first I want to make the general point that failures to acknowledge these differences have produced a number of major errors in the empirical literature on intimate partner violence. By extension, until a broad program of research investigates differences among the causes and consequences of the various types of intimate partner violence, scholars and clinicians won't know how widespread the errors are. Two examples will illustrate the basic processes by which such errors are produced.

First, when researchers inadvertently aggregate different types of violence under one label, they produce data that are an "average" of the characteristics or correlates of the types that are aggregated. For example, a recent meta-analysis of the literature on the relationship between growing up in a violent home and subsequently becoming part of a violent marital relationship indicates quite small effects (Stith et al., 2000). This calls into question what is often claimed to be one of the best-established phenomenon in the literature on intimate-partner violence, often referred to as the "intergenerational transmission of violence." However, those who have conducted research supporting the intergenerational transmission claim do not distinguish among types of violence, instead examining the effects of childhood experiences of any sort of violence in the home on any adult perpetration of intimate partner violence. This would not be a problem if the effects of childhood experiences on different types of adult violence were the same, but a recent study differentiating among the types finds that intimate terrorism is strongly related to childhood experiences of violence but that situational couple violence is not (Johnson & Cares, 2004). The "average" relationship, dominated by situational couple violence, does not represent the relationship that is of most interest, the effect of childhood experiences of family violence on the likelihood of becoming a wife beater—an intimate terrorist.

Second, sometimes research on one type of intimate partner violence is used to draw conclusions about quite a different type. For example, in the late 1970s Suzanne Steinmetz used data from general survey samples that were dominated by situational couple violence (Johnson, 1995, 2001) as evidence about the nature of intimate terrorism (Steinmetz, 1977–78), which led her to the incorrect conclusion that that there were as many battered husbands as battered wives. This is the error that produced the decades-long and continuing debate over the gender symmetry of domestic violence.

The typology of intimate partner violence presented below has its roots in this debate about gender symmetry. For decades, feminist theorists have argued that domestic violence is largely male perpetrated and rooted in the patriarchal traditions of the Western family (Dobash & Dobash, 1979). In contrast, family violence theorists have argued that domestic violence is rooted in the everyday tensions and conflicts of family life and that women are as violent as men in intimate relationships (Straus, 1999). As it turns out, they were studying different phenomena, one largely male perpetrated, the other roughly gender symmetric. On one hand, feminist theorists, using agency samples, were studying the types of intimate partner violence that are rooted in large part in the dynamics of patriarchal control (intimate terrorism and violent resistance). On the other hand, family violence theorists, using general survey data, were studying situational couple violence, which is rooted in the dynamics of family conflict.

INTIMATE TERRORISM

In intimate terrorism, the perpetrator uses violence in the service of gaining and holding general control over his or her partner. The "control" that is the defining feature of intimate terrorism is more than the specific, short-term control that is often the goal of violence in other contexts. The mugger wants to control you only briefly in order to take your valuables and move on, hopefully never to see you again. In contrast, the control sought in intimate terrorism is general and long-term. Although each particular act of intimate violence may have any number of short-term, specific goals, the violence is embedded in a larger pattern of coercive control that permeates the relationship. This is the kind of violence that comes to mind when most people hear the term *domestic violence*, and in heterosexual relationships it is largely male perpetrated.

Figure 5.1 is a widely used graphic representation of intimate partner violence deployed in the service of general control. This diagram and the understanding of domestic violence that lies behind it were developed over a period of years from the testimony of battered women that convinced the staff of the Duluth Domestic Abuse Intervention Project that the most important characteristic of the violence they encountered was that it was embedded in a general pattern of coercive control (Pence & Paymar, 1993).

Patterns of coercive control cannot, of course, be identified by looking at violent incidents in isolation. They can only be identified from more general information about the relationship—information about the use of multiple tactics to control one's partner. A brief tour of the wheel might clarify the pattern of intimate terrorism that Catherine Kirkwood calls a "web" of abuse (Kirkwood, 1993).

It is not unusual for an intimate terrorist to deprive his[2] partner of control over economic resources. He controls all the money. She is allowed no bank account and no credit cards. If she works for wages, she has to turn over her paychecks to him. He keeps all the cash, and she has to ask him for money when she needs to buy groceries or clothes for herself or their children. He may require a precise accounting of every penny, demanding to see the grocery bill and making sure she returns every bit of the change.

This economic abuse may be justified through the next form of control, male privilege: "I am the man of the house, the head of the household, the king in my castle." Of course, this use of male privilege can cover everything. As the man of the house, his word is law. He doesn't have to explain. She doesn't disagree with him. She is to do his bidding without question. And she doesn't talk back. All this holds even more rigidly in public, where he is not to be humiliated by back-talk from "his woman" (Dobash & Dobash, 1979).

How does he use the children to support his control? First of all, they too know he is the boss. He makes it clear that he controls not only them but their mother as well. He may use them to back him up, to make her humiliation more complete by forcing them into the room to assist him as he confronts her, asking them if he isn't right, and making

Figure 5.1   Domestic Violence/Intimate Terrorism

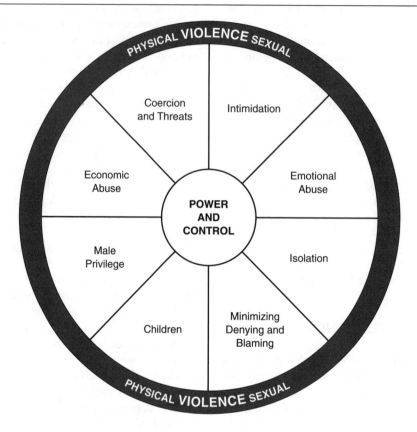

Source: Adapted from Pence and Paymar (1993).

them support his control of her. He may even have convinced them that he should be in charge, that he does know what is best (father knows best), and that she is incompetent or lazy or immoral. In addition, he may use her attachment to the children as a means of control, by threatening to take them away from her or hurt them if she isn't a "good wife and mother" (Dobash & Dobash, 1979). Of course, being a good wife and mother means doing as he says.

He may also use isolation to keep her away from everyone else and make himself her only source of information, of support, of money, of everything. In a rural setting, he might be able to literally isolate her, moving to a house trailer in the woods, with one car that he controls, no phone, keeping her there alone. In an urban setting, or if he needs her to go out to work, he can isolate her less literally, by driving away her friends and relatives and intimidating the people at work so that she has no one to talk to about what's happening to her (Pence & Paymar, 1993).

When she is completely isolated, and what he tells her about herself is all she ever hears about herself, he can tell her over and over again that she's worthless—humiliating her, demeaning her, emotionally abusing her. She's ugly, stupid, a slut, a lousy wife, an incompetent mother. She only manages to survive because he takes care of her. She'd be helpless without him. And who else is there to tell her otherwise? Maybe he can convince her that she can't live without him (Chang, 1996; Kirkwood, 1993).

If she resists, he intimidates her to show her what might happen if she doesn't behave. He may scream at her, swear at her, smash things, let her see his rage. He may kick her cat, hang her dog, threaten to hit her or beat her or pull her hair out or burn her or tell her he'll kill her and maybe the kids, too.

Putting all these means of control together, or even a few of them, the abuser entraps and enslaves his partner. If she manages to thwart one means of control, there are others at his disposal. Wherever she turns, there is another way he can control her. Sometimes she is ensnared by multiple strands. She can't seem to escape—she is trapped. But with the addition of violence there is more than entrapment. There is terror.

For this reason, the diagram does not include the violence as just another means of control, another spoke in the wheel. The violence is depicted, rather, as the rim of the wheel, holding all the spokes together. When violence is added to such a pattern of coercive control, the abuse becomes much more than the sum of its parts. The ostensibly nonviolent tactics that accompany that violence take on a new, powerful, and frightening meaning, controlling the victim not only through their own specific constraints but also through their association with the general knowledge that her partner will do anything to maintain control of the relationship, even attack her physically. Most obviously, the threats and intimidation are more than idle threats if he has physically assaulted her before. His "request" to see the grocery receipts becomes a "warning"; his calling her a stupid slut may signal the potential for a vicious physical attack. As battered women often report, "All he had to do was look at me that way, and I'd jump." What is for most of us the safest place in our world—home—is for her a place of constant fear.

VIOLENT RESISTANCE

What is a woman to do when she finds herself terrorized in her own home? At some point, most women in such relationships do fight back physically. For some, this is an instinctive reaction to being attacked, and it happens at the first blow—almost without thought. For others, it doesn't happen until it seems the assaults will be endless if she doesn't do something to stop him—so she fights back. However, for most heterosexual women, the usual size difference between them and their partner ensures that violent resistance won't help and may make things worse, so they abandon violence and turn to other means of coping. For a few, eventually it seems that the only way out is to kill their partner.

The critical defining pattern of violent resistance is that the resistor, faced with an intimate terrorist, uses violence, but not in an attempt to take general control over her partner or the relationship. Violence in the face of intimate terrorism may arise from any of a variety of motives (Swan & Snow, 2002; Walker, 1989). She may (at least at first) believe that she can defend herself, that her violent resistance will keep him from attacking her further. That may mean that she thinks she can stop him right now, in the midst of an attack, or it may mean that she thinks that if she fights back often enough he will eventually decide to stop attacking her physically.

Even if she doesn't think she can stop him, she may feel that he shouldn't be allowed to attack her without getting hurt himself. This desire to hurt him in return even if it won't stop him can be a form of communication—"What you're doing isn't right, and I'm going to fight back as hard as I can." Or it may be a form of retaliation or payback, along the lines of "He's not going to do that without paying some price for it." In a few cases, she may be after serious retaliation, attacking him when he is least expecting it and doing her best to do serious damage, even killing him. But there is another, more frequent motive for such premeditated attacks—escape. Sometimes, after years of abuse and entrapment, a victim of intimate terrorism may feel that the only way she can escape from this horror is to kill her tormenter.

SITUATIONAL COUPLE VIOLENCE

The first two types of intimate partner violence may be what most of us think of when we hear the term domestic violence, but the most common type of intimate partner violence does not involve any attempt on the part of either partner to gain general control over the relationship. The violence is situationally provoked, as the tensions or emotions of a particular encounter lead someone to react with violence. Intimate relationships inevitably involve conflicts, and in some relationships one or more of those conflicts may escalate to violence. The violence may be minor and singular, with one argument at some point in the relationship escalating to the level that someone pushes or slaps the other, is immediately remorseful, apologizes and never does it again. Or it could be a chronic problem, with one or both partners frequently resorting to violence, minor or severe.

The motives for such violence vary. A physical attack might feel like the only way one's extreme anger or frustration can be expressed. It may even be intended to do serious injury as an expression of anger. It may primarily be an attempt to get the attention of a partner who doesn't seem to be listening. There can be a control motive involved, albeit not one that is part of a general pattern of coercive control. One partner may simply find that the argument is not going well for him or her, and decide that one way to win this is to get physical.

The separate violent incidents of situational couple violence may look exactly like those involved in intimate terrorism or violent resistance. The difference is in the general power and control dynamic of the relationship, not in the nature of any or all assaults. In situational couple violence, there is no general pattern of exerting coercive control. It is simply that one or more disagreements have resulted in violence. The violence may even be frequent if the situation that provokes the violence is recurring, as when one partner frequently feels that the other is flirting and the confrontations over that issue regularly

lead one or the other of them to lash out. And the violence may be quite severe, even homicidal. What makes it situational couple violence is that it is rooted in the events of a particular situation rather than in a relationship-wide attempt to control.

HOW DO WE KNOW ABOUT THESE TYPES?

The descriptions of the three types of partner violence that you have just read are derived from 30 years of social science research on violence between intimate partners, research that generally did not make the distinctions that I describe. How, then, can we manage to come to conclusions about these different types of partner violence from research that doesn't distinguish among them? There are two answers to that question. First, some of the more recent research does operationalize the distinctions. Second, there are ways to tease out of the research that didn't make distinctions information regarding the different types of partner violence. One way is based on the sampling biases of the two major types of domestic violence research. The violence in general survey research is almost entirely men's and women's situational couple violence. Thus, any general survey research that compares violent with nonviolent men or women—or victims with nonvictims—can be assumed to tell us mostly about situational couple violence. In contrast, the violence in agency samples is primarily men's intimate terrorism and women's violent resistance. Thus, agency-based studies can be used to inform us regarding those two types of violence. Another way to discern types in research that didn't explicitly note them is to look for patterns associated with violence that show the characteristics of each of the types. Here is an example. Recent research that has operationalized the distinctions has shown consistently that intimate terrorism is more likely than situational couple violence to be frequent and severe (Graham-Kevan & Archer, 2003,

2005; Johnson, 2001, in press; Johnson & Leone, 2005; Leone, Johnson, & Cohan, 2003; Leone, Johnson, Cohan, & Lloyd, 2004). It follows that violence that is frequent and severe is likely to be intimate terrorism and violence that is infrequent and mild is likely to be situational couple violence. Thus, if studies show that anger management therapy is effective only in the treatment of men whose violence is infrequent and mild, we have indirect support for the conclusion that it is effective for situational couple violence but not effective for intimate terrorism. With these strategies in mind, we can examine the literature on communication in violent relationships.

◆ *Communication Within Violent Intimate Relationships*

There is a sizable literature on communication patterns in violent intimate relationships. Like research on intimate partner violence conducted in other disciplines, that done in communication is limited in two ways. First, the majority of research by communication scholars does not recognize or distinguish among different types of intimate partner violence. For reasons explained previously, it is likely that most of the violence among the couples involved in this research was situational couple violence, and I make that assumption in reviewing the literature. The important issue of applicability to intimate terrorism will have to be handled much more speculatively.

Second, most of the research does not focus specifically on communication during violent incidents. It involves either self-reports of general patterns of communication and conflict in the relationship or observation of communication patterns in laboratory settings that are unlikely to be reasonable facsimiles of what happens during incidents that actually involve violence. Situational couple violence may well be rooted in patterns of communication during conflict that facilitate or at least do not

inhibit an escalation to violence. In contrast, the communication involved in intimate terrorism is less likely to be exhibited in the laboratory context or during normal conversation or conflict. Thus, both caveats suggest that we view the research primarily as informing us about situational couple violence.

COMMUNICATION PATTERNS IN SITUATIONAL COUPLE VIOLENCE

It has long been observed that physically violent relationships almost always also include verbal aggression, defined as an attack on a person's self-concept, including character attacks, competence attacks, physical appearance attacks, and so on (Infante & Wigley, 1986) and that verbal aggression can be devastating to individuals and to relationships (Sabourin, 1996; Straus & Sweet, 1992). In studies of the communication patterns of violent couples, the relationship between verbal and physical aggression is most often treated as causal, the most common model being some version of the catalyst hypothesis (Roloff, 1996) in which a hostile predisposition turns to violence when provoked by verbal aggression. It has also been noted, however, that verbal aggression does not inevitably lead to violence, for a number of reasons. For example, Infante's model presumes that verbal aggression leads to violence only when it sets off a hostile predisposition in the recipient. In the absence of such hostility, the verbal aggression may be "ignored or viewed as good-natured kidding" (Infante, Chandler, & Rudd, 1989, p. 166). More recently, Roloff (1996) has made effective use of the general literature on the interaction processes involved in violence (Felson, 1984) to identify four general factors that "might cause verbal aggression to lead to physical aggression" (Roloff, 1996, p. 23), implying that when these factors are missing, verbal aggression may not escalate to violence. The first factor is face loss, especially when the verbal aggression involves central aspects of the individual's self-concept and when the attack is public and seen as illegitimate and unmitigated. The second is desire to control, about which I will have more to say in the later section on intimate terrorism. The third escalating factor is violence potential (experience with and willingness to use violence), and the fourth is anger.

Roloff's (1996) discussion of factors that might influence verbal aggression to escalate to violence does not inform us of the source of the verbal aggression in the first place. Although Infante and his colleagues (1989) did discuss a number of possible reasons for verbal aggression, their major focus has been on argumentative skill deficiency. The basic scenario involves a disagreement in which one or both of the partners "[lacks] the verbal skills for dealing with social conflict constructively" (p. 166). This skill deficiency leads the deficient partner to turn to verbal aggression as a means of winning the argument. A general norm of reciprocity in relationships then contributes to escalation, as each partner responds to verbal aggression with more verbal aggression (negative reciprocity). Such an escalation is most likely when both partners have skill deficiencies.

Indeed, there is considerable evidence from work done in this tradition that situationally violent couples are more verbally aggressive and deficient in argumentative skills than are nonviolent couples (Infante, Myers, & Buerkel, 1994; Infante & Rancer, 1996; Sabourin, 1996). Similarly, Feldman and Ridley (2000; Ridley & Feldman, 2003), working in a family conflict tradition, find that both men and women in violent relationships show more unilateral verbal aggression, more mutual verbal aggression, less constructive relative to destructive communication, and less problem solving.

The primary model constructed from this line of research most closely resembles what we know about situational couple violence. It is not very gendered and seems to involve an almost inadvertent escalation of conflict into violence. The core problem is one of communication skill deficiencies for which an individual compensates with verbal aggression that then escalates into violence. All we need to do to intervene is to improve the couple's communication skills through methods such as cognitive restructuring or argumentative skills training (Sabourin, 1996, pp. 215–217).

As is common in the literature on domestic violence in other disciplines, work done by communication scholars does not make any distinctions among types of violence, nor does it consider the possibility that for some couples the verbal aggression is not a causal factor in violence, but one among a variety of tactics that one partner is using to control the other (as in intimate terrorism). The samples on which the research is based often draw their violent respondents from shelters or programs for batterers and therefore almost certainly include not only situational couple violence but also intimate terrorism. There is a hint of that possibility in Ridley and Feldman's results, in which they find a greater likelihood of a male demand/female withdrawal pattern among their violent couples (Feldman & Ridley, 2000; Ridley & Feldman, 2003). This is the opposite of the typical pattern for distressed heterosexual couples, in which it is more likely that women make demands and men withdraw. The male demand/female withdrawal pattern could be showing up in these data as a function of a few couples in which a pattern of intimate terrorism has led the women to defensively withdraw when their partner makes demands on them. This possibility raises the question of whether the skill deficiency model applies to all violent relationships.

Most work in this area simply compares violent couples with nonviolent couples, lumping together violent couples who might be quite different from each other and creating an "average" communication pattern for comparison with nonviolent couples. Olson's (2002) work demonstrates the importance of abandoning this approach and differentiating among types of violence.

She conducted in-depth interviews with individuals involved in aggressive and violent relationships. She identified three different communication patterns, one that suggests conditions under which verbal aggression will not escalate to violence, one that I would argue represents situational couple violence, and one that probably represents intimate terrorism.

Twelve of Olson's (2002) 31 couples were involved in what she called an aggressive relationship. Although they did reciprocate verbal aggression, generally they were not violent, and "their relationships were more democratic, and, overall, their communication was healthier" (p. 120). For example, many of them had conversations with their partners about what they would not tolerate during a conflict. Although there is risk that these relationships might escalate to situational couple violence, the couples' low tolerance for aggression and their communication about the nature of their conflict reduces the likelihood they will escalate to physical violence.

The second couple type identified in this study, violent relationships, does involve an escalation into situational couple violence and seems to embody the process described above as negative reciprocity. Olson (2002) describes these relationships as having "a dyadic pattern of control . . . [in which] the shared control fluctuated back and forth between partners. . . . As a result, these relationships were fraught with power struggles, resulting in reciprocated aggression and violence" (p. 118). She also points out that these couples described a typical wife demand/husband withdraw pattern, often involving the wife's use of aggression to get her withdrawing partner's attention.

Olson's (2002) discussion of these first two groups supports a model in which verbal aggression functions as a catalyst to provoke violence from the target of that aggression—if the target already has a hostile predisposition and is prone to violence, especially when the couple is likely to engage in negative reciprocity of communication. However, she identifies a third

group that does not fit that model at all, a group that clearly embodies what I have called intimate terrorism.

COMMUNICATION PATTERNS IN INTIMATE TERRORISM

Olson's third group, abusive relationships, is "characterized by power imbalances in which the control, maintained by one partner, permeated the entire relationship" (Olson, 2002, p. 117). She reports that these relationships exhibited domineering-submissive communication patterns, and she quotes one respondent clearly indicating a husband demand/wife withdraw pattern such as those found in other studies of violent couples (Babcock, Waltz, Jacobson, & Gottman, 1993; Feldman & Ridley, 2000; Ridley & Feldman, 2003). This pattern has also been described as having a "chilling effect" by Roloff and his colleague (Cloven & Roloff, 1993; Roloff & Cloven, 1990), in which the recipients of violence become more and more reluctant to speak their mind in the relationship.

The dangers of aggregating all violent couples and comparing their averages to those of nonviolent couples are clear from the results of Olson's (2002) nuanced analysis. If one were to combine her two violent types into one, the pattern one would see would closely resemble the work on verbal aggression cited above, with relatively high verbal aggression, less constructive communication patterns, a relatively normal wife demand/husband withdraw pattern, and a high husband demand/wife withdraw pattern. The reality is quite different, however, consisting of two groups of violent couples showing quite distinct communication patterns, one of which corresponds to situational couple violence, the other to intimate terrorism.

Roloff's useful discussion of the conditions under which verbal aggression (what he calls coercive communication) will lead to violence elaborates on the patterns likely to be found in situational couple violence, but it also includes a section on desire to control that is clearly relevant to intimate terrorism (Roloff, 1996, pp. 27–30). In this type of aggressive interaction, resistance is critical. The partner's refusal to comply with a coercive communication challenges the aggressor's sense of control, leading him or her to escalate to the use of violence. Roloff makes the connection to Infante's skill deficiency model, arguing that coercive partners will be more likely to use violence if they do not have the communication skills that allow them to gain compliance. It is important to note, however, that the causal chain in this case is quite different from that hypothesized in the typical argumentative skill deficiency model, in which the incompetent communicator turns to verbal aggression which in turn sets off the *partner's* violence. Roloff's (1996) discussion, in contrast, suggests that the incompetent communicator first uses verbal aggression to attempt to gain compliance, then turns to physical violence when verbal attacks are ineffective. The model here is intimate terrorism, in which a variety of control tactics are used to take general control over the relationship.

More concrete, less abstract analyses of the nature of the communication involved in intimate terrorism focus on two major areas. First, there is a huge literature on the nature of the psychological abuse often involved in intimate terrorism (Arias & Pape, 1999; Chang, 1996; Marshall, 1996; O'Leary & Maiuro, 2001; Tolman, 1992). One of the major control tactics used by intimate terrorists involves breaking down the self-esteem of their partner, in part to convince her that acceding to the control of her partner is in her best interests, in part to convince her that she is so worthless that her current relationship is the only option available to her.

Second, there is a literature that focuses on the rhetoric that intimate terrorists use to seduce and entrap their partners (Rosen, 1996). In related work, Lloyd and her colleagues have done very useful analyses of the ways in which the rhetoric of romance

sometimes justifies violence (Lloyd & Emery, 2000a, 2000b). It is also useful to situate this work in the context of long-standing feminist analyses of romance as a "cover" for the domination of women (Firestone, 1970, pp. 146–155; Jackman, 1994; Millett, 1970; Rose, 1985). Finally, the language of patriarchy legitimizes men's control over "their" women (Adams, Towns, & Gavey, 1995; Dobash & Dobash, 1979; Major, 1987).

In sum, the evidence regarding the communication patterns in intimate terrorism suggests two general scenarios—one in which the controlling partner (usually the husband) needs to use both verbal aggression and violence to take control over his partner, and a second in which the husband's control is well-enough established that what we see is husband's demands and wife's withdrawal or submission. In addition, the content of the communication will often involve psychologically demeaning messages about the victim of the violence and a rhetoric of romance and patriarchy that justifies the control exercised by the intimate terrorist.

◆ Gender and Communication in Different Types of Intimate Partner Violence

It is clear from the work of Olson (2002, 2004a) that communication scholars must make distinctions among types of intimate partner violence if they are to understand the nature of communication processes associated with each type. However, in most cases communication researchers do not make these distinctions, choosing instead to simply compare violent with nonviolent relationships. Thus, the distinctions discussed above are not well established in the communication literature.

The ambiguities created by aggregation of different types of violence are serious indeed. Average differences found between the communication patterns of violent and nonviolent couples could be produced by differences in only a subset of violent couples, and various specific differences could be produced by different subsets. Within one study, patterns that correspond to the "argumentative skill deficiencies produce verbal aggression that provokes violence" model might be produced by a subset of the violent couples involved in situational couple violence, while an increase in husband demand/wife withdraw patterns is produced by a different subset that is involved in intimate terrorism.

We need research that routinely investigates the possibility that samples of violent relationships include different types of violence with quite different communication patterns. There are three major tactics by which typologies could be applied in such research. First, operationalizations of theory-based typologies could be developed. Second, cluster analysis or related quantitative data-analytic techniques could be used to develop empirically derived typologies. Third, qualitative analysis could be used to develop empirically based typologies. My colleagues and I have used the first two approaches (Johnson, 2001; Johnson & Leone, 2005; Leone et al., 2004). Olson has used the third (Olson, 2002) and has also developed a theory-based typology that could be operationalized (Olson, 2004a).

What can we say at this point about the gendering of communication processes in the different types of violent relationships? I think we can say a good deal—tentatively. Tentatively, I have suggested that the argumentative deficiency/verbal aggression/negative reciprocity model might describe, explain, and predict situational couple violence. The literature on this pattern does not generally distinguish between male and female violence, implying that the patterns are relatively ungendered. The work of Feldman and Ridley (Feldman & Ridley, 2000; Ridley & Feldman, 2003) more directly asserts that much the same model is applicable to both men and women. However, before drawing that conclusion,

we need more qualitative research that focuses on differences in communication within the category of situational couple violence. We should not risk repeating the mistake of assuming that something is a unitary phenomenon without first determining that it is. To choose an example that is particularly relevant to issues of gender and communication, the general literature on situational couple violence indicates that men's violence is much more likely than women's to produce injuries and that women's violence is likely to be perceived as less serious (Straus, 1999). Thus, I would expect couple communication about violent incidents to involve quite a different dynamic following male violence than it would following female violence. Ironically, it may be the case that couples are less likely to get involved in metacommunication to prevent another escalation if the violence was the less frightening women's violence. And this pattern might be relevant to Olson's (2002, 2004a) distinction between aggressive and violent couples. Although I did not place her aggressive group in the category of situational couple violence because it was not clear that they had ever experienced physical violence, Olson sees aggressive and violent couples as variations of situational couple violence,[3] and she might be right. Some of these couples may have experienced physical violence and dealt with it in a manner that prevented a recurrence.

When it comes to intimate terrorism, I have suggested that a male demand/female withdraw pattern may be typical and that communication that involves the assertion of control will be endemic. Furthermore, the content of the communication will often involve psychological abuse, the assertion of male privilege, and a rhetoric of romance that justifies the violence.

I have essentially said nothing about the patterns of communication involved in violent resistance because as far as I know there is no communication research that focuses on it. We really do not know what types of communication encourage or inhibit violent resistance to intimate terrorism.

◆ Communication About Violent Relationships

In addition to research on communication patterns within violent relationships, communication scholars have addressed various aspects of communication about violent relationships, and analyses of the general themes of romance, patriarchy, masculinity, and femininity discussed previously in the section on communication within violent relationships are also relevant here (Christopher & Lloyd, 2000; Dobash & Dobash, 1979; Lloyd & Emery, 2000b; Wood, 2001, 2004). Thus, the placement of that discussion is somewhat arbitrary, as is the distinction I make below between private and public speech about violent relationships.

PRIVATE SPEECH ABOUT VIOLENT RELATIONSHIPS

A number of scholars, including communication scholars, have looked into the nature of the narratives created by both victims and perpetrators of intimate partner violence. Most of this work has been carried out on samples that are likely to be dominated by intimate terrorism and violent resistance. We know much less about the narratives that couples create about their situational couple violence.

Perpetrators. Work on the narratives of men who perpetrate violence has generally been carried out with samples from batterers programs or prison populations (Adams et al., 1995; Dobash & Dobash, 1998; Hearn, 1998; Ptacek, 1988; Stamp & Sabourin, 1995; Wood, 2004), and is thus probably dominated by accounts of intimate terrorism. Similarly, work on *violent* women has focused to a large extent on those imprisoned for attacks on their abusive partners (Browne, 1987; O'Keefe, 1997; Richie, 1996; Roberts, 1996; Walker, 1989), thus applying primarily to violent resistance. To my knowledge, none

of this work on either men or women has made distinctions among types of violence in order to investigate how perpetrators' narratives might differ across those types. The work on violent men discusses rationalizations, justifications, minimization, and contradictions. Wood's (2004) recent work ties these rhetorical tactics substantively to contradictory narratives of masculinity. The work on violent women who have attacked abusive partners identifies themes of terror, hopelessness, and entrapment. Clearly, we need more work on the narratives of men and women who are involved in situational couple violence.

Victims. With regard to the victims of domestic violence, in some sense much of what we know in general about intimate terrorism is based on the narratives of women who have survived it. Most of the research on intimate terrorism is carried out with agency samples, sometimes based on questionnaire responses, but more often involving in-depth interviewing (Dobash & Dobash, 1979; Kirkwood, 1993; Pence & Paymar, 1993). Although most of this work is presented as data on the nature of domestic violence rather than as analyses of women's narratives, some research is explicitly couched in narrative terms (Ferraro, 1996; Olson, 2001, 2004b; Riessman, 1992; Winkelmann, 2004; Wood, 2000, 2001).

Help seeking. One important area of private speech about domestic violence has received very little attention. Considerable evidence indicates that victims of intimate terrorism are quite resourceful in seeking help, both formal and informal, from others (Gondolf & Fisher, 1988; Leone et al., 2003). Unfortunately, there is also evidence that their pleas for help often go unheeded. We need research on the nature of the communication between victims and the friends, family, and agency representatives from whom they seek help. Perhaps we could uncover clues about the nature of effective help seeking regarding domestic violence.

PUBLIC SPEECH ABOUT VIOLENT RELATIONSHIPS

Public discourses about relationship violence are critical determinants of the resources that victims have available to them, and a number of scholars have analyzed the nature of such public discussions. Some of these analyses are embedded in histories of the battered women's movement (Dobash & Dobash, 1992; Schechter, 1982). Others provide explicit analyses of the rhetoric that turned relationship violence from a private problem to a public policy matter (Ferraro, 1996; Fineman & Mykitiuk, 1994) and finally into a general human rights issue (Heise, 1996). A few deal with the nature of media rhetoric regarding domestic violence (Meyers, 1997). All these analyses are heavily gendered, addressing the means by which domestic violence has been framed as an issue of violence against women. As I have argued elsewhere, in public discourse the term domestic violence has come to represent intimate terrorism, the most gendered form of intimate partner violence (Johnson, 2005). There is now developing, however, a powerful counterdiscourse that has yet to be analyzed, the discourse of the men's and fathers' rights movements that frames domestic violence as a couples problem. Their rhetoric is rooted in the same problem I have identified in the scholarly literature: the assumption that domestic violence is a unitary phenomenon. They cite the same survey research as evidence that women are as violent as men, not realizing, or not caring, that those data tell us little about the nature of true wife abuse or husband abuse.

◆ Conclusion: The Gendering of Communication Within and About Violent Relationships

From this literature review, it is clear that (1) communication within and about intimate partner violence is heavily gendered and that (2) the nature of that gendering cannot be understood without making distinctions among types of such violence. Intimate terrorism is largely male perpetrated and involves communication patterns that establish men's dominance over "their" women. Violent resistance is, as a result, largely enacted by women and involves communication patterns about which we know very little but that presumably involve women's resistance to subordination and their conclusion that violence is a viable tactic for such resistance. Situational couple violence is to some extent gender symmetric and involves communication patterns that contribute to the escalation of the inevitable conflicts of intimate relationships into verbal aggression and violence. In many cases, incidents of situational couple violence are followed by communication that effectively de-escalates the violence. Public and private discourses about domestic violence are also heavily gendered, focused on the differences between men and women and the gendered aspects of society that are implicated in domestic violence.

It is very important, however, to recognize the extent to which the blinders of heterosexism constrain these analyses. I have chosen to contribute to some extent to this narrowness of vision by saying nothing to this point about intimate partner violence in lesbian and gay relationships so that I could end on the following note. We face a deeply problematic confounding of gender and sexual orientation in much of this literature. Although there is a developing literature on the nature of violence in gay and lesbian relationships (Giorgio, 2002; Island & Letellier, 1991; Renzetti, 1992; Renzetti & Miley, 1996), the vast majority of studies are focused on heterosexual relationships, making it impossible for us to untangle the effects of heterosexuality from the effects of gender. For example, are men the primary perpetrators of intimate terrorism because heterosexuality is rooted in male dominance over women, or is it because men (both gay and straight) are more likely than women to feel a need to control their partners (male or female)? We need to expand our research to include violence in gay and lesbian relationships not only to be able to intervene more effectively in same-sex intimate partner violence but also to better understand the nature of intimate partner violence in general (Merrill, 1996).

◆ Notes

1. There is a fourth type, *mutual violent control*, that comprises two intimate terrorists vying for control of their relationship. This type appears in very small numbers in some samples and there is some debate about whether it is a true type or an artifact of the constraints of imperfect operationalization.

2. I use gendered pronouns because the vast majority of intimate terrorists are men terrorizing female partners. That does not mean that women are *never* intimate terrorists. A small number of women do terrorize their male partners (Steinmetz, 1977–78), and there are also women in same-sex relationships who terrorize their female partners (Renzetti, 1992).

3. Olson also treats her abusive couples as a type of situational couple violence. It seems clear to me that, on the contrary, they are experiencing intimate terrorism. It appears from her discussion that she did not consider that possibility because one of her abusive partners was a woman, and she was working with an early version of my framework that somewhat single-mindedly emphasized the patriarchal roots of intimate terrorism (Johnson, 1995).

◆ References

Adams, P., Towns, A., & Gavey, N. (1995). Dominance and entitlement: The rhetoric men use to discuss their violence toward women. *Discourse and Society, 6,* 387–406.

Arias, I., & Pape, K. T. (1999). Psychological abuse: Implications for adjustment and commitment to leave violent partners. *Violence and Victims, 14*(1), 55–67.

Babcock, J. C., Waltz, J., Jacobson, N. S., & Gottman, J. M. (1993). Power and violence: The relationship between communication patterns, power discrepancies, and domestic violence. *Journal of Consulting & Clinical Psychology, 61*(1), 40–50.

Browne, A. (1987). *When battered women kill.* New York: Free Press.

Chang, V. N. (1996). *I just lost myself: Psychological abuse of women in marriage.* Westport, CN: Praeger.

Christopher, F. S., & Lloyd, S. A. (2000). Physical and sexual aggression in relationships. In S. S. Hendrick & C. Hendrick (Eds.), *Close relationships: A sourcebook* (pp. 331–343). Thousand Oaks, CA: Sage.

Cloven, D. H., & Roloff, M. E. (1993). The chilling effect of aggressive potential on the expression of complaints in intimate relationships. *Communication Monographs, 60*(3), 199–219.

Dobash, R. E., & Dobash, R. P. (1979). *Violence against wives: A case against patriarchy.* New York: Free Press.

Dobash, R. E., & Dobash, R. P. (1992). *Women, violence and social change.* New York: Routledge.

Dobash, R. E., & Dobash, R. P. (1998). Violent men and violent contexts. In R. E. Dobash & R. P. Dobash (Eds.), *Rethinking violence against women* (pp. 141–168). Thousand Oaks, Ca: Sage.

Feldman, C. M., & Ridley, C. A. (2000). The role of conflict-based communication responses and outcomes in male domestic violence toward female partners. *Journal of Social and Personal Relationships, 17*(4–5), 552–573.

Felson, R. B. (1984). Patterns of aggressive social interaction. In A. Mummendey (Ed.), *Social psychology of aggression: From individual behavior to social interaction* (pp. 108–126). New York: Springer-Verlag.

Ferraro, K. J. (1996). The dance of dependency: A genealogy of domestic violence discourse. *Hypatia, 11*(4), 77–91.

Fineman, M. A., & Mykitiuk, R. (Eds.). (1994). *The public nature of private violence: The* discovery of domestic abuse. New York: Routledge.

Firestone, S. (1970). *The dialectic of sex: The case for feminist revolution.* New York: Bantam.

Giorgio, G. (2002). Speaking silence: Definitional dialogues in abusive lesbian relationships. *Violence Against Women, 8*(10), 1233–1259.

Gondolf, E. W., & Fisher, E. R. (1988). *Battered women as survivors: An alternative to treating learned helplessness.* Lexington, MA: D.C. Heath.

Graham-Kevan, N., & Archer, J. (2003). Intimate terrorism and common couple violence: A test of Johnson's predictions in four British samples. *Journal of Interpersonal Violence, 18*(11), 1247–1270.

Graham-Kevan, N., & Archer, J. (July, 2005). *Using Johnson's domestic violence typology to classify men and women in a nonselected sample.* Paper presented at the 9th International Family Violence Conference, Durham, NH.

Hearn, J. (1998). *The violences of men: How men talk about and how agencies respond to men's violence to women.* Thousand Oaks, CA: Sage.

Heise, L. L. (1996). Violence against women: Global organizing for change. In J. L. Edleson & Z. C. Eisikovits (Eds.), *Future interventions with battered women and their families* (pp. 7–33). Thousand Oaks, CA: Sage.

Infante, D. A., Chandler, T. A., & Rudd, J. E. (1989). Test of an argumentative skill deficiency model of interspousal violence. *Communication Monographs, 56*(2), 163–177.

Infante, D. A., Myers, S. A., & Buerkel, R. A. (1994). Argument and verbal aggression in constructive and destructive family and organizational disagreements. *Western Journal of Communication, 58*(2), 73–84.

Infante, D. A., & Rancer, A. S. (1996). Argumentativeness and verbal aggressiveness: A review of recent theory and research. In B. R. Burleson (Ed.), *Communication yearbook 1996* (pp. 319–351). Thousand Oaks, CA: Sage.

Infante, D. A., & Wigley, C. J. (1986). Verbal aggressiveness: An interpersonal model and measure. *Communication Monographs, 53*(1), 61–69.

Island, D., & Letellier, P. (1991). *Men who beat the men who love them: Battered gay men and domestic violence.* New York: Haworth Press.

Jackman, M. R. (1994). *The velvet glove: Paternalism and conflict in gender, class, and race relations.* Berkeley: University of California Press.

Johnson, M. P. (1995). Patriarchal terrorism and common couple violence: Two forms of violence against women. *Journal of Marriage and the Family, 57*(2), 283–294.

Johnson, M. P. (2001). Conflict and control: Symmetry and asymmetry in domestic violence. In A. Booth, A. C. Crouter, & M. Clements (Eds.), *Couples in conflict* (pp. 95–104). Mahwah, NJ: Lawrence Erlbaum.

Johnson, M. P. (2005). Domestic violence: It's not about gender—or is it? *Journal of Marriage and Family, 67*(5), 1126–1130.

Johnson, M. P. (in press). Conflict and control: Gender, symmetry, and asymmetry in domestic violence. *Violence Against Women.*

Johnson, M. P., & Cares, A. (2004, November). *Effects and non-effects of childhood experiences of family violence on adult partner violence.* Paper presented at the National Council on Family Relations annual meeting, Orlando, FL.

Johnson, M. P., & Leone, J. M. (2005). The differential effects of intimate terrorism and situational couple violence: Findings from the National Violence Against Women Survey. *Journal of Family Issues, 26*(3), 322–349.

Kirkwood, C. (1993). *Leaving abusive partners: From the scars of survival to the wisdom for change.* Newbury Park, CA: Sage.

Leone, J. M., Johnson, M. P., & Cohan, C. L. (2003, November). *Help-seeking among women in violent relationships: Factors associated with formal and informal help utilization.* Paper presented at the National Council on Family Relations annual meeting, Vancouver, British Columbia.

Leone, J. M., Johnson, M. P., Cohan, C. M., & Lloyd, S. (2004). Consequences of male partner violence for low-income, ethnic women. *Journal of Marriage and Family,* 66(2), 471–489.

Lloyd, S. A., & Emery, B. C. (2000a). The context and dynamics of intimate aggression against women. *Journal of Social and Personal Relationships,* 17(4–5), 503–521.

Lloyd, S. A., & Emery, B. C. (2000b). *The dark side of courtship: Physical and sexual aggression.* Thousand Oaks, CA: Sage.

Major, B. (1987). Gender, justice, and the psychology of entitlement. In P. Shaver & C. Hendrick (Eds.), *Sex and gender. Review of personality and social psychology* (Vol. 7. pp. 124–148). Newbury Park, CA: Sage.

Marshall, L. L. (1996). Psychological abuse of women: Six distinct clusters. *Journal of Family Violence,* 11(4), 379–409.

Merrill, G. S. (1996). Ruling the exceptions: Same-sex battering and domestic violence theory. In C. M. Renzetti & C. H. Miley (Eds.), *Violence in gay and lesbian domestic partnerships* (pp. 9–21). New York: Haworth Press.

Meyers, M. (1997). *News coverage of violence against women: Engendering blame.* Thousand Oaks, CA: Sage.

Millett, K. (1970). *Sexual politics.* New York: Doubleday.

O'Keefe, M. (1997). Incarcerated battered women: A comparison of battered women who killed their abusers and those incarcerated for other offenses. *Journal of Family Violence,* 12(1), 1–19.

O'Leary, K. D., & Maiuro, R. D. (Eds.). (2001). *Psychological abuse in violent domestic relations.* New York: Springer.

Olson, L. N. (2001). Survival narratives: A feminist analysis of women's stories of disengagement. *Speech Communication Annual,* 15, 53–79.

Olson, L. N. (2002). Exploring "common couple violence" in heterosexual romantic relationships. *Western Journal of Communication,* 66(1), 104–128.

Olson, L. N. (2004a). Relational control-motivated aggression: A theoretically-based typology of intimate violence. *Journal of Family Communication,* 4(3/4), 209–233.

Olson, L. N. (2004b). The role of voice in the (re)construction of a battered woman's identity: An autoethnography of one woman's experiences of abuse. *Women's Studies in Communication,* 27(1), 1–23.

Pence, E., & Paymar, M. (1993). *Education groups for men who batter: The Duluth model.* New York: Springer.

Ptacek, J. (1988). Why do men batter their wives? In K. Yllo & M. Bograd (Eds.), *Feminist perspectives on wife abuse* (pp. 133–157). Newbury Park, CA: Sage.

Renzetti, C. M. (1992). *Violent betrayal: Partner abuse in lesbian relationships.* Newbury Park, CA: Sage.

Renzetti, C. M., & Miley, C. H. (1996). *Violence in gay and lesbian domestic partnerships.* New York: Haworth Press.

Richie, B. (1996). *Compelled to crime: The gender entrapment of battered black women.* New York: Routledge.

Ridley, C. A., & Feldman, C. M. (2003). Female domestic violence toward male partners: Exploring conflict responses and outcomes. *Journal of Family Violence,* 18(3), 157–170.

Riessman, C. (1992). Making sense of marital violence: One woman's narrative. In G. Rosenwald & R. Ochberg (Eds.), *Storied lives: The cultural politics of self understanding.* New Haven, CT: Yale University Press.

Roberts, A. R. (1996). Battered women who kill: A comparative study of incarcerated participants with a community sample of battered women. *Journal of Family Violence,* 11(3), 291–304.

Roloff, M. E. (1996). The catalyst hypothesis: Conditions under which coercive communication leads to physical aggression. In D. D. Cahn & S. A. Lloyd (Eds.), *Family violence from a communication perspective* (pp. 20–36). Thousand Oaks, CA: Sage.

Roloff, M. E., & Cloven, D. H. (1990). The chilling effect in interpersonal relationships: The reluctance to speak one's mind. In D. D. Cahn (Ed.), *Intimates in conflict: A communication perspective* (pp. 49–76). Hillside, NJ: Erlbaum.

Rose, S. (1985). Is romance dysfunctional? *International Journal of Women's Studies,* 8(3), 250–265.

Rosen, K. H. (1996). The ties that bind women to violent premarital relationships: Processes of seduction and entrapment. In D. D. Cahn & S. A. Lloyd (Eds.), *Family violence from a communication perspective* (pp. 151–176). Thousand Oaks, CA: Sage.

Sabourin, T. C. (1996). The role of communication in verbal abuse between partners. In D. D. Cahn & S. A. Lloyd (Eds.), *Family violence from a communication perspective* (pp. 199–217). Thousand Oaks, CA: Sage.

Schechter, S. (1982). *Women and male violence: The visions and struggles of the battered women's movement.* Boston: South End Press.

Stamp, G. H., & Sabourin, T. C. (1995). Accounting for violence: An analysis of male spousal abuse narratives. *Journal of Applied Communication Research, 23*(4), 284–307.

Steinmetz, S. K. (1977–78). The battered husband syndrome. *Victimology, 2*(3-4), 499–509.

Stith, S. M., Rosen, K. H., Middleton, K. A., Busch, A. L., Lundeberg, K., & Carlton, R. P. (2000). The intergenerational transmission of spouse abuse: A meta-analysis. *Journal of Marriage and the Family, 62*(3), 640–654.

Straus, M. A. (1999). The controversy over domestic violence by women: A methodological, theoretical, and sociology of science analysis. In X. B. Arriaga & S. Oskamp (Eds.), *Violence in intimate relationships* (pp. 17–44). Thousand Oaks, CA: Sage.

Straus, M. A., & Sweet, C. (1992). Verbal/symbolic aggression in couples: Incidence rates and relationship to personal characteristics. *Journal of Marriage and the Family, 54*(2), 346–357.

Swan, S. C., & Snow, D. L. (2002). A typology of women's use of violence in intimate relationships. *Violence Against Women, 8*(3), 286–319.

Tolman, R. M. (1992). Psychological abuse of women. In R. T. Ammerman & M. Hersen (Eds.), *Assessment of family violence: A clinical and legal sourcebook* (pp. 291–310). New York: John Wiley.

Walker, L. E. (1989). *Terrifying love: Why battered women kill and how society responds.* New York: Harper & Row.

Winkelmann, C. L. (2004). *The language of battered women: A rhetorical analysis of personal theologies.* Albany: State University of New York Press.

Wood, J. T. (2000). That wasn't the real him: Women's dissociation of violence from the men who enact it. *Qualitative Research in Review, 1,* 1–7.

Wood, J. T. (2001). The normalization of violence in heterosexual romantic relationships: Women's narratives of love and violence. *Journal of Social and Personal Relationships, 18*(2), 239–261.

Wood, J. T. (2004). Monsters and victims: Male felons' accounts of intimate partner violence. *Journal of Social and Personal Relationships, 21*(5), 555–576.

PART II

GENDER AND COMMUNICATION IN ORGANIZATIONAL CONTEXTS

Introduction

◆ Dennis K. Mumby

T he relationship between gender and organization studies has traditionally been rather tenuous and uneasy. While the study of "gender in organizations" has been the focus of scholarly attention for at least three decades, efforts to develop a sustained, programmatic, and interdisciplinary approach to "gendered organizing" have, at least until recently, proven largely unproductive. Indeed, since the early 1980s, critical organization scholars have regularly lamented the lack of systematic attention to the intersection of gender and organization (e.g., Acker, 1990; Hearn & Parkin, 1983; Mills, 1988); Wilson's (1996) claim that organization studies is "tenaciously blind and deaf to gender" (p. 825) is perhaps the apotheosis of this lament. Such has been the apparent apathy of fields such as management and organizational sociology toward the study of gender and organizing that Martin and Collinson (2002) have been moved to argue that gender scholars should "strike out" on their own and establish a separate field of gendered organization studies.

Given this historical context, it is not unreasonable to ask what has happened in the last 10 years or so to transform this research terrain. From a position of marginality, the gender question has become a central problematic in organization studies. In many respects, the essays in this section are both medium and product of this shift; that is, they could only have been written in the wake of the changing research terrain of organization studies, but at the same time they provide a frame for future research in gendered organization studies. In this brief introductory essay, I want to address some of the factors that have converged to make the study of the relationships among gender, communication, and organization a particularly rich and compelling vein of research, as well as to position the essays in this section within this body of research.

Of course, as I intimated above, it's rather specious to suggest that organization studies has been completely "blind and deaf" to gender, given that it has been a focal point of research in organization-related fields for many years. What is true, however, is that a rather narrow conception of the relationship between gender and organization has prevailed in research over the last 30 years. While I have no wish to

recapitulate the 30 years of research in gender and organization (see, e.g., Ashcraft, 2005; Buzzanell, 1994; Fine, 1993, for excellent overviews), there are certain recurrent themes that characterize the early work in this area.

First, most of the early research was concerned with "women in management," with a clear focus on efforts to understand the changing character of the workplace as women began to rise to positions of leadership in corporations. Researchers focused predominantly on gender as an independent variable, and attempted to identify how women managers both differed from and were similar to their male counterparts, particularly with regard to leadership abilities (e.g., Eagly & Johannesen-Schmidt, 2001; Eagly & Johnson, 1990). Some studies (not necessarily particularly well-grounded in empirical data) even argued for the superiority of "women's ways" of leadership (e.g., Rosener, 1990). Given the novelty of women in corporate leadership roles 30 years ago, this focus made some sense, with the feeling that "adding" women leaders might well significantly impact "business-as-usual" in daily organizational life. Indeed, Kanter's (1977) classic study suggests that this concern was not misplaced, as she shows how women managers posed a challenge to the process of "homosocial reproduction" (i.e., male managers continually recreating the corporate environment in their own image through hiring practices, internal appointments, communication styles, etc.), and disrupted the putative seamlessness of the masculine corporate world. In some ways, then, much of the early research on gender and organizations is not so much about gender per se as it is about accounting for women as other and exotic amid the homogeneity of daily corporate life.

Second, consistent with the widespread tendency in academe to regard gender as a code word for women (see Dow & Wood's introduction to the *Handbook*), early studies of gender in organizations focused almost exclusively on women and, more specifically, women of a particular class and race. Almost without exception, the study of gender was (and to a large extent still is) about the ways in which white middle-class women negotiate(d) a world that was largely male (and white, middle-class, able-bodied, and heterosexual). In this sense, there was a certain essentialism to much of the early "gender as variable" research in that the very notion of the feminine (and the masculine as an absent presence) was treated as unproblematic and monolithic. Gender was thus a rather stable and taken-for-granted concept that was mostly synonymous with sex. The idea that gender is constructed and negotiated in an ongoing, quotidian fashion was mostly foreign to this early work. By extension, *women in management* functioned as an umbrella term that stood for an undifferentiated group who confronted a broad set of issues and concerns in male-dominated modern corporate life. The term itself suggests an "entryist" orientation in which women are understood as an identifiable, empirical phenomenon that has destabilized and changed—and therefore must be assimilated into—the dynamic of the management environment.

Third, much of this early work adopted—either explicitly or implicitly—a liberal feminist perspective in which the goal was to identify the issues and problems that mitigate against the successful assimilation of women into the management world. The goal was to create a level playing field upon which women could compete with men. For the most part, this level playing field was understood as being attainable by providing women with a set of strategic tools that overcome men's advantage. Focus, then, was on corporate life at the individual or, at most, interpersonal level. While women generally were seen as disadvantaged by a male-dominated corporate culture, relatively little attention was paid to the larger, structural issues of organizational life that militate against women's success. Interestingly, Kanter's (1977) early study did address structural impediments to women's corporate progress, but she read this larger structure as gender neutral,

arguing that as women enter the workforce in greater numbers, the kinds of obstacles they face will recede.

Finally, because early gender research focused mainly on interpersonal dynamics (between, for example, women managers and male subordinates), it is mostly insensitive to larger issues of power and gender. The idea that the organizing process is itself fundamentally gendered and therefore a metacommunicative context for interpreting interpersonal dynamics (see Mills & Chiaramonte, 1991) means that these broader questions of power are rarely addressed.

Acker's (1990) now classic article was the first to articulate clearly the idea that organizations are fundamentally gendered and thus to make explicit the connections among gender, organizing, and power:

> To say that an organization . . . is gendered means that advantage and disadvantage, exploitation and coercion, action and emotion, meaning and identity, are patterned through and in terms of a distinction between male and female, masculine and feminine. Gender is not an addition to ongoing processes, conceived as gender neutral. Rather, it is an integral part of those processes, which cannot be properly understood without an analysis of gender. (p. 146)

In this conception, gender and organizing are not separate phenomena but exist rather as co-constitutive and mutually implicative. Furthermore, and of particular importance for communication scholars, Acker positions gender as a discursive, interpretive process where the character of gendered identities involves a struggle over meaning. From this perspective, gender identities are not even particularly stable but are rather a product of competing discourses that attempt to shape the social, political, and cultural context within which gender identities take on meaning. In a very important way, then, Acker identifies the gendering of organizational life as a communicative process to be understood through perspectives that are sensitive to the contested, constructed, dynamic, and conflicted character of the very notion of gender.

The essays in this section take on some variation of this view of gender, exploring a number of ways that we can come to grips with the complex articulations of the gender-organization dynamic. In the remainder of this introduction, I situate these essays within the contemporary research terrain as well as in relation to the conception of gendered organizing articulated above.

◆ Organizing Gender: A Contemporary Perspective

Taken together, the four chapters in this section provide an interesting snapshot of just how far the study of gender and organization has come in the last 15 years. Absent are any discussions of gender in organizations. Missing are references to women in management. Instead, we are treated to textured and nuanced discussions of a number of contemporary debates in the literature. Let me briefly adumbrate a few conceptual and empirical threads that I see running through these chapters.

It is clear that the theoretical and conceptual terrain of current research is vastly more sophisticated now than 20 years ago. Several of the chapters draw extensively on, for example, poststructuralism, feminist standpoint theory, globalization theory, Foucauldian analytics, and so on. Such a shift is not merely a case of the kind of rampant "paradigm proliferation" that a number of scholars have criticized over the last 20 years (e.g., Pfeffer, 1993). Rather, it reflects what I see as a dialectic between theory and the empirical phenomena under study, and represents an effort to provide accounts that do justice to the complexity of the relationship between gender and organization. In Foucault's sense, each of these chapters attempts to "think otherwise" about that relationship and reconceptualize it in ways that set potentially fruitful

research agendas. Karen Ashcraft (Chapter 6) takes up the well-worn notion of "gender difference" and reconceptualizes it in a way that bears little resemblance to early efforts to empirically examine whether men and women really behave differently in the workplace. This increased theoretical sophistication both gives us more elegant accounts of gendered organizing and allows us to actually see a different phenomenon. For example, the influence of poststructuralist theory has enabled us to appreciate and study gendered identities as relatively unstable, complex, contextually situated communicative accomplishments. Such a conception has led to investigations of identity management in the workplace, for example, that were barely conceivable within the women-in-management literature.

A second thread that runs through at least three of the essays in this section is what Conquergood (1991) referred to as "the return of the body" in communication research (see also Dow & Wood, Bell & Blaeuer, and Stormer in this volume). At first glance, such a notion appears to fly in the face of the dramatic and ongoing shift in many areas of the field toward discursive approaches to communication phenomena—a shift significantly enabled by developments in poststructuralism and critical theory. Recent studies of gendered workplace identities, however, have argued that discourse-based approaches frequently overlook the "em-bodied" character of work and the extent to which such identities depend on bodily performance. Bringing the body back in to organization studies is not to return to essentialist conceptions of gender; rather, it is to recognize that the body itself is inflected with cultural, political, and economic interests. Thus, when Ashcraft, citing Connell, argues that "the sweat cannot be excluded," she is precisely making the case that the effort to understand organizations as discursive constructions has tended to overlook what people actually do at work—that is, they engage in various forms of labor that place a number of demands on the body.

Trethewey, Scott, and LeGreco (Chapter 7) address head-on the idea of gendered professional identity as an embodied performance. Drawing on poststructuralism, they are particularly interested in the worker's body as a site of struggle. In what ways do organizations attempt to control the body? How is the body as a potential site of control inflected with discourses of race, class, and sexuality? What are the possible ways in which the body can enact forms of workplace resistance? To what extent are professional identities "em-bodied?" Trethewey et al.'s discussions of "dirty work" (e.g., firefighters, correctional officers, nurses and so on), illustrate how workers in such professions are extremely adept at managing and maintaining professional, gendered identities in the face of the taint associated with such work. Townsley (Chapter 8) is equally attentive to issues of the body, situating her analysis in the context of globalization processes. Two aspects of her chapter are particularly intriguing. First, she directly addresses topics (love and sex) that traditionally have received scant attention in the organization studies literature (and in this sense directly responds to a call by Ashcraft in her chapter for more research on these topics). Second, she takes on these issues in ways that illustrate how, far from being marginal organizational concerns, they are widely implicated in daily organizing processes. For example, her discussion of nannying as a form of domestic labor paints a stark and compelling picture of how, under current globalization practices, even apparently natural concepts like "love" and "mothering" are caught up in political "webs of meaning" that empower Northern women and disenfranchise Southern women.

A third thread woven throughout these chapters involves what might be called—to blatantly steal from a recent book title that's close to my heart—reworking gender difference (Ashcraft & Mumby, 2004). The notion of difference, a defining element of research on gender and organization from its inception, has been radically reconceptualized in recent years. In brief, the major shift in this regard has been from conceptualizing difference as located in specific male and female traits that are manifest in varying communication skills, to seeing gender difference as negotiated, contested, and relatively unstable. Current research (including the chapters in this section) is interested not so much in the product (measurable gender differences) as in the process (how do we investigate the dynamics through which difference is produced, and what are the differences that make a difference in this production process).

This conceptual shift has far-reaching implications. It focuses attention on the notion that difference as an ongoing, negotiated process is both meaning based and intensely political. It is also arbitrary; that is, the only differences that are meaningful are those constructed by communities of people. But of course, we are all held accountable within this constructed, arbitrary system of differences that make a difference (West & Fenstermaker, 1995; West & Zimmerman, 1987). And the chapters in this section address the organization of gendered difference in several ways.

A central issue for Ashcraft is how the construction of gendered difference is both medium and outcome of hierarchized professional identities. For example, once it has been socially constructed and reified through cultural, political, and economic structures, by what discursive and nondiscursive mechanisms is the (usually white, male) identity of the professional airline pilot maintained and reproduced? Furthermore, once such a hegemonic identity is challenged and exposed as arbitrary, what counter identities arise and how are they resisted and/or accommodated? Trethewey, Scott, and LeGreco address the construction of gendered difference in a number of ways but in particular by examining the central role of the performative organizational body. They are especially interested in the body as it "figures" in the increasingly entrepreneurial character of the post-Fordist workplace, where both men and women must harness (both literally and figuratively) their bodies to create a professional, sometimes resistant, identity.

Gender difference has also been reworked through finer grained, more dynamic analyses of femininities and masculinities. Current research has moved away from the incipient essentialism of earlier, variable analyses and toward the study of how multiple forms of femininity and masculinity are negotiated and performed as constitutive features of daily organizing. The old saw regarding women's versus men's workplace communication styles has largely given way to the idea that gendered organizational identities are socially constructed and that these processes of construction are political, routine, and at the very core of the dialectics of power and resistance that characterize organizational life. The chapters in this section beautifully exemplify this discourse-based conception of identity construction, whether in discussions of firefighting as a form of hegemonic masculinity or in framing *career* as a discursive construct.

Finally, many gender researchers recognize the need to examine intersections of gender, class, race, sexuality, and so on in the organizing process. As a community of researchers, we are still not doing a particularly good job of empirically studying these intersections, although awareness of these issues has risen considerably in the past few years. While gender continues to be a principal point of articulation for scholars in organization studies, many recognize that it is difficult—if not impossible—to address gender as somehow separable from other social constructs. The essays here do take up the question of intersectionality. Townsley carefully explores globalization processes as imbued with raced, classed, gendered, and sexed discourses. Buzzanell and Lucas show how career makes no sense as an abstract construct until it is contextualized in terms of the (gendered, classed, raced, etc.) lived realities of organization members. In her evocation of standpoint theory, Ashcraft clearly sees gender as but one element in the discourses

of professional identity construction. Trethewey, Scott, and LeGreco position the body as organized and disciplined through the multiple and intersecting discourses of gender, race, class, and sexuality.

◆ Conclusion

In this brief essay I have tried to contextualize the current state of research on gender and organizations. An overly simple but convenient way of summarizing the evolution of this area of study is to suggest that it has shifted from a focus on gender/women in organizations to exploring the complexities and contradictions of the gendered organizing process. Such a shift not only complicates and textures our understanding of gender, but also draws attention to how messy and precarious is the organizing process itself. Communication scholarship is particularly well positioned to explore the ongoing dynamics of gendered organizing, and in recent years scholars in our field have developed an exciting, diverse, and innovative research agenda that paints a vivid picture of this process. The four chapters in this section mark a coming of age of this agenda and point it in important new directions.

◆ References

Acker, J. (1990). Hierarchies, jobs, bodies: A theory of gendered organizations. *Gender and Society, 4,* 139–158.

Ashcraft, K. L. (2005). Feminist organizational communication studies: Engaging gender in public and private. In S. K. May & D. K. Mumby (Eds.), *Engaging organizational communication theory and research: Multiple perspectives* (pp. 141–169). Thousand Oaks, CA: Sage.

Ashcraft, K. L., & Mumby, D. K. (2004). *Reworking gender: A feminist communicology of organization.* Thousand Oaks, CA: Sage.

Buzzanell, P. M. (1994). Gaining a voice: Feminist organizational communication theorizing. *Management Communication Quarterly, 7,* 339–383.

Conquergood, D. (1991). Rethinking ethnography: Toward a critical cultural politics. *Communication Monographs, 58,* 179–194.

Eagly, A. H., & Johannesen-Schmidt, M. C. (2001). The leadership styles of women and men. *Journal of Social Issues, 57,* 781–797.

Eagly, A. H., & Johnson, B. (1990). Gender and leadership style: A meta-analysis. *Psychological Bulletin, 108,* 233–256.

Fine, M. (1993). New voices in organizational communication: A feminist commentary and critique. In S. Bowen & N. Wyatt (Eds.), *Transforming visions: Feminist critiques in communication studies* (pp. 125–166). Cresskill, NJ: Hampton Press.

Hearn, J., & Parkin, W. (1983). Gender and organizations: A selective review and critique of a neglected area. *Organization Studies, 4,* 219–242.

Kanter, R. M. (1977). *Men and women of the corporation.* New York: Basic Books.

Martin, P. Y., & Collinson, D. (2002). "Over the pond and across the water": Developing the field of "gendered organizations." *Gender, Work and Organization, 9,* 244–265.

Mills, A. J. (1988). Organization, gender and culture. *Organization Studies, 9,* 351–369.

Mills, A. J., & Chiaramonte, P. (1991). Organization as gendered communication act. *Canadian Journal of Communication, 16,* 381–398.

Pfeffer, J. (1993). Barriers to the advance of organizational science: Paradigm development as a dependent variable. *Academy of Management Review, 18,* 599–620.

Rosener, J. B. (1990). Ways women lead. *Harvard Business Review, 68,* 119–125.

West, C., & Fenstermaker, S. (1995). Doing difference. *Gender & Society, 9,* 8–37.

West, C., & Zimmerman, D. (1987). Doing gender. *Gender & Society, 1,* 125–151.

Wilson, F. (1996). Organizational theory: Blind and deaf to gender? *Organization Studies, 17,* 825–842.

BACK TO WORK

Sights/Sites of Difference in Gender and Organizational Communication Studies

◆ Karen Lee Ashcraft

G ender has enjoyed a long presence in organizational communication scholarship, though it has worn many masks and spent much time in the shadows. This chapter traces key ways in which organizational communication scholars have seen gender over the years and proposes a new way of seeing. The primary lens, I argue, has accentuated gender difference. Diverse conceptions and vital developments notwithstanding, scholars of organizational communication remain focused on difference at the organization level, supported by a turn toward analyses of "gendered organizations" (Acker, 1990), as well as a disciplinary tendency to cling to at least some shards of the container metaphor of organization (Carlone & Taylor, 1998; Putnam, Phillips, & Chapman, 1996). I suggest the merits of another way of seeing difference, in and beyond specific organization sites: namely, the gender division and hierarchy of actual labor—of tasks, jobs, and occupations. Organizational communication scholars have largely sidelined the meaning and significance of the actual work people perform. In this sense, my argument merges parallel calls to "bring work back in" to organization studies (Barley, 1996; Barley & Kunda, 2001) and to "include the sweat" in gender studies (Connell, 1995). Accordingly, I draw the contours of a long-standing interdisciplinary inquiry into gendered jobs. My aim is to (1) acquaint communication audiences with this literature, (2) initiate dialogue about how we might learn from and contribute to it, and (3) build a case for the particular promise of studying the multifaceted relationship between difference and occupational identity. My hope is that attending to alternative sites of difference can enhance our vision of the "work" difference does.

◆ Difference in Site: Seeing Gender in Organizational Communication Studies

Elsewhere, I have more extensively considered the development of feminist theory in organizational communication studies (Ashcraft, 2005a), as well as common ways of framing the relationship among gender, discourse, and organization (Ashcraft, 2004). Here, I condense and rework those analyses to provide a historical glance at key visions of gender in organizational communication studies, most of which converge around what I refer to as "difference in site."

EARLY VISIONS OF GENDER DIFFERENCE AT WORK: CONTRARY COMMUNICATION STYLES

Initially, gender appeared in organizational communication studies as it did in other areas of communication research—as "sex," a binary, anatomical variable associated with differences in communication predispositions and practices (Canary & Hause, 1993). Of central concern to this literature was the empirical existence of gender differences at work; the source or production of difference was largely ignored. Later difference studies integrated theoretical developments in gender identity, moving beyond the notion of fixed or intrinsic traits linked to biological sex categories and toward cultural theories of

difference as acquired outcome or social product (Wood, 2003). Much of this work implied strong connections between symbolic and empirical realms—that is, between socially constructed images of femininity and masculinity and the "real-life" behaviors of women and men.

One strand of organizational research that illustrates such development is the study of gender differences in leadership. For over three decades, this research has largely addressed the empirical question: Do men and women lead differently? Scholars have developed diverse approaches to the matter, ranging from variable-analytic studies of leadership perceptions and behavior (see Eagly & Johnson, 1990; Eagly & Karau, 1991; Eagly, Makhijani, & Klonsky, 1992), to projects articulating the distinctive ethos of so-called masculine and feminine leadership (e.g., Natalle, 1996), to research on how actual discourse among women leaders reflects gendered style (e.g., Fairhurst, 1993). Although 30 years of scholarship has generated increasingly complex conceptions of how sex and gender might matter to leading, it has not yielded clear answers to the empirical question of difference (Butterfield & Grinnell, 1999; Walker, Ilardi, McMahon, & Fennell, 1996; Wilkins & Anderson, 1991). Still, many scholars drop confident references to "women's ways" of leading, periodically nodding to the fact that not all people live up to gender expectations (e.g., Nelson, 1988). The dominant empirical focus has long been accompanied by murmurs about the effects of gendered leadership on women's professional success. Eventually, scholars invoked claims of gender difference, however empirically suspect, to accomplish multiple aims—to expose the masculine bias of managerial and professional communication, to suggest resulting dilemmas and barriers faced by women seeking advancement (e.g., "double binds" and "glass ceilings"), and even to bill women's alleged leadership differences as a business opportunity or "feminine advantage" (e.g., Bass & Avolio, 1994; Helgesen, 1990; Loden, 1985; Rosener, 1990).

As the example of leadership research suggests, gender difference studies in organizational communication perform competing ideological functions. Such functions are less visible in empirical projects with positivist leanings (e.g., the sex-variable approach), which tend to suppress moral and political premises by aspiring to a value-neutral stance. Nonetheless, these projects serve to reify a model of gender wherein difference appears as a stable, binary phenomenon that can be known independent of intersections with race, class, sexuality, relationship, institution, and other contextual factors. Most gender difference studies in organizational communication depict difference free from its historical, cultural, political, and structural context (Ashcraft, 2004); and most examine white, middle-class professionals, fueling the problematic assumption that contemporary norms among this population adequately reflect universal perceptions and practices (Calás & Smircich, 1996). By failing to interrogate such factors, most studies miss how current constructions of difference are fraught with inequality and dysfunction, not to mention how easily both different-but-equal and different-but-superior logics can slip into rationales for control and exclusion (Ashcraft, 1999; Ashcraft & Pacanowsky, 1996; Buzzanell, 1995; Calás & Smircich, 1993). That said, it is also the case that gender difference research in organizational communication studies paved the way for the politicization of gender at work. As the leadership literature illustrates, difference studies—however flawed and inconclusive—set the stage for the now customary argument that professional communication tends to favor masculine orientations, engendering difficulties for many women and marginalized men (e.g., Murphy & Zorn, 1996).

DIFFERENCE IN SHARPER FOCUS: POLITICS, PERFORMANCE, AND MASCULINITY

Contemporary turns in the study of gender difference and organizational communication redress that ideological conflict—namely, the tendency to investigate difference as if in a vacuum yet utilize difference findings to activate political consciousness. Two particular developments illustrate the diversity of responses. A first turn entails the rise of feminist standpoint theory (FST) in organizational communication studies (e.g., Allen, 1996, 1998; Dougherty, 1999). FST underscores the "location" of particular gendered identities and rejects the notion of gender as an isolated theoretical construct or empirical phenomenon. In this way, it illuminates contextual factors suppressed by conventional difference research, highlighting the relational, political, material, temporal, and spatial character of identity positions, as well as the particular importance of intersections among gender, race, and class. Some FST authors, for example, consider how the embodied experience of gendered labor fosters distinctive ways of knowing and being in the world (e.g., Aptheker, 1989; Harding, 1991; Smith, 1987). As I elaborate later, FST scholars in organizational communication have yet to pick up on this dimension of "material life," but they do tend to concur with other FST authors on this point: politically located, marginalized perspectives can yield critical standpoints from which to generate alternative knowledge. In this sense, FST casts difference as epistemology and moral politics (e.g., Alcoff, 1988; Alcoff & Potter, 1993; Wood, 1993).

Whereas FST is often said to reflect a critical modernist orientation, a second turn follows a poststructuralist impulse to conceptualize gender as an ongoing, local performance that yields agentic, yet also precarious, subjectivities (Alcoff, 1988; Ashcraft & Mumby, 2004; Gherardi, 1995). The traditional empirical question (Do men and women communicate differently at work?) is thus turned on its head, and the focus becomes not the existence but the appearance of order and its communicative (re)production (How are available social constructions of gender invoked in particular interactions, and how do these performances preserve and/or challenge the fiction of gender dualisms?). Like more conventional difference studies, this perspective acknowledges connections between symbolic and empirical dimensions of gender but presumes fragility instead of stability, asking how the feminine-masculine binary is negotiated in everyday life. While this view has a long theoretical lineage (e.g., Butler, 1990; Kondo, 1990; Weedon, 1987), the work of West and colleagues (e.g., Fenstermaker & West, 2002; West & Fenstermaker, 1995; West & Zimmerman, 1987) is particularly influential in the context of organizational communication studies. Their work challenges psychological models of difference by theorizing gender as something we do together—the situated management of interaction in response to dominant expectations for gender difference. Particular settings supply a variety of resources and enable creative improvisations; thus, we have some room to imaginatively engage social scripts. By expanding the model from "doing gender" to "doing difference," West and Fenstermaker (1995) integrate concerns for the intersectionality (of race, class, and so on) inherent to identity performances. Applying this framework, many organizational scholars now examine how people "do difference" in varied work contexts (Ashcraft & Mumby, 2004; Gherardi, 1994).

Despite such important moves to complicate difference, research on gender difference at work continued to underscore implications for women, with several conflicted consequences. Even as it usefully marked work challenges faced by women, this focus had the effect of casting women as deviant or "special" organization characters. Meanwhile, corresponding privileges associated with masculinity received less attention, and men as gendered figures remained mostly invisible. The female emphasis also implied that feminist organizational communication scholarship was the concern and domain of women. Scholars began to challenge these messages at a conceptual level, suggesting attention to gender relations, or the ways in which women/femininities and men/masculinities

are constructed against one another (e.g., Alvesson & Billing, 1992; Ashcraft & Pacanowsky, 1996; Mumby, 1993). By the mid-1990s, however, few had published related empirical projects. Reflecting a larger surge of cultural interest in masculinity, scholars beyond the field of communication, and particularly from the European gender and organization studies community, began to confront the intersection of work and masculinity (e.g., Collinson & Hearn, 1994). Today, a rapidly growing literature explores the construction of masculinity in organizational life (e.g., Cheng, 1996; Collinson & Hearn, 1996b). Concern for masculinity took hold in the organizational communication literature toward the late 1990s and remains a growing research interest (e.g., Mumby, 1998). Still, few communication scholars have examined how masculinities and femininities are co-constructed in the context(s) of organizing (Ashcraft & Mumby, 2004).[1]

Difference, then, is a primary way that organizational communication scholars have seen gender. Perspectives vary, ranging from a focus on the biological variable of sex to the behavioral outcomes of early cultural socialization to the interplay of abstract symbolism and mundane life. More recently, FST and "doing difference" models represent divergent efforts to complicate difference, supplanting static dualisms with a sense of multiplicity-in-flux by incorporating relational, cultural, political, material, historical, and other situational factors. The "doing difference" approach is particularly friendly to the recent study of men as gendered actors, as it underscores how we are all held accountable to gender. It also shows how dominant scripts for gender performance tend to equate the accomplishment of masculinities and femininities with doing dominance and doing deference, respectively (West & Zimmerman, 1987). Amid these developments, much gender difference research continues to mark individuals and interactions—not organizations—as the pivotal units of analysis.

A SHIFT IN SIGHT: GENDERED ORGANIZATIONS

In the early 1990s, organizational communication studies encountered another way of seeing gender. Mobilized by Acker's (1990) influential essay articulating "a theory of gendered organizations," as well as other works in sociology and political science (e.g., Ferguson, 1984; Kanter, 1975, 1977), communication scholars began to shift focus away from individuals and inter-actions *in* organizational settings and toward the premise that organizational forms function as "meta-communication" about gender relations (Mills & Chiaramonte, 1991) or as "gendered discourse communities" (Mumby, 1996). In other words, structures like bureaucracy were seen to supply preferred narratives of gender, power, and work relations, which then shape the everyday process of organizing. Accordingly, scholars began to examine how bureaucratic discourse controls and devalues femininities by promoting hierarchy, impersonal relations, and distrust of "private" concerns in the name of rationality and objectivity (e.g., Martin, 1990; Morgan, 1996; Mumby & Putnam, 1992; Savage & Witz, 1992).

The shift toward organization-level analyses sparked awareness that meaningful social change requires more than creative individual and interpersonal performances of gender; it also requires alternative institutional forms. Scholars thus began to contribute to a growing interdisciplinary interest in feminist forms of organization (Ferree & Martin, 1995). Several authors now approach feminist organizing as the ongoing negotiation of "alternative discourse communities" that seek emancipatory discourses of gender, power, and work amid cultural and material constraints (Fraser, 1990-1991; Mumby, 1996). These scholars investigate the discursive strategies through which members manage the contradictions of alternative organizing, as well as the larger forms of organization implied by their tactics (e.g., Ashcraft, 2000, 2001; Gottfried & Weiss, 1994; Iannello, 1992; Maguire & Mohtar, 1994).

It is difficult to overstate the significance of the turn toward gendered organization. For one thing, the move signaled the rise of systemic and structural (i.e., organization-level) analyses in the literature on gender and organizational communication. Preoccupation with gendered people and practices *at* work gave way to the more profound insight that gender relations premised on difference are deeply institutionalized. Put bluntly, gender difference is not simply imported by individuals into the workplace; nor is it a handy complement to or an incidental side effect of bureaucratic control. Rather, gender difference functions as a pivotal organizing mechanism that is actively—even strategically—deployed by founders, managers, and coworkers. The field of organization studies has seen a virtual explosion of research premised on this insight (Britton, 2000; Ely & Meyerson, 2000), as well as the steady growth of an international, interdisciplinary community devoted to the study of gendered organization (Martin & Collinson, 2002). Communication scholars have contributed abundantly to this effort.[2]

Indeed, the shift toward gendered organization greatly influenced the shape of gender scholarship in organizational communication. Like scholars in the larger interdisciplinary community, communication researchers began to focus overwhelmingly on gendered organizational form and culture in physical sites of work. In other words, we took *organization* as a tangible work*place* where gender relations are accomplished and gendered cultures produced. This literal and limited reading is not surprising, for it already enjoyed the institutional support of our home field, long dominated by an image of organization as a container in which communication occurs (Putnam et al., 1996). As Carlone and Taylor (1998) contend, even after much criticism of the container metaphor, organizational communication scholarship continues to privilege one articulation of organization and culture (i.e., culture *in* or *of* organizational sites) amid other promising articulations (e.g., the formation of working subjectivities in popular/public culture).

To be sure, site-bound approaches yield vital insights, exposing the accomplishment of gendered control and resistance in the micropractices of work life, as well as the ways in which gendered organizational structures, policies, and narratives assume local shape. And yet, I argue, to overemphasize organization- or site-level analyses of form and culture is to downplay parallel discursive formations that also organize gender and labor. Preoccupation with site minimizes other readings of organization—for instance, how gendered work, workers, and workplaces are (dis)organized across diverse sites of social activity, such as professional or union activities or even popular culture. Simply put, site-bound studies overlook equally important ways in which difference "works."

To date, then, organizational communication scholars have seen gender mostly in terms of individuals, interactions, and institutions. They have exposed multiple ways in which gender difference becomes a core organizing principle of personal identity, mundane communication, and organizational system design. But by limiting the scope of research to "difference in site," they have eclipsed other sights (i.e., ways of seeing) and sites (i.e., locations) of gendered organizing. To build a case for the timeliness and promise of a shift in focus toward the organization of gendered jobs, I look beyond the organizational communication literature.

◆ Out of Site: Gender Difference and the Division of Labor

Scholars have not always depicted relations among gender, difference, and work as a matter "contained" in physical sites of organization. Nor is it the case that all contemporary research on gender and labor fails to look beyond the workplace. My aim

in this section is to characterize an alternative site of difference largely overlooked by organizational communication studies: the gendered division of labor.

EARLY ACCOUNTS OF OCCUPATIONAL SEGREGATION BY SEX

Although gender initially surfaced in organizational communication studies as a matter of different professional interaction styles, scholars in other fields saw gender and work differently. Economists, sociologists, and political scientists, for instance, have long considered how gender difference is articulated with societal divisions of labor. Prominent among the abiding themes of this work is the tenacity of job segregation, or the strikingly persistent separation of men's from women's work and the associated concentration of women in lower-end, service-oriented jobs (e.g., Anker, 1998; Bradley, 1989; Cockburn, 1985; Crompton & Sanderson, 1990; Hakim, 1992; Kemp, 1994; Mies, 1986; Reskin & Hartmann, 1986). Phillips and Taylor (1980) put it bluntly: "Everywhere we turn, we see a clear distinction between 'men's work' and 'women's work,' with women's work almost invariably characterized by lower pay, lack of craft traditions, weak union organization, and—above all—unskilled status" (p. 79).

In their pioneering essay, Phillips and Taylor (1980) pay particular notice to the role of skill in producing "ghettoes of 'women's work'" (p. 80), arguing that skill is an ideological tool "saturated with sex," that "the sex of those who do the work, rather than its content . . . leads to its identification as skilled or unskilled" (p. 85). Indeed, as male workers have struggled against trends toward de-skilling, "craft has been increasingly identified with masculinity, with the claims of the breadwinner, with the degree of union strength. Skill has been increasingly defined *against* women—skilled work is work that women don't do" (p. 86). Similarly, other early works documented how male-dominated trade unions defend their skilled status by resisting the twin threats of technology and female labor reserves (e.g., Armstrong, 1982; Cockburn, 1983; Coyle, 1982). Concurring with Phillips and Taylor (1980) that assessments of skill depend on the body performing the task, Hearn (1982) contends that jobs once considered the domain of women are deemed more professional when men take them on. Otherwise, the "semi-professions," populated by women and managed by men, become "handmaidens" to the professions, performing undesirable labor while serving as the lowly foil against which the professions appear elite. Hearn concludes that professionalization projects amount to patriarchal instruments for extending male control over arenas once female-dominated, like reproductive and emotional labor. Elaborating this point, Carrigan, Connell, and Lee (1985) argue that the division of labor serves not only to affirm men's control over women, but also to reproduce inequalities among men. In their view, hegemonic masculinity is "embedded in the dynamics of institutions . . . quite as much as the personality of individuals" (p. 591).

Early scholarship on gender and labor beyond communication studies thus theorized how sexed bodies are entwined with the societal division and valuation of work. Here, the separation *and* relation of jobs became relevant: Tasks are not just divided along sex lines; their worth is often measured in accordance with the bodies performing them. As Acker (1990) would later note, "Individual men and particular groups of men do not always win in these processes, but masculinity always seems to symbolize self-respect for men at the bottom and power for men at the top, while confirming for both their gender's superiority" (p. 145). Applied here, the various "collars" workers wear are meaningful only in relation to each other, and the devaluation of so-called pink-collar work serves to shore up the worth of white- and blue-collar labor. Phillips and Taylor (1980) anticipate the irony of this apparent gender

victory: In celebrating the manliness of skill, men "recreate for capital a group of 'inferior' workers who can be used to undercut them" (p. 87). Attesting to this threat is the devaluation of once male-dominated fields, such as clerical work, librarianship, and public relations, when a critical mass of women entered these occupations (e.g., Calás & Smircich, 1993; Garrison, 1972-1973; Touhey, 1974). Abundant scholarship has elaborated these initial conceptual efforts with empirical investigations of sex-segregated work.

EMPIRICAL STUDIES OF "WOMEN'S WORK"

Until fairly recently, empirical examinations of job segregation overwhelmingly stressed features of feminized jobs and/or women's labor. Here, I characterize the more contemporary face of the massive literature that resulted. Continuing the legacy of research on secretarial work, for example, Sotirin and Gottfried (1999) demonstrate how the practice of "bitching" among secretaries simultaneously serves to reify stereotypes of gender difference, disrupt imperatives for professional deference, and temporarily claim status as knowledge workers. Similarly concerned with the simultaneity of control and resistance, Kennelly (2002) compares logics of difference among women in clerical work and furniture sales—jobs that are, respectively, female-dominated and sex-integrated. Whereas the furniture saleswomen adopted a liberal sameness stance that devalued "other" women, most secretaries pushed a cultural difference position bent on revaluing women's "otherness." Yet both tactics upheld the gender order of occupations. Only a third perspective, voiced mostly by African American secretaries, aligned with other women yet challenged conventional gender categories. Such projects suggest an array of possible articulations of difference, as well as their conflicted consequences.

To date, Pringle (1989a, 1989b) offers one of the most complex portraits of secretarial work. Her research investigates both the ethos of the occupation (i.e., expectations for the performance of white, middle-class, heterosexual femininity) and its place in organizational life (i.e., the bureaucratic institutionalization of boss-secretary relations). Pringle also brings sexuality into the mix, inviting a nuanced understanding of how women actively negotiate their identities as sexual objects *and* subjects, even in the context of highly feminized, typically sexualized labor.

More recently, scholars have extended studies of secretarial work to consider the case of temporary clerical workers and their heightened susceptibility to organizational and occupational controls (e.g., Gottfried, 1994; Henson, 1996; Rogers, 2000). In particular, Rogers and Henson (1997) undermine Pringle's hope for sexual agency, showing how the structural vulnerability and gendered subtext of temporary secretarial jobs collide to compel deferential feminine performances and compromise resistance to sexual harassment.

Sexuality is a recurring theme in many studies of feminized labor, in which the tacit sexual contract endemic to all employment often becomes more visible (Gherardi, 1995). Mills (1997), for example, demonstrates how flight attendants in the British airline industry were crafted around the "dueling discourses" of desexualization and eroticism. The latter came to prevail as British airlines, largely in response to international trends, began to reverse their common practice of hiring mostly male flight attendants. Revitalizing Pringle's (1989a) interest in irony and sexual agency, Linstead (1995) examines how flight attendants embroiled in a labor dispute effectively utilized their institutionalized sexual objectification to mobilize public opinion in their favor, illustrating the "liberating repression of subjectivity" (p. 205). In a similar vein, other scholars observe how women workers can deploy the very feminized sexualities used to subordinate them,

embracing but also reworking logics of difference as a resistance tactic (e.g., Edley, 2000; Hossfeld, 1993; Young, 1989).

Emerging from this literature are common challenges that characterize feminized work, such as expectations for deference, emotional service, and sexualized labor, as well as the ambivalent responses of many women. Simultaneously, studies of feminized jobs capture the notable diversity of women's experience, illustrating the FST claim that particular cultural and material situations matter. Many of the secretarial studies reviewed above, for instance, take care to elucidate the intersection of race, class, and gender hierarchies, demonstrating how white, middle-class, heterosexual feminine performances are aligned with front-office space, while "other" femininities are often tucked out of sight (e.g., Pringle, 1989b; Rogers & Henson, 1997). Other authors attend to the gender, race, class, and sexuality dynamics of "dirtier" work, such as factory labor, restaurant service, and cleaning jobs (e.g., Ehrenreich, 2001; Hossfeld, 1993). Rollins (1997), for example, explores the contradictory identity dance of domestic labor, wherein invisibility can cultivate hyper-consciousness of and resistance toward those served, as well as deferential job performances that naturalize class and race privilege. Adib and Guerrier (2003) provide a powerful demonstration of the multiplicity and fluidity of job identity among hotel cleaning laborers, who marked and denied the salience of various identity features as they struggled to negotiate power and difference. Also emerging from this literature, then, is a refusal of any monolithic account of femininity at work.

A final consensus across this literature is that women are disadvantaged—at the very least, economically—by their subordinate status in both horizontal and vertical segregation. In short, women are not only crowded into the least valued occupations (i.e., horizontal); wherever they work, they are also concentrated toward the bottom of job hierarchies (i.e., vertical). Because conventional economic theories, which assume that rational individuals seek to maximize their lifetime earnings, inadequately account for segregation (Jacobs, 1999), many scholars debate alternative explanations.[3] One account maintains that gender socialization develops distinctive orientations or strengths, such that women are likely to feel more skilled at and comfortable with pursuits like the caring professions. A variant of that answer accentuates women's distinctive motivations and needs, such as those for less demanding or time-consuming work due to their domestic responsibilities.[4] Some authors combine such logics to acknowledge personal satisfaction with individual choice amid cultural socialization (e.g., Hakim, 1992, 1995; Marshall & Wetherell, 1989; Marshall, 1989). Turning away from a focus on women's complicity, other accounts look to subtle processes of institutional discrimination that reproduce subordinate status in the labor market. This vein of explanation has been expanded to include more individual agency, for example, in projects that consider how women variously interact with educational messages and peer cultures (e.g., Eisenhart & Holland, 1992). Other analyses of institutional discrimination stress social and historical context (Greene, Ackers, & Black, 2002) and weigh the possibility, elaborated below, that institutional discrimination emanates as much from embedded masculine symbolism as it does from actual men (Faulkner, 2000; Hinze, 1999).

EMPIRICAL STUDIES OF "MEN'S WORK"

A second major branch of the empirical literature investigates masculinized occupations and/or men's labor. Although much newer to the scene than studies of feminized work (Jackson, 1999), this research has quickly grown to contemplate masculinity in relation to a range of occupations. One common focus is the social construction of blue-collar labor and working-class

identities. Just as sexuality is a core concern in the literature on feminized work, so the body has become a prominent theme in the literature on men's manual labor. This emphasis both reflects and interrogates popular associations of working-class men with images of raw physicality—with grueling work performed by sweaty bodies exuding a primal, even savage sexuality (e.g., Collinson, 1992; Fine, Weis, Addelston, & Marusza, 1997; Gherardi, 1995; Willis, 1977). In a move to develop "embodied sociology," for example, Monaghan (2002) examines identity work stemming from the commodification of blue-collar bodies in the private security industry. His analysis specifically probes how nightclub bouncers craft competency in relation to corporeal performance amid the perpetual threat of violence.

Like studies of feminized labor, this literature attends to discursive practices surrounding workers' bodies and to the multiplicity of gendered subjectivities as simultaneously raced, classed, sexualized, aged, and so on. In response to Collinson and Hearn's (1994, 1996a) call for the study of "multiple masculinities" at work, many authors strive to explicate diverse connections between masculinities and occupations. Their work takes seriously the insight afforded by concepts like hegemonic masculinity (Carrigan et al., 1985; Connell, 1993; Donaldson, 1993): that gender inequality is not merely binary (i.e., men/masculinity over women/femininity) but also entails dynamic hierarchies *among* men and women (i.e., dominant and subordinate masculinities/femininities).

Scholars have thus considered the gender coding of managerial and professional identities as well and, specifically, how competing masculinities assist the symbolic and material division of mental (i.e., white-collar) from manual (i.e., blue-collar) labor. For instance, against masculine images of working-class physicality, "professional" figures appear as refined masculine subjects who rein in bodily excess to perform the higher-order work of the mind (Mumby,

1998). These dependent images supply both characters with resources and vulnerabilities at the meeting of class and gender (Ashcraft & Flores, 2003). Blue-collar masculinities are susceptible to appearing uncivilized, but their "primal" subjectivities enable a kind of rule over the "soft" bodies of women and white-collar superiors. Despite its intellectual and institutional privilege over blue-collar identities, professional masculinity is vulnerable to feminization, given its bureaucratic sterility, suppression of the body, self-imposed discipline, and obligatory ingratiation (Bederman, 1995; Ferguson, 1984). In such ways, working masculinities play off one another in ongoing political struggle. As this discussion suggests, a growing body of work conceives of management as a relatively coherent occupation, however contextually variable (e.g., Aaltio-Marjosola & Lehtinen, 1998; Kerfoot & Knights, 1993; Kerfoot & Whitehead, 2000; Linstead, 1997; Roper, 1996). Common to this work is the claim that organization scholars have long treated managerial professionals as gender-free characters; hence, it is high time to examine "men as managers, managers as men" (Collinson & Hearn, 1996b).

Complicating any simplistic notion that men's work comes only in two collars, scholars have investigated other masculinized fields of work as well (e.g., Wright, 1996). Hodgson (2003) considers how the masculine ethos of sales jobs influences forms of organizational resistance. His analysis shows how the particular breed of manly individualism associated with the salesman image enabled some resistance to technocratic surveillance, even as it disabled resistance to other controls by institutionalizing isolation and dependence on managerial affirmation. In another analysis focused on the intersection of occupation and organization, Mills (1998) examines multiple masculinities as they emerged in conjunction with certain jobs at British Airways—namely, the pilot as professional hero, the engineer as technical scientist, the steward as boy or small (and later gay) male servant,

and the indigenous male worker as "native boy" employed in menial tasks. Taking a closer look at the formation and maintenance of airline pilot identity, my own work has also begun to explore the merging of conflicted class symbolism and the resulting "anti-managerial professional" embodied in the work of airline pilots (e.g., Ashcraft, 2005b; Ashcraft & Mumby, 2004). Such projects indicate the often fuzzy lines that demarcate mental from manual, professional from non-professional, and skilled from unskilled labor.

As reviewed thus far, studies of feminized and masculinized jobs simultaneously embrace and challenge binary conceptions of gender. A binary model persists to the extent that men's work and women's work have generally been analyzed in isolation, but dualistic visions are concurrently shattered by findings of diverse experiences within sex groupings. The literature has also stepped beyond binary conceptions in two other ways: (1) studies of the co-construction of masculine and feminine work and (2) studies of "crossover" attempts.

GENDER RELATIONS: THE CO-CONSTRUCTION OF MASCULINE AND FEMININE JOBS

The rise of interest in masculinity and job segregation has entailed a promising turn toward analyses of the co-construction of occupational masculinities and femininities. In an early example, Collinson and Knights (1986) begin their analysis of job segregation with the gendered symbolism of skill in the insurance industry. Moving to an organizational level of analysis, they reveal how management practices of recruitment, supervision, and promotion interacted with members' defensive identity work to reproduce a gendered labor divide. Similarly, Morgan and Knights (1991) contend that job segregation is best understood within the political, industrial, and organizational economies wherein divisions of labor are enacted. They urge particular consideration of how corporate strategy development shapes local divisions of labor. Such pleas for organization site analyses read rather oddly now, but only in the wake of the striking shift in scholarly attention from gendered jobs to gendered organizations. Most importantly, the authors depict men and women vying over visions of difference at work, which change in relation to one another and in response to particular managerial strategies.

Several scholars have since taken up the study of job segregation and gender relations, particularly at the organization level. For example, Mills (1995) draws on his research with British Airways to show how images portrayed in corporate texts minimize occupational integration by aligning specific demographic profiles with certain jobs, while Pierce (1995) describes the construction of "Rambo litigators" against "mothering paralegals" in a large law firm. Alvesson (1998) puzzles over the strict gender division of labor in an advertising firm that subscribed to a feminine ethos and minimized bureaucracy. His analysis of the complex interplay among masculinities and femininities indicates how local constructions of gender can depart from global images; it also suggests a looser connection between the domination of masculinities and domination by men. Taking heed of calls for analyses situated in organizational and larger political economies, Greene et al. (2002) interpret resistance to job integration in two manufacturing firms in light of the social and material history of familial relations in the surrounding community. Looking beyond organizational sites to understand interaction within them, this analysis powerfully reveals how men and women become deeply invested in the gender division of labor.

Jackson (1999) provides one of the most direct articulations yet of a gender relations perspective on work segregation, arguing that the conventional focus on women's/feminized labor neglects the interdependency of femininities and masculinities. She proposes an innovative agenda for the study of masculinity and work that underscores embodied labor, probes how men *and* women make use of hegemonic masculinity, and takes seriously the point that "male domination is relational and comes at a price," as in the case of poor men whose struggle to achieve manly ideals can involve "risks of bodily self-exploitation, high mortality and morbidity risks" (p. 104). Faulkner (2000) also illustrates how gender difference is employed to maintain hierarchies of masculinity among engineers and to support occupational dualisms like technical/social and specialist/generalist.

Other scholars have also strayed from the organization level, stressing gender configurations in the context of particular occupations. Lawson (1999) explains how job segregation persists amid increasing demand for women workers in the Ecuadoran garment industry: The "tailor" is distinguished from the "seamstress," and the former's artisan status rests on the latter's susceptibility to domestic duties. Hinze (1999) examines the social construction of specialty prestige in the medical profession. No matter which bodies do the work, she says, gender symbolism characterizes and rationalizes perceptions of difficulty and value within the profession, such that surgical specialties associated with strong, intervening hands and "balls" trump specialties like pediatrics and psychiatry. This work supports Alvesson's (1998) claim of a loose link between male and masculine domination and complicates early claims that gendered assessments of skill stem mainly from the body performing the work (e.g., Phillips & Taylor, 1980).

Across these projects emerges a sobering portrait of gendered job segregation as a ubiquitous, tenacious division that organizes the labor process, traversing time and culture, cutting across and within occupations and organizations. With pervasive ideological and institutional support, the divide has been shored up time and again by the identity work of men and women facing the complex political and material realities of labor. Pointing to trade education as a vital site of both institutional support and identity work, Prokos and Padavic (2002) analyze the "hidden curriculum" of police academy training, which teaches recruits that a certain breed of masculinity is essential to job performance and not easily enacted by women. They highlight how the presence of a few women in male-dominated work serves up a visible foil against which manliness can be defined and elevated. In doing so, they join a large crowd of scholars watching what happens when the gender lines of labor are crossed.

OUT OF PLACE: TRANSGRESSING THE LABOR DIVIDE

The gender divide may be crossed in a variety of ways (Bradley, 1989; Morgan, 1992). As already noted above, jobs deemed the domain of one sex may become the terrain of the other, as in the feminization of clerical and public relations work or the masculinization of midwifery and spinning. Studies documenting such reversals in the majority population tend to bring a historical lens to an occupational level of analysis. Another stream of studies investigates the experience of "minorities" in gendered jobs—those attempting to buck the divide. Rather than stress occupational makeovers, these studies examine individual job infiltration.

Of particular relevance to the literature on infiltration is Kanter's (1977) account of tokenism, which anticipates largely negative consequences suffered by individuals in the numerical minority. For example, a wealth of research examines the experience of women in male-dominated jobs (e.g., Davey & Davidson, 2000; Fletcher, 1999; Jorgenson, 2002; Martin, 1994; Miller, 2002; Spencer & Podmore, 1987). Particularly since management has been long been men's turf, the extensive women-in-management literature can be read as perhaps the most copious illustration.[5] As hinted by the sheer volume of this literature, most studies of women entering men's work emphasize white,

upper-middle-class women and men in the context(s) of white-collar labor. In the spirit of the token thesis, such work tends to highlight subtle barriers (e.g., the "glass ceiling") women encounter as they attempt hierarchical advancement and managerial work.

The tokenism premise predicts that men in female-dominated work would suffer similar adverse effects, and a recent wave of research on men who do women's work enables empirical consideration of that claim (e.g., Williams, 1993). Young and James (2001) are among the few still supporting the primacy of demographic composition. They find that Kanter's (1977) three perceptual conditions of tokenism—exaggerated contrasts between majority and minority members, minorities' high visibility, and related assimilation pressures—negatively influenced the work attitudes of male flight attendants, though with some mediating variables. In contrast, most of the research on men in women's jobs complicates the significance of token status and underscores the gendered direction of infiltration. Long ago, for instance, Segal (1962) concluded that male nurses encountered negative experiences, not only because they were few in number but also due to status contradictions stemming from feminized work, since "many common ways of using one's occupation as an expression of virility in our culture . . . are closed to male nurses" (p. 38). Nearly 30 years later, Heikes's (1991) study of male nurses similarly challenged Kanter's (1977) theory of proportions, arguing that gender norms and other socio-cultural factors appreciably influence group interaction patterns.

Abundant research supports the claim that token experiences are distinctively gendered. Indeed, it appears that gender may even reverse the effects of tokenism, such that men in feminized jobs often enjoy benefits denied to women. The leading proponent of this argument is Williams (1989, 1992, 1993, 1995), whose research with male nurses, elementary teachers, social workers, and librarians suggests that men who do women's work face gendered threats *and* enjoy subtle privileges. White men in particular seem to ride a "glass escalator" to the top of feminized occupations, concentrated as they are in specialties with higher pay and status. For example, Evans's (1997) study of male nurses demonstrates how feminized work can entail a high valuation of men and masculinity, facilitating men's disproportionate rise to administrative positions. Aided by gendered institutions and even some female colleagues, many men effectively achieve distance from both the women with whom they work and the hazards of occupational femininity.

Such findings raise the question of whether crossing the gendered lines of labor reflects a move toward equality or more of the same. In particular, scholars have debated the conflicted meanings of men performing traditionally women's work. Bradley (1993), for example, suggests that men's movement toward female-dominated occupations, compelled by the decline in jobs associated with masculine skill, subjects men to the stigmas of feminized labor and, thus, represents an opportunity to undermine the history of gendered labor relations. Donaldson (1993) seems to concur, arguing that the degradation of so-called masculine work opens possibilities for even relatively elite men to criticize hegemonic masculinity. Calás and Smircich (1993) also imply grounds for unrest in their analysis of the feminization of management, which reveals how women's difference gets invoked to exacerbate class disparities. In varied ways, then, these authors grapple with the political implications of Phillips and Taylor's (1980) initial insight that sex segregation creates "a group of 'inferior' workers who can be used to undercut" men's privileged labor status (p. 87).

Following Williams' (e.g., 1995) lead, other scholars caution that men's presence in feminized labor is far from transformative. For example, Cross and Bagilhole's (2002) interviews with men employed in caring, cleaning, and teaching occupations suggest that men's efforts at remasculinization "have

enhanced their career opportunities over women" and that "men's entry into non-traditional jobs does not necessarily signal a change in men's dominance as a sex" (p. 223). Hence, "any investigation of possible sites of changing masculinities should not ignore or disguise the continuing material dominance of men over women . . . even in female-dominated occupations" (p. 224). In a similar interview project, Lupton (2000) calls attention to the contradictory position of men doing women's work, at once beneficiaries of the so-called glass escalator and targets of considerable gender assessment. He examines how men perceive and respond to this conflict, ultimately reframing their work in ways that downplay feminine associations or recrafting their masculinity to fit a female-dominated work setting.

Henson and Rogers (2001) treat male temporary clerical workers as a particularly telling case that confronts the divergent conclusions of Kanter (1977) and Williams (e.g., 1995). Such men face a profoundly gendered tokenism wherein their efforts to align with hegemonic masculinity become especially tricky, given the absence of secure employment with a clear occupational hierarchy. And yet, even without "a real job" and its "glass escalator," male clerical temps find ways to "strike a hegemonic bargain, retracing the lines of occupational segregation and reinvigorating hegemonic masculinity and its domination over women and subaltern men" (Henson & Rogers, 2001, p. 236). Specifically, participants affirmed the feminine character of the job yet rejected its application to them by reframing their work, distancing themselves from it with a "cover story," and resisting expectations of deference.

Such research indicates serious limits to the transformative promise of transgressing the gendered labor divide. Clearly, the conventional gender coding of labor can be revised to maintain strands of masculine privilege when women or feminized men enter male-dominated work (Ashcraft, 2005b; Britton, 1997), and even men employed in the most vulnerable forms of feminized labor can reinscribe the traditional gender order (Henson & Rogers, 2001). Thus far, then, individual job infiltration seems more likely to yield re-segregation (i.e., gendered divisions and hierarchies of labor within occupations) than de-segregation, while occupational makeovers (e.g., the feminization of clerical work) simply redraw the boundaries of segregation. In either case, the gender balance of power remains tipped in favor of men and masculinity. Simply put, small- *and* large-scale shifts appear to yield more of the same. It is equally clear, however, that reproducing the gendered division of labor is no tidy process. Extensive research on women and men in non-traditional jobs indicates the complex, situated contradictions entailed in crossing over; and the responses of tokens and colleagues function mostly to accommodate, but also to resist, gendered occupational systems.

Whereas most studies stress identity work among token members, particularly men's discursive efforts to maintain "workable" masculinities, Sargent's (2000) examination of elementary teachers is rare for its attention to "structural impediments that exist from the perspective of the men who might choose to cross over" (p. 430). In addition to facing ambiguous expectations for role modeling and for hyper-performance of physical and disciplinary tasks, men working with children encounter close institutional scrutiny, based on the embedded assumption that "women's laps are places of love. Men's are places of danger" (p. 416). Such work serves as an important reminder of the continued need for sensitivity to gendered organization, or the ways in which institutional contexts facilitate certain kinds of identity work.

It is interesting to note that, unlike the literature on women's work, empirical studies of male-dominated labor are not generally accompanied by debates about how or why men come to such work. Likewise, analyses of gender job segregation tend to seek explanations for women's subordinate status, not men's dominant

position (e.g., Jacobs, 1999). However, an emerging body of research has begun to ask how men arrive in female-dominated occupations (e.g., Chusmir, 1990). Perhaps the formulation of "relevant" research questions reflects our own participation as scholars in naturalizing the gendered division of labor.

It has not been my aim here to provide an exhaustive review of the literature on gendered jobs. Even the lengthy review provided, of necessity, omits much. My intent was to render an accessible portrait of an interdisciplinary arena of inquiry for a communication audience accustomed to seeing gender, difference, and work in other ways. I painted the literature in broad strokes, highlighting early conceptual themes and their development across four interrelated streams of research: (1) women's work, (2) men's work, (3) gender relations and the maintenance of the labor divide, and (4) crossover attempts. Across all of these streams emerges a resounding conclusion: Though in different ways, and to different degrees, work tasks appear to be divided along gender lines around the globe, within and across occupations and organizations. Again and again, aided by men and women colleagues and gendered institutions, certain men and/or masculinities rise to the top of job hierarchies (which, importantly, means that many men occupy the middle and bottom as well). As Cross and Bagilhole (2002) declare,

> Gender segregation in the labour market operates horizontally and vertically; not only are men and women allocated qualitatively different types of jobs, the labour market is marked with women overwhelmingly concentrated at the lower levels of the occupational hierarchy in terms of wages or salary, status and authority. (p. 206)

Their summary echoes the observation made almost 25 years earlier by Phillips and Taylor (1980), with which this section began. And, if recent statistical analyses are any measure, little hope for gender occupational integration waits on the horizon. Segregation decline rates seem to be stagnating, while the wage gap appears to be reaching a plateau (Jacobs, 1999). Organizational communication scholars have yet to confront the magnitude and persistence of these material realities. It is time for another vision of difference—the gendered division and hierarchy of labor—to move into our line of sight.

◆ Back to Work: Alternative Sites of Difference in Organizational Communication Studies

In many respects, this chapter is part of a larger movement to "bring work back in" to organization studies (Barley, 1996; Barley & Kunda, 2001). My ultimate purpose is to find a foothold in organizational communication studies for Connell's (1995) claim that "the sweat cannot be excluded" (p. 51). As Jackson (1999) observes,

> "Including the sweat" is a good idea, not as a means to validate male strength, since women's work also involves considerable physical effort, but as an approach which offers a fuller understanding of the gendered experience of work and equity in labor sharing. (p. 97)

Here, I wish to build on this momentum and sketch a new sight/site of (gender) difference for organizational communication scholars: the organization of occupation.

Attention to the evolution of occupational identity across arenas of social activity holds particular promise. In foregrounding occupational identity, I mean to encompass a wide range of phenomena entailed in the dynamic relation between the abstract image and actual role performance of a job. By *image*, I refer to larger, public discourses of occupational identity, manifest in popular, trade, and even mundane conversational representations of the essence of a job and the people who perform it. I use *role* to refer to enacting a job, to the micropractices of actually performing the work. Of course, both (and other possible) dimensions of identity entail performance, but I associate "image" and "role" with different kinds of realities. The latter negotiates the former in the context of everyday work life, as people try on occupational selves and carry out job responsibilities.

Central to this chapter is how the study of occupational identity, broadly conceived, can enrich our understanding of work as a fundamentally gendered performance. Thus far, organizational communication scholars have devoted their attention to gendered identity work in particular organizations or to the gendering functions of particular organizational forms.[6] By and large, the workplace has become our overwhelming focus, while the actual tasks getting done— not to mention the impact of occupational messages and (sub)cultures within and beyond specific organization sites—have fallen to the periphery. We have not yet begun to explore the full range of Acker's (1990) original formulation of gendered organizational processes, and the literature on gendered jobs forcefully exposes what Acker hints in passing: Gender is an organizing principle of occupational identity, which, in turn, is a vital means of reproducing the division and hierarchy of labor.

Occupational identity traverses sites of organizing (e.g., workplaces, labor associations, regulatory agencies, trade education, family socialization, and popular culture) as a host or carrier of narratives regarding what counts as legitimate and valued work, who "naturally" belongs in certain lines of work, and so forth. In particular, occupational image supplies an emotional and rational grounding for assigning value (i.e., social, political, material standing) to and pursuing (i.e., job choice and related identity work) particular kinds of labor, whereas occupational role performances suggest the practical limits, tensions, variability, and negotiability of image discourse. For example, Faulkner (2000) concludes that descriptions of jobs are often more gendered than the actual work entailed, thereby increasing the likelihood of traditional occupational choice in response to "unrealistic" job previews. As this suggests, examining the communicative (re)production of occupational identity across sites of organizing can clarify how the gender division and hierarchy of labor is or was accomplished.

For organizational communication scholars, this requires expanding the current focus on how organizations, as physical sites or structural forms, are gendered. The bigger question becomes what "work" gender does in the organization of labor. In other words, where (including and exceeding workplace sites) and how does gender (and related axes of difference) play into the material configurations of work, such as who does what job, with what sort of bodily performance, at what social and economic value? With its eye for dialectical relations between discursive and material processes and products, such a question is sufficiently expansive to facilitate dialogue across critical modernist and postmodernist feminist stances (Ashcraft & Mumby, 2004).

Specifically, the question invites multiple and complex stances on difference. Returning to the two theoretical developments described earlier, organizational communication scholars might take up the insights of FST theorists (Aptheker, 1989; Harding, 1991; Smith, 1987) by exploring labor activity (i.e., sustained engagement with certain occupations and tasks) as a critical nexus of "material life" that engenders different standpoints. Or, through the more postmodern lens of "doing gender," scholars might ask how discourses of difference are woven together to distinguish "professions" from "semi-professions," to naturalize occupational borders, to regulate laboring bodies, to produce the intense pleasure and pain of doing and resisting work. Clearly, these stances hinge on some competing assumptions. For example, FST maintains that

different realities are produced by the lived experience of different cultural and material conditions, whereas "doing gender" holds difference as an unstable fiction, the "truth" of which social actors secure through shifting, situated performances. Yet both perspectives can inform gendered occupational identity, variously illuminating its discursive generation and tangible effects.

Despite their tensions, FST and "doing gender" also share some assumptions about difference—points of convergence that can be further cultivated in the study of occupational identity. First, both stances recognize gender difference as a relational construction. Not only are femininities and masculinities constructed in terms of one another, but also in relation to multiple discourses of identity and difference. For example, even as the gendered jobs literature demarcates "women's work" from "men's jobs," it undermines the viability of a dualistic account, marking the simultaneous significance of class, sexuality, race, and so on. Careful attention to the intersectionality of occupational identity can usefully challenge easy references to "male domination" or "the pink ghetto." Such attention can even reveal how narratives of difference are strategically invoked to police and resist occupational borders (Ashcraft & Mumby, 2004).

A second common interest follows from a shared commitment to intersectionality. Though in varied ways, both stances are concerned with the relation between discourse and the working body. The study of occupational identity marks the embodied character of work—the physical, mental, emotional, and even sexual "sweat" entailed in labor activity. In particular, the gendered jobs literature points to the ways in which managerial and professional discourse works to conceal the body and suppress the presence of sweat (literally and figuratively), whereas labor aligned with many femininities, non-white racial identities, and working-class subjectivities tends to at once demand and censure the heightened visibility of the body.

Finally, both stances increasingly call for dialectical and historically informed perspectives on mundane work activity. For the most part, the gendered jobs literature portrays the division and hierarchy of labor as an unfolding accomplishment—the ongoing struggle of real people to make conflicted choices amid institutional contradictions. Most studies model the complex interplay of control and resistance; some conduct diachronic analyses of shifts in job segregation (e.g., Frehill, 2004; Gray, 1991; Milkman, 1987); and a few have begun to consider how occupational identities are crafted in response to political and economic exigencies (e.g., Ashcraft & Mumby, 2004; Witz, 1990, 1992). Arguably, with its sensitivity to multiple sites and levels of organizing activity over time, the study of occupational identity requires a research sensibility that blends concern for mundane, discursive identity work with an institutional, historical consciousness.

The specific proposal of this chapter, then, is that organizational communication scholars draw on these productive tensions and alliances to examine how "difference matters" (Allen, 2003) to the organization of occupation. Such a charge invites at least two specific shifts in focus: (1) organization site-level analyses can take work (i.e., task, job, occupation) more seriously; and (2) extra-organizational analyses can clarify other sites and ways in which difference and work organize one another. On the first shift, the gendered jobs literature clearly indicates that workplaces are a pivotal site for enacting and negotiating the division of labor; it also avows that organizational forms and contexts can shape members' identity work. For these reasons alone, it makes little sense to trade organization-level for occupation-level analyses. Yet as others have argued, there is much we miss when we forget the job being done (Barley, 1996; Barley & Kunda, 2001; Bloor & Dawson, 1994), including the ways that (gender) difference is integral to the organizing process.

But the gendered jobs literature is equally clear that the organization of occupation exceeds particular sites of work. The division of labor is accomplished far beyond the walls of organizational sites, in what communication scholars might call settings of "anticipatory socialization" (e.g., Clair, 1996)—familial configurations of work, career advice from family and friends, messages in various educational settings, popular representations of work, and occupational recruitment or public relations campaigns, to name a few. Two decades ago, Hearn (1982) noted a growing scholarly tendency to examine the division of labor as manifest in the workplace and urged the devotion of similar energy to the gender dynamics of professionalization projects—historical moments wherein occupational members exercise collective agency, strategically representing their jobs and selves in a struggle for legitimacy, monopoly, and membership closure (e.g., Macdonald, 1995; Witz, 1990, 1992).

Davies (1996) updates the call for more systematic theorizing of the relation between gender and profession. Drawing on parallel insights from the study of gendered organization (e.g., Acker, 1990; Savage & Witz, 1992), she suggests an alternative to the usual focus (reviewed above) on token women seeking a place in male-dominated professions: The current preoccupation with many women's exclusion from elite men's work obscures the equal import of inclusion. Women have long served as silent partners in professionalism, she argues, pointing to the dependence of much professional practice on feminized adjunct labor in ill-defined, non- or semi-professional support roles. Hence, professionalization projects are fundamentally gendered, entailing "a specific historical and cultural construction of masculinity" (Davies, 1996, p. 661). Such conceptual work paves the way for organizational communication scholars like me, who wish to explore occupational formations beyond the usual boundaries of organization (e.g., Ashcraft & Mumby, 2004).

As that last sentence implies, this chapter serves twin functions. On the one hand, it invites a shift that I sincerely believe can enrich understanding. Simultaneously, the chapter marks—and even builds an initial case for the significance of—turns in my own research. It is not surprising, of course, that these moves go together. At some level, scholarly writing is just another occupational representation, rife with identity work. I mention that now because I want to conclude with a "wish list" of sorts for our field, should we choose to engage occupational research. The list is meant to invite reflection on the politics of such research and, in so doing, brings my own way of seeing more explicitly to the table.

Wish 1: Scholars of gendered jobs seem highly cognizant of the costs of segregation, especially for women. May we also consider the costs for men and prove just as willing to confront the pains of integration. The gendered jobs literature hints at such costs. Greene et al. (2002) illustrate how men and women become deeply invested in segregation. Jackson (1999) draws attention to the corporeal costs of segregation for marginalized men, as well as to the possibility that some women strategically utilize hegemonic masculinity. In an arresting pair of reports, Wharton and Baron (1987, 1991) find that women in male-dominated work settings expressed the most job satisfaction; meanwhile, men in integrated work environments experienced significantly lower job satisfaction and self-esteem and higher job-related depression than men in male-dominated or female-dominated work. My own research with commercial airline pilots has begun to explore some men's fears about the diversification of pilot identity (Ashcraft, 2005b; Ashcraft & Mumby, 2004). Even as a feminist member of an increasingly feminized field, I understand their concerns for the tangible, material consequences of de-segregation.

A related second wish: Scholars of gendered jobs seem comfortable with studies of men's efforts to maintain masculinity when performing women's work. May we also welcome studies of men's identity work when women enter male-dominated professions (e.g., Britton, 1997). In my airline pilot project, for example, I have begun to examine men's narratives of declining privilege and

the largely neglected tactics of resistance they engender (Ashcraft, 2005b). More broadly, may we embrace studies that investigate not only the experiences of token members, but also the (often politically unpopular) perspectives of majority members encountering crossover attempts or de-segregation.

Wish 3: For all our interest in the sexuality of organization (e.g., Hearn, Sheppard, Tancred-Sheriff, & Burrell, 1989), scholars of gendered jobs and of organizational communication seem reticent to research sex work[7]—a trend that likely reflects disciplined assumptions about "legitimate" labor, not to mention feminist ambivalence about the multiple and slippery meanings of terms like *working women* or *professional women*. As we expand empirical studies of sexuality *at* work, may we confront latent anxieties and engage the study of sexual labor. Importantly, such study could complicate dualisms (and entailed values) of central interest to feminist organizational inquiry—such as public and private, love and labor, power and pleasure, economy and emotion—while also exposing and challenging the subtext of feminist inquiry (e.g., Zatz, 1997). Put plainly, may we step beyond current theoretical accounts and examine the myriad ways in which sex "services" the organization of work.

A final wish: However we opt to see, in whatever sites we choose, may we develop useful visions of the "work" of difference—as it is, and as it could be.

◆ Notes

1. For an example of an exception, see Alvesson (1998).

2. For more extensive reviews, see Ashcraft and Mumby (2004) and Mumby and Ashcraft (2006).

3. See Collinson and Knights (1986) for a review of key explanations through the early 1980s.

4. For more on such explanations, see reviews in Eisenhart and Holland (1992) and Hinze (1999).

5. See, for example, Burke and McKeen (1992) and Fagenson (1993).

6. For examples of exceptions, see Holmer Nadesan and Trethewey (2000) and Trethewey (2001).

7. For exceptions, see Brewis and Linstead (2000a, 2000b), Murphy (2003), and Townsley, this volume.

◆ References

Aaltio-Marjosola, I., & Lehtinen, J. (1998). Male managers as fathers? Contrasting management, fatherhood, and masculinity. *Human Relations, 51,* 121–136.

Acker, J. (1990). Hierarchies, jobs, bodies: A theory of gendered organizations. *Gender & Society, 4,* 139–158.

Adib, A., & Guerrier, Y. (2003). The interlocking of gender with nationality, race, ethnicity and class: The narratives of women in hotel work. *Gender, Work, & Organization, 10,* 413–432.

Alcoff, L. (1988). Cultural feminism versus post-structuralism: The identity crisis in feminist theory. *Signs, 13,* 405–436.

Alcoff, L., & Potter, E. (Eds.). (1993). *Feminist epistemologies.* New York: Routledge.

Allen, B. J. (1996). Feminist standpoint theory: A black woman's (re)view of organizational socialization. *Communication Studies, 47,* 257–271.

Allen, B. J. (1998). Black womanhood and feminist standpoints. *Management Communication Quarterly, 11,* 575–586.

Allen, B. J. (2003). *Difference matters: Communicating social identity in organizations.* Prospects Heights, IL: Waveland.

Alvesson, M. (1998). Gender relations and identity at work: A case study of masculinities and femininities in an advertising agency. *Human Relations, 51,* 969–1005.

Alvesson, M., & Billing, Y. D. (1992). Gender and organization: Toward a differentiated understanding. *Organization Studies, 13,* 73–102.

Anker, R. (1998). *Gender and jobs: Sex segregation of occupations in the world.* Geneva: International Labour Office.

Aptheker, B. (1989). *Tapestries of life: Women's work, women's consciousness, and the meaning of daily experience.* Amherst: University of Massachusetts Press.

Armstrong, P. (1982). If it's only women it doesn't matter so much. In J. West (Ed.), *Work, women and the labour market.* London: Routledge & Kegan Paul.

Ashcraft, K. L. (1999). Managing maternity leave: A qualitative analysis of temporary executive succession. *Administrative Science Quarterly, 44,* 240–280.

Ashcraft, K. L. (2000). Empowering "professional" relationships: Organizational communication meets feminist practice. *Management Communication Quarterly, 13,* 347–392.

Ashcraft, K. L. (2001). Organized dissonance: Feminist bureaucracy as hybrid form. *Academy of Management Journal, 44,* 1301–1322.

Ashcraft, K. L. (2004). Gender, discourse, and organization: Framing a shifting relationship. In D. Grant, C. Hardy, C. Oswick, & L. L. Putnam (Eds.), *The Sage handbook of organizational discourse* (pp. 275–298). London: Sage.

Ashcraft, K. L. (2005a). Feminist organizational communication studies: Engaging gender in public and private. In S. May & D. K. Mumby (Eds.), *Engaging organizational communication theory and research: Multiple perspectives* (pp. 141–169). Thousand Oaks, CA: Sage.

Ashcraft, K. L. (2005b). Resistance through consent? Occupational identity, organizational form, and the maintenance of masculinity among commercial airline pilots. *Management Communication Quarterly, 19,* 67–90.

Ashcraft, K. L., & Flores, L. A. (2003). "Slaves with white collars": Decoding a contemporary crisis of masculinity. *Text and Performance Quarterly, 23,* 1–29.

Ashcraft, K. L., & Mumby, D. K. (2004). *Reworking gender: A feminist communicology of organization.* Thousand Oaks, CA: Sage.

Ashcraft, K. L., & Pacanowsky, M. E. (1996). "A woman's worst enemy": Reflections on a narrative of organizational life and female identity. *Journal of Applied Communication Research, 24*, 217–239.

Barley, S. R. (1996). Technicians in the workplace: Ethnographic evidence for bringing work into organization studies. *Administrative Science Quarterly, 41*, 404–441.

Barley, S. R., & Kunda, G. (2001). Bringing work back in. *Organization Science, 12*, 76–95.

Bass, B. M., & Avolio, B. (1994). Shatter the glass ceiling: Women make better managers. *Human Resource Management, 33*, 549–560.

Bederman, G. (1995). *Manliness and civilization: A cultural history of gender and race in the United States, 1880–1917*. Chicago: University of Chicago Press.

Bloor, G., & Dawson, P. (1994). Understanding professional culture in organizational context. *Organization Studies, 15*, 275–295.

Bradley, H. (1989). *Men's work, women's work*. Minneapolis: University of Minnesota Press.

Bradley, H. (1993). Across the great divide: The entry of men into women's jobs. In C. L. Williams (Ed.), *Doing "women's work": Men in nontraditional occupations* (pp. 10-27). Thousand Oaks, CA: Sage.

Brewis, J., & Linstead, S. (2000a). "The worst thing is the screwing" (1): Consumption and the management of identity in sex work. *Gender, Work and Organization, 7*, 84–97.

Brewis, J., & Linstead, S. (2000b). "The worst thing is the screwing" (2): Context and career in sex work. *Gender, Work and Organization, 7*, 168–180.

Britton, D. M. (1997). Gendered organizational logic: Policy and practice in men's and women's prisons. *Gender and Society, 11*, 796–818.

Britton, D. M. (2000). The epistemology of the gendered organization. *Gender and Society, 14*, 418–434.

Burke, R. J., & McKeen, C. A. (1992). Women in management. In I. T. Robertson (Ed.), *International review of industrial and organizational psychology* (Vol. 7, pp. 245–283). New York: John Wiley.

Butler, J. (1990). *Gender trouble: Feminism and the subversion of identity*. New York: Routledge.

Butterfield, D. A., & Grinnell, J. P. (1999). "Re-viewing" gender, leadership, and managerial behavior: Do three decades of research tell us anything? In G. N. Powell (Ed.), *Handbook of gender and work* (pp. 223–238). Thousand Oaks, CA: Sage.

Buzzanell, P. M. (1995). Reframing the glass ceiling as a socially constructed process: Implications for understanding and change. *Communication Monographs, 62*, 327–354.

Calás, M. B., & Smircich, L. (1993). Dangerous liaisons: The "feminine-in-management" meets "globalization." *Business Horizons, 36*, 71–81.

Calás, M. B., & Smircich, L. (1996). From "the woman's point of view": Feminist approaches to organization studies. In W. R. Nord (Ed.), *Handbook of organization studies* (pp. 218–257). Thousand Oaks, CA: Sage.

Canary, D. K., & Hause, K. S. (1993). Is there any reason to study sex differences in communication? *Communication Quarterly, 41*, 129–144.

Carlone, D., & Taylor, B. (1998). Organizational communication and cultural studies. *Communication Theory, 8*, 337–367.

Carrigan, R., Connell, R., & Lee, J. (1985). Toward a new sociology of masculinity. *Theory and Society, 14*, 551–604.

Cheng, C. (Ed.). (1996). *Masculinities in organizations*. Thousand Oaks, CA: Sage.

Chusmir, L. H. (1990). Men who make nontraditional career choices. *Journal of Counseling & Development, 69*, 11–16.

Clair, R. P. (1996). The political nature of the colloquialism "A real job": Implications for organizational socialization. *Communication Monographs, 63*, 249–267.

Cockburn, C. (1983). *Brothers: Male dominance and technological change*. London: Pluto Press.

Cockburn, C. (1985). *Machinery of dominance: Women, men and technical know-how*. London: Pluto Press.

Collinson, D. (1992). *Managing the shop floor: Subjectivity, masculinity, and workplace culture*. New York: De Gruyter.

Collinson, D., & Hearn, J. (1994). Naming men as men: Implications for work, organization and management. *Gender, Work, & Organization, 1*, 2–22.

Collinson, D., & Hearn, J. (1996a). "Men" at "work": Multiple masculinities/multiple workplaces. In M. Mac an Ghaill (Ed.), *Understanding masculinities: Social relations and cultural arenas* (pp. 61–76). Buckingham, UK: Open University Press.

Collinson, D., & Hearn, J. (Eds.). (1996b). *Men as managers, managers as men: Critical perspectives on men, masculinities and managements*. London: Sage.

Collinson, D., & Knights, D. (1986). "Men only": Theories and practices of job segregation in insurance. In H. Willmott (Ed.), *Gender and the labour process* (pp. 141–178). Aldershot, UK: Gower.

Connell, R. W. (1993). The big picture: Masculinities in recent world history. *Theory and Society, 22*, 597–623.

Connell, R. W. (1995). *Masculinities*. Berkeley: University of California Press.

Coyle, A. (1982). Sex and skill in the organisation of the clothing industry. In J. West (Ed.), *Work, women and the labour market*. London: Routledge & Kegan Paul.

Crompton, R., & Sanderson, K. (1990). *Gendered jobs and social change*. London: Unwin Hyman.

Cross, S., & Bagilhole, B. (2002). Girls' jobs for the boys? Men, masculinity and non-traditional occupations. *Gender, Work, & Organization, 9*, 204–226.

Davey, C. L., & Davidson, M. J. (2000). The right of passage? The experiences of female pilots in commercial aviation. *Feminism & Psychology, 10*, 195–225.

Davies, C. (1996). The sociology of professions and the profession of gender. *Sociology, 30*, 661–678.

Donaldson, M. (1993). What is hegemonic masculinity? *Theory and Society, 22*, 643–657.

Dougherty, D. S. (1999). Dialogue through standpoint: Understanding men's and women's standpoints of sexual harassment. *Management Communication Quarterly, 12*, 436–468.

Eagly, A. H., & Johnson, B. (1990). Gender and leadership style: A meta-analysis. *Psychological Bulletin, 108*, 233–256.

Eagly, A. H., & Karau, S. J. (1991). Gender and the emergence of leaders: A meta-analysis. *Journal of Personality and Social Psychology, 60*, 685–710.

Eagly, A. H., Makhijani, M. G., & Klonsky, B. G. (1992). Gender and the evaluation of leaders: A meta-analysis. *Psychological Bulletin, 111*, 3–22.

Edley, P. P. (2000). Discursive essentializing in a woman-owned business: Gendered stereotypes and strategic subordination. *Management Communication Quarterly, 14*, 271–306.

Ehrenreich, B. (2001). *Nickel and dimed: On (not) getting by in America*. New York: Metropolitan Books.

Eisenhart, M. A., & Holland, D. C. (1992). Gender constructs and career commitment: The influence of peer culture on women in college. In B. V. Reid (Ed.), *Gender constructs and social issues* (pp. 142–180). Urbana: University of Illinois Press.

Ely, R. J., & Meyerson, D. E. (2000). Theories of gender in organizations: A new approach to organizational analysis and change. *Research in Organizational Behaviour, 22*, 103–151.

Evans, J. (1997). Men in nursing: Issues of gender segregation and hidden advantage. *Journal of Advanced Nursing, 26*, 226-231.

Fagenson, E. A. (Ed.). (1993). *Women in management: Trends, issues, and challenges in managerial diversity*. Newbury Park, CA: Sage.

Fairhurst, G. (1993). The leader-member exchange patterns of women leaders in industry: A discourse analysis. *Communication Monographs, 60*, 321–351.

Faulkner, W. (2000). Dualisms, hierarchies and gender in engineering. *Social Studies of Science, 30*(5), 759–792.

Fenstermaker, S., & West, C. (Eds.). (2002). *Doing gender, doing difference: Inequality, power and institutional change*. New York: Routledge.

Ferguson, K. (1984). *The feminist case against bureaucracy*. Philadelphia: Temple University Press.

Ferree, M. M., & Martin, P. (Eds.). (1995). *Feminist organizations: Harvest of the new women's movement*. Philadelphia: Temple University Press.

Fine, M., Weis, L., Addelston, J., & Marusza, J. (1997). (In)secure times: Constructing white working class masculinities in the late 20th century. *Gender and Society, 11*, 52–68.

Fletcher, J. (1999). *Disappearing acts: Gender, power, and relational practice at work*. Cambridge: MIT Press.

Fraser, N. (1990-1991). Rethinking the public sphere: A contribution to the critique of actually existing democracy. *Social Text, 25/26*, 56–80.

Frehill, L. M. (2004). The gendered construction of the engineering profession in the United States, 1893–1920. *Men and Masculinities, 6*, 383–403.

Garrison, D. (1972–1973, Winter). The tender technicians: The feminization of public librarianship, 1876–1905. *Journal of Social History*, 221–249.

Gherardi, S. (1994). The gender we think, the gender we do in our everyday organizational lives. *Human Relations, 47*, 591–610.

Gherardi, S. (1995). *Gender, symbolism and organizational cultures*. London: Sage.

Gottfried, H. (1994). Learning the score: The duality of control and everyday resistance in the temporary-help service industry. In W. R. Nord (Ed.), *Resistance and power in organizations* (pp. 102–127). London: Routledge.

Gottfried, H., & Weiss, P. (1994). A compound feminist organization: Purdue University's Council on the Status of Women. *Women and Politics, 14*, 23–44.

Gray, B. L. (1991). Organizational struggles of working women in the nineteenth century. *Labor Studies Journal, 16*, 16–34.

Greene, A.-m., Ackers, P., & Black, J. (2002). Going against the historical grain: Perspectives on gendered occupational identity and resistance to the breakdown of occupational segregation in two manufacturing firms. *Gender, Work, & Organization, 9*, 266–285.

Hakim, C. (1992). Explaining trends in occupational segregation: The measurement, causes, and consequences of the sexual division of labour. *European Sociological Review, 8*, 127–152.

Hakim, C. (1995). Five feminist myths about women's employment. *British Journal of Sociology, 46*, 101–118.

Harding, S. (1991). *Whose science? Whose knowledge? Thinking from women's lives*. Ithaca, NY: Cornell University Press.

Hearn, J. (1982). Notes on patriarchy: Professionalization and the semi-professions. *Sociology, 16*, 184–202.

Hearn, J., Sheppard, D., Tancred-Sheriff, P., & Burrell, G. (Eds.). (1989). *The sexuality of organization*. London: Sage.

Heikes, E. J. (1991). When men are the minority: The case of men in nursing. *Sociological Quarterly, 32*, 389–401.

Helgesen, S. (1990). *The female advantage: Women's ways of leadership*. New York: Doubleday.

Henson, K. D. (1996). *Just a temp*. Philadelphia: Temple University Press.

Henson, K. D., & Rogers, J. K. (2001). "Why Marcia you've changed!" Male clerical temporary workers doing masculinity in a feminized occupation. *Gender & Society, 15*, 218–238.

Hinze, S. W. (1999). Gender and the body of medicine or at least some body parts: (Re)constructing the prestige hierarchy of medical specialties. *Sociological Quarterly, 40*, 217–239.

Hodgson, D. (2003). "Taking it like a man": Masculinity, subjection and resistance in the selling of life assurance. *Gender, Work, & Organization, 10*(1), 1–21.

Holmer Nadesan, M., & Trethewey, A. (2000). Performing the enterprising subject: Gendered strategies for success (?). *Text and Performance Quarterly, 20*, 223–250.

Hossfeld, K. J. (1993). "Their logic against them": Contradictions in sex, race, and class in Silicon Valley. In P. S. Rothenberg (Ed.), *Feminist frameworks: Alternative theoretical accounts of the relations between women and men* (pp. 346–358). New York: McGraw-Hill.

Iannello, K. P. (1992). *Decisions without hierarchy: Feminist interventions in organizational theory and practice*. London: Routledge.

Jackson, C. (1999). Men's work, masculinities and gender divisions of labour. *Journal of Development Studies, 36*, 89–108.

Jacobs, J. A. (1999). The sex segregation of occupations: Prospects for the 21st century. In G. N. Powell (Ed.), *Handbook of gender and work* (pp. 125–141). Thousand Oaks, CA: Sage.

Jorgenson, J. (2002). Engineering selves: Negotiating gender and identity in technical work. *Management Communication Quarterly, 15*, 350–380.

Kanter, R. M. (1975). Women and the structure of organizations: Explorations in theory and behavior. In R. M. Kanter (Ed.), *Another voice: Feminist perspectives on social life and social science* (pp. 34–74). Garden City, NY: Anchor Books.

Kanter, R. M. (1977). *Men and women of the corporation.* New York: Basic Books.

Kemp, A. A. (1994). *Women's work: Degraded and devalued.* Englewood Cliffs, NJ: Prentice Hall.

Kennelly, I. (2002). "I would never be a secretary": Reinforcing gender in segregated and integrated occupations. *Gender & Society, 16*, 603–624.

Kerfoot, D., & Knights, D. (1993). Management, masculinity and manipulation: From paternalism to corporate strategy in financial services in Britain. *Journal of Management Studies, 30*, 659–677.

Kerfoot, D., & Whitehead, S. (2000). Keeping all the balls in the air: Further education and the masculine/managerial subject. *Journal of Further and Higher Education, 24*, 183–201.

Kondo, D. K. (1990). *Crafting selves: Power, gender, and discourses of identity in a Japanese workplace.* Chicago: University of Chicago Press.

Lawson, V. (1999). Tailoring is a profession, seamstressing is work: Resisting work and reworking gender identities among artisanal garment workers in Quito. *Environment and Planning A, 31*, 209–227.

Linstead, S. (1995). Averting the gaze: Gender and power on the perfumed picket line. *Gender, Work, & Organization, 2*, 192–205.

Linstead, S. (1997). Abjection and organization: Men, violence, and management. *Human Relations, 50*, 1115–1145.

Loden, M. (1985). *Feminine leadership, or how to succeed in business without being one of the boys.* New York: Times Books.

Lupton, B. (2000). Maintaining masculinity: Men who do "women's work." *British Journal of Management, 11*, 33–48.

Macdonald, K. M. (1995). *The sociology of the professions.* London: Sage.

Maguire, M., & Mohtar, L. F. (1994). Performance and the celebration of a subaltern counterpublic. *Text and Performance Quarterly, 14*, 238–252.

Marshall, H., & Wetherell, M. (1989). Talking about career and gender identities: A discourse analysis perspective. In S. Skevington & D. Baker (Ed.), *The social identity of women* (pp. 106–129). London: Sage.

Marshall, J. (1989). Re-visioning career concepts: A feminist invitation. In B. Lawrence (Ed.), *Handbook of career theory* (pp. 275–291). Cambridge, UK: Cambridge University Press.

Martin, J. (1990). Deconstructing organizational taboos: The suppression of gender conflict in organizations. *Organization Science, 1*, 339–359.

Martin, P. Y., & Collinson, D. (2002). "Over the pond and across the water": Developing the field of "gendered organizations." *Gender, Work and Organization, 9*, 244–265.

Martin, S. E. (1994). "Outsider within" the station house: The impact of race and gender on black women police. *Social Problems, 41*, 383–400.

Mies, M. (1986). *Patriarchy and accumulation on a world scale: Women in the international division of labour.* London: Zed Books.

Milkman, R. (1987). *Gender at work: The dynamics of job segregation by sex during World War II.* Urbana: University of Illinois Press.

Miller, G. E. (2002). The frontier, entrepreneurialism, and engineers: Women coping with a web of masculinities in an organizational culture. *Culture and Organization, 8*, 145–160.

Mills, A. J. (1995). Man/aging subjectivity, silencing diversity: Organizational imagery in the airline industry. The case of British Airways. *Organization, 2*, 243–269.

Mills, A. J. (1997). Dueling discourses: Desexualization versus eroticism in the corporate framing of female sexuality in the British airline industry, 1945–1960. In A. Prasad (Ed.), *Managing the organizational melting pot: Dilemmas of workplace diversity* (pp. 171–198). Thousand Oaks, CA: Sage.

Mills, A. J. (1998). Cockpits, hangars, boys and galleys: Corporate masculinities and the development of British Airways. *Gender, Work, & Organization, 5,* 172–188.

Mills, A. J., & Chiaramonte, P. (1991). Organization as gendered communication act. *Canadian Journal of Communication, 16,* 381–398.

Monaghan, L. F. (2002). Hard men, shop boys and others: Embodying competence in a masculinist occupation. *Sociological Review, 50,* 334–355.

Morgan, D. (1996). The gender of bureaucracy. In J. Hearn (Ed.), *Men as managers, managers as men* (pp. 61–77). Thousand Oaks, CA: Sage.

Morgan, D. H. J. (1992). *Discovering men.* London: Routledge.

Morgan, G., & Knights, D. (1991). Gendering jobs: Corporate strategy, managerial control and the dynamics of job segregation. *Work, Employment & Society, 5,* 181–200.

Mumby, D. K. (1993). Feminism and the critique of organizational communication studies. In S. Deetz (Ed.), *Communication yearbook 16* (pp. 155–166). Newbury Park, CA: Sage.

Mumby, D. K. (1996). Feminism, postmodernism, and organizational communication: A critical reading. *Management Communication Quarterly, 9,* 259–295.

Mumby, D. K. (1998). Organizing men: Power, discourse, and the social construction of masculinity(s) in the workplace. *Communication Theory, 8,* 164–183.

Mumby, D. K., & Ashcraft, K. L. (2006). Striking out from the backwater: Organizational communication studies and gendered organization (a response to Martin and Collinson). *Gender, Work and Organization, 13,* 68–90.

Mumby, D. K., & Putnam, L. L. (1992). The politics of emotion: A feminist reading of bounded rationality. *Academy of Management Review, 17,* 465–486.

Murphy, A. G. (2003). The dialectical gaze: Exploring the subject-object tension in the performances of women who strip. *Journal of Contemporary Ethnography, 32,* 305–335.

Murphy, B. O., & Zorn, T. (1996). Gendered interaction in professional relationships. In J. T. Wood (Ed.), *Gendered relationships* (pp. 213–232). Mountain View, CA: Mayfield.

Natalle, E. J. (1996). Gendered issues in the workplace. In J. T. Wood (Ed.), *Gendered relationships* (pp. 253–274). Mountain View, CA: Mayfield.

Nelson, M. W. (1988). Women's ways: Interactive patterns in predominantly female research teams. In A. Taylor (Ed.), *Women communicating: Studies of women's talk* (pp. 199–232). Norwood, NJ: Ablex.

Phillips, A., & Taylor, B. (1980). Sex and skill: Notes toward a feminist economics. *Feminist Review, 6,* 79–88.

Pierce, J. L. (1995). *Gender trials: Emotional lives in contemporary law firms.* Berkeley: University of California Press.

Pringle, R. (1989a). Bureaucracy, rationality and sexuality: The case of secretaries. In G. Burrell (Ed.), *The sexuality of organization* (pp. 158–177). Newbury Park, CA: Sage.

Pringle, R. (1989b). *Secretaries talk: Sexuality, power and work.* London: Verso.

Prokos, A., & Padavic, I. (2002). "There oughtta be a law against bitches": Masculinity lessons in police academy training. *Gender, Work, & Organization, 9,* 439–459.

Putnam, L., Phillips, N., & Chapman, P. (1996). Metaphors of communication and organization. In S. R. Clegg, C. Hardy, & W. R. Nord (Eds.), *Handbook of organization studies* (pp. 375–408). London: Sage.

Reskin, B., & Hartmann, H. (1986). *Women's work, men's work: Sex segregation on the job.* Washington, DC: National Academy Press.

Rogers, J. K. (2000). *Temps: The many faces of the changing workplace*. Ithaca, NY: Cornell University Press.

Rogers, J. K., & Henson, K. D. (1997). "Hey, why don't you wear a shorter skirt?" Structural vulnerability and the organization of sexual harassment in temporary clerical employment. *Gender & Society, 11*, 215–237.

Rollins, J. (1997). Invisibility, consciousness of the other, *ressentiment*. In P. Zavella (Ed.), *Situated lives: Gender and culture in everyday life* (pp. 255–270). New York: Routledge.

Roper, M. (1996). "Seduction and succession": Circuits of homosocial desire in management. In J. Hearn (Ed.), *Men as managers, managers as men* (pp. 210–226). Thousand Oaks, CA: Sage.

Rosener, J. B. (1990). Ways women lead. *Harvard Business Review, 68*, 119–125.

Sargent, P. (2000). Real men or real teachers? Contradictions in the lives of men elementary teachers. *Men and Masculinities, 2*, 410–433.

Savage, M., & Witz, A. (Eds.). (1992). *Gender and bureaucracy* (Vol. 39). Oxford, UK: Blackwell/Sociological Review.

Segal, B. E. (1962). Male nurses: A case study in status contradiction and prestige loss. *Social Forces, 41*, 31–38.

Smith, D. (1987). *The everyday world as problematic: A feminist sociology*. Boston: Northeastern University Press.

Sotirin, P., & Gottfried, H. (1999). The ambivalent dynamics of secretarial "bitching": Control, resistance, and the construction of identity. *Organization, 6*, 57–80.

Spencer, A., & Podmore, D. (Eds.). (1987). *In a man's world: Essays on women in male-dominated professions*. London: Tavistock.

Touhey, J. C. (1974). Effects of additional women professionals on ratings of occupational prestige and desirability. *Journal of Personality and Social Psychology, 29*, 86–89.

Trethewey, A. (2001). Reproducing and resisting the master narrative of decline: Midlife professional women's experiences of aging. *Management Communication Quarterly, 15*, 183–226.

Walker, H. A., Ilardi, B. C., McMahon, A. M., & Fennell, M. L. (1996). Gender, interaction, and leadership. *Social Psychology Quarterly, 59*, 255–272.

Weedon, C. (1987). *Feminist practice and post-structuralist theory*. Oxford, UK: Basil Blackwell.

West, C., & Fenstermaker, S. (1995). Doing difference. *Gender & Society, 9*, 8–37.

West, C., & Zimmerman, D. (1987). Doing gender. *Gender & Society, 1*, 125–151.

Wharton, A. S., & Baron, J. N. (1987). So happy together? The impact of gender segregation on men at work. *American Sociological Review, 52*, 574–587.

Wharton, A. S., & Baron, J. N. (1991). Satisfaction? The psychological impact of gender segregation on women at work. *Sociological Quarterly, 32*, 365–387.

Wilkins, B. M., & Anderson, P. A. (1991). Gender differences and similarities in management communication. *Management Communication Quarterly, 5*, 6–35.

Williams, C. L. (1989). *Gender differences at work*. Berkeley: University of California Press.

Williams, C. L. (1992). The glass escalator: Hidden advantages for men in the "female" professions. *Social Problems, 39*, 253–267.

Williams, C. L. (Ed.). (1993). *Doing "Women's work": Men in non-traditional occupations*. London: Sage.

Williams, C. L. (1995). *Still a man's world: Men who do women's work*. Berkeley: University of California Press.

Willis, P. (1977). *Learning to labor: How working class kids get working class jobs*. New York: Columbia University Press.

Witz, A. (1990). Patriarchy and professions: The gendered politics of occupational closure. *Sociology, 24*, 675–690.

Witz, A. (1992). *Professions and patriarchy*. London: Routledge.

Wood, J. T. (1993). Gender and moral voice: Moving from women's nature to standpoint epistemology. *Women's Studies in Communication, 15*, 1–24.

Wood, J. T. (2003). *Gendered lives: Communication, gender, and culture* (5th ed.). Belmont, CA: Thomson/Wadsworth.

Wright, R. (1996). The occupational masculinity of computing. In C. Cheng (Ed.), *Masculinities in organizations* (pp. 77–96). Thousand Oaks, CA: Sage.

Young, E. (1989). On the naming of the rose: Interests and multiple meanings as elements of organizational culture. *Organization Studies, 10,* 187–206.

Young, J. L., & James, E. H. (2001). Token majority: The work attitudes of male flight attendants. *Sex Roles, 45,* 299–319.

Zatz, N. D. (1997). Sex work/sex act: Law, labor and desire in constructions of prostitution. *Signs, 22,* 277–308.

7

CONSTRUCTING EMBODIED ORGANIZATIONAL IDENTITIES

Commodifying, Securing, and Servicing Professional Bodies

◆ Angela Trethewey, Cliff Scott,
and Marianne LeGreco

In spite of the considerable emphasis placed on bodies at work—how they should look, feel, and act in the workplace—the body remains an absent presence in contemporary organizational theory. Through everyday organizational processes and practices, social discourses of power are appropriated, reproduced, and/or transformed in ways that enable and constrain how members enact and embody professional identities. It is often through organizations that "we come to understand who we are and who we might become," and the body plays an important and gendered role in this process (Trethewey, 1997, p. 218). In this chapter we explore and critique particular processes, including those we title *commodifying, risking/securing,* and *servicing,* through which the bodies of organizational members are made professional in gendered ways. Furthermore, we examine the gendered (and often classed) consequences of those constructions for both professional and nonprofessional employees.

◆ *Theorizing the Professional Body at Work*

There is a variety of practical reasons for organizational communication scholars to study the body. Employee bodies are both the medium and the outcome of practice and knowledge. Nurses' understandings of patients, for example, may be mediated by touch (Shakespeare, 2003, p. 54). Employees' relationships with other professionals and clients may be facilitated or hindered by embodied expressions of professionalism, care, or expertise. Health and safety concerns often focus on employee bodies. The study of bodies at work can tell us how employees "use their bodies in a competent way and how do they use their bodies to show they are competent" (Shakespeare, 2003, p. 54). Examining the discursive construction of the professional body can help answer questions about the relationship between work and identity.

We deploy poststructuralist and feminist theories that conceive of the body as both a product and process of discourse. How our bodies become meaningful in everyday work life is a partial product or effect of the discursive structures that comprise our social worlds. And yet, as we perform our sense of who we are or wish we could be at work, we actively draw upon and occasionally attempt to resist (in more or less privileged ways) these very structures. White middle-class professional women come to experience and understand their aging bodies through the cultural master narrative of decline in which aging is associated with the loss of face, body, and sexuality. Yet these women simultaneously resist the master narrative, largely through class-based consumption, and attempt to craft professionally viable bodies and identities (Trethewey, 2001).

We assume that meanings for professional bodies and, indeed, professional bodies themselves, are largely discursively constituted. Social discourses of power, including gender, race, class, and entrepreneurialism, work in concert to constitute particular organizational subject positions. As Weedon (1997) explains,

Discourses are more than ways of thinking and producing meaning. They constitute the "nature" of the body, unconscious and conscious mind and emotional life of the subjects they seek to govern. Neither the body nor thoughts and feelings have meanings outside of their discursive articulation, but the ways in which discourses constitute the minds and bodies of individuals is always part of a wider network of power relations, often with institutional bases. (p. 105)

To say that embodied identities are discursively constituted does not mean that individuals are determined by discourse. Instead, agency is manifest when social actors reflexively choose among, creatively combine, and/or resist the subject positions offered by various discourses of power in circulation at a particular historical moment. While discourses often attempt to fix the meaning of a subject position, they can never do so completely or finally because they are conflictual, contradictory, and contested (Trethewey & Ashcraft, 2004). A discourse may offer a preferred identity, but its "very organization will imply other subject positions and the possibility of reversal" (Weedon, 1997, p. 106). The discursive construction of public, masculine work as a primary and preferred site of identity negotiation for professional employees is largely accomplished through differentiating public, paid employment from less valued private, feminine, home and family activities. And yet, because the distinctions between public and private and masculinity and femininity are discursively constructed and constantly shifting, individuals are afforded opportunities to enact embodied identities in keeping with, in opposition to, and in the interstices of those competing subject positions (Alvesson, 1998; Mumby, 1998; Murphy, 1998).

A focus on the discursive construction of the body is not meant to deny its materiality.

We believe the relationship between discourse and the material world can be understood as a dialectic tension such that discourse cannot explain every aspect of the material world and material conditions do not simply determine discourse (Ashcraft & Mumby, 2004). Hands, breasts, and varicose veins exist outside of texts and embodied discourse yet are understood through discourses that are written upon bodies in specific ways. Bodies are things that have physical presence, but they become meaningful as "residues of discourse that can only be understood through discourse" (p. 56). Thus, our embodied experiences involve a complex negotiation of both physical and discursive space (Gillies et al., 2004). Attempts to accomplish a professional self often imbue embodied identities with asymmetrical, gendered value (Holmer Nadesan & Trethewey, 2000; Trethewey, 1999). Discourses not only position gendered (and classed) bodies but often do so with material consequences.

The ways we adorn, pose, sculpt, feed, ignore, and obsess about our bodies have very real consequences for our personal, organizational, and societal well-being. Yet, organizational communication research has developed "an epistemological blindspot . . . wherein the extent to which organizations exert tangible effects on real, flesh-and-blood people gets frequently overlooked" (Ashcraft & Mumby, 2004, p. 78). Scholars' tendency to reduce organizations to text or discourse has, however, unintentionally, neglected the embodied, material consequences of discourse that members face as they negotiate their everyday lives.

A sustained exploration of the discourses that work to construct our symbolic and material selves is warranted. Indeed, we begin this essay by outlining how discourses of gender and entrepreneurialism position the body as a feature of one's identity to be assembled, improved, and monitored. As Giddens (1992) claims, "the body is less and less an extrinsic 'given,' functioning outside the internally referential systems of modernity, but becomes itself reflexively mobilized" (p. 7). Contemporary organizations

are the site of that embodied mobilization. Gendered, professional identities are "a product always in progress" that need further empirical investigation in organizational life (Ashcraft & Mumby, 2004, p. 9).

We find it ironic that scholars of organizational communication have largely ignored embodied experience, even though organizational discourse has long been occupied with members' bodies as a locus of social control. Frederick Taylor's (1911) drive to find the "one best way" to execute tasks was meant to ensure that workers' bodies would be used in the most efficient way possible. His scientific management posited a managerially prescribed system for the ways in which a worker could use his/her body. In short, head work—the conception of work—was left to managers, while body work—implementation of managerial work design—was left to employees (Braverman, 1974). "The managerial principles of scientific management meant that the working body (as a source of skill) came to be the object of inquiry in order that the human body (as the source of effort) could become the object of more exacting control" (Hancock & Tyler, 2000, p. 87). Townley (1994) catalogues the variety of ways that employees' tasks and, by implication, bodies are still codified, organized, and controlled through contemporary human resource management (job analysis, performance appraisals).

Contemporary organizational discourse and practice still treats the employee's working body as an entity that can be rationalized, disciplined, regulated, and tested (random drug tests; personality tests) (Holmer Nadesan, 1996, 1997; Townley, 1994). This extends into the symbolic when organizations make explicit the symbolic force they want organizational bodies to exert. Management's interest in shaping corporate culture derives from the desire to have workers' bodies "speak" the organization's "core values" (Peters & Waterman, 1982). Dress codes and other nonverbal markers, including employee demeanor and style, come to represent the organization literally and figuratively. Control of employee bodies is now more insidious because it is often self-imposed. The disciplinary power of discourse "seeps into the very grain of individuals, reaches right into their bodies, permeates their gestures, their posture," their being (Foucault, 1980, quoted in Martin, 1988, p. 6). As we will argue, this is particularly true for women and other marginalized groups whose bodies and identities are stigmatized in organizational life.

The professional body is not a fixed, stable entity. It is a discursively constituted process and product. In this chapter we pay particular attention to how discourses of gender and entrepreneurialism and their attendant classed implications work to shape both the bodies of professional employees and their non-professional counterparts. We articulate how gender and entrepreneurialism are two primary discourses at work on professional bodies. We then address the commodification, risking/securing, and servicing through which professional bodies are enacted. Finally, we discuss the ways in which organizational scholars may contribute to reforming organizational bodies.

GENDERED ORGANIZING

Organizational discourse is gendered. It tends to reflect and reproduce preferred modes of being that ascribe asymmetrical value to masculinity and femininity. Specifically, it articulates masculinity/femininity as a difference that makes a difference in organizational life such that hegemonic masculinity is typically preferred. This argument has been made powerfully and persuasively by organizational scholars (Acker, 1990; Ashcraft, 2004; Ashcraft & Mumby, 2004; Buzzanell, 2000; Marshall, 1993; Mumby & Putnam, 1992), so we will draw attention here to the ways organizational discourse privileges that which has historically been linked to masculinity.

Organizational discourse tends to value rationality, the public sphere, and the mind, all of which have been socially constructed as masculine and tends to marginalize that which is associated with femininity, namely: emotionality, the private sphere, and the body. Acker (1990) suggests that organizational discourse, far from being neutral, offers a masculine version of the ideal worker, one whose body is free from the demands of childbearing, menstruating, and emoting. While "women's bodies are ruled out of order, or sexualized and objectified, in work organizations, men's bodies are not" (p. 152). Women's bodies are often suspect or marginal in professional contexts, leaving women to engage in struggles to negotiate their bodies and their identities (Mumby, 1997; Trethewey, 1999). These struggles for identity create additional burdens for professional women and their nonprofessional counterparts (Acker, 1990).

ENTERPRISING SUBJECTS

If gendered discourses assume that women's bodies are essentially unfit for the professional world, entrepreneurial ones offer all women, indeed all employees, an increasingly ubiquitous, market-driven, and market-located mode of "fixing" their bodies and gendered identities in ways that align better with a preferred, organizational ideal (Tracy & Trethewey, 2005). Employees are increasingly encouraged to treat the self as an enterprise, so work is primarily where they enact an enterprising identity (du Gay, 1996). Through the consumption and subsequent performance of training courses, seminars, self-help literature, professional attire, and other symbols of organizational and social status (BlackBerrys, PDAs, automobiles), employees often seek to manifest a successful, professional identity. Much of this consumption plays out in asymmetrical ways wherein otherwise functional/healthy, typically feminine bodies are pathologized (Gullette, 1997; Tavris, 1992; Trethewey, 1999). Garsten and Grey's (1997) analysis suggests that enterprising subjects are focused on skill acquisition and self-discipline where the underlying assumption is that "control of the self can lead to control of the world" (p. 217).

However empowering the discourse of enterprise may at first appear to be, it exerts control by creating needs through advertising and public relations rather than imposing norms. It replaces the disciplinary gaze of the supervisor with autosurveillance, and rather than repressing its subjects, it constructs and entices them. The subject becomes, above all, self-regulating and self-disciplining (du Gay, 1996). Not all subjects are equally able to enact enterprise, despite the apparent availability of the discourse. While consumption may be a strategy employed to craft preferred identities, the entrepreneurial project of the self remains gendered and classed (Bourdieu, 1984; Jagger, 2000; Holmer Nadesan, 1999; Holmer Nadesan & Trethewey, 2000). Organizational contexts add yet another layer of complexity to women's attempts to craft an enterprising self and body. When women enter the public sphere of work, masculine expectations for professionalism, or what Holmer Nadesan (1999) calls an "aestheticized masculinity," create another set of gaps for women whose bodies are viewed as repositories of emotions and sexuality and other devalued and marginalized traits.

Here again, women rely upon strategies of consumption to master their unruly selves. In order to overcome their emotionality, women purchase popular success texts or invest in other therapeutic technologies to learn to better manage their emotions and present a more professional (read: masculine?) self (Holmer Nadesan & Trethewey, 2000). To present a more professional and enterprising (read: less feminine?) image/body, women consume a variety of products. At work they often find themselves in a never-ending and ultimately impossible quest to reach the entrepreneurial ideal and to get their professional identities and bodies "right" (Holmer Nadesan & Trethewey, 2000). While both men and women are impacted by discourses of enterprise that create an ideal no one can ultimately achieve, women's difficulties are more pronounced because gendered discourses articulate their bodies in terms of a "debased otherness" (Holmer Nadesan & Trethewey, 2000).

Gender is not the only discourse that impacts a subject's ability to embody an enterprising, professional self. The ability to consume is determined by purchasing power or socioeconomic status and, as a result, our bodies bear the imprint of class tastes (Bourdieu, 1984). All consumers, regardless of purchasing power, use and appropriate commodities and services as identity signs and symbols. Goods and services have both an instrumental use value and an identity value such that consumption is a means to express and reproduce social differences. Bourdieu (1984) argues that classed differences are produced when consumers develop "*habitus*": taken-for-granted preferences for and a sense of appropriateness regarding cultural goods and services. These habituated preferences, or classed taste differences, which are born of material conditions, are inscribed onto consumers' bodies such that each class has a "clearly identifiable relationship with its body" manifest in body size, shape, posture, ways of eating, walking, drinking and moving (Jagger, 2000, p. 53). Working-class individuals may treat their bodies instrumentally and thus prefer to engage in weight lifting or other activities that build strength rather than the slimming and sculpting that reproduce fit middle-class bodies. These embodied distinctions are not fixed or universal; rather, the body is a form of cultural capital and a site of struggle that is often enacted through consumption and entrepreneurialism.

The discourses of gender and entrepreneurialism are two of the primary forces that work in concert to position members' bodies as professional or, conversely, as lacking professionalism. An exhaustive exploration of embodied professionalism would include race, sexuality, class, age, and so on. In the following sections, where we make gender and entrepreneurialism prominent, we also suggest how other facets of identity might figure into the professional body.

◆ Embodying Professionalism

Social discourses of power, gender, and entrepreneurialism reinforce the notion that professional bodies are skillfully crafted. Professionalism is a feature of one's identity that can be managed and manipulated by enterprising subjects. Organizational communication scholars have begun to empirically explore the ways gendered organizational discourses affect how women's bodies are literally and discursively positioned at work, in "real" or "professional" jobs.

The dominant vision of the professional body today is aligned with our culturally preferred and ideologically constructed meanings for a real job. According to Clair (1996), a "real job" (read: professional position) "pays well, holds the possibility of 'advancement,' includes being a part of 'management,' allows for 'independence' and 'your own office,' is 'full-time' at '40 hours' with 'benefits' and with a 'reputable company'" (p. 257). These jobs have historically been the province of men. Thus, it is no surprise that our scholarly discussion of the construction of the professional body has focused on challenges faced by professional women struggling to succeed. Trethewey (1999), following Bartky (1988) and Bordo (1989), indicates that white middle-class women make use of, understand, and craft their professional bodies in very particular ways.

The professional body is physically and emotionally fit. Women who are not physically fit are viewed as being out of control and less able to endure the demands of work. Second, white middle-class women treat their bodies as a text to be read by others. They use nonverbal behaviors (ways of sitting, walking, and moving) and other performative strategies to display a body that is confident, not threatening; engaging, not available; and feminine, but not excessively so. Nevertheless, women's abilities to embody professionalism are compromised because their bodies are constructed as excessive. Professional women describe their bodies and those of other women in terms of spillage, slips, and leaks. Pregnancy, menstruation, emotional responses to work, and the inadvertent (and nearly unavoidable, given our cultural construction's of women's sexuality) sexualized display of the body are all cast as potential liabilities. Women experience, describe, and constantly monitor their seemingly excessive bodies because they may, at any moment, unintentionally reveal their inappropriateness, their femaleness, their otherness. Among professional women, "the response, therefore, is to keep the body in check, to prevent leaks, in short to discipline and control the body" (Trethewey, 1999, p. 445). Women's own participation in rendering their professional bodies docile through self-surveillance works to normalize and individualize the politics in current gendered constructions of professionalism.

Acker (1990) reminds us that while female bodies certainly have difficulty embodying the organizational ideal, some (most?) male bodies may not have equal access to the abstract ideal either. The male body which a woman assumes to be hegemonic is not only gendered, but raced and classed as well (see p. 154).

The ability of working-class men and/or men of color to embody professionalism is also compromised (Collinson, 1992). As Ashcraft and Allen (2003) argue, "At least in the U.S., we depend on the convergence of raced and classed divisions of labor to concentrate people of color in 'cheap,' 'dirty,' 'invisible,'—at minimum, devalued—support roles" (p. 22). Indeed, the absence of men and women of color in the upper levels of organizational hierarchies suggests that whiteness is not only normalized but privileged in ways that suggest real jobs are not just figuratively white but literally so. Those with nonwhite bodies face the difficult task of negotiating their identities themselves so they are not read as "unruly others" or not "really" professional (Holmer Nadesan, 1999, p. 216; see also Allen, 2001; Spellers, 1998).

While organizational scholars have often theorized in ways that assume that "white (collar) workplaces and work/ers constitute 'universal' settings, identities, and practices," this is clearly not the case (Ashcraft & Allen, 2003, p. 25). Although these workers, their work, and their contexts may be the culturally preferred or dominant models, they are certainly not the most common or most real. That fewer and fewer individuals are actually employed in such positions has not yet diminished the ideological power of this model that serves as an ideal(ized) and normalizing standard by which other positions and the workers who occupy them are (de)valued (Ashforth & Kreiner, 1999). And yet, embodying professionalism may have more to do with performing whiteness, an (idealized and normative) subject position that is also classed (see Ashcraft & Allen, 2003; Trethewey, 2001). Thus, the ideological standards we use to evaluate real professionals are not only gendered, raced, and classed but also affect employees' abilities to embody professionalism at work. In the following sections we take up the specific processes employees engage in their struggles to embody professionalism.

COMMODIFYING BODIES

Discourses of entrepreneurialism, which, as we've suggested, are not unrelated to discourses of whiteness, encourage professional employees to treat their bodies as sites of intervention through consumption. As organized individuals attempt to make projects of themselves through this discourse, they turn to the body as an easily malleable commodity. The body, especially for women, becomes a site for enacting technologies that change or alter its appearance in ways that, increasingly, make it more marketable. From the application of makeup to more permanent strategies like cosmetic surgery, these technologies are used by individuals as a form of "bodily capital" in which the "physical body is an economic asset" (Monaghan, 2002, p. 337). Exotic dancers epitomize workers who engage in a variety of body technologies to

achieve a successful performance. These women often go to great lengths to achieve, or at least perform, the contemporary (often impossible) ideal of feminine attractiveness marked by a thin, lithe body, large breasts, blonde hair and white skin (Wesely, 2003). Strippers find that this Barbie doll look gets the most attention and financial rewards from the (mostly male) customers. Doing the work involved in achieving this ideal is no small accomplishment. Wesely (2003) reports that dancers employ a variety of strategies to "manage" their weight, including taking addictive and illegal drugs, undergoing liposuction, developing eating disorders, and exercising obsessively. Dancers also shave their body hair, dye their hair, choose to have their bodies—particularly their genitalia—pierced, make their hips and breasts prominent when they walk, and often undergo cosmetic surgery to more closely replicate the fantasy image expected of them because, as one explained, "the bigger your boobs, the more table dances you got" (Wesely, 2003, p. 654). While these technologies do provide dancers with greater material rewards, they are certainly not without danger. Ingesting drugs, undergoing elective surgery, and binging and purging, for example, are clearly risky. The dancers' identities are also at risk when they are objectified and reduced to their physical attributes.

While exotic dancers may seem to embody an extreme form of femininity/sexuality, their strategies are in keeping with those that professional employees practice routinely. As we have indicated, for many women, "sexuality is an unspoken component of their work. Their jobs do not have to require them to take their clothes off for them to feel that to be successful they must shape and discipline their bodies toward a prescribed feminine image" (Murphy, 2003, p. 309; see also Cockburn, 1991).

While exotic dancers may treat their commodified bodies as assets, other women may use similar consumption strategies to attempt to prevent theirs from becoming professional liabilities. In a culture that celebrates youth and understands aging in the context of an ideological master narrative of "decline" (Gullette, 1997), professional women adopt a variety of entrepreneurial workplace strategies to better manage their aging process and the loss/lack associated with it. To counter or mitigate the effects of graying hair, menopause, lined faces, or changing bodies on their professional identities, at midlife women often attempt to pass as younger. They color their hair, hire personal trainers, wear expensive clothing, and are supportive of those who make the "personal choice" to undergo cosmetic surgery to sustain or regain their youthful appearance (Gullette, 1997, p. 203).

Organizational and cultural discourses encourage women to treat their aging bodies as an individual(ized) problem "best 'managed' through 'enterprising' choices" (Trethewey, 2001, p. 214) rather than as a social problem constituted by corporations, health care organizations, the media, and other institutional discourses. Such an entrepreneurial approach to aging enables some, particularly white middle-class women, to continue to be successful professionals. These strategies may enable some professional women to combat the master decline narrative; however, they simultaneously "absolve privileged women of the responsibility for recognizing and fighting against other types of oppression that affect [aging] women such as poverty, racism and homophobia" (Grimes, 2000, p. 3). Thus, entrepreneurial strategies that feature consumption reproduce the social construction of whiteness and reinscribe white (middle-class) privilege (Trethewey, 2001). Simultaneously, entrepreneurialism enables those who age less "successfully," who are left without the benefit of pensions, who are downsized, who are passed over for someone more hungry to be explained away by their lack of entrepreneurial savvy.

All sorts of employees are positioned by entrepreneurial discourses as manifest in the rapid and pervasive increase in cosmetic surgeries. White middle-class men are one of the fastest growing segments of the cosmetic surgery market. Top executives, for example, are electing to undergo liposuction, Botox injections, face-lifts, and other procedures to stay competitive in a labor market that places a premium on youth. Gay men are increasingly targeted as niche consumers and, indeed, their identities are "increasingly dependent upon consumer practices for their expression" (Holt, 2003, p. 47).

Although discourses that commodify our bodies tend to constrain professional identities and practices, they might also enable opportunities for resistance. Authors du Gay, Hall, Janes, MacKay, and Negus (1997) argue that meaning is always made in usage. Consumers have the ability to resist and reframe discourses of commodification because of their power to appropriate a variety of meanings.

By resisting the passivity that often accompanies consumption, consumers reclaim the power of demand, exercise agency, and participate more actively in practices of organization (Twitchell, 2000). As we consider potential sites of resistance to commodification, we must search for the spaces where organized individuals have exercised their agency as consumers to challenge more pervasive discourses (LeGreco, 2005). In doing so, organizational scholars may extend research concerning the body to consider practices of appropriation (du Gay et al., 1997). For example, Zoller's (2003a, 2003b) research regarding the proliferation of on-site fitness centers has suggested that organizations have become increasingly interested in the health of their workers. As suggested above, this desire to produce fit members might be a covert discourse of commodification; however, it has been argued that our analysis cannot end with commodification (du Gay et al., 1997). We must explore how workers use or appropriate these fitness centers to fulfill a variety of needs.

While producers/organizations might design a product, like a fitness center, to better control the bodies of their workers, these workers also reap the material benefits of reduced blood pressure, lower stress levels, and improved general health. As they use such products, they might be better positioned to make demands that the organization provide healthier food or more choices within their health care plans. Perhaps the best resistance to the commodification of the body is the commodification of the workplace. Such actions and the analysis of them must attend carefully to the operations of social class, because workers lacking job security and status may have less agency to make demands on their organizations. Exploring the dialogue between commodification and appropriation presents us with a fresh perspective on the choices and resources available to workers in the construction of professional identities and bodies.

SECURING BODIES

It is often said that ours is an age of complexity, fragmentation, and insecurity. In the workplace, "individuals confront the realities of hypercompetitive marketplaces, technologically mediated relationships, inconsistent empowerment, and economic insecurity" (Pratt & Doucet, 2000, p. 204). Risk has always been a key feature of the relationship between individuals and their organizations. Workers bring their bodies to work and put them at risk through labor in exchange for tangible (money) and intangible (identity, meaning, control) benefits that are often unstable and can easily be withdrawn. Professional bodies are often the medium and product of gendered efforts to resolve this insecurity. Everyday performances of gender at work can be viewed as embodied attempts to resolve insecure subjectivities, and this communication often reflects and reproduces social and material risks to the body. Thus, by interrogating our understanding of our bodies in relation to organized risks we may better understand the role of communication in the construction of gendered workplace meanings (Acker, 1990; Hassard, Holliday, & Willmott, 2000; Trethewey, 2000). The embodied doing of gender is therefore meaningfully

(and problematically) accomplished in the context of insecurity and risk.

In the absence of other sources of security, the workplace increasingly functions as a site of identity formation where we engage in the more individualistic pursuits of success, achievement, enterprise, and consumption often as a means of securing preferred gender identities (du Gay, 1996; Holmer Nadesan & Trethewey, 2000). Insecurities may function as sources of gender identities that are more or less preferred. Following Collinson (2003), we define insecurity as "an irreducible ambiguity at the heart of identity construction" that emerges as a discursive medium and outcome of efforts to fix meanings of the self. Insecurity is tied to a "dual experience of the self" in which members are "active agents in the world" (subjects) who also reflexively monitor how others see them (objects) (p. 532; see also Giddens, 1991). Yet, as we will suggest, insecurities may also be considered sites where the doing of gender is accomplished through micropractices that draw upon and often reproduce discourses that attempt to fix the meanings of gender asymmetrically.

Everyday understandings of what it means to be a man or woman at work are often accomplished in relation to personal risks. Many of us go to work not just to earn a living but to find meaning, belonging, and identity. These collective resources cannot be obtained autonomously. Structures of power shape the means by which members must discipline themselves, including their bodies. To avoid the risks of rejection, identity loss, and insecurity, we often submit to a normalization (Foucault, 1977, 1980) in which "the eccentricities of human beings, in their behavior, appearance, and beliefs, are measured and if necessary corrected" (Collinson, 2003, p. 528). While we can withhold thoughts and (particularly negative) feelings from others (Hochschild, 1983; Kramer & Hess, 2002), our bodies can be gazed upon, evaluated, and disciplined asymmetrically. As we seek security in the senses of belonging, identity, and control that can be obtained through conformity with local expectations, organizational discourse provides resources for accomplishing gender in embodied ways (Trethewey, 1999, 2000). As such, our embodied attempts at resolving gendered insecurity have the potential to reproduce the structures of insecurity to which we respond (Collinson, 2003; Giddens, 1984). Collinson's (1992) study of male shop floor employees demonstrates how their efforts to resolve or even resist the insecurities produced by the discourses of working-class masculinity often had the unintended consequence of reproducing the very structures of meaning that alienated these workers from both management and one another.

Enacting gendered professionalism at work involves our ability to draw upon, reproduce, and occasionally resist contradictory extra-organizational discourses about bodily appearance. Trethewey's (2000) study of women's bodies at work demonstrates how these professionals often consider their bodies objects on display. Although women have traditionally been the objects (and subjects) of discourses about dressing for success, the male professional body—once relatively invisible—is now arguably the object of mounting expectations for fitness as well. Thus, both women and men may experience insecurity about their bodies, and attempt to perform as secure subjects in order to resolve those ambiguities.

In addition to providing standards by which our gendered performances are judged, insecurities also provide sites at which to accomplish gender (Collinson, 2003). Since insecurities threaten a preferred sense of self, embodying gender in locally appropriate ways often requires that we craft our bodies in opposition to these threats. The varied, gendered meanings of professionalism are thus carried out in organizational practices through which we attempt to comport, position, and otherwise discipline our bodies in relation to interpersonal and material hazards. As a case in point, the accommodation and negotiation of risk has long been a resource for the performance of masculinity. While

this performance takes on different forms, depending on the class of masculinity being enacted (Willis, 1977), a willingness to decisively take on risk has long been a precondition for the believable performance of masculine organizational roles (Collinson, 1999; Zoller, 2003a).

Our bodies are often cast as professional regarding in relation to risks through communication that relies upon and reproduces gendered and classed notions of how bodies should appear at work. The very idea of looking professional ("dress for success") connotes a secure, usually male, middle- and upper-class body far removed from the taint of physical labor. Suits and designer shoes are only practical when our bodies are isolated from many physical dangers and we do not have to work with our hands. Thus, professional dress calls upon and reproduces class divisions. It is ironic that increasingly informal workplace dress codes ("business casual" or "blue jean Fridays") have emerged in the United States during a historical moment in which risky physical labor is considered by many either distant or irrelevant due to global outsourcing and an increasingly service- and information-based economy.

While many seek a sense of professionalism through isolation from bodily risks, others seek security through isolation from professionalism. Empirical studies of gender in blue-collar contexts have documented how some employees position their own personal, organizational, and occupational identities against notions of professionalism, preferring instead to engage in skilled manual labor and/or jobs designed for the daily negotiation of risk (Collinson, 1992, 1999; Haas, 1977; Knights, 1990). Many studies of blue-collar workplace masculinity describe men's discursive efforts to collectively construct notions of self that ascribe asymmetrical value to types of work that are more or less embodied; where, for example, working with one's hands is a pursuit worthy of real men and paper pushing is feminized. Collinson (1988, 1992), in his study of male shop floor employees, documents the efforts of members to engage in discursive practices that construct their collective identity in opposition to management, an emasculated other that they construct in feminine terms ("Nancy boy"). For them, what would be gained by adopting a more professional identity is outweighed by the risks of aligning one's self and body with the feminized managers who are viewed as literally afraid to dirty their hands. Similarly, Scott (2005) describes the efforts of municipal firefighters to secure masculine workplace identities (being "real" firefighters) by violating safety procedures and risking their bodies in pursuit of hypermasculine badges of honor. When fire conditions became so extreme that incident commanders ordered firefighters out of burning structures, some younger firefighters disobeyed so that they could melt and disfigure parts of their helmet, a seemingly sure means of passing as an authentic firefighter.

When the accommodation of bodily risk is integral to efforts to stabilize and secure preferred identity, embodied acts of resistance to managerial discourse (resisting or disobeying rules intended to protect employees) may be employed to secure identity even as they may also threaten one's physical safety. Scholars must move beyond romanticizing such acts of resistance to consider their unintended consequences (Collinson, 1992), particularly when they are directed at the resolution of insecurity. In her analysis of the biometric surveillance of the body, Ball (2005) argues that retinal scans and fingerprint technology have emerged in workplaces to secure the body as a source of truth and an anchor for identity. Ball, however, suggests that the body is always changing and often unstable. Organizational practices that attempt to fix the body often instill us with a false sense of security. Indeed, there is little evidence to suggest that insecurities are ever fully resolved. Scholars should explore the material, embodied consequences of security and insecurity at work and the discourses that work to produce them.

SERVICING BODIES

In their quest to craft a secure identity, professional employees often rely upon others to service their bodies (and those of their family members). For professional employees, especially women, these service providers enable and maintain the seamless performance required by the entrepreneurial self. Professional women often rely upon a cadre of others to care for, attend to, and fine-tune their bodies to better respond to the symbolic and material demands of work. The services of hair stylists, colorists, manicurists, fitness trainers, aestheticians, personal shoppers, massage therapists, plastic surgeons, health care professionals, and others are required to keep the gendered professional body in working order. These apparent requirements of the professional body are, of course, discursive effects of commodification, entrepreneurialism, medicalization, gender, and class.

Those who do the work of maintaining others' professional bodies are rarely among the professional class. Indeed, "to maintain a certain distance from one's own body, and especially from those of others, has developed as an important sign of hierarchical position in western societies" (Hancock & Tyler, 2000, p. 98). Work that involves touching others' bodies is often stigmatized, and those who do it are often physically or socially "tainted" (Ashforth & Kreiner, 1999) in gendered and classed ways. For example, nurses who do bodywork or lots of touching are looked down upon, as "touching is not considered 'real work' by others" (Van Dongen & Elema, 2001, p. 161). Nurses manage this tainted activity by describing bodywork as an art or a calling, crafting for themselves a more preferred identity. Their doing so is in stark contrast to the masculine "ideology of excellence" practiced by medical students. Scheibel (1996) describes how medical students learn to appropriate female bodies mechanistically. One way they manage the potential taint associated with touching patients' bodies is to construct their work as technical, skilled, and not at all touchy-feely. They describe performing gynecological exams with language that is detached and mechanical. One doctor described an unconscious woman patient as a "vending machine"; each student "walks up and sticks a hand in" (p. 318).

The management of taint and the doing of gender and class may intersect and function as communicative activities that mutually constitute one another. In their comparative study of taint management among correctional officers and municipal firefighters, Tracy and Scott (in press) note that the highly masculine image afforded firefighters gave them a "status shield" that enabled them to ward off the taint of certain tasks ("shit work") and clients ("shit bums"). Firefighters were also able in this way to employ performances of masculinity and sexuality to manage taint through discursive techniques that were less available to correctional officers.

Not only do professionals engage in a variety of strategies to maintain their bodies and professional images, they also regularly hire others to attend to the unsavory aspects of their own bodily functions or those of their loved ones. In so doing, they free themselves to pursue preferred work identities. Indeed, "many of the gains of professional-class working women have been leveraged on the backs of poor women" (Flanagan, 2004, p. 128). In her exposé of how professional women are able to become "liberated," Flanagan makes it clear that middle-class professionals often employ teams of working-class, often Third World women to tend to their literal and figurative "shit" work, including cleaning their toilets and changing dirty diapers. Barbara Ehrenreich (2001) reminds us that "shit happens," and it happens "to a cleaning person every day" (p. 93). It was not always this way. White second-wave feminists were loath to enlist the aid of their black counterparts as domestics, and many encouraged alternative means to attend to domestic matters while they entered the workforce, including advocating wages for housework, men's participation in it, and communal living. Today, most of those alternatives appear to have fallen away, as the first world has "been flooded with immigrant domestic workers" in the past 20 years (Flanagan, 2004, p. 114), and professional women's "equivocations about the moral justness of white women's employing dark-skinned women to do their shit work simply evaporated" (p. 114).

It is possible to resist the current arrangements in which bodies are serviced. Greater awareness about how feminine bodies are tainted or pathologized may empower women and men to find new ways of creatively maintaining and displaying the body to their satisfaction. As consumers, we can also inquire about the wages and working conditions of those who serve us and spend money reflectively rather than reactively. Gender may also be employed positively in the seemingly inevitable practices of taint management. Tracy and Scott (2003) conclude with "cautious optimism" that some performances of gender and sexuality have the capacity to manage taint in ways that could uphold rather than stigmatize so-called dirty occupations. They demonstrate how firefighters employed performances of masculinity and heterosexuality to reorganize tainted and feminized dimensions of identity-threatening job tasks, including serving clients that they deem unworthy (who were not experiencing a "real" emergency). They note, however, that such performances were less available to correctional officers, the other occupation represented in their sample.

◆ Reforming the Body: An Action Agenda for Organizational Communication Research

We began this chapter by arguing that, whether professional or unprofessional, the body remains an absent presence in the study of organizations. We have reviewed a number of studies that do, but they are exceptions that prove the rule. Most organization studies are predicated on the unacknowledged modernist assumption that organizational processes are mental, that the social practices that make up the experience of organizing are enacted without passion, pain, pleasure, hunger, or joy. They have often dissociated mind and body and have tended to psychologize embodied experience (Acker, 1990; Deetz, 2003; Hassard et al., 2000). It would be nice if that this scholarly disregard for the body had only scholarly consequences. Unfortunately, however, the mind/body dualism in the academy is related to a similar tendency in everyday workplace discourse, which has life-and-blood implications for the embodied experiences of people at work, implications that our discipline has often failed to acknowledge. Thus, research and pedagogy have perpetuated the myth that organizing is a disembodied process, even as it "assumes and celebrates particular bodily performances" (Sinclair, 2005, p. 89).

We have largely failed to study the discursive constitution and material effects of working-class bodies. Studies documenting the discursive constitution of working-class identities are numerous (Collinson, 1992; Connell, 1995; Willis, 1981), but missing from nearly all of them is a theoretical account of the material implications of such identity work for workers' bodies. Sixty percent of the U.S. workforce makes less than what is considered a living wage and experience chronic and acute distress as a result (Ehrenreich, 2001). Their embodied experience of work centers less on identity management and more on survival.

We think it is troubling, for example, that, to date, there have been no critical studies in our field of Wal-Mart. One of the nation's largest employers, Wal-Mart has a dubious record in its relations with its largely low-wage, part-time employees. Discrimination against its female employees has been alleged in a recent class action suit,

the largest workplace bias case in U.S. history. It was brought by six female employees who claim the company has systematically denied women promotion and paid them less than men (Greenhouse & Hays, 2004). Wal-Mart can be viewed as an artifact of current material, economic, and (embodied) experiential trends in the workplace. Indeed, some have coined the Wal-Martization of the economy to explain a general downward pressure on wages. Wal-Mart

pays its full-time hourly workers an average of $9.64, about a third of the level of union [grocery] chains. It also shoulders much less of its workers' annual health insurance costs than rivals, leaving 53% of its 1.2 million employees uncovered by the company plan. (Conlin & Bernstein, 2004, p. 64)

A former manager at Wal-Mart describes how he would routinely "'load workers into my truck to take them down to United Way'" for support services. He kept on file the telephone numbers of local homeless shelters, food banks, and soup kitchens because his employees, "couldn't make it on their paychecks" (p. 64). If we are true to the fundamental tenets of our discipline, the communicative basis for these material conditions will be explored and the possibilities for change theorized, even enacted.

We believe it would be a mistake to lay the blame for the current situation only on institutions, such as corporations or universities. Scholars have probably also been constrained by their own theoretical concepts. For example, much of the extant scholarship on organized bodies is predicated on the work of Foucault (1977, 1980). While Foucault's conceptualizations of the relationships among discourse/power, identity, and the body have led to great developments in the study of bodies and identities in organizations, the ongoing appropriation of Foucault may have had the unintended consequence of a kind of "text positivism" in which the body is just another text (Ashcraft & Mumby, 2004). Here, the tendency is to focus on the discursive and cultural consequences to identity work without attending to the very real, embodied experiences that make up the texture of work.

This critique does not aim at Foucauldian analyses per se, but rather argues for a more direct consideration of the capacity of discourse to enable the production of positive and negative material realities. Consider the embodied conditions of the working female poor and their children. Single women are overrepresented among the working poor, for whom wages often do not cover child care costs or barely do so. Women are overrepresented in low-wage service jobs that often lack health insurance or pension coverage. It is not surprising, then, that the "U.S. has the highest child-poverty rate in the industrialized world. 'Our low-income mothers work twice as hard as those in any other industrial country—but their kids are worse off'" (Conlin & Bernstein, 2004, p. 64). To what extent do organizational communication studies of women at work address these material realities and the processes of organizational communication that draw upon gendered societal discourses to produce them? To what extent is our work instead overwhelmingly biased toward the experiences and perspectives of white upper-middle-class managers who are privileged to be able to focus on middle-class gender issues such as enterprising selves, image management, and glass ceilings because they don't have to worry about paying the rent, getting day care for their kids and health insurance?

Reforming our research on professional bodies will require several shifts in our disciplinary practice. First, if the body remains an absent presence in organizational theory, existing lines of research should be revised and extended to account for embodiment. Second, scholars should pay greater attention to the material conditions that produce and are produced by embodied organizational discourse. Third, the research on organized bodies cannot be taken seriously until it considers how discourses of race, class, and sexuality function as resources for doing gender and/or professionalism. Finally, we urge that scholars pay careful attention to how their own research, whether or not it is intended to address gender, disembodies the very research subjects it intends to empower. Doing so requires greater methodological self-reflexivity. They could consider how their own research designs and other scholarly practices function to accommodate, resist, or supplant mind/body dualism.

As we contemplate how to enact such scholarship, perhaps the study of organizational policy provides us with an opportunity to explore alternative forms of organizing that focus on embodied needs. Organizations often enact policy as a "documented posture of the organization, revealing the essential tension, contradiction, and struggle between rights granted and privileges withheld" (Peterson & Albrecht, 1999, p. 170). As individuals construct their professional personas, these policies operate as a discursive guide to make sense of the material conditions of our organized bodies.

Policies pertaining to health insurance, workers' compensation, and parental leave provide employees with a framework to interpret their bodies when they fall ill, get hurt, or choose to have children. Policy statements illustrate a relationship between organization and individual that hinges on trust, vulnerability, and dependence (Goold, 1998). Policies rely on the allure of stability and security to control the meanings and actions of workers, especially in terms of their health (Conrad & McIntush, 2002). When our bodies align with socialized expectations, we fabricate a sense of mastery or control over our more primitive desires (Bordo, 1993). The idea that we take personal responsibility for the health of our bodies, particularly as they operate in the workplace, fuels the discourses of professionalism and the need for policy to provide clear courses of action.

While policies might provide workers with key resources to interpret and construct their organizational experiences, they often function communicatively to conflate the gendered needs of bodies. As Martin (1990) illustrated in her analysis of pregnancy in organizations, a male executive's heart attack differs greatly from a female executive's childbearing both in their embodied experiences and in the discourses used to construct them. Organizations and individuals negotiate a preferred posture for making sense of embodied needs. We must realize that efforts to secure organizational policies are always implicated in the gendered organization of work. Workmen's compensation, for example, was developed when white male workers dominated the labor market. It was designed to accommodate the needs and experiences of this specific group (Boris & Kleinberg, 2003). Other policies were designed to protect the worker from harm, suggesting that work placed the (male) body at risk. Women's emergence into the labor force marked a notable change in the construction of social and organizational policies concerning women and work (Rose, 1991). Women's bodies were constructed as problematic within the traditional worker paradigm. Policies derived from women's experiences often drew from and sustained the otherness of their bodies through the justification for initiatives like parental leave (Boris & Kleinberg, 2003). These gendered discourses positioned the leaky, protruding female body as placing the work at risk. As a result, organizations and individuals tend to view the material needs of a woman's body as cumbersome to professional advancement.

Policies may reify the worker's position of powerlessness, as they dictate how workers should interpret their gendered, raced, classed, and aged experiences. For example, Clair (1993) argues that sexual harassment policies that advocate a "say-no" approach or a "keep-a-record" solution further disempower victims and privatize issues by keeping grievances out of our daily public discourses. At the same time, however, policies also present workers with public possibilities for resistance by providing structural resources for holding organizations accountable for their safety, security, and well-being. As Clair further demonstrated, when victims draw from alternative resources by,

for example, making policy procedures, brochures, and punishments more visible, they resisted the dominant practices of silencing and marginalizing. When they hold their colleagues, superiors, and organizations accountable for benefits and safety accorded through policies, they make these issues a part of our public organizational discourses. Moreover, they open a dialogue for ensuring the needs and rights of the worker. When we let the organization set the sole terms of participation, we abdicate our individual needs in the service of that organization. In doing so, we enable the organization and the policies that it enacts to define our needs, interpret our experiences, and understand our bodies for us.

In their current state, the majority of organizational policies reflect the motivations of managerialism—the reproduction of working-class dependence on the organization to define needs and dictate practice (LeGreco, 2002). In more critical incarnations of research, we might continue to look at the disjunctures between policy and practice (Kirby, 2000; Kirby & Krone, 2002) as they both enable and constrain the actions of the working class. At the same time, more participatory forms of research hold a great deal of promise for transcending the constraints of policy and reframing organizational practice. Scholars will continue to praise increased employee participation (Deetz, 1992) and call for bold research projects that engage socially significant problems in practical ways (Cheney, Wilhelmsson, & Zorn, 2002; Tracy, 2002; Trethewey, 2002). We argue that the applied study of policy serves as a starting point to translate our scholarship into material benefits for the individuals we study. If we enabled a discussion between management and working-class families regarding parental leave, family health programs, and child care, for example, we could build new organizational policies from the ground up that reflect the embodied needs of working families. In doing so, we might more effectively bridge the gap between our research concerning organized bodies and those that actually do the work.

Organizational communication scholars are well positioned to stake a claim among those on the forefront of the effort to reform organizational bodies. We can document the experience of both professional employees and the working poor, who often enable professional bodies to thrive. We can serve as advocates not only of professional women, but also of working-class employees. We can critique the organizational discourses and policies that reinforce the glass ceiling and make family leave difficult as well as those that enable and perpetuate low-wage work, unsafe working conditions, and the growing crisis in health insurance. And we can celebrate organizational best practices that serve a variety of professional and nonprofessional bodies.

◆ References

Acker, J. (1990). Hierarchies, jobs, bodies: A theory of gendered organization. *Gender & Society, 4,* 139–158.

Allen, B. J. (2001). Gender, race and communication in professional environments. In L. P. Arliss & D. Borisoff (Eds.), *Women and men communicating: Challenges and changes* (pp. 212–231). Prospect Heights, IL: Waveland Press.

Alvesson, M. (1998). Gender relations and identity at work: A case study of masculinities and femininities in an advertising agency. *Human Relations, 51,* 969–1005.

Ashcraft, K. L. (2004). Gender, discourse and organization. In D. Grant, C. Hardy, C. Oswick, & L. Putnam (Eds.), *The Sage handbook of organizational discourse* (pp. 275–291). London: Sage.

Ashcraft, K. L., & Allen, B. J. (2003). The racial foundation of organizational communication. *Communication Theory, 13,* 5–38.

Ashcraft, K. L., & Mumby, D. K. (2004). *Reworking gender: A feminist communicology of organization.* Thousand Oaks, CA: Sage.

Ashforth, B. E. (2001). *Role transitions in organizational life: An identity-based perspective.* Mahwah, NJ: Erlbaum.

Ashforth, B. E., & Kreiner, G. (1999) "How can you do it?" Dirty work and the challenge of constructing a positive identity. *Academy of Management Review 24,* 413–34.

Ball, K. (2005). Organization, surveillance and the body: Towards a politics of resistance. *Organization, 12,* 89–108.

Bartky, S. L. (1988). Foucault, femininity, and the modernization of patriarchal power. In I. Diamond & L. Quinby (Eds.), *Feminism and Foucault: Reflections on resistance* (pp. 61–86). Boston: Northeastern University Press.

Boris, E., & Kleinberg, S. J. (2003). Mothers and other workers: (Re)conceiving labor, maternalism, and the state. *Journal of Women's History, 15,* 90–116.

Bordo, S. (1993). *Unbearable weight.* Berkeley: University of California Press.

Bordo, S. (1989). The body and the reproduction of femininity. In A. Jaggar & S. Bordo (Eds.), *Gender, body, knowledge* (pp. 13–33). New Brunswick, NJ: Rutgers University Press.

Bourdieu, P. (1984). *Distinction.* (Trans., R. Nice). London: Routledge.

Braverman, H. (1974). *Labor and monopoly capital.* New York: Monthly Review Press.

Buzzanell, P. M. (2000). *Rethinking organizational and managerial communication from feminist perspectives.* Thousand Oaks, CA: Sage.

Cheney, G., Wilhelmsson, M., & Zorn, T., Jr. (2002). 10 strategies for engaged scholarship. *Management Communication Quarterly, 16,* 92–100.

Clair, R. P. (1993). The bureaucratization, commodification, and privatization of sexual harassment through institutional discourse. *Management Communication Quarterly, 7,* 123–157.

Clair, R. P. (1996). The political nature of colloquialism, a "real job": Implications for organizational socialization. *Communication Monographs, 63,* 249–267.

Cockburn, C. (1991). *In the way of women: Men's resistance to sex equality in organization.* Ithaca, NY: ILR Press.

Collinson, D. (1988). Engineering humour: Masculinity, joking and conflict in shopfloor relations. *Organization Studies, 9,* 181–199.

Collinson, D. (1992). *Managing the shopfloor: Subjectivity, masculinity and workplace culture*. Berlin: de Gruyter.

Collinson, D. L. (1999). "Surviving the rigs": Safety and surveillance on North Sea oil installations. *Organization Studies, 20*, 579–600.

Collinson, D. (2003). Identities and insecurities: Selves at work. *Organization, 10, 527–547.*

Conlin, M., & Bernstein, A. (2004, May 31). Working . . . and poor. *Business Week*, pp. 58–68.

Connell, R. W. (1995). *Masculinities*. Berkeley: University of California Press.

Conrad, C., & McIntush, H. G. (2003). Organizational rhetoric and healthcare policymaking. In T. L. Thompson, A. M. Dorsey, K. I. Miller, & R. Parrott (Eds.), *Handbook of health communication* (pp. 403–443). Mahwah, NJ: Erlbaum.

Deetz, S. (1992). *Democracy in an age of corporate colonization*. Albany: State University of New York.

Deetz, S. (2003). Reclaiming the legacy of the linguistic turn. *Organization, 10, 421–429.*

du Gay, P. (1996). *Consumption and identity at work*. London: Sage.

du Gay, P., Hall, S., Janes, L., Mackay, H., & Negus, K. (1997). *Doing cultural studies: The story of the Sony Walkman*. Thousand Oaks, CA: Sage.

Ehrenreich, B. (2001). *Nickel and dimed: On not getting by in America*. New York: Metropolitan.

Flanagan, C. (2004, March). How serfdom saved the women's movement: Dispatches from the nanny wars. *Atlantic Monthly*, 109–128.

Foucault, M. (1977). *Discipline and punish: The birth of the prison*. (Trans., A. Sheridan). New York: Vintage.

Foucault, M. (1980). *The history of sexuality*. (Trans., R. Hurley). New York: Vintage.

Garsten, C., & Grey, C. (1997). How to become oneself: Discourses of subjectivity in post-bureaucratic organizations. *Organization, 4*, 211–228.

Giddens, A. (1984). *The constitution of society*. Berkeley: University of California Press.

Giddens, A. (1991). *Modernity and self-identity*. Stanford, CA: Stanford University Press.

Giddens, A. (1992). *The transformation of intimacy*. Cambridge: Polity Press.

Gillies, V., Harden, A., Johnson, K., Reavy, P., Strange, V., & Willig, C. (2004). Women's collective constructions of embodied practices through memory work: Cartesian dualism in memories of sweating and pain. *British Journal of Social Psychology, 43*, 99–112.

Goold, S. D. (1998). Money and trust: Relationships between patients, physicians, and health plans. *Journal of Health Politics, Policy and Law, 23*, 687–696.

Greenhouse, S., & Hays, C. L. (2004, June 23). Wal-Mart sex bias suit given class-action status. *New York Times*, A1.

Grimes, D. S. (2000). Essentialism and difference in community building. *Electronic Journal of Radical Organisation Theory, 6*, 1–12.

Gullette, M. M. (1997). *Declining to decline: Cultural combat and the politics of midlife*. Charlottesville: University Press of Virginia.

Haas, J. (1977). Learning real feelings: A study of high steel ironworkers' reactions to fear and danger. *Sociology of Work and Occupations, 4*(2), 147–170.

Hancock, P., & Tyler, M. (2000). Working bodies. In P. Hancock, B. Hughes, E. Jagger, K. Patterson, R. Russell, E. Tulle-Winton, & M. Tyler (Eds.), *The body, culture and society: An introduction* (pp. 84–100). Buckingham, UK: Open University Press.

Harter, L. M. (2004). Masculinity(s), the agrarian frontier myth, and cooperative ways of organizing: Contradictions and tensions in the experience and enactment of democracy. *Journal of Applied Communication Research, 32*, 89–118.

Hassard, J., Holliday, R., & Willmott, H. (2000). *Body and organization*. London: Sage.

Hochschild, A. (1983). *The managed heart: Commericialization of human feeling*. Berkeley: University of California Press.

Holmer Nadesan, M. (1996). Organizational identity and space of action. *Organizational Studies, 17*, 49–81.

Holmer Nadesan, M. (1997). Constructing paper dolls: The discourse of personality testing in organizational practice. *Communication Theory, 7*, 189–218.

Holmer Nadesan, M. (1999). The popular success literature and "A brave new Darwinian workplace." *Consumption, Markets and Culture, 3*, 27–60.

Holmer Nadesan, M., & Trethewey, A. (2000). Enterprising subjects: Gendered strategies of success. *Text and Performance Quarterly, 20*, 1–28.

Holt, M. (2003). Consumption, reflexibility, and the production of lesbian and gay identities. *Australian Journal of Psychology, 55* (Suppl.), 47.

Jagger, E. (2000). Consumer bodies. In P. Hancock, B. Hughes, E. Jagger, K. Patterson, R. Russell, E. Tulle-Winton, & M. Tyler (Eds.), *The body, culture and society: An introduction* (pp. 45–63). Buckingham, UK: Open University Press.

Kirby, E. (2000). Should I do as you say, or do as you do? Mixed messages about work and family (Article 3400). *Electronic Journal of Communication, 10.* Retrieved February 24, 2002, from www.cios.org/getfile/KIRBY_V10N3400

Kirby, E., & Krone, K. (2002). "The policy exists but you can't really use it": Communication and the structuration of work-family politics. *Journal of Applied Communication Research, 30*, 50–77.

Knights, D. (1990). Subjectivity, power and the labour process. In D. Knights & H. Willmott (Eds.), *Labour process theory* (pp. 297–335). London: Macmillan.

Kramer, M. W., & Hess, J. (2002). Communication rules for the display of emotions in organizational settings. *Management Communication Quarterly, 16*, 66–80.

LeGreco, M. (2002). *The politics of organizing public and private: A case study of the first governor-mom.* Unpublished master's thesis, Arizona State University, Tempe.

LeGreco, M. (2005, February). *Playing with our food: Consumption as communication in the constitution of culture.* Paper presented at the annual meeting of the Western States Communication Association, San Francisco, CA.

Martin, B. (1988). Feminism, criticism and Foucault: In I. Diamond & L. Quinby (Eds.), *Feminism and Foucault: Reflections on resistance* (pp. 3–19). Boston: Northeastern University Press.

Martin, J. (1990). Deconstructing organizational taboos: The suppression of gender conflict in organizations. *Organization Science, 1*, 339–359.

Marshall, J. (1993). Viewing organizational communication from a feminist perspective. A critique and some offerings. In S. Deetz (Ed.), *Communication yearbook* (Vol. 16, pp. 122–143). Newbury Park, CA: Sage.

Monaghan, L. F. (2002). Hardmen, shop boys and others: Embodying competence in a masculinist occupation. *Sociological Review, 50*, 334–355.

Mumby, D. K. (1997). The problem of hegemony: Rereading Gramsci for organizational communication studies. *Western Journal of Communication, 61*, 343–375.

Mumby, D. K., (1998). Organizing men: Power, discourse, and the social construction of masculinity(s) in the workplace. *Communication Theory, 8*, 164–183.

Mumby, D. K., & Putnam, L. L. (1992). The politics of emotion: A feminist reading of bounded rationality. *Academy of Management Review, 17*, 465–486.

Murphy, A. G. (1998). Hidden transcripts of flight attendant resistance. *Management Communication Quarterly, 11*, 499–535.

Murphy, A. G. (2003). The dialectical gaze: Exploring the subject-object tension in the performances of women who strip. *Journal of Contemporary Ethnography, 32*, 305–335.

Peters, T. J., & Waterman, R. H. (1982). *In search of excellence.* New York: Harper & Row.

Peterson, L. W., & Albrecht, T. (1999). Deconstructing organizational maternity leave policy. *Journal of Management Inquiry, 8*, 168–181.

Pratt, M., & Doucet, L. (2000). Ambivalent feelings in organizational relationships. In S. Fineman (Ed.), *Emotions in organizations* (2nd ed., pp. 204–226). Thousand Oaks, CA: Sage.

Rose, S. O. (1991). "From behind the women's petticoats": The English Factory Act of

1874 as a cultural production. *Journal of Historical Sociology, 4,* 33–51.

Scheibel, D. (1996). Appropriating bodies: Organ(izing) ideology and cultural practice in medical school. *Journal of Applied Communication Research, 24,* 310–331.

Scott, C. W. (2005). *The discursive organization of workplace safety and risk.* Unpublished doctoral dissertation, Arizona State University, Tempe.

Shakespeare, P. (2003). Nurses' bodywork: Is there a body of work? *Nursing Inquiry, 10,* 47–56.

Sinclair, A. (2005). Body and management pedagogy. *Gender, Work and Organization, 12,* 89–104.

Spellers, R. E. (1998). Happy to be Nappy: Embracing an Afrocentric Aesthetic of Beauty. In J. N. Martin, T. K. Nakayama, & L. A. Flores (Eds.), *Readings in cultural contexts* (pp. 70–78). Mountain View, CA: Mayfield.

Tavris, C. (1992). *The mismeasure of woman.* New York: Touchstone.

Townley, B. (1994). *Reframing human resource management: Power, ethics and the subject at work.* London. Sage.

Tracy, S. J. (2002). Altered practice — altered stories — altered lives: Three considerations for translating organizational communication scholarship into practice. *Management Communication Quarterly, 16,* 85–91.

Tracy, S. J., & Scott, C. W. (in press). Sexuality, masculinity and taint management among firefighters and correctional officers: Getting down and dirty with "America's heroes" and the "scum of law enforcement. *Management Communication Quarterly.*

Tracy, S. J., & Trethewey, A. (2005). Fracturing the real-self ←→ fake-self dichotomy: Moving toward "crystallized" organizational discourses and identities. *Communication Theory, 15,* 168–195.

Trethewey, A. (1997). Resistance, identity, and empowerment: A postmodern feminist analysis of a human service organization. *Communication Monographs, 64,* 281–301.

Trethewey, A. (1999). Disciplined bodies: Women's embodied identities at work. *Organization Studies, 20,* 423–450.

Trethewey, A. (2000). Revisioning control: A feminist critique of disciplined bodies. In P. M. Buzzanell (Ed.), *Rethinking organizational and managerial communication from feminist perspectives* (pp. 107–126). Thousand Oaks, CA: Sage.

Trethewey, A. (2001). Reproducing and resisting the master narrative of decline: Midlife professional women's experience of aging. *Management Communication Quarterly, 15,* 183–226.

Trethewey, A. (2002). Translating scholarship into practice. *Management Communication Quarterly, 16,* 81–84.

Trethewey, A., & Ashcraft, K. L. (2004). Practicing disorganization: The development of applied perspectives on living with tension. *Journal of Applied Communication Research, 32,* 81–88.

Twitchell, J. (2000). Two cheers for materialism. In J. B. Schor & D. B. Holt (Eds.), *The consumer society reader* (pp. 281–290). New York: New Press.

Van Dongen, E., & Elema, R. (2001). The art of touching: The culture of "body work" in nursing. *Anthropology & Medicine, 8,* 149–162.

Willis, P. (1981). *Learning to labor: How working class kids get working class jobs.* New York: Columbia University Press.

Weedon, C. (1997). *Feminist practice and poststructuralist theory* (2nd ed.). London: Blackwell.

Wesely, J. K. (2003). Exotic dancing and the negotiation of identity: The multiple uses of body technologies. *Journal of Contemporary Ethnography, 32,* 643–669.

Zoller, H. M. (2003a). Health on the line: Identity and disciplinary control in occupational health and safety discourse. *Journal of Applied Communication Research, 31,* 118–139.

Zoller, H. M. (2003b). Working out: Managerialism in workplace health promotion. *Management Communication Quarterly, 17,* 171–205.

8

LOVE, SEX, AND TECH IN THE GLOBAL WORKPLACE

◆ Nikki C. Townsley

*N*ew York Times* columnist and author Thomas Friedman (2005) recently declared, "The world is flat." Friedman was struck with this epiphany while interviewing Nandan Nilekani, CEO of Infosys Technologies, for his documentary on outsourcing in Bangalore, India, one of the world's high-tech capitals. While the two were conversing in the Infosys video-conferencing room complete with a wall-size, flat-screen TV capable of projecting all members of the company's global supply chain simultaneously, Nilekani proclaimed, "Tom, the playing field is being leveled."

This statement led Friedman to explore further how globalization has opened business opportunities to nonwhite, non-Western, Southern, or third world populations. Since 2000, he contends, a variety of "flatteners" such as outsourcing, "offshoring," and "supply-chaining" have facilitated a "global, Web-enabled playing field that allows for multiple forms of collaboration on research and work in real time, without regard to geography, distance, or in the near future, even language." According to Friedman (2005), the globalists' dream of open access has been fulfilled: "You can innovate without having to emigrate."

Proponents of globalization repeatedly espouse tales of a newfound, global prosperity. Multinational firms operate in foreign locales in abundance, providing jobs and wages where there were none. Traditional

◆ 143

state-run services are increasingly becoming deregulated and privatized, opening formerly sacrosanct public institutions to new market players. Services and knowledge-based work are replacing manufacturing, facilitating more innovation in work design and meeting consumer demands. Information technology communications continue to dismantle time, space, and even cultural boundaries, allowing faster, more responsive, and ultimately more effective business cycles. Yet, while some scholars and lay authors alike point to these neoliberal arguments as proof the digital divide is dead and the market is a panacea, the extent to which globalization actually flattens power relations and facilitates equal access and opportunity remains questionable. In fact, some scholars suggest just the opposite.

Critics argue that the rise in high-level professionals in service-related firms, for example, contributes significantly to socioeconomic inequality among workers and nations alike (Sassen, 2000). The free-agent professional sector full of individuals who travel from firm to firm across the globe, sharing their continually refined "portfolio" of knowledge has grown in concert with the "informalization" of production activities necessary to support the former (Sassen, 2005). Globalization entails a "whole infrastructure of activities, firms, and jobs which are necessary to run the advanced corporate economy" (p. 31), including networks of subcontractors, home workers, and night workers whose contributions underpin the more trendy and talked about shifts in today's global workplace.

In this chapter, I explore three oft-neglected work industries that make up the behind-the-scenes work of globalization. I hope to reiterate the importance of a gendered lens for studying changes in the global division of labor. Whether global commerce embodies, maintains, and/or contests discrimination based on gender, race, class, ethnicity, sexuality, religion, and nationality continues to motivate my own thinking about the relationship among gender, work,

and globalization. Who benefits in the global labor market? Whose interests dominate? How are those interests gendered? And while the limited scope of this paper prevents any definitive answers to these questions, scholarship has begun to provide insight into the complex processes and practices that constitute the popular yet misunderstood subjects of globalization and global work trends. By examining this interdisciplinary research, we begin to see globalization and the global division of labor as a set of relationships among institutions, states, organizations, and populations—relationships that clearly draw upon long-standing, traditional assumptions of gender in their shaping of new forms and types of work as well as newly articulated representations of it in what is being called the New Economy. I will review some of the recent, compelling research on gender, work, and globalization in the hope of expanding the scope of gendered organizational communication studies to include what I refer to as love, sex, and tech in the global workplace.

◆ Globalizing Gendered Organizational Communication Studies

The long-standing tradition of treating *organization* as a composite of hierarchy and distinct job roles within a constant sociohistorical context has led organization scholars to rethink the term. Wanting to dismantle the bricks-and-mortar metaphor whereby organizational communication is "contained" within four walls, scholars have started to "bring work back in" (Barley & Kunda, 2001) and to refocus attention on occupation (see Ashcraft this volume). Yet, as Ashcraft notes, when occupation has been the starting point for analysis, our attention has been primarily limited to professional work in traditionally male-dominated fields. Even the most recent analyses of occupation assume a professional self for whom choice is a given and not a product of changing institutional, economic, and cultural conditions.

Other research points to the contemporary rise in alternative work arrangements that traverse traditional conceptions of organization, occupation, career, and work history (see Buzzanell, 2000). *Contingent labor,* an umbrella term that refers to a continuum of employment contracts and relations, provides an apt context in which to examine substantive changes in work organization. The term references a range of employment relationships: part-time, temporary, leased, contract, and outsourced contracts. Yet while the label provides a useful linguistic handle to help grasp the elusive nature of contemporary work, it also obscures the complexities of it, particularly the gendering of emerging trends in labor and work organization.

Much scholarly attention has been given to the global economy, particularly from an economic or managerial framework. As feminist scholars have noted, globalization studies have overwhelmingly focused on the economic restructuring of global capital in universal markets or the primacy of information technology in a global economy (Susser, 1997). Sassen (2000) notes the overwhelming focus on upper circuits of capital. Drawing on Spivak's "capitalocentrism," Bergeron (2001) challenges "globalocentric" perspectives that take the inevitable, deterministic, and unified presumption of globalization for granted. In response, many feminist scholars are reasserting the centrality of gender to globalization studies (Acker, 2004).

While there has always been diversity within feminist theory, early theorizing often drew upon *woman* as a construct as part of the effort to establish solidarity as well as credibility in the academy. However, as women of color as well as multicultural and global feminists have pointed out, Woman as a rallying cry has actually been politically divisive and exclusionary. They argue that the power of gender relations is precisely that—relational. We can only understand gender oppression in relationship to other axes of power such as race, ethnicity, religion, class, occupation, marital status, education, and nationality. Furthermore, these interlocking systems must be analyzed within their specific political, social, economic, cultural, and historical contexts. They must be understood in relation to the multinationals, nongovernmental organizations, nation states, and regional networks of which they are a part. Astute analyses even question whether the concept of the nation state holds water at this historical juncture as compared with other conceptual boundaries, such as North-South, developed-developing, or first world-third world, and their relationship to gender (Kim-Puri, 2005).

We can trace an evolution within gender studies. Its focus has shifted from gender as a sex binary to its being dynamic and communicatively constructed through interaction with others (Townsley, 2003). Gender relations are produced and sustained at multiple levels of production; the cases that follow show that they produce global divisions of labor that reflect local and regional meanings. The complex networks within a gendered political economy are continually being remade, and the dimensions of these transformations can be globally mapped as well (Steans, 1999).

It is important to note the limits of a structural approach to the emerging gendered, global division of labor, an approach that minimizes actors' (women's) agency and ability to fashion (or refashion) transformative identities and subjectivities in otherwise constrained conditions. Feminist scholars in particular have shifted their focus to places where women are both actors and beneficiaries of globalizing processes, including, for example, informal-sector work that challenges or disrupts multinational capital (Bergeron, 2001). From their perspective, the discourse and practice of flexibility so prevalent in contemporary work organization provides both risk *and* opportunity for the workforce (Smith, 1997). The integral flexibility of contingent labor may indeed benefit one worker yet displace another; thus, our theorizing about it must be flexible enough to account for the mixed and uneven results of processes of globalization that unfold across and within continents, countries, and constituents.

In what follows, I explore three areas of so-called women's work, conceived through the frame of love, sex, and tech. To do so is to risk reifying global femininities. Mohanty (2002) warns of reproducing clichéd representations of the

> ubiquitous global teenage girl factory worker, the domestic worker, and the sex worker. There is also the migrant/immigrant service worker, the refugee, the victim of war crimes, the woman-of-color prisoner who happens to be mother and drug user, the consumer-housewife, and so on. There is also the mother-of-the-nation/religious bearer of traditional cultural and morality. (p. 527)

My goal is not to reify accounts of globalization that stymie the complexity of "woman". I agree with Mohanty (2002) that "all women are workers, mothers, or consumers in the global economy, but we are also all those things simultaneously" (p. 527). Rather than simply theorizing about sex work as women's work, it is important to map the power relations that constitute the networks of these gendered industries whereby divisions of worker/consumer, public/private, local/global, and masculinity/femininity are problematized.

Postmodern feminists have actively resisted the binaries of public/private, third/first world, global/local, and Western/non-Western by mapping circuits of power in global politics. Their work seeks to undermine the conflation of the global with the masculine and economic, the local with the feminine and culture (Freeman, 2001) by analyzing the interrelationships between and within these categories and focusing on the flows not just of capital but of people. Sassen (2000) refers to cross-border circuits or flows of migration and illegal trafficking in people as "counter-geographies of globalization."

By counter-geographies, Sassen suggests that networks of workers are simultaneously a dominant, even institutionalized component of the global market and part of the unassuming shadow economy as well. Sassen would shift the focus away from the mobile professionals who jet around the globe to the reproductive work that is necessary to support their time-space flexibility (Willis & Yeoh, 2000). Immigrant and migrant women, for example, move to what Sassen (2005) calls the "global cities" to provide the food, clothing, hotel, dry cleaning, child care, and sex services that professional workers demand. According to Sassen, it is precisely these circuits or flows of persons and services that need to be examined, right alongside the knowledge workers, as the work of globalization. Not only are these circuits underrepresented in discourses of globalization (as well as organizational communication research), but women's strategies for survival actually constitute major dynamics within the context of economic globalization. For example, in the Philippines, state-sponsored emigration programs abound as a means to address foreign debt and unemployment, and women's remittances from work abroad (both formal and informal) as domestic workers, nurses, entertainers, and even mail-order brides represent well over a third of the state's revenue (Sassen, 2005).

We are witnessing the expansion and development of a new, international, gendered division of labor. What the United Nations Human Development Program has termed the "globalization of care" (see Ehrenreich, 2002) demonstrates the gendering of work and the globalizing of gendered work. Multiple actors (institutional and informal) at multiple scales—the home to the supranational organization—continually interact to produce circuits of survival. Rather than focus solely on the effects of globalization, such as how men and women are treated differently in global restructuring, more interesting analyses are shifting their lenses to discourses that themselves constitute the practices and processes of globalization. Rather than taking globalization (or gender) as a given, static reality, Larner (2002) refocuses toward discursive analyses of "the forms of expertise and practices through which new political-economic objects and subjects are constituted . . . [and in particular how] feminized labour forces are constituted in the name of 'globalization'" (p. 651). She elaborates further, "the globalizing of economies, and the labour forces that emerge, are likely to involve multiple actors, novel techniques, and more idiosyncratic processes than is often recognized" (p. 655). It is precisely these communicative processes that I explore in the following cases of love, sex, and tech in the global workplace.

COMMODIFYING LOVE: THE GROWTH OF A GLOBAL INDUSTRY OF CARE

"Oh, congratulations!" a friend exclaimed. Sarah, a white upper-class American professional, grabbed my arms and urged, "You must consider hiring a nanny now that you'll have *two* babies under 2 years old!"

"Ah, I don't know if I want to be a part of a system that . . . ," I interjected while backing up slightly.

As if on a crusade, Sarah moved forward and continued, "First of all, you need time to write. You need to think of your career. Try an au pair. These women are looking for sponsors to come to the U.S. to earn a living and get an education. And you can hire one for less than the cost of day care for two kids!"

"Perhaps, but the idea of hiring another woman to care for my kids is, well, unsettling for me, particularly as a feminist," I countered, wishing she'd hear my concerns.

"Hogwash," Sarah admonished, "you need the time to work, and they need the work. It's a win-win situation. Look at my friend Elsa who hired an older Mexican woman to care for her three kids. Elsa wanted her children to be bilingual, and the nanny, I think her name was Esmeralda, helped teach the kids Spanish. Elsa also paid Esmeralda to return to Mexico several times a year so she could visit her own family. It was so clear when I visited that Esmeralda *loved* Elsa's babies as if they were her own."

As Sarah continued to extol the benefits of employing an international nanny, I found myself confronted with the politics of globalization in my own living room. The discourse of global care work had become so naturalized that even my progressive friends were parroting the arguments. Nannies earn more money working abroad than they ever could at home. Their birth children depend upon their wages for food and shelter. Employers' children benefit from special nanny love, and they learn a foreign language. And the nanny's presence allows the employer to pursue career success without the constraints of daily child care. In this discourse, both women—the employer and the nanny—are discursively positioned as beneficiaries in a global exchange. Yet, racist and essentialist claims about women are reified. While some women may indeed benefit, the discourse of global care work obscures the larger politics of global migration.

Global neoliberalism is often described as a dualistic system of Northern creditors and Southern debtors in which the "global indentured servitude" of the South to the North is produced and maintained, often through the World Bank and the International Monetary Fund (IMF). Southern women may leave their families to work as paid domestic laborers for Northern women and their children.[1] These care workers often migrate through informal networks of acquaintances, friends, and family, or via state-sponsored programs that seek to maximize remittances from female migrants to develop otherwise stagnant national economies or fill weak labor pools. Indeed, both home families and nation states alike wait in anticipation of the growing wealth to be made from this form of global servitude.

Labor migration is not new, and the growth of female migrants is astonishing.

Females now are 60% to 80% of legal migrants deployed to other countries from, for example, the Philippines, Indonesia and Sri Lanka (Asis, Huang, & Yeoh, 2004, p. 203). Female Filipino migrants have risen from being 12% of those deployed in 1975 to being the majority today (Asis et al., 2004). Because of national initiatives meant to ameliorate labor shortages, some East and Southeast Asian countries such as Singapore and Hong Kong (along with Canada and the United States) have become top destinations for Filipino migrants. Overwhelmingly, the specific jobs taken up by migrant women are domestic and care-based.

Lan's (2003) conception of domestic labor is particularly helpful here. She urges scholars to reconsider the feminization of domestic labor across public and private spheres by treating unpaid household labor and waged domestic work as existing on the same continuum. Her research on Filipina migrant workers in Taiwan demonstrates the fragility of treating both paid and unpaid labor as binaries. Filipinas work as paid domestic laborers but must also fulfill strict gendered responsibilities in their home family in the Philippines as well; they traverse the roles of housewife and breadwinner. Even single Filipinas who migrate for work are faced with familial responsibilities such as the sponsorship of their younger siblings' education. These women also must weigh and evaluate the roles of unpaid labor and waged work when contemplating marriage proposals from employers. Fully aware that they will be required to do domestic chores as a wife, as they did as a maid (or nanny), without an income, many still choose marriage because of the social or nonmaterial benefits of international marriages. The women shift from waged labor to a labor of love. As Lan notes, "migrant domestic workers not only travel across national borders but also march through the public-private divide of domestic labor, struggling with the unsolvable equation of money and love" (p. 205). Thus, the global care industry depends on both the geographic mobility of Southern women and the commodification of love for its continued success.

While many industries market care, be they major health institutions or local day care centers, nanny work is differentiated by its occurrence within a private home and its status as an ongoing relationship of pseudo-maternal love and intimacy (Tronto, 2003). In this sense it is sequestered from the work-a-day world of the marketplace by its geography and its normative rules for engagement. Whereas the market demands alienation and competition, nannies' work is the fragile performance of love and devotion, performed as a family member, as it were. As Hochschild (2002) demonstrates in her research on Filipina nannies in California, nanny love, particularly in the United States, is not the imported resource of "happy peasant mothering" often described by Anglo American women. It is "a love that partly develops on American shores, informed by an American ideology of mother-child bonding and fostered by intense loneliness and longing for their own children" (Hochschild, 2002, p. 24). As one of her participants in the nanny study, María Gutierrez, says about her employer's child, "I love Ana more than my own two children. Yes, more! It's strange, I know. But I have time to be with her. I'm paid. I am lonely here. I work 10 hours a day, with one day off. I don't know any neighbors on the block. And so this child gives me what I need" (Hochschild, 2002, p. 24). María's narrative contextualizes the production of nanny love and challenges the very gendered and racist assumptions built into the discourse of global care work. Maria's mother, having lost four babies to miscarriage and death and having worked on a farm all her life, was less than warm. Maria didn't know the tale of maternal love until she manufactured it herself in America. According to Hochschild, imperialism resurfaces in this exchange, whereby "love and care become the new gold" (p. 26).

Geographers are also unearthing the politics of the growing mobile-care industry. Pratt (1999), for example, applies a poststructuralist lens to the enduring question of choice; namely, what occupational options do women have in the global labor market? She examines how university-educated Filipina nurses who travel to Vancouver, British Columbia through the Canadian Live-In Caregiver program end up occupationally segregated. Pratt identifies three particular discursive constructions—"supplicant, preimmigrants," "inferior housekeepers," and "husband stealers"—which, in addition to the "historical geographies of colonialism and racism" (p. 229), coalesce to circumscribe particular subject positions of marginality for Filipinas in Vancouver. That is, despite their training as registered nurses, domestic work was immediately inscribed on Filipina bodies by employers and the state alike. As one of Pratt's research participants, Joergie, states, "It's really difficult to integrate . . . So at the bus stop, because we're people of color . . . they'll ask you: so you're a nanny, right? . . . I find that racist, really" (Pratt, 1998, p. 289).

Pratt (1998) reveals counter discourses that "disrupt and repair" these imposed identities, including those of martyrdom and consumerism. She argues that the practice of Filipina domestic workers' remitting substantial portions of their income to their families in the Philippines helps detract from racist treatment by reaffirming their self-identity as martyr, or one who endures condescending, racist treatment by employers and society for the sake of others. She describes the martyrdom in terms of "the cultural norm of *utang na loob,*" debts of gratitude paid to kin caregivers to watch the household while the woman is overseas (Lan, 2003). Pratt (1998) also argues that other Filipina women assume confidence and self-assurance through discursive practices of consumerism, using earned income to partake in the spectacle of weekend mall shopping. While the practice of shopping could be easily be interpreted as reaffirming dominant cultural and gendered identities, Pratt's focus on resistant strategies affirms the varied and complex ways by which

women simultaneously affirm and rewrite discourses that shape labor market segregation across the globe.

Clearly the migration of female domestic labor challenges conceptions of what constitutes work in the so-called New Economy. As discussed above, migrant women traverse a variety of work and family roles, complicating traditional, bounded notions of both workplace and family. They perform family across borders and space, and for a variety of others, such as their birth family and their employer's family. They also negotiate a complex range of gendered, cultural, and raced identities along with their dual roles of breadwinner and mother. But it is not just their performances that must be considered when we examine the larger discourse of global care work. Indeed, this discourse relies upon and reflects longstanding meanings of *woman* that are classed and raced, and these meanings are produced in local contexts. Southern women hire nannies themselves and/or pay family members to care for their own children. And implicit throughout the framework are the absent-but-always-present fathers who contribute to the taken-for-granted gendered division of labor—in the home and the workplace. Thus, global care work must be examined through all of its networked links: the households who produce and employ care workers; the organizations that demand so much of professionals' time that they need help to balance work and family responsibilities; the nation-states that promote global migration; and the international organizations that govern global trade and regulations. All are implicated in the production and maintenance of the discourse and practices of gendered global care work.

MANUFACTURING DESIRE: MAPPING THE GLOBAL SEX WORK INDUSTRY

"Slim, sunburnt, and sweet, they love the white man in an erotic and devoted way.

They are masters of the art of making love by nature, an art that we Europeans [Whites, Westerners] do not know" (Life Travel [company], as cited in Bales, 2002, p. 226).

> Viola, a young Albanian, was 13 when she started dating 21-year-old Dilin, who proposed to marry her, then move to Italy where he had cousins who could get him a job. Arriving in Italy, Viola's life changed forever. Dilin locked her in a hotel room and left her, never to be seen again. A group of men entered, and began to beat Viola. Then, each raped her. The leader informed Viola that Dilin had sold her and that she had to obey him or else she would be killed. For seven days Viola was beaten and repeatedly raped. Viola was sold a second time to someone who beat her head so badly she was unable to see for two days She was told if she didn't work as a prostitute, her mother and sister in Albania would be raped and killed. Viola was forced to submit to prostitution until police raided the brothel she was in. She was deported to Albania. (U.S. Department of State, 2005)

My juxtaposition here of an advertisement for Swiss sex tourism and a personal narrative of trafficking demonstrate the complex and varied positions within another gendered, global discourse—sex work. Also referred to as trafficking in women, global sex work involves both the forced and voluntary movement of women and children within and across borders. Although some form of prostitution has always existed whereby an actor exchanges a sexual service for money or other valuables, the growth, magnitude, and the dispersed yet interconnected form of the contemporary global sex trade is unprecedented. According to U.S. State Department's 2005 *Trafficking in Persons* report, over a million children are exploited in the global sex trade. It is anticipated that hundreds of thousands of women and children will join the 10 million who are already caught every year in a global web of prostitution, sex slavery, and other forms of commercialized sexual exploitation. While some women and children find themselves trafficked unwillingly or unknowingly, others migrate in search of sex work in order to survive in otherwise failing economies. The practice of having to pay escorts to help them cross borders often binds these women to an unforgivable debt. Traffickers then demand payment by forcing the women into a brothel or street prostitution.

The geography of the global sex trade is far-reaching. Every continent and region has ties to it, with most nation states serving as sources, transit places, or destinations for sex workers. At the same time, parallels between the supplier and consumer states mirror larger divisions of global inequity. Central and Eastern Europe, Southeast Asia, South Korea, the Philippines, and Thailand remain dominant sources while Westerners remain leading consumers of sex tourism. Further, gendered and raced discourses about Southern women (e.g., they love in an erotic and devoted way; they are masters of making love by nature; they are sweet) also shape and are shaped by the production and maintenance of the global sex industry. Nevertheless, the women themselves resist classification. Their choices and navigation of the sex industry demonstrate the communicative tensions between what is considered voluntary or forced, prostitute or wife, local or global.

Yea's (2004) ethnographic research on Filipina entertainers in U.S. military camps in South Korea demonstrates the dynamic tensions that women cope with as they attempt to transition from identities as trafficked entertainers to runaway brides. Yea contends that research on transnational migrants, particularly Southeast Asian women, must "[re]focus on transformations and negotiations *between* migrants' roles, positions, identities and identifications" (p. 182). Trafficked Filipinas are more than a part of a particular labor regime (illegal, legal, and so on) or a particular role (bride, entertainer). Rather, they are women who face "anxieties of identity" as they continually traverse multiple subject positions globally. Filipinas do not want to return to their country of origin for fear of being stigmatized as sexually trafficked. At the same time, being labeled trafficked entertainers in Korean camp towns enhances their opportunities to develop relationships that could lead to marriage and a visa by encouraging GIs to enact the masculine ritual of the knight in shining armor. This identity, however, threatens these relationships because of the contradictory meanings that GIs hold of entertainer and bride.

Yea's (2004) research demonstrates the importance of local context in understanding the meanings and practices of global sex work. It shows how women are both subjugated *and* empowered by sex work discourse. Tambiah's (2005) research confirms women's tendency to be both objects and agents of gendered behaviors and sexualities. In response to a call by the women's wing of an authoritarian guerilla army to preserve Tamil culture through appropriate women's dress, Tambiah found that local women supported nationalist struggle, but some chose to resist rigid gender performances. Women simultaneously drew upon discourses of motherhood and domesticated femininity, transgressed these discourses through sex work or work as combatants. At the same time, the state stepped up its surveillance of brothels and sex workers in the name of protecting the morality of its culture, while also turning a blind eye to the use of prostitutes by the Sri Lankan armed forces. Multiple tensions contribute to the contradictory meanings and practice of sex work in Sri Lanka, demonstrating again the importance of local context in shaping global discourse.

Indeed, one of the greatest challenges in researching abstract forces or broad trends associated with globalization is localizing the discourse (see Burawoy et al., 2000). In an exemplary study of global sex tourism, Wonders and Michalowski (2001) demonstrate how "the actual practice of sex work reflects the positionality of each city within the global economy" (p. 565). Rather than focus on women as the problem, they trace the global connections among migration, tourism, and national economies to illustrate how these links facilitate "the commodification of both male desire and women's bodies within the global capitalist economy" (p. 546). Mobile sex workers (largely poor, Southern women) meet mobile sex consumers (mostly privileged Northern males) in global cities, reflecting and reconstituting (male) desire in moments of emotional, sensual, and sexual labor. Wonders and Michalowski adeptly illustrate the ways that mediating institutions, such as culture, tourism, the labor market, public policy and law, coalesce to shape local instantiations of global sex work. Their analysis leads them to suggest that

> what is new and noteworthy about global sex tourism is not "sex," "sex work," or even the commodification of bodies, but the extent to which sex work in specific locales is over-determined by broader global forces . . . [L]ocal infrastructures that shape the possibilities for sex tourism in Amsterdam and Havana increasingly reflect global, rather than local forces. (p. 565)

While sex work may appear different in practice and ideology depending on its location, identifiable, consistent global forces converge at these sites, including gendered and raced discourses of sexuality.

Although organizational scholars have examined the sexuality of organization, gendered global labor flows reiterate the need to expand the scholarly lens to include research on the global organization of sex work. Just as nanny work relies upon and is constituted through informal and formal networks at multiple scales, sex work has expanded owing to global forces of economics, labor, and law. It serves as a developmental strategy for states and households eager to generate revenue and/or foreign currency flows. Nations and supranational organizations such as the IMF also encourage particular practices as a solution to debt relief, indirectly increasing sex trade production. At the same time, nongovernmental organizations such as the Coalition Against Trafficking in Women work with other human rights as well as supranational organizations, such as the U.N., to combat sexual abuses and trafficking. Thus, the development, maintenance, and transformation of the global sex work industry clearly involve many actors, organizations, and nations and rely upon longstanding, taken-for-granted gendered and raced discourses of sexuality. Thai sex tourism provides an interesting sociohistorical example.

The sex trade in Thailand has grown out of collaborations between the United States and Thai militaries, the IMF, the World Bank, and the United Nations. The signing of the 1967 Recreation and Relaxation Contract, also referred to as the R&R, by Robert S. McNamara, the U.S. secretary of defense at that time, has been cited as a key step in the development of the Thai sex industry (Rogers, 1999). According to Rogers, the contract provided vacation furloughs for American soldiers fighting in Vietnam, resulting in Thailand's first sex-tour agency, Tommy Tours. Rogers explains that although the U.S. military did not cause the Thai sex industry to come to be; it contributed to the expansion of an already established, legal, localized practice. When the United States made plans to withdraw from Vietnam, the Thai government sought assistance from the World Bank to assuage economic collapse from the disappearance of tourist monies. When McNamara later became president of the World Bank, Thailand, with aid from the World Bank, the IMF, and private investors, became a global, tourist hotbed complete with its own airlines, hotels, and sex industry brokers. The prospect of dark, exotic women available to serve hard-working white men raised tourists' expectations. When the state became dependent upon dollars as a consequence and its economy collapsed in 1997, sex tourism became even cheaper for foreigners, leading to lower wages for workers.

In an interesting dialogue among an academician, policy advisor, agency coordinator, and sex worker representative, concepts involved in the organization of sex work were explored (see Brewis & Linstead, 2002). Types of work sites (parlors or brothels, street work and curb-crawling, and toleration zones) were discussed, and the identity of prostitute as worker was explored. They questioned whether prostitutes should be theorized as employees, asking how prostitution could be a job if workers' freedom and choice were limited? I find the question both interesting and disturbing.

Critical scholarship has long tried to understand how workers negotiate their identities and needs in relation to organizational interests and demands (Ashcraft, 1998; Ashcraft & Pacanowsky, 1996; Holmer Nadesan, 1996; Trethewey, 1997). Prostitutes are among those who negotiate their identities and struggle over the meanings of their work. But as much of the research attests, not all Southern women feel constrained by the conditions or available means of employment. In fact, many see the newfound global opportunities as simply that—opportunities in an otherwise economically constrained environment. Sex workers engage in practices and counter-discourses that challenge dominant perceptions, including, for example, discursively constructing sex work as simply a means to provide for their families, not as immoral or unjust (Steinfatt, 2002). As Sanders (2005) argues, sex workers "capitalize" on their sexuality for their personal economic gain through "calculated" efforts to manufacture the hetero-erotic identity that male clients seek. In the words of one of her participants, "It's just acting." Indeed, it is the gendered performances of the self, evinced in global nanny and sex work, that reappear yet again in global "phone work."

◆ Giving Good Phone: Organizing Gender in the Global Call Center

"Does she give good phone?" he asks nonchalantly.

I look up from my bowl of pasta with surprise. "Did he really just say that?" I think to myself. "I'm sorry. I was engrossed with my meal. Would you mind repeating that?" I ask the American software industry executive, John, sitting across the table from me.

"No problem. I was saying that we have a common question that we use in the industry to evaluate a person's ability to work as a telesales representative," he explains.

"And that question is, Does she give good phone?" I offer, hoping to be wrong.

"Correct!" John shouts a little too loudly for the restaurant patrons nearby. "That's it. Does she give good phone? After all, if she doesn't sound nice on the phone, she won't be able to woo our customers, and we'll lose money. It all starts with that first call."

I place my utensils down so I can give full attention to the man across the table. John explains that the expression she gave good phone refers to women's unique communication style.

He elaborates: "Women sound nice on the phone. Women talk with a lilt. They have a song-like quality to their voice. They have a softer approach, a softer language than men, and as a result are better able to establish a rapport with their audience."

I had asked John to dinner to discuss his firm's use of contingent labor, but I found myself engrossed in his gendered tales of recruitment. His reference to bottom-line business results (e.g., rapport with customers) seemed to justify the explicit practice of hiring women for telesales positions. Rather than being embarrassed or worried about the organization's blatant sexism, he naturalized the norm by essentializing women as naturally sweet-sounding and empathetic, and thus profitable. However, when pushed further, John assured me that he never asked women directly whether or not they gave good phone; this shop floor talk remained within the boundaries of the boys' club at work. Thus, while he reifies women in pursuit of profit, he also recognizes that this discourse ought to stay "in the company of men." In that way, organizational goals are furthered as they are hidden so that the firm is protected from lawsuits based on gender or sexual harassment.

Giving good phone clearly extends the gendered meaning of smiling down the phone to include sexuality. The linguistic efficiency of this second phrase simultaneously confers a persona of women as naturally nice (virgins) and permits men's fantasy of the naughty female (the whore on the 1-900 line) to exist simultaneously. Hence, normative heterosexuality is confirmed in the business setting. As John told me, "I have a man as my telesales rep, but I would never ask, 'Does he give good phone?'" The question would never arise, for it would shatter the natural imagery of female-to-male sexuality and threaten organizational masculinities with unnatural homoeroticism. A seemingly simple question discursively produces and reflects the gendered and (hetero)sexed meanings of telesales work—a newly expanding work trend illustrated in the global call center organization.

Global call centers have only recently begun to receive both academic and lay attention. They can be described as technology-intensive offices where customer service is done over the phone instead of in face-to-face interactions. Call centers are part of the spectrum of services associated with a range of industries, including health care, tourism, and sales, in both public and private sectors worldwide (Glucksmann, 2004). Call centers are diverse in their operations, though scholars note the uniformity of their organization (Frenkel, Tam, Korczynski, & Shire, 1998). These researchers address how call centers exemplify the rise of services over production, and some praise them as "nurseries of a new form of work," particularly in their technological applications (Wickham & Collins, 2004, p. 1). The Automated Call Distribution System (ACDS), for example, routes customer calls to available call center operatives, also called agents, in a computerized effort to minimize customer waiting and regulate agents' use of organizational scripts (Frenkel et al., 1998). We are familiar with ACDS routing: "Welcome to

[X corporation]. If you would like to speak to a customer service representative, please press 1" as we seek help in making reservations, fixing computer glitches, and even disputing parking tickets!

While the U.S. media debate the offshoring of American labor, Western multinational organizations continue to move more telephone customer services to remote sites. Taylor and Bain's (2005) analysis suggests that cost reduction and language are driving the rise of offshore call center organization. They argue that India has become a popular call center relocation destination in part because businesses save 40% to 60% after migrating work processes to cities such as Bangalore or Mumbai. English language education through their primary and secondary schools prepares Indians to manage customer service interactions with other English speakers. Taylor and Bain also note, however, that recent research contradicts the notion of seamless communication based on a shared language between Indian call center agents and Western or Northern customers. Nevertheless, the business mind-set favoring offshore customer service captures multiple elements of work in the new economy.

Call center work demonstrates the fragile boundaries between consumption and production, space and place (Glucksmann, 2004). Customers communicate with call center agents in different lands, languages, and time zones, breaking down the boundaries of time and space. Phone performance involves interactive service work that sells the self. Both the process and the product are being sold, much like nanny and sex work performances. Agents often adopt an American accent, an American name, and perform a script to construct a particular service identity sought by Western customers. Some go so far as to suggest that their ability to smile down the phone is more paramount than skill or product knowledge in call center work. Personality, emotionality, and sociality are cited as requisite traits for service positions and are operationalized by management in order to measure sales effectiveness (Taylor & Bain,

1999). Yet, although the emotional labor necessary for these performances may appear natural for women, this construction requires extra emotion work for all call center agents, male and female. Heavy workloads and the banality of work tasks are part of why customer service interactions have been found to contribute to emotional stress and exhaustion in call center work (Deery, Iverson, & Walsh, 2002). While they place great emphasis on providing emotional support, organizations continue to devalue the skills in customer services compared with the technical skills in support jobs typically held by men (Belt, Richardson, & Webster, 2002).

Research confirms the gendering of recruitment in call centers discussed earlier. Women are indeed sought and hired for agent positions due in part to the perception of feminine abilities (Belt et al., 2002; Collinson, 1987). According to research by Belt et al. (2002), managers and workers both report highly gendered assumptions about females' and males' abilities to communicate and handle highly controlled and routinized jobs. Despite the gendered meanings that are embodied, practiced, and even manipulated in this global trend, little research has examined the gendering of call center work organization (for an exception see Belt & Richardson, 2000). Research on power and control and on the dialectic of power and resistance could prove fruitful for future gendered analyses in call center organization.

Tayloristic or traditional control methods have been cited as central to call center organization. Using panoptical forms of surveillance, management watches the open office and listens in on service calls (Bain & Taylor, 2000; Wickham & Collins, 2004). Scholars note the use of point systems and even standardized tests to measure agents' product knowledge as other forms of control at work (Winiecki, 2004). Just as we are familiar with being asked to press a number on our telephones to receive a service, we also know the warning that "your call may be monitored," supposedly to improve customer service. The agent's "footprint" on a call is measured for target times and results, which are then tallied and publicized on an electronic call center wallboard for all agents and managers to see (Wickham & Collins, 2004, p. 5). The work can be likened to a virtual relationship between caller and agent that occurs "down the telephone" and is mediated by high speed data links that collect information to be used by management to refine service and discipline workers (Marshall & Richardson, 1996).

Recent research on call centers has shifted from a focus on power as surveillance to studies of concertive control. In this sense, control is achieved as agents come to positively identity with organizational goals and objectives, while some go so far as to regulate call quality by monitoring peers as well (Knights & McCabe, 2003). These studies illustrate how traditional command-and-control practices work with teamwork and other forms of concertive control in the post-bureaucratic call center organization (Callaghan, 2001; van den Broek, 2004). These studies may shed light on the omnipresent question in organization studies: what is new about New Economy work? From a power perspective, traditional and concertive forms of control coexist and even work in concert in contemporary call centers. What is old continues but in new and complex forms. At the same time, workers are not mere cogs in the machine. Research suggests that call center agents actively resist the attempts of organizational control at the individual, even collective level.

Mulholland's (2004) study explores how Irish call center workers engage in a variety of everyday practices to resist inequitable structures of the organization. Called *scammin,'* through tactics of work avoidance such as smoking, absenteeism, and faking sales calls (by simply talking to answering machines and recording these as sales), workers resist the amount of value that management might otherwise seek to extract from them. Their informal, collective actions

therefore challenge contemporary theories that stress the "increasing individualization of worker experience" in new economy work (p. 720). If they are fined for straying too far from the scripted sales formulas even in, ironically, successful customer calls, workers reacted by "working to rule" or withdrawing their emotional labor and giving perfunctory performances (p. 717). Callaghan and Thompson (2001) also document how call center agents resist organizational control through customer communications. In each of these studies, one can see that a dualistic understanding of control and resistance is tacitly maintained. Acts of resistance are heralded, while call center work organization continues and larger power relations remain intact. As Mumby (2005) states, current research on control and resistance tends to "adopt an incipient functionalism" that depicts subjects as pseudo-heroes in their subordinate roles while still ineffectual in their ability to efface changes to dominant systems of power (p. 37). Given the growth and ubiquity of control and surveillance in new economy work regimes as exemplified in call center organization (Wickham & Collins, 2004), Mumby (2005) calls for "the study of resistance as a set of situated discursive and nondiscursive practices that are simultaneously enabling and constraining, coherent and contradictory, complex and simple, efficacious and ineffectual" (p. 38). For example, Ashcraft's study of commercial airline pilots demonstrates how male professionals negotiate narratives of decline in a changing industry by actively maintaining historical images or identities of pilot as (hyper)masculine. They simultaneously resist control through the masculinization of their work as they consent to contemporary industry mandates. Ashcraft's study reveals not merely the ways professionals (a seemingly privileged occupational group) resist, but how gendered discourses of work are always malleable and unstable, and thus subject to change.

While call centers have been defined as nurseries of work innovation that utilize combinations of Tayloristic control through automated distribution technologies, surveillance through visual as well as technical panoptic tactics, and market-supervision and emotional labor through customer call performances (Wickham & Collins, 2004), analyses of the gendered discourses of call center work remain largely absent. As I outlined, this omission is odd given the prevalence of women in the field as well as the gendered assumptions that constitute service work in the first place. Rapid growth and global expansion coupled with the travel or export of gendered beliefs of women's abilities demand further attention. What has been studied confirms the former software executive's narrative. The intensity of recruitment processes that target particular social skills, such as bubbly personalities, reflects the feminized trend of seeking and hiring women to give good phone in call center work—despite national place! Women agents themselves have come to internalize and reproduce these gendered assumptions of skill and ability: they confess to invoking "femininity on the phone" in order to manipulate customers (Belt et al., 2002). Management and agents alike maintain the value of women's superior "people skills," and at the same time report frustration with their limited ability to use such skills in a fast paced, neo-assembly-line call center environment (Belt et al., 2002). Thus, women are simultaneously rewarded in the new economy with the opportunity for new (call center) jobs, only to find themselves pigeonholed into highly constrained, routinized work that offers relatively low financial rewards (compared to other avenues of new economy work). One is quickly reminded of the claim that the global playing field is now level. Indeed, in all of the aforementioned forms of women's work, possibilities are held as the proverbial carrot. Upon further analysis, the contradictions embedded within these opportunities reveal themselves, demonstrating the promise and peril, risk and opportunity, and infinite contradictions for contemporary women workers.

◆ Considering the Future of Global, Gendered Organization Studies

The literature review suggests a need for further analysis. Glucksmann (2004) calls for a new perspective on call centers that "can position and contextualize them within the overall configuration of production/distribution/exchange/consumption of which they are a part" (p. 798). I would argue that the same perspective could and should be adopted for all New Economy work relationships. While I have focused on three particular occupations, more research is necessary to understand the political, social, cultural, and economic interconnections and interdependencies between and across categories of exchange. If gender and other axes of power are to be understood *relationally,* an explicit focus on the men and masculinities that co-constitute love, sex, and tech work must accompany studies of global gender-divisions of labor. As Jackson (1999) notes, the Western ideal of a unitary individual with rights to work fails conceptually in societies where work and the lack thereof is conceived and enacted in more social terms. For example, how do Southern men negotiate a sense of work identities when their wives and mothers leave the birth family to care for Northerners' children, particularly when economic conditions leave them with fewer opportunities for employment than the women? What Northern masculinities contribute to the demand for Southern nannies in the first place? Does women's and/or men's enactment of agency contribute to the maintenance and/or challenge of traditional gender divisions of labor (Connell, 2000)?

Clearly, women's work is a highly contested category. The phrase has served to reify particular tasks as more feminine and subsequently less valued in the overall political economy of work. One of the major problems of categorizing work by sex is that the labels mirror the larger hierarchy whereby men and men's work are more highly valued societally and financially. Yet, even the gendered hierarchy of power so taken for granted in Western theories of dominance becomes unstable in global accounts. This is where gendered organization scholarship offers particular value in being able to parse out the locally situated discursive practices that constitute larger global discourses of hope and despair in the New Economy. At the same time, organizational scholars must heed the call to frame their analyses within the larger political economies, societies, and cultures of which their studies are but a part. Only then can we explore the interconnections of power, context, and histories that constitute a range of contemporary alternative work arrangements in both the dominant global economy and the shadow infrastructure that supports it.

Several interconnections have been identified in this chapter on love, sex, and tech in the global workplace. The gendered discourses of care, desire, and communication arise not only out of local contexts and practices but from traditional understandings of women's work and from contemporary shifts in the global labor market and economy. These insights provide distinct challenges (and opportunities!) for future studies. I want to focus on two scholarly avenues—communicating gendered economics and gendered (in)visibility—that should be further pursued.

Throughout the studies of global nanny work, sex work, and call center labor, economics continues to be a central shaper of occupational choice. Women are migrating in search of work and are leaving their families, becoming indebted to smugglers and/or being subjected to Western cultural mores. The material experience and talk of money clearly shapes how individual women as well as their respective home communities make sense of migration within the larger global economy. Yet these narratives are often lost in (scholarly?) translation, or simply minimized as opportunity. How women (and men) experience dislocation or relocation, however, must be understood

within the larger economic and often state-sponsored relationships that facilitate and encourage such migratory shifts.

In addition to the materiality of capital, physical geography plays another key role in the gendering of global work. As I was reading and rereading the literature used for this chapter, I was struck not only by the invisibility of these forms of work in discourses of globalization or even in the scholarship in organization studies but by the sequestering of nanny, sex, and call center work geographically. Nannies work in private homes. Sex workers take to back alleys and perform nighttime economies. Call centers are located in remote, often rural locations. In this sense, these jobs represent Sassen's (2000) "counter-geographies of globalization" twice removed. Not only do they constitute the backdrop of services that maintain the infrastructure of global cities, they are mobile and transient as well. As Larner (2002) explained, new labor forces are comprised of multiple actors, for example, the informal networks that foster off-the-map work choices such as nanny and sex work. Not only is the work they do invisible, the gendering of these counter-geographies is missing as well. As Acker (2004) states, gender is a "hidden commodity" in globalization, masked by the implicit masculinization of macro-global structures (p. 19). Unexamined in the focus on the high-capital professions in global cities are important discussions of capitalist globalizing processes, and our understanding of gender processes is biased as a result.

By refocusing on the gendering processes that shape global work, organization scholars begin to "expose the discontinuities between the realities of women and men's lives and mainstream scholarly work about global processes" (Acker, 2004, p. 20). We then problematize the Western construct of choice that pervades occupation, work, and organization studies, as well as extant understandings of agency so often framed in terms of either-or. We begin to see women's identities as multiple, shifting, and even contradictory; and as outgrowths of how economics and place are communicated and internalized across workers' life spans. And we begin to empirically explore whether or not the global playing field is indeed being leveled for men and women alike.

◆ Note

1. Throughout this chapter, I use the term, *Southern*, rather than the highly disputed *third world* or *developing* monikers, to reference women from nations experiencing long periods of economic decline.

◆ References

Acker, J. (2004). Gender, capitalism, and globalization. *Critical Sociology, 30,* 17–41.

Ashcraft, K. L. (1998). "I wouldn't say I'm a *feminist,* but . . .": Organizational micropractice and gender identity. *Management Communication Quarterly, 11,* 587–597.

Ashcraft, K. L. (2005). Resistance through consent? Occupational identity, organizational form, and the maintenance of masculinity among commercial airline pilots. *Management Communication Quarterly, 19,* 67–90.

Ashcraft, K. L., & Pacanowsky, M. E. (1996). "A woman's worst enemy": Reflections on a narrative of organizational life and female identity. *Journal of Applied Communication Research, 24,* 217–239.

Asis, M. M. B., Huang, S., & Yeoh, B. S. A. (2004). When the light of the home is abroad: Unskilled female migration and the Filipino family. *Singapore Journal of Tropical Geography, 25,* 198–215.

Bain, P., & Taylor, P. (2000). Entrapped by the "electronic panopticon"? Worker resistance in the call centre. *New Technology, Work, and Employment, 15,* 2–19.

Bales, K. (2002). Because she looks like a child. In B. Ehrenreich & A. R. Hochschild (Eds.), *Global woman: Nannies, maids, and sex workers in the new economy* (pp. 207–229). New York: Metropolitan Books.

Barley, S. R., & Kunda, G. (2001). Bringing work back in. *Organization Science, 12,* 76–96.

Belt, V., & Richardson, R. (2000). Women's work in the information economy. *Information, Communication, & Society, 3,* 366–385.

Belt, V., Richardson, R., & Webster, J. (2002). Women, social skill, and interactive service work in telephone call centres. *New Technology, Work, and Employment, 17,* 20–34.

Bergeron, S. (2001). Political economy discourses of globalization and feminist politics. *Signs: Journal of Women in Culture and Society, 26,* 983–1006.

Brewis, J., & Linstead, S. (2002). Managing the sex industry. *Culture and Organization, 8,* 307–326.

Burawoy, M., Blum, J. A., George, S., Gille, Z., Gowan, T., Haney, L., et al. (2000). *Global ethnography: Forces, connections, and imaginations in a postmodern world.* Berkeley: University of California Press.

Buzzanell, P. M. (2000). The promise and practice of the new career and social contract: Illusions exposed and suggestions for reform. In P. M. Buzzanell (Ed.), *Rethinking organizational and managerial communication from feminist perspectives* (pp. 209–235). Thousand Oaks, CA: Sage.

Callaghan, G. (2001). Edwards revisited: Technical control and call centres. *Economic and Industrial Democracy, 22,* 13–37.

Collinson, D. L. (1987). "Picking women": The recruitment of temporary workers in the mail order industry. *Work, Employment, & Society, 1,* 371–387.

Connell, R. W. (2000). *The men and the boys.* Berkeley: University of California Press.

Deery, S., Iverson, R., & Walsh, J. (2002). Work relationships in telephone call centres: Understanding emotional exhaustion and employee withdrawal. *Journal of Management Studies, 39,* 471–496.

Ehrenreich, B. (2002). *Global woman: Nannies, maids, and sex workers in the New Economy.* New York: Metropolitan Books.

Freeman, C. (2001). Is local:Global as feminine:Masculine? Rethinking the gender of globalization. *Signs: Journal of Women in Culture and Society, 26,* 1007–1037.

Frenkel, S. J., Tam, M., Korczynski, M., & Shire, K. (1998). Beyond bureaucracy? Work organization in call centres. *The International Journal of Human Resource Management, 9,* 957–979.

Friedman, T. L. (2005). *It's a flat world, after all.* Retrieved April 3, 2005, from www .nytimes.com/2005/04/03/magazine/03DO MINANCE.html

Glucksmann, M. A. (2004). Call configurations: Varieties of call centre and divisions of labour. *Work, Employment and Society, 18,* 795–811.

Hochschild, A. R. (2002). Love and gold. In B. Ehrenreich & A. R. Hochschild (Eds.), *Global woman: Nannies, maids, and sex workers in the new economy* (pp. 15–30). New York: Metropolitan Books.

Holmer Nadesan, M. (1996). Organizational identity and space of action. *Organization Studies, 17,* 49–81.

Jackson, C. (1999). Men's work, masculinities, and gender divisions of labour. *The Journal of Development Studies, 36,* 89–108.

Kim-Puri, H. J. (2005). Conceptualizing gender-sexuality-state-nation: An introduction. *Gender & Society, 19,* 137–159.

Knights, D., & McCabe, D. (2003). Governing through teamwork: Reconstituting subjectivity in a call centre. *Journal of Management Studies, 40,* 1587–1619.

Lan, P.C. (2003). Negotiating social boundaries and private zones: The micropolitics of employing migrant domestic workers. *Social Problems, 50,* 525–549.

Larner, W. (2002). Globalization, governmentality, and expertise: Creating a call centre labour force. *Review of International Political Economy, 9,* 650–675.

Marshall, J., & Richardson, R. (1996). The impact of "telemediated" services on corporate structures: The example of "branchless" retail banking in Britain. *Environment and Planning A, 28,* 1845–1856.

Mohanty, C. T. (2002). "Under Western eyes" revisited: Feminist solidarity through anticapitalist struggles. *Signs: Journal of Women in Culture and Society, 28,* 500–535.

Mulholland, K. (2004). Workplace resistance in an Irish call centre: Slammin,' scammin,' smokin' an' leavin.' *Work, Employment and Society, 18,* 709–724.

Mumby, D. K. (2005). Theorizing resistance in organization studies: A dialectical approach. *Management Communication Quarterly, 19,* 19–44.

Pratt, G. (1998). Inscribing domestic work on Filipina bodies. In H. J. Nast & S. Pile (Eds.), *In places through the body* (pp. 283–304). London: Routledge.

Pratt, G. (1999). From registered nurse to registered nanny: Discursive geographies of Filipina domestic workers in Canada. *Economic Geography, 75,* 215–237.

Rogers, B. (1999, October-November). Bitter harvest. *Ms.* Retrieved January 24, 2006, from www.msmagazine.com/oct99/bitter harvest.asp

Sanders, T. (2005). "It's just acting": Sex workers' strategies for capitalizing on sexuality. *Gender, Work, and Organization, 12,* 319–342.

Sassen, S. (2000). Women's burden: Counter-geographies of globalization and the feminization of survival. *Journal of International Affairs, 53,* 503–524.

Sassen, S. (2005). The global city: Introducing a concept. *Brown Journal of World Affairs, 11,* 27–44.

Smith, V. (1997). New forms of work organization. *Annual Review of Sociology, 23,* 315–339.

Steans, J. (1999). The private is global: Feminist politics and global political economy. *New Political Economy, 4,* 113–128.

Steinfatt, T. M. (2002). *Working at the bar: Sex work and health communication in Thailand.* Westport, CT: Ablex Publishing.

Susser, I. (1997). The flexible woman: Regendering labor in the informational society. *Critique of Anthropology, 17,* 389–402.

Tambiah, Y. (2005). Turncoat bodies: Sexuality and sex work under militarization in Sri Lanka. *Gender & Society, 19,* 243–261.

Taylor, P., & Bain, P. (1999). "An assembly line in the head": Work and employee relations in the call centre. *Industrial Relations Journal, 30,* 101–118.

Taylor, P., & Bain, P. (2005). "India calling to the far away towns": The call centre labour process and globalization. *Work, Employment and Society, 19,* 261–282.

Townsley, N. C. (2003). Looking back, looking forward: Mapping the gendered theories, voices, and politics of organization. *Organization, 10,* 617–630.

Trethewey, A. (1997). Resistance, identity, and empowerment: A postmodern feminist analysis of clients in a human service organization. *Communication Monographs, 64,* 281–301.

Tronto, J. C. (2003). The nanny question in feminism. *Hypatia, 17,* 34–25.

U.S. Department of State. (2005). *Trafficking in persons.* Report retrieved October 13, 2005, from www.state.gov/g/tip/rls/tiprpt/2005/46903.htm

van den Broek, D. (2004). "We have the values": Customers, control and corporate ideology in call centre operations. *New Technology, Work, and Employment, 19,* 2–13.

Wickham, J., & Collins, G. (2004). The call centre: A nursery for new forms of work organisation? *Service Industries Journal, 24,* 1–18.

Willis, K. D., & Yeoh, B. S. A. (2000). Gender and transnational household strategies: Singaporean migration to China. *Regional Studies, 34,* 253–264.

Winiecki, D. J. (2004). Shadowboxing with data: Production of the subject in contemporary call centre organisations. *New Technology, Work, and Employment, 19,* 78–94.

Wonders, N. A., & Michalowski, R. (2001). Bodies, borders, and sex tourism in a globalized world: A tale of two cities—Amsterdam and Havana. *Social Problems, 48,* 545–571.

Yea, S. (2004). Runaway brides: Anxieties of identity among trafficked Filipina entertainers in South Korea. *Singapore Journal of Tropical Geography, 25,* 180–197.

9

GENDERED STORIES OF CAREER

Unfolding Discourses of Time, Space, and Identity

◆ Patrice M. Buzzanell and Kristen Lucas

At a conference sponsored by the National Bureau of Economic Research in January 2005, Lawrence H. Summers, president of Harvard University, sparked national attention when he addressed the issue of the underrepresentation of women in tenured faculty positions in science and engineering at top universities and research institutions (Summers, 2005). Summers proposed that women are not subject to overt sex discrimination in hiring and promotion practices. Differences in intelligence, gendered socialization, and, ultimately, personal preferences, Summers said, lead many women to opt out of pursuing high-paying, high-powered jobs. He concluded that "what's behind all of this . . . is the general clash between people's legitimate family desires and employers' current desire for high power and high intensity." He maintained that most women simply do not desire high-power, successful careers in science and engineering, and, to a lesser extent, are not equipped (motivationally or as a matter of aptitude) to succeed in them at the same level as men.

Women, indeed, are grossly underrepresented in science, technology, engineering, and math (also known as the STEM disciplines). Only 8.3% of tenured or tenure track professors in those fields are women (Nelson,

2005). In business and government, their representation is disproportionate as well. Among Fortune 500 companies, less than 16% of corporate officers are women (Catalyst, 2005b), and only one quarter work in line positions that have control over core business operations (Catalyst, 2005a). In government, only one third of the top-ranking policy leaders are women (Center for Women in Government, 2004).

Ostensibly, the laws passed by the Equal Employment Opportunity Commission have banned discrimination in hiring and promotion. So, if discrimination is no longer permitted and there is legal recourse now when it does occur, could there be some substance to Summers's (2005) claims? Could it be that the cause of the disparity is that women simply choose not to pursue high-profile careers (those characterized by high earnings, status, and perquisites), whether those careers are in science, engineering, business, government, or elsewhere? Summers's remarks tapped into some longstanding beliefs about differences in men's and women's abilities, interests, and desires. These beliefs play out daily in career processes and outcomes when, for example, an employer wonders silently or asks out loud if a young female interviewee is planning to have a family or if a man is groomed for management instead of an equally capable woman.

To his credit, Summers (2005) admitted that he could be wrong and encouraged research that examines his "high-power job hypotheses." However, the problem with his remarks was that he presented them as "causes" that legitimate and naturalize the underrepresentation of women in high-profile careers. In some cases, women may choose to pursue low-profile careers or temporary jobs. In others there may be visible and invisible barriers as well as limited and/or forced choices that exclude women from careers at the top of their fields. In contrast to Summers's tack of locating the problem in women and sex/gender differences, we place normative career models and assumptions at the center of the debate.

We argue that the gendered construction of *career* acts to discriminate against women (and other members of traditionally underrepresented groups).

In this chapter we review career literature from a variety of perspectives to provide an overview of salient issues and research trends at the intersections of gender, career, and communication. We argue that there are material, psychological, and discursive factors that make the nature and enactment of career difficult for many women. We problematize career by highlighting and critiquing three of its prominent dimensions (see MacDermid, Roy, & Zvonkovic, 2005). This critique identifies who is harmed by and who benefits from normalized processes within these dimensions as well as by normative conceptions of career itself. In this way we can show that the career experiences of women are different from—not inferior to—the normative (male) model. We begin by discussing career discourses as contextual and gendered constructions. Next we highlight gendered career communication theory and research within the key dimensions of time, space, and identity. Finally, we pose some directions for future research.

◆ Contextual and Gendered Discourses of Career

Career derives from the medieval and Latin words *carraria* (a road for vehicles) and *carrus* (car), respectively. It is defined as "a field for or pursuit of consecutive progressive achievement especially in public, professional, or business life" or "a profession for which one trains and which is undertaken as a permanent calling" (*Merriam-Webster Online Dictionary*, www.m-w.com). In essence, then, a career can be considered to be the journey individuals take over the course of their lifetimes—one that involves advancement and competencies acquired with time and training. While the journey motif is used most often as a metaphor for career (Inkson & Amundson, 2002), it does not reflect how career discourse and practices have changed based on when and where career has been examined (contextual constructions) and whose is being discussed (gendered story).

CONTEXTUAL CONSTRUCTIONS OF CAREER

Career theory, research, and practice are interdisciplinary and shaped by specific historical, economic, and cultural events (Arthur, Hall, & Lawrence, 1989). As bureaucratic models became prominent at the beginning of the 20th century, the notion of career became a means of viewing the movements of organizational members from their initial entry into the workforce through various forms of training and assessment all the way to retirement (see Hall, 2002; Miles & Snow, 1996). As McKinlay (2002) notes, a modern career was based on promise—"the vow that an organization makes to the individual [man] that merit, diligence and self-discipline would be rewarded by steady progress through a pyramid of grades" (p. 596). From recruitment to retirement, then, career involved individuals' conformity to procedural and behavioral codes as well as a careful monitoring of self-presentation, especially of appearance (McKinlay, 2002).

After World War II, during an era of unprecedented economic growth in the United States, the so-called silent generation contented itself with control, predictability, loyalty, stability, and long-term membership in a single organization (Kratz, 2004; Sheehy, 1995). Career models were linear and oriented upward (Buzzanell & Goldzwig, 1991). Career research and advice focused on the advancement of white males in managerial and/or professional occupations within hierarchically organized companies through fast-track identification systems, executive development programs, position competitions in internal labor markets, and formal or informal mentoring and networking

(Arthur et al., 1989; Miles & Snow, 1996; Ragins & Cotton, 1999; Rosenbaum, 1989). Because career emphasized linearity, exclusionary processes, certain preferred outcomes and members, and competition, it was imbued with traditionally masculine qualities (Buzzanell, 1994; Marshall, 1989).

By the mid-1970s, however, the stable world of the organization man was shattered by the uncertainties of international competition and economic stagnation-inflation that gave way to reorganizations, outsourcings, and network structures in the 1980s (Kratz, 2004; Miles & Snow, 1996; Smith, 2001) and emphasis on self-management of career in the 1990s (Sterns & Huyck, 2001). Contingent or temporary work became more prominent, benefits that many workers took for granted (e.g., health insurance) were eliminated, and temporary staffing company Manpower became one of the largest corporations in the United States (Gossett, 2003; Smith, 2001). Workers, including managers and professionals, experienced unemployment, underemployment, downward mobility, and successive downsizings with some workforce segments, such as people of color and working-class members, being disproportionately harmed by such trends (Buzzanell, 2000; Fairhurst, Cooren, & Cahill, 2002; Heckscher, 1995; Hirsch, 1987; Newman, 1993).

The world of the organization man also changed as women and people of color joined managerial and professional ranks (Calás & Smircich, 1996). Academic and popular materials recounted individual strategies that contributed to white women's success at climbing the corporate ladder (e.g., Harragan, 1977). Whether women could even have managerial and professional careers was debated with the male career model being the lens by which women's careers were evaluated (Bell & Nkomo, 2001). Other materials addressed the structural barriers, double binds, and gendered societal expectations women faced and continue to face (e.g., Acker,

1990; Buzzanell, 1995; Kanter, 1977; Wood & Conrad, 1983). Over time, treatment of career, class, race, gender, and other group membership intersections became more complex and grounded in members' own discourse, identity constructions, and material circumstances. This turn toward the intersectionality of gender and other identity constructions meant that researchers no longer delved solely into sex differences and structural barriers but also examined how women (and men) described and performed their careers over time and space. They used survey and life history analysis to investigate black and white women's professional, classed, racialized, and gendered identities and to reveal how their striving for success and dignity in their workplaces was similar and different (Bell & Nkomo, 2001). Black and white working-class men's constructions of self-worth and social hierarchy are gleaned from interviews probing into their views on jobs, society, class boundaries, racism, and immigration patterns in the United States and France (Lamont, 2000). Meanings of career, success, and life in Native American culture display the difficulties of using alternative criteria for career fulfillment and well-being (Juntunen et al., 2001). Among girls and boys born in poverty, it became clear that hope diminishes over time, leading researchers to question educational interventions and the salience of career as traditionally defined for these children and the working poor (Weinger, 1998; see also Ehrenreich, 2001).

THE GENDERED STORY OF CAREER

Besides historical influences, other ways in which the career is constructed are gendered. Not all women or men adhere to feminine or masculine career approaches but some ways of framing and enacting career are gendered.

Women and men often frame career narratives differently (Gergen & Gergen, 1993; see also the "Dream" or life vision in Kittrell, 1998; Levinson, 1996). "Manstories" are focused on a quest. They are linear narratives progressing toward greater work achievement and success (Gergen, 1990). The quest is guided by mentors and by an occupational dream or vision men create in their 20s (Levinson, 1986). Masculine or traditional careers focus on external manifestations of success and require that individuals be perceived as ideal workers who are willing to put in long hours, fashion a promotable image, acquire the necessary human and social capital, and privilege work over family and personal time (Buzzanell, 2001; Holmer Nadesan & Trethewey, 2000; Perlow, 1998, 1999; Williams, 2000). The traditional career requires that individuals demonstrate enterprising qualities so that they and their organizations become winners. They are "to cultivate their self, to realize their dreams, and at the same time contribute to, and share in, the enchantment of organizational excellence" (Fournier, 1998, p. 56; see also Holmer Nadesan, 1999). In this competition between winners and losers, workers engage in personal branding in which self-promotion strategies are turned into "an ideological understanding of the corporate world capable of an embracing influence over workers' very sense of self" (Lair, Sullivan, & Cheney, 2005, p. 309).

Individuals enacting the masculine, enterprising career are expected to project a fit and youthful image, valorize appearance and personality over substance, and commodify themselves and their relationships (Lair et al., 2005; Holmer Nadesan, 1999; Holmer Nadesan & Trethewey, 2000; Trethewey, 2000). Optimally, these men have wives and children because that family structure is associated with higher income and salary progression (Schneer & Reitman, 2002). The masculine career still leaves little room for alternative career routes, family, leisure, and community service.

"Womanstories" tend to be fluid, shifting, and embodied—interweaving life aspects, allegiances and relationships (Gergen, 1990; see also Bateson, 1989). These stories become manifest in a feminine career form that combines employment, marriage or partnerships, and motherhood or caregiving in phases but also marks a "sense of responsibility to wider contextual needs" (Marshall, 1989, p. 286) or a strengthening of self in relation to others over the course of a lifetime (Gallos, 1989). Their broader context or responsibilities may include civic engagement, such as working on community-centered projects (Tonn, 2003), or the vow black women take to give back to their communities of origin (Bell & Nkomo, 2001). Because a feminine career cannot be understood without examining multiple commitments and nonwork experiences (Arthur, Inkson, & Pringle, 1999; Powell & Mainiero, 1992), this career has been labeled relational and kaleidoscopic to emphasize career decisions that are "part of a larger and intricate web of interconnected issues, people, and aspects that had come together in a delicately balanced package" (Mainiero & Sullivan, 2005, p. 111).

The feminine career form appears discontinuous compared with traditional, linear models. So-called irregularities emerge because of the various ways women enact careers. They may opt out of the labor force, downplay career ambitions, relocate based on partners' employment opportunities, stay at home permanently or take temporary leaves of absence to care for dependent children or aging parents, pursue contingent, temporary, and flexible work arrangements, become entrepreneurs, and/or imbue a high profile career with nurturing, power sharing, and community involvement (Arthur et al, 1999; Arthur & Rousseau, 1996; Bell & Nkomo, 2001; Cunningham & Murray, 2005; Edley, 2004; Fels, 2004; Helgesen, 1990; Hewlett & Luce, 2005; Hylmö & Buzzanell, 2002; Mainiero & Sullivan, 2005).

SUMMARY

Contextual and gendered overviews of career supply societal narratives from which individuals draw to craft their career identities and outcomes. Although these societal narratives seem to direct the formation of particular gendered identities, they also are contradictory, flexible, and subject to change as women and men resist, refashion, adopt, reject, and revise aspects of contemporary careers. Indeed, scholars try both to expose the ways in which career systematically excludes anyone who does not fit the profile of the ideal entrepreneurial worker and to create a vision for workplace change (Bailyn, 1993, 2004; Buzzanell, 1995, 2000; Fels, 2004; Kirby & Krone, 2002; Lair et al., 2005; Perlow, 1998; Williams, 2000). When career dimensions are problematized, tensions within discourses and practices can be explored productively.

◆ Gendered Career Dimensions

Career is actualized through individuals' identity constructions along the lines of key career dimensions. Of these interrelated dimensions, the spatiotemporal dialectic is the most prominent in career discourse and practices. It also is gendered, insofar as masculine approaches and values are more aligned with the prominent linear career: "The male principle is more closely associated with time, with linear progress in a given direction, and the female principle with space and a more cyclic pattern of change and transformation" (Marshall, 1989, p. 280). We distinguish among and analyze gendered career communication within each interrelated dimension (time, space, and identity) separately.

TIME

Arthur and colleagues (1999) say that "career theory emphasizes the time perspective through which unfolding experiences come about" (p. 3). Time is embedded in, constructed by, and manifest (in meaning) through discourse in particular cultural and organizing processes. Although socially constructed and experienced in different ways (e.g., cyclical, linear, biological, seasonal, project oriented, social times; see Bailyn, 1993), the prominent career time is linear. In Western thinking and practices, time is clock time—objective, standardized, commodified, simplistic, measurable, and independent of objects, events, people, and contexts (for an overview see Crossan, Cunha, Vera, & Cunha, 2005). Marshall (1989) points out that this linear orientation is masculine insofar as it admits no deviation. However, the linear temporal orientation by which individuals classify and evaluate themselves and others has differential effects on the lives of women and men. It also establishes discursive closure by which alternative ways of talking and thinking about time are either inadmissible or are considered naïve or trivial (Deetz, 1992).

According to Buzzanell and Goldzwig (1991), a primary issue is the metaphorical association of time and directionality that plays out in career discourse. Time is elevated as the "unalterable criterion for classification. . . . What is different about traditional career model metaphorical extensions or analogies is the extent to which such spatiotemporal terms privilege 'promotability' and 'worth' in the particular hierarchy" (p. 482). Not only does individuals' positional time in internal labor markets signify worth and success but their use of time indicates correct priorities (see Bailyn, 1993; Perlow, 1998, 1999). U.S. workers are expected to spend incredibly long hours at work. This time is measured through presence or "face time" in the office, hours engaged in paid activities, diminished leisure time, and prioritization of work over family time (Bailyn, 1993; Bonebright, Clay, & Ankenmann, 2000; Hochschild, 1997; Schor, 1992).

Masculine conceptualizations of time with regard to career can be detrimental to members of both sexes but particularly to women. Women and their careers can be negatively affected by the competing demands of work and biological clocks, the loss of skills accumulation due to time-based discontinuities, and the inaccurate perceptions of their commitment to career caused by family-based constraints on face time at work. Early-career phases are marked by a steep accumulation of skills, the development of important organizational networks, and an establishment of professional reputation. However, this stage occurs when women are in their most fertile, childbearing years. To perform the tasks necessary for high profile careers (putting in extra hours at work, relocating, and traveling for business purposes), women are staying single longer and delaying childbirth. Ultimately, these delays make it more difficult to find a partner and have a baby, and many career-focused women (33% in the U.S., overall; 42% in corporate America) are childless. Instead of *choosing* to be child free, their situation becomes a "creeping nonchoice" (Hewlett, 2002, p. 66; see also Sheehy, 1995). There are long-term emotional consequences for women desiring fulfillment in dimensions of life other than work.

For women who do choose to have children, lost time can also have serious consequences. As children are typically born during women's early-career stages, the discontinuity in their careers may mean that they are not able to develop their reputations to the fullest extent possible. In technical fields, a leave of absence of even a year or two could mean falling behind in necessary technical know-how. In a variety of careers, even brief leaves of absence (maternity leave) often are associated with penalties in long-term earning power (Hewlett & Luce, 2005). They could also create and/or increase gaps in wages, promotions, and so on among women with children, those without, and men. A woman who recently took advantage of family-friendly policies to have two children was initially denied tenure on the grounds that she did not meet her university's standards of productivity. Although the university had promised to "stop the tenure clock" by not counting the time she was on leave when evaluating her productivity, she was granted tenure only after a 3-year legal battle (Inside Higher Ed, 2005). This example demonstrates the differences between official and actual policy implementation (see Kirby & Krone, 2002).

Face time, one's physical presence at the workplace, remains a critical indicator of commitment to the organization and to career development (Bailyn, 1993; Perlow, 1998). Women (and men) who desire meaningful personal relationships are disadvantaged because they often cannot, or choose not to, put in the long hours and the appearance of single-minded dedication to their companies that high-profile careers demand (Bailyn, 2004; Buzzanell, 2000; Lair et al., 2005). Because women also continue to bear the burden for second-shift duties (child care, housework), their attention to outside commitments—regardless of their productivity and efficiency at work—often is attributed to a lack of commitment to organization and career.

Traditional time-based conceptualizations and assessments of career, along with the prioritization of work time over other life aspects, can have economic, relational, and psychological effects that are detrimental to many people, especially women. Furthermore, the loss of talent when some women (and men) opt out, downshift, become disillusioned, or start their own businesses is of increasing concern to U.S. businesses (Berger, 2000; Chaker, 2003; Hewlett & Luce, 2005; Saltzman, 1991). Using a gendered lens, researchers have examined the ideological underpinnings and material consequences of career so that they can offer alternative ways for individuals and organizations to frame and enact the temporal dimension of career.

SPACE

Space, as a dimension of career, also has physical, social, and discursive aspects. Physical space is important because individual movements and locations connote

power. Levels of organizational prestige and authority are associated with whether employees occupy a cubicle or an office, if their assigned work space is large or small, or even if it is on lower or higher floors. Social space focuses on the ways individuals experience their work roles in larger occupational contexts (Arthur et al., 1989): Work experiences can include location in a structural-organizational or a chain-of-command hierarchy. They can be linked with individuals' centrality to decision-making units in the organizations or to the extent of employees' engagement in communicative networks that span organizational boundaries. Discursive space may shape and be shaped by public argument such that the privilege to talk is reconfigured to accommodate new voices (Mumby, 2000). Like time, space is a symbolic process that is "fully implicated in engaging, constraining, producing, and maintaining discursive practices" (McKerrow, 1999, p. 272). Some spatial features—access, appropriation, domination—relate directly to gendered career processes and outcomes (McKerrow, 1999). Each of these is described below.

Access addresses the structures by which movement among different spaces and networks is formed or regulated. The discourse and practices surrounding access, such as internal labor markets and career networks, can influence quality of work life and career possibilities. Padavic and Reskin (2002) demonstrate how an internal labor market of separate career ladders in a grocery store limited women's advancement opportunities. Although women were not explicitly discriminated against, top management positions were linked to initial career paths in the produce department (dominated by men), whereas departments dominated by women (cashier, bakery) had short career ladders without bridges to management ladders. Padavic and Reskin (2002) also argue that short career ladders encourage high rates of turnover, which then can be used to keep wages low for people who occupy those positions.

Professional networks have been shown to facilitate employees' career advancement, increase the success of their socialization, and make important organizational knowledge accessible. Networks, however, also are gendered. Analysis indicates that the uses and effects of informal networks are gendered and racialized. Women seem to be as adept as men at forming them, but their networks are not well integrated into organizational power centers (Powell & Mainiero, 1992). Managers of color are less likely to have intimate informal relationships than white managers of either sex (Ibarra, 1995). Black women find informal social networks less accessible (Bell & Nkomo, 2001; Combs, 2003).

Appropriation addresses the ways in which privilege is protected through the acquisition and use of space. Occupations are gendered in ways that ensure the allotment and perpetuation of more prestigious, "difficult," and highly paid occupations to privileged members of society (Ashcraft & Mumby, 2004; Cejka & Eagly, 1999; Leidner, 1991). This feature is best illustrated by the sex segregation of jobs. Although great strides have been made in opening career choices to both sexes (women firefighters, men flight attendants), considerable sex segregation persists. Women are more likely to occupy "front space" jobs (receptionist, customer service) that emphasize communication with customers and demand high levels of emotional labor. Men are more likely to occupy "back space" jobs (repair technician) that center on technical know-how and hands-on work. What is even more troublesome is that the feminization of particular occupations (when women are the numerical majority) leads to lower wages and prestige.

Appropriation can also occur through the placement of employees in core and peripheral positions. This process is gendered in that men are more likely than women to be in core or line positions that have direct control over business operations. Women and minorities are more likely to have peripheral, or staff, positions

outside of the core business (human resources, public relations, diversity services; Padavic & Reskin, 2002). Among *Fortune* 500 companies, women are dramatically underrepresented in key executive positions (Catalyst, 2005a, 2005b). Research by Catalyst indicates that women in top ranks disproportionately hold peripheral positions. Men hold 85% of key executive positions and 90% of core executive positions. Half of male officers work in core positions; only one quarter of women with key positions do so.

Focusing on career as a set of discursive and technical practices rather than on careers as vocationally and occupationally situated enables researchers to demonstrate how workers are constructed, and construct themselves, as core and peripheral organizational members. Fournier (1998; see also Collinson & Collinson, 1997) displays how the discourse of enterprise (discipline, self-empowerment, and enchantment) creates a discursive space in which career and identity are produced such that there are some members who are located at the core (the "enterprising self") and some who are at the margins (the "fatalistic self"). Those at the core create narratives of careering or self-directed development; those at the margins describe exploitation and structural constraints. These narratives align with members' identity constructions: "Through the new career discourse, employees are seduced into inventing their self and desires in ways conducive to the pursuit of organizational excellence" (Fournier, 1998, p. 60).

Domination examines how space is regulated and who controls different types of it. Domination can occur in a variety of ways and can subordinate diverse people who are "othered." The surge of women into the workplace in the 1960s and 1970s was accompanied by (attempts at) the domination of work spaces by men. Women have been subjected to invisible barriers that limit access to the top of organizations (glass ceilings; see Buzzanell, 1995). Minority women also experience "concrete walls" that serve to isolate them within the organization. Unlike glass ceilings, where women can still see who and what is going on above them, these walls block minority women from seeing and being seen (Bell & Nkomo, 2001). They continue to ensure that top organizational positions, including academic positions, still are white-male dominated (Bell & Nkomo, 2001; Buzzanell, 1995).

Another way in which domination of space occurs in the workplace is through the gendering of work spaces. Even if a majority of employees are supportive of women in the workplace, a few exceptions can drastically reframe the space as a male domain. A male coworker can shift a neutral workplace into a hostile environment by telling profane jokes or making sexual references to or advances on women. Gendered displays such as these emphasize differences between women and men and lay claim to the space belonging to men by making women feel uncomfortable and/or unwelcome.

Domination also can occur by attempts to insulate the sphere of work from competing spheres of home or life. Making the work space off-limits to talk about family or to attend to family needs (talking on the phone to a child's teacher) can ostracize people who want to integrate their lives. Because women bear the burden for issues such as child care (see Hochschild, 1997), the separate spheres of work and home can be difficult, if not impossible, to balance in day-to-day practice, and women can be led to reconsider career choices that would allow more time for family commitments.

As a whole, communication scholars offer insight into diverse career processes and practices relating to gender and space. Some have found that discourses of the new career obfuscate material consequences for particular segments of the labor force, most notably for white women and men with less education, geographic mobility, and resources, and for people of color (Buzzanell, 2000). With regard to sex-segregated occupations, women may engage in complex discursive practices that enlarge (and constrict) their abilities to work

effectively in different kinds of jobs (blue-collar positions; see Conn, 2004). Individuals and their family members construct their gendered identities and career possibilities differently based on work arrangements, such as telecommuting (Hylmö, 2004), on entrepreneurial work (Edley, 2004), and in job loss situations (Buzzanell & Turner, 2003). The admissibility of discourse in different realms is explored in gender and family talk at work, where mothers are discouraged from and silence themselves in this talk (Farley-Lucas, 2000; Jorgenson, 2002) and where men and women are discouraged from taking family leaves through colleagues' comments, managers' mixed messages, and negative career consequences (Hochschild, 1997; Kirby, 2000; Kirby & Krone, 2002). As Bailyn (1993) puts it, there seems to be "a real taboo on talking, or even thinking, about children and parenting at work" (p. 25). She wonders if this is a way "to delegitimize the private sphere, to keep the separation of public and private in place. One wonders, too, what the emotional cost of such a taboo might be" (p. 25). Because many temporary, part-time, or contingent workers are female, research on the impact of temporary workers on the permanent work environment (Gossett, 2001) as well as on their complex identifications with organizations (Gossett, 2003; Jordan, 2003) is salient to communication research on gender career.

IDENTITY

In career literature, identity is described in two ways. It is considered to be a key tension or problematic in career discourse and practice (Kirby, Golden, Medved, Jorgenson, & Buzzanell, 2003) that involves shifting and seemingly contradictory identities and discourses. Identity also functions as a metacompetency or essential facet of career construction about which individuals seek to craft a coherent story (Arthur et al., 1999; Hall, 2002; Ibarra, 2003).

As a communication *problematic,* identity, according to Kirby and colleagues (2003), concerns the ways in which individuals (re)constitute themselves as family and workplace members and how they would describe and enact their life priorities. As such, identity is an ongoing process with different manifestations in different contexts. In work-family literature, it is linked to gendered understandings of and conflicts within work or family roles and realms (Kirby et al., 2003). When it is viewed as a discursive process, however, the focus changes to ongoing processes of negotiation by which individuals craft themselves as gendered and embodied (see Holmer Nadesan & Trethewey, 2000). Researchers have discussed how individuals form their understandings of themselves in relation to their work over time and how these identities shift as individuals face particular career and/or life changes. Some of these changes are workplace pregnancy and relationships with supervisors and subordinates, job loss, the processes of employment interviewing and organizational assimilation which underrepresented members undergo, and midcareer and/or midlife identity (re)constructions (Allen, 2000; Ashcraft, 1999; Buzzanell, 1999; Liu & Buzzanell, 2006; Meisenbach, 2004; Trethewey, 2000, 2001). Most of this literature describes tensions among varied identity contradictions as individuals attempt to resolve these contradictions.

As a *metacompetency* or essential facet of career construction, identity is viewed as "a higher-order capability that enables the person to acquire other skills" (Hall, 2002, p. 32), with identity growth and career effectiveness requiring the two elements of feedback about one's self and self-awareness. Hall (2002) advocates the construction of a clear and internally consistent identity, saying that it "then, is a measure of wholeness—of how well integrated the person's life is" (p. 133). Given Western mandates to know oneself and to focus on the coherent self as the source of career success, it is not surprising that Hall would

consider identity as the most important aspect of career development from the individual's viewpoint.

There are numerous theories about and means of assessing career identity awareness and (re)construction which typically advise individuals to know themselves and their central life interests or anchors as starting points to viable and satisfying careers (see Hall, 2002; Butler & Waldroop, 1999; Schein, 1990). However, recent counseling advice recommends that individuals not start with extensive self-analysis, but rather network with weak ties and try different kinds of work (Ibarra, 2003). Through the performance of possible identities, individuals can then craft different stories of their careers—particularly during times of transition—for different audiences (Ibarra & Lineback, 2005). The doing of career identity work involves individuals' engagement in varied work activities and in iterative storying about their work, careers, and identity(ies). These and other materials from the literature on career counseling talk about forming career identities out of many possible selves using a winnowing process that then attempts to fix a coherent identity for a particular time and place. The focus is on appropriate person-career fit, identity coherence, and career counseling processes.

Besides discourses and prescriptions about routes toward personalized career identity work, communication researchers have explored another source of successful career identity constructions; namely, popular societal discourses. Holmer Nadesan (1999) found that self-help or popular success literature "promise[s] self-fulfillment through the consumption of products and through strategic identification with corporate identities and/or cultures" (p. 39). Lair and colleagues (2005) noted that popular discourses of personal branding offer routes to success in a turbulent economic environment. Yet, these and other materials on the new career promise success without consideration of detrimental consequences for women and others who cannot assume a universal standard (ideal worker, typically male) (Buzzanell, 1995, 2000; Lair et al., 2005; Holmer Nadesan & Trethewey, 2000). Identity is complicated by the management of invisible social identities, such as those formed through race, chronic illness, disability, sexual orientation, religion, and age (Clair, Beatty, & MacLean, 2005). In cases such as these, individuals appear to have choice in revealing their often stigmatized identities, but their identity struggles are much more complex than "choice" to reveal or "pass" would suggest (Lair et al., 2005; Spradlin, 1998).

In problematizing identity, we turn to communication researchers who have contrasted the search for "real" coherent selves advocated by many career theorists and self-help writers with the "fake" or inauthentic selves by which individuals perform career identities that are inconsistent with their personal feelings and interests but beneficial to their organizations (Tracy & Trethewey, 2005). Instead of promoting coherent real identity constructions, Tracy and Trethewey suggest that the poststructuralist image of a crystallized self might better capture the politicized and layered ways in which career, gender, race, discourse, and identity intersect. Embracing the shifting nature of identity(ies) can enrich and expand gendered discourses on career standards, occupational participation, and the crafting of productive career narratives.

◆ Discussion

We began this chapter by summarizing Summers's (2005) remarks about women's underrepresentation in science and engineering careers in institutions of higher education. In general, career developmental processes, practices, and consequences are gendered globally with inequitable career patterns situating women in less prominent, more caregiving, and less economically viable occupations and work-life choices (Burke,

2000; Maume, 1999; Townsley, this volume). As a result, Summers's assumptions about women's choices, socialization, and biological predispositions are replicated in gendered career patterns.

The issue, however, is not simply that many men and women have different career patterns that often disadvantage women. Rather, it is that career discourses are fundamentally gendered in subtle ways and that career research has insufficiently problematized career and its dimensions of time, space, and identity within their historical and gendered complexities.

Career discourses and practices are fundamentally gendered. Contemporary career materials encourage self-discipline, personal branding, use of self-help literature, development of enterprising careers, and adherence to the new employment contract as sensible approaches for sustained employability (Buzzanell, 2000; Fournier, 1998; Lair et al., 2005; Holmer Nadesan & Trethewey, 2000). However, the long-term consequences for individuals, families, and communities have not been broached fully in research or practice (Han & Moen, 1999; Kirby et al., 2003; Lucas & Buzzanell, 2006; Williams, 2000). Reflection on these trends indicates that they would disadvantage every workforce member (anyone who ever has dependents, who ages, whose appearance is not in top form, and who has illnesses or disabilities). Moreover, a focus on appearance, image, and 24/7 paid labor may divert attention from substantive career issues that warrant sustained attention. These issues include the use of economic criteria as the primary rationale for work-family decisions; an increasing economic divide between those with and without career resources and opportunities; the continuing sex segregation of occupations; and unfinished work on gendered equity in work and family practices, relationships, and policies (Bailyn, 2004; Fine, Weiss, Addelston, & Marusza, 1997; Gilbert & Brownson, 1998; Millman, 2005; Williams, 2000).

More expansive theory and research has constructed alternative career stories and models that all workforce members can embrace (see Arthur et al., 1999; Bailyn, 2004; Buzzanell & Ellingson, 2005; Gomez et al., 2001; Kirby & Krone, 2002; Lucas & Buzzanell, 2004; Mainiero & Sullivan, 2005). Taken together, these contradiscursive moves highlight intersections among discourse, gender, and career. They expand the career dimensions of time, space, and identity. They engage in dialogue about shifting career, gender, and professional identities and identifications. They can support the admissibility of arguments bridging work and life domains. They can encourage greater understanding of the career and life cycle intersections within particular contexts and for specific cohorts in societies. Finally, they contribute to the inclusion of the values, needs, and approaches of various workforce segments into career models, policies, and organizational practices. As these discourses and visions of inclusive career research and practice continue, they expand the ways in which people are active participants and initiators of change. These processes of gender and career transformation focus on incremental changes in micropractices through governmental policies as well as radical change in gendered relationships and organizing. They maximize the dialectical processes of agency by which positions and possibilities, discourse and materiality, masculinities and femininities, and power and resistance come into play (Ashcraft & Mumby, 2004; McNay, 1999). It is this work to which communication researchers attend and to which they will continue to make distinct contributions.

Surfacing career assumptions and practices as fundamentally gendered is only an initial step in problematizing career (see MacDermid et al., 2005). We encourage further analyses of the three career dimensions in which gender inequities play out. These analyses should incorporate mixed methods and use different theoretical approaches to deal with the complexities of the gendered career. They also can help

develop career communication research and interventions that address the interests and well-being of all workforce members.

Because career discourses and contexts change constantly, these problematizations should occur repeatedly over time and for each generational cohort. Data gathering and analytic approaches that have been underutilized in career communication research are the life history interview and the life course method (through which life choice patterns are studied as embedded in historical-social-political contexts and as constraining or encouraging agency). Researchers can use life history interviews and grounded theory to find out how individuals interpret their life course (sequence of roles and events as well as their enactment over time) within certain historical and sociocultural contexts (Bell & Nkomo, 2001). Questions of particular importance for life course researchers interested in gendered career communication are these: What accounts for social trends, norms, and ideals about a worthy life and career? How do individuals change cultural and gendered career scripts? How does each new cohort replicate and/or transform existing notions about career (see Giele, 1998)?

In short, by problematizing career, communication researchers can create awareness about assumptions, inequities, and potential solutions. They can reinforce an inclusive conceptualization of career as *an expansive discourse through which work acquires coherence and meaning in individuals' lives.* Using our definition, researchers, practitioners, and organizational members can rearticulate career as a means of enhancing quality of work (and nonwork) life. We hope that future research from multiple disciplines, particularly communication, will respond fully and effectively to Summers's (2005) attempt to be provocative when he said, "[My hypotheses] may be all wrong. I will have served my purpose if I have provoked thought on this question and provoked the marshalling of evidence to contradict what I have said."

◆ References

Acker, J. (1990). Hierarchies, jobs, bodies: A theory of gendered organizations. *Gender & Society, 4*, 139–158.

Allen, B. J. (2000). "Learning the ropes": A black feminist standpoint analysis. In P. M. Buzzanell (Ed.), *Rethinking organizational and managerial communication from feminist perspectives* (pp. 177–208). Thousand Oaks, CA: Sage.

Arthur, M. B., Hall, D. T., & Lawrence, B. S. (1989). Generating new directions in career theory: The case for a transdisciplinary approach. In M. B. Arthur, D. T. Hall, & B. S. Lawrence (Eds.), *Handbook of career theory* (pp. 7–25). Cambridge, UK: Cambridge University Press.

Arthur, M. B., Inkson, K., & Pringle, J. K. (1999). *The new careers: Individual action and economic change.* London: Sage.

Arthur, M. B., & Rousseau, D. M. (Eds.). (1996). *The boundaryless career: A new employment principle for a new organizational era.* New York: Oxford University Press.

Ashcraft, K. (1999). Managing maternity leave: A qualitative analysis of temporary executive succession. *Administrative Science Quarterly, 44,* 240–280.

Ashcraft, K. L., & Mumby, D. K. (2004). *Reworking gender: A feminist communicology of organization.* Thousand Oaks, CA: Sage.

Bailyn, L. (1993). *Breaking the mold: Women, men, and time in the new corporate world.* New York: The Free Press.

Bailyn. L. (2004). The Hughes Award: Time in careers—careers in time. *Human Relations, 57,* 1507–1521.

Bateson, M. C. (1989). *Composing a life.* New York: Plume.

Bell, E. L. J., & Nkomo, S. M. (2001). *Our separate ways: Black and white women and the struggle for professional identity.* Boston: Harvard Business School Press.

Berger, B. (2000). Prisoners of liberation: A psychoanalytic perspective on disenchantment and burnout among career women lawyers. *JCLP/In Session: Psychotherapy in Practice, 56,* 665–673.

Bonebright, C. L., Clay, D. L., & Ankenmann, R. L. (2000). The relationship of workaholism and work-life conflict, life satisfaction, and purpose in life. *Journal of Counseling Psychology, 47,* 469–477.

Burke, R. J. (2000). Career priority patterns among managerial women: A study of our countries. *Psychological Reports, 86,* 1264–1266.

Butler, T., & Waldroop, J. (1999). Job sculpting: The art of retaining your best people. *Harvard Business Review, 77*(5), 144–152.

Buzzanell, P. M. (1994). Gaining a voice: Feminist perspectives in organizational communication. *Management Communication Quarterly, 7,* 339–383.

Buzzanell, P. M. (1995). Reframing the glass ceiling as a socially constructed process: Implications for understanding and change. *Communication Monographs, 62,* 327–354.

Buzzanell, P. M. (1999). Tensions and burdens in employment interviewing processes: Perspectives of non-dominant group applicants. *The Journal of Business Communication, 36,* 134–162.

Buzzanell, P. M. (2000). The promise and practice of the new career and social contract: Illusions exposed and suggestions for reform. In P. M. Buzzanell (Ed.), *Rethinking organizational and managerial communication from feminist perspectives* (pp. 209–235). Thousand Oaks, CA: Sage.

Buzzanell, P. M. (2001). Gendered practices in the contemporary workplace: A critique of what often constitutes front page news in the *Wall Street Journal. Management Communication Quarterly, 14,* 518–538.

Buzzanell, P. M., & Ellingson, L. (2005). Contesting narratives of workplace maternity. In L. M. Harter, P. Japp, & C. Beck (Eds.), *Narratives, health, and healing: Communication theory, research and practice.* (pp. 277–294). Hillsdale, NJ: Erlbaum.

Buzzanell, P. M., & Goldzwig, S. R. (1991). Linear and nonlinear career models: Metaphors, paradigms, and ideologies. *Management Communication Quarterly, 4,* 466–505.

Buzzanell, P. M., & Turner, L. H. (2003). Emotion work revealed by job loss discourse: Backgrounding-foregrounding of feelings, construction of normalcy, and (re)instituting of traditional masculinities. *Journal of Applied Communication Research, 31,* 27–57.

Calás, M. B., & Smircich, L. (1996). From "the woman's" point of view: Feminist approaches to organization studies. In S. R. Clegg, C. Hardy, & W. R. Nord (Eds.), *Handbook of organization studies* (pp. 218–257). London: Sage.

Catalyst. (2005a). *Women and minorities on Fortune 100 boards.* Retrieved September 27, 2005, from www.catalystwomen.org/pressroom/press_releases/5_11_05%20%20ABD%20report.pdf

Catalyst. (2005b). *Women in the Fortune 500.* Retrieved September 27, 2005, from www.catalystwomen.org/pressroom/press_releases/2–10–05%20Catalyst%20Female%20CEOs%20Fact%20Sheet.pdf

Cejka, M. A., & Eagly, A. H. (1999). Gender-stereotypic images of occupations correspond to the sex segregation of employment. *Personality and Social Psychology Bulletin, 25,* 413–423.

Center for Women in Government. (2004). *Appointed policy makers in state government five-year trend analysis: Gender, race and ethnicity.* Retrieved September 27, 2005, from www.cwig.albany.edu/APMSG-advancecopy.pdf

Chaker, A. M. (2003, December 30). Luring moms back to work. *Wall Street Journal,* pp. D1, D2.

Clair, J. A., Beatty, J. E., & MacLean, T. L. (2005). Out of sight but not out of mind: Managing invisible social identities in the workplace. *Academy of Management Review, 30,* 78–95.

Collinson, D. L., & Collinson, M. (1997). "Delayering managers": Time-space surveillance and its gendered effects. *Organization, 4,* 375–407.

Combs, G. M. (2003). The duality of race and gender for managerial African American women: Implications of informal social networks on career advancement. *Human Resource Development Review, 2,* 385–405.

Conn, C. E. (2004). *Blue-collar women at work: A poststructuralist feminist reading of gendered identities and materiality.* Unpublished dissertation, Purdue University, West Lafayette, IN.

Crossan, M., Cunha, M. P. E., Vera, D., & Cunha, J. (2005). Time and organizational improvisation. *Academy of Management Review, 30,* 129–145.

Cunningham, C. R., & Murray, S. S. (2005). Two executives, one career. *Harvard Business Review, 83*(2), 125–131.

Deetz, S. (1992). *Communication in an age of corporate colonization.* Albany, NY: SUNY Press.

Edley, P. (2004). Entrepreneurial mothers' balance of work and family: Discursive constructions of time, mothering, and identity. In P. M. Buzzanell, H. Sterk, & L. H. Turner (Eds.), *Gender in applied communication contexts* (pp. 255–273). Thousand Oaks, CA: Sage.

Ehrenreich, B. (2001). *Nickel and dimed: On (not) getting by in America.* New York: Henry Holt.

Fairhurst, G. T., Cooren, F., & Cahill, D. J. (2002). Discursiveness, contradiction, and unintended consequences in successive downsizings. *Management Communication Quarterly, 15,* 501–540.

Farley-Lucas, B. (2000). Communicating the (in)visibility of motherhood: Family talk and the ties to motherhood with/in the workplace. *Electronic Journal of Communication/La Revue Electronique de Communication, 10*(3). (Available at www.cios.org/www/ejcrec2.htm)

Fels, A. (2004). Do women lack ambition? *Harvard Business Review, 82*(4), 50–60.

Fine, M., Weiss, L., Addelston, J., & Marusza, J. (1997). (In)secure times: Constructing white working-class masculinities in the late 20th century. *Gender & Society, 11,* 52–68.

Fournier, V. (1998). Stories of development and exploitation: Militant voices in an enterprise culture. *Organization, 5,* 55–80.

Gallos, J. V. (1989). Exploring women's development: Implications for career theory, practice, and research. In M. B. Arthur,

D. T. Hall, & B. S. Lawrence (Eds.), *Handbook of career theory* (pp. 110–132). Cambridge, UK: Cambridge University Press.

Gergen, M. (1990). Baskets of reed and arrows of steel: Stories of chaos and continuity. In S. Srivastva (Ed.), *Symposium: Executive and organizational continuity.* Cleveland, OH: Case Western Reserve University.

Gergen, M., & Gergen, K. (1993). Narratives of the gendered body in popular autobiography. In R. Josselson & A. Lieblich (Eds.), *The narrative study of lives* (Vol. 1, pp. 191–218). Newbury Park, CA: Sage.

Giele, J. Z. (1998). Innovation in the typical life course. In J. Z. Giele & G. H. Elder, Jr. (Eds.), *Methods of life course research: Qualitative and quantitative approaches* (pp. 231–263). Thousand Oaks, CA: Sage.

Gilbert, L. A., & Brownson, C. (1998). Current perspectives on women's multiple roles. *Journal of Career Assessment, 6,* 433–448.

Gomez, M. J., Fassinger, R. E., Prosser, J., Cooke, K., Mejia, B., & Luna, J. (2001). Voces abriendo caminos (voices forging paths): A qualitative study of the career development of notable Latinas. *Journal of Counseling Psychology, 48,* 286–300.

Gossett, L. M. (2001). The long–term impact of short–term workers: The work life concerns posed by the growth of the contingent workforce. *Management Communication Quarterly, 15,* 115–120.

Gossett, L. (2003). Kept at arm's length: Questioning the desirability of member identification. *Communication Monographs, 69,* 385–404.

Hall, D. T. (2002). *Careers in and out of organizations.* Thousand Oaks, CA: Sage.

Han, S.-K., & Moen, P. (1999). Work and family over time: A life course approach. *The ANNALS of the American Academy of Political and Social Science, 562,* 98–110.

Harragan, B. L. (1977). *Games mother never taught you: Corporate gamesmanship for women.* New York: Warner.

Heckscher, C. (1995). *White-collar blues: Management loyalties in an age of corporate restructuring.* New York: Basic Books.

Helgesen, S. (1990). *The female advantage: Women's ways of leadership.* New York: Doubleday.

Hewlett, S. A. (2002). Executive women and the myth of having it all. *Harvard Business Review, 80*(4), 66–73.

Hewlett, S. A., & Luce, C. B. (2005). Off-ramps and on-ramps: Keeping talented women on the road to success. *Harvard Business Review, 83*(3), 43–54.

Hirsch, P. (1987). *Pack your own parachute: How to survive mergers, takeovers, and other corporate disasters.* Reading, MA: Addison-Wesley.

Hochschild, A. (1997). *The time bind: When work becomes home and home becomes work.* New York: Metropolitan Books.

Holmer Nadesan, M. (1999). The popular success literature and "A Brave New Workplace." *Consumption, Markets and Culture, 3,* 27–60.

Holmer Nadesan, M., & Trethewey, A. (2000). Performing the enterprising subject: Gendered strategies for success (?). *Text & Performance Quarterly, 20,* 223–250.

Hylmö, A. (2004). Women, men, and changing organizations: An organizational culture examination of gendered experiences of telecommuting. In P. M. Buzzanell, H. Sterk, & L. H. Turner (Eds.), *Gender in applied communication contexts* (pp. 47–68). Thousand Oaks, CA: Sage.

Hylmö, A., & Buzzanell, P. M. (2002). Telecommuting as viewed through cultural lenses: An empirical investigation of the discourses of utopia, identity, and mystery. *Communication Monographs, 69,* 329–356.

Ibarra, H. (1995). Race, opportunity, and diversity of social circles in management networks. *Academy of Management Journal, 38,* 673–703.

Ibarra, H. (2003). *Working identity: Unconventional strategies for reinventing your career.* Boston: Harvard Business School Press.

Ibarra, H., & Lineback, K. (2005). What's your story? *Harvard Business Review,* Managing Yourself special issue reprint #R0501F, pp. 1–8.

Inkson, K., & Amundson, N. E. (2002). Career metaphors and their application in theory and counseling practice. *Journal of Employment Counseling, 39*, 98–108.

Inside Higher Ed. (2005). *Faux Family Friendly?* Retrieved September 27, 2005, from www.insidehighered.com/news/2005/09/15/ucsb

Jordan, J. W. (2003). Sabotage or performed compliance: Rhetorics of resistance in temp worker discourse. *Quarterly Journal of Speech, 89*, 19–40.

Jorgenson, J. (2002). Engineering selves: Negotiating gender and identity in technical work. *Management Communication Quarterly, 15*, 350–380.

Juntunen, C. L., Barraclough, D. J., Broneck, C. L., Seibel, G. A., Winrow, S. A., & Morin, P. M. (2001). American Indian perspectives on the career journey. *Journal of Counseling Psychology, 48*, 274–285.

Kanter, R. M. (1977). *Men and women of the corporation.* New York: Basic Books.

Kirby, E. L. (2000). Should I do as you say, or do as you do? Mixed messages about work and family. *Electronic Journal of Communication/La Revue Electronique de Communication, 10*(3). (Available at www.cios.org/www/ejcrec2.htm)

Kirby, E., Golden, A., Medved, C., Jorgenson, J., & Buzzanell, P. M. (2003). An organizational communication challenge to the discourse of work and family research: From problematics to empowerment. In P. Kalbfleisch (Ed.), *Communication yearbook 27* (pp. 1–44). Mahwah, NJ: Lawrence Erlbaum.

Kirby, E. L., & Krone, K. (2002). "The policy exists but you can't really use it": Communication and the structuration of work-family policies. *Journal of Applied Communication Research, 30*, 50–77.

Kittrell, D. (1998). A comparison of the evolution of men's and women's dreams in Daniel Levinson's theory of adult development. *Journal of Adult Development, 5*, 105–115.

Kratz, E. F. (2004, December 13). The gray flannel office. *Fortune, 150*(12), 152–160.

Lair, D. J., Sullivan, K., & Cheney, G. (2005). Marketization and the recasting of the professional self: The rhetoric and ethics of personal branding. *Management Communication Quarterly, 18*, 307–343.

Lamont, M. (2000). *The dignity of working men: Morality and the boundaries of race, class, and immigration.* Cambridge, MA: Harvard University Press.

Leidner, R. (1991). Serving hamburgers and selling insurance: Gender, work, and identity in interactive service jobs. *Gender & Society, 5*, 154–177.

Levinson, D. (1986). *The seasons of a man's life.* New York: Knopf.

Levinson, D. (1996). *The seasons of a woman's life.* New York: Knopf.

Liu, M., & Buzzanell, P. M. (2006). When workplace pregnancy highlights difference: Openings for detrimental gender and supervisory relations. In J. H. Fritz & B. L. Omdahl (Eds.), *Problematic relationships in the workplace* (pp. 47–68). New York: Peter Lang.

Lucas, K., & Buzzanell, P. M. (2004). Blue-collar work, career, and success: Occupational narratives of *sisu. Journal of Applied Communication Research, 32*, 273–292.

Lucas, K., & Buzzanell, P. M. (2006). Employees "without" families: Discourses of family as an external constraint to work-life balance. In L. H. Turner & R. West (Eds.), *Family communication sourcebook* (pp. 335–352). Thousand Oaks, CA: Sage.

MacDermid, S. M., Roy, K., & Zvonkovic, A. M. (2005). Don't stop at the borders: Theorizing beyond dichotomies of work and family. In V. L. Bengston, A. C. Acock, K. R. Allen, P. Dilworth-Anderson, & D. M. Klein (Eds.), *Sourcebook of family theory and research* (pp. 493–516). Thousand Oaks, CA: Sage.

Mainiero, L. A., & Sullivan, S. E. (2005). Kaleidoscope careers: An alternate explanation for the "opt-out" revolution. *Academy of Management Executive, 19*(1), 106–123.

Marshall, J. (1989). Re-visioning career concepts: A feminist invitation. In M. B. Arthur, D. T. Hall, & B. S. Lawrence (Eds.), *Handbook of career theory* (pp. 275–291). Cambridge, UK: Cambridge University Press.

Maume, D. J., Jr. (1999). Occupational segregation and the career mobility of white men and women. *Social Forces, 77,* 1433–1459.

McKerrow, R. E. (1999). Space and time in the postmodern polity. *Western Journal of Communication, 63,* 271–290.

McKinlay, A. (2002). "Dead selves": The birth of the modern career. *Organization, 9,* 595–614.

McNay, L. (1999). Subject, psyche and agency: The work of Judith Butler. *Theory, Culture & Society, 16,* 175–193.

Meisenbach, R. J. (2004). *Framing fund raising: A poststructuralist analysis of higher education fund raisers' work and identities.* Unpublished dissertation, Purdue University, W. Lafayette, IN.

Miles, R. E., & Snow, C. C. (1996). Twenty-First-Century careers. In M. B. Arthur & D. M. Rousseau (Eds.), *The boundaryless career: A new employment principle for a new organizational era* (pp. 97–115). New York: Oxford University Press.

Millman, J. (2005, June 6). Promotion track fades for those starting at bottom. *Wall Street Journal,* pp. A1, A5.

Mumby, D. K. (2000). Communication, organization, and the public sphere: A feminist perspective. In P. M. Buzzanell (Ed.), *Rethinking organizational and managerial communication from feminist perspectives* (pp. 3–23). Thousand Oaks, CA: Sage.

Nelson, D. J. (2005). *A national analysis of diversity in science and engineering faculties at research universities.* Norman, OK. Retrieved September 13, 2005 from http://cheminfo chem.ou.edu/~djn/diversity/briefings/Diversity %20Report%20Final.pdf

Newman, K. S. (1993). *Declining fortunes: The withering of the American dream.* New York: Basic Books.

Padavic, I., & Reskin, B. (2002). *Women and men at work* (2nd ed.). Thousand Oaks, CA: Pine Forge Press.

Perlow, L. A. (1998). Boundary control: The social ordering of work and family time in a high-tech corporation. *Administrative Science Quarterly, 43,* 328–357.

Perlow, L. A. (1999). The time famine: Toward a sociology of work time. *Administrative Science Quarterly, 44,* 57–81.

Powell, G. N., & Mainiero, L. A. (1992). Cross-currents in the river of time: Conceptualizing the complexities of women's careers. *Journal of Management, 18,* 215–237.

Ragins, B. R., & Cotton, J. L. (1999). Mentor functions and outcomes: A comparison of men and women in formal and informal mentoring relationships. *Journal of Applied Psychology, 84,* 529–550.

Rosenbaum, J. E. (1989). Organization career systems and employee misperceptions. In M. B. Authur, D. T. Hall, & B. S. Lawrence (Eds.), *Handbook of career theory* (pp. 329–353). Cambridge, UK: Cambridge University Press.

Saltzman, A. (1991). *Downshifting: Reinventing success on a slower track.* New York: HarperCollins.

Schein, E. H. (1990). *Career anchors: Discovering your real values.* San Francisco: Jossey-Bass Pfeiffer.

Schneer, J. A., & Reitman, F. (2002). Managerial life without a wife: Family structure and managerial career success. *Journal of Business Ethics, 37,* 25–38.

Schor, J. B. (1992). *The overworked American: The unexpected decline of leisure.* New York: Basic Books.

Sheehy, G. (1995). *New passages: Mapping your life across time.* New York: Random House.

Smith, V. (2001). *Crossing the great divide: Worker risk and opportunity in the new economy.* Ithaca, NY: ILR Press.

Spradlin, A. (1998). The price of "passing:" Lesbian perspectives on authenticity in organizations. *Management Communication Quarterly, 11,* 598–605.

Sterns, H. L., & Huyck, M. H. (2001). The role of work in midlife. In M. E. Lachman (Ed.), *Handbook of midlife development* (pp. 447–486). New York: John Wiley & Sons.

Summers, L. H. (2005, January 14). *Remarks at NBER Conference on Diversifying the Science & Engineering Workforce.* Retrieved February 18, 2005, from www.president .harvard.edu/speeches/2005/nber.html

Tonn, J. C. (2003). *Mary P. Follett: Creating democracy, transforming management.* New Haven, CT: Yale University Press.

Tracy, S. J., & Trethewey, A. (2005). Fracturing the real-self←—→fake-self dichotomy: Moving toward "crystallized" organizational discourses and identities. *Communication Theory, 15,* 168–195.

Trethewey, A. (2000). Revisioning control: A feminist critique of disciplined bodies. In P. M. Buzzanell (Ed.), *Rethinking organizational and managerial communication from feminist perspectives* (pp. 107–127). Thousand Oaks, CA: Sage.

Trethewey, A. (2001). Reproducing and resisting the master narrative of decline: Midlife professional women's experiences of aging. *Management Communication Quarterly, 15,* 183–226.

Weinger, S. (1998). Children living in poverty: Their perception of career opportunities. *Families in Society: The Journal of Contemporary Human Services, 79,* 320–330.

Williams, J. (2000). *Unbending gender: Why family and work conflict and what to do about it.* New York: Oxford University Press.

Wood, J. T., & Conrad, C. (1983). Paradox in the experience of professional women. *Western Journal of Speech Communication, 47,* 305–322.

PART III

GENDER AND COMMUNICATION IN RHETORICAL CONTEXTS

Introduction

◆ Karlyn Kohrs Campbell

S urveying the study of gender and rhetoric is a potentially enormous enterprise because rhetoric is one of the oldest areas in the field of communication. Although the five chapters in this section concern central topics in the study of gender and rhetoric, several more could have been included if space were available. Moreover, the terms *gender* and *rhetoric* are challenging because both have had different meanings at different times. Because men have long been the norm and women the "other" (de Beauvoir, 1952), the study of men or masculinity has only recently become a part of the study of gender. Likewise, the study of rhetoric long focused almost exclusively on oratory, but recent scholarship, as two chapters in this section illustrate, has turned toward the intersections of rhetoric and mass media.

In most scholarship before the late 20th century, gender was generally used to refer to women's "difference" from men rather than to refer to something that both possessed, and the history of rhetorical studies is no different. Women were thought to embody gender while men did not, in much the same way that African Americans embodied race, while whiteness remained invisible. As a result, the body of work investigating women's rhetorical theories and practices, with a specific focus on the role of gender, is much larger than that investigating men's. That is, although men's rhetorical activities have received far more attention from scholars, the role of gender in those activities usually remained invisible.

The chapters in this section reflect this reality, which the authors acknowledge in different ways. The role of masculinity in rhetorical action, for instance, remains understudied; consequently, it is not a major focus in this section. Although the *Handbook* focuses on gender and communication rather than women and communication, most research discussed in this section concerns women, reflecting rhetorical scholars' concerted efforts over the last several decades to remediate the longstanding emphasis on the discourses of powerful white men and to recover women's rhetorical history.

Despite the long-standing derogation of women's public discourse, efforts to preserve U.S. women's rhetoric predate the emergence of the discipline of communication or of public address as an object of study. From the beginning, women who spoke for social causes worked to create a historical record of their discursive efforts, dramatically illustrated by the creation of the six-volume *History of Woman Suffrage* (1881, 1882, 1886, 1902, 1922). Accordingly, some of the public activism by the early advocates of

woman's rights, abolitionists and civil rights activists, suffragists, dress reformers, birth control champions, and others has been preserved in out-of-print books, yellowing newspapers, and convention proceedings, as well as in their papers.

The effort to bring this work to the attention of communication scholars began in the 1930s when Doris G. Yoakam completed her doctoral dissertation, *An Historical Survey of the Public Speaking Activities of American Women, 1828–1860,* at the University of Southern California in 1935, and Harriet E. Grim completed her three-volume dissertation, *Susan B. Anthony: Exponent of Freedom,* at the University of Wisconsin in 1937. The essays and chapters that Yoakam subsequently published, "Pioneer Women Orators of America" (1937), "Women's Introduction to the American Platform" (1943), and "Susan B. Anthony" (1955), brought some of these materials to the attention of the field.

In 1952, Lillian O'Connor completed a dissertation at Columbia University, inspired by Yoakam's work, that won the Pi Lambda Theta award for research on the professional advancement of women. Published as *Pioneer Women Orators: Rhetoric in the Ante-Bellum Reform Movement* (1954), it was a work of scholarly import that used primary sources to identify 27 women who spoke prior to 1860 and whose texts could be located, beginning with speeches by Frances Wright (1828) and Maria W. Miller Stewart (1832) and ending with those of Caroline Healy Dall (1859) and Martha Coffin Wright (1860). Repeating a pattern that has recurred often in women's history (Lerner, 1993), these pioneering efforts had little or no impact on the study of public address in the United States, which continued to conceive of public discourse as an almost exclusively male activity, as reflected in anthologies (Campbell, 1985).

Ultimately, the sustained study of women's rhetoric, like that of women's history generally, is linked to the rise of the second wave of feminism in the 1960s. Of note, however, is Eleanor Flexner's history of the early U.S. woman's rights movement, originally published in 1959. Similarly, Wilmer A. Linkugel's 1960 dissertation on the Rev. Dr. Anna Howard Shaw at the University of Wisconsin, which collected her extant speech texts, predated the second wave, and his essay, "The Woman Suffrage Argument of Anna Howard Shaw" (1963), was the first critical study of women's rhetoric to appear in the *Quarterly Journal of Speech* after Yoakam's 1937 essay. Subsequent scholarship focused on the second wave of feminism (Campbell, 1973; Foss, 1979; Hancock, 1972; Hope, 1975; Solomon, 1979). Following that were works challenging the canon of male orators with criticisms that illuminated outstanding works by such great women speakers as Elizabeth Cady Stanton (Campbell, 1980; Waggenspack, 1989); Angelina Grimké (Browne, 1996, 1999; Daughton, 1995; Japp, 1985); Sarah Moore Grimké (Vonnegut, 1995); Susan B. Anthony (Campbell, 1983); Ida B. Wells, Mary Church Terrell, and Sojourner Truth (Campbell, 1986); Emma Goldman (Solomon, 1988); Frances E. Willard (Slagell, 1992); Lucy Stone (Kerr, 1992); Olympia Brown (Greene, 1983); Ernestine Potowski Rose (Bodensteiner, 2000), Matilda Joslyn Gage (Brammer, 2000), and Mary Harris "Mother" Jones (Tonn, 1996), among others.

Nearly all white women who were activists in the 19th century absorbed the racism that has permeated U.S. culture from its beginnings. Elizabeth Cady Stanton, Susan B. Anthony, and others made racist comments in response to the ratification of 14th and 15th amendments, which not only denied suffrage to women but inserted the word *male* into the Constitution (*History of Woman Suffrage,* 1882, pp. 188–189, 270; see also Davis, 1981). Because of white racism, a distinct rhetorical tradition began in 1831 with the efforts of Maria W. Miller Stewart to galvanize Boston's African Americans to self-help action and to shame whites into living up to the principles espoused in the nation's

founding documents (Richardson, 1987). Exclusionary practices dismissed or ignored the activities of the National Association of Colored Women's Clubs and the rhetorical efforts of Mary Church Terrell and Ida B. Wells-Barnett, who fought against the evils of racism in all its forms and for the civil rights of all (Giddings, 1984; Terborg-Penn, 1998). Bacon, in Chapter 12, describes how the recovery of African American women's rhetoric, the history of their activism, and the development of distinctive critical perspectives has been chiefly the work of African American theorists and critics, energized by the civil rights movement and by African American feminists/ womanists.

Feminist theory and/or theory that incorporates gender issues has developed as well, although much remains to be done. The *Handbook* includes essays on gender in Greco-Roman theorizing and on gender and contemporary rhetorical theory. Other noteworthy efforts include Blair's (1992) critique of rhetorical historiography, the special edition of the *Western Communication Journal* on histories of rhetoric (Blair & Kahl, 1990), and Ratcliffe's (1996) *Anglo-American Challenges to the Rhetorical Tradition*, in which she attempts to educe feminist rhetorical theory from the practices of Mary Daly, Adrienne Rich, and Virginia Woolf.

The essays in this section survey the scholarship in five areas and identify some of the challenges facing scholars. Keremidchieva and I (Chapter 10) trace the history of public address as an object of study and the scholarly traditions that prompted recovery of the history of women's public activism, disciplinary traditions that affect the study of gender, problems created by definitions of public and private, and research on alternative rhetorical practices that interact with and affect what has traditionally been considered public address. Such redefinitions may suggest the possibility of a feminine public sphere. Visual mass communication technologies also pose new challenges for students of gender and public address. The rhetorics of oppressed groups must become hyperembodied to gain attention. As the site and substance of their messages, these bodies challenge the assumption that argument is ever and always verbal. Moreover, because the "Oprahesque" female style emphasizing conversation, emotionality, and self-reflection is particularly suited to television, male politicians are constrained to adapt to its feminine norms. In requiring that they enact an effeminate style of disclosure and pseudo-intimacy, television effectively "queers" men's public address.

Beasley (Chapter 11) claims that second-wave feminism set the agenda for much of recent social scientific and humanistic research on gender and political communication. The difficulties in defining either the second wave or political communication complicate any assessment of their relationships. Studies of political communication from these differing disciplinary traditions reflect conflicting methods and differing views of activism and even of what constitutes "politics." Beasley compares and contrasts the scholarship emerging from these traditions and affirms the value of both but indicates strongly that each would be strengthened significantly by more attention to the research in the other.

Bacon (Chapter 12) surveys the scholarship that explores the intersection and interaction of race/ethnicity and gender. Theorists and critics of color challenge traditional methods as inimical to the discursive practices of those who are not white males and identify the non-oratorical but important rhetorical practices of women and men of color. In particular, scholars have explored the dual oppression of women of color as well as the ways that concepts of masculinity can oppress men of color. Accordingly, an emphasis on the intersectionality of race/ethnicity, class, gender, and nationality becomes essential to analyzing the rhetorical praxis of women and men of color. Of note, too, in the dynamics of race/ethnicity and gender are the dynamics and effects of privilege on white women and men, which are often unrecognized and unacknowledged. Critical methods grounded in signifying and

Afrocentricity have emerged out of the lived experiences and history of African Americans.

Glenn and Collings Eves (Chapter 13) detail research on rhetoric and gender in ancient Greece and Rome. They identify the impact of scholarship that takes gender into account, the power of gender binaries to discipline Greek and Roman males as well as females, and the effort to recover the traces and texts of such ancient women as Aspasia, Sappho, Hipparchia, Hortensia, and others. They also examine the binary that required elaborate systems of gender identification, including the notion that signs of effeminacy were indicative of defective character, which was linked to control of the body in delivery. Finally, they suggest possibilities for alternate readings of this material and for extending studies of gender and rhetoric in cultures other than those dominant in Greece and Rome.

Stormer (Chapter 14) surveys the conflicts that bedevil contemporary theorizing about gender and rhetoric; in particular, the sense in which the embodiment of rhetoric has been repressed in order for theorizing to occur. He interrogates the common assumption of widely differing rhetorical theorists that lived experience produces rhetorical knowledge and urges attention to the challenge posed by seeing gender as living in a sexed body. He stimulates us to theorize from an understanding that being gendered and being rhetorical are reciprocal and interactive, and he challenges us to think differently, asking, "What if we take the body as a rhetorical situation?"

These chapters offer a portrait of the contexts, assumptions, and goals that have animated the study of gender and rhetoric in the discipline of communication. As they make clear, the intersections of gender and rhetoric span centuries. They can be traced from the rhetorical practices and theories of antiquity to women's emergence on the public platform in the 19th century in the United States to current theories of gender performativity. Equally as important as these authors' recognition of the depth and breadth of this field of study is their articulation of new directions in which to move and new questions to ponder as research continues to develop. Taken as a whole, they constitute our effort to describe the state of scholarship on gender and rhetoric in 2005 and to imagine its future.

◆ References

Beauvoir, S. de (1952). *The second sex* (H. M. Parshley, Trans.). New York: Knopf.

Blair, C. (1992). Contested histories of rhetoric: The politics of preservation, progress, and change. *Quarterly Journal of Speech, 78,* 403–428.

Blair, C., & Kahl, M. L. (1990). Introduction [to special issue]: Revising the history of rhetorical theory. *Western Journal of Speech Communication, 54,* 148–159.

Bodensteiner, K. A. (2000). *The rhetoric of Ernestine L. Rose with collected speeches and letters* (3 vols.). Doctoral dissertation, University of Kansas.

Brammer, L. R. (2000). *Excluded from suffrage history: Matilda Joslyn Gage, nineteenth-century American feminist.* Westport, CT: Greenwood Press.

Browne, S. H. (1996). Encountering Angelina Grimké: Violence, identity, and the creation of radical community. *Quarterly Journal of Speech, 82,* 55–73.

Browne, S. H. (1999). *Angelina Grimké: Rhetoric, identity, and the radical imagination.* Lansing: Michigan State University Press.

Campbell, K. K. (1973). The rhetoric of women's liberation: An oxymoron. *Quarterly Journal of Speech 59,* 74–86.

Campbell, K. K. (1980). Stanton's "Solitude of Self": A rationale for feminism. *Quarterly Journal of Speech, 66,* 304–312.

Campbell, K. K. (1983). Contemporary rhetorical criticism: Genres, analogs, and Susan B. Anthony. In J. I. Sisco, (Ed.), *The Jensen lectures: Contemporary communication studies* (pp. 117–132). Tampa: University of South Florida.

Campbell, K. K. (1985). The communication classroom: A chilly climate for women? *ACA Bulletin #51,* 68–72.

Campbell, K. K. (1986). Style and content in the rhetoric of early Afro-American feminists. *Quarterly Journal of Speech, 72,* 434–445.

Condit [Railsback], C. (1984). The contemporary American abortion controversy: Stages in the argument. *Quarterly Journal of Speech, 70,* 410–424.

Daughton, S. M. (1995). The fine texture of enactment: Iconicity as empowerment in Angelina Grimké's Pennsylvania Hall address. *Women's Studies in Communication, 18,* 19–43.

Davis, A. Y. (1981). *Women, race and class.* New York: Vintage/Random House.

Flexner, E. (1959). *Century of struggle: The woman's rights movement in the United States.* Cambridge, MA: Belknap/Harvard University Press.

Foss, S. K. (1979). Equal Rights Amendment controversy: Two worlds in conflict. *Quarterly Journal of Speech, 65,* 275–288.

Giddings, P. (1984). *When and where I enter: The impact of black women on race and sex in America.* New York: William Morrow.

Greene, D. (1983). *Suffrage and religious principle: Speeches and writings of Olympia Brown.* Metuchen, NJ: Scarecrow Press.

Hancock, B. R. (1972). Affirmation by negation in the women's liberation movement. *Quarterly Journal of Speech, 58,* 264–271.

History of woman suffrage, 6 vols. (1881, 1882, 1886, 1902, 1922/ rpt. edition, 1985). Ed. Elizabeth Cady Stanton, Susan B. Anthony, & Matilda Joslyn Gage (vols. 1–3); Susan B. Anthony & Ida Husted Harper (vols. 4–6). Salem, NH: Ayer.

Hope, D. S. (1975). Redefinition of self: A comparison of the rhetoric of the women's liberation and black liberation movements. *Today's Speech, 23,* 17–25.

Japp, P. M. (1985). Esther or Isaiah? The abolitionist-feminist rhetoric of Angelina Grimké. *Quarterly Journal of Speech, 71,* 335–348.

Kerr, A. M. (1992). *Lucy Stone: Speaking out for equality.* New Brunswick, NJ: Rutgers University Press.

Lerner, G. (1993). *The creation of feminist consciousness: From the Middle Ages to eighteen-seventy*. New York: Oxford University Press.

Linkugel, W. A. (1963). The woman suffrage argument of Anna Howard Shaw. *Quarterly Journal of Speech, 49*, 165–174.

O'Connor, L. (1954). *Pioneer women orators: Rhetoric in the ante-bellum reform movement*. New York: Vantage Press.

Ratcliffe, K. (1996). *Anglo-American feminist challenges to the rhetorical traditions: Virginia Woolf, Mary Daly, Adrienne Rich*. Carbondale: Southern Illinois University Press.

Richardson, M. (Ed.). (1987). *Maria W. Stewart, America's first black woman political writer: Essays and speeches*. Bloomington: Indiana University Press.

Slagell, A. R. (1992). *A good woman speaking well: The oratory of Frances E. Willard*. Doctoral dissertation, University of Wisconsin.

Solomon, M. (1979). The positive woman's' journey: A mythic analysis of the rhetoric of STOP ERA. *Quarterly Journal of Speech, 65*, 262–274.

Solomon, M. (1988). Ideology as rhetorical constraint: The anarchist agitation of "Red Emma" Goldman. *Quarterly Journal of Speech, 74*, 184–200.

Terborg-Penn, R. (1998). *African American women in the struggle for the vote*. Bloomington: Indiana University Press.

Tonn, M. B. (1996). Militant motherhood: Labor's Mary Harris "Mother" Jones. *Quarterly Journal of Speech, 82*, 1–21.

Vonnegut, K. S. (1995). Poison or panacea? Sarah Moore Grimké's use of the public letter. *Communication Studies, 46*, 73–88.

Waggenspack, B. M. (1989). *The search for self-sovereignty: The oratory of Elizabeth Cady Stanton*. New York: Greenwood.

Yoakam, D. G. (1943). Women's introduction to the American platform. In W. N. Brigance (Ed.), *History and criticism of American public address* (Vol. 1, pp. 153–192). New York: Longmans, Green.

Yoakam, D. (1937). Pioneer women orators in America. *Quarterly Journal of Speech, 23*, 251–259.

Zaeske, S. (1995). The "promiscuous audience" controversy and the emergence of the early woman's rights movement. *Quarterly Journal of Speech, 81*, 191–207.

10

GENDER AND PUBLIC ADDRESS

◆ Karlyn Kohrs Campbell and
Zornitsa Keremidchieva

eminist scholars long have debated the usefulness of gender as an
analytic category, questioning whether it can avoid renaturalizing
sex differences (Hawkesworth, 1997) or be used to analyze issues other
than those related to women. Addressing the challenges of writing history through the lens of gender, Scott (1997) argues that uses of gender
related to "women, children, families, and ideologies," shield topics
such as "war, diplomacy, and high politics" from critical scrutiny
(p. 156) and "endorse a certain functionalist view ultimately rooted in
biology and [that] perpetuate the idea of separate spheres (sex and politics, family and nation, women and men) in the writing of history" (p.
157). Although this usage captures the social construction of sex relations, it cannot explain their historical and cultural particularity, their
internal mechanisms, and the forces that transform them.

Rhetorical scholarship faces similar challenges. Although rhetoric has
been practiced and studied since antiquity, public address as an object of
study begins with Brigance's (1943) *A History and Criticism of American
Public Address,* in which he claims that "the emergence of women on the
American platform was so distinctive a phase of history that it seemed
best to give it fitting emphasis in a separate chapter" (p. viii). Thus, while
acknowledging women's oratorical history, Brigance inaugurated a scholarly pattern: discussions of gender would be associated primarily with
women's rhetorical practices, whose traditions would be considered separate and distinct, hence not immediately relevant to mainstream theorizing about public address as a cultural and political form.

Public address had been studied as oratory. Wrage's (1947) *Public Address: A Study in Social and Intellectual History* codified a shift from the study of speech performances to the study of speech texts, marking the decline of elocution and oral performance and the rise of textualism (Parrish, 1957; Rosteck, 1998). In textualizing oratorical performance as a history of ideas, Wrage (1947) posited a claim fundamental to public address scholarship, that "from the speeches given by many men, it is possible to observe the reflections of prevailing social ideas and attitudes" (p. 456). Such study illuminated the nature of society: "A speech is an agency of its time, one whose surviving record provides a repository of themes and their elaborations from which we may gain insight into the life of an era as well as into the mind of a man" (Wrage, pp. 455–456). Public address gained eminence as scholarship that represented disparate cultural experiences, a synthesis underwritten by gendered assumptions.

Yoakam's (1943) study of women's public address in Brigance's *A History and Criticism of American Public Address* presupposed the dominant notions of publicness: (a) public speech is a practice that constitutes U.S. democracy; hence, public speaking is a means of governance of inherent political significance; (b) public and private speech differ, a conceptual distinction between political and apolitical speech and a spatial distinction between public forum and private occasion. Significantly, the public domain was seen as the terrain of men's activities, whereas women were associated with the private sphere.

Yoakam (1943) claimed that the early 19thcentury woman, clearly white and middle-class, was confined to a "woman's sphere," centered in the home, where "it was believed she could yield to society the greatest returns" (p. 153). Women, however, found numerous points of contact with the world outside, particularly as audiences at public lectures and organizers of abolitionist bazaars and fairs. Those activities fell "within the dictates of the sphere . . . to be of service in the cause of humanity" (p. 157). Yet women soon aspired to the public platform. Their methods were

> too slow for the time, for the need. All the pent-up energies, all the rebellion against degradation and submission, all the desires to effect radical changes could no longer be held in submission. [Women], too, must use the public platform to disseminate their ideas, to create and stimulate a public sentiment so strong that eradication of oppression and inequality could be the only ultimate result. (p. 157)

Implicit in Yoakam's depiction is that public speaking has an effectivity unmatched by other means of social engagement. Her positing of an idealized public sphere as an engine of progress is consistent with Brigance's (1943) emphasis on public address as a technology of influence and (progressive) citizenship (Hance, 1958; O'Neill, 1941; Temple, 1947; Timmons, 1942). Adopting a context of spheres necessitates a narrative of inclusion in which the story of women's public speaking will always be about women moving from (politically insignificant) female space to a (proper, singularly important politically) male sphere, although separate spheres risks an androcentric understanding of the democratic process. When incorporated into evaluations, it risks "a tedious predictability, offering us but two basic findings: women talk differently from men, and all existing discourse is patriarchal" (Condit, 1997, p. 112), which calls into question its descriptive, analytic, and explanatory utility. If, following Butler (1990), scholarship also is understood as an "apparatus of production" (p. 7), then public address scholarship produces culturally available conceptions of the natural order. Gender underwrites its history and the ways in which public address has been studied.

Our purpose is to locate gender as a conceptual foundation from which to evaluate what public address has been and/or needs to be as a communicative phenomenon and as an object and tradition of scholarship. In what follows, a dual inquiry—into the state of scholarship on gender in public address and on the gendered underpinnings of the field's theory and methods—leads to further inquiry into the interplay of rhetoric and gender in the constitution of communal practices, modes of knowledge, and means of governance.

◆ Gender and the Public(s) of Public Address

During the cold war, Wrage's argument that speeches are a history of cultural ideas permitted scholars to emphasize public speaking as a distinctively democratic practice and to assert the discipline's relevance in a context marked by the anxieties of war. Often reiterated (Baker & Eubanks, 1960; Dearin, 1980; Haring, 1952; Lang, 1951; Wallace, 1954), the claim that studying public address is a means to understand national character and promote "patriotism" (O'Brien, 1951) culminated in Lucas's (1988) insistence that "[the major oratorical texts] are unsurpassed historical and cultural documents of the first order. Central to our country's mythic heritage and historical experience, they merit interrogation as quintessentially American documents" (p. 247). In Lucas's extension of Wrage's argument, public speaking defined the norms of U.S. democracy, and public address scholarship documented national ideas and values, thus becoming part of the project of U.S. exceptionalism (Greene & Kuswa, 2002).

Public speaking and citizenship were interdependent, a link that Dearin (1980) claims "is by no means encompassed by the genre called oratory or 'public speaking,' in the United States, as well as in certain other Western societies, it is epitomized by this genre. To ignore speeches is to ignore an important determinant of history" (p. 355).

Dearin echoes Brigance (1943), who insisted that personal influence and social status, not artistry, guided his choice of speakers, which presupposes that those who speak in national forums are the kinds of citizens worthy of critical attention. Requiring that scholars study works of national significance encouraged analysis of the speeches of U.S. presidents, leaders of national movements, and eminent churchmen, although the nationalization of politics was historically specific to the late 19th and the early 20th centuries (Beasley, 2001). As an assumption it treats "what were life and death concerns affecting a majority of the population . . . as frivolous, minor, and largely irrelevant to our rhetorical past" (Campbell, 1989d, p. 218). Apart from studies of women's participation in the suffrage, antislavery, and prohibition movements and in Equal Rights Amendment activities, the local and municipal politics traditionally more densely populated with and engaged in by women would not meet the so-called national significance test (Mattingly, 2002; Ryan, 1992). Thus, interrogating what is public in public address scholarship challenges the "privileging of one sphere over the other and the kinds of discourses that get valued or marginalized as a result" (Griffin, 1996).

Scholars of gender and public address have had a variety of responses to the problems presented by the gendering of the public platform. Generally, however, they have been united by an emphasis on recovering and revalorizing women's rhetorical activities, both public and private, thus understanding gender as the difference represented by women. As we discuss below, one dominant trend has been scholars' emphasis on the inclusion of women in public address studies, a project that details the contexts for resistance to women's public discourse as well as women's rhetorical responses to that resistance. This emphasis has produced a body of scholarship designed to highlight women's rhetorical contributions in disparate public contexts.

RECOVERING HISTORICAL WOMEN'S VOICES

Scholars researching women's activities have made sustained efforts to democratize public address. The project of recovering women's rhetorics was launched to counteract the gender bias at the core of the rhetorical canon; its initial focus centered on the rhetorical activities of 19th- and early 20th-century women rhetors in the United States (Campbell, 1985, 2001). Campbell (1998a) argues that "women's ignorance of their history, of their invention, has placed a double burden on them, compelling them to reinvent over and over again the spaces and selves that have given them voice" (p. 117). Although not without its skeptics (Ballif, 1992; Biesecker, 1992; Hopkins, 1989), recovery of women's public address has appealed to feminist scholars despite the challenges posed by a lack of texts, a phenomenon attributable to structural biases against archiving and reproducing women's documents, especially those written by women who were not educated or affluent (Campbell, 2002). The recovery project has produced a number of collections of women's historical and contemporary public discourse, including those by O'Connor (1954), Kennedy and O'Shields (1983), Anderson (1984), as well as Campbell's (1989a, 1989b) two-volume commentary and reader on historical feminist rhetoric (see also Campbell, 1993, 1994). In addition, scholars in composition and rhetoric have produced a number of book-length critical anthologies treating women's rhetoric and rhetorical theory (Donawerth, 2002a; Lunsford, 1995; Mattingly, 2001; Miller & Bridwell-Bowles, 2005; Ritchie & Ronald, 2001; Wertheimer, 1997), as well as other work on women's historical rhetorical education (Bacon & McClish, 2000; Donawerth, 2002b; Eldred & Mortensen, 1993; Hobbs, 1995; Mattingly, 1995; Rothermel, 2002).

A primary emphasis in this critical scholarship has been understanding women rhetors' responses to the restrictions on their public speech, restrictions which historians attribute to such cultural mythologies as the "cult of domesticity" (Kraditor, 1968), the "cult of true womanhood" (Welter, 1976), and "republican motherhood" (Kerber, 1980). Campbell's (1989a) observation that women overcame considerable obstacles to speak was based on study of the woman's rights movement. Another significant strain of scholarship has examined the rhetoric of historical women on behalf of themselves and other marginalized groups in movements advocating abolition, woman's rights, temperance, birth control, and labor reform (see Browne, 1999; Carlson, 1992, 1994; Conrad, 1981; Croy, 1998; Daughton, 1995; Dow, 1991; Hayden, 1999a, 1999b; Henry, 1995; Hogan & Solomon, 1995, 1996, 2000; Japp, 1985; Kendall & Fisher, 1974; Kowal, 2000; Linkugel & Solomon, 1991; Mattina, 1994; McCleary, 1994; Miller, 1999; Powell, 1995; Ray, 2003; Shepler & Mattina, 1999; Sillars, 1995; Solomon, 1988; Tonn, 1996; Triece, 2000; Waggenspack, 1989; Zulick & Leff, 1995). Much of this work focuses on the inventive strategies employed by women rhetors to respond to the difficult historical contexts they faced as "public" women advocating social change (Campbell, 1998a).

More recent scholarship has identified specific cultural and political forces contributing to women's exclusion by demonstrating that gender becomes a public concern as means of resolving other political exigencies. Zaeske's (1995) narrative of the emergence of the "promiscuous audience," the forbidding of women to address audiences of men and women, notes that Frances Wright, among the first to address mixed audiences, was not so attacked despite "creating a sensation by lecturing in public about politics" (p. 194). The tour by the abolitionist Grimké sisters, which attracted men and women, prompted the General Association of the Massachusetts Congregational Churches to issue a written order against women speaking to mixed-gender audiences on public topics. Containment of women's right to speak was articulated in the political agenda of thwarting abolitionist activism (see also Morris, 2001).

Indeed, scholars have argued that women's responses to the rhetorical problems they faced were sensitive to the political and historical contexts in which they operated, even at the risk of compromising feminist goals. Zaeske (1995) demonstrates that early feminists, such as the Grimké sisters, Abby Kelley, and Lucretia Coffin Mott, argued for women's right to address promiscuous audiences from the standpoint of a "gendered morality that emphasized the special nature of female benevolence and the social utility of exercising that benevolence through the spoken word" (p. 192; see also Carlson, 1992). This rhetoric reinforced a view of women as citizens of a different kind. By the 1848 Seneca Falls convention, speakers derived arguments from the philosophy of natural rights (Campbell, 1989a), reflecting the rise of modern liberalism, which has proved ill equipped to address the structural bases of women's exclusion from public life. In the 1870s, arguments from expediency, which linked woman's rights to social benefits, began to predominate (Campbell, 1989a; Dow, 1991), often reinforcing contemporary political anxieties about immigration, racial equality, and industrial labor disputes (see, e.g., Murphy, 1990).

Studies of historical women's discourse have focused on the activities of white women, although critical anthologies have tended to include a chapter or two on African American women's experiences and discourse (see, e.g., Campbell, 1989a; Logan, 1997). A few essays in communication journals have examined their historical rhetoric (Behling, 2002; Campbell, 1986). In recent years, however, a number of books have initiated a recovery project for African American women's rhetoric that parallels the project described in this chapter (see Bacon, 2002; Houston & Davis, 2002; Logan, 1999; Peterson, 1995; Royster 2000). Bacon's essay in Chapter 12 describes that project and explores the intersections of race/ethnicity and gender in rhetorical action.

GENDER AND THE DISCIPLINING OF PUBLIC ADDRESS

Recent public address scholarship that goes beyond a focus on historical women continues to examine the ways in which disciplining gender becomes a tool for political suppression. Morris (2002) demonstrates that intensified investments in gendered speech norms often constitute a response to political and social crises. His study of the sex crime panic launched by J. Edgar Hoover traces the transformation of the homosexual from "pansy into menace" following the Great Depression. Through historically contingent networks of political exigencies, such studies suggest that gender, itself intensely historical, comes to underwrite norms of rhetorical access. Gender, then, is a regime of power that produces norms and forms of public address and regulates who can enact them (see also Brookey, 1998; Campbell, 1995; Hiltner, 1999; Miller, 1998), a conclusion that is borne out in studies of the public discourse of contemporary women (see, e.g., Campbell, 1998b; Jamieson, 1995).

Public address scholarship on their rhetorical activities, although it has retained some focus on women's efforts in movements for social change, such as the second wave of feminism, generally has tended to emphasize the role of women's discourse in organized political contexts, as Beasley does in Chapter 11. For example, continuing in the tradition of "great women speakers" inaugurated by scholars of historical public address, researchers have created a stream of scholarship on the rhetoric of U.S. first ladies (Anderson, 2002; Campbell, 1996, 1998b; Edwards & Chen, 2000; Parry-Giles & Blair, 2002; Wertheimer, 2003). Much of the rhetoric of second-wave feminism, particularly radical feminism, does not lend itself to the same kind of treatment as historical women's rhetoric because much of it did not emerge on the public platform in the same fashion. Instead, as Campbell (1973) has described, second-wave feminism was characterized by writings that emerged from consciousness-raising. Such discourse was highly personal and thus resists traditional modes of analysis that analyze rhetoric addressing public issues. Even so, a small body of scholarship has emerged on feminist rhetoric—and responses to it—from this period, although much of it focuses on visible public issues, such as the Equal Rights Amendment or abortion rights (Condit, 1990; Foss, 1979; Hancock, 1972; Pearce, 1999; Perkins, 1989; Solomon, 1979).

◆ Engendering Alternatives to Dominant Modes of Public Address

Like women rhetors on the public platform, scholars of gender and public address have had to face the rhetorical/critical/theoretical implications of the gender-based dichotomy between public and private, a dichotomy manifested in the rhetorical spaces, modes of address, and subject matter that they study (Kerber, 1988; Matthews, 1992). In recent decades, researchers have explored the ways that the gap between private and public is bridged through inventive rhetorical styles and genres as well as through the rhetorical functions of discursive practices that stretch the traditional boundaries of public address.

THEORIZING GENDER, GENRE, AND STYLE IN PUBLIC DISCOURSE

Struggles to overcome the limitations of available rhetorical means are addressed in scholarship investigating intersections of gender, genre, and style (Ritchie & Ronald, 2001; Shugart, 1997). Proceeding from her claim that the rhetoric of women's liberation was a distinctive genre that required unconventional means of analysis, Campbell (1989a) later coined the phrase "feminine style" to encapsulate the means women speakers developed to "cope with the conflicting demands of the podium" (p. 12). It included maintaining a personal tone, relying on personal experience and inductive forms of reasoning, and addressing the audience as peers. Through consciousness-raising, the goal was to empower audience members to see themselves as "agents of change." Significantly, feminine style is not essential to women's communication, but can be enacted by anyone (Campbell, 1989a, 1989b; Dow, 1995; Jamieson, 1988).

Subsequent scholarship enlarges the functions of feminine style. Zurakowski (1994) finds that speakers' use of feminine style encouraged audience participation and helped to sustain female commitment to the abortion rights movement. A similar effect of creating membership cohesion is reported in Hayden's (1997) study of the Boston Women's Health Book Collective. Mattina's (1994) work on Leonora O'Reilly, a Progressive Labor reformer and paid organizer and recruiter for the Women's Trade Union League, suggests that the possibilities and perils of feminine style were relevant to working-class reformers. Hayden (2003) also explores its strengths and weaknesses for a contemporary movement for social change.

Dow and Tonn (1993) extend feminine style by arguing that its elements appear in mainstream political discourse. They also contend that it produces a substantive effect by challenging the available grounds for political judgment. Based on examination of five presidential campaign films, however, Parry-Giles and Parry-Giles (1996) warn that feminine style can fall short as a transformative strategy for female political candidates, given that political image construction still relies on the "traditionally masculine myths, icons, and character traits derived from participation in male-based institutions" (p. 350).

EXPLORING ALTERNATIVE RHETORICAL PRACTICES AND THE ROLE OF THE "PUBLIC"

In other efforts to interrogate traditional conceptions of the private and public spheres, scholars have enlarged what counts as public address by investigating women's diverse rhetorical practices that are equally valuable in creating and sustaining public opinion (Foss, 1996; Foss & Foss, 1991; Mattingly, 1999; Torrens, 1997; Williams, 1994). In various reform campaigns, men and women have employed print, forms of association, correspondence, and visual rhetorics as alternative means that challenge the narrow definition of citizenship through public speaking and open the possibility for appreciating women's activities as more than time fillers for do-gooders. An illustrative case is Williams's (1994) study of quilts as examples of women's protest rhetoric: the Secession Quilt made by Jemima Cook in 1860, the Woman's Christian Temperance Union's Crusade Quilt of 1876, and the 1989 Eugene Peace Quilt made by residents of Eugene, Oregon. Quilts, Williams argues, gave some women "a vehicle for speech" (p. 21). Woman suffragists also used non-traditional means, such as parades (Borda, 2002), cartoons (Ramsey, 2000), *tableaux vivante,* "living speeches" or storyboards in shop windows that activists would slowly turn, picketing the White House, and burning President Wilson in effigy in order to disseminate their message (Baumgartner, 1994).

Solomon (1991) notes that, although public speaking was important in the woman's rights movement, "workers themselves recognized the vital importance of another rhetorical medium: the periodical edited and published by sympathizers. Through this channel, the movement could reach, educate, and inspire scores of women who could not be tapped by other means" (p. 3). Gring-Pemble (1998), in addressing "how women, like those who ultimately united in Seneca Falls and who have limited access to public space, locate a transitional space for exchanging ideas and discussing public matters prior to a public formal declaration" (p. 44), uses the correspondence between Antoinette Brown Blackwell and Lucy Stone to highlight the "pre-genesis" stage of women's rights (see Voss & Rowland, 2000). Mattingly (1995) focuses on 19th-century women's recruitment into activism via "women teaching other women" (p. 45; see also Gale & Griffin, 1998).

These authors suggest that women created zones to discuss matters of collective concern. Their use of print, alternative forms of public discourse, and organizing strategies suggests the possibility that their public sphere had distinct internal norms of stranger sociability (Freedman, 1979). Study has been shifted from the internal dynamics of women's social movements to identifying the social and political impact of women's activism. Publics are bigger than movements, but movements affect the rhetorical culture of a public. In this sense, the affiliative forms developed by women and the influence of various women's movements in raising issues deliberated by the larger culture reflect a key characteristic of a public; namely, "individuals who are personally strangers derive the core of common meanings that enable them to inhabit the same world" (Hauser, 1987, p. 438). By accounting for the captive and accidental audiences of women's rhetorics, including the responses of those who were opposed or passive or skeptical yet also remained in contact with women's issues, we gain a fuller sense of how discourses of and about women circulate and how investments in regulating women constitute public culture.

The public need not equal the political. Recent scholarship details the popular encounters of men and women of different classes at lecture halls, dinner parties given by women's clubs, on street corners, in charity clubs and reform meetings. Mead's (1951), Bode's (1956), Campbell's (1989c), Hogan and Hogan's (2003), and Ray's (2004, 2005) studies of the lyceum and of debating clubs historicize the moments when public speaking, gender, and class intersected in specific cultural locations. Nineteenth-century parlor rhetorics offer a glimpse into women's space not considered public but exhibiting oratorical performance (Johnson, 2002; see also Martin, 1987). Adopting a spatial conception of the public/private distinction risks conflating gender with class because politics is not always public, and men sometimes find political capital in the private sphere. Ryan (1992) notes:

> The political formulations of the late nineteenth century seemed only to reverse the spatial ordering, if not the power relations, of public life: the lower classes claimed open public spaces as the sites of political resistance, while their social superiors retreated into private recesses to exert power behind the scenes, in reform associations or bureaucratic channels. (pp. 277–278)

Private acts can become political actions. Theodore's (2002) work on women's first national petition campaign against forcible removal of the Cherokees and other tribes and Zaeske's (2002, 2003) studies of the evolution of women's petitioning call attention to the ways that signing petitions as private individuals became self-reflective performances of citizenship.

Finally, women's appeals to the state for rights posit a significant challenge to our view of the (male) public sphere as the zone par excellence of democratic governance. Following Habermas (1962/2000), Hauser (1987) describes a public sphere located between "the private realm of the personal, business, professional and special interests on the one hand and the domain of state action on the other" (p. 438). At the same time, Hauser fears that "at the institutional level, where the public sphere mediates between society and the state and is thus attached to a formal structure of authority, there is great susceptibility for degeneration of the public sphere as a discursive space"

(p. 439). A public sphere ensures a zone where "as words and deeds are publicly enacted without restraints, humans attending to communication experience freedom to discover their interests. As restraints are imposed," Hauser warns, "interests become distorted" (p. 438).

Historically, such free humans could only have been propertied white males. Pace Griffin (1996), this alone does not make the public sphere essentially male. Much research reveals that women have contributed greatly to the invention, dissemination, and regulation of public opinion and to topics of public debate. The question is whether to adopt Habermas's thesis about deterioration of the public sphere as a de facto loss of democracy to instrumental rationality. In Habermas's (1962/2000) narrative, the decline of the bourgeois public sphere coincides with the rise of the modern, liberal, constitutional state followed by the social welfare state. In the process, "the free exercise of the autonomy of private persons through norms of critical rationality is replaced by the instrumental logics of the state" (p. 225).

One way to address concerns about the decline of deliberative democracy is to apply historiographic rigor in investigating whether Habermas's narrative applies to the U.S. context (Ryan, 1992). Another is to consider whether our use of *public* and *private* confuses an analytic with a historical distinction (Kerber, 1988). Finally, historians and political theorists long have recognized women's historical role as state builders (Mink, 1990; Sklar, 1993; Wilkinson, 1999), given their efforts to obtain rights from the state, thus granting the state new relevance. Without underestimating the problematic gender dynamics of state politics, scholars should consider the ways in which concern about the deterioration of the public sphere reflects anxiety about the undermining of foundational, exclusive, and unencumbered male rights. Feminism is indeed "a scandal" that brings the personal into public life (Deem, 1999).

◆ Conclusion

Technological developments pose still other challenges. In theory and practice, performance, the way public address is enacted, grows in significance as it increasingly emerges through visual mass communication technologies that invite, even require, "image-based politics" (Parry-Giles, 1998, p. 460). To capture attention, nondominant rhetorics must become hyperembodied in visually saturated mass media landscapes. Such bodies are not "merely flags to attract attention . . . but the site and substance of the argument itself" (DeLuca, 1999, p. 10; see also Pezzullo, 2003), a claim that challenges argument as a singularly linguistic form and demands reevaluation of what counts as evidence in public address scholarship.

In a regime of visibility, the body becomes the text and voice of public address, and the visual medium frames its expressive capacity. In her study of public address in the electronic age, Jamieson (1988) concludes that gendered aesthetics govern visual representations. She argues that the personal female style is particularly suited to television because of its emphasis on conversation, appearance, emotionality, and self-expression. In demanding that male politicians adapt to its feminine norms of appearance and conversation; in reducing their male bodies to the two-dimensional surface of the screen; in requiring that they enact the "effeminate" style of disclosure and pseudo-intimacy, television effectively "queers" men's public address. Put differently, the male body performs the discursive demands of the medium in drag.

Our assessment of gender in public address scholarship and of our discipline's mode of inquiry leads us to conclude that the disciplinary embrace of the public/private and mind/body splits, particularly in an age dominated by visual media, constitute major challenges.

We are entering a new stage in the conversation about the place of gender in public address scholarship, shifting from the gendered constitution of identities toward the gendered constitution of practices, forms, sites, and bodies, a movement further explored in Stormer's (this volume) essay on gender and rhetorical theory. Such scholarship is fostered by recognition that the character of public address and of our knowledge about it have always depended on the implicit and explicit work of gender. Substantively, as it offers new ways to appreciate the politics of women's artistry and the discursive force of corporeality, work on gender has been instrumental in democratizing public address. It has added vitality to public address as a political practice and as an object of inquiry. Gender is also a powerful analytic to destabilize the heteronormative assumptions of the dichotomous public(male)/private(female) model of discursive constitution; as such, gender challenges our theory and methods.

◆ References

Anderson, J. (1984). *Outspoken women: Speeches by American women reformers, 1635–1935*. Dubuque, IA: Kendall/Hunt.

Anderson, K. V. (2002). Hillary Rodham Clinton as "Madonna": The role of metaphor and oxymoron in image restoration. *Women's Studies in Communication, 25*, 1–24.

Bacon, J. (2002). *The humblest may stand forth: Rhetoric, empowerment, and abolition*. Columbia: University of South Carolina Press.

Bacon, J., & McClish, G. (2000). Reinventing the master's tools: Nineteenth-century African American literary societies of Philadelphia and rhetorical education. *Rhetoric Society Quarterly, 30*, 19–47.

Baker, V. L., & Eubanks, R. T. (1960). Democracy: Challenge to rhetorical education. *Quarterly Journal of Speech, 46*, 72–78.

Ballif, M. (1992). Re/dressing histories: Or, on re/covering figures who have been laid bare by our gaze. *Rhetoric Society Quarterly, 22*, 91–98.

Baumgartner, L. M. (1994). *Alice Paul, the National Woman's Party, and a rhetoric of mobilization*. Doctoral dissertation, University of Minnesota.

Beasley, V. B. (2001). Making diversity safe for democracy: American pluralism and the presidential local address, 1885–1992. *Quarterly Journal of Speech, 87*, 25–40.

Behling, L. L. (2002). Reification and resistance: The rhetoric of Black womanhood at the Columbian Exposition, 1893. *Women's Studies in Communication, 25*, 173–196.

Biesecker, B. (1992). Coming to terms with recent attempts to write women into the history of rhetoric. *Philosophy and Rhetoric, 25*, 140–161.

Bode, C. (1956). *The American lyceum: Town meeting of the mind*. New York: Oxford University Press.

Borda, J. L. (2002). The woman suffrage parades of 1910–1913: Possibilities and limitations of an early feminist rhetorical strategy. *Western Journal of Communication, 66*, 25–52.

Brigance, W. N. (1943). *A history and criticism of American public address* (Vols. 1–2). New York: McGraw-Hill.

Brookey, R. A. (1998). Keeping a good wo/man down. Normalizing Deborah Sampson Gannett. *Communication Studies, 49*, 73–85.

Browne, S. H. (1999). *Angelina Grimké: Rhetoric, identity, and the radical imagination*. East Lansing: Michigan State University Press.

Butler, J. (1990). *Gender trouble: Feminism and the subversion of identity*. New York: Routledge.

Campbell, K. K. (1973). The rhetoric of women's liberation: An oxymoron. *Quarterly Journal of Speech, 59*, 74–86.

Campbell, K. K. (1985). The communication classroom: A chilly climate for women? *ACA Bulletin, 51*, 68–72.

Campbell, K. K. (1986). Style and content in the rhetoric of early Afro-American feminists. *Quarterly Journal of Speech, 72*, 434–445.

Campbell, K. K. (1989a). *Man cannot speak for her: A critical study of early feminist rhetoric*. Westport, CT: Praeger.

Campbell, K. K. (1989b). *Man cannot speak for her: Key texts of the early feminists*. Westport, CT: Praeger.

Campbell, K. K. (1989c). La Pucelle D'Orleans becomes an American girl: Anna Dickinson's "Jeanne d'Arc." In M. C. Leff & F. J. Kauffield (Eds.), *Texts in context: Critical dialogues on significant episodes in American political rhetoric* (pp. 91–112). Davis, CA: Hermagoras Press.

Campbell, K. K. (1989d). The sound of women's voices [Book review]. *Quarterly Journal of Speech, 75*, 212–258.

Campbell, K. K. (Ed.). (1993). *Women public speakers in the United States, 1800–1925: A bio-critical sourcebook*. Westport, CT: Greenwood Press.

Campbell, K. K. (Ed.). (1994). *Women public speakers in the United States, 1925–1993: A bio-critical sourcebook*. Westport, CT: Greenwood Press.

Campbell, K. K. (1995). Gender and genre: Loci of invention and contradiction in the earliest speeches by U.S. women. *Quarterly Journal of Speech, 81*, 479–495.

Campbell, K. K. (1996). The rhetorical presidency: A two-person career. In M. Medhurst (Ed.), *Beyond the rhetorical presidency* (pp. 179–195). College Station: Texas A&M University Press.

Campbell, K. K. (1998a). Inventing women: From Amaterasu to Virginia Woolf. *Women's Studies in Communication, 21*, 111–126.

Campbell, K. K. (1998b). The discursive performance of femininity: Hating Hillary. *Rhetoric & Public Affairs, 1*, 1–19.

Campbell, K. K. (2001). Rhetorical feminism. *Rhetoric Review, 20*, 9–10.

Campbell, K. K. (2002). Consciousness-raising: Linking theory, criticism, and practice. *Rhetoric Society Quarterly, 32*, 45–64.

Carlson, A. C. (1992). Creative casuistry and feminist consciousness: A rhetoric of moral reform. *Quarterly Journal of Speech, 78*, 16–32.

Carlson, A. C. (1994). Defining womanhood: Lucretia Coffin Mott and the transformation of femininity. *Western Journal of Communication, 58*, 85–97.

Condit, C. M. (1990). *Decoding abortion rhetoric: Communicating social change.* Urbana: University of Illinois Press.

Condit, C. M. (1997). In praise of eloquent diversity: Gender and rhetoric as public persuasion. *Women's Studies in Communication, 20,* 91–116.

Conrad, C. (1981). The transformation of the "old feminist" movement. *Quarterly Journal of Speech, 67,* 284–97.

Croy, T. D. (1998). The crisis: A complete critical edition of Carrie Chapman Catt's 1916 presidential address to the National American Woman Suffrage Association. *Rhetoric Society Quarterly, 28,* 49–73.

Daughton, S. M. (1995). The fine texture of enactment: Iconicity as empowerment in Angelina Grimké's Pennsylvania Hall Address. *Women's Studies in Communication, 18,* 19–43.

Dearin, R. D. (1980). Public address history as part of the communication discipline. *Communication Education, 29,* 348–356.

Deem, M. (1999). Scandal, heteronormative culture, and the disciplining of feminism. *Critical Studies in Mass Communication, 16,* 86–93.

DeLuca, K. M. (1999). Unruly arguments: The body rhetoric of Earth First!, ACT UP, and Queer Nation. *Argumentation & Advocacy, 36,* 9–21.

Donawerth, J. (Ed.). (2002a). *Rhetorical theory by women before 1900: An anthology.* Lanham, MD: Rowman & Littlefield.

Donawerth, J. (2002b). Nineteenth-century United States conduct book rhetoric by women. *Rhetoric Review, 21,* 5–21.

Dow, B. J. (1991). The "womanhood" rationale in the woman suffrage rhetoric of Frances E. Willard. *Southern Communication Journal, 56,* 298–307.

Dow, B. J. (1995). Feminism, difference(s), and rhetorical studies. *Communication Studies, 46,* 106–117.

Dow, B. J., & Tonn, M. B. (1993). "Feminine style" and political judgment in the rhetoric of Ann Richards. *Quarterly Journal of Speech, 79,* 286–302.

Edwards, J. L., & Chen, H.R. (2000). The First Lady/First Wife in editorial cartoons:

Rhetorical visions through gendered lenses. *Women's Studies in Communication, 23,* 367–391.

Eldred, J. C., & Mortensen, P. (1993). Monitoring Columbia's daughters: Writing as gendered conduct. *Rhetoric Society Quarterly, 23,* 46–69.

Foss, S. K. (1979). Equal Rights Amendment controversy: Two worlds in conflict. *Quarterly Journal of speech, 65,* 275–288.

Foss, S. K. (1996). Re-sourcement as emancipation: A case study of ritualized sewing. *Women's Studies in Communication, 19,* 55–76.

Foss, K. A., & Foss, S. K. (1991). *Women speak: The eloquence of women's lives.* Prospect Heights, IL: Waveland.

Freedman, E. (1979). Separatism as strategy: Female institution building and American feminism, 1870–1930. *Feminist Studies, 3,* 512–529.

Gayle, B. M., & Griffin, C. L. (1998). Mary Ashton Rice Livermore's relational feminist discourse: A rhetorically successful feminist model. *Women's Studies in Communication, 21,* 55–76.

Greene, R. W., & Kuswa, K. D. (2002). Governing balkanization at home: Liberalism and the rhetorical production of citizenship. *Controversia: An international Journal of Debate and Democratic Renewal, 1,* 16–33.

Griffin, S. (1996). The essentialist roots of the public sphere: A feminist critique. *Western Journal of Communication, 60,* 21–39.

Gring-Pemble, L. (1998). Writing themselves into consciousness: Creating a rhetorical bridge between the public and private spheres. *Quarterly Journal of Speech, 84,* 41–61.

Habermas, J. (2000). *The structural transformation of the public sphere: An inquiry into a category of bourgeois society.* Cambridge: MIT Press. (Originally published 1962)

Hance, K. G. (1958). Some values of a study of rhetoric and public address in a liberal or general education. *Southern Speech Journal, 23,* 179–188.

Hancock, B. R. (1972). Affirmation as negation in the women's liberation movement. *Quarterly Journal of Speech, 58,* 264–272.

Haring, D. G. (1952). Cultural contexts of thought and communication. *Quarterly Journal of Speech, 37,* 161–172.

Hauser, G. A. (1987). Features of the public sphere. *Critical Studies in Mass Communication, 4,* 437–441.

Hawkesworth, M. (1997). Confounding gender. *Signs: Journal of Women in Culture and Society, 22,* 649–685.

Hayden, S. (1997). Re-claiming bodies of knowledge: An exploration of the relationship between feminist theorizing and feminine style in the rhetoric of the Boston Women's Health Book Collective. *Western Journal of Communication, 61,* 127–163.

Hayden, S. (1999a). Negotiating femininity and power in the early twentieth century West: Domestic ideology and feminine style in Jeannette Rankin's suffrage rhetoric. *Communication Studies, 50,* 83–102.

Hayden, S. (1999b). Reversing the discourse of sexology: Margaret Higgins Sanger's What every girl should know. *Southern Communication Journal, 64,* 288–306.

Hayden, S. (2003). Family metaphors and the nation: Promoting a politics of care through the Million Mom March. *Quarterly Journal of Speech, 89,* 196–216.

Henry, D. (1995). Text in context: Lucretia Coffin Mott's "Discourse on woman." *Rhetoric Society Quarterly, 25,* 11–19.

Hiltner, J. R. (1999). "Like a bewildered star": Deborah Sampson, Herman Mann, and Address, delivered with applause. *Rhetoric Society Quarterly, 29,* 5–23.

Hobbs, C. (Ed.). (1995). *Nineteenth-century women learn to write.* Charlottesville: University of Virginia Press.

Hogan, L. S., & Hogan, M. J. (2003). Feminine virtue and practical wisdom: Elizabeth Cady Stanton's "Our Boys." *Rhetoric & Public Affairs, 6,* 415–436.

Hogan, L., & Solomon, M. (1995). Extending the conversation, sharing the inner light. *Rhetoric Society Quarterly, 25,* 32–46.

Hopkins, M. F. (1989). Critical response to the panel on diversity as scholarly enrichment. *Women's Studies in Communication, 12,* 21–28.

Houston, M., & Davis, O. I. (Eds.). (2002). *Centering ourselves: African American feminist and womanist studies of discourse.* Cresskill, NJ: Hampton Press.

Huxman, S. S. (1996). Mary Wollstonecraft, Margaret Fuller, and Angelina Grimké: Symbolic convergence and a nascent rhetorical vision. *Communication Quarterly, 44,* 16–28.

Huxman, S. S. (2000). Perfecting the rhetorical vision of woman's rights: Elizabeth Cady Stanton, Anna Howard Shaw, and Carrie Chapman Catt. *Women's Studies in Communication, 23,* 307–336.

Jamieson, K. H. (1988). *Eloquence in an electronic age: The transformation of political speechmaking.* New York: Oxford University Press.

Jamieson, K. H. (1995). *Beyond the double bind: Women and leadership.* New York: Oxford University Press.

Japp, P. M. (1985). Esther or Isaiah? The abolitionist-feminist rhetoric of Angelina Grimké. *Quarterly Journal of Speech, 71,* 335–348.

Johnson, N. (2002). *Gender and rhetorical space in American life, 1866–1910.* Carbondale: Southern Illinois University Press.

Kendall, K. E., & Fisher, J. Y. (1974). Frances Wright on women's rights: Eloquence versus ethos. *Quarterly Journal of Speech, 60,* 58–68.

Kennedy, P. S., & O'Shields, G. H. (Eds.). (1983). *We shall be heard: Women speakers in America, 1828-present.* Dubuque: IA: Kendall/Hunt.

Kerber, L. K. (1980). *Women of the republic: Intellect and ideology in revolutionary America.* Chapel Hill: University of North Carolina Press.

Kerber, L. K. (1988). Separate spheres, female worlds, woman's place. The rhetoric of women's history. *Journal of American History, 75,* 9–39.

Kowal, D. M. (2000). One cause, two paths: Militant vs. adjustive strategies in the British and American women's suffrage movement. *Communication Quarterly, 48,* 240–255.

Kraditor, A. S. (1968). *Up from the pedestal: Selected writings in the history of American feminism.* Chicago: Quadrangle.

Lang, W. C. (1951). Public Address as a force in history. *Quarterly Journal of Speech, 37,* 31–34.

Linkugel, W. A., & Solomon, M. (1991). *Anna Howard Shaw: Suffrage orator and social reformer*. New York: Greenwood Press.

Logan, S. W. (1997). Black women on the speaker's platform (1832–1899). In M. M. Wertheimer (Ed.), *Listening to their voices: The rhetorical activities of historical women* (pp. 150–173). Columbia: University of South Carolina Press.

Logan, S. W. (1999). *"We are coming:" The persuasive discourse of nineteenth-century black women*. Carbondale: Southern Illinois University Press.

Lucas, S. E. (1988). The renaissance of American public address: Text and context in rhetorical criticism. [Book review]. *Quarterly Journal of Speech, 74*, 241–260.

Lunsford, A. (Ed.). (1995). *Reclaiming Rhetorica: Women in the rhetorical tradition*. Pittsburgh, PA: University of Pittsburgh Press.

Martin, T. P. (1987). *The sound of our own voices: Women's study clubs, 1860–1910*. Boston: Beacon Press.

Matthews, G. (1992). *The rise of public woman: Woman's power and woman's place in the United States, 1630–1970*. New York: Oxford University Press.

Mattina, A. F. (1994). "Rights as well as duties": The rhetoric of Leonora O'Reilly. *Communication Quarterly, 42*, 196–205.

Mattingly, C. (1995). Woman-tempered rhetoric: Public presentation and the WCTU. *Rhetoric Review, 14*, 44–61.

Mattingly, C. (1999). Friendly dress: A disciplined use. *Rhetoric Society Quarterly, 29*(2), 25–43.

Mattingly, C. (Ed.). (2001). *Water drops from women writers: A temperance reader*. Carbondale: Southern Illinois University Press.

Mattingly, C. (2002). Telling evidence: Rethinking what counts in rhetoric. *Rhetoric Society Quarterly, 32*, 99–108.

McCleary, K. E. (1994). "A tremendous awakening": Margaret H. Sanger's speech at Fabian Hall. *Western Journal of Communication, 58*, 182–200.

Mead, D. (1951). *Yankee eloquence in the Middle West: The Ohio lyceum, 1850–1870*. East Lansing: Michigan State College Press.

Miller, D. H. (1998). *Freedom to differ: The shaping of the gay male and lesbian struggle for civil rights*. New York: New York University Press.

Miller, D. H. (1999). From one voice a chorus: Elizabeth Cady Stanton's 1860 address to the New York state legislature. *Women's Studies in Communication, 22*, 152–189.

Miller, H., & Bridwell-Bowles, L. (Ed.). (2005). *Rhetorical women: Roles and representations*. Tuscaloosa: University of Alabama Press.

Mink, G. (1990). The lady and the tramp: Gender, race, and the origins of the American welfare state. In L. Gordon (Ed.), *Women, the state, and welfare* (pp. 92–122). Madison: University of Wisconsin Press.

Morris, C. E. (2001). "Our capital aversion": Abigail Folsom, madness, and radical antislavery praxis. *Women's Studies in Communication, 24*, 62–89.

Morris, C. E. (2002). Pink herring and the fourth persona: J. Edgar Hoover's sex crime panic. *Quarterly Journal of Speech, 88*, 228–244.

Murphy, J. M. (1990). "To create a race of thoroughbreds": Margaret Sanger and The Birth Control Review. *Women's Studies in Communication, 13*, 24–45.

O'Brien, J. F. (1951). A re-examination of state and local oratory as a field for study. *Quarterly Journal of Speech, 37*, 71–76.

O'Connor, L. (1954). *Pioneer women orators: Rhetoric in the ante-bellum reform movement*. New York: Columbia University Press.

O'Neill, J. M. (1941). Professional maturity. *Quarterly Journal of Speech, 27*, 173–182.

Parrish, W. M. (1957). Elocution: Definition and a challenge. *Quarterly Journal of Speech, 43*, 1–11.

Parry-Giles, S. J. (1998). Image based politics, feminism and the consequences of their convergence. *Critical Studies in Mass Communication, 15*, 460–468.

Parry-Giles, S. J., & Blair, D. M. (2002). The rise of the rhetorical first lady: Politics, gender ideology, and women's voice, 1789–2002. *Rhetoric & Public Affairs, 5*, 566–599.

Parry-Giles, S. J., & Parry-Giles, T. (1996). Gendered politics and presidential image construction: A reassessment of the "feminine style." *Communication Monographs, 63*, 337–353.

Pearce, K. C. (1999). The radical feminist manifesto as generic appropriation: Gender, genre, and second wave resistance. *Southern Communication Journal, 64*, 307–315.

Perkins, S. (1989). The rhetoric of androgyny as revealed in *The Feminine Mystique*. *Communication Studies, 40*, 69–80.

Peterson, C. L. (1995). *"Doers of the word": African-American women speakers and writers in the North (1830–1880)*. New York: Oxford University Press.

Pezzullo, P. C. (2003). Resisting "National Breast Cancer Awareness Month": The rhetoric of counterpublics and their cultural performances. *Quarterly Journal of Speech, 89*, 345–365.

Powell, K. A. (1995). The Association of Southern Women for the Prevention of Lynching: Strategies of a movement in the comic frame. *Communication Quarterly, 43*, 86–99.

Ramsey, E. M. (2000). Inventing citizens during World War I: Suffrage cartoons in *The Woman Citizen*. *Western Journal of Communication, 64*, 113–147.

Ray, A. G. (2003). Representing the working class in early U.S. feminist media: The case of Hester Vaughn. *Women's Studies in Communication, 26*, 1–26.

Ray, A. G. (2004). The permeable public: Rituals of citizenship in antebellum men's debating clubs. *Argumentation & Advocacy, 41*, 1–16.

Ray, A. G. (2005). *The lyceum and public culture in the 19th century United States*. East Lansing: Michigan University Press.

Ritchie, J., & Ronald, K. (Eds.). (2001). *Available means: An anthology of women's rhetoric(s)*. Pittsburgh, PA: University of Pittsburgh Press.

Rosteck, T. (1998). Form and cultural context in rhetorical criticism: Re-reading Wrage. *Quarterly Journal of Speech, 84*, 471–490.

Rothermel, B. A. (2002). A sphere of noble action: Gender, rhetoric, and influence at a nineteenth-century Massachusetts state normal school. *Rhetoric Society Quarterly, 33*, 35–64.

Royster, J. J. (2000). *Traces of a stream: Literacy and social change among African American women*. Pittsburgh: University of Pittsburgh Press.

Ryan, M. P. (1992). Gender and public access: Women's politics in nineteenth-century America. In C. Calhoun (Ed.), *Habermas and the public sphere* (pp. 259–288). Cambridge: MIT Press.

Scott, J. W. (1997). Gender: A useful category of historical analysis. In J. Scott (Ed.), *Feminism and history* (pp. 152–180). Oxford, UK: Oxford University Press.

Shepler, S. R., & Mattina, A. F. (1999). "The revolt against war": Jane Addams' rhetorical challenge to the patriarchy. *Communication Quarterly, 47*, 151–165.

Shugart, H. A. (1997). Counterhegemonic acts: Appropriation as a feminist rhetorical strategy. *Quarterly Journal of Speech, 83*, 210–229.

Sillars, M. O. (1995). From romantic idealism to enlightenment rationalism: Lucretia Coffin Mott responds to Richard Henry Dana, Sr. *Rhetoric Society Quarterly, 25*, 47–55.

Sklar, K. K. (1993). The historical foundations of women's power in the creation of the American welfare state, 1830–1930. In S. Koven & S. Michel (Eds.), *Mothers of a new world: Maternalist politics and the origins of welfare states* (pp. 1–42). New York: Routledge.

Solomon, M. (1979). The "positive woman's" journey: A mythic analysis of the rhetoric of STOP-ERA. *Quarterly Journal of Speech, 65*, 262–274.

Solomon, M. (1988). Ideology as rhetorical constraint: The anarchist agitation of "Red Emma" Goldman. *Quarterly Journal of Speech, 74*, 184–200.

Solomon, M. (1991). The role of the suffrage press in the woman's rights movement. In M. M. Solomon (Ed.), *A voice of their own: The woman suffrage press, 1840–1910* (pp. 1–16). Tuscaloosa: University of Alabama Press.

Temple, W. J. (1947). Serviceable speech in a democracy. *Quarterly Journal of Speech, 33*, 489–492.

Theodore, A. (2002). "A right to speak on the subject:" The U.S. women's antiremoval petition campaign, 1829–1831. *Rhetoric & Public Affairs, 5*, 566–599.

Timmons, W. M. (1942). Public address to provoke thought. *Quarterly Journal of Speech, 23*, 301–305.

Tonn, M. B. (1996). Militant motherhood: Labor's Mary Harris "Mother" Jones. *Quarterly Journal of Speech, 82*, 1–21.

Torrens, K. M. (1997). All dressed up with no place to go: Rhetorical dimensions of the nineteenth-century dress reform movement. *Women's Studies in Communication, 20*, 189–210.

Triece, M. E. (2000). Rhetoric and social change: Women's struggles for economic and political equality, 1900–1917. *Women's Studies in Communication, 23*, 238–260.

Voss, C. R., & Rowland, R. C. (2000). Preinception rhetoric in the creation of a social movement: The case of Frances Wright. *Communication Studies, 51*, 1–14.

Waggenspack, B. M. (1989). *The search for self-sovereignty: The oratory of Elizabeth Cady Stanton.* New York: Greenwood Press.

Wallace, K. R. (1954). The field of speech, 1953: An overview. *Quarterly Journal of Speech, 40*, 117–129.

Welter, B. (1976). *Dimity convictions: The American woman in the nineteenth century.* Athens: Ohio University Press.

Wertheimer, M. M. (1997). *Listening to their voices: The rhetorical activities of historical women.* Columbia: University of South Carolina Press.

Wertheimer, M. M. (Ed.). (2003). *Inventing a voice: The rhetoric of selected American first ladies of the twentieth century.* New York: Rowman & Littlefield.

Wilkinson, P. (1999). The selfless and the helpless: Maternalist origins of the U.S. welfare state. *Feminist Studies, 25*(3), 571–597.

Williams, M. R. (1994). A reconceptualization of protest rhetoric: Women's quilts as rhetorical forms. *Women's Studies in Communication, 17*, 20–44.

Wrage, E. J. (1947). Public address: A study in social and intellectual history. *Quarterly Journal of Speech, 33*, 451–457.

Yoakam, D. G. (1943). Woman's introduction to the American platform. In W. N. Brigance (Ed.), *A history and criticism of American public address* (pp. 153–192). New York: McGraw-Hill.

Zaeske, S. (1995). The "promiscuous audience" controversy and the emergence of the early woman's rights movement. *Quarterly Journal of Speech, 81*, 191–207.

Zaeske, S. (2002). Signatures of citizenship: The rhetoric of women's antislavery petitions. *Quarterly Journal of Speech, 88*, 147–168.

Zaeske, S. (2003). *Signatures of citizenship: Petitions, antislavery, and women's political identity.* Chapel Hill: University of North Carolina Press.

Zulick, M. D., & Leff, M. (1995). Time and the "true light" in Lucretia Coffin Mott's "Discourse on woman." *Rhetoric Society Quarterly, 25*, 20–31.

Zurakowski, M. M. (1994). From doctors and lawyers to wives and mothers: Enacting "feminine style" and changing abortion rights arguments. *Women's Studies in Communication, 17*, 45–68.

11

GENDER IN POLITICAL COMMUNICATION RESEARCH

The Problem With Having No Name

◆ Vanessa B. Beasley

When Betty Friedan (1963) published *The Feminine Mystique*, she stirred a political revolution by writing about "the problem that has no name" (p. 15). Friedan wrote about women like herself:

> On an April morning in 1959, I heard a mother of four, having coffee with four other mothers in a suburban development fifteen miles from New York, say in a tone of quiet desperation, "the problem." And the others knew, without words, that she was not talking about a problem with her husband, or her children, or her home. Suddenly they realized that they all shared the same problem, the problem that has no name. (p. 19)

For Friedan, the problem was a "sense of dissatisfaction, a yearning," the asking Is this all? when the roles women were repeatedly told would bring them personal satisfaction did not (p. 15). Although their talk began cautiously and their middle-class problems were only part of a growing tide of women's concerns, such discussions contributed to the political movement that historians have called the second wave of feminism in the United States.

I argue that the second wave set the agenda for much of the research on gender and political communication in the social sciences and the humanities. The results of that research, however, look very different because conceptualizations of gender vary as do implicit definitions of politics. These differences are telling and reveal the limits of each tradition. Just as Friedan foreshadowed the problems second-wave feminists would have in defining their concerns, so current differences between these types of research make it difficult for scholars of gender and political communication to share their findings.

◆ The Second Wave of Feminism and Political Communication Research

I begin with an overview of second-wave feminism and offer three reasons it was situated to influence research on gender in the burgeoning area of political communication. I highlight some key moments in the development of social scientific and rhetorical lines of inquiry and show how political communication has one foot firmly planted on each side of the methodological divide. I then describe the lines of research that dominate scholarship in political communication in the United States roughly within the last decade. Within the social scientific tradition, two primary areas of gender-oriented scholarship are voter mobilization and mediated representation. The rhetorical tradition is dominated by "great woman" case studies and the gendering of issues. Of necessity, the references for each of these represent only a partial view into each line of inquiry, and these four categories do not include all current research on gender in political communication. Nevertheless, my review of recent scholarship suggests that they contain the major themes and central research questions guiding the field today.

THE TROUBLE WITH NAMES: SOME OPERATIONAL DEFINITIONS

As terms, both *second wave* and *political communication research* are notoriously difficult to define. As Enke (2003) notes, "The second wave . . . may be understood not so much as a set of ideas that define a select group of women but rather as a *bid for coherence* around *multiple* challenges to the gendered, raced organization of social spaces" (p. 661). There is general consensus that the second wave began in the middle of the 20th century (Evans, 2003; Rosen, 2000). It is commonly differentiated from the first wave of women's activism, dating back at least to the 1830s (Campbell, 1989; Ryan, 1992), which dissipated after the ratification of the 19th Amendment in 1920 (see Andersen, 1996; Buechler, 1990).

Just as the first wave is associated with the fight for women's suffrage, the second wave is associated with the failed effort to ratify the Equal Rights Amendment. The second wave is characterized as "pursuit of multiple goals through very diverse organizational forums" (Buechler, 1990) and by a divisive lack of consensus about the inclusion of women and men of multiple classes, races, and sexual orientations. However intensely such debates played out among diverse activists (Flannery, 2001), they were often portrayed as occurring between two camps: liberal or "reform" feminists primarily interested in eliminating gender discrimination in education, employment, and other institutional settings and "radical" feminists engaged in the critique of patriarchy and traditional sex roles (Dow, 1996, p. 28; Ryan, 1992, p. 40). As symbolic distinctions between liberal and radical feminists gained traction with the general public during the second wave and its "backlash," feminism became more difficult to define. Was its cause NOW-style "equal pay for equal work?" Or was it more subversive and antifamily, as opponents repeatedly charged?

"Political communication research" also can mean different things. Swanson and

Nimmo (1990) define it as research that "makes claims about the relationships between communication processes and political processes" (p. 7), while Stuckey (1996) suggests that the "task of political communication scholars . . . is to analyze the creation, dissemination, and absorption of the symbolic messages that comprise our political life" (p. viii). Given these definitions, there is room for diverse methods, questions, and objects of study in this research; nevertheless, two characteristics define political communication research as a distinct field of study.

First, most political communication research either falls on the social scientific side, which is associated with quantitative methods that correspond with those used in cognate areas such as political science, psychology, and sociology, or the rhetorical side, with its more ancient roots in the Western philosophical tradition and its contemporary association with interpretive, critical, and historical methods. Whatever their differences, researchers agree that both have contributed to foundational lines of inquiry (Denton & Woodward, 1985; Swanson & Nimmo, 1990; Stuckey, 1996). Second, all political communication researchers tend to define "politics" in traditional ways. With some exceptions, these researchers study politics as practiced within statist, governmental, or other institutional contexts; thus, they study communicative practices and processes in social or electoral campaigns, debates, mediated representations of political issues, and so on. These researchers seem to agree with Jacoby (1996) that "when everything is political, nothing is" (p. B2) and tend not to include the more ambiguous realm of "cultural politics."

As portrayed here, second-wave feminism and political communication research seem riddled with binary tensions between liberal versus radical activism, social scientific and rhetorical methods, and even statist politics and cultural politics. There are three reasons to pay close attention to these tensions. Because political communication research

was in its infancy during feminism's second wave, so it was influenced by how and why political communication scholars initially became interested in gender.

SHARED INSTITUTIONAL, INTELLECTUAL, AND IDEOLOGICAL HISTORIES

The rise and fall of the second wave roughly coincided with the adolescence of broadcast media when their impact on U.S. politics was becoming increasingly obvious. Like other social movements of the 1960s and 1970s, the second wave was covered by mainstream print and broadcast media, with the "first sustained attempts by the national media to treat the themes and interpret the implications of the women's movement" being made in 1970 (Dow, 1996, p. 27). At roughly the same time, scholars in the social sciences were increasingly concerned with political coverage in the news, especially following the influential work of Edelman (1964) and Lasswell (Lasswell & Leites, 1949).

Edelman was one of the first theorists to write about the ways in which symbolic constructions of mediated politics affected material outcomes, while Lasswell offered social scientists a critical argument that such language was important and a method— content analysis—through which they could gauge its significance. Finding a scientific way to measure political language was not a concern for rhetorical scholars, however. A foundational premise of this tradition is the Aristotelian notion that the end of persuasion is decision making, which, when accompanied by Aristotle's definition of rhetoric as "all of the available means of persuasion," emboldened rhetorical critics to explore specific case studies situated within communicative, cultural, and other types of constraints. Although Edelman was influential for rhetoricians, Burke's (1962, 1968, 1969) emphasis on the role of drama in social relations equipped scholars with new ways of understanding symbolic representations of social conflict and hierarchy. Generally, then, the simultaneous development of these three components throughout the 1970s—a movement, mass media, and the beginnings of an area of scholarship—gave rise to mediated contexts, methods, and critical vocabularies through which communication scholars could begin to study gender and politics.

Many of the central concerns motivating second-wave feminists were shared by political scientists and communication scholars. Although the goals of the movement were self-consciously "multiple," gender roles were a key concern (Nicholson, 1997). This focus suited communication scholars interested in political science, with its traditional emphasis on institutions, public policies, and voting patterns typically associated with sex role differentiation. Indeed, some of the first articles on gender and political communication in the social scientific literature explored the impact of sex roles on political beliefs and preferences, especially in response to specific campaign messages (Flora & Lynn, 1974; Hedlund, Freeman, Hamm, & Stein, 1979; Krauss, 1974; Shabad & Andersen, 1979).

Meanwhile, scholars from multiple fields were researching the civil rights and student rights movements. Because many second-wave leaders drew upon their personal experiences with these movements, the women's movement was ripe for study about the ways it paralleled and differed from them. As rhetorical scholars responded to this need, articles on the so-called women's liberation movement were among the first to address gender issues within politics in communication journals (Campbell, 1973; Hancock, 1972; McPherson, 1973; Rosenwasser, 1972).

Before the second wave confronted the socioeconomic differences among women, Friedan's (1963) emphasis on the problems of middle-class "housewives and mothers—previously nonpolitical and largely white" (Tobias, 1997, p. 72) was an important stimulus for the movement and the middle-class

scholars who were among the first to study it. In a sense, Friedan's (1963) discussion of the "problem" invited a communicative analysis. Although the core, salient political issue for middle-class suburban white women in the 1950s and 1960s may have been as yet unspeakable even by the women themselves, it is perhaps no surprise that in the 1980s and 1990s scholars from multiple disciplines were repeatedly asking definitional questions about feminism and its impact on their intellectual and other professional habits (see Blair & Brown, 1994; Campbell, 1988; Tompkins, 1987). What exactly were "women's problems," and what did it mean to be a feminist?

Social scientists typically turned to overtly political texts—political advertising, campaign events, media coverage of campaigns—to ask such questions, which included framing and priming research by asking which, when, how, and why specific policy dilemmas have been defined as women's issues. Rhetorical scholars also asked how women's problems and gender have been defined. Often they both used case studies and historical research to investigate the strategies women have used in public discourse to advance political causes. Campbell's *Man Cannot Speak for Her* (1989) offers a paradigmatic rationale and a model for the recovery of women's voices in public address in the United States, paying specific attention to messages and campaigns designed to affect public policy. Other rhetorical scholars examine contemporary discourses that fall outside the campaign-driven model—movies and television shows, for example—to show how cultural messages can reinforce particular gender roles and/or disarm their would-be challengers (see Dow, 1996).

In other words, the second wave occurred at the right time and asked the right questions in the right places from the 1970s to 1990s to prompt interest in research on gender and political communication. In the next two sections I review recent research from each tradition and discuss two main research areas representing contemporary lines of inquiry. Read in light of the intellectual and institutional history above, my review suggests that the traditions have methodological and topical differences and employ different notions of politics and gender.

Many social scientists conceptualize politics in terms of what Swanson and Nimmo (1990) have called the "voter persuasion paradigm," which views "communication in election campaigns . . . [as] the field's paradigm case" (p. 8). The campaign model defines the political in terms of the types of messages worthy of study and their assumed outcomes, which are limited to specific electoral changes, policy changes, or both. Likewise, this model typically views gender as a biological category or variable through which to identify the possible impact of sex differences on political preferences and/or behaviors. In general, when these researchers invoke the term *gender*, they are usually referring to women only (or at least situations in which women are salient), a tendency that positions maleness as the political norm.

The rhetorical tradition, which includes research informed by the voter persuasion paradigm, is likely to use a broader definition of "the political," one that more obviously embraces the second-wave mantra that "the personal is political" and ranges from ongoing social movements (which may or may not have a clear agenda) to everyday social relations. Likewise, the rhetorical tradition tends to conceptualize gender as more than biological sex differences and to incorporate social constructions, cultural practices, and feminist ideology.

◆ *Gender in Social Scientific Research: Female Voters and Mediated Representations*

Social scientific research on political communication follows the "voter persuasion model" in which communicative phenomena are assumed to be part of a campaign

for policy or electoral change. Change cannot come about without a perceived reason for it, however. For second-wave feminists like Friedan, identifying the problem was part of the struggle. After the ratification of the 19th Amendment, it became more difficult for feminists to mobilize male and female voters, leading to the suggestion, lamented by Friedan (1963) herself, that "the 'woman problem' in America no longer existed" (p. 19).

In political science this difficulty can be explained by the theory of the mobilization of bias, which holds that political systems are maintained by a fundamental set of beliefs, values, and procedures that promote certain groups while constraining others. According to the classic theory of E. E. Schattschneider (1956), such systems inherently favor the status quo, and systemic constraints become especially obvious when subgroups try to increase their participation in order to change public policy (p. 71). For the politically disadvantaged, the primary communicative challenges are identifying and mobilizing potentially supportive voters and then making issues salient for them in order to win elections. Much recent social scientific research in political communication continues to discuss how gender might be salient and/or instrumental in relation to these challenges, viewing it primarily as one variable that can influence the course and outcome of political campaigns.

FEMALE VOTER MOBILIZATION

One common method of identifying potential voters involves public opinion research, which is linked through its institutional and intellectual history to research in mass communication and political science. Two central premises of public opinion research—the desirability of measuring attitudes and the potential of attitudes to change—are closely related to studies on attitude formation and attitude change that have been part of communication research since the mid-20th century.

A major use of public opinion research concerns the *gender gap*, a term used by scholars and journalists to explain "differences between men and women in their party identification and voting choice" (Norris, 2003, p. 147). In this usage, gender refers to a biological category similar to sex. The gender gap has been a topic in public opinion research on presidential elections since 1980 (see Chaney, Alvarez, & Nagler, 1998), although Norris (2003) argues that it was influential long before that (pp. 149–154; see also Mansbridge, 1985). Recent research supports a continued belief in such a gap through longitudinal studies that often focus on the role of communication (Atkeson & Rapoport, 2003; Carlson, 2001; Norrander, 1997; Trevor, 1999). Other social scientists interested in the gender gap have used public opinion data to ascertain voters' attitudes toward specific political figures (see Burden, 1999), while still others discuss gender as a variable influencing voters' exposure to talk radio and other genres of mass communication as sources of political information (Bennett, 2002; Kaid & Holtz-Bacha, 2000; Kern & Just, 1997; Kohut & Parker, 1997; Pfau, Cho, & Chong, 2001).

A second type of voter mobilization research concentrates on voters' reactions to messages and presentational strategies used by female candidates during campaigns. I distinguish this line of research from studies that primarily concern media coverage of a female candidate. The former is consistent with voter mobilization research because they are geared toward understanding communicative strategies purposefully employed by campaigns to appeal to voters. The latter contributes to a body of work referred to below as "issue representation" because it typically concerns choices made by third parties (i.e., editors and reporters).

Much research on message-oriented voter mobilization concerns political advertisements (see Kern & Edley, 1994). Scholars have asked, for example, if negative advertising is effective in mobilizing support for female candidates (Gordon, Shafie, &

Crigler, 2003; Robertson & Froemling, 1999). Robertson and Froemling found that education and family were more likely to be themes in advertisements for female than for male candidates, while Hitchon, Chang, and Harris (1997) measured subjects' reactions to perceptions of emotion in advertisements by female and male candidates. Other research asks questions about perceptions of gendered style in candidates' presentational strategies (Bystrom & Miller, 1999; Dolon & Kropf, 2004), campaign literature (Larson, 2001), and overall campaign strategies (Berstein, 2000; Black & Erickson, 2000; Plutzer & Zipp, 1996).

MEDIATED REPRESENTATIONS

Two influential concepts in social scientific political communication research are *priming* and *framing*. Priming "focuses on the standards or criteria that people use to make political evaluations" (Kenski, 1996, p. 72); framing refers to ways in which issues and "choice problems" are selectively presented, emphasizing some aspects while drawing attention from others (Iyengar, 1991, p. 11). These concepts can be especially salient for researchers interested in political issues related to gender. Indeed, one of the challenges during the second wave was to persuade men and women to view topics such as pay equity, gender discrimination, and reproductive rights not as women's issues but as public policy issues with implications for all citizens. Rhetorical scholars also study issue representation, as I discuss below. Yet my review of recent social scientific literature suggests that although some scholars are interested in the framing of feminism as a social movement with implications for public policy, others pay considerable attention to how media frame specific female candidates.

Recent studies concerned with how feminism has been portrayed in the U.S. media include Ashley and Olson (1998); Costain, Braunstein, and Bergren (1997); Dow (1999); Huddy (1997); and Lind and Salo

(2002). Likewise, Barker-Plummer (2002) has investigated how feminist activists themselves used the media to further their cause. Social scientific researchers increasingly have also asked framing and priming questions about media portrayals of female candidates (see Chang & Hitchon, 1997). Such analyses include virtually all levels of electoral contests in which women are candidates (see Aday & Devitt, 2001; Banwart, Bystrom, & Robertson, 2003; Bystrom, Robertson, & Banwart, 2001; Splichal & Garrison, 2000). The guiding assumption in virtually all of this research is that male and female candidates are treated unequally in U.S. media coverage (see Smith, 1997).

Scholars interested in how individual women are framed in media coverage do not always focus only on the candidates but have also taken an interest in coverage of candidates' spouses. For example, Bystrom, McKinnon, and Chaney (1999) compared media coverage of Elizabeth Dole, then a would-be first lady, and counterpart Hillary Clinton in the 1996 presidential race, when both were running as presidential spouses. Winfield and Friedman (2003) conducted a similar analysis in 2000. For her part, Hillary Rodham Clinton has repeatedly been the subject of content analysis (see Corrigan, 2000; Nichols & Wolf, 2000; Gardetto, 1997). Finally, a related if smaller body of research asked whether the presence of female journalists has affected how media frame politics (Mills, 1997; Richardson & Moss, 1995; Weaver, 1997).

◆ Gender in Rhetorical Research: Great Women and Gendered Issues

As I have noted, one difference between social scientific and rhetorical research is method. Some rhetorical scholars have adapted the spirit of the voter persuasion or campaign model in order to develop historical case studies of women's rhetoric as U.S. political activism. Many studies concern the

fight for suffrage and other political crusades in which women participated during the 19th century, most notably those on abolition and temperance. Choosing these examples of women's public discourse as a point of origin for rhetorical research on gender in political communication is fitting because, as Campbell (1989) reminds us, "a central element in women's oppression was the denial of her right to speak" (p. 9).

The model of politics in this rhetorical research seems conventional in the sense that it involves more-or-less organized campaigns for public policy reforms, yet it relies on a slightly different model of gender than that usually applied in social scientific research. To be sure, women in the 19th century were women because of biology, but they also were above and outside politics because of their culture. They were above politics because of the traditional split between the public and private spheres, with women inhabiting the latter so as not to be sullied by the former. At the same time, they were outside politics because they were disenfranchised. Such mixed cultural messages about womanhood were strong then as now (see Beasley, 2002), and in the scholarly tradition of researching great women in politics, authors continue to note the ways in which contemporary women still face a "double bind" (Jamieson, 1995) that is especially evident in political contexts. In this section on the rhetorical tradition, I begin with the "great women" studies, followed by a related theme in recent rhetorical research: studies of the gendering of political issues and images.

GREAT WOMEN ORATORS

Research published over the last 10 years indicates continued interest in the great women orators of the late 19th and early 20th centuries. Scholars have asked new questions about the rhetoric of Angelina and Sarah Grimké (Browne, 1996, 1999; Carlacio, 2002; Daughton, 1995; Huxman,

1996; Vonnegut, 1995); Elizabeth Cady Stanton (Hogan & Hogan, 2003; Huxman, 2000; Miller, 1999; Strange, 2002); and other leading suffragists (see Hayden, 1999; Slagell, 2001). In addition, rhetorical scholars shed new light on the rhetorical constraints and opportunities these women faced (Borda, 2002; Campbell, 1995; Ramsey, 2000; Ray, 2003; Zaeske, 1995, 2003).

In some studies, the reader gains a sense that the political is used by rhetorical scholars to refer to the cultural barriers these women were trying to challenge as well as to campaigns for specific causes. Ray (2003), for example, discusses how the choices made by woman's rights activists left them in a precarious rhetorical and ideological position in 1868, particularly with regard to their inability to speak compellingly to working-class audiences. Strange (2002) analyzed a lecture that Elizabeth Cady Stanton repeatedly delivered to lyceum audiences on traditional gender roles in the family. Hogan and Hogan (2003) examined another of Stanton's lyceum speeches in which she criticized organized religion and the education system. There is evidence then that even during the first wave of feminism, the personal could be political.

These and other "great women" paved the way for future women to have political influence in the United States. Indeed, when Lucas and Medhurst (1999) issued their compilation of the top 100 speeches of the 20th century, they noted that 23 were delivered by women. Of these 23, however, only four were by women who had been elected to public office, which suggests that women have had more political influence outside than inside government offices. Nevertheless, rhetorical scholars continue to study the relationship between gender and the rhetoric of elected officials; in fact, there has been continued debate about male and female rhetors' use of "feminine style" in contemporary U.S. politics (Blankenship & Robson, 1995; Dow & Tonn, 1993; Parry-Giles & Parry-Giles, 1996; Robson, 2000; Scheckels, 1997). Campbell (1989) describes

this style as being characterized by personal tone, inductive structure, recognition of the audience as peers, and efforts at identification with the audience—qualities that she notes historically have been associated with women's "passivity, submissiveness, and patience" (p. 13). To speak of the role of gender in political communication, then, is not always to ask how women learn to speak more like men but whether the opposite also has been true, particularly in a mediated age.

Finally, one additional category of great women is U.S. first ladies. Although some have investigated other presidential spouses (see Blair, 2001; Edwards & Huey, 2001; Parry-Giles & Blair, 2002; Wertheimer, 2003), rhetorical studies during the past decade of first ladies most frequently concern Hillary Rodham Clinton (Anderson, 2002; Campbell, 1998; Parry-Giles, 2000, 2001; Templin, 1999; Winfield, 1997). Clinton's eight years in that role provoked mercurial reactions from Americans; accordingly, she reinvigorated the study of this unelected political position, especially with regard to how its rhetorical demands and constraints compare to those of other political offices (see Bostdorff, 1998).

GENDERED ISSUES

In the 1970s and 1980s, rhetorical scholars studied gender in the context of women's liberation as a social movement. In the past decade, no similar level of scholarship on social movements has appeared; instead, scholars have asked how particular issues have been discussed, either by media commentators or by the candidates. Some of these studies have addressed overtly political issues. Beasley (2002) asked how suffrage was explained to public audiences by presidents, while Triece (2000) shows the ways that women's political and economic gains have been constrained by public discourse. Daughton (1994) investigates instances in which "gender-related problems" posed challenges in modern presidential campaigns.

These authors note the inherently conservative nature of U.S. politicians' discussions of women's problems. Indeed, as Dow (2004) recently commented, even as the second wave of feminism was unfolding, mass media were framing the women's liberation movement in ways likely to inhibit the capacity for social change.

Other rhetorical scholars have examined specific public events and controversies to see how traditionally gendered issues are portrayed. Hayden's (2003) discussion of the Million Mom March comes closest to being political in the traditional sense, yet the case of the march involves an organized effort to impact public sentiment rather than a specific vote. Hayden argues that the "nation-as-family" metaphor implicitly used by activists may have some political efficacy in promoting "motherist politics" (p. 197). Lay's research (2003; Lay & Wahlstrom, 1996) on the rhetoric of midwifery has revealed the state's interest in controlling women's experiences in childbirth (see also Miller, 1999). As these studies indicate, the rhetorical tradition's notion of the political is broad enough to incorporate social issues, with Hayden's work (2003) showing that rhetorical constructions of the feminine as maternal can potentially alter the political paradigm itself.

◆ Conclusion

Rhetoricians and social scientists interested in political communication continue to identify aspects of the problem that has no name but in different ways. Social scientific research on political communication remains rooted in the campaign model of political discourse; for these researchers, politics means elections and gender means women. Gender research in this tradition often explores differences in perception, judgment, and interpretation that presumably are based in sex differences, with men as the presumed normative standard. These studies also include numerous content analyses of media representations of feminism as well as specific female political agents. Rhetorical research also focuses on campaigns, yet it has tended to generate more historical case studies of first-wave feminists and their public activism. Rhetorical studies of historical and contemporary political campaigns and female political leaders have interpreted politics to include traditional electoral concerns as well as more ephemeral yet consequential cultural practices. For rhetoricians, gender can refer to the biological indicators of sex and/or the social and rhetorical construction of issues, practices, and speaking styles as feminine and/or masculine.

In a sense, then, social scientific research has come closer to adopting the institutionally oriented worldviews of Friedan and the reformist liberal feminists of the second wave. By focusing on how and why women vote as well as on how women and women's issues are portrayed in media, these researchers implicitly ask if and how institutional practices of gender-based discrimination are sustained and/or mitigated via the democratic process. Rhetorical scholars also have studied institutional practices and their constraints on women's political activism, yet they seem to have adopted some of the assumptions of the radical feminists; namely, that sexism is perpetuated by cultural meanings that exist within institutions and individuals. Rhetoricians also seem more likely to accept the notion that gender has performative aspects and is not solely determined by sex chromosomes.

Clearly, both traditions of this research are vital. We need to know more about electoral processes and cultural practices, and we need research that combines the best of both traditions. To produce such work, however, we shall have to transcend our distinctive vocabularies and assumptions in order to speak to each other across methodological and epistemological divides. In the process, we also need to pay attention to what these two traditions share— namely, the tendency to view gender and politics primarily as Friedan herself did: as the province of middle-class white heterosexual U.S. women. The next wave of political communication researchers interested in gender will surely have to be more inclusive and imaginative.

◆ References

Aday, S., & Devitt, J. (2001). Style over substance: Newspaper coverage of Elizabeth Dole's presidential bid. *Harvard International Journal of Press/Politics, 6,* 52–73.

Andersen, K. (1996). *After suffrage: Women in partisan and electoral politics before the New Deal era.* Chicago: University of Chicago Press.

Anderson, K. V. (2002). From spouses to candidates: Hillary Rodham Clinton, Elizabeth Dole, and the gendered office of the U.S. president. *Rhetoric & Public Affairs, 5,* 105–132.

Ashley, L., & Olson, B. (1998). Constructing reality: Print media's framing of the women's movement. *Journalism & Mass Communication Quarterly, 75,* 263–278.

Atkeson, L. R., & Rapoport, R. B. (2003). The more things change, the more they stay the same: Examining gender differences in political attitude expression. *Public Opinion Quarterly, 67,* 495–522.

Barker-Plummer, B. (2002). Producing public voice: Resource mobilization and media access in the National Organization for Women. *Journalism & Mass Communication Quarterly, 79*(1), 188–205.

Banwart, M. C., Bystrom, D. G., & Robertson, T. (2003). From the primary to the general election: A comparative analysis of candidate media coverage in mixed-gender 2000 races for governor and U.S. Senate. *American Behavioral Scientist, 46,* 658–676.

Beasley, V. B. (2002). Engendering democratic change: How three U.S. presidents discussed female suffrage. *Rhetoric & Public Affairs, 5,* 79–103.

Bennett, S. E. (2002). Predicting Americans' exposure to political talk radio in 1996, 1998, and 2000. *Harvard International Journal of Press/Politics, 7,* 9–23.

Berstein, A. G. (2000). The effects of message theme, policy explicitness, and candidate gender. *Communication Quarterly, 48,* 159–173.

Black, J. H., & Erickson, L. (2000). Similarity, compensation, or difference? A comparison of female and make office-seekers. *Women and Politics, 21,* 1–38.

Blair, C., & Brown, J. R. (1994). Disciplining the feminine. *Quarterly Journal of Speech, 80,* 383–400.

Blair, D. M. (2001). No ordinary time: Eleanor Roosevelt's address to the 1940 Democratic National Convention. *Rhetoric & Public Affairs, 4,* 203–222.

Blankenship, J., & Robson, D. A. (1995). The "feminine style" in political discourse: An exploratory essay. *Communication Quarterly, 43,* 353–366.

Borda, J. L. (2002). The woman suffrage parades of 1910–1913: Possibilities and limitations of an early feminist rhetorical strategy. *Western Journal of Communication, 66,* 25–53.

Bostdorff, D. M. (1998). Hillary Rodham Clinton and Elizabeth Dole as running "mates" in the 1996 campaign: Parallels in the rhetorical constraints of First Ladies and Vice Presidents. In R. E. Denton, Jr. (Ed.), *The 1996 presidential campaign: A communication perspective* (pp. 199–227). Westport, CT: Praeger.

Browne, S. H. (1996). Encountering Angelina Grimké: Violence, identity, and the creation of radical community. *Quarterly Journal of Speech, 82,* 55–74.

Browne, S. H. (1999). *Angelina Grimké: Rhetoric, identity, and the radical imagination.* East Lansing: Michigan State University Press.

Buechler, S. M. (1990). *Women's movements in the United States.* New Brunswick, NJ: Rutgers University Press.

Burden, B. C. (1999). Public opinion and Hillary Rodham Clinton. *Public Opinion Quarterly, 63,* 237–250.

Burke, K. (1962). *A Grammar of motives.* Cleveland, OH: World Publishing Company.

Burke, K. (1968). *Counter-statement.* Berkeley: University of California Press.

Burke, K. (1969). *A rhetoric of motives.* Berkeley: University of California Press.

Bystrom, D. G., McKinnon, L. M., & Chaney, C. (1999). First Ladies and the Fourth Estate: Media coverage of Hilary Clinton and Elizabeth Dole in the 1996 presidential campaign. In L. L. Kaid & D. G. Bystrom (Eds.), *The electronic election: Perspectives on the 1996 campaign communication* (pp. 81–97). Mahwah, NJ: Erlbaum.

Bystrom, D., & Miller, J. L. (1999). Gendered communication styles and strategies in Campaign 1996: The videostyles of women and men candidates. In L. L. Kaid & D. G. Bystrom (Eds.), *The electronic election: Perspectives on the 1996 campaign communication* (pp. 293–302). Mahwah, NJ: Erlbaum.

Bystrom, D. G., Robertson, T. A., & Banwart, M. C. (2001). Framing the fight: Analysis of media coverage of female and male candidates in primary races for governor and U.S. Senate in 2000. *American Behavioral Scientist, 44*, 1999–2013.

Campbell, K. K. (1973). The rhetoric of women's liberation: An oxymoron. *Quarterly Journal of Speech, 59*, 74–86.

Campbell, K. K. (1988). What really distinguishes and/or ought to distinguish feminist scholarship in communication studies? *Women's Studies in Communication, 88*, 4–6.

Campbell, K. K. (1989). *Man cannot speak for her: A critical study of early feminist rhetoric.* Westport, CT: Greenwood.

Campbell, K. K. (1995). Gender and genre: Loci of invention and contradiction in the earliest speeches of U.S. women. *Quarterly Journal of Speech, 81*, 479–495.

Campbell, K. K. (1998). The discursive performance of femininity: Hating Hillary. *Rhetoric & Public Affairs, 1*, 1–19.

Carlacio, J. (2002). "Ye knew your duty but ye did it not": The epistolary rhetoric of Sarah Grimké. *Rhetoric Review, 21*, 247–264.

Carlson, T. (2001). Gender and political advertising across cultures: A comparison of male and female political advertising in Finland and the US. *European Journal of Communication, 16*, 131–155.

Chaney, C., Alvarez, R., & Nagler, J. (1998). Explaining the gender gap in U.S. presidential elections, 1980–1992. *Political Research Quarterly, 51*, 311–339.

Chang, D., & Hitchon, J. (1997). Mass media impact on voter responses to women candidates: Theoretical developments. *Communication Theory, 7*, 29–52.

Corrigan, M. (2000). The transformation of going public: President Clinton, the First Lady, and health care reform. *Political Communication, 17*, 149–168.

Costain, A., Braunstein, R., & Bergren, H. (1997). Framing the women's movement. In P. Norris (Ed.), *Women, media, and politics* (pp. 205–220). New York: Oxford University Press.

Daughton, S. M. (1994). Women's issues, women's place: Gender-related problems in presidential campaigns. In K. E. Kendall (Ed.), *Presidential campaign discourse: Strategic communication problems* (pp. 221–240). Albany: State University of New York Press.

Daughton, S. M. (1995). The fine texture of enactment: Iconicity as empowerment in Angelina Grimké's Pennsylvania Hall address. *Women's Studies in Communication, 18*, 19–44.

Denton Jr., R. E., & Woodward, G. C. (1985). *Political communication in America.* New York: Praeger.

Dolon, J., & Kropf, J. S. (2004). Credit claiming for the U.S. House: Gendered communication styles? *Harvard International Journal of Press/Politics, 9*, 41–59.

Dow, B. J. (1996). *Prime time feminism.* Philadelphia: University of Pennsylvania Press.

Dow, B. J. (1999). Spectacle, spectatorship, and gender anxiety in television news coverage of the 1970 Women's Strike for Equality. *Communication Studies, 50*, 143–158.

Dow, B. J. (2004). Fixing feminism: Women's liberation and the rhetoric of television documentary. *Quarterly Journal of Speech, 90*, 53–80.

Dow, B. J., & Tonn, M. B. (1993). Feminine style and political judgment in the rhetoric of Ann Richards. *Quarterly Journal of Speech, 79*, 286–303.

Edelman, M. J. (1964). *Symbolic uses of politics.* Urbana: University of Illinois Press.

Edwards. J. L., & Huey, R. C. (2000). The First Lady/First Wife in editorial cartoons:

Rhetorical visions through gendered lenses. *Women's Studies in Communication, 23,* 367–392.

Enke, A. (2003). Smuggling sex through the gates: Race, sexuality, and the politics of space in second wave feminism. *American Quarterly, 55,* 635–667.

Evans, S. (2003). *Tidal wave: How women changed America at century's end.* New York: Free Press.

Flannery, K. T. (2001). The passion of conviction: Reclaiming polemic for a reading of second-wave feminism. *Rhetoric Review, 20,* 113–129.

Flora, C. B., & Lynn, N. B. (1974). Women and political socialization: Considerations on the impact of motherhood. In J. Jaquette (Ed.), *Women in politics* (pp. 37–43). New York: Wiley.

Friedan, B. (1963). *The feminine mystique.* New York: Norton.

Gardetto, D. C. (1997). Hillary Rodham Clinton, symbolic gender politics, and *The New York Times,* January–November 1992. *Political Communication, 14,* 225–240.

Gordon, A., Shafie, D. M., & Crigler, A. N. (2003). Is negative advertising effective for female candidates? An experiment in voters' use of gender stereotypes. *Harvard International Journal of Press/Politics, 8,* 35–53.

Hancock, B. R. (1972). Affirmation by negation in the women's liberation movement. *Quarterly Journal of Speech, 58,* 264–271.

Hayden, S. (1999). Negotiating femininity and power in the early twentieth century west: Domestic ideology and feminine style in Jeanette Rankin's suffrage rhetoric. *Communication Studies, 50,* 83–102.

Hayden, S. (2003). Family metaphors and the Nation: Promoting a politics of care through the Million Mom March. *Quarterly Journal of Speech, 89,* 196–206.

Hedlund, R. D., Freeman, P. K., Hamm, K. E., & Stein, R. M. (1979). The electability of women candidates: The effects of sex role stereotypes. *Journal of Politics, 41,* 513–524.

Hitchon, J. C., Chang, C., & Harris, R. (1997). Should women emote: Perceptual bias and opinion change in response to political ads for candidates of different genders. *Political Communication, 14,* 49–69.

Hogan, L. S., & Hogan, M. J. (2003). Feminine virtue and practical wisdom: Elizabeth Cady Stanton's "Our Boys." *Rhetoric & Public Affairs, 6,* 415–436.

Huddy, L. (1997). Feminists and feminism in the news. In P. Norris (Ed.), *Women, media, and politics* (pp. 183–204). New York: Oxford University Press.

Huxman, S. S. (1996). Mary Wollstonecraft, Margaret Fuller, and Angelina Grimké: Symbolic convergence and a nascent rhetorical vision. *Communication Quarterly, 44,* 16–29.

Huxman, S. S. (2000). Perfecting the rhetorical vision of woman's rights: Elizabeth Cady Stanton, Anna Howard Shaw, and Carrie Chapman Catt. *Women's Studies in Communication, 23,* 307–337.

Iyengar, S. (1991). *Is anyone responsible? How television frames political issues.* Chicago: University of Chicago Press.

Jacoby, R. (1996, April 2). America's professoriate: Politicized, yet apolitical. *Chronicle of Higher Education,* B1–B2.

Jamieson, K. H. (1995). *Beyond the double bind: Women and leadership.* New York: Oxford University Press.

Kaid, L. L., & Holtz-Bacha, C. (2000). Gender reactions to TV political broadcasts. *Harvard International Journal of Press/Politics, 5,* 17–29.

Kenski, H. C. (1996). From agenda-setting to priming and framing. In M. E. Stuckey (Ed.), *The theory and practice of political communication research* (pp. 67–83). Albany: State University of New York Press.

Kern, M., & Edley, P. P. (1994). Women candidates going public: The 30-second format. *Argumentation and Advocacy, 31,* 80–96.

Kern, M., & Just, M. (1997). A gender gap among voters? In P. Norris (Ed.), *Women, media, and politics* (pp. 99–112). New York: Oxford University Press.

Kohut, A., & Parker, K. (1997). Talk radio and gender politics. In P. Norris (Ed.), *Women, media, and politics* (pp. 221–234). New York: Oxford University Press.

Krauss, W. R. (1974). Political implications of gender roles: A review of the literature. *American Political Science Review, 68,* 1706–1723.

Larson, S. G. (2001). "Running as women?" A comparison of female and male Pennsylvania assembly candidates' campaign brochures. *Women and Politics, 22,* 107–124.

Lasswell, H. D., & Leites, N. (1949). *Language of politics: Studies in quantitative semantics.* New York: G. W. Stewart.

Lay, M. M. (2003). Midwifery on trial: Balancing privacy rights and health concerns after *Roe v. Wade. Quarterly Journal of Speech, 89,* 60–78.

Lay, M. M., & Wahlstrom, B. J. (1996). The rhetoric of midwifery: Conflicts and conversations in the Minnesota home birth community in the 1990s. *Quarterly Journal of Speech, 82,* 383–402.

Lind, R. A., & Salo, C. (2002). The framing of feminist and feminism in news and public affairs programs in U.S. electronic media. *Journal of Communication, 52,* 211–219.

Lucas, S. E., & Medhurst, M. J. (1999). *The top 100 American speeches in the 20th century.* Retrieved January 30, 2005, from www .americanrhetoric.com/newtop100speeches .htm

Mansbridge, J. J. (1985). Myth and reality: The ERA and the gender gap in the 1980 election. *Public Opinion Quarterly, 49,* 164–178.

McPherson, L. (1973). Communication techniques of the women's liberation front. *Communication Quarterly, 21,* 33–38.

Miller, D. H. (1999). From one voice a chorus: Elizabeth Cady Stanton's 1860 address to the New York state legislature. *Women's Studies in Communication, 22,* 152–190.

Mills, K. (1997). What difference do women journalists make? In P. Norris (Ed.), *Women, media and politics* (pp. 41–55). New York: Oxford University Press.

Nichols, S., & Wolf, M. A. (2000). News media construction of womanhood in the 1990s: A feminist critique of the rhetorical contest between Hillary Clinton and Elizabeth Dole for First Lady during the 1996 presidential campaign. *Women & Language, 23,* 47–60.

Nicholson, L. (Ed.). (1997). *The second wave: A reader in feminist theory.* New York: Routledge.

Norrander, B. (1997). The independence gap and the gender gap. *Public Opinion Quarterly, 61,* 464–477.

Norris, P. (2003). The gender gap: Old challenges, new approaches. In S. J. Carroll (Ed.), *Women and American politics: New questions, new directions* (pp. 146–172). New York: Oxford University Press.

Parry-Giles, S. J. (2000). Mediating Hillary Rodham Clinton: Television news practices and image-making in the postmodern age. *Critical Studies in Media Communication, 17,* 205–226.

Parry-Giles, S. J. (2001). Political authenticity, television news, and Hillary Rodham Clinton. In R. P. Hart & B. H. Sparrow (Eds.), *Politics, discourse, and American society: New agendas* (pp. 211–227). Lanham, MD: Rowman & Littlefield.

Parry-Giles, S. J., & Blair, D. (2002). The rise of the rhetorical First Lady: Politics, gender ideology, and women's voice, 1789–2002. *Rhetoric & Public Affairs, 5,* 565–600.

Parry-Giles, S. J., & Parry-Giles, T. (1996). Gendered politics and presidential image construction: A reassessment of the "feminine style." *Communication Monographs, 63,* 337–354.

Pfau, M., Cho, J., & Chong, K. (2001). Communication forms in U.S. presidential campaigns: Influences on candidate perceptions and the democratic process. *Harvard International Journal of Press/Politics, 6,* 88–106.

Plutzer, E., & Zipp, J. F. (1996). Identity politics, partisanship, and voting for women candidates. *Public Opinion Quarterly, 60,* 30–58.

Ramsey, E. M. (2000). Inventing citizens during World War I: Suffrage cartoons in *The Woman Citizen. Western Journal of Communication, 64,* 113–148.

Ray, A. G. (2003). Representing the working class in early U.S. feminist media: The case of Hester Vaughn. *Women's Studies in Communication, 26,* 1–27.

Richardson, R., & Moss, C. (1995). "Just between you and me:" "Feminine style" and "feminine coze" in Connie Chung's interview with the parents of Newt Gingrich. *Speaker and Gavel, 32,* 26–37.

Robertson, T., & Froemling, K. (1999). Sex, lies, and videotape: An analysis of gender in campaign advertisements. *Communication Quarterly, 3,* 333–342.

Robson, D. C. (2000). Stereotypes and the female politician: A case study of Senator Barbara Mikulski. *Communication Quarterly, 48,* 205–223.

Rosen, R. (2000). *The world split open: How the women's movement changed America.* New York: Penguin Books.

Rosenwasser, M. J. (1972). Rhetoric and the progress of the women's liberation movement. *Communication Quarterly, 20,* 45–56.

Ryan, B. (1992). *Feminism and the women's movement: Dynamics of change in social movement, ideology and activism.* New York: Routledge.

Schattschneider, E. E. (1956). *The semisovereign people.* New York: Holt, Rinehart & Winston.

Shabad, G., & Andersen, K. (1979). Candidate evaluations by men and women. *Public Opinion Quarterly, 50,* 42–61.

Slagell, A. R. (2001). The rhetorical structure of Frances E. Willard's campaign for woman suffrage, 1876–1896. *Rhetoric & Public Affairs, 4,* 1–23.

Smith, K. B. (1997). When all's fair: Signs of parity in media coverage of female candidates. *Political Communication, 14,* 71–83.

Splichal, S., & Garrison, B. (2000). Covering public officials: Gender and privacy issue differences. *Journal of Mass Media Ethics, 15,* 167–180.

Strange, L. S. (2002). Dress reform and the feminine ideal: Elizabeth Cady Stanton and the "coming girl." *Southern Communication Journal, 68,* 1–13.

Stuckey, M. E. (1996). *The theory and practice of political communication research.* Albany: State University Press of New York.

Swanson, D., & Nimmo, D. (1990). *New directions in political communication.* Newbury Park, CA: Sage.

Templin, C. (1999). Hillary Clinton as threat to gender norms: Cartoon images of the First Lady. *Journal of Communication Inquiry, 23,* 20–37.

Tobias, S. (1997). *Faces of feminism: An activist's reflection on the women's movement.* Boulder, CO: Westview Press.

Tompkins, J. (1987). Me and my shadow. In R. R. Warhol & D. P. Herndl (Eds.), *Feminisms: An anthology of literary theory and criticism* (pp. 1079–1092). New Brunswick, NJ: Rutgers University Press.

Triece, M. E. (2000). Rhetoric and social change: Women's struggles for economic and political equality. *Women's Studies in Communication, 23,* 238–260.

Trevor, M. C. (1999). Political socialization, party identification, and gender gap. *Public Opinion Quarterly, 63,* 62–89.

Vonnegut, K. S. (1995). Poison or panacea? Sarah Moore Grimké's use of the public letter. *Communication Studies, 46,* 73–89.

Weaver, D. (1997). Women as journalists. In P. Norris (Ed.), *Women, media and politics* (pp. 21–40). New York: Oxford University Press.

Wertheimer, M. M. (Ed.). (2003). *Inventing a voice: The rhetoric of selected American first ladies of the twentieth century.* New York: Rowman & Littlefield.

Winfield, B. H. (1997). The making of an image: Hillary Rodham Clinton and American journalism. *Political Communication, 14,* 241–253.

Winfield, B. H., & Friedman, B. (2003). Gender politics: News coverage of the candidates' wives in Campaign 2000. *Journalism & Mass Communication Quarterly, 80,* 548–568.

Zaeske, S. (1995). The "promiscuous audience" controversy and the emergence of the early women's rights movement. *Quarterly Journal of Speech, 81,* 191–207.

Zaeske, S. (2003). *Signatures of citizenship: Petitions, antislavery, and women's political identity.* Chapel Hill: University of North Carolina Press.

12

THE INTERSECTIONS OF RACE AND GENDER IN RHETORICAL THEORY AND PRAXIS

◆ Jacqueline Bacon

M any issues confront rhetoricians studying intersections of gender and race in discourse. What counts as rhetoric? How does it affect power and agency? What methods and perspectives best elucidate the impact of race and gender on discursive practices? When do rhetors adopt or reject traditional rhetorical strategies, and how are they oppressed and/or empowered, silenced and/or privileged by race and gender?

Critics have proposed new texts and critical methods to account more fully for the discursive influences of race and gender. Tensions between dominant and alternative paradigms,[1] the use of conventional strategies for radical ends, and the ways gender and race constrain and empower rhetors have generated innovative studies of discursive practices. In this chapter, I consider theoretical/conceptual questions underlying this scholarship, examine scholars' critical methods, and suggest directions for research. Throughout, I highlight the ways that intersections of race and gender illuminate, challenge, and expand theoretical and critical approaches to discourse.

◆ Theoretical Issues and Challenges

THE NATURE OF RHETORIC

Feminists Gearheart (1979) and Foss, Griffin, and Foss (1997), and African American scholars Asante (1987) and Karenga (2003) argue that rhetoric in the Western tradition is patriarchal and inimical to those who are not white men. They argue that it justifies antagonism, coercion, domination, even potential violence. Karenga (2003) argues for an Afrocentric conception of rhetoric as "communal deliberation, discourse, and action, oriented toward that which is good for the community and the world" (p. 3; see also Alkebulan, 2003). McPhail (2003) notes that "it is not rhetoric per se that is foreign to the African ethos, but the conceptual framework that limits rhetoric to a representational view of language" in contrast to a perspective in which "the word" has "creative and constitutive power" and is connected to "morality, spirituality, and social responsibility" (p. 103). Foss, Foss, and Griffin (1999) offer theory and practice concerned with the ways that "individuals create worlds, perspectives, and identities" (p. 7). These alternative formulations also occasion criticism. Dow (1995) and Condit (1997) suggest that definitions that claim that rhetoric is inherently patriarchal rely on essentialist notions of differences between men and women or of innate traits within certain groups.

Whatever their views of persuasion, most scholars argue for a broad definition of what constitutes rhetorical action. Scholars of African American rhetoric such as Nero (1995) and Jackson and Richardson (2003) advocate the inclusion of rhetorical acts other than those by orators addressing audiences. Davis (2002) redefines African American women's rhetoric to encompass a "discourse of experience" that "celebrates the construction of knowledge and meaning of African American women and situates rhetoric as a site of struggle for inclusion and survival" (p. 38). Others include discourses that have been considered private, such as poetry, epistles, or conversation (Donawerth, 2002; Flores, 1996; Garrett, 2002).

◆ Feminism, Womanism, and Masculinity

Beginning with groundbreaking work in the 1970s (e.g., Campbell, 1973; Hancock, 1972; Linkugel, 1974), feminism has had a significant impact on rhetorical studies. Scholars claimed that women's discourse merited attention and needed to be assessed on its own terms rather than with criteria suited to the rhetoric of white men. Other scholars and activists, particularly women of color, critiqued the exclusionary and often racist aspects of feminism and challenged feminist critics to look beyond the practices of white women. Foss et al. (1997) "acknowledge that when [they] . . . began to employ feminist perspectives," their use of such terms as "women's perspective, women's communication, and women's voices . . . did not reflect the differences that exist among women" (p. 120; see also Darlington & Mulvaney, 2002; Dow, 1995, p. 109). Crenshaw (1997b) notes that "feminist rhetorical critics are increasingly sensitive to interdisciplinary feminist scholarship that values pluralized differences among women and seeks to understand how these differences are ideologically valued or devalued in the texts we examine" (p. 220).

Some African American female scholars developed alternatives based on womanism or black feminism. Although these differ,[2] Collins (1996) explains that both recognize that "black women's particular location provides a distinctive angle of vision on oppression," attend to the "over-arching issue of analyzing the centrality of gender in shaping a range of relationships within African-American communities," and explore "the diverse ways that black women have been affected by interlocking systems of oppression" (pp. 15–16). In other words, "certain core themes shape African American women's rhetoric and rhetorical behavior," particularly "a legacy of struggle" against various forms of oppression, "the search for voice," "the interdependence of thought and action," and "empowerment in the context of everyday life" (Hamlet, 2000, p. 422; see also Davis, 1999).

Some scholars consider manhood as well as womanhood as "a historical, ideological process" through which individuals position themselves within cultural ideas about "who men are, how they ought to behave, and what sorts of powers and authorities they may claim" (Bederman, 1995, p. 7). Rhetorical critics have begun to examine the ways that gender affects the practices of male rhetors. "Masculinity is a rule-governed practice," that is "performed and maintained—culturally and individually—through and in terms of preset rhetorical arguments" (Catano, 2001, p. 2). Foss et al. (1997) note that masculinity is not synonymous with patriarchy—"a system of power relations that privileges and accords power to the white, heterosexual male"—and that patriarchy can and does harm men (pp. 121–122; see also Hantzis, 1998, p. 224). Although certain expressions of masculinity often are presented as normative (Catano, 2001, p. 2), masculinity is not a fixed category, but is constructed by discourse and manifested in multiple ways (see Condit, 1997, p. 103; Spitzack, 1998, pp. 141–142).

Because constructions of manhood often assume and bolster white supremacy, racial constructions of masculinity can exclude and oppress men of color (Bederman, 1995; Booker, 2000; Hine & Jenkins, 1999; Horton & Horton, 1993a; Wilder, 2001). Just as feminist and womanist theorists have stressed that womanhood must be seen as part of the larger context of gender and community relationships, scholars emphasize the political and communal implications of masculinity for men of color. Because resistance to white oppression often is seen as essential to self-determination, traditionally masculine ideals, such as authority in the family and community and physical strength, frequently are linked to resistance, freedom, equality, and racial power (Booker, 2000; Graham, 2001; Hammerback, Jensen, & Gutierrez, 1985, pp. 74–75, 93–94; Hine & Jenkins, 1999; Horton & Horton, 1993b; Wilder, 2001).

Links between masculinity and racial power can be problematic for women of color, suggesting that they should privilege race over gender (Guy-Sheftall, 1992; hooks, 1981; White, 1999). Carby's (1987) work on African American women novelists, however, suggests that doing so must be viewed in terms of strategic, historically specific concerns (pp. 67–68). Other scholars note that the equation of manhood and racial uplift need not imply patriarchy and that masculinity can be understood in ways that empower men and women (Allen, 1995; Estes, 2000). Hammerback and Jensen (1998) argue that César Chávez linked manliness to nonviolence (pp. 116–117).

◆ Intersectionality, Identity, and Difference

Scholars agree that the notion of *intersections* is key to understanding the ways that race and gender influence rhetorical identity and praxis. Those who study women of color stress that it is not enough just to add them to analyses of the discourse of white women or men of color (Houston & Davis, 2002, p. 3; Turner, 1998, p. 331). Nor can the relative or disparate influence of race and gender be identified (Powell, 1995; Trinh, 1989, p. 106). Instead, racism and sexism—and other forms of oppression—interact, creating a complex subject position.[3] The notion of *intersectionality*, articulated by African American feminist scholars Collins (1990) and Crenshaw (1991), posits that African American women's perspectives are shaped by "intersecting systems of race, class, gender, sexual, and national oppression" that should be viewed with a "both/and conceptual orientation" (Collins, 1990, pp. 11–12, 29).

Similar claims apply to women of other ethnic groups. Flores (1996) and Mao (2004) rely on Anzaldúa's (1987) concept of "borderlands" to theorize the ways that women of color (Chicanas and Asian Americans) negotiate aspects of their identity. Women who occupy a literal and/or figurative border, Anzaldúa maintains, "live in the interface" between two cultures (p. 37). In their rhetoric, she proposes, "the dominant culture's traditional, conventional narratives" coexist in a "struggle" with "other counter narratives" (cited in Lunsford, 1999, p. 48). However the interactions of race and gender are characterized, employing "an intersectional method" means more "than just 'covering all the categories'"; critics must "trace them to their intersections" and understand how "oppressive ideologies intersect in mutually reinforcing ways" (Crenshaw, 1997b, p. 230).

The identities and rhetorics of white women and men also are shaped by intersections. As scholars have begun to study whiteness, which, like masculinity, has been unexamined or undertheorized, they have probed its influence on the rhetoric of white women and men (Cramer, 2003; Crenshaw, 1997a; Jackson, 1999). Understanding the influences of gender and race includes understanding the ways that both advantage and oppress (Bacon, 2002; Powell, 1995; Rowe, 2000; Zaeske, 2003). Individuals can adopt "contradictory subject positions" that permit "the interplay of privilege and alterity" as "part of both a dominant culture and a marginalized one" (Friedman, 1995, p. 15; see also Rowe, 2000).

Essentializing the experiences, perspectives, or rhetorical strategies of groups such as African American women and relying on binaries such as white women/nonwhite women are tempting but dangerous critical traps (Allen, 2002, p. 23; Buzzanell, 2000; Friedman, 1995, p. 5; McPhail, 1991). As Dow (1995) asserts, critics naturally wish to "create an identity for whom we study and what we do," and "difference theories"

are useful in "explaining the experiences of some women" (pp. 108–109). Dow and others advocate self-reflexivity about groupings and divisions. Crenshaw (1991) claims that it is "more fruitful" to understand identity as created "at the site where categories intersect" than to challenge "the possibility of talking about categories at all" (p. 1299).

Rhetorical critics also interrogate the conventional frameworks used to discuss diversity. Difference is not a problem to be overcome, a struggle with winners or losers, or an obstacle to unity within and between groups. McPhail (1991) advocates models "in which differences might be complementary, and not merely antagonistic" (p. 8). Olson (1997) identifies the rhetoric of Audre Lorde as a model of a discursive practice that "acknowledg[es] and bridg[es] differences" (p. 63). "Although difference often translates into division in U.S. culture," Olson (1998) asserts, "Lorde's rhetorical technique endeavors to build identifications among diverse subordinated communities by focusing upon commonalities in oppressive, relational practices across differences" (p. 454).

AGENCY AND EMBODIMENT

Agency, which Campbell (2005) defines as "a sense that language matter[s], that influence through symbolic action in speech and/or writing [is] possible and occur[s]" (p. 2), has particular connotations for speakers marginalized by race, gender, or both. Royster's (2000) description of agency as created in African American women's writing can be a model for others: "The act of claiming creative and intellectual authority over information and experience and thereby, with a sense of vision and agency, using literacy both well and with persuasive attempt" allows African American women "to empower themselves" and "to operate with vision, insight, passion, and compassion in making sense of their lives and seeking to improve their conditions" (p. 61).

Leff and Utney (2004) explain that black rhetors' "efforts to overcome a system that repressed and demeaned them require rhetorical instruments sufficient not only to serve immediate political ends but also to constitute a new conception of themselves and their fellow African Americans" (p. 38).

Agency, as Campbell (2005) explains, is complex, multifaceted, and often ambiguous. Her view of agency as "communal and participatory, hence, both constituted and constrained by externals that are material and symbolic" (p. 2) speaks to the ways that race and gender are manifested in discourse. Rhetors must "accept, negotiate, and resist the subject-positions available to them at given moments in a particular culture"; and these "culturally available subject-positions are, simultaneously, obstacles and opportunities" (p. 4; see also Triece, 2000, pp. 242–243). Race and gender demarcate potential locations, and rhetors simultaneously invent their roles and negotiate the constraints and expectations that race and gender place on them. Campbell's assertion that agency is communal also points to contexts that empower various groups rhetorically. For African American women, "rhetorical prowess has been intertwined historically with the artful ways in which they have participated as agents of change in community life" (Royster, 1995, p. 176).

Rhetorical agents choose and enact different subject-positions, and embodiment creates authority in distinctively non-verbal ways. People of color and white women never are disembodied; their physical presence always carries racialized and/or gendered meanings. Although physical presence shapes and constrains symbolic action, it can also be marshaled, as Leff and Utney (2004) demonstrate, to allow rhetors to perform and convey experience in "ways that no propositional argument could accomplish" (p. 45) or even to claim alternative and empowering definitions of their physicality (Painter, 1996, pp. 139–142; see also Bacon, 2002; Fanuzzi, 1999; Peterson, 1995).

♦ The Master's Tools: Complicity, Resistance, or Both?

Critics who study marginalized rhetors who use traditional strategies confront African American feminist poet and essayist Lorde's (1984) famous words in her 1979 speech to the Second Sex Conference in New York: *"The master's tools will never dismantle the master's house.* They may allow us temporarily to beat him at his own game, but they will never enable us to bring about genuine change" (p. 112). Can rhetors who use such tools practice resistance?

Some scholars have investigated the ways that marginalized groups create alternative rhetorics—strategies and forms developed in order to respond to a marginalized group's needs. Flores (1996) posits that a "rhetoric of difference" allows "Chicana feminists" to "construct an identity that runs counter to that created for them by either Anglos or Mexicans" and to defy "other-created images" (pp. 143, 146); Davis (1998) proposes that "a rhetoric of humanity underscores an African cosmology of harmony and time" (p. 80). These alternatives vary, yet they share a focus on everyday experience, a rejection of external definitions, and openness to diversity within a community.

Many marginalized rhetors rely on conventional techniques, and the practices of some do reinforce the master's privilege. In various contexts, white women have silenced women of color or reinforced stereotypes of them (Bacon, 2002, pp. 124–135; Cramer, 2003; Powell, 1995; Zaeske, 2003, pp. 62–66); Asian women use terms that suggest essentialist differences between the sexes (Wu, 2001). As Sutherland (1999) warns, critics must take care not to "search for ourselves" by assuming that the history of any group to which the critic belongs will follow the critic's "preferences and political agendas" (p. 14; see also Garrett, 2002, pp. 92–93).

Conventional strategies can be used to resist oppression and patriarchy. Campbell

(1998b) asserts that "what seem to be the master's tools" not only allow "a female voice" to "emerge" but also can challenge "received wisdom" and "undermine, even sabotage, the master's house" (pp. 112–114). Illo (1966/1972) and Walker (1992) demonstrate that African American speakers rely on classical oratorical tropes, even in explicitly radical discourse. Using the master's tools can be an act of appropriation and reinvention, a refashioning that turns them into weapons against oppression (Bacon & McClish, 2000, p. 21). What hooks (1994) asserts about slaves' appropriation of language applies to the master's tools generally: "This language would need to be possessed, taken . . . seized and spoken by the tongues of the colonized . . . re-hear[d] . . . as a potential site of resistance" (pp. 169–170). Nineteenth-century African American women, for example, accepted and challenged aspects of the "cult of true womanhood" (Bacon, 1999b, 2002; Behling, 2002; Campbell, 1989; White & Dobris, 2002). Antebellum African American women drew on dominant tropes in order to reinvent themselves in potentially revolutionary ways (Bacon, 2002; Bacon & McClish, 2000). Ouyang (2001) examines the "manipulation of dominant language" (p. 204) in the texts of the Eaton sisters, who were of Chinese and English descent. (For African Americans, appropriation and revision includes signifying, explored below.) Flores (1996) asserts that Chicana feminists take the "very acts that are used to denigrate Chicanas, such as the use of Spanglish," and marshal them as "tributes to the uniqueness of Chicanas" or reinvent the symbol of the Virgin Mary to transform her from "passive idol to be worshipped to active strong woman" (p. 148).

Rhetors do not make either/or choices between so-called traditional and alternative tactics; they use whatever is available. Ritchie and Ronald (2001) maintain that throughout history women have "connect[ed] with and depart[ed] from the rhetorical tradition" and "redefined and subverted traditional means and ends of argument" (p. xvii). Rhetors also adapt to contexts; for example, indirection is common in Chinese discourse (Mao, 2004; Wu, 2001) as well as in that of white women, African American women, and African American men (Bacon, 2002). Choices vary with the rhetor's position in society and the cultural and social factors constraining his or her discourse.

◆ Critical Methods

Analyzing the discourse of those seeking social change is a challenge to critical methods (Campbell, 1971). Some critical methods develop out of the distinctive experiences of marginalized people. Others urge that conventional tools be redefined. Foss et al. (1997) maintain that instead of abandoning "the notion of *ethos,*" rhetoricians should consider how it might be developed from a perspective that accounts for "the communication of marginalized groups" (p. 130). Methods based on the distinctive features of discursive practice have demonstrated their value (Bacon, 2002, p. 9; Davis, 1998, pp. 82–83; Pennington, 2003, p. 305).

◆ Close Readings, Historical Foundations

Accordingly, many critics ground their work in analysis designed to identify what is distinctive through close readings of texts.[4] Paying attention to historical context—often challenging conventional assumptions—critics ask how the constructions of gender and race in a particular time and place shape a rhetor's choice of strategies. Close readings allow critics to focus meticulously on the textual manifestations of the intersections of race and gender. Horton and Horton (1993a, 1993b) and Forbes (2003) examine the ways that militancy and resistance influenced the activism of 19th-century African American men.

Brown's (1995) research demonstrates that African American women in the postemancipation South participated in public meetings, challenging widespread assumptions about separate public and private spheres, and it explores the complex public roles these women played. Campbell (1986, 1989, 2005), Logan (1995, 1999), Nero (1995), and Royster (2000), for example, explore the historical contexts of discursive acts by African American women, scrutinizing the circumstances that shape a text's production.

Some texts present special challenges. Rhetors who are illiterate have their words transcribed by others, editors may intervene, and oral discourses may exist only in accounts by journalists. Scholars have determined that Lydia Child edited and, to some extent, altered *Incidents in the Life of a Slave Girl* (Jacobs, 1861, cited in Mills, 1992) describing the ways in which Child's assumptions about race and gender may have shaped the final narrative (see also Yellin, 1987). The 1850 *Narrative of Sojourner Truth,* transcribed by white female abolitionist Olive Gilbert because Truth never learned to read or write, includes observations that Gilbert identifies as her own. Critical analysis of Truth's 1851 speech at a woman's rights convention in Akron, Ohio, includes the ways that the prejudices or assumptions of Gilbert and other transcribers might introduce inaccuracies and the variations among different versions (Bacon, 2002; Campbell, 2005; Fitch & Mandziuk, 1997; Lipscomb, 1995; Mabee & Newhouse, 1993; Painter, 1996; Stetson & David, 1994). Murray (1991) identifies the ways that the oratory of Native Americans was recorded by whites for white readers with particular cultural expectations.

◆ Traditional Methods

Students of 19th-century African American rhetoric recognize that it is appropriate to draw on classical as well as 18th-century models in analyzing this discourse because many African American rhetors were trained in these traditions (Bacon & McClish, 2000; Kates, 2001, pp. 53–74; McClish, 2005; McHenry, 2002). At the same time, the influences of gender and/or race on a rhetor's work suggest that conventional categories must be adapted, reinvented, or challenged. African American oratory cannot always be easily classified as either epideictic or deliberative (Walker, 1992, p. 2). Bacon and McClish show that concepts from 18th-century Scottish faculty psychology were modified by 19th-century African American female literary society members in arguments for women's activism and education.

Modern theoretical perspectives have proved useful. Burke's (1945/1969a; 1950/1969b) explorations of the power of hierarchy, division, identification, and mystery and his attention to the ways in which language creates association and stratification have been appropriated to analyze the influences of race and/or gender (Bacon, 2002; Carlson, 1999; Lee, 2002; Logan, 1999). Logan (1999) adopts concepts from Perelman and Olbrechts-Tyteca's *New Rhetoric* (1969) to analyze African American women's rhetoric, noting that their work describes "the kind of communication nineteenth-century black women engaged in to address the pressing needs of people of African descent" (p. xvi). I have found it an appropriate framework for analyzing arguments that engage "the realm of values and interpretation," including argument about "exegesis, particularly that which advocates alternative scriptural interpretations" (Bacon, 1999a, p. 9; Bacon, 2002, pp. 141–150).

Walker (1992) combines classical categories with elements of Hart's (1990) cultural criticism, praising Hart's attention to "cultural and mythic referents" invoked by speakers (p. 408). Dangerfield (2003) uses Hart's framework to analyze the lyrics of hip-hop musician Lauryn Hill, which includes "the influence of culture" and links "individual experience, social connected-ness, and cultural particularity" (p. 212). Logan (1999) and Wu (2001) apply Bitzer's (1968) rhetorical situation to the discourse of late-19th-century African American women and post-Mao Chinese feminist rhetors respectively.

◆ Alternative Approaches

Scholars apply intersectionality and "both/and" to explore the ways race and gender shape the rhetorical practices of African American women (Bacon, 2002; Crenshaw, 1997b; Davis, 2002). Standpoint theory has been used to analyze the way that such intersections affect the epistemology and praxis of African American women (Bell, Orbe, Drummond, & Camara, 2000; McClish & Bacon, 2002; Orbe, 1998). As articulated by social scientists, such as Harding (1991) and Hartsock (1983), standpoint theory posits that epistemology emerges out of "socially situated knowl-edge" (Harding, 1991, p. 138). Research about women, Harding proposes, must be based on "the perspective of women's lives" rather than on "assumptions and practices that appear natural or unremark-able from the perspective of the lives of men in the dominant groups" (p. 150). Orbe uses standpoint theory to illuminate the ways that differences and commonalities shape discourse (p. 7). McClish and Bacon use standpoint theory to analyze the dis-course of African American and white women; however, any standpoint is expressed in language, and "the connection of language to power means that the medi-ating role of language is always a defining factor in shaping the discourse of the oppressed" (p. 32).

Some critics draw on Afrocentric con-cepts. Stanford (2004) examines the influ-ence of an Afrocentric worldview on the poetry of a female inmate-student in a writing workshop in the Cook County Jail (Chicago). Dagbovie (2004) analyzes

Afrocentric themes in the writings of 19th- and 20th-century African American women. Langley (2001) examines the impact of African epistemologies and the concept of *nommo*—"the generative and productive power of the spoken word" (Asante, 1987, p. 17)—on the 18th-century griot Lucy Terry Prince. In an analysis of the rhetoric of *Essence* editor Susan L. Taylor, Hamlet (2000) relies on "womanist episte-mology," which "combines Afrocentric and feminist consciousness with the uniqueness of African American female history, culture, and experiences" (p. 425). Significantly, Hamlet cautions that "a female Afrocentric standpoint might be different from a male Afrocentric standpoint because Afrocentric theories have marginalized African American women's history and experiences just as tra-ditional feminist theories have done" (p. 423). Jackson (1997) foregrounds gender in his exploration of Afrocentric conceptions of masculinity.

Signifying, a body of strategies linked to African religion and narrative, also has been used to analyze the discourse of African American women and men (Bacon, 2002, pp. 97–108, 215–218; Zafar, 1999). Described by scholars such as Gates (1987, 1988) and Mitchell-Kernan (1973), signify-ing subsumes tropes that exploit linguistic ambiguity and indeterminacy, such as the repetition and revision of dominant forms, the invocation of multiple linguistic mean-ings, and irony and ironic reversal.

Critics appropriate the notion of perfor-mance to consider rhetoric in which race and gender intersect. Race and gender are performed in discourse; moreover, discourse is a performance, and as Peterson (1995) notes, "speaking and writing" can be "a form of doing, of social action" (p. 3). Peterson analyzes the ways that 19th-century African American women such as Sojourner Truth and Frances Ellen Watkins Harper performed discursively while draw-ing on, recreating, and undermining racial-ized and gendered notions of their bodies and creating authority as they engaged "the performative power of the word—both written and spoken" (p. 3). Scholars have analyzed as performance the rhetoric of Deborah Sampson Gannett (Brookey, 1998; Campbell, 1995, pp. 485–490), Nelson Mandela (Zagacki, 2003), Native North American orators (Clements, 2002), and U.S. first ladies (Campbell 1998a; Parry-Giles & Blair, 2002). In addition, critics have begun to explore the performance of masculinity and/or whiteness (Gingrich-Philbrook, 1998; Warren, 2001a, 2001b).

◆ **Directions for Research**

Although many scholars have considered intersections of race and gender in analyses of the rhetorics of women of color, critics sometimes have overlooked gender in studying the discourse of men of color, particularly the ways that manhood is expressed. Just as scholars have discovered that many of the tools used to study womanhood and women's discourses were developed using the white female as a standard and, thus, cannot be applied to the lives and texts of women of color, so notions of masculinity must be reconsidered for men of color. As Jackson (1997) notes, many "paradigms" of masculinity have been "constructed with the European American male as the exemplary subject" (p. 743).

Whiteness increasingly is featured in analyses of the rhetorics of white women, but the influence of privileges and opportunities dependent on race are less often noted. Lack of attention to intersections of race and gender is most apparent in analyses of the rhetoric of white men. There is some attention to gender in analyses of white men's rhetoric; yet, with some notable exceptions (Bostdorff, 2004; Ware, 1997; Wellman, 1997), critics rarely acknowledge that they are focusing on *white* masculinity. In so doing, they illustrate the "exemplary subject" trap Jackson (1997) describes and fail to challenge white privilege or the dominance of European American perspectives. Two recent volumes on the Promise Keepers

(Claussen, 1999, 2000), for example, include analyses of the movement's rhetoric. Race is mentioned in relation to the Promise Keepers' stated goals of racial reconciliation and inclusion, yet only one chapter (Hawkins, 2000) discusses the impact of whiteness on the movement's mainly white middle-class participants.[5]

Although some theoretical treatments of Afrocentricity and Afrocentric analyses of discourse foreground gender, more are needed. Some scholars analyze discursive representations of Afrocentric masculinity, yet as Hamlet (2000) demonstrates, the rhetorical use of Afrocentricity by African American women differs from, modifies, or challenges that of their male colleagues. As noted, some work addresses the interaction of gender and race in the rhetorics of women and men from other ethnic backgrounds, but more is needed.

New methods and histories emerge as critics expand the range of texts they analyze by men and women of different ethnic backgrounds. The academy, including rhetorical studies, remains dominated by white scholars. Rhetoricians must dedicate themselves to changing their disciplinary complexion, advocating educational and social policies that will increase diversity in order to appreciate and celebrate the range of discourses in which race and gender intersect in journals, anthologies, and classrooms.

◆ **Notes**

1. Although not a completely satisfactory term, I use *alternative* throughout this chapter to denote both theoretical models and discursive approaches that contrast with those derived from or explained by Western rhetorical theories or categories.

2. The particulars of the distinctions between the two are beyond the scope of this chapter; interested readers should see Collins (1996), Houston and Davis (2002), and Taylor (1998).

3. Although race and gender are the focus of this chapter, they are not the only forces that can restrict or privilege a rhetor's discourse. Variables such as class and sexual orientation also constitute interlocking, interdependent aspects of identity that shape rhetorical praxis.

4. Indeed, close reading should not be seen (as it often is) as opposed to theoretical approaches; it rests on certain analytical assumptions that a critic brings to the text (see, for example, Browne, 1996; Leff, 1992; Lucas, 1988).

5. Hawkins does not explicitly draw on scholarly or theoretical treatments of whiteness, yet he takes into account the ways that the rhetoric of white Promise Keepers is influenced by their race.

◆ References

Alkebulan, A. A. (2003). The spiritual essence of African American rhetoric. In R. L. Jackson & E. B. Richardson (Eds.), *Understanding African American rhetoric: Classical origins to contemporary innovations* (pp. 23–40). New York: Routledge.

Allen, B. J. (2002). Goals for emancipatory communication research on Black women. In M. Houston & O. I. Davis (Eds.), *Centering ourselves: African American feminist and womanist studies of discourse* (pp. 21–34). Cresskill, NJ: Hampton Press.

Allen, R. L. (1995). Racism, sexism, and a million men. *Black Scholar, 25*(4), 24–26.

Anzaldúa, G. (1987). *Borderlands/La frontera: The new mestiza.* San Francisco: Aunt Lute Books.

Asante, M. K. (1987). *The Afrocentric idea.* Philadelphia: Temple University Press.

Bacon, J. (1999a). "God and a woman": Women abolitionists, biblical authority, and social activism. *Journal of Communication and Religion, 22,* 1–39.

Bacon, J. (1999b). The *Liberator*'s "Ladies' Department," 1832–37: Freedom or fetters? In M. G. Carstarphen & S. C. Zavoina (Eds.), *Sexual rhetoric: Media perspectives on sexuality, gender, and identity* (pp. 3–19). Westport, CT: Greenwood Press.

Bacon, J. (2002). *The humblest may stand forth: Rhetoric, empowerment, and abolition.* Columbia: University of South Carolina Press.

Bacon, J., & McClish, G. (2000). Reinventing the master's tools: Nineteenth-century African-American literary societies of Philadelphia and rhetorical education. *Rhetoric Society Quarterly, 30*(4), 19–47.

Bederman, G. (1995). *Manliness & civilization: A cultural history of gender and race in the United States, 1880–1917.* Chicago: University of Chicago Press.

Behling, L. L. (2002). Reification and resistance: The rhetoric of Black womanhood at the Columbian Exposition, 1893. *Women's Studies in Communication, 25,* 173–196.

Bell, K. E., Orbe, M. P., Drummond, D. K., & Camara, S. K. (2000). Accepting the challenge of centralizing without essentializing: Black feminist thought and African American women's communicative experiences. *Women's Studies in Communication, 23,* 41–62.

Bitzer, L. F. (1968). The rhetorical situation. *Philosophy & Rhetoric, 1,* 1–14.

Booker, C. B. (2000). *"I will wear no chain!" A social history of African American males.* Westport, CT: Praeger.

Bostdorff, D. M. (2004). The Internet rhetoric of the Ku Klux Klan: A case study in web site community building run amok. *Communication Studies, 55,* 340–361.

Brookey, R. A. (1998). Keeping a good wo/man down: Normalizing Deborah Sampson Gannett. *Communication Studies, 49,* 73–85.

Brown, E. B. (1995). Negotiating and transforming the public sphere: African American political life in the transition from slavery to freedom. In the Black Public Sphere Collective (Eds.), *The black public sphere* (pp. 111–150). Chicago: University of Chicago Press.

Browne, S. H. (1996). Encountering Angelina Grimké: Violence, identity, and radical community. *Quarterly Journal of Speech, 82,* 55–73.

Burke, K. (1969a). *A grammar of motives.* Berkeley: University of California Press. (Original work published 1945)

Burke, K. (1969b). *A rhetoric of motives*. Berkeley: University of California Press. (Original work published 1950)

Buzzanell, P. M. (2000). Commentary about Aimee M. Carillo Rowe's "Locating feminism's subject: The paradox of white femininity and the struggle to form feminist alliances." *Communication Theory, 10*, 81–89.

Campbell, K. K. (1971). The rhetoric of radical Black nationalism: A case study in self-conscious criticism. *Central States Speech Journal, 22*, 151–160.

Campbell, K. K. (1973). The rhetoric of women's liberation: An oxymoron. *Quarterly Journal of Speech, 59*, 74–86.

Campbell, K. K. (1986). Style and content in the rhetoric of early Afro-American feminists. *Quarterly Journal of Speech, 72*, 434–445.

Campbell, K. K. (1989). *Man cannot speak for her* (2 vols.). Westport, CT: Greenwood Press.

Campbell, K. K. (1995). Gender and genre: Loci of invention and contradiction in the earliest speeches by U.S. women. *Quarterly Journal of Speech, 81*, 479–495.

Campbell, K. K. (1998a). The discursive performance of femininity: Hating Hillary. *Rhetoric & Public Affairs, 1*, 1–20.

Campbell, K. K. (1998b). Inventing women: From Amaterasu to Virginia Woolf. *Women's Studies in Communication, 21*, 111–126.

Campbell, K. K. (2005). Agency: Promiscuous and protean. *Communication and Critical/Cultural Studies, 2*, 1–19.

Carby, H. V. (1987). *Reconstructing womanhood: The emergence of the Afro-American woman novelist*. New York: Oxford University Press.

Carlson, A. C. (1999). "You know it when you see it": The rhetorical hierarchy of race and gender in *Rhinelander v. Rhinelander*. *Quarterly Journal of Speech, 85*, 111–128.

Catano, J. V. (2001). *Ragged dicks: Masculinity, steel, and the rhetoric of the self-made man*. Carbondale: Southern Illinois University Press.

Claussen, D. S. (1999). *Standing on the promises: The Promise Keepers and the revival of manhood*. Cleveland, OH: Pilgrim Press.

Claussen, D. S. (2000). *The Promise Keepers: Essays on masculinity and Christianity*. Jefferson, NC: McFarland.

Clements, W. M. (2002). *Oratory in Native North America*. Tucson: University of Arizona Press.

Collins, P. H. (1990). *Black feminist thought: Knowledge, consciousness, and the politics of empowerment*. New York: Routledge.

Collins, P. H. (1996). What's in a name? Womanism, Black feminism, and beyond. *Black Scholar, 26*(1), 9–17.

Condit, C. M. (1997). In praise of eloquent diversity: Gender and rhetoric as public persuasion. *Women's Studies in Communication, 20*, 91–116.

Cramer, J. M. (2003). White womanhood and religion: Colonial discourse in the U.S. Women's Missionary Press, 1869–1904. *Howard Journal of Communications, 14*, 209–224.

Crenshaw, C. (1997a). Resisting whiteness' rhetorical silence. *Western Journal of Communication, 61*, 253–278.

Crenshaw, C. (1997b). Women in the Gulf War: Toward an intersectional feminist rhetorical criticism. *Howard Journal of Communications, 8*, 219–235.

Crenshaw, K. (1991). Mapping the margins: Intersectionality, identity politics, and violence against women of color. *Stanford Law Review, 43*, 1241–1299.

Dagbovie, P. D. (2004). Black women historians from the late 19th century to the dawning of the civil rights movement. *Journal of African American History, 89*, 241–61.

Dangerfield, C. N. (2003). Lauryn Hill as lyricist and womanist. In R. L. Jackson & E. B. Richardson (Eds.), *Understanding African American rhetoric: Classical origins to contemporary innovations* (pp. 209–221). New York: Routledge.

Darlington, P. S. E., & Mulvaney, B. M. (2002). Gender, rhetoric, and power: Toward a model of reciprocal empowerment. *Women's Studies in Communication, 25*, 139–172.

Davis, O. I. (1998). A Black woman as rhetorical critic: Validating self and violating the space of otherness. *Women's Studies in Communication, 21*, 77–89.

Davis, O. I. (1999). In the kitchen: Transforming the academy through safe spaces of resistance. *Western Journal of Communication, 63,* 364–381.

Davis, O. I. (2002). Theorizing African American women's discourse: The public and private spheres of experience. In M. Houston & O. I. Davis (Eds.), *Centering ourselves: African American feminist and womanist studies of discourse* (pp. 35–51). Cresskill, NJ: Hampton Press.

Donawerth, J. (Ed.). (2002). *Rhetorical theory by women before 1900: An anthology.* Lanham, MD: Rowman & Littlefield.

Dow, B. J. (1995). Feminism, difference(s), and rhetorical studies. *Communication Studies, 46,* 106–117.

Estes, S. (2000). I *am* a man! Race, masculinity, and the 1968 Memphis sanitation strike. *Labor History, 47,* 153–170.

Fanuzzi, R. (1999). The trouble with Douglass's body. *American Transcendental Quarterly, 13,* 27–49.

Fitch, S. P., & R. M. Mandziuk. (1997). *Sojourner Truth as orator: Wit, story, and song.* Westport, CT: Greenwood Press.

Flores, L. A. (1996). Creating discursive space through a rhetoric of difference: Chicana feminists craft a homeland. *Quarterly Journal of Speech, 82,* 142–156.

Forbes, E. (2003). Every man fights for his freedom: The rhetoric of African American resistance in the mid-nineteenth century. In R. L. Jackson & E. B. Richardson (Eds.), *Understanding African American rhetoric: Classical origins to contemporary innovations* (pp. 155–170). New York: Routledge.

Foss, K. A., Foss, S. K., & Griffin, C. L. (1999). *Feminist rhetorical theories.* Thousand Oaks, CA: Sage.

Foss, S. K., Griffin, C. L., & Foss, K. A. (1997). Transforming rhetoric through feminist reconstruction: A response to the gender diversity perspective. *Women's Studies in Communication, 20,* 117–135.

Friedman, S. S. (1995). Beyond white and other: Relationality and narratives of race in feminist discourse. *Signs, 21,* 1–49.

Garrett, M. M. (2002). Women and the rhetorical tradition in premodern China: A preliminary sketch. In X. Lu, W. Jia, & D. R. Helsey (Eds.), *Chinese communication studies: Contexts and comparisons* (pp. 87–100). Westport, CT: Ablex.

Gates, H. L., Jr. (1987). *Figures in black: Words, signs, and the "racial" self.* New York: Oxford University Press.

Gates, H. L., Jr. (1988). *The signifying monkey: A theory of Afro-American literary criticism.* New York: Oxford University Press.

Gearheart, S. M. (1979). The womanization of rhetoric. *Women's Studies International Quarterly, 2,* 195–201.

Gingrich-Philbrook, C. (1998). On masculinity: Disciplinary violation as gender violation: The stigmatized masculine voice of performance studies. *Communication Theory, 8,* 203–220.

Graham, H., III. (2001). Black, and Navy too: How African-American sailors of the Vietnam era asserted manhood through Black Power militancy. *Journal of Men's Studies, 9,* 227–241.

Guy-Sheftall, B. (1992). Breaking the silence: A Black feminist response to the Thomas/Hill hearings (for Audre Lorde). *Black Scholar, 22*(1–2), 35–37.

Hamlet, J. D. (2000). Assessing womanist thought: The rhetoric of Susan L. Taylor. *Communication Quarterly, 48,* 420–436.

Hammerback, J. C., & Jensen, R. J. (1998). *The rhetorical career of César Chávez.* College Station: Texas A&M University Press.

Hammerback, J. C., Jensen, R. J., & Gutierrez, J. A. (1985). *A war of words: Chicano protest in the 1960s and 1970s.* Westport, CT: Greenwood Press.

Hancock, B. R. (1972). Affirmation by negation in the women's liberation movement. *Quarterly Journal of Speech, 58,* 264–271.

Hantzis, D. M. (1998). Good questions, persistent challenges: The promise of masculinity studies in communication. *Communication Theory, 8,* 221–235.

Harding, S. (1991). *Whose science? Whose knowledge? Thinking from women's lives.* Ithaca, NY: Cornell University Press.

Hart, R. P. (1990). *Modern rhetorical criticism.* Glenview, IL: Scott, Foresman/Little, Brown.

Hartsock, N. C. M. (1983). The feminist standpoint: Developing the ground for a specifically feminist historical materialism. In S. Harding & M. B. Hintikka (Eds.), *Discovering reality: Feminist perspectives on epistemology, metaphysics, methodology, and philosophy of science* (pp. 283–310). Dordrecht, Holland: D. Reidel.

Hawkins, B. (2000). Reading a Promise Keepers event: The intersection of race and religion. In D. S. Claussen (Ed.), *The Promise Keepers: Essays on masculinity and Christianity* (pp. 182–193). Jefferson, NC: McFarland.

Hine, D. C., & Jenkins, E. (Eds.). (1999). *A question of manhood: Vol. 1. "Manhood of rights": The construction of Black male history and manhood, 1750–1870.* Bloomington: Indiana University Press.

hooks, b. (1981). *Ain't I a woman: Black women and feminism.* Boston: South End Press.

hooks, b. (1994). *Teaching to transgress: Education as the practice of freedom.* New York: Routledge.

Horton, J. O., & Horton, L. E. (1993a). The affirmation of manhood: Black Garrisonians in antebellum Boston. In D. M. Jacobs (Ed.), *Courage and conscience: Black & white abolitionists in Boston* (pp. 127–153). Bloomington: Indiana University Press.

Horton, J. O., & Horton, L. E. (1993b). Violence, protest, and identity: Black manhood in antebellum America. In J. O. Horton, *Free people of color: Inside the African American community* (pp. 80–96). Washington, DC: Smithsonian Institution Press.

Houston, M., & Davis, O. I. (2002). Introduction: A Black woman's angle of vision on communication studies. In M. Houston & O. I. Davis (Eds.), *Centering ourselves: African American feminist and womanist studies of discourse* (pp. 1–18). Cresskill, NJ: Hampton Press.

Illo, J. (1966/1972). The rhetoric of Malcolm X. In A. L. Smith (Ed.), *Language, communication, and rhetoric in Black America* (pp. 158–175). New York: Harper & Row.

Jackson, R. L., II. (1997). Black "manhood" as xenophobe: An ontological exploration of the Hegelian dialectic. *Journal of Black Studies, 27,* 731–750.

Jackson, R. L., II. (1999). White space, white privilege: Mapping discursive inquiry into the self. *Quarterly Journal of Speech, 85,* 38–54.

Jackson, R. L., II, & Richardson, E. B. (2003). Introduction. In R. L. Jackson II & E. B. Richardson (Eds.), *Understanding African American rhetoric: Classical origins to contemporary innovations* (pp. xiii–xix). New York: Routledge.

Karenga, M. (2003). Nommo, Kawaida, and communicative practice: Bringing good into the world. In R. L. Jackson II & E. B. Richardson (Eds.), *Understanding African American rhetoric: Classical origins to contemporary innovations* (pp. 3–22). New York: Routledge.

Kates, S. (2001). *Activist rhetorics and American higher education, 1885–1937.* Carbondale: Southern Illinois University Press.

Langley, A. (2001). Lucy Terry Prince: The cultural and literary legacy of Africana womanism. *Western Journal of Black Studies, 25,* 153–162.

Lee, L.-L. (2002). Creating a female language: Symbolic transformation embedded in *Nushu.* In X. Lu, W. Jia, & D. R. Helsey (Eds.), *Chinese communication studies: Contexts and comparisons* (pp. 101–118). Westport, CT: Ablex.

Leff, M. C. (1992). Things made by words: Reflections on rhetorical criticism. *Quarterly Journal of Speech, 78,* 223–231.

Leff, M., & Utney, E. A. (2004). Instrumental and constitutive rhetoric in Martin Luther King Jr.'s "Letter from Birmingham Jail." *Rhetoric & Public Affairs, 7,* 37–51.

Linkugel, W. A. (1974). The rhetoric of American feminism: A social movement course. *Speech Teacher, 23,* 121–130.

Lipscomb, D. R. (1995). Sojourner Truth: A practical public discourse. In A. A. Lunsford (Ed.), *Reclaiming Rhetorica: Women in the rhetorical tradition* (pp. 227–245). Pittsburgh, PA: University of Pittsburgh Press.

Logan, S. W. (1995). *With pen and voice: A critical anthology of nineteenth-century African-American women*. Carbondale: Southern Illinois University Press.

Logan, S. W. (1999). *"We are coming": The persuasive discourse of nineteenth-century Black women*. Carbondale: Southern Illinois University Press.

Lorde, A. (1984). "The master's tools will never dismantle the master's house." In *Sister outsider: Essays & speeches by Audre Lorde* (pp. 110–113). Freedom, CA: Crossing Press.

Lucas, S. E. (1988). The renaissance of American public address: Text and context in rhetorical criticism. *Quarterly Journal of Speech, 74,* 241–260.

Lunsford, A. A. (1999). Toward a Mestiza rhetoric: Gloria Anzaldúa on composition and postcoloniality [interview with Gloria Anzaldúa]. In G. A. Olson & L. Worsham (Eds.), *Race, rhetoric, and the postcolonial* (pp. 43–78). Albany: State University of New York Press.

Mabee, C., & Newhouse, S. M. (1993). *Sojourner Truth: Slave, prophet, legend*. New York: New York University Press.

Mao, L. (2004). Uniqueness or borderlands? The making of Asian-American rhetorics. In K. Gilyard & V. Nunley (Eds.), *Rhetoric and ethnicity* (pp. 46–55). Portsmouth, NH: Boynton/Cook.

McClish, G. (2005). William G. Allen's "Orators and Oratory": Inventional amalgamation, pathos, and the characterization of violence in African-American abolitionist rhetoric. *Rhetoric Society Quarterly, 35*(1), 47–72.

McClish, G., & Bacon, J. (2002). "Telling the story her own way": The role of feminist standpoint theory in rhetorical studies. *Rhetoric Society Quarterly, 32*(2), 27–55.

McHenry, E. (2002). *Forgotten readers: Recovering the lost history of African American literary societies*. Durham, NC: Duke University Press.

McPhail, M. L. (1991). Complicity: The theory of negative difference. *Howard Journal of Communications, 3,* 1–13.

McPhail, M. L. (2003). The politics of (in)visibility in African American rhetorical scholarship: A (re)quest for an African worldview. In R. L. Jackson & E. B. Richardson (Eds.), *Understanding African American rhetoric: Classical origins to contemporary innovations* (pp. 99–113). New York: Routledge.

Mills, B. (1992). Lydia Maria Child and the endings to Harriet Jacobs's *Incidents in the life of a slave girl. American Literature, 64,* 255–272.

Mitchell-Kernan, C. (1973). Signifying. In A. Dundes (Ed.), *Mother wit from the laughing barrel: Readings in the interpretation of Afro-American folklore* (pp. 310–328). Englewood Cliffs, NJ: Prentice Hall.

Murray, D. (1991). *Forked tongues: Speech, writing and representation in North American Indian texts*. London: Pinter.

Nero, C. I. (1995). "Oh, what I think I must tell this world!" Oratory and public address of African-American women. In K. M. Vaz (Ed.), *Black women in America* (pp. 261–275). Thousand Oaks. CA: Sage.

Olson, L. C. (1997). On the margins of rhetoric: Audre Lorde transforming silence into language and action. *Quarterly Journal of Speech, 83,* 49–70.

Olson, L. C. (1998). Liabilities of language: Audre Lorde reclaiming difference. *Quarterly Journal of Speech, 84,* 448–470.

Orbe, M. P. (1998). From the standpoint(s) of traditionally muted groups: Explicating a co-cultural communication theoretical model. *Communication Theory, 8,* 1–26.

Ouyang, H. (2001). Rewriting the butterfly story: Tricksterism in Onoto Watanna's *A Japanese Nightingale* and Sui Sin Far's "The smuggling of Tie Co." In L. Gray-Rosendale & S. Gruber (Eds.), *Alternative rhetorics: Challenges to the rhetorical tradition* (pp. 203–217). Albany: State University of New York Press.

Painter, N. I. (1996). *Sojourner Truth: A life, a symbol*. New York: Norton.

Parry-Giles, S. J., & Blair, D. M. (2002). The rise of the rhetorical first lady: Politics, gender ideology, and women's voice, 1789–2002. *Rhetoric & Public Affairs, 5,* 565–599.

Pennington, D. L. (2003). The discourse of African American women: A case for extended paradigms. In R. L. Jackson II & E. B. Richardson (Eds.), *Understanding African American rhetoric: Classical origins to contemporary innovations* (pp. 293–307). New York: Routledge.

Perelman, C., & Olbrechts-Tyteca, L. (1969). *The new rhetoric: A treatise on argumentation* (J. Wilkinson & P. Weaver, Trans.). Notre Dame, IN: University of Notre Dame Press.

Peterson, C. L. (1995). *"Doers of the word": African-American women speakers and writers in the North (1830–1880).* New York: Oxford University Press.

Powell, K. A. (1995). United in gender, divided by race: Reconstruction of issue and identity by the Association of Southern Women for the Prevention of Lynching. *Communication Studies, 46,* 34–44.

Ritchie, J., & Ronald, K. (Eds.). (2001). *Available means: An anthology of women's rhetoric(s).* Pittsburgh, PA: University of Pittsburgh Press.

Rowe, A. M. C. (2000). Locating feminism's subject: The paradox of white femininity and the struggle to form feminist alliances. *Communication Theory, 10,* 64–80.

Royster, J. J. (1995). To call a thing by its true name: The rhetoric of Ida. B. Wells. In A. A. Lunsford (Ed.), *Reclaiming Rhetorica: Women in the rhetorical tradition* (pp. 167–184). Pittsburgh, PA: University of Pittsburgh Press.

Royster, J. J. (2000). *Traces of a stream: Literacy and social change among African American women.* Pittsburgh, PA: University of Pittsburgh Press.

Spitzack, C. (1998). Theorizing masculinity across the field: An intradisciplinary conversation. *Communication Theory, 8,* 141–143.

Stanford, A. F. (2004). More than just words: Women's poetry and resistance at Cook County Jail. *Feminist Studies, 30,* 277–301.

Stetson, E., & David, L. (1994). *Glorying in tribulation: The lifework of Sojourner Truth.* East Lansing: Michigan State University Press.

Sutherland, C. M. (1999). Women in the history of rhetoric: The past and the future. In C. M. Sutherland & R. Sutcliffe (Eds.), *The changing tradition: Women in the history of rhetoric* (pp. 9–31). Calgary, Canada: University of Calgary Press.

Taylor, U. Y. (1998). Making waves: The theory and practice of Black feminism. *Black Scholar, 28*(2), 18–28.

Triece, M. E. (2000). Rhetoric and social change: Women's struggles for economic and political equality, 1900–1917. *Women's Studies in Communication, 23,* 238–260.

Trinh, T. M. (1989). *Woman, native, other: Writing postcoloniality and feminism.* Bloomington: Indiana University Press.

Turner, K. J. (1998). Rhetorical studies in the twenty-first century: Envisioning the possibilities. *Southern Communication Journal, 63,* 330–336.

Walker, R. J. (1992). *The rhetoric of struggle: Public address by African American women.* New York: Garland.

Ware, V. (1997). Island racism: Gender, place, and white power. In R. Frankenberg (Ed.), *Displacing whiteness: Essays in social and cultural criticism* (pp. 283–310). Durham, NC: Duke University Press.

Warren, J. T. (2001a). Doing whiteness: On the performative dimensions of race in the classroom. *Communication Education, 50,* 91–108.

Warren, J. T. (2001b). The social drama of a "rice burner": A (re)constitution of whiteness. *Western Journal of Communication, 65,* 184–205.

Wellman, D. (1997). Minstrel shows, affirmative action talk, and angry white men: Marking racial otherness in the 1990s. In R. Frankenberg (Ed.), *Displacing whiteness: Essays in social and cultural criticism* (pp. 311–331). Durham, NC: Duke University Press.

White, C. L., & Dobris, C. A. (2002). The nobility of womanhood: "Womanhood" in the rhetoric of 19th century black club women. In M. Houston & O. I. Davis (Eds.), *Centering ourselves: African American feminist and womanist studies of discourse* (pp. 171–185). Cresskill, NJ: Hampton Press.

White, D. G. (1999). *Too heavy a load: Black women in defense of themselves, 1894–1994.* New York: Norton.

Wilder, C. S. (2001). *In the company of black men: The African influence on African American culture in New York City.* New York: New York University Press.

Wu, H. (2001). The alternative feminist discourse of post-Mao Chinese writers. In L. Gray-Rosendale & S. Gruber (Eds.), *Alternative rhetorics: Challenges to the rhetorical tradition* (pp. 219–234). Albany: State University of New York Press.

Yellin, J. F. (1987). Introduction. In H. A. Jacobs & L. M. Child (Eds.), *Incidents in the life of a slave girl: Written by herself* (pp. xiii–xxxiv). Cambridge, MA: Harvard University Press.

Zaeske, S. (2003). *Signatures of citizenship: Petitioning, slavery, and women's political identity.* Chapel Hill: University of North Carolina Press.

Zafar, R. (1999). The signifying dish: Autobiography and history in two Black women's cookbooks. *Feminist Studies, 25,* 449–469.

Zagacki, K. S. (2003). Rhetoric, dialogue, and performance in Nelson Mandela's "Televised Address on the Assassination of Chris Hani." *Rhetoric & Public Affairs, 6,* 709–735.

13

RHETORIC AND GENDER IN GRECO-ROMAN THEORIZING

◆ Cheryl Glenn and Rosalyn Collings Eves

istorical maps are necessarily exclusionary: to be comprehensible, they require selecting certain details at the expense of others. In Burkean terms, historiographies are a selection, reflection, and deflection of potential interpretations (Burke, 1966, p. 45). Our perspective on rhetoric's disciplinary landscape has been shaped predominantly by a view of rhetoric that is male, aristocratic, and Western, which has made it difficult for scholars to see terrains or rhetorical practices that do not fall neatly within these terms (Royster, 2003). Therefore, any and every interpretation comes at some cost. Our focus here is on gender and rhetoric in a Greco-Roman context, which is only one of several possible interpretations of that context. Our focus necessarily obscures other important considerations of gender in ancient rhetorics: rhetorics that are not Greco-Roman, ancient Near Eastern (including biblical), Egyptian, Asian, or even of Christians during the Roman republic.

In this chapter, we seek to identify theories and research on rhetoric and gender in Greco-Roman theorizing and to identify gaps in this knowledge. Accordingly, we examine the central research topics in this area and the primary theories and methods that inform research in this area. We provide an overview of existing research and, finally, potential sites for future research.

◆ General Research Trends

Until the appearance of feminist and other revisionary historiographies in the last 15 years or so, the history of rhetoric had been gendered masculine: predominantly a history of male historians writing about aristocratic male rhetors. Thus, men composed the default audience for rhetorical strictures and practices. When Plato talks about the value of true rhetoric to lead the soul toward good, it is an unquestionably masculine soul (trans. 1925). When Aristotle offers a rudimentary audience psychology in his *Rhetoric*, it is for an audience of men (trans. 1991, Book. II). And when Cicero (trans. 1942) describes the ideal orator as one combining wisdom and eloquence, his definition rests on that individual's ability to participate in the public sphere of civic action—a sphere closed to women. Because men have been the default rhetors described in Greco-Roman texts and initial secondary scholarship, much early work focused on establishing alternative gendered models for rhetoric and rhetors (e.g., Glenn 1997b; Jarratt 1993). Such work, as Glenn states in the introduction to *Rhetoric Retold* (1997b), seeks to recover historical women rhetors and recuperate their rhetorical practices and contributions. Zaeske (2002) similarly argues that such recovery work acknowledges women's contributions to rhetorical theory. These studies assume that gender informs rhetorical performance and that gender, far from being natural and inevitable, is socially constructed.

One of the earliest research trends entailed comparing the rules of discourse for physical bodies inscribed as masculine and feminine (McClure, 1999, "Introduction"). Other studies have deduced gendered rhetorical theories from the rhetorical practices of historical men and women. However, since neither rhetoric nor gender remains a stable category (let alone a master narrative) over time or space, more recent studies have focused on close readings of individual rhetors.

Knowing full well that gender is neither transparent nor natural, some scholars have turned their attention to the ways masculinity and femininity are constructed in rhetorical treatises and how writers use language alternately to (re)enforce or question traditional gender norms (Ballif, 2001; duBois, 1982, 1995; Graver, 1998). Such studies also consider how rhetors are constructed by the gender norms evinced in rhetorical theorizing. According to Gleason (1995), "Rhetoric was a calisthenics of manhood" for Roman men (p. xxii).

A current research strand situates itself beyond any masculine/feminine divide to concentrate, instead, on alternative constructions of masculinity (Gleason, 1995; Graver, 1998), disrupting the notion of a stable self and its concomitant dual gender system by exploring the treatment of figures sexed male but construed as nonmasculine (if not feminine). Because gender has become increasingly understood to be a marker of power differential (rather than a social construct affixed to a sexed body), gendered rhetorics are now based on issues of class, foreignness, effeminacy, and the like. Similarly, scholars are trying to understand alternative representations of femininity, as in Glenn (1997a) and Henry's (1995) studies of Aspasia, McClure's (2003) theorizing of courtesan and hetaerae rhetorics, O'Higgins (2001) work on women's cultic joking, Maurizio's (2001) work on Delphic priestesses, and others.

A final research trend involves recent moves to identify sites of gender that are not traditional, aristocratic, male, and/or Western. Such studies include Zaeske's (2002) work on the rhetoric of Esther; Lesko's (1997) and Lipson's (2003) work on women's rhetoric in ancient Egypt; Royster's (2003) preliminary work on Enheduanna, a Sumerian high priestess; and work on nonelite groups within the Greek or Roman empires, such as Kennedy's (1999) work on Hipparchia the Cynic (whose embodied practices were themselves rhetorical). Whatever their specific goal, a central issue for all of these researchers has become understanding the social conditions in which rhetoric is produced, the conditions that dictate who can speak—for whom, to whom, in what manner, and in what context (Berlin, 1993; Campbell, 2002; Glenn, 1997b).

◆ Theories and Methods

Campbell (2002) argues that traditional theories and methods in rhetoric are insufficient to the task of feminist recuperation because they rely on male-gendered norms. Her warning suggests that any investigation of gender and rhetoric must be guided by contemporary theories and methodologies that successfully undo what Burke calls the "trained incapacity" (1984, p. 7) that has long elided gender within a masculine norm. Rhetorical historiographers working with classical texts now regularly rely on theories and methods that highlight gender and other social disparities, drawing on gender studies, postmodernism, feminism, material Marxism, and postcolonialism.

These studies rely on gender studies' recognition that gender is a socially and historically contingent construct imposed on a sexed body (Glenn 1997b). Construed along a differential of power, gender can be concomitant with but not limited to sexual difference. Halsall (2004) explains gender "as a performed identity," one that "crosscuts and is crosscut by all the other possible factors that constitute an individual's identity: ethnicity, age, social class or rank, religion, family, or kin group" (p. 19). If gender operates along power differentials, and rhetoric, according to Berlin (1993), is "a set of strictures regarding the way language is to be used in the service of power" (p. 142), then discussions of rhetoric (and therefore power) are inevitably about gender.

The association of power with rhetoric and gender is largely a legacy of those aforementioned theoretical approaches, all of which draw scholarly attention to disparities of power in society as it is shaped through discourse. Along with Foucauldian notions of power, postmodernism also shapes our understanding that any truth

(such as social concepts of gender or rhetoric) is relative and socially, politically, and economically contingent. Feminist studies of rhetoric and gender focus on the forces that have historically prevented women (as both gendered and sexed bodies) from speaking (Glenn, 1997a). Marxist theorists demonstrate the necessity of considering alternate, nonelite dissenting voices that helped constitute historical rhetorics (Poulakos, 1993). Postcolonialism, similarly, creates an exigence for studying non-Western rhetorics that also have been devalued or co-opted by traditional rhetorics.

These various theoretical underpinnings operate to differing degrees in historiographical methods. Historiography recognizes that no grand narrative reconstruction of the past is ever possible, that history is always contingent and always interested (Glenn, 1997b). Thus, histories of rhetoric and gender are particularly complex because both are historically contingent constructs and, therefore, doubly subject to context. As such, they are shaped by the needs of their own era and our own. Revisionary historiography looks for traces and absences in the rhetorical record in order to create multilayered, multiperspectival, polyphonic accounts of the past that better approximate historical truths (Sutherland, 2002).

Perhaps most vexing for scholars working with issues of rhetoric and gender in antiquity is the paucity of texts. McClure (2001) describes the difficulty of extracting women's voices from fragments, especially from male-authored texts. The solution for some has been to read against the grain, to read as much for what is not there as for what is. For example, Glenn (1997b) describes reconstructing the Periclean-era (fifth-century BCE) female rhetor Aspasia through careful readings of the Sophists and knitting together the existing strands of her rhetorical contributions in order to shape the context of her work's disappearance. Similarly, Poulakos (1993) advocates negotiating between Marxist and poststructuralist approaches to disrupt the contexts in which the voices of nonelite speakers would have been silenced. When texts are available, scholars read them closely, tapping a range of interpretive methods, including discourse analysis, which reveals gendered speech patterns in written texts by men and women (McClure, 2001). Enos (2002) has suggested that a fuller understanding of rhetorical traditions and contexts requires discovering new sources of primary evidence, including nontextual sources, by adopting and adapting archeological methods. Although classical scholars often rely on art and artifacts in addition to textual sources, such studies in rhetoric are rare.

◆ Gender and Rhetoric in Greece[1]

Because gender constructions are historically contingent (e.g., our current understanding of gender expectations in Greek antiquity is mostly limited to the fourth and fifth centuries BCE), Jarratt (2002) admonishes scholars about applying a single set of gender expectations across multiple historical periods. In her study of Sappho, Jarratt claims that gender expectations were less rigid in archaic Greece than in the later classical era and women had more freedom to move about in society. Glenn (1997b) suggests the possibility of women's education in schools like those Sappho established. However, there is considerably less scholarship on the understanding of gender in archaic Greece than in the classical era.

The golden era of rhetoric in classical Greece was marked by increasing codification of gender lines, which duBois (1982) explains by the shift from narrative discourse to increasingly polarized philosophical discourse over the course of the sixth through fourth centuries BCE. Thus, the Greek male in the fifth century was described in terms of difference: "not-animal, not-barbarian, not-female" (p. 4), and the *polis*, the public sphere of aristocratic male citizens, was founded on the exclusion of foreigners, slaves, and women (Glenn, 1997b). Because women were confined to the *oikos*, the domestic sphere, men became the default norm in the public sphere and its discourse.

By our contemporary standards, a woman's role was paradoxical in that women were essential to marriage, the domestic economy, and the perpetuation of society but were excluded from public life, educational opportunity, and legal rights and protection (duBois, 1982; Bizzell & Herzberg, 2001). In addition, class hierarchy exacerbated differences among women of various social classes (Glenn, 1997b), despite a gendered system of limited engagement in leading religious rituals and in domestic responsibility. By the second and first centuries BCE, aristocratic women gained limited power in terms of holding public office (Bizzell & Herzberg, 2001). Nonetheless, only prostitutes and hetaerae—not respectable women—appeared in public or participated in the *polis* (Cape 1997; McClure, 1999).

This gender binary was codified in discourse. Both philosophy and rhetoric (in imitation of philosophy) "emphasiz[ed] reliance on rational argument and universals and understating the role of emotion, belief, style" (Campbell, 2002, p. 49). This position reinforced binary distinctions by privileging a masculine rationality over a feminine emotionality. DuBois (1993) argues that early philosophers of rhetoric distinguished themselves from women, barbarians, and slaves by their lack of emotion and that this distinction was maintained in their public discourse.

Cultural and philosophical beliefs about biology also reinforced these gender constructions. As Glenn (1997b) points out, the Aristotelian belief in the superiority of the male helped naturalize social hierarchies. The Greeks perceived sexuality in gendered terms as well, specifying differences in sexuality on the basis of role (active or passive) rather than biological sex. And as naturally finer beings, only masculine males had the right to participate in public discourse (Glenn, 1997b).

◆ *Displaying Gender in Greek Rhetorical Discourse*

In an era when hereditary power and language were used to influence the community, language became a marker of status, defining elite members of the polis as well as barbarians, or those who "babble" (duBois, 1982). *Areté,* the highly nuanced understanding of virtue essential to masculinity and available only to upper-class males, was demonstrated only through rhetorical prowess in the *agon*, the arena for public disputes (Hawhee, 2002). As the instantiation of societal power differentials, the deployment of language was inevitably informed by gender expectations.

Just as social masculinity was figured in terms of what it was not (duBois, 1982), so was rhetorical masculinity. Masculine speech was to be straightforward, rational, and unadorned; adornment was equated with femininity (Plato, 1925). Similarly, speech that aimed at pleasing, like that of many Sophists, was suspect for its feminine associations (Ballif, 2001). When Hellenistic oratory became increasingly florid and ornamental, this "Asianist" style was read as a sign of the increasing degeneracy of classical oratory (Walker, 2000).

Masculine discourse was considered the transparent norm, so most ancient commentary on gendered discourse patterns focused on deviant (usually feminine) speech, which could be found in the dramatic performances of female characters (Glenn, 1997b). Although Greek actors relied more on costume and gesture than language to indicate sex, female characters exhibited distinctively female patterns of speech: "lyric expression of fear and grief; prayers to the gods for help; . . . references to domestic activities . . . ; references to the intimate relations between child and mother or between sexual partners" (Griffith, 2001, p. 123). Although not necessarily characteristic of actual women, such patterns were culturally coded feminine with the most distinctive sign of femininity being the failure to speak at all: "a silence that would be shameful or cowardly in a man might . . . confer an ideal air of 'modesty' and 'good sense' upon a woman" (Griffith, 2001, p. 123).

◆ *Rhetorical Constructs of Gender*

In addition to the ways that gender expectations inform rhetorical practices, scholars also have examined the ways in which gender is constructed explicitly in rhetorical texts, most commonly in Plato's and Aristotle's works. As mentioned above, duBois (1982) critiques Platonic philosophy for its debilitating binaries of reason and emotion, masculine and feminine. Ballif (2001) argues that Plato's philosophic rhetoric in *Phaedrus* equates purity of soul with masculinity and recasts women as the inferior gender by associating them with sophistry. Jarratt and Ong (1995) argue that Plato's promotion of autochthonous birth—the birth of warriors directly from the land—in the *Menexenus* enacts a fantasy that men do not need women, displacing women from one of their few socially valued roles.

Similarly, scholars critique Aristotle for promulgating the biological inferiority of women and for explaining the accomplishments of extraordinary women like Sappho by suggesting that they are somehow more or other than women (Glenn, 1997b). In fact, because of the widespread assaults by feminists on Plato's and Aristotle's depictions of gender (particularly the feminine), feminist philosophers have issued two scholarly collections attempting to rehabilitate the Greek philosophers' work (Tuana, 1994; Freeland, 1998).

◆ *Rhetorical Practices of Gendered Individuals*

By far the largest body of scholarship on gender and rhetoric in Greek contexts explores rhetorical practices of rhetors gendered differently from the norm. Often driven by feminist goals, this scholarship mostly focuses on female rhetors, women (such as Sappho, Aspasia, Diotima, and Hipparchia) who must compensate by moving beyond "the available means of persuasion" (Aristotle, trans. 1991, Book I, ii) to transform or otherwise adapt the spaces and circumstances in which they find themselves. However, as indicated below, Roman (and Greco-Roman) rhetoric offers examples of alternatively gendered male speakers as well.

Perhaps the most distinguished of those female rhetors is Sappho, whose existence can be re-membered from extant poetic fragments (unlike Aspasia, who must be reconstructed from fragments, and Diotima, who appears in writings by men). DuBois (1995) argues that Sappho's writings disrupt many of our notions about antiquity:

> She is a woman but also an aristocrat, a Greek, but one who turned toward Asia, a poet who writes as a philosopher before philosophy, a writer who speaks of sexuality that can be identified neither with Michel Foucault's account of Greek sexuality nor with many versions of contemporary lesbian sexuality. (p. 25)

In Sappho, Glenn (1997b) finds evidence for female literacy and a gendered rhetoric: Sappho's poetry reveals her skill in and resistance to traditional, male-approved forms and subjects, such as epithalamium, epiphany, and priamel (epigrammic catalog). Similarly, Lardinois (2001) argues that "the poetry of Sappho was closely modeled on the public speech genres of women in ancient Greece," which included prayers to female goddesses, laments, and the praise of young brides (p. 75). In her comparison of Sappho with Alcaeus, another sixth-century lyric poet from Lesbos, Jarratt (2002) discovers in Sappho a gendered form of memory that actively constructs feminine desire and later influences Cicero's and Quintilian's formulations of rhetorical memory.

Aspasia also has a long, albeit contested, history. Henry (1995) argues that, next to Sappho and Cleopatra, "Aspasia's is the longest and richest female biographical tradition to come down to us from the Greco-Roman past" (p. 6). As Glenn (1997a, 1997b) and Jarratt and Ong (1995) have demonstrated, Aspasia's ability as a rhetor was extraordinary: despite her position as a non-Athenian woman, she transgressed gendered boundaries and established herself as an eloquent rhetor (she is said to have written Pericles's funeral oration), as a possible teacher of Socrates, and as a potential inventor of the Socratic method.

Scholars interested in gendered rhetoric also have recovered the rhetoric of women such as Diotima of Mantinea and Hipparchia the Cynic. Some dispute the existence of Diotima (see Halperin, 1990), who appears only in Plato's dialogues. Swearingen (1995) and Glenn (1997b) counter that Plato was not known to use purely fictional characters. Diotima demonstrates the ability of a gendered figure to speak, and she makes an argument about love that emphasizes the unity of spirit and body and transcends the typical sensual-spiritual (and, by extension, feminine-masculine) dichotomy that so often characterizes Plato's work. Kennedy (1999) suggests that Hipparchia the Cynic can teach us useful things about a feminist rhetoric and ethic of embodiment. A highborn woman in Hellenistic Greece who deliberately embraced social exile when she married a Cynic, Hipparchia offers a historical precedent for the ways that women can find spaces for an embodied rhetoric that espouses ethical principles and for the use of exile to critique cultural institutions.

Recent studies have also attempted to work out uniquely feminine rhetorics by examining the speech patterns of particular groups of women, including women's cultic groups and Delphic priestesses. O'Higgins (2001) examines women's cultic joking and mocking in secret Demeter cults by reading often derogatory male references to such joking through a gendered lens. McClure

(2003) also works toward a feminine gendered rhetoric in her study of representations of courtesans in Book 13 of Athenaeus, where the riddles of the hetaerae are shown to allow them to control access to meaning and gain the upper hand in discourse. Maurizio (2001) argues that the Pythian or Delphic oracles deliberately adopted ambiguity to meet their clients' expectations and to resist straightforward (one word/one meaning) masculine writing.

Other potential sites for studies of gendered rhetorical practices include philosophic groups whose positions were gendered in opposition to the dominant Platonic and Aristotelian rhetorics. Such studies include Ballif's (2001) and Jarratt's (1991) work on the Sophists, but they might also include groups more often overlooked in rhetorical studies, including the Cynics, the Epicureans, and the Pythagoreans. Kennedy's (1999) work on the Cynics suggests the potential for further gendered analysis of their embodied discourse. The Pythagoreans also merit study for their contributions to the conceptualization of rhetoric; their female members—Theano, Phintys of Sparta, and Perictyone—helped spread the Pythagorean philosophy of *harmonia* and adapted it to the microcosm of the home (Glenn, 1997b).

◆ Gender and Rhetoric in Rome

Gold (1998) suggests that, in antiquity, gender and sexuality intersected in interesting ways: gender categories were not set up as rigid binaries, but often were constructed through the performance of individuals. Gleason (1995) similarly suggests that, within the Greco-Roman era of the Second Sophistic, gender was not bound to anatomical sex. Although qualities of masculinity and femininity were highly polarized, an individual might register anywhere along the spectrum between them. Because the culture was highly dimorphic in terms of gender and humans are only weakly so,

Greco-Roman cultures developed an elaborate system of gender identifications.

Masculine ideals in the Roman empire were strongly influenced by Stoic ideals, which posited that men should represent a union of mind and body; the ideal man's noble birth could be read in his bodily deportment and his character (Gold, 1998). Men were often defined by continence and self-control, in opposition to women and barbarians (Halsall, 2004). Gleason (1995) notes that the Second Sophistic (second century CE) was a time of some cultural anxiety. A rhetorical display of *paideia*[2] was used to increase the distance between the educated elite and others and to make their superiority appear "natural" (p. xix). In particular, those involved in government required education and familiarity with rhetoric to demonstrate their civic virtue and masculinity (Halsell, 2004). Before the fall of the Roman Empire in the fifth century CE, masculinity allied martial virtue with civic engagement, but as the empire began to break apart, the army began to develop its own identity, projecting a masculinity that was more fierce, non-Roman, and animalistic (Halsall, 2004), with the worst characterization for a man being androgynous (rather than feminine).

Despite changing cultural contexts, the feminine ideal appeared much the same for women in Rome as in Greece. Cape (1997) suggests that well-born Roman girls were less confined and better educated than Greeks, even in rhetorical precepts, as they were often educated alongside boys and that they also were allowed to speak in courts. Elite Roman women could occasionally appear publicly to advertise the family's wealth and influence (Skinner, 1997). However, women were still expected to adhere to the domestic ideal of the influential Roman matron (Glenn, 1997b). Quintilian (trans. 2001) praises in his *Institutes of Oratory* the educated mother who influences her son's ability to speak well. Women were not entirely valorized. They were still denied full access to public spaces (Richlin, 1997), and, in contrast to masculine seamlessness, their bodies were held to represent a mind/body split (Gold, 1998).

◆ Displaying Gender in Roman Rhetorical Discourse

According to Gleason (1995), Richlin (1997),[3] and Gunderson (2000), rhetoric was an integral part of male socialization during the Roman Empire, with schools and performance halls providing significant opportunities for the construction, development, and performance of manhood; in Cato's words, *vir bonus dicendi peritus,* the orator was *vir bonum.* As Gunderson tells us, the Latin word *vir* refers to a man who is a husband and a soldier; "a man in Latin is a real man, a manly man" (p. 7). Thus, a man's rhetorical style revealed not only his masculinity but his character. Rhetors with defective (i.e., effeminate) style were also morally defective (Graver, 1998; Gunderson, 2000; Richlin, 1997).

Rhetorical performance was measured not simply in formal style and speech, but in physical voice and deportment as well. Summing up rhetorical treatises, Gleason (1995) explains that "the orderly man . . . reveals his self-restraint through his deportment: he is deep voiced and slow stepping, and his eyes, neither fixed nor rapidly blinking, hold a certain indefinably courageous gleam" (p. 61). Gunderson (2000) describes Quintilian's ideal masculine orator as one who is restrained in his movements. Such restraint differentiated rhetoric, and its association with truth and spirit, from acting, which was associated with deception and the body. Enders's (1997) work on delivery is a fascinating study of the way rhetoricians—in Greece but predominantly in Rome—tried to police gender and genre lines by discouraging aspiring orators from theatricality in their delivery.

Rhetorical handbooks also indicated that gender could be read in the presentation of the body, according to types of dress and degrees of adornment. Masculinity and virile character could be read in clothing. An orator should be neither disheveled nor dandified (Gunderson, 2000). Adornment became associated with feminine fraud, deception, and illicit sexuality (Richlin, 1995)—or worse with femininity because, like the Greeks, Romans viewed sexuality in terms of role rather than partners (Gunderson; Skinner, 1997). Thus, a male rhetor who offered listening pleasure to others was vulnerable to taking on the label of feminine. When Demosthenes was denounced for dress deemed too elaborate, the denunciation took the form of sexual slurs; his attackers accused him of performing oral sex on other men (Gunderson). In terms of rhetorical presentation (stylistic, behavioral, or physical), masculinity was the default norm. And as Gunderson argues, masculinity, embedded in the delivery of one's text as well as of one's body, was always negotiated in relation to other texts and bodies—the feminine, the foreign, the slave.

◆ Rhetorical Constructs of Gender

As the preceding section suggests, much of the rhetorical work of gender construction was accomplished in rhetorical handbooks. In particular, scholars have studied the way prominent rhetoricians—Cicero, Seneca (both the elder and younger), Tacitus, and Quintilian—implicitly have configured gender in their instructions on the presentation of a rhetorical self.

For instance, in her study of masculinity during the Second Sophistic, Gleason (1995) makes her case for the rhetorical construction of masculinity by drawing on the Roman belief that physiognomy coded gender and, therefore, Roman rhetoricians stressed that association. Cicero's rhetor should control his eye movements, as the eyes were an important indicator of internal thought. He should also attend to vocal variety, which was important for maintaining the audience's interest, but too much variety was dangerous because it risked betraying the rhetor as unmanly. For the elder Seneca, depraved or overly smooth speech was an indicator of depraved morals.

Graver (1998) argues that the younger Seneca takes his father's position one step further, suggesting that if speech and behavior indicate internal character, so do writing and other personal characteristics. In particular, she examines Seneca's attacks on Maecenas for his departure from a "virile" style. From his writing, Seneca concludes that Maecenas himself is *mollis* (soft), a reference to sexual deviance as well as to a "failure to discipline oneself" (Graver, p. 611). For Seneca, rhetorical failure stems ultimately from flawed character—a failure to discipline oneself, to be(come) a man.

According to Gunderson (2000), Quintilian believes that a good, masculine man (vir bonus) reveals his character through his physical presentation. This ideal, however, is constantly threatened by the rhetor's body, which may signify independently of the speaker if not closely disciplined. Thus, rhetorical success, like successful masculine performativity, requires constant vigilance and a restrained physical presentation. Enders (1997) argues that the discourses of Quintilian and Tacitus link theatrics, bad rhetoric, and effeminacy. This tactic, she charges, "marginalized women, homosexuals, bad oratory, and theater by casting certain types of speakers and speech as perverse and disempowered" (p. 253). For Quintilian, good rhetoric (and masculinity) is best described by what it is not—it is "not dull, coarse, exaggerated ... *soft* or effeminate" (Enders, p. 260). This rule of masculine rhetoric relied on what Gunderson calls the "mythology of decorum"—a mythology that protected rhetorical provinces from women and from nonelite males, who might find it difficult to adopt a style for which there are no rules.

◆ Rhetorical Practices of Gendered Individuals

Because rhetoric and masculinity were mutually constructed, feminine rhetors (sexed female or male) were always already barred from full participation. To speak at all, they had to reconfigure their words and appearance to a speaking moment. Their difficulties are illustrated by Gaia Afrania, whose attempts to speak in public courts were ridiculed, and by Amasia Sentia, who was praised only for presenting her argument like a man (Cape, 1997; Glenn, 1997b; Richlin, 1997).

One of the few women to successfully speak in public was Hortensia, the daughter of Quintilian's rival, Quintus Hortensius. She spoke to the triumvirs in the Forum in Rome (Cape, 1997; Glenn 1997b), arguing that women should not have to give money for war efforts when they could not participate in politics. Her successful public speaking was condoned only because she was her father's daughter, because she spoke for other women, and because this was an isolated instance.

Cape (1997) suggests that although women did not regularly participate in public oration, they successfully participated in private conversations or *sermo*. Both Glenn (1997b) and Cape (1997) describe the widely reputed epistolary eloquence of Cornelia, mother of the Graccus brothers (Tiberius and Gaius). Glenn describes additional Roman women who found their way into the historical record by virtue of their education and family connections—Verginia, Sempronia, Fulvia, Octavia. Still, upon entering the public sphere, they were vulnerable to attacks on their virtue, honor, and families.

Gleason's (1995) study is one of the few that focuses on alternative masculine rhetorics. She describes the rhetorical rivalry over gender correctness that existed between the ultramasculine Polemo and the sexually ambiguous Favorinus. Favorinus was multiply disadvantaged as a Sophist, a Gaul, a congenital eunuch, and effeminate in physical appearance and voice. Yet he fascinated audiences with a self-conscious presentation that refigured his liabilities as advantages. Gleason's study underscores the interdependency of gender and rhetoric: gender is necessarily rhetorical, and rhetoric, as it deals with issues of power, is necessarily gendered.

◆ Conclusion

Despite its relatively recent emergence,[4] scholarship on rhetoric and gender in antiquity displays numerous strengths, the most obvious being the facility and creativity scholars have shown in locating alternate sites for rhetorical work and in learning to reread male-centered texts for alternative perspectives. Particularly powerful are the studies of specific women rhetors in Greece and the studies of Roman masculinity. Because these sites are fairly recent, it is difficult to offer a widespread critique of the field, but we believe that many of the existing gaps and problems in the field will be resolved with time and additional scholarship. However, some of the more prevalent weaknesses include insufficient understanding of rhetorical masculinity in Greek culture[5]; insufficient studies of alternative gendered positions, such as class, ethnicity, age, or disability; and a Western bias that privileges the origin of rhetoric in classical Greco-Roman culture. In addition, the field faces an interdisciplinary challenge—although studies on masculinity and rhetoric are conducted within classics and rhetorical studies, there is not yet a rich interchange between the two.

The possibilities for future studies in gender and rhetoric in antiquity are exciting. We began by suggesting that this chapter presents only one possible reading of gender and rhetoric in Greco-Roman theorizing. We would like to close by inviting alternative readings to complement and complicate this reading. Royster (2003)

suggests three powerful means of shifting our focus on the rhetorical landscape to illuminate unexplored terrain: shift where we stand, shift the rhetorical subject, and shift the circle of practice.

To shift our stance we need to explore rhetorics that are not male, elite, or Western in the rhetorical practices of contemporary or even preexisting cultures. For example, Wells (2003) points out that the Sumerian Epic of Gilgamesh and the writings of Enheduanna predate Homer, yet few scholars have explored their rhetorical possibility. Other Near Eastern rhetorics have also been neglected; Zaeske's (2002) study of the biblical Queen Esther's rhetoric offers a productive model.

Egyptian rhetoric offers another possibility for the study of rhetoric and gender. Although scholarship on Egyptian rhetoric is gradually increasing (Hutto, 2002), scholarship on gendered rhetorical practices is still sparse. Some exceptions include Lesko's (1997) study of women's rhetoric in ancient Egypt and Lipson's (2003) rhetorical study of hieroglyphics (including those of the female pharaoh Hatshepsut). Similarly, the first section of Jackson and Richardson's (2003) recent collection shifts the scholarly focus from classical Greco-Roman rhetoric by exploring the Egyptian origins of African American rhetoric.

Another place rhetoric and gender in antiquity could be explored is in Asian rhetoric. Wu (2002) argues that feminist historiography in Chinese rhetoric is problematic: studies of Chinese women are not rhetorical, and studies of Chinese rhetoric ignore women. Royster (2003) suggests that rhetoricians could study the work of Pan Chao (48–117 CE), "a royal historiographer, librarian, and teacher during the great Han empire in China" (p. 156; see also Donawerth, 2002).

Shifting our stance might also include looking at rhetorics within Greco-Roman culture that exemplify other gendered positions: class, geography, and so on. Cribiore (2001) offers a preliminary glimpse of

Greek women writers in the second century CE from the Egyptian cities of Hermopolis and Heptakomia. Although Cribiore offers tentative theorizing about these women's writings, other readings, interpretations, and theorizings are still possible.

Other neglected rhetors of this period include Christians and Jews. Augustine's Christianization of rhetorical practices opened the way for later Christian women such as Julian of Norwich and Margery Kempe to claim divine inspiration as their justification for public speaking, and it is surprising that more rhetorical work on Christian rhetoric in this era is lacking. Burrus (1996), Cameron (1994), and Clark (1994) explore rhetorical strategies in early Christian male writings about women. Harvey's (2001) study of biblical woman in Syriac tradition argues that Syriac homilies and hymns gave women a rhetorical voice lacking in biblical narratives. But much of the work on gender constructions in early Christianity, including voluminous research in Paul's New Testament epistles, has been done by religious scholars (see Penner & Stichele, 2004), not by rhetoricians. Contemporary Jewish rhetorics (including Old Testament rhetorical practices) are another promising research topic.

A final option for the study of rhetorics within Greco-Roman culture involves marginalized philosophical groups. Much work has been done recently on reclaiming the Sophists (Ballif, 2001; Jarratt, 1991; Schiappa, 2003). Other studies have suggested the association between Stoicism and masculinity (Graver, 1998). Schilb (1994) suggests the need to move beyond the conventional opposition of Sophists versus Platonists by including the Cynics, Epicureans, or Pythagoreans. Kennedy (1999) and Glenn (1997b) have identified preliminary options for rhetoric and gender work among these philosophic movements. Branham and Goulet-Cazé's (1997) edited collection on the Cynics and Gordon's (1996) work on Epicurus might offer other useful starting points for rhetorical work.

Royster (2003) also asks us to shift our perspective by shifting the rhetorical subject and "focus on the recovery of specific women rhetors within these territories and time frames" (p. 152). Although many of the studies surveyed in this article do just that, there is still work for feminist rhetorical historiography, as Plant's (2004) recent anthology demonstrates. In addition, scholars might identify rhetorical subjects who are gendered in other ways. For example, most of the descriptions of rhetoric in this era assume an able-bodied, voiced individual. With the exception of Gleason's (1995) study of Favorinus, there are few models of rhetorical practices for physically nonnormative individuals. Just as masculinity is figured as healthy, it is also perennially youthful (or at least, not old). We need more studies exploring the impact of aging on rhetorical and gendered practices.

Gleason's (1995) conclusion suggests that the focus on masculine definition in rhetorical sources too often disguises issues of social class. Finding ways to study the rhetorical practices of nonelite individuals would also be a valuable contribution. The collection of essays in *Women and Slaves in Greco-Roman Culture* (Joshel & Murnaghan, 1998), which attempts to excavate the gendered experiences of women and slaves, is one such contribution.

Royster's final suggestion is to shift our circle of practice, to reconsider what counts as rhetoric. Many of the potential projects described here fall partially under the purview of this option. As Lu (1998) notes, Chinese rhetorical practices were not as self-consciously theorized as those of Greco-Roman writers, but they were no less "rhetorical." Biesecker (1993) suggests a need for increased study of community rhetorics that disrupt the predominantly individual-centered narratives of rhetorical study. Here again, Kennedy's (1999) study of the Cynics seems to present a productive option. We offer these suggestions in lieu of closure as an invitation to further discussion.

◆ Notes

1. Any distinction between Greek and Roman rhetoric is artificial. Greek and Roman rhetors overlapped considerably, as Gleason's (1995) study of masculinity among Greek rhetors living within the Roman Empire during the Second Sophistic demonstrates.

2. Traditionally, *paideia* has meant an educational system, broadly conceived, that shaped Greek character.

3. Although Richlin's (1997) study focuses primarily on "the socialization of Roman citizen boys into manhood through the study of rhetoric" (p. 91), she suggests other issues in the study of gender and rhetoric in Roman contexts: (a) how rhetorical handbooks encourage gender construction, (b) the content of these rhetorical guides, (c) the correlation between gender and geography in the Atticist-Asianist debate, (d) the contrast between Greek and Roman definitions of rhetoric, and (d) the ways that womanhood is constructed in Roman culture through its exclusion from rhetoric.

4. General classical scholarship on women in antiquity did not become widespread until the 1970s and 1980s, with publication of scholars such as Foley (1981), Hallett (1984), Keuls (1985), and Pomeroy (1975).

5. Foxhall and Salmon's (1998a, 1998b) companion volumes address in detail different aspects of masculinity in Greek culture. These volumes lack, however, a thorough explanation of the way masculinity and rhetoric are mutually shaped in Greek rhetorical discourse—no study of Greek rhetoric exists on the scale of Gleason's (1995) or Gunderson's (2000) studies.

◆ References

Aristotle. (1991). *On rhetoric: A theory of civic discourse* (G. A. Kennedy, Trans.). New York: Oxford University Press.

Ballif, M. (2001). *Seduction, sophistry, and the woman with the rhetorical figure.* Carbondale: Southern Illinois University Press.

Berlin, J. (1993). Revisionary history: The dialectical method. In T. Poulakos (Ed.), *Rethinking the history of rhetoric: Multidisciplinary essays on the rhetorical tradition* (pp. 135–152). Boulder, CO: Westview.

Biesecker, B. (1993). Coming to terms with recent attempts to write women into the history of rhetoric. In T. Poulakos (Ed.), *Rethinking the history of rhetoric: Multidisciplinary essays on the rhetorical tradition* (pp. 153–172). Boulder, CO: Westview.

Bizzell, P., & Herzberg, B. (Eds.). (2001). *The rhetorical tradition: Readings from classical times to the present* (2nd ed.). Boston: Bedford/St. Martin's.

Branham, R. B., & Goulet-Cazé, M. (Eds.). (1997). *The cynics: The cynic movement in antiquity and its legacy.* Berkeley: University of California Press.

Burke, K. (1966). *Language as symbolic action: Essays on life, literature, and method.* Berkeley: University of California Press.

Burke, K. (1984). *Permanence and change: An anatomy of purpose* (3rd ed.). Berkeley: University of California Press.

Burrus, V. (1996). Reading Agnes: The rhetoric of gender in Ambrose and Prudentius. *Journal of Early Christian Studies, 4,* 461–475.

Cameron, A. (1994). Early Christianity and the discourse of female desire. In L. J. Archer, S. Fischler, & M. Wyke (Eds.), *Women in ancient societies: "An illusion of the night"* (pp. 152–168). New York: Routledge.

Campbell, K. K. (2002). Consciousness-raising: Linking theory, criticism, and practice. *Rhetoric Society Quarterly, 32,* 45–64.

Cape, R. W., Jr. (1997). Roman women in the history of rhetoric and oratory. In M. M. Wertheimer (Ed.), *Listening to their voices: The rhetorical activities of historical women* (pp. 112–132). Columbia: University of South Carolina Press.

Cicero. (1942). Of oratory (E. W. Sutton & H. Rackham, Trans.). In *Cicero: De Oratore, Vol. III.* Loeb Classical Library. Cambridge, MA: Harvard University Press.

Clark, E. A. (1994). Ideology, history, and the construction of "woman" in late ancient Christianity. *Journal of Early Christian Studies, 2,* 155–184.

Cribiore, R. (2001). Windows on a woman's world: Some letters from Roman Egypt. In A. Lardinois & L. McClure (Eds.), *Making silence speak: Women's voices in Greek literature and society* (pp. 223–239). Princeton, NJ: Princeton University Press.

Donawerth, J. (2002). *Rhetorical theory by women before 1900: An anthology.* Lanham, MD: Rowman & Littlefield.

duBois, P. (1982). *Centaurs and amazons: Women and the pre-history of the great chain of being.* Ann Arbor: University of Michigan Press.

duBois, P. (1993). Violence, apathy, and the rhetoric of philosophy. In. T. Poulakos (Ed.), *Rethinking the history of rhetoric: Multidisciplinary essays on the rhetorical tradition* (pp. 119–134). Boulder, CO: Westview.

duBois, P. (1995). *Sappho is burning.* Chicago: University of Chicago Press.

Enders, J. (1997). Delivering delivery: Theatricality and the emasculation of eloquence. *Rhetorica, 15,* 253–278.

Enos, R. L. (2002). The archaeology of women in rhetoric: Rhetorical sequencing as a research method for historical scholarship. *Rhetoric Society Quarterly, 32,* 65–79.

Foley, H. P. (1981). *Reflections of women in antiquity.* New York: Gordan & Breach.

Foxhall, L., & Salmon, J. (Eds.). (1998a). *Thinking men: Masculinity and its self-representation in the classical tradition.* London: Routledge.

Foxhall, L., & Salmon, J. (Eds.). (1998b). *When men were men: Masculinity, power, and identity in classical antiquity.* London: Routledge.

Freeland, C. A. (Ed.). (1998). *Feminist interpretations of Aristotle.* University Park: Pennsylvania State University Press.

Gleason, M. (1995). *Making men: Sophists and self-presentation in ancient Rome.* Princeton, NJ: Princeton University Press.

Glenn, C. (1997a). Locating Aspasia on the rhetorical map. In M. M. Wertheimer (Ed.), *Listening to their voices: The rhetoric of historical women* (pp. 19–41). Columbia: University of South Carolina Press.

Glenn, C. (1997b). *Rhetoric retold: Regendering the tradition from antiquity through the Renaissance.* Carbondale: Southern Illinois University Press.

Gold, B. K. (1998). "The house I live in is not my own": Women's bodies in Juvenal's *Satires. Arethusa, 31,* 369–386.

Gordon, P. (1996). *Epicurus in Lycia: The second-century world of Diogenes of Oenoanda.* Ann Arbor: University of Michigan Press.

Graver, M. (1998). The manhandling of Maecenas: Senecan abstractions of masculinity. *American Journal of Philology, 119,* 607–632.

Griffith, M. (2001). Antigone and her sister(s): Embodying women in Greek tragedy. In A. Lardinois & L. McClure (Eds.), *Making silence speak: Women's voices in Greek literature and society* (pp. 117–136). Princeton, NJ: Princeton University Press.

Gunderson, Erik. (2000). *Staging masculinity: The rhetoric of performance in the Roman world.* Ann Arbor: University of Michigan Press.

Hallett, J. (1984). *Fathers and daughters in Roman society: Women and the elite family.* Princeton, NJ: Princeton University Press.

Halperin, D. M. (1990). Why is Diotima a woman? Platonic *Eros* and the figuration of gender. In D. M. Halperin, J. J. Winkler, and F. Zeitlin (Eds.), *Before sexuality: The construction of erotic experience in the ancient Greek world.* (pp. 257–308). Princeton, NJ: Princeton University Press.

Halsall, G. (2004). Gender and the end of empire. *Journal of Medieval and Early Modern Studies, 31,* 17–39.

Harvey, S. A. (2001). 2000 NAPS presidential address: Spoken words, voiced silence: Biblical women in Syriac tradition. *Journal of Early Christian Studies, 9,* 105–131.

Hawhee, D. (2002). Agonism and areté. *Philosophy and Rhetoric, 35,* 185–207.

Henry, M. M. (1995). *Prisoner of history: Aspasia of Miletus and her biographical tradition.* New York: Oxford University Press.

Hutto, D. (2002). Ancient Egyptian rhetoric in the old and middle kingdoms. *Rhetorica, 20,* 213–233.

Jackson, R. L., & Richardson, E. (Eds.). (2003). *Understanding African American rhetoric:*

Classical origins to contemporary innovations. New York: Routledge.

Jarratt, S. C. (1991). *Rereading the sophists: Classical rhetoric refigured.* Carbondale: Southern Illinois University Press.

Jarratt, S. C. (1993). Sapphic pedagogy: Searching for women's difference in history and in the classroom. In T. Enos (Ed.), *Learning from the histories of rhetoric: Essays in honor of Winifred Bryan Horner* (pp. 75–90). Carbondale: Southern Illinois University Press.

Jarratt, S. C. (2002). Sappho's memory. *Rhetoric Society Quarterly, 32,* 11–43.

Jarratt, S. C., & Ong, R. (1995). Aspasia: Rhetoric, gender, and colonial identity. In A. Lunsford (Ed.), *Reclaiming Rhetorica: Women in the rhetorical tradition* (pp. 9–24). Pittsburgh, PA: University of Pittsburgh Press.

Joshel, S.R., & Murnaghan, S. (Eds.). (1998). *Women and slaves in Greco-Roman culture: Differential equations.* London: Routledge.

Kennedy, K. (1999). Hipparchia the cynic: Feminist rhetoric and the ethics of embodiment. *Hypatia, 14,* 48–71.

Keuls, E. C. (1985). *The reign of the phallus: Sexual politics in ancient Athens.* New York: Harper & Row.

Lardinois, A. (2001). Keening Sappho: Female speech genres in Sappho's poetry. In A. Lardinois & L. McClure (Eds.), *Making silence speak: Women's voices in Greek literature and society* (pp. 75–92). Princeton, NJ: Princeton University Press.

Lesko, B. S. (1997). The rhetoric of women in Pharaonic Egypt. In M. M. Wertheimer (Ed.), *Listening to their voices: The rhetorical activities of historical women* (pp. 89–111). Columbia: University of South Carolina Press.

Lipson, C. S. (2003). Recovering the multimedia history of writing in the public texts of ancient Egypt. In M. E. Hocks & M. R. Kendrick (Eds.), *Eloquent images* (pp. 89–115). Cambridge: MIT Press.

Lu, X. (1998). *Rhetoric in ancient China fifth to third century* B.C.E.: *A comparison with classical Greek rhetoric.* Columbia: University of South Carolina Press.

Maurizio, L. (2001). The voice at the center of the world: The Pythias' ambiguity and authority. In A. Lardinois & L. McClure (Eds.), *Making silence speak: Women's voices in Greek literature and society* (pp. 38–54). Princeton, NJ: Princeton University Press.

McClure, L. (1999). *Spoken like a woman: Speech and gender in Athenian drama.* Princeton, NJ: Princeton University Press.

McClure, L. (2001). Introduction. In A. Lardinois & L. McClure (Eds.), *Making silence speak: Women's voices in Greek literature and society* (pp. 3–16). Princeton, NJ: Princeton University Press.

McClure, L. (2003). Subversive laughter: The sayings of courtesans in book 13 of Athenaeus' *Deipnosophistae. American Journal of Philology, 124,* 259–294.

O'Higgins, D. M. (2001). Women's cultic joking and mockery: Some perspectives. In A. Lardinois & L. McClure (Eds.), *Making silence speak: Women's voices in Greek literature and society* (pp. 137–160). Princeton, NJ: Princeton University Press.

Penner, T. C., & Stichele, C. V. (Eds.). (2004). *Contextualizing acts: Lucan narrative and Greco-Roman discourse.* Leiden, The Netherlands: Brill.

Plant, I. M. (2004). *Women writers of ancient Greece and Rome: An anthology.* Norman: University of Oklahoma Press.

Plato. (1925). Gorgias. In *Plato* (Vol. III; W. R. M. Lamb, Trans.). Loeb Classical Library 166. Cambridge, MA: Harvard University Press.

Pomeroy, S. (1975). *Goddesses, whores, wives and slaves: Women in classical antiquity.* New York: Schocken.

Poulakos, T. (1993). Human agency in the history of rhetoric: Gorgias' *Encomium of Helen.* In V. J. Vitanza (Ed.), *Writing histories of rhetoric* (pp. 59–80). Carbondale: Southern Illinois University Press.

Quintilian. (2001). *The orator's education* (D. A. Russell, Trans.). Cambridge, MA: Harvard University Press.

Richlin, A. (1995). Making up a woman: The face of Roman gender. In H. Eilberg-Schwartz &

W. Doniger (Eds.), *Off with her head! The denial of woman's identity in myth, religion, and culture* (pp. 185–213). Berkeley: University of California Press.

Richlin, A. (1997). Gender and rhetoric: Producing manhood in the schools. In W. J. Domink (Ed.), *Roman eloquence: Rhetoric in society and literature* (pp. 90–110). London: Routledge.

Royster, J. J. (2003). Disciplinary landscaping, or contemporary challenges in the history of rhetoric. *Philosophy and Rhetoric, 36,* 148–167.

Schiappa, E. (2003). *Protagoras and Logos: A study in Greek philosophy and rhetoric.* Columbia: University of South Carolina Press.

Schilb, J. (1994). Future historiographies of rhetoric and the present age of anxiety. In V. Vitanza (Ed.), *Writing histories of rhetoric* (pp. 128–138). Carbondale: Southern Illinois University Press.

Skinner, M. B. (1997). Introduction. In J. Hallett & M. B. Skinner (Eds.), *Roman sexualities* (pp. 3–25). Princeton, NJ: Princeton University Press.

Sutherland, C. M. (2002). Feminist historiography: Research methods in rhetoric. *Rhetoric Society Quarterly, 32,* 109–122.

Swearingen, C. J. (1995). A lover's discourse: Diotima, logos, and desire. In A. Lunsford (Ed.), *Reclaiming Rhetorica: Women in the rhetorical tradition* (pp. 25–51). Pittsburgh, PA: University of Pittsburgh Press.

Tuana, N. (Ed.). (1994). *Feminist interpretations of Plato.* University Park, PA: Pennsylvania State University Press.

Walker, J. (2000). *Rhetoric and poetics in antiquity.* Oxford, UK: Oxford University Press.

Wells, C. (2003). Toward a fragmatics, or improvisionary histories of rhetoric, the eternally ad hoc. *Philosophy and Rhetoric, 36,* 277–300.

Wu, H. (2002). Historical studies of rhetorical women here and there: Methodological challenges to dominant interpretive frameworks. *Rhetoric Society Quarterly, 32,* 81–97.

Zaeske, S. (2002). Unveiling Esther as a pragmatic radical rhetoric. *Philosophy and Rhetoric, 33,* 193–220.

14

A VEXING RELATIONSHIP

Gender and Contemporary Rhetorical Theory

◆ Nathan Stormer

G iven communication scholars' attention to the history and criticism of women's rhetorical discourse as well as to discourses of sexuality, one might expect ongoing debate about the theoretical significance of gender in rhetoric. Yet, despite substantial attention to gender in rhetorical studies, conversation about gender in contemporary rhetorical theory is thin. Begun in the 1970s (Campbell, 1973; Kramer, 1974), discussion of the intersections of gender and theory intensified in the late 1980s and early 1990s (Campbell, 1989, 1995; Foss, 1989; Foss & Griffin, 1992; Rakow, 1987; Spitzack & Carter, 1987), but by the turn of the century, the debate had almost ceased. Assuming that women's rhetorical practices were different from those of men due to their distinctive rhetorical situations, discussions of gender and rhetoric most commonly appeared in analyses that recovered the forgotten discourse of historical and contemporary women, a stream of scholarship that Campbell and Keremidchieva describe in their essay on "Gender and Public Address" in this volume. Within this scholarship, an implicit theoretical paradigm operationalized "gender" as women's "difference," such that the liberal goal of incorporating women into rhetorical traditions, and forcing those traditions to account for women, took precedence.

The recovery of women's voices was complicated by scholars who strove to account for differences among women as well as for women's differences from men, a development detailed by Bacon in her chapter, "The Intersections of Race and Gender in Rhetorical Theory and Praxis," in this volume. In addition to their attention to race, critics also have complicated the idea of gender through analyses of specific rhetors whose sexuality challenges the normative views of man and woman (Brookey, 1998; Deem, 1999; Morris, 2002; Shugart, 2003; Sloop 2004). Throughout the 1990s, liberal, cultural, and poststructural feminists interrogated the liberal assumptions of scholarship on gender and rhetoric. They instigated debate about the meaning of gender itself and on how it is enacted and produced through rhetorical action, as well as how it is to be defined in relation to race, class, nationality, sexuality and the unsatisfying horizon of "etc." (Biesecker, 1992; Bruner, 1996; Buzzanell, 2000; Campbell, 1993; Condit, 1997; Dow 1995, 1997; Downey, 1997; Foss, Griffin, & Foss, 1997). In the wake of debates over difference, scholars have continued to make excellent reclamations of women's contributions to the history of rhetoric (Bridwell-Bowles, 2005; Donawerth, 2002; Lunsford, 1995; Ritchie & Ronald, 2001; Wertheimer, 1997), as well as have examined the role of gender in classical rhetorical theory, as Glenn and Collings Eves describe in their chapter, "Rhetoric and Gender in Greco-Roman Theorizing," in this volume. Thus, over time, gender has held different implicit and explicit meanings within the theory of rhetoric. It has meant, simply, biological women or has been treated as a variable in a rhetorical situation and in human identity or as a concept, lacking fixed meaning, that is rhetorically constituted. Yet, after 30-plus years of scholarship, direct conversation between communication researchers about gender and contemporary rhetorical theory has broken down.

One complication is that although gender originally was not a feminist concept (Moi, 1999), it has become so central to feminism that to discuss gender invites the assumption that one is discussing feminist theory, and vice versa. Gender has ceased to be a peculiarly feminist concept, as it has been taken up in queer studies, in masculinity studies, and absorbed, albeit unevenly, into scholarship across the academy. Nonetheless, it still retains its pedigree as a mark of feminist theorizing, even within contemporary rhetorical theory. Gender analysis in rhetorical studies could be taken as a rough index of the state of feminism in the field. As a result, a false sense of engagement and coherence clings to any attention to gender, as if its use in rhetorical history or criticism signals a sustained theoretical project.

An initial dialogue splintered into ad hoc innovations, yet the sense that gender refers to feminism bestows a misleading sense of unity. Consequently, taking stock of the relationships between these sprawling entities—gender and rhetorical theory—is a vexing prospect. Rather than extend older themes that have lost their centripetal force or pretend that current research coheres around any specific theme, I wish to introduce a new point of stasis. I shall reframe the initial debates in terms of a single predicate: gendered experience as the origin of rhetorical theory. This begs the question of how the substance of that experience is rhetorically constituted. Is gender an effect or cause? To untangle this knot, I propose that we think of gender as the repressed rhetoric of materiality within theory, or rather that we consider how the embodiment of gender has been repressed to allow theory to be written. Thinking of gender as a rhetoric of materiality allows theorists to study the ways that it generates and is generated by theory. Theorists must then view gender as a historical condition of possibility and impossibility for theory rather than its cause or effect. Many have moved in this direction but have not yet been appreciated.

Because of all the potentially relevant scholarship, I will not summarize theories per se. I focus as much on contemporary gender theory as on contemporary rhetorical theory. In so doing, I try to enable theorists to see commonalities and differences where they might not have seen them before and, I hope, to re-engage a dialogue about gender and rhetorical theory.

◆ Gender as Experiential Origin of Rhetorical Theory

As part of the effort to redress the historical exclusion of women from rhetorical studies, feminist scholars made gender an issue in rhetorical theory, contending that different theories are required to recognize and value women's rhetorical practices. As the first feminist statement in contemporary rhetorical theory, Campbell's (1973) landmark essay, "The Rhetoric of Women's Liberation: An Oxymoron," is the perfect indicator. Campbell argued that women's liberation discourse was

> a genre without a rhetor, a rhetoric in search of an audience, that transforms traditional argumentation into confrontation, that "persuades" by "violating the reality structures" but that presumes a consubstantiality so radical that it permits the most intimate of identifications. (p. 86)

Women's liberation was a radical discourse that contained "distinctive substantive-stylistic features" (p. 84) that the received wisdom of rhetoric was incapable of explaining. In addition, canonical views of a good rhetor as self-reliant, self-confident, and independent contradict traditional feminine norms of behavior (p. 75), indicating that rhetorical theory not just favors but imagines only idealized masculine rhetors. The challenge to rhetorical theorists was to explain the difference gender makes.

GENDER AS A CAUSE OF RHETORICAL THEORY

In that vein, a guiding assumption in contemporary rhetorical theory has been that the gender of practitioners is a cause of their rhetorical theories, whether explicitly elaborated or as tacit, operative theories. Two of the most commonly debated ideas about gender and rhetorical theory, Campbell's (1989a) feminine style and Foss and Griffin's (1995) invitational rhetoric, presuppose that theory flows from gendered experience. Discussing the history of women's public advocacy, Campbell (1989a) describes feminine style as an outgrowth of craft-learning experiences common to women in traditional, gender-complementary Western culture. The skills and relationships developed in such semi-segregated, interdependent, domestic contexts cultivate contingent reasoning, participatory modes of interaction, and trust in lived experience. This experiential basis promotes a rhetorical style marked by inductive structures, anecdotal evidence, personal experience, personal tone, calls for audience participation, and attempts to identify with the audience as peers (1989a, p. 13). Several scholars have applied and qualified feminine style in contemporary contexts (Blankenship & Robson, 1995; Dow & Tonn, 1993; Parry-Giles & Parry-Giles, 1996).

Feminine gender, defined tacitly as the experience of being a woman in modern Western cultures, has produced an operative theory of style according to Campbell. Condit (1997), however, questions how representative a singular feminine style is of people's diverse gender experiences, and Bruner (1996) argues that the assumptions made about craft learning reify gender. Campbell (1989a) is careful to stipulate that feminine style is not located in biology and that men can and do adopt a feminine style. Parry-Giles and Parry-Giles (1996) caution that feminine style is not necessarily empowering because it can be used by political candidates to reinforce hegemonic masculinity. With feminine style, Campbell revises the common assumption that rhetorical theory develops from the experiential needs of the rhetor. She has insisted, however, that the gendered difference of that experience be attended to and that women, because of a history of regulated subservience to men, have a common existence on which to build. In that sense, "feminine style is as much a product of *power* as it is a product of *gender*" (Dow, 1995, p. 109) or of gender as experienced in unequal power relationships. Campbell (1989a) embraces rather than rejects traditional theories, seeing the rhetorical tradition as valuable to oppressed and oppressor alike yet seeking to explain how gendered experience should modify its masculinized assumptions.

Foss and Griffin (1995) offer a different theory with a similar premise. Invitational rhetoric is "an invitation to understanding as a means to create a relationship rooted in equality, immanent value, and self-determination. Invitational rhetoric constitutes an invitation to the audience to enter the rhetor's world and to see it as the rhetor does" (p. 5). Relying on Gearheart's (1979) indictment of the "intent to persuade [as] an act of violence" (p. 195), Foss and Griffin contrast invitational rhetoric with persuasion, which they treat as a single, conglomerate theory that embodies patriarchy. For them, persuasion is a coercive attempt to change others that inherently dominates and devalues by treating people as instruments of power (pp. 3–4). Invitational rhetoric shifts rhetorical theorizing from a study of change to a study of understanding (presuming that understanding is not a special case of change). Scholars have noted the ways in which Foss and Griffin's critique of persuasion as domination implies that the substance of rhetorical theory is linked to sex, sometimes using essentialist language about woman's nature similar to that for which Wood (1992) criticizes Gilligan (1982). Indeed, Foss and Griffin's implied sexism has invited significant criticism.

Noting their use of Gearheart's essentialist prose, Dow (1995) labels invitational rhetoric gynocentric because it promotes traditional femininity as a balm for masculinist domination (p.110), a reversal of value within traditional gender complementarity but a reinvestment in it as well. Condit (1997) contends that the great breadth of gendered experience makes Foss and Griffin's position suspect. Bruner (1996) argues that they reify gender stereotypes. Although they disavow essentialism (Foss, 1989; Foss & Foss, 1991; Griffin, 1996), in their most recent work, Foss, Foss, and Griffin (1999, 2004) foreground as feminist certain rhetorical theorists such as Daly, Starhawk, Gunn Allen, S. Johnson, and Gearheart, all of whom naturalize inherent differences between men and women.

In response, Foss, Griffin, and Foss (1997) make explicit the place of gender in generating theory, arguing that women's communication practices offer alternatives to exploitative, patriarchal theories (p. 131). Hence, dominating theories of persuasion are incumbent with patriarchal communication and alternative, egalitarian theories of rhetoric are incumbent with women's communication. Patriarchy is defined as a "system of power relations that privileges and accords power to the white, heterosexual male" (121). Foss, Griffin, and Foss suggest a nonbiological frame for gender, particularly when they qualify theories derived from women with the caveat that such theories also come from "other marginalized groups" (p. 131). Accordingly, theory is a function of one's position in a hierarchy in which power-up theories enable male domination and exploitation; power-down theories enable equity and harmony. Advocates of invitational rhetoric sometimes define gender as a power relationship and sometimes imply that it is inherent to man and woman, but what is socially derived and what is inherent remains unclear. Whatever the extent of their essentialism, by rejecting change-centered persuasion Foss and Griffin (1995) ask that rhetorical theory be devoted to explaining how to build relationships across differences through ways of communicating common to women and what they call others.

Whereas Campbell (1989a) seeks to explain the ways that rhetorical tools should be conceptualized through gendered experience, Foss and Griffin (1995) embrace a vision of women's experience as a feminist corrective to rhetorical theory. Nonetheless, a crucial similarity between feminine style and invitational rhetoric is the emphasis on experience as the origin of theory. Neither Campbell nor Foss and Griffin refer to standpoint theory, yet both assume its basic tenet: one's lived experience is a prime source of one's thinking. Or, more specific to rhetoric, theory is an effect of social position. Women learn to produce rhetoric differently because of their experiences, and in those different practices lie operative theories of rhetoric.

STANDPOINT THEORY AND RHETORICAL THEORY

Standpoint theory comes in many guises, from reductive visions of men's and women's lives to highly variable, contextual explanations of epistemology. It seeks a localized epistemology grounded in point of view, a "fractured optics" as Haraway (1989) calls it, as opposed to the masculinized, omniscient position of objectivity that feminists have dissected (Bordo, 1986; Irigaray, 1985; Lloyd, 1994). Key works in standpoint theory emerged in the early 1980s (Hartsock, 1983; Jaggar, 1983; Rose, 1983), and other important works followed. Smith (1987) calls attention to class differences in women's standpoints, and Collins (1990) insists that racial experience contributes uniquely to epistemology. Harding (1991), Longino (1990), and Haraway (1991) successfully move the concept of a standpoint away from being an encomium to women's lives and toward an alternative, pluralistic concept of objectivity, or "situated knowledge." Spivak (1993) offered the

concept of "strategic essentialism" as a way to negotiate the tension between the exclusionary potential of *woman* and the political value of solidarity in identity. Although communication scholars have engaged with standpoint theory (see Bell, Orbe, Drummond, & Camara, 2000; Darlington & Mulvaney, 2002; Durham, 1998; Hallstein, 1999, 2000; Wood, 1998), there is no substantial citation of standpoint scholarship in contemporary rhetorical theory. Instead, a shared premise connects these literatures: lived experience produces knowledge (in this case, of rhetoric) that gains validity because of the partiality of its perspective.

A problem attends the so-called standpoint premise that gendered experience is an origin of rhetorical theory in both invitational rhetoric and feminine style. Citing Harding's (1993, p. 155) warning that women's experience is not synonymous with feminist knowledge, Dow (1997) cautions that reductive uses of personal experience risk making social position identical with the limit of one's voice, and equating one's race, class, and sexuality with what one can know and the meaning of what one says. However, the risk of overstating the limits of difference rests on the more significant problem of explaining materiality. What of biology and the sex/gender system? An antecedent to thinking about gender in rhetorical theory has been a fairly common endorsement of a sex/gender binary, first defined by Rubin (1975) in "The Traffic in Women." She argued that a sex/gender system organizes social structure, so that sex contrasts with gender as nature contrasts with culture, and she offered second-wave feminists a new tool for severing the dictates of sexual biology from the acculturation of gender when analyzing the lines of power between men and women. Campbell (1973, 1989a, 1995, 1998) endorses this distinction, though not Rubin's essay specifically. Foss, Griffin, and Foss (1997; Foss, Foss, & Griffin, 1999) also assume this distinction. In each case, adherents face questions about ironically reductive, exclusionary tendencies in their theories.

Nicholson (1994) argues that although the sex/gender distinction explicitly dismisses biological determinism, it endorses "biological foundationalism," which can admit degrees of essentialism. "Many who would endorse the understanding of sex identity as socially constructed still think of it as a cross-cultural phenomenon," she says, or that universally there is a "similar social response to some 'deeper' level of biological commonality" between women and between men. "Linking this position and thinking of sex as independent of gender is the idea that distinctions of nature, at some basic level, ground or manifest themselves in human identity" (p. 82). Embedded in the definition of gender as the experience of being a man or a woman, not the possession of sexual organs, is the assumption that being a man or a woman means living in that kind of body, not just engaging in gendered roles. What is gender if not the experience of living in a sexed body? Ask yourself whether feminine style or invitational rhetoric would be accepted as explanations of *women*'s ways of communicating if they were predicated *solely* on the experience of cross-dressers or transsexuals. If you answered no, you understand the biological foundationalism of rhetorical theory that treats gendered experience as originary. To what extent does a shared biology inflect the experience of gender and what does that mean for rhetorical theories that presume gendered experience as their foundation?

◆ *Gendered Experience as Rhetorical Effect*

A sex/gender distinction creates circularity in rhetorical theory because gendered experience, the source of theory, is also an effect of rhetoric. The rhetorical dimension of gender's materiality is repressed in two ways.

QUESTIONING THE SEX/ GENDER DISTINCTION

First, extending Nicholson's (1994) argument, the concept of gendered experience has depended on sex to unify but not determine gender. To fulfill its unifying function, however, the rhetorical constitution of sexual materiality and its necessary linkage to gender remains unacknowledged. As a natural, socially nonbinding fact of life, the truth about sex is that it does not control identity, a claim that requires sex to have an inarguably inessential nature. The biological foundation that supposedly explains the commonality of gender hierarchies across cultures implicitly depends on a rhetorical naturalization of sex difference, but it is a difference that should not matter. Ignorance about the truth of sex becomes the pretext for male dominance. In the face of historical arguments that sex rightly determines social position, sex/gender theorists argue that sex gives no rights. They endorse the naturalness of sex but reverse its impact—it is naturally irrelevant rather than naturally definitive. The sex/ gender distinction does not sever one from the other but links them in a necessarily nondetermining way. For gender to be socially changeable, biological determinism must be contained, so sex must be specified as naturally, factually marginal to gender. Gender as experience is not independent of the materiality of sex; it depends on sex being a particular, inconsequential materiality. "[G]ender can become a metaphor for biology just as biology can become a metaphor for gender" (Flax, 1987, p. 637).

The idea of heterosexual difference and of what is natural to sexuality, however indifferent we should be to whatever that difference is, has been rhetorically constituted over millennia. Foucault (1990) spurred a scholarly revolution by treating sex as historical, arguing that homosexuals and heterosexuals emerged as biological beings in the 19th century, and that a modern science of sex became a vector of power. Owing to her reconsideration of binary thinking and the influence of Foucault, Rubin (1984; see also Rubin & Butler, 1994, pp. 70–72) abandoned a sex/gender distinction and called for a history of sexuality. Butler's (1990, 1993, 2004) theory that gender performativity constitutes sexual identity has been highly influential across the humanities; she has called for a history of bodies "doing" gender to document the embodiment of sexuality. Historians such as Gilman (1985), Laqueur (1990), and Schiebinger (1993) demonstrate that what is apparently natural to sex is culturally contingent. Gilman's (1985) account of the intersections of sexuality, race, and medical pathology remains a pivotal piece of scholarship. Laqueur's (1990) similarly influential work details the shift in Western anatomy and biomedicine over less than five centuries from the one-sex model of ancient Greece to the current two-sex model. Equally significant, Schiebinger (1993) demonstrates that early modern taxonomic principles constituted natural order in terms of gender complementarity. Historical work continues apace whether scholars analyze the rhetorical history of the gay gene (Brookey, 2002), the technological and economic context of modern theories of reproductive heterosexuality (McGrath, 2002), or the role of modern anthropology in racializing sexuality (Lyons, 2004).

Although arguing that sex does not determine gender is effective in refuting biologically determinist traditions of excluding women from rhetorical studies, it makes reflexive critique of ideological assumptions difficult, such as heteronormative assumptions about human sexuality. Scott (1991) contends that experience cannot be understood outside of historical narrative. Otherwise, ideologies that organize experience into what seems to be common sense are reproduced rather than critiqued in those narratives, particularly ideologies defining the limits of sexual and racial variability. How flexibly someone understands sex and sexuality is crucial for how they chronicle the experience of gender. This holds true for biomedical stories about the facts of life or personal stories about one's own sexuality. The sexed body at the center of gendered experience has never stood still, and what we know sex to be, and how we know it, changes more rapidly today than ever. The claim that sexual nature is inessential to gender identity does not stand outside this history or escape from it. It is another important move in a long series of efforts to rhetorically constitute the materiality of gender. In Fausto-Sterling's (2000) apt phrasing, "sexuality *is* a somatic fact *created* by a cultural effect" (p. 21).

QUESTIONING THE MATERIALITY OF EXPERIENCE, THEORY, AND PRACTICE

The concept of gendered experience depends on a second level of repressed rhetoric about materiality. In contemporary theory about gender, the events, practices, and norms that make up experience have often been treated as embodied theories, yet as somehow extrarhetorical. If asked, I doubt any rhetorician would claim that writing theory is not a rhetorical effort, but when one turns to experience as operative theory, whether that experience is a kind of rhetoric is less clear. For instance, Campbell (1989a, 1992), Foss and Foss (1991), Biesecker (1992), and Condit (1997) all define rhetoric as some kind of communication practice, but their notions of practice vary. Rejecting traditional public persuasion, Foss and Foss look at communication practices in women's daily lives rather than in the public arena. From a different theoretical posture, Biesecker critiques a female canon as replicating the racial, ethnic, and socioeconomic exclusions of a male canon, asking instead that we study the "plurality of practices that constitute the everyday" (p. 157). Foss and Foss and Biesecker agree that nontraditional theory enables us to recognize as rhetoric what the tradition has marked as unworthy or illegitimate; however, Foss, Foss and Griffin (1999) pursue that through a strong version of cultural feminism and Biesecker through poststructuralism.

In response to Biesecker (1992), Campbell (1993) vigorously defends the study of excellence in public persuasion, arguing that such work is not inherently exclusionary and that there is little rhetorical value in analyzing everyday practices rather than individuals' texts. Indeed, it would erase women once more (p. 158), echoing feminist criticism that poststructuralism wrongly de-emphasizes women as individuals (Alcoff, 1988; Benhabib, 1992; Hartsock, 1983; Webster, 2000). Regarding cultural feminism, Condit (1997) defends the study of public persuasion against the charge that it is inherently dominating (Foss & Griffin, 1995). Although she does not rule out study of nontraditional practices, Condit (1997) reasserts the value of public eloquence and calls for its redefinition to accommodate a multiplicity of genders and to abandon the "tedious predictability" of explaining that men and women talk differently (p. 112).

These exchanges illustrate confusion between theory and practice as well as rhetoric and nonrhetoric. If rhetorical practice refers generally to public speaking and writing, as Campbell (1989a, 1995) and Condit (1997) imply, then experience exists apart from rhetoric and only informs it. Yet if giving speeches is part of one's gendered experience, then some experience is unequivocally rhetorical, as Campbell (1998) argues. If gender is socially constructed through discourse, as all these scholars agree, then practices beyond public speaking and writing also must be rhetorical. To claim that experience is shaped by gendered discourse but is not rhetorical is like saying the audience is in a less rhetorical situation than the rhetor. If you do away with traditional notions of theory and practice, there is no good way to separate experience from rhetorical practice from rhetorical theory because, materially, they are all coincident with each other. Where does rhetoric based in experience end and experience begin? Should there be a distinction?

If rhetorical practice is limited to practices other than persuasive speaking and writing, as Foss and Griffin (1995) ask, one gains no

advantage. Communication practices remain informed by a socially constructed gender, which is a kind of communication that embodies theory. If it is difficult to explain material differences between theory as practice, practice as experience, and experience as theory in public discourse, then marking which everyday communication practices create understanding but are not persuasive is even more daunting.

If, as Biesecker (1992, 1993) advises, rhetoric includes the everyday practices by which people acquire subjectivity and position, in or out of public spaces, then the outcome of gendered experience is limited to the formation of identity. Hers is a more assertive version of Condit's (1997) call to view gender as an outcome of rhetoric, using a combination of Derrida's supplementarity and Foucault's archaeology as tools to explain how subjectivity is produced. That is, Biesecker reverses gender from an origin to gender as an outcome too neatly. We move from studying how difference in daily life organizes knowledge and power to studying how power-knowledge organizes *différance* in daily life. Biesecker (1993) argues that we can do both, but how is not clear because the basic understanding of everyday life and its place in rhetorical studies are not the same.

Part of the project of turning to experience as a source of theory is to enable marginalized populations to have a place in the history of rhetoric. The challenge was to disrupt the traditions that preordained whose experiences mattered, what was and was not real theory, and whose practices were worthy of study. Neither of these repressed rhetorics about materiality constitute a reason to abandon thinking about the experience of gender, although they do justify thinking about it differently.

◆ Gender as a Condition of Possibility and Impossibility

The logic of cause and effect will not resolve the problems of analyzing gender as experience or the impact of that experience on rhetorical theory. Taking a particular, historical model of sexuality as the biological foundation of gender represses theorists' rhetoric that naturalizes that specific model. It also precludes the scholar from understanding that other, radically different models of sexuality are part of people's experience as gendered beings and, hence, part of their rhetorical theories. Further, making gendered experience either an extradiscursive resource for theory or a consequence of discourse represses theorists' rhetoric about the material differences that presumably distinguish experience, rhetorical practice, and rhetorical theory from one another. The nettle of cause/effect thinking is that gendered experience must be reified, understood as a thing that has its most profound impact either before one engages in rhetoric or after. Rather than treat gender as a thing that anchors rhetorical theory, either as what embodies theory or what theory seeks to explain, I suggest that gender be understood as a condition of possibility and impossibility.

SEPARATING GENDER THEORY AND IDENTITY POLITICS

One rightly asks, a condition of what (im)possibilities? The topic here is gender and contemporary rhetorical theory, not gender and feminism, and the difference is crucial. Identity politics has made the discussion of gender a referendum on how to understand difference and subjectivity in feminism. The late 1990s witnessed substantial scholarship about the state of gender difference as a concept in feminism (Cheah & Grosz, 1998a; Cheah & Grosz, 1998b; Braidotti, 1997; Felski, 1997; Frye, 1996; Hawkesworth, 1997; Heinämaa, 1997; Moi, 1999; Scott, 1999; Webster, 2000). The following interrelated series of disagreements brought the discussion of difference to a crisis: (a) the white racism of second-wave feminists (Collins, 1990; Davis, 1989; hooks, 1981); (b) the heterosexism of feminist theory (Butler, 1990; Rich, 1980; Rubin, 1984); (c) the neocolonial relationship of

first world feminism to third world women (Minh-ha, 1986; Mohanty, 1991; Sandoval, 1991; Spivak, 1988); (d) replacing *woman* with *gender* as a category of historical analysis (Downs, 1993; Gordon, 1991; Scott, 1988, 1993); and (e) the political merits of modernist versus poststructuralist theories of agency (Alcoff, 1988; Benhabib, 1992; Butler, 1995; Fraser, 1995). The challenge to the coherence of woman, then gender, then feminism "can be seen as a logical outcome of the concept of 'difference' itself, which endlessly proliferates into a multiplicity of sometimes conflictual forms" (Cheah & Grosz, 1998a, p. 3). In feminist studies, the consequence of this challenge was that theories of gender became focused on explaining the formation of the self as a sexed, raced, classed, culturally hybridized being.

In rhetorical studies, the crisis of ever-proliferating notions of difference had a similar profile in the dialogue about gender and rhetorical theory. Biesecker's (1992) and Bruner's (1996) critiques of the use of gender in feminist scholarship are symptomatic. Biesecker champions a need to understand the multiple ways that women come to be speaking subjects. Similarly, Bruner promotes Butler's (1990) performativity theory as a way to explain gender identity without stereotyping women. Although I am sympathetic to critiques of modernist assumptions, Biesecker and Bruner mistake the political problem of difference in feminism for the conceptual problem of gender in rhetorical theory. As they attempt to redress elitism in the history of women rhetors and replace the reductive, predictable claim that women and men talk differently, they fail to displace the idea that gender is principally about identity politics. The value of gender as a concept to rhetorical theory is not strictly as an explanation of subjectivity, nor should rhetorical critique be limited to studies of normative or subversive gender enactments. Rhetorical studies absorbed the boundaries of dispute from feminism too well.

The insights from rethinking rhetorical theory in terms of gender are not synonymous with feminism's ability to maintain political salience, even as we benefit from the rich discussion of gender difference in feminism. We should think of gender as a condition of possibility and impossibility for rhetorical theory, not for feminism. An underappreciated consequence of the collapse of gendered experience, rhetorical theory, and practice is that theorizing becomes an embodied process, not an abstract mental art. Rhetorical theory is always a rhetorical practice embedded in our lived experience. Rhetorical theory is immanent to what it explains, as a product and productive of experience (Scott, 1991). This pushes the poststructuralist criticism of feminine style and invitational rhetoric to a more useful conclusion. Leaving behind a dialectical either/or problem of cause and effect, of making gendered experience a thing that generates or results from rhetoric, a poststructuralist logic of both/and allows us to appreciate that gender is always antecedent to, always a consequence of theorizing rhetoric, and more. Being gendered is part of the process of being rhetorical and vice versa. One does not beget the other.

CONSIDERING THE BODY AS SITUATION

A historically grounded view of gender performativity, a material philosophy of process, and a multicultural perspective on the relationship of culture, experience, and power are important to understand gender as a condition immanent in all rhetorical theory without preordaining what gender or rhetorical theory must be. Butler (1990, 1993) famously argued that gender is performative, that corporeal styles of masculinity and femininity, when normalized, ground our sense that sexuality is deeply rooted in our nature. Sexual nature, an effect of gender, becomes the cause of gender. The persistent complaint about performative views of gender is that they make the body too elastic. Zita (1998) addresses

what may be the best a fortiori argument for the pliable body, the male lesbian. For a male who identifies lesbian, adopts the pronominal she, and participates in lesbian communities, there is always a "stubborn return of the body's sex" (p. 107), not because of a failure of imagination in the "charmed circle" of friends, but because

> privileges and points of access granted to male bodies and not to female bodies may be rejected or "disowned" later in life or variously distributed among males early in life, but they cannot be denied or discounted in the life experiences that generally mark male somatic existence. Flesh so named makes a difference. (p. 106)

The "historical gravity of the sexed body" (p. 106) is contingent, but it is not "lightweight and detachable" (p. 107). In that sense, one's somatic experience cannot be detached; thus, all knowledge of rhetoric emerges from experience that is overdetermined by its sexual gravity. This does not mean that sex is essential, that gender is biologically determined in the end. It means that sex has an unavoidable historical weight and that sex and gender are interrelated culturally.

An alternative understanding of materiality as lived process, not as object, is also necessary. The emphasis on embodied experience as knowledge is an effort to dislodge "thought from its Cartesian homeliness" (Colebrook, 2000, p. 89; Cheah, 1996). The mind/body dichotomy is attended by an understanding of materiality as dumb object and abstract thought as immaterial ether. Countless scholars have taken Descartes to task for this binary. A persistent problem is how to understand thought as part of the body when the materiality of mind and body is historically dynamic. In the language of Grosz (1994, 1999), materiality involves diverse events of *becoming*. Along with Gatens (1996) and Lloyd (1994), she has been exploring an alternate view of embodiment in which the body is neither pregiven substance nor discursively constructed but a situation in which thought and substance develop together in relation to other bodies and forces. Together they build from a number of sources, but Spinoza's *Ethics* (James, Lloyd, & Gatens, 2000) is primary, and as Gatens (2000) observed, "A Spinozist will insist that to think differently is, by definition, to exist differently: one's power of thinking is inseparable from one's power of being and *vice versa*" (p. 63). The body is not synonymous with current wisdom about biology, nor is it defined generally by the surface of one's skin. Defining the body as situation allows the meaning of human embodiment to alter greatly over time (Colebrook, 1999; Dale, 1999; Gatens, 2000).

The body as situation is no panacea. The risk of singular purpose common to theories of identity persists. One studies how a person becomes a subject in order to explain how like people become subjects, but if that is the only value to studying the relation of gendered experience and rhetorical theory, it can seem tautological. To avoid the tunnel vision of identity politics (Shome & Hegde, 2002), one needs a perspective on the interaction of power, culture, and experience. Certain themes of postcolonial studies are helpful. The emphasis on global multicultural history and on power relationships that organize the constitution of culture and experience are welcome correctives (Shome, 1996; Shome & Hegde, 2002). Historically, colonialism and its aftermath offer many challenges to the self-evidence of Western gendered experience (Mohanram, 1999; Stoler, 2002). Significantly, there is a robust analysis of how the diverse materiality of experience is reduced and universalized in the production of cultural identity (Appadurai, 1996; Spivak, 1999). Adopting a global critique of modernity increases sensitivity to the ways that everyday life is universalized and globalized and is important so theorists can place their own thinking in a larger context.

With a healthy appreciation of the historical gravity of the experience of embodiment, understanding the body as a situation

has two benefits for rhetoric scholars concerned with gender. First, the broad objective of introducing gender difference into rhetorical theory is realized, but not as a preset category with a preset purpose. Experience and embodiment and theorizing are mutually defining aspects of "becoming"; ontology is simultaneously a way of thinking and being. Becoming a speaking subject involves the experience of becoming gendered (as man, woman, trans-, or as yet unimagined genderings), such that essential to living in a body are ways of being rhetorical and thinking about rhetoric. Further, becoming gendered will be fused with race, age, class, and so forth as specific experiences constitute their interrelation. Because experience and the materiality of one's body are changeable, a scholar cannot assume that gender explains theory or that theory explains gender. To change one is to change the other. Theory is not indigenous to experience; no experience has theory that is *native* to it, only what develops in situation.

Second, experience is not exclusive; it is relational. This is not a call for hyperindividualism in which all experiences are atomized islands of unique, irreplaceable knowledge. There is no inherent difference that cannot be mimed and undone by someone else's "becoming." Halberstam (1998) explores the historic and contemporary constitution of masculine identity by females. Sloop (2004) studies the way that recent controversies over transgenderism have been contained by mainstream discourses (see also his chapter, "Critical Studies in Gender/Sexuality and Media," in this volume). The experience of masculinity is lived by males and females, as is the experience of femininity, and neither exists exclusively in the situation of a female or male body (Condit, 1997). In rhetorical theory, no ways of thinking that emerge from becoming gendered belong only to that style of becoming. This means that masculinity is embedded in invitational rhetoric and that feminine style is not reducible to the sex of the rhetors.

◆ Conclusion

The conversation about gender and contemporary rhetorical theory has atrophied. The limits of cause/effect logic and efforts to account for the diffusion of subjectivities have constricted dialogue. If a resumption is desired, I suggest we attempt to think of the body as a situation in which gender and theory are materially codependent in lived experience. This offers a steep challenge to theoretical traditions that repress their own embodiment. In effect, theory would become an aesthetic history of performance (Pollack, 1998). It would spur scholars to ask what difference gender makes to rhetoric beyond establishing the subject position of the rhetor. There are no specific models to point to, only suggestive possibilities.

Johnson (2002) studies the gendered space of rhetorical practice and training in U.S. postbellum culture, in which part of gendered embodiment was rhetorical training and its appropriate spatial location. Further, an idealized domestic sphere was produced in conjunction with women's proper oratorical practices. Gender is not strictly about identity but about cultural geography. Further, theories develop to support rhetorical effects other than persuasion. Peterson (1995) analyzes the way that 19th-century black women developed operative theories of representation in relation to their racialized embodiment of gender. Although Peterson (1995) and Johnson (2002) do not translate these performance histories into modifications of existing theoretical traditions, they provide the groundwork. Further, some have begun to study how classical rhetorical theories were produced through masculinized embodiment (Gunderson, 2000, 2003), but what of more recent history? What of practices not associated with traditional notions of rhetoric, as Biesecker (1992) asked? What if we take the body as a rhetorical situation? What happens to gender and rhetorical theory then?

◆ References

Alcoff, L. (1988). Cultural feminism versus poststructuralism. *Signs: Journal of Women in Culture and Society, 13*, 405–436.

Appadurai, A. (1996). *Modernity at large: Cultural dimensions of globalization.* Minneapolis: University of Minnesota Press.

Bell, K. E., Orbe, M. P., Drummond, D. K., & Camara, S. K. (2000). Accepting the challenge of centralizing without essentializing: Black feminist thought and African American women's communicative experiences. *Women's Studies in Communication, 23*, 41–62.

Benhabib, S. (1992). *Situating the self: Gender, community and postmodernism in contemporary ethics.* New York: Routledge.

Biesecker, B. (1992). Coming to terms with recent attempts to write women into the history of rhetoric. *Philosophy & Rhetoric, 25*, 140–161.

Biesecker, B. (1993). Negotiating with our tradition: Reflecting again (without apologies) on the feminization of rhetoric. *Philosophy & Rhetoric, 26*, 236–242.

Blankenship, J., & Robson, D. C. (1995). A "feminine style" in women's political discourse: An exploratory essay. *Communication Quarterly, 43*, 353–366.

Bordo, S. (1986). The Cartesian masculinization of thought. *Signs: Journal of Women in Culture and Society, 11*, 439–456.

Braidotti, R., (1997). Comments and reply: Comments on Felski's "The doxa of difference": Working through sexual difference. *Signs: Journal of Women in Culture and Society, 23*, 23–40.

Braidotti, R., with Butler, J. (1994). Feminism by any other name. *differences: A Journal of Feminist Cultural Studies, 6*, 27–61.

Bridwell-Bowles, L. (Ed.). (2005). *Rhetorical women: Roles and representations.* Tuscaloosa: University of Alabama Press.

Brookey, R. A. (1998). Keeping a good wo/man down: Normalizing Deborah Sampson Gannett. *Communication Studies, 49*, 73–85.

Brookey, R. A. (2002). *Reinventing the male homosexual: The rhetoric and power of the gay gene.* Bloomington: Indiana University Press.

Bruner, M. L. (1996). Producing identities: Gender problematization and feminist argumentation. *Argumentation and Advocacy, 32,* 185–198.

Butler, J. (1990). *Gender trouble: Feminism and the subversion of identity.* New York: Routledge.

Butler, J. (1993). *Bodies that matter: On the discursive limits of "sex."* New York: Routledge.

Butler, J. (1995). Contingent foundations. In S. Benhabib, J. Butler, D. Cornell, N. Fraser, & L. Nicholson, *Feminist contentions: A philosophical exchange* (pp. 35–57). New York: Routledge.

Butler, J. (2004). *Undoing gender.* New York: Routledge.

Buzzanell, P. (2000). Commentary about Aimee M. Carrillo Rowe's "Locating feminisms subject: The paradox of white femininity and the struggle to forge feminist alliances." *Communication Theory, 10,* 81–89.

Campbell, K. K. (1973). The rhetoric of women's liberation: An oxymoron. *Quarterly Journal of Speech, 59,* 74–86.

Campbell, K. K. (1989). *Man cannot speak for her: A critical study of early feminist rhetoric* (Vol. 1). New York: Praeger.

Campbell, K. K. (1989b). *Man cannot speak for her: Key texts of the early feminists* (Vol. 2). New York: Praeger.

Campbell, K. K. (1993). Biesecker cannot speak for her either. *Philosophy & Rhetoric, 26,* 153–159.

Campbell, K. K. (1995). Gender and genre: Loci of invention and contradiction in the earliest speeches by U.S. women. *Quarterly Journal of Speech, 81,* 479–495.

Campbell, K. K. (1998). Inventing women: From Amaterasu to Virginia Woolf. *Women's Studies in Communication, 21,* 111–126.

Cheah, P. (1996). Mattering. *diacritics, 26,* 108–139.

Cheah, P., & Grosz, E. (1998a). Of being-two: Introduction. *Diacritics, 28,* 3–18.

Cheah, P., & Grosz, E. (1998b). The future of sexual difference: An interview with Judith Butler and Drucilla Cornell. *Diacritics, 28,* 19–41.

Colebrook, C. (1999). A grammar of becoming: Strategy, subjectivism, and style. In E. Grosz (Ed.), *Becomings: Explorations in time, memory, and futures* (pp. 117–140). Ithaca, NY: Cornell University Press.

Colebrook, C. (2000). From radical representations to corporeal becomings: The feminist philosophies of Lloyd, Grosz, and Gatens. *Hypatia, 15,* 76–93.

Collins, P. H. (1990). *Black feminist thought: Knowledge, consciousness, and the politics of empowerment.* Boston: Unwin Hyman.

Condit, C. M. (1997). In praise of eloquent diversity: Gender and rhetoric as public persuasion. *Women's Studies in Communication, 20,* 91–116.

Dale, C. M. (1999). A queer supplement: Reading Spinoza after Grosz. *Hypatia, 14,* 1–12.

Darlington, P. S., & Mulvaney, B. M. (2002). Gender, rhetoric, and power: Toward a model of reciprocal empowerment. *Women's Studies in Communication, 25* (2), 139–172.

Davis, A. Y. (1989). *Women, culture, & politics.* New York: Random House.

Deem, M. (1999). Scandal, heteronormative culture, and the disciplining of feminism. *Critical Studies in Mass Communication, 16,* 86–93.

Donawerth, J. (Ed.). (2002). *Rhetorical theory by women before 1900: An anthology.* Lanham, MD: Rowman & Littlefield.

Dow, B. J. (1995). Feminism, difference(s), and rhetorical studies. *Communication Studies, 46,* 106–117.

Dow, B. J. (1997). Politicizing voice. *Western Journal of Communication, 61,* 243–251.

Dow, B. J., & Tonn, M. B. (1993). "Feminine style" and political judgment in the rhetoric of Ann Richards. *Quarterly Journal of Speech, 79,* 286–302.

Downey, S. (1997). Rhetoric as balance: A dialectical feminist perspective. *Women's Studies in Communication, 20,* 137–150.

Downs, L. L. (1993). If "woman" is just an empty category, why am I afraid to walk alone at night? Identity politics meets the postmodern subject. *Comparative Studies in Society & History, 35,* 414–437.

Durham, M. G. (1998). On the relevance of standpoint epistemology to the practice of journalism: The case for "strong objectivity." *Communication Theory, 8,* 117–140.

Fausto-Sterling, A. (2000). *Sexing the body: Gender politics and the construction of sexuality.* New York: Basic Books.

Felski, R. (1997). The doxa of difference. *Signs: Journal of Women in Culture and Society, 23,* 1–21.

Flax, J. (1987). Postmodernism and gender relations in feminist theory. *Signs: Journal of Women in Culture and Society, 12,* 621–643.

Foss, K. A. (1989). Feminist scholarship in speech communication: Contributions and obstacles. *Women's Studies in Communication, 12,* 1–10.

Foss, K. A., & Foss, S. K. (1991). *Women speak: The eloquence of women's lives.* Prospect Heights, IL: Waveland.

Foss, K. A., Foss, S. K., & Griffin, C. L. (1999). *Feminist rhetorical theories.* Thousand Oaks, CA: Sage.

Foss, K. A., Foss, S. K., & Griffin, C. L. (Eds.). (2004). *Readings in feminist rhetorical theory.* Thousand Oaks, CA: Sage.

Foss, S. K., & Griffin, C. L. (1992). A feminist perspective on rhetorical theory: Toward a clarification of boundaries. *Western Journal of Communication, 56,* 330–349.

Foss, S. K., & Griffin, C. L. (1995). Beyond persuasion: A proposal for an invitational rhetoric. *Communication Monographs, 62,* 1–18.

Foss, S. K., Griffin, C. L., & Foss, K. A. (1997). Transforming rhetoric through feminist reconstruction: A response to the gender diversity perspective. *Women's Studies in Communication, 20,* 117–135.

Foucault, M. (1990). *The history of sexuality, vol. 1: An introduction* (R. Hurley, Trans.). New York: Vintage.

Fraser, N. (1995). False antitheses: A response to Seyla Benhabib and Judith Butler. In S. Benhabib, J. Butler, D. Cornell, N. Fraser, & L. Nicholson (Eds.), *Feminist contentions: A philosophical exchange* (pp. 59–74). New York: Routledge.

Frye, M. (1996). The necessity of differences: Constructing a positive category of women. *Signs: Journal of Women in Culture and Society, 21,* 991–1010.

Gatens, M. (1996). *Imaginary bodies: Ethics, power, and corporeality.* London: Routledge.

Gatens, M. (2000). Feminism as "password": Re-thinking the "possible" with Spinoza and Deleuze. *Hypatia, 15,* 59–75.

Gearheart, S. M. (1979). The womanization of rhetoric. *Women's Studies International Quarterly, 2,* 195–201.

Gilligan, C. (1982). *In a different voice: Psychological theory and women's development.* Cambridge, MA: Harvard University Press.

Gilman, S. (1985). *Difference and pathology: Stereotypes of sexuality, race, and madness.* Ithaca, NY: Cornell University Press.

Gordon, L. (1991). On "difference." *Genders, 10,* 91–111.

Griffin, C. (1996). The essentialist roots of the public sphere: A feminist critique. *Western Journal of Communication, 60,* 21–39.

Grosz, E. A. (1994). *Volatile bodies: Toward a corporeal feminism.* Bloomington: Indiana University Press.

Grosz, E. A. (1999). Thinking the new: Of futures yet unthought. In E. A. Grosz (Ed.), *Becomings: Explorations in time, memory, and futures.* Ithaca, NY: Cornell University Press.

Gunderson, E. (2000). *Staging masculinity: The rhetoric of performance in the Roman world.* Ann Arbor: University of Michigan Press.

Gunderson, E. (2003). *Declamation, paternity, and Roman identity: Authority and the rhetorical self.* New York: Cambridge University Press.

Halberstam, J. (1998). *Female masculinity.* Durham, NC: Duke University Press.

Hallstein, D. L. O. (1999). A postmodern caring: Feminist standpoint theories, revisioned caring, and communication ethics. *Western Journal of Communication, 63,* 32–57.

Hallstein, D. L. O. (2000). Where standpoint stands now: An introduction and commentary. *Women's Studies in Communication, 23,* 1–15.

Haraway, D. J. (1989). *Primate visions: Gender, race, and nature in the world of modern science.* New York: Routledge.

Haraway, D. J. (1991). *Simians, cyborgs, and women: The reinvention of nature.* New York: Routledge.

Harding, S. (1991). *Whose science? Whose knowledge? Thinking from women's lives.* Ithaca, NY: Cornell University Press.

Harding, S. (1993). Reinventing ourselves as other: More new agents of history and knowledge. In L. Kaufman (Ed.), *American feminist thought at century's end* (pp. 140–164). Cambridge, MA: Blackwell.

Hartsock, N. (1983). *Money, sex, and power: Toward a feminist historical materialism.* New York: Longman.

Hawkesworth, M. (1997). Confounding gender. *Signs: Journal of Women in Culture and Society, 22,* 649–685.

Heinämaa, S. (1997). What is a woman? Butler and Beauvoir on the foundations of the sexual difference. *Hypatia, 12,* 20–39.

hooks, b. (1981). *Ain't I a woman: Black women and feminism.* Boston: South End Press.

Irigaray, L. (1985). *Speculum of the other woman.* Ithaca, NY: Cornell University Press.

Jaggar, A. (1983). *Feminist politics and human nature.* Totowa, NJ: Rowman & Allenheld.

James, S., Lloyd, G., & Gatens, M. (2000). The power of Spinoza: Feminist conjunctions. *Hypatia, 15,* 40–58.

Johnson, N. (2002). *Gender and rhetorical space in American life, 1866–1910.* Carbondale: Southern Illinois University Press.

Kramer, C. (1974). Women's speech: Separate but unequal? *Quarterly Journal of Speech, 60,* 14–24.

Laqueur, T. (1990). *Making sex: Body and gender from the Greeks to Freud.* Cambridge, MA: Harvard University Press.

Lloyd, G. (1993). *The man of reason: "Male" and "female" in Western philosophy* (2nd ed.). Minneapolis: University of Minnesota Press.

Lloyd, G. (1994). *Part of nature: Self-knowledge in Spinoza's* Ethics. Ithaca, NY: Cornell University Press.

Longino, H. (1990). *Science as social knowledge: Values and objectivity in scientific inquiry.* Princeton, NJ: Princeton University Press.

Lunsford, A. (Ed.). (1995). *Reclaiming Rhetorica: Women in the rhetorical tradition.* Pittsburgh, PA: University of Pittsburgh Press.

Lyons, A. P. (2004). *Irregular connections: A history of anthropology and sexuality.* Lincoln: University of Nebraska Press.

McGrath, R. (2002). *Seeing her sex: Medical archives and the female body.* New York: Manchester University Press.

Minh-ha, T. (1986). Difference: A special third world women's issue. *Discourse, 8,* 11–37.

Mohanram, R. (1999). *Black body: Women, colonialism, and space.* Minneapolis: University of Minnesota Press.

Mohanty, C. T. (1991). Cartographies of struggle: Third world women and the politics of feminism. In C. T. Mohanty, A. Russo, & L. Torres (Eds.), *Third world women and the politics of feminism* (pp. 1–47). Bloomington: University of Indiana Press.

Moi, T. (1999). *What is a woman? And other essays.* Oxford, UK: Oxford University Press.

Morris III, C. E. (2002). Pink Herring & The Fourth Persona: J. Edgar Hoover's sex crime panic. *Quarterly Journal of Speech, 88,* 228–244.

Nicholson, L. (1994). Interpreting gender. *Signs: Journal of Women in Culture and Society, 20,* 79–105.

Parry-Giles, S. J., & Parry-Giles, T. (1996). Gendered politics and presidential image construction: A reassessment of the "feminine style." *Communication Monographs, 63,* 337–353.

Peterson, C. (1995). *"Doers of the word": African American women speakers & writers in the North (1830–1880).* New Brunswick, NJ: Rutgers University Press.

Pollack, D. (1998). Introduction: Making history go. In D. Pollack (Ed.), *Exceptional spaces: Essays in performance & history* (pp. 1–45). Chapel Hill: University of North Carolina Press.

Rakow, L. F. (1987). Looking to the future: Five questions for gender research. *Women's Studies in Communication, 10,* 79–86.

Rich, A. (1980). Compulsory heterosexuality and lesbian experience. *Signs: Journal of Women in Culture and Society, 5,* 631–660.

Ritchie, J., & Ronald, K. (Eds.). (2001). *Available means: An anthology of women's rhetoric(s)*. Pittsburgh, PA: University of Pittsburgh Press.

Rose, H. (1983). Hand, brain, and heart: A feminist epistemology of science. *Signs: Journal of Women in Culture and Society, 9*, 73–90.

Rubin, G. (1975). The traffic in women: Notes on the "political economy" of sex. In R. R. Reiter (Ed.), *Toward an anthropology of women* (pp. 157–210). New York: Monthly Review.

Rubin, G. (1984). Thinking sex: Notes for a radical theory of the politics of sexuality. In C. S. Vance (Ed.), *Pleasure and danger: Exploring female sexuality* (pp. 267–319). Boston: Routledge.

Rubin, G., & Butler, J. (1994). Sexual traffic. *differences, 6*, 62–99.

Sandoval, C. (1991). U.S. third world feminism: The theory and method of oppositional consciousness in the postmodern world. *Genders, 10*, 1–24.

Schiebinger, L. (1993). *Nature's body: Gender in the making of modern science*. Boston: Beacon Press.

Scott, J. W. (1988). *Gender and the politics of history*. New York: Columbia University Press.

Scott, J. W. (1991). The evidence of experience. *Critical Inquiry, 17*, 773–797.

Scott, J. W. (1993). The tip of the volcano. *Comparative Studies in Society & History, 35*, 438–443.

Scott, J. W. (1999). *Gender and the politics of history* (Rev. ed.). New York: Columbia University Press.

Shome, R. (1996). Postcolonial interventions in the rhetorical canon: An "other" view. *Communication Theory, 6*, 40–59.

Shome, R., & Hegde, R. S. (2002). Postcolonial approaches to communication: Charting the terrain, engaging the intersections.

Shugart, H. A. (2003). Performing ambiguity: The passing of Ellen DeGeneres. *Text & Performance Quarterly, 23*, 30–54.

Sloop, J. (2004). *Disciplining gender: Rhetorics of sex identity in contemporary U.S. culture*. Amherst: University of Massachusetts Press.

Smith, D. (1987). *The everyday world as problematic: A feminist sociology*. Boston: Beacon Press.

Spitzack, C., & Carter, K. (1987). Women in communication studies: A typology for revision. *Quarterly Journal of Speech, 73*, 401–423.

Spivak, G. C. (1988). *In other worlds: Essays in cultural politics*. New York: Routledge.

Spivak, G. C. (1993). *Outside the teaching machine*. New York: Routledge.

Spivak, G. C. (1999). *A critique of postcolonial reason: Toward a history of the vanishing present*. Cambridge, MA: Harvard University Press.

Stoler, A. L. (2002). *Carnal knowledge and imperial power: Race and the intimate in colonial rule*. Berkeley: University of California Press.

Webster, F. (2000). The politics of sex and gender: Benhabib and Butler debate subjectivity. *Hypatia, 15*, 1–22.

Wertheimer, M. M. (1997). *Listening to their voices: The rhetorical activities of historical women*. Columbia: University of South Carolina Press.

Wood, J. T. (1992). Gender and moral voice: Moving from woman's nature to standpoint epistemology. *Women's Studies in Communication, 15*, 1–24.

Wood, J. T. (1998). Ethics, justice, and the "private sphere." *Women's Studies in Communication, 21*, 127–149.

Zita, J. (1998). *Body talk: Philosophical reflections on sex and gender*. New York: Columbia University Press.

PART IV

GENDER AND COMMUNICATION IN MEDIATED CONTEXTS

Introduction

◆ Bonnie J. Dow

When I began to study media images of gender almost two decades ago as a doctoral student, the first scholarly project I undertook was an analysis of *The Mary Tyler Moore Show* (1970–77), a situation comedy widely touted as the first television program focusing on an independent, unmarried, working woman. *The Mary Tyler Moore Show* debuted in 1970, and reflected cultural themes that had gained public visibility as a result of the onset of the second wave of feminism in the late 1960s. My interest in the program was as personal as it was scholarly. I had grown up watching it on Saturday nights with my family, and Mary Richards, the main character, was a kind of heroine for me when I was a girl. She represented possibilities for life as an adult woman that I rarely saw on television or as one of several children being raised by a stay-at-home mother. Mary Richards was not a wife, a mother, a teacher, or a nurse, and thus fell outside the major categories of female role models to which I had been exposed. I found her fascinating.

Yet when I turned a critical eye on *The Mary Tyler Moore Show* in graduate school, more than a decade after it left prime time, I offered an assessment of it that emphasized the timidity of its feminist vision and that critiqued the ways in which Mary Richards's freedom had been domesticated by the portrayal of her as a kind of office wife to male characters (see Dow, 1990). To me, that assessment did not negate the value the program had for me as a girl. Rather, it complicated it in useful ways, revealing the complexities of mediated depictions of gendered identity and the need for critical analysis that investigates their potential meanings. The chapters in this section take up that charge, exploring the implications of the mediation of gender in a variety of contexts.

The idea that gender is mediated is certainly not unique to this section of *The Handbook of Gender and Communication*—all experiences of gender are mediated in some way. The performative turn in studies of gender, which we discuss in the introduction and which is exemplified in each section in different ways, makes clear that gender comes into being and takes on meaning through communicative practices in interpersonal, organizational, rhetorical, and cultural contexts. This section focuses on mass media constructions of gender and their intersections with race, ethnicity, class, sexuality, and nationality. Like the other sections, this one is guided by the general assumption that gender is contingent and contextual and is always in the process of construction, performance, and reiteration. Specifically, however, the authors in this section focus on how the production, dissemination, consumption, and use of media messages and technologies play a major role in that process. Thus, the study of media and gender is generally guided by this question: How do mass media both communicate and challenge dominant norms and expectations related to gender?

◆ The Development of Scholarship on Gender and Media

Like the investigation of the role of gender in communication generally, early attempts to investigate it in media were spurred by the rise of the second wave of feminism in the United States. As Angharad Valdivia and Sarah Projansky note in Chapter 15, "Feminism and/in Media," future second-wave leader Betty Friedan's best-selling analysis of the images of women in magazines in *The Feminine Mystique* (1963) was an early recognition of the power of mass media to define gender roles, an issue that feminist activists continued to address. For example, one of the first public protests by second-wave feminists was mounted at the 1968 Miss America pageant in Atlantic City, a televised cultural ritual that feminists, in their press release, charged with exercising "thought control . . . to enslave us all the more in high-heeled, low-status roles; to inculcate false values in young girls; to use women as beasts of buying; to seduce us to prostitute ourselves before our own oppression" ("No More Miss America," 1970, p. 588). Clearly referencing mass media's role in influencing definitions of gender, the press release further maintained that "the Pageant contestants epitomize the roles we are all forced to play as women" and that "Miss America is a walking commercial for the Pageant's sponsors. Wind her up and she plugs your product on promotion tours and TV" (p. 586). In the 1970s, the National Organization for Women began to engage in systematic activism about media practices and images. Its (National Organization for Women, 1966) statement of purpose had announced: "In the interests of the human dignity of women, we will protest and endeavor to change the false image of women now prevalent in the mass media" (p. 101; see also Barker-Plummer, 2002; Bradley, 2003).

Feminist activists' recognition of the power of mass media to communicate gender ideology soon was echoed in academic researchers' efforts to track the representation of "sex roles" in mass media, primarily television, although there also was early attention to magazines, newspapers, and advertising. Reflecting a pattern prevalent in much early research on gender and communication, such research tended not to use the term gender, but instead studied "sex roles," which generally meant "women's roles." Focusing on the quantity and types of representations of women, it posited that media representations should be measured against "real world" conditions (e.g., the numbers and types of women on television should reflect their numbers in the population) as well as posited that media consumers, especially young ones, consume and "model" media representations in fairly direct ways. Another important characteristic of this early work was its embrace of a liberal feminist perspective that held that lack of representation or negative representation in media was a form of discrimination that, if corrected, would lead to improvements in women's lives off the screen or the page. *Hearth and Home: Images of Women in the Mass Media* (Tuchman, Daniels, and Benét, 1978), the key collection of 1970s research on media and gender, is a good indicator of these characteristics (see also Franzwa, 1976; King & Stott, 1977). For example, in her introduction to this classic work, Tuchman concludes that

> the mass media perform two tasks at once. First . . . they reflect dominant values and attitudes in the society. Second, they act as agents of socialization, teaching youngsters in particular how to behave. Watching lots of television leads children and adolescents to believe in traditional sex roles: Boys should work; girls should not. (p. 37)

Primarily social scientific in its approach, *Hearth and Home* set an agenda for work on gender and media in the early years, and it is especially noteworthy for its attention

to racial difference, particularly the disparate portrayals of black and white women on television. The book's detailing of the "symbolic annihilation" (p. 8) of women in mass media and of the generally limited and demeaning portrayals of women in television, magazines, newspapers, and advertising set the stage for the development of critically oriented approaches that would probe the textual and symbolic dynamics of mass media representations of gender.

THE RISE OF CRITICAL/ CULTURAL RESEARCH ON GENDER AND MEDIA

Academic work on gender and media in the 1970s tended toward the social scientific, using quantitative methodologies and primarily content analysis. Yet as Valdivia and Projansky note, influential books using critical approaches to analyze images of women in film were published by commercial presses in the early 1970s (e.g., Haskell, 1974; Rosen, 1973). Along with early works on women in film history, they brought a humanistic, critical lens to bear on mediated constructions of gender. Although quantitative work continued, as it does today (e.g., Andsager & Roe, 1999), providing useful information about levels and types of representation, within the communication discipline it has become less influential than critically oriented forms of inquiry. The chapters in this section of the *Handbook* focus on what can be termed *critical/cultural* approaches to the analysis of media and gender, because they have been the primary source for theoretical and methodological developments in this area since the 1980s. For example, early work on media effects, which used quantitative measures to investigate how media exposure alters beliefs, attitudes, and/or values (see, e.g., Gross & Jeffries-Fox, 1978), has been challenged by the development of reception studies (also called "audience studies") by critical/cultural researchers. Using combinations of textual analysis, ethnography, and interview data, they try to understand how viewers make meaning from media as they incorporate it into their daily lives (see, e.g., Press, 1991).

Critical/cultural approaches generally emphasize the symbolic qualities of gender representation and their relationship to ideology. This kind of work leads scholars to analyze foci such as aesthetics, genre and narrative form, character development and relationships, spectatorship and reception, while relating mass media to gendered identities within cultural contexts. By the early 1980s, the critical media study of gender was still focused primarily on women and primarily those who were white, heterosexual, educated, able-bodied, middle-class and upper-class. It was being heavily influenced by the international development of cultural studies, which was broadly understood as being "concerned with the relations between forms of culture and forms of power" and with "the ways in which culture interacts with social inequalities" (Schiach, 1999, p. 3). Cultural studies scholarship, which includes but is not limited to much work on media, understands culture as "the circulation of sense, meaning, and consciousness," in ways that are always already political; that is, constitutive of power relations (Hartley, 2002, p. 51).

Cultural studies became a powerful presence in the field of communication in the 1980s as scholars began to turn their attention to how ideology is circulated in public discourse, especially media. Because the study of media and gender had political roots, cultural studies would appear to be a natural home for work on gender and feminism, but this was not the case initially (see Schiach, pp. 3–4). Although Valdivia and Projansky offer a narrative about the central role that feminist theorizing and critique played in film study, work on gender, especially from a feminist perspective, was not embraced in the early years of cultural studies. The preferred foci of analysis then were more likely to be class and race, with little attention to how gender inflected and was inflected by those identity categories.

Feminist cultural studies has flourished, however, and its influence on the critical study of gender and media has been profound. A central contribution of cultural studies is its move away from sex as an unproblematic indicator of gender and toward understanding gender as a social construction, experience, and performance that is always shaped by power relations. The study of gender and media also has paralleled cultural studies in that it has always been interdisciplinary. Media texts are studied, but so are the contexts of reception and production, and the work is driven by political commitments. More so than in some other areas of gender study in communication, critical work on gender and media has at its base some level of commitment to gender justice; that is, to working toward a world in which definitions of gender are not used to create and preserve social inequities. Valdivia and Projansky discuss research that evidences a belief in the political work of both media representation and media critique. Dwight Brooks and Lisa Hébert (Chapter 16) also specifically note that the work they discuss on the intersections of race and gender in mass media emphasizes "media's role in the production and reproduction of inequity and in the development of more equitable and democratic societies."

Likewise, Lisa Cuklanz's chapter on gendered violence in media (Chapter 18) makes clear that feminist beliefs fuel research on representations of violence against women and that women's subordination is reflected and reproduced thereby and should be challenged. In his chapter on gender and sexuality in media, John Sloop (Chapter 17) maintains that "queer scholarship works against the ways in which gender/sexuality is disciplined ideologically and institutionally and works toward a culture in which a wider variety of genders/sexualities might be performed." Mia Consalvo, in her chapter on gender and new media (Chapter 19), is least explicit on this issue, perhaps because, as she notes, new media study is still trying to determine "how gender 'matters' or

comes to matter in relation to new media."
Even so, as she also notes, feminist theory is
a major influence on gender and new media
research.

DIVERSE THEORETICAL DEVELOPMENTS AND SHARED THEORETICAL CONCERNS

Even under a general critical/cultural
rubric, however, the research discussed in
the chapters in this section demonstrates
the diversity of theoretical and critical
approaches used to analyze interactions
between media and gender since the 1970s.
Valdivia and Projansky, for example, note
the importance of psychoanalytic theories
to the initial stage of feminist film study in
the 1970s and 1980s, particularly through
the theorization of the "male gaze" as a
central issue in film spectatorship. Yet psychoanalytic approaches are generally not
used in the study of other media, and
feminist film study has expanded since the
1980s to include myriad theoretical directions. Similarly, early approaches to critical
television study were heavily influenced by
semiotics and by Marxism (e.g., Fiske &
Hartley, 1978) but have since developed
in directions that reflect the influence of
poststructuralism and theories of gender
performativity.

In their chapter, Brooks and Hébert note
that studies of the intersections of race and
gender in media have tended to focus on the
constitution of racial difference in representations of "women of color"; scholarship
analyzing media tendencies toward, for
example, the hypersexualization of African
American women (Hill-Collins, 2004) has
been heavily influenced by black feminist
thought. Brooks and Hébert also point to
newer strains of theorizing that are influencing work on media, race, and gender,
such as critical race theory and theories
of whiteness in research on mediated
masculinities. Cuklanz, in her chapter on
gender and violence, traces theoretical
developments in the study of violence,
making a persuasive case that representations of violence against women long have
been a central concern of academic media
and gender scholars just as television violence has been for researchers of media
effects. Contemporary scholars argue that
representations of gendered violence are
not merely a kind of plot device but constitute "forms and properties of the media
themselves" (Caputi, 1987, p. 169) and
provide key components of the masculine
and feminine subjectivities created by mass
media.

Sloop's chapter clearly explicates the
turn toward theories of gender performativity in media and gender study. He maintains that the use of such theories has
emerged most visibly in analysis of media
representations of lesbians, gays, and the
transgendered, because they most visibly
trouble traditional gendered binaries and
the definitions of masculinity and femininity that arise from them. The notion that
gender is performed rather than innate also
is central to research on gender and new
media, as Consalvo notes in her chapter,
particularly because of "early rhetoric that
stated new media such as the Internet
created a space where bodies (including
their relative genders, races, classes, sexual
identities, and so on) could be easily left
behind." Thus it was a major task of gender
scholars to argue that gender did indeed
matter in new media, not just in terms of
representation and performance in online
environments, but also in terms of usage,
access, production, and the creation of
online communities. To address such issues,
gender and new media scholars have made
use of and developed a wide array of theories that do not surface elsewhere in this
section—theories of the social shaping and
construction of technology, of identity construction, and of the role of the body in new
media contexts.

Even with the theoretical diversity
prompted by the various forms, genres, and
uses of media that the authors in this section
address, there are overarching issues for
research on gender and media. One is the

degree to which messages and technologies are hegemonic, creating and/or sustaining oppressive gender ideologies and gendered subjectivities for their audiences that ultimately serve racist, classist, heterosexist, and patriarchal interests. Much research on texts or reception argues strongly for media's hegemonic function (Condit, 1989; Cloud, 1996; Dow, 2001; Rockler, 1999; Sender, 1999; Shugart, 2003). Other scholars offer resistant or oppositional readings in arguing that media texts contain progressive meaning possibilities that consumers can use to resist dominant norms and to further their own marginalized subjectivities (Cooper, 2002; Cooper & Pease, 2002). Similarly, scholars studying reception or media use claim that audiences/users actively use media to serve their own interests (Bobo, 1995; Bryson, 2004). Although their attention initially focused on white female consumers, particularly of "women's genres" such as romances or soap operas (Brunsdon, 1982; Radway, 1984), it has since expanded to include issues of racial, sexual, and class identity (Bird & Jorgenson, 2002; Sender, 1999; Watts & Orbe, 2002), as well as international contexts (Acosta-Alzuru, 2003). Indeed, as all authors in this section note, a second central concern for gender and media researchers, particularly in the last decade, is that previous theorizing about gender and media interaction must be revised and expanded to incorporate the ways that media texts and reception/usage are inflected by race, class, ethnicity, sexuality, and nationality, as well as by the increasingly global reach of mass media.

EMERGING AREAS FOR GENDER AND MEDIA RESEARCH

Two of the chapters in this section specifically focus on areas of gender and media research that can be fairly characterized as recent in their emergence: Sloop's chapter on gender and sexuality and Consalvo's chapter on gender and new media. Although the former treats a newly visible representational theme in long-existing forms and genres of media, and the latter treats the varied implications of new technologies, a critical mass of research in these two areas has only emerged in the last decade or so. Other emerging areas in gender and media research, such as the study of masculinity and the study of the gendered implications of media globalization, are discussed within broadly focused chapters. For example, both Cuklanz's chapter on gendered violence and Brooks and Hébert's chapter on gender and race in media offer sustained discussion of research on media and masculinity. Although gender and media researchers initially focused almost exclusively on critiquing media representations of women and femininity, by the late 1980s many of them recognized that the interdependence of gendered identities required a parallel examination of masculinity, countering a tendency in some feminist work to view masculinity "as a homogenous and monolithic force, while attention is turned instead to the careful theorizing of women's experiences and perspectives" (Mandziuk, 2000, p. 105). Generally, research on media and masculinity has developed from feminist premises and "is geared toward analyzing the ways in which masculinity is deployed against women's/feminist interests in cultural messages" (Dow & Condit, 2005, p. 460) or offers progressive possibilities for women/feminism (for examples of each, see Battles & Hilton-Morrow, 2002; Cooper, 2002; Cuklanz, 1998), although scholars are focusing on the implications of representations of masculinity for racial politics as well (e.g., Orbe, 1998; Watts & Orbe, 2002).

Linked to the development of cultural studies along a U.S./U.K./Australian axis, the study of gender and media has always been somewhat international, particularly theoretically, and collections of research on gender and media frequently feature analyses of English-language media from beyond U.S. borders (e.g., Baehr & Gray, 1996; Brunsdon, D'Acci, & Spigel, 1997).

However, research on gender and media in global contexts, especially South Asian and South American contexts, has grown rapidly in recent years, as Valdivia and Projansky take care to address in their chapter (for examples of such research, see La Pastina, 2004; Luthra, 1999), and this scholarship shows the importance of recognizing the challenges and possibilities that global production, dissemination, and reception present for the study of gender and media.

◆ Organization of Chapters

With the exception of Consalvo's chapter on gender and new media, the chapters in this section are organized around themes (feminism, race, violence, sexuality) rather than genre or type of medium. A thematic approach makes sense for the first four chapters in the section because theoretical and methodological practices within these themes are often applied across media types and genres. For example, as Brooks and Hébert point out, black feminist thought has been influential across the study of film, television, and music. Similarly, as Sloop's chapter demonstrates, theories of gender performativity and queer theories have been brought to bear on both entertainment and news media, in both broadcast and print. Thus, a thematic approach seemed the most likely to minimize certain kinds of repetition. However, authors of two chapters, on feminism and on violence, chose to organize their chapters at least partially along the lines of genre and/or medium. Ultimately, in all four of the thematic chapters, research on film and television receives the greatest share of attention, simply because those are by far the most developed areas in the academic study of gender and media, particularly in terms of theoretical and methodological growth over the past three decades.

The chapter on new media departs from the thematic approach characterizing the other four chapters for three reasons. First, the technologies, communicative practices, and messages that constitute "new media study" are new enough and definitionally diffuse enough that they deserve the kind of sustained explication that a focused chapter can provide. Second, because of the unique nature of new media and its interactive possibilities, the distinctions between producers, consumers, and users are blurred. Because the other chapters generally emphasize themes within media representation, simply including relevant examples of new media research within them would omit those important areas of new media research that focus on access, usage, and production as they relate to gender. Third, and related, many of the theories developed and invoked by new media scholars are theories concerning the social functions of technologies that are not discussed elsewhere in the *Handbook* but are crucial to understanding the interaction of gender and new media.

◆ Conclusion

Media technologies, environments, and messages are proliferating at staggering speed in the 21st century. From iPods to BlackBerries, from reality shows to "niche networks," and from Web pages to blogs, the ever-expanding range of media products, programming, and participants is overwhelming, threatening to make the conclusions of media research obsolete almost as soon as they are published. Thus, in one sense, the chapters in this section are simply snapshots of the status of research on media and gender at this point in time. Yet, as much changes, much remains the same, and these essays also reveal the cultural resilience of mediated constructions of gender, as well as the continuing relevance of the questions media scholars ask of and about them and the theories they bring to bear in that process.

For example, I opened this introduction with a brief discussion of *The Mary Tyler*

Moore Show, a television program that left prime time in 1977 yet has lived on as a kind of yardstick for measuring the progress of women on television. As recently as 2003, journalists were comparing Mary Richards to Carrie Bradshaw, the heroine of HBO's successful series *Sex and the City* (1998–2003) in ways that implied that there had been little progress in televisual representations of women (Heldenfels, 2003; Orenstein, 2003). The deeper question this provokes for a gender and media scholar, however, is, Why do journalists measure the progress of representations of women on television through a focus on the depiction of the lives of single white heterosexual career women? What does such a focus say about the race, class, and sexuality blinders that operate across mass media, whether in journalism or series television? (see Dow, 2005). These are the deeper issues that animate the chapters in this section. Ultimately, they demonstrate the importance of mass media analysis to the development of knowledge about the role of gender and communication in our lives.

◆ References

Acosta-Alzuru, C. (2003). "I'm not a feminist, I only defend women as human beings": The production, representation, and consumption of feminism in a *Telenovela. Critical Studies in Media Communication, 20,* 269–294.

Andsager, J. L., & Roe, K. (1999). Country music video in country's Year of the Woman. *Journal of Communication, 49,* 69–82.

Baehr, H., & Gray, A., Eds. (1996). *Turning it on: A reader on women and the media.* New York: Arnold.

Barker-Plummer, B. (2002). Producing public voice: Resource mobilization and media access in the National Organization for Women. *Journalism and Mass Communication Quarterly, 79,* 188–205.

Battles, K., & Hilton-Morrow, W. (2002). Gay characters in conventional spaces: Will and Grace and the situation comedy genre. *Critical Studies in Media Communication, 19,* 87–105.

Bird, S. E., & Jorgenson, J. (2002). Extending the school day: Gender, class and the incorporation of technology in everyday life. In M. Consalvo & S. Paasonen (Eds.), *Women and everyday uses of the Internet: Agency and identity* (pp. 255–274). New York: Peter Lang.

Bobo, J. (1995). *Black women as cultural readers.* New York: Columbia University Press.

Bradley, P. (2003). *Mass media and the shaping of American feminism, 1963–1975.* Jackson: University of Mississippi Press.

Brunsdon, C. E. (1982). *Crossroads:* Notes on soap opera. *Screen, 22*(4), 32–37.

Brunsdon, C., D'Acci, J., & Spigel, L. (Eds.). (1997). *Feminist television criticism: A reader.* New York: Oxford University Press.

Bryson, M. (2004). When Jill jacks in: Queer women and the net. *Feminist Media Studies, 4,* 239–254.

Caputi, J. (1987). *The age of sex crime.* Bowling Green, OH: Bowling Green University.

Cloud, D. (1996). Hegemony or concordance? The rhetoric of tokenism in "Oprah" Winfrey's rags-to-riches biography. *Critical Studies in Mass Communication, 13,* 115– 137.

Condit, C. M. (1989). The rhetorical limits of polysemy. *Critical Studies in Mass Communication, 6,* 103–122.

Cooper, B. (2002). *Boys Don't Cry* and female masculinity: Reclaiming a life & dismantling the politics of normative heterosexuality. *Critical Studies in Media Communication, 19,* 44–63.

Cooper, B., & E. C. Pease. (2002). "Don't want no short people 'round here": Confronting heterosexism's intolerance through comic and disruptive narratives in *Ally McBeal. Western Journal of Communication, 66,* 300–318.

Cuklanz, L. (1998). The masculine ideal: Rape on prime-time television, 1976–78. *Critical Studies in Media Communication, 15,* 423–48.

Dow, B. J. (1990). Hegemony, feminist criticism, and *The Mary Tyler Moore Show*. *Critical Studies in Mass Communication, 7,* 261–274.

Dow, B. J. (2001). Ellen, television, and the politics of gay and lesbian visibility. *Critical Studies in Media Communication, 18* (2), 123–140.

Dow, B. J. (2005). "How will you make it on your own?" Feminism and television since 1970. In J. Wasko (Ed.), *A companion to television* (pp. 379–394). London: Blackwell.

Dow, B. J., & Condit, C. M. (2005). The state of the art in feminist scholarship in communication. *Journal of Communication, 55,* 448–478.

Fiske, J., & Hartley, J. (1978). *Reading television*. London: Methuen.

Franzwa, H. (1976). *The image of women in television: An annotated bibliography*. Washington, DC: U.S. Commission on Civil Rights.

Friedan, B. (1963). *The feminine mystique*. New York: Norton.

Gross, L., & Jeffries-Fox, S. (1978). "What do you want to be when you grow up, little girl?" In G. Tuchman, A. K. Daniels, & J. Benét (Eds.), *Hearth and home: Images of women in the mass media* (pp. 240–265). New York: Oxford University Press.

Hartley, J. (2002). *Communication, cultural, and media studies: The key concepts* (3rd ed.). London: Routledge.

Haskell, M. (1974). *From reverence to rape: The treatment of women in the movies*. New York: Penguin.

Heldenfels, R. D. (2003, June 26). Is "Sex in the City" this generation's "Mary Tyler Moore Show"? *The Oregonian*, p. E10.

Hill-Collins, P. (2004). *Black sexual politics: African Americans, gender, and the new racism*. New York: Routledge.

Hobson, D. (1982). *Crossroads: The drama of a soap opera*. London: Methuen.

King, J., & Stott, M. (1977). *Is this your life? Images of women in the media*. London: Virago.

La Pastina, A. (2004). *Telenovela* reception in rural Brazil: Gendered readings and sexual mores. *Critical Studies in Media Communication, 21,* 162–181.

Luthra, R. (1999). The women's movement and the press in India: The construction of female foeticide as a social issue. *Women's Studies in Communication, 22,* 1–24.

Mandziuk, R. M. (2000). Necessary vigilance: Feminine critiques of masculinity. *Critical Studies in Media Communication, 17,* 105–108.

National Organization for Women. (1966). Statement of purpose. In M. Schneir (Ed.), *Feminism in our time: The essential writings, World War II to the present* (pp. 103–107). New York: Vintage Books.

"No more Miss America." (1970). In R. Morgan (Ed.), *Sisterhood is powerful: An anthology of writings from the women's liberation movement* (pp. 584–588). New York: Vintage.

Orbe, M. P. (1998). Constructions of reality on MTV's *The Real World:* An analysis of the restrictive coding of black masculinity. *The Southern Communication Journal, 64,* 32-47.

Orenstein, C. (2003, September 5). What Carrie could learn from Mary. *New York Times,* p. A19.

Press, A. L. (1991). *Women watching television: Gender, class, and generation in the American television experience*. Philadelphia: University of Pennsylvania Press.

Radway, J. (1984). *Reading the romance: Women, patriarchy, and popular literature*. Chapel Hill: University of North Carolina Press.

Rockler, N. (1999). From magic bullets to shooting blanks: Reality, criticism, and *Beverly Hills, 90210. Western Journal of Communication, 63,* 72–94.

Rosen, M. (1973). *Popcorn Venus: Women, movies, and the American dream*. New York: Avon.

Schiach, M. (1999). Introduction. In M. Schiach (Ed.), *Feminism & cultural studies* (pp. 107). New York: Oxford.

Sender, K. (1999). Selling sexual subjectivities: Audiences respond to gay window advertising. *Critical Studies in Mass Communication, 16,* 172–196.

Shugart, H. A. (2003). Reinventing privilege: The new (gay) man in contemporary popular media. *Critical Studies in Media Communication, 20,* 67–91.

Tuchman, G. (1978). Introduction: The symbolic annihilation of women by the mass media. In G. Tuchman, A. K. Daniels, & J. Benét (Eds.), *Hearth and home: Images of women in the mass media* (pp. 3–38). New York: Oxford University Press.

Tuchman, G., Daniels, A. K., and Benét, J. (Eds.). (1978). *Hearth and home: Images of women in the mass media.* New York: Oxford University Press.

Watts, E. K., & Orbe, M. P. (2002). The spectacular consumption of "True" African American culture: "Whassup" with the Budweiser guys? *Critical Studies in Media Communication, 21,* 1–20.

15

FEMINISM AND/IN MASS MEDIA

◆ Angharad N. Valdivia and Sarah Projansky

F eminist media scholarship is a rich and diverse body of work that has been discussed and organized in a variety of ways by previous scholars (e.g., Baehr & Gray, 1996; Carter & Steiner, 2004; Farrell, 1995; Florence & Reynolds, 1995; Gallagher, 1981, 2001, 2003; Johnson, 1995; Rakow & Wackwitz, 2004; Ross & Byerly, 2004; Tuchman, Daniels, & Benét, 1978; Valdivia, 1995; Van Zoonen, 1994); indeed, Van Zoonen (1994) characterizes this scholarship as having "enormous heterogeneity" (p. 2).

Our perspective in this chapter reflects the following three assumptions. First, as with all types of feminist studies, feminist media scholarship draws upon a broad range of diverse and sometimes contradicting methodological and theoretical paradigms, from the liberal feminist goals that characterize early positivist/quantitative studies of female representation on television to the more recently developed highly interpretive approaches exemplified by the psychoanalytic focus of feminist film studies and the poststructuralist and postcolonial emphases of much contemporary work on global media products. Second, feminist media scholarship addresses a staggering variety of media forms, including mass market books, popular music, newspapers and magazines, television (both news and entertainment), film (fictional, documentary, and experimental), advertising, radio, and new media, including the Internet and computer games. Third, feminist media scholarship is an explicitly political enterprise in a way that not all research on gender and communication is.

There is disagreement, however, as to the specific relationship between feminist academic work and feminist political activism. Gallagher (2003) asserts that "the defining characteristic of this body of work is its explicitly political dimension" (p. 19; see also Gallagher, 2001). Rakow and Wackwitz (2004) delineate what "feminist communication theory ought to be good for: to help us understand the conditions of our lives, to help us name our experiences and make them stories for the telling, to give strategies for achieving justice" (p. vii). Van Zoonen (1991) agrees that feminist media research contains "a reciprocal relation between theory, politics and activism, the commitment of feminist academics to have their work contribute to a larger feminist goal" (p. 34). After more than 30 years of dedicated research on feminism and the media, scholars agree that not all research on gender and the media is feminist and that a commitment to gender justice must be a standard that unites research identified as feminist. Moreover, efforts toward gender justice must be mindful of issues of diversity, such as race and ethnicity, class, sexuality, national origin, and ability (Doty, 1993; Dow & Condit, 2005; Fregoso, 2003; hooks, 1992; Nakamura, 2002; Shohat, 1998).

The large number of permutations resulting from these assumptions accounts for the diversity and unwieldiness of feminist media research. Thus, this chapter reflects particular emphases that we have chosen in order to make our task manageable. We attempt to do justice to major themes in the historical, theoretical, and methodological development of feminist media studies and to discuss research that treats specific forms of media, as well as to discuss dominant directions in recent feminist work on media. Although we note the contribution of quantitative studies to the development of feminist media research, our overwhelming emphasis is on work utilizing a critical, interpretive approach, as the majority of explicitly feminist contemporary work on media emerges from this perspective. Finally, some strains of feminist media research, including those treating gendered violence, sexuality, the

intersections of race and gender in a U.S. context, and new media, receive less attention in this chapter because they are the primary focus of other chapters in the media section of the *Handbook*. We do, however, offer a particular emphasis on the global dimensions of feminist media study, as such a focus does not appear elsewhere in the media section of the *Handbook,* although it does surface in various ways in the "Gender and Communication in Intercultural and Global Contexts" section.

◆ Historical Development of Feminist Media Studies

Within mainstream media studies in the United States, the history of feminist research is commonly traced to Friedan's *The Feminine Mystique* (1963). In that central text in the development of second-wave U.S. feminism, she foregrounded mass media as a site for struggle over the sign of woman. Looking at women's magazines for an analysis of prewar and postwar representations, Friedan noted the historical contingency of these images and argued that femininity and gender roles were neither natural nor eternal. As such, she was a pioneer of feminist analysis of the media and in the political battle over feminism to be waged through the media.

We begin with this historical tale because it is so indicative of both the highlights and the omissions in much of the research and received history of feminist media studies. Located in the United States as we both are, it is no surprise that we trace our history to a U.S. author and publication. Nevertheless, we know that this type of early research and activism occurred in a variety of additional locations and contexts. First, one of the markers of oppression is the disappearing history of oppressed and/or marginalized groups. Feminist research and politics predate the 1960s, yet that history keeps getting lost and needs to be rescued. Rakow (1986) notes that "recovery" was one of four major strategies in a feminist approach to the study of popular culture. This is especially important for oppressed peoples, for whom the loss of memory is a root of oppression (Gunn Allen, 2004). Second, if global research has not been circulated, the imperial routes of publication, not its quality, are to blame. The rich debates held throughout the United Nations International Decade for Women (1975–85), which culminated in a conference held in China and in Gallagher's groundbreaking *Unequal Opportunities* (1981), demonstrated the broad interest in and need for such global and comparative research. Feminist scholars in Latin America produced highly influential work, such as Santa Cruz and Erazo's *Compropolitan* (1980), a scathing critique of the transnational marketing of *Cosmopolitan* in particular and of commodified sexuality in general. In North America, Tuchman, Daniels, and Benét (1978) produced an early collection whose relevance extends until today. Feminist media research can be found throughout the world, in many languages, even if we as U.S. scholars are usually more familiar with the Anglocentric material of the U.S.-U.K.-Australian triangle, South Africa being an occasional inclusion. In fact many recent collections that claim global reach have been criticized precisely because their Anglo-American lines belie an international perspective (Cere, 2005).

Early attempts at feminist media research were, like all research, products of their time. Located in 1960s and 1970s liberal feminist politics, these attempts, including Friedan's, sought to document gender discrimination and to propose a politics to remedy it. In the United States the positivist social scientific climate inflected the exploration of cognitive, attitudinal, and behavioral components of sex roles and their representation in mass media (Busby, 1975; Tedesco, 1974). As Dow and Wood discuss in the introduction to the *Handbook,* during this period sex and biology, not gender and culture, were still the reigning concepts. Friedan's intervention focused on mainstream U.S. media and came out of white middle-class gender politics and its focus on the oppression of middle-class housewives. Friedan was a privileged, educated, and well-connected professional whose contacts enabled the rapid distribution of her book and ideas. Concepts of race, ethnicity, class, ability, national origin, and sexuality were missing from her formulation but would soon be included in the debate from a number of positions. Yet it is difficult to locate precisely when and where such interventions from the margins were made, as the center is far better documented. In that respect, feminist media studies share much with other literatures.

◆ Content/Textual Analysis Research

Throughout the 1970s in the United States, scholarship measuring frequency of coverage, especially "first woman to" projects along with cognitive effects and sex role socialization approaches, dominated the nascent area of feminist media studies and remained the dominant paradigms in the field of communication and media studies. Especially in content and representation analysis, "images of women" research implicitly or explicitly proposed a mimetic process of reflection. The extension of this scholarship implied that a change in images would lead to a change in women's status and social change at large.

One major finding in content analysis was symbolic annihilation (Goffman, 1976; Tuchman, Daniels, & Benét, 1978): Women were underrepresented in the media and were likely to be trivialized, victimized, or ridiculed when they were represented. Symbolic annihilation was found across a broad range of media, from news coverage to general interest magazines. Women, however, were overrepresented in particular forms of media such as pornography and in particular genres within journalism such as the human interest section and, of course, fashion, society, and food pages. In television and film, melodramatic genres also overrepresented women. Advertising, which became a major focus of feminist research, was not surprisingly found to be a major site of gendered representation.

Building on earlier work by Goffman (1976), a number of scholars set about documenting advertising portrayals and their impact on children, while others began to try to make links between advertising and learning about sex roles, self-esteem, body image, and violence against children and women (Courtney, 1983; Courtney & Whipple, 1974; Kilbourne, 1979; Shields, 1996). Not all research, however, followed a social scientific model. Berger (1973), for example, provided a template for extending art history research into the study of advertisements. Similarly, Goffman's decidedly qualitative approach was extended by Williamson (1978) and Coward (1985) in their critical studies. (For an exhaustive review of the gender and advertising literature, see Shields 1996.)

Although we now reinterpret that body of work as limited in theory and methodology, early content analytical scholarship yielded information and knowledge that has proven to be an enduring component of feminist media studies, documenting the low level of representation of women in media products as well as providing a sense of the dominant types of representation that did exist. Importantly, however, this work was undeniably focused on white, middle class gender politics, and research on working-class women and/or women of color was virtually nonexistent. As Dow explains in her introduction to the media section of the *Handbook,* and as is evident below in the sections focusing on feminist research on specific media, the early emphasis on content analysis has generally given way to an emphasis on critical/cultural approaches.

◆ Production Research

One of the lessons learned from content analysis was that no direct correlation exists between content and the gender (or race) of those producing it. An increase in the number of women journalists or advertising personnel did not change gendered narratives

(Ferguson, 1990; Rakow & Kranich, 1991). Scholars began to explore additional factors— for instance, how critical mass and degrees of agency in a media organization might generate changes. Another finding in the area of media production was the so-called glass ceiling, that invisible set of barriers that prevents women and minorities from moving up within an organization (Beasley & Gibbons, 1993; Beasley & Silver, 1977; Mills, 1988). In many media organizations, women could be found only in secretarial or janitorial positions! Feminist media scholars found that entry-level access did not translate into upward mobility regardless of education or experience. There were relative differences, however, as both journalism and advertising were pink-collar occupations (i.e., the majority of entry-level workers were women, resulting in a loss of skill, prestige, and real wages), as opposed to film production, where the glass ceiling was and remains much lower and impenetrable for most female workers. In women's magazines, the bulk of the labor force is female, yet the pay scale differs drastically from general and male-oriented magazines, despite, in some cases, comparable circulation and more than comparable advertising content. Glass ceiling issues focused on hiring and promotion, especially for higher positions. The women of the *New York Times,* for example, formed a caucus and fought to have jobs posted and for open interview policies (Robertson, 1992). Production codes and conventions were also found to be gendered. For instance, reporters whose schedules matched 9 to 5 press conferences were less likely to cover after-hours events, yet this was the time when many women, people of color, and working-class people could meet (see Tuchman, 1978). Moreover, the normalization of the white middle-class male subject meant that coverage of women was presented in terms of its difference from normative masculinity.

Although early production research focused primarily on the role of women as media workers, particularly in journalism, more recent production studies by feminist scholars focus on the ways that feminist ideology is negotiated in the process of producing ostensibly progressive media products, such as television series featuring strong female characters (e.g., D'Acci, 1994), the programming offered on "women's networks" such as Lifetime Television (e.g., Meehan & Byars, 2000), or women directors working in Hollywood (Lane, 2000).

◆ Audience Research

Audience research is a more recent component of media studies that draws on a number of related paradigms to make interpretive, cultural, and individual contexts central in understanding meaning making. From the functionalist perspective still being used by media industries, the question is who is watching and for how long. In this administrative paradigm, women are central because marketing data demonstrate that they make most consumer decisions in most Western households. Thus it becomes important to understand them as members of the audience. Mass communication research developed uses and gratifications as a paradigm that at least sought to position the audience as making some decisions on a personal or cultural basis. Very little of this scholarship, however, considered gender as an important variable.

The turn to culture, through ethnographic and other qualitative approaches that have been much more often connected to issues of gender, has strongly influenced contemporary feminist research on the media. Certainly, many (e.g., Nightingale, 1996; Parameswaran, 2003) have warned about the "celebratory tenor of ethnographic projects, which have claimed that readers'/viewers' interpretive creativity offers evidence of subversive political resistance in audiences' everyday lives" (Parameswaran, 2003, p. 311). Valdivia (2000) has criticized the paradigm of pleasure as the only or the most foregrounded response to an interpretive effect of media content in much

of the mainstream feminist reception literature. She has noted as well the need to study different segments of the audience without, for instance, assuming that all women of color will have similar interpretive strategies. The promise of this paradigm remains the possibility of making the politics of gender, race, and class serious and central aspects of feminist media studies.

Classics in this paradigm include Radway's *Reading the Romance* (1984), Brundson's work on soap opera (1982), Brown's *Soap Opera and Women's Talk* (1994), as well as Press's *Women Watching Television* (1991). Radway's focus on readers of romance novels opened the door to feminists exploring interpretive practices of women in a wide range of media. Press's (1991) study added the variables of class and age to the developing paradigm (see also Heide, 1995), but it was not until Bobo (1988, 1995) explored different potential readings of the female African American audience in relation to *The Color Purple* that race became central to such studies. Brooks and Hébert discuss additional contemporary examples of reception analysis focusing on race and gender in their chapter in this volume.

Although this account foregrounds U.S. and British scholars, much earlier, Mattelart (1977, 1986) conducted reception analysis on soap opera interpretations in the politicized barrios of Allende's Chile. Contemporary research extends this focus to Latinas (Rojas, 2004) as well as to the reception of South American *telenovelas* (Acosta-Alzuru, 2003a, 2003b; La Pastina, 2004). Parameswaran (2003) warns that global audience research must be careful not to rely on "regressive models of 'native' women's identities and reversed binaries of 'us' versus 'them' [because that] only reproduces the epistemological legacies of colonial modernity" (p. 334) and fails to interrogate the "models and practices of global capitalism" (p. 316). Hegde focuses on such issues in her chapter in this volume. Postcolonial feminist scholarship on reception is a growing and noteworthy area in communication. Acosta-Alzuru (2005), among others, interrogates her own position as a native informant in her country of origin, and Hegde (1998), Parameswaran (1999, 2003, 2005), Shohat (1998), Shohat and Stam (1994), and Shome (1996, 2000) repeatedly interrogate transnational, global, and multicultural issues of reception and gender. Women and gender as/in the audience is a complex area: Hermes' (2003) asserts that "its value for feminism has been to provide an empirical means to question established notions of femininity and masculinity, and to provide new theorizations of gender" (2003, p. 382; see also Hermes 2005).

◆ *Medium-Specific Research*

In addition to taking up a methodological emphases such as content analysis, production studies, and audience reception, scholars have focused on medium-specific issues as well as on particular genres within those media. In what follows, we focus on journalism and the news, radio, film, television, and women's magazines and advertising, generally highlighting noteworthy critical/cultural scholarship about them and keeping in mind that the extent and emphases of scholarship in these areas differs significantly.

JOURNALISM AND THE NEWS

Feminist work on journalism and the news is seen as a crucial area of study because, philosophically and legally, the press has the burden and responsibility to provide knowledge and information that will lead to informed decision-making and the promise of democracy. Friedan's loose content analysis of women's magazines was followed by rigorous analyses of newspapers and news on women's topics, women's bylines, women in photographs, women as sources, women in the newsroom, gendered news narratives, and so on. Tuchman's (1978) excellent work on the gendered

aspect of news routines presaged Rakow and Kranich's (1991) study of news as a gendered narrative. Feminist media research has influenced a symbolic change away from the labeling of women in the news as "wife or relative of," decorative object, or "first woman to," and led to some substantial coverage of domestic violence, rape, body politics, and political representation. In newsrooms such as at the *New York Times*, women, after both scholarship and lawsuits, have gained some mobility beyond the lower rung of beginning reporter. Both in print and especially in broadcasting, women journalists have sometimes broken through the glass ceiling as reporters and much less often also as editors or producers. The fact that journalism is now a pink-collar occupation makes still largely male editorships relevant as a topic for continuing feminist research and activism. Steiner (1998) explores "stories of quitting" to explain why some women journalists leave the newsroom. Clearly it remains an embattled workplace in terms of gender issues.

Contemporary critical/interpretive feminist studies of news coverage often appear outside the rubric of journalism studies perhaps because journalism journals prefer quantitative methodologies (Parameswaran, 2005). Nonetheless, excellent examples of contemporary feminist critical scholarship about news exist. For instance, the essays collected in Carter, Branston, and Allan (1998) treat representation, employment, and production issues related to gender and the news in the United States and Britain. Other scholars have offered critical analysis of news coverage of what are popularly perceived and presented as women's issues, such as the 1991 Hill-Thomas hearings or women's participation in electoral politics (Byerly, 1999; Lubiano, 1992; Parry-Giles, 2000; Steiner, 1999; Vavrus, 1998, 2002). Moreover, a growing body of research analyzes mainstream news coverage of feminism itself, much of it focusing on the visibility of the second wave of U.S. feminism in the 1970s. Although some of this scholarship is primarily about representational politics (Douglas, 1994; Dow, 1999, 2003, 2004,

Poirot, 2004), some of it combines analysis of representation with the study of feminist media strategies and/or the study of production contexts (see, e.g., Barker-Plummer, 1995, 2002; Bradley, 2003).

Importantly, with very few exceptions (see, e.g., Meyers, 2004), commercial news coverage of women, women's issues, and feminism overwhelmingly offers representations of white middle-class heterosexual women. Although scholars often note this bias, the available scholarship also tends to emphasize white middle-class heterosexual gender politics. Moreover, although scholars have produced a body of literature on the treatment of African Americans in the news, such research often does not explicitly foreground the intersections of race and gender (see, e.g., the essays in Means Coleman, 2002). Noteworthy studies do treat such intersections in news coverage of Latinas and Latinos, an especially important focus now that they are the most numerous minority in the United States. For example, Vargas (2000) argues that Latinos are marginalized and gendered in the news—rendered feminine and less valuable— Molina Guzmán (2005), in a case study of the Elián Gonzalez spectacle, finds that the coverage racialized and gendered the previously "exceptional ethnic" Cubans into a brown, feminine space.

Generally, critical work on journalism and the news deserves further development within feminist media studies, particularly with regard to the intersections of gender, race, and ethnicity. Another area that warrants further development is the study of self-identified feminist news media in their historical and contemporary forms. Few such studies exist, although exceptions include Farrell's (1998) and Thom's (1997) studies of *Ms.* magazine (see also Barker-Plummer, 2002; McCracken, 1993; McKinnon, 1995; Pearson, 1999).

RADIO

Although radio is much less studied by Western feminists than either print or broadcast journalism, it remains the medium of choice and access in much of the world (for exceptions see Douglas, 2004; Hilmes, 1999). Roth, Nelson, and Davis (1995) provide a noteworthy example of research on Western radio, however, in their exploration of the takeover of a radio station by First Nation women in Canada who fought to secure rights and concessions from local governments using a radio station as the vehicle for resistance and change. The essay highlights the fact that pockets of third world resistance exist in first world countries and that some women in them use radio as a tool for empowerment. Generally, however, radio studies focus on non-Western women (Mitchell, 2004; Riaño, 1994; Thompson, Anfossi Gómez, & Suárez Soto, 2005). Radio research finds collective action in the creation and operation of programs and entire stations such as Costa Rica's FIRE (Suárez Soto, 2000). From Centro Flora Tristan in Lima, Peru, to La Casa Morada in Santiago, Chile, radio is a major component throughout the world of a feminist media activism based on feminist research. Radio can be and has been used for health campaigns dealing specifically with women's issues (see McKinley & Jensen, 2003) as well as for revolutionary and system-challenging programs, both established and pirate, as Downing (2001) documents. These efforts deserve further study.

FILM

Feminist film studies emerged in the academy in the late 1960s and early 1970s, a particularly unique moment for at least two reasons. First, academic feminist approaches to film grew out of, contributed to, and depended on the larger social movements for women's rights taking place at the time. Many of the young feminist film scholars were activists and many of the women working in documentary and experimental film conceived of their filmmaking as part of a movement for equality. Thus, feminist film studies was deeply connected to social activism at the same time that it began to become prominent in scholarly contexts. While that was also true for feminist scholars working in other areas, a second aspect of this historical moment is relatively unique to film studies. At that time, film studies was not yet well established as an independent area. Unlike feminist scholarship in, for example, literary studies, sociology, psychology, and even communication studies—which emerged out of and in the context of well-established but also arguably patriarchal fields—feminist film studies took root nearly simultaneously with film studies as a field. As a result, film studies, nearly since its inception, has been deeply influenced by feminist thought. One could even argue that feminist scholarship—which was gaining ground in many academic fields at the time—helped bring legitimacy to film studies, rather than vice versa.

Early work in feminist film studies included two books published by nonacademic presses: Rosen's *Popcorn Venus: Women, Movies, and the American Dream* (1973) and Haskell's *From Reverence to Rape: The Treatment of Women in the Movies* (1974). Both books offered a feminist perspective on the depiction of women in film over time, were written in an accessible style and meant for a lay audience, and both were reprinted by much larger mainstream presses within a year. In the academy, influential early work focused on questions of film history (Higashi, 1978), representation and semiotics (Cook & Johnston, 1988; Cowie, 2000), the political possibilities of feminist filmmaking (Johnston, 2000; Lesage, 1990), and what it would mean for understandings of representation and women's voice to recover women filmmakers who had been ignored by film studies' attention to the *auteur* (Cook, 1988; Johnston, 1988). These feminist scholars were engaging many of the questions that had been dominant in film studies: questions about Marxism, semiotics, representation, and authorship. However, they were also interested in the specifically political dimension of these theories—including the

possibility of a "progressive text" that could be "read against the grain" to reveal ideology and contradiction and thereby to "make strange" gender ideologies (see, e.g., Gledhill, 1984)—and the possibility of activist filmmaking as a source of theoretical knowledge and as a vehicle for social change.

The most influential early feminist film scholarship by far was Mulvey's essay "Visual Pleasure and Narrative Cinema" (1975). Mulvey argued that the psychoanalytical spectator that scholars such as Metz (2000) had been theorizing without any attention to gender difference was, in fact, a male spectator. Specifically, she used psychoanalytic theories as a "radical weapon" to point out that the cinematic gaze was organized through structures of fetishism, scopophilia, and castration anxiety, producing an active male gaze and passive female object-to-be-looked-at. Mulvey's essay helped to encourage a great deal of psychoanalytic work in feminist film studies, much of it theorizing spectatorship. Doane (1982) responded to Mulvey in an essay in which she moved away from Freudian and Lacanian psychoanalysis to theorize a female gaze through the concept of the masquerade. Other challenges to Mulvey followed, including Gaines's (1986) critique of both the maleness and whiteness of the way psychoanalysis had been used in scholarship.

Although psychoanalysis was a particularly dominant theoretical model in the late 1970s and early 1980s, by the mid-1980s and into the 1990s, scholars began asking about genre, in particular about reclaiming melodrama, a derided form of popular culture associated primarily with women spectators (e.g., Doane, 1987; Kaplan, 1990; López, 1994; Williams, 1990). Scholars also interrogated film's relationship to popular culture more generally—e.g., fan magazines, advertising, and fashion—and asked how that relationship might more profitably illuminate how women engage with and are represented in film (Gaines, 1990; Hansen, 1986). Others addressed the intersection of race and gender in representation (e.g., Lesage, 1981; Tajima, 1989), as well as how filmmaking could be used to shift that history (e.g., Attille & Blackwood, 1986; Gibson-Hudson, 1994). Still others were concerned with the role of race in spectatorship and how a shift away from psychoanalysis and toward ethnography might offer a more nuanced understanding of black women's experience as filmgoers (e.g., Bobo, 1988; hooks, 1992). Some scholars examined gender and representation, spectatorship, and filmmaking in global cinema, including Latin American, Chinese, and various European cinemas (e.g., Bruno & Nadotti, 1988; Flitterman-Lewis, 1990; Hershfield, 1996; Knight, 1992; Martin-Márquez, 1999; Zhang, 1996). Others focused on sexuality and lesbianism in spectatorship (e.g., Weiss, 1992), authorship (e.g., Mayne, 1994), and film production (e.g., Holmlund & Fuchs, 1997).

The 1980s and early 1990s marked a moment when feminist approaches became standard and when feminist scholars participated in opening up film studies more generally beyond the "high theory" of the 1970s. The 1980s also marked a moment of "taking stock," when a series of veteran scholars paused to reflect on where feminist film studies had been and where it was going (e.g., de Lauretis, 1984; Gledhill, 1984; Kaplan, 1983, 1986; Kuhn, 1982, Mayne, 1985, 1990; Penley, 1989; more recently, see Mellencamp, 1995).

Since the 1990s, both film studies and feminist film studies have remained relatively eclectic, drawing on a variety of disciplinary approaches and building on work from the 1980s that turned to cultural context and audience and ethnography. Film as a category of analysis has become more contested, as scholars have looked to multimedia spectacles, the increasingly fluid boundaries between film and video, the growth of the Internet, and the place of film in that mediated context and in the larger context of globalization. Additionally, feminist film scholars have taken up theoretical concepts and concerns more generally,

including attention to masculinity (e.g., Cohan & Hark, 1993; Jeffords, 1994; Penley & Willis, 1993; Tasker, 1993), whiteness (e.g., Negra, 2001), transnationalism and Eurocentrism (e.g., Kaplan, 2004; Shohat & Stam, 1994), the anthropological gaze (e.g., Rony, 1996; Trinh, 1989), and queer theory (e.g., Straayer, 1996; White, 1999). They also have turned to history (along with a good portion of the larger field of film studies), looking again at silent U.S. cinema in particular in order to add to ongoing, revisionist debates about how to understand the place of film in society and in larger mass-mediated contexts (e.g., Bean & Negra, 2002; Rabinovitz, 1998; Staiger, 1995; Stamp, 2000; Studlar, 1996). Others have looked at racialization and the star system, both then (e.g., Feng, 2000; Liu, 2000) and now (e.g., Valdivia, 1996), as well as at culturally grounded film movements and histories, such as Fregoso's (1993, 2003) work on Chicana/o film. Finally, some scholars have looked again at issues of authorship, focusing on how questions of intersectional identities overlap with production context, the economy, globalization, and social change (see Bobo, 1995; Foster, 1997; Hamamoto & Liu, 2000; Heung, 1995; hooks, 1989; hooks & Dash, 1992; Kennedy, 1992; Lane, 2000; Oishi, 2000; Projansky, 2001; Smith, 1992; Wallace, 1988).

As feminist film studies moves into the 21st century, it is grappling with the ongoing growth and complexity of feminist theories, as well as with the shifting boundaries around film as a category and with its relationship to other media and to other aspects of popular culture (see the recent forum in *Signs* [2004], including essays by Jayamanne, Kaplan, Kuhn, Mayne, and Spigel).

TELEVISION

Feminist television studies are interconnected with feminist film studies, although they arguably emphasize different issues. Audience and pleasure, industry and production (given the more extensive role of women in mainstream TV production than in mainstream film), and canonical and cult shows are all foci of feminist television studies. Like feminist film studies, feminist television studies have also become more eclectic, addressing, for example, issues of social space, the changing structure of media technology, history and memory, and feminist and postfeminist discourses on television.

In the 1980s, work on audience often focused on television soap operas. Like melodrama, soap operas had been denigrated as a form of popular culture, assumed to be empty narratives used to distract women and to define them as passive consumers. Early work challenged these assumptions, looking carefully at both soap operas and women viewers as worthy of study and explicitly linking soap opera to theories of melodrama (e.g., Ang, 1985; Brunsdon, 1982; Feuer, 1984, 1989; Kuhn, 1984; Modleski, 1984; Nochimson, 1992). One of the most influential arguments to come out of this work was the idea that soap operas matched the flow of a woman's day. In other words, the commercial interruptions, the repetition of information, and the emphasis on talk all allowed a woman who was working in the house— ironing, cooking, cleaning, caring for children—to move in and out of the space the television occupied without losing her connection with the program. This argument did much to shift the ways in which television narrative, representation, and spectatorship were theorized, but it nevertheless contains what is now seen as an obvious class bias—most women do not work only within the home during the day. Nevertheless, this theory linking a representational form to the specificity of a woman's experience was an important insight, and it influenced subsequent work on daytime television, such as talk shows (e.g., Masciarotte, 1991; Morse, 1990; Shattuc, 1997).

Within communication studies, questions about polysemy and the possibility of oppositional or resistant readings emerged in relation to theories of audience and spectatorship.

Fiske's 1987 book, *Television Culture*, was highly influential in this area, as was a published exchange between Condit (1989) and Cloud (1992). Both argued that the audience could not make any meaning it wanted, and Condit drew on audience members' responses to a television show about abortion to make her point. She showed that while pro-choice and pro-life viewers came to different conclusions about the value of a story, each generally agreed on the ideological position of a show. Through her study of the detective drama *Spenser for Hire,* Cloud argued for even more containment of meaning by the text, basing her argument primarily on textual analysis. In theorizing audience, many scholars emphasize ethnography much more than do Fiske, Condit, and Cloud (Jenkins, 1992; Press, 1991; Seiter, 1995). In her study of *Cagney and Lacey,* D'Acci (1994) combined audience reception work with textual analysis and production history, providing an important example of feminist work that insists it is never enough to study just the text, the audience, or the production history.

D'Acci's work is also an example of feminist television research that looks to cult or canonical shows, primarily (but not exclusively) sitcoms: *I Love Lucy,* 1951–1957 (Desjardins, 1999; Mellencamp, 1986); *Julia,* 1968–1971(Bodroghkozy, 1992); *The Mary Tyler Moore Show,* 1970–1977 (Bathrick, 1984; Dow, 1996); *Laverne and Shirley,* 1976–1983 (Doty, 1993); *Cagney and Lacey,* 1982–1988 (D'Acci, 1994); *Kate and Allie,* 1984–1989 (Deming, 1992; Rabinovitz, 1989); *L.A. Law,* 1986–1994 (Mayne, 1988); *thirtysomething,* 1987–1991 (Mumford, 1994–95; Probyn, 1990; Torres, 1989); *A Different World,* 1987–1993 (Gray, 1995); *Roseanne,* 1988–1997 (Rowe, 1990); *Murphy Brown,* 1988–1998 (Dow, 1996; Rabinovitz, 1999; Walkowitz, 1993); *Twin Peaks,* 1990–1991 (Lafky, 1999); *Living Single,* 1993–1998 (Smith-Shomade, 2002); *The X-Files,* 1993–2002 (Badley, 2000); *My So-Called Life,* 1994–1995 (Byers, 1998); *Xena: Warrior Princess,* 1995–2001 (Helford, 2000; Jones, 2000); *Ally McBeal,* 1997–2002

(Dubrofsky, 2002; Vavrus, 2000); *Buffy the Vampire Slayer,* 1997–2003 (Early, 2001; Ono, 2000; Wilcox, 1999); and the *Star Trek* franchise, 1966–present (Harrison et al., 1996; Jenkins, 1992; Joyrich, 1996; Roberts, 2000). These shows have become the texts that feminist film scholars return to repeatedly. In part, these scholars are asking about the feminist possibilities of television. How feminist are these shows? What happens to feminism when it is depicted on these shows and through these characters? What does it mean to read feminism "back into" shows such as *I Love Lucy?* What happens to feminism and gender representation when questions of both gender and race are engaged within the shows? What are the possibilities for powerful women working in television?

Although questions about feminism on television do run throughout this collective body of work, each scholar, of course, raises other issues as well, and contemporary work indicates the myriad directions in which feminist television studies are developing. For example, Doty (1993), Byers (1998), and Helford (2000) look at questions of queer reading and queer representation, and Bodroghkozy (1992), Gray (1995), Ono (2000), and Smith-Shomade (2002) address intersections of gender and race in shows centering women. In their chapter in this volume, Brooks and Hébert address the growing work on masculinity. Some scholars (Meehan, 2001; Meehan & Byars, 2000) have looked at narrowcasting, especially as cable has developed, using both textual analysis and production studies to show how women are constructed and targeted by the industry and the text. Lifetime Television has been a special object of study in this area. Some scholars have turned to relatively recent genres such as music television (Kaplan, 1987; Lewis, 1990; Smith-Shomade, 2002) and reality shows (Dubrofsky, in press), or more limited ones such as natural history programs (Crowther, 1995). McCarthy (2001) looks at television in social space, comparing, for example, its place in 1950s taverns (a primarily masculine space) with department

stores (a primarily feminine space). She draws on Spigel's (1992) work on how advertisements early on worked to position television within domestic space. McCarthy's and Spigel's work also relates to the relationship between television texts and other social discourses as varied as bridal magazines (Rabinovitz, 1992) and public policy (Haralovich, 1989). Spigel (1995) has combined textual analysis and ethnography to think about the role of reruns in how her female college students define the past from which they then distance themselves. Some scholars work on the links between film and television. They argue for the specificity of each, but they also emphasize that because cultural discourses flow across both, we need to think about them together (Leibman, 1995; Projansky, 2001). White (1992) has looked at ways therapeutic discourse emerges and even predominates on television.

White's work also helps to rethink television itself. She suggests that television as a whole might be linked to the therapeutic, just as work on soap opera suggested that television could be understood as melodramatic and engaged in modes of distraction, and just as work on representations of feminism suggests television may be particularly suited to feminist and postfeminist discourses. Thus, feminist television studies have contributed and continue to contribute to the rethinking of television studies as a whole.

MAGAZINES AND ADVERTISING

Following early work by Berger (1973), Goffman (1976), Williamson (1978), Santa Cruz and Erazo (1980), and Coward (1985), feminist research on magazines and advertising continues to be a fruitful area of study. Following Millium's (1975) work on images of women in advertising, Winship (1987) has provided a classic cultural studies approach to the analysis of magazines, gender, feminism, and popular culture. Other important studies include Barthel (1988) and Ferguson (1983). Wolf (1991) extended this work to focus on beauty, foregrounding advertisements. Kitch (2001) has worked on the historical development of visual stereotypes. Research even has included the analysis of advertising within feminist media (McCracken, 1993; McKinnon, 1995; Steinem, 1990). Some focuses as much on the Internet as on print and television (Nakamura, 2002), and much of it emerges under the broader rubric of gender and consumer culture, both contemporary and historical (Cronin, 2000; Scanlon, 1995, 2002), including the examination of clothing slogans as an instance of resexualization (Gill, 2003).

Contemporary research also addresses girls as a generation worth studying and examines the construction of girl culture. Two readers on the subject, *Growing Up Girls* (Mazzarella & Pecora, 1999) and *Girl Wide Web* (Mazzarella, 2005), extend previous research such as that mapped out by McRobbie (1991, 2000; see also Driscoll, 2002; Harris, 2004a, 2004b). Both of these collections include chapters on class and ethnicity. Mastronardi (in press) extends Shields (2003) on space, body, and self-image to the adolescent female population.

The role of gendered ethnicity in advertising and magazines is attracting some attention from scholars exploring new attempts to exploit the "girl market" (Acosta-Alzuru & Kreshel, 2002; Acosta-Alzuru & Lester Roushanzamir, 2003) in ways that expand the ethnic register to relationally position whiteness as central and Latinas as the eternal outsiders. Jennifer Lopez has been examined in terms of her relation to and difference from Penelope Cruz (Valdivia, 2005), as narratives of Latinidad do seem to differentiate between those with European (read as white and pure) and those with Latin American roots (read as brown and polluted). Consequently these two celebrities are used to advertise different types of products. Shields (2002) explores not only how advertising affects self-image but also (2003) how it links feminine power to the decreased amount of space women are supposed to occupy. Johnson (2003) and Johnson, David, and

Huey (2004) relate these themes to Latinas and their self image as inflected by advertisements in magazines, while Martinez (2004) looks at *Latina* magazine as an effort to construct a panethnic gendered identity. Many other feminist scholars link themes surrounding magazines and advertising to a global context. Williamson (1978) links advertising to themes of gendered postcoloniality, and Moorti (2003) examines fashion marketing as a transnational strategy to market ethnic style.

◆ Contemporary/Emerging Approaches to Feminist Media Study

In this final section, we discuss two of the many contemporary themes in feminist media studies. We choose these themes not because they are the most dominant or important, but because they resonate well with our own work. We mean them only as examples of the kind of varied topics and methodologies employed by contemporary feminist media scholars.

POSTFEMINISM AND MASS MEDIA

In the early 1980s, popular media in the United States began using the term *postfeminism* (see Bolotin, 1982). Media drew attention to the defeat of the ERA in 1982 and the continuing increase of middle-class women in higher education and professional occupations and then defined these social changes as evidence of the success of feminism. Popular media began to assume feminism was no longer needed and women were now beyond (i.e., "post") the need for feminist activism. Feminist media scholars soon began writing about this concept, finding it not only in newspaper and magazine articles that literally used the term postfeminism, but also in films and television shows that may not have used the term but still implied that feminism was somehow in the past (see Dow, 1996; Jones, 1992; Lotz, 2001; Probyn, 1993; Projansky,

2001; Vavrus, 2000; Walters, 1995). Probyn theorized the idea of *choiceoise* as part of postfeminism. She argued that many films and television shows represented women as having choice (a key feminist concept) between and among marriage, children, and career. Nevertheless, as Probyn points out, the specific choices to which women supposedly have access remain limited. Most postfeminist texts represent women as choosing only among marriage, children, and career. Questions about alternative ways to (choose to) organize one's life are thus nonexistent in postfeminism (see also Jones, 1992).

Modleski (1991) describes representations of masculinity in postfeminism in her book, *Feminism Without Women*. She argues that many popular texts use postfeminism to define men as better feminists than women. The logic of these texts goes something like this: if feminism has been successful and men and women are now equal, then men can be feminists just like women. Modleski's argument, however, is that this idea displaces women and returns men to the center of concern (see also Cuklanz, 2000; Projansky, 2001).

Several scholars also have pointed to a blindness to race, class, and sexuality in postfeminism, emphasizing that media's typical postfeminist woman is white, heterosexual, and middle class (Dow, 1996; Holmlund, 2005; Projansky, 2001). The experiences of most women in the United States—who are not white, heterosexual, and/or middle class—are written out of media's discussion of women's lives today. Moreover, the complexity of feminist history and theory disappears. Issues that are central to contemporary scholarly and activist feminism—e.g., intersectionality, queerness, labor activism, transnational coalitions—simply cease to exist in postfeminist media representations of feminism.

More recently, some scholars, particularly those working in the United Kingdom, have built on this previous work to articulate an alternative response to postfeminism. Rather than ultimately taking a stand against whatever postfeminist representations they analyze or arguing that there is a difference between feminism (which is by definition politicized and a continuing movement) and postfeminism (which is by definition depoliticized), these scholars emphasize the now undeniable and pervasive discursive presence of the latter in popular culture and the role those discourses play in producing a mainstream definition of feminism. Their goal is more often to ask what pleasures and social changes are (and are not) available to women as a result of their engagement with postfeminist media representations (see McRobbie, 2004; Negra & Tasker, in press; Tasker & Negra, 2005).

GLOBAL AND DIVERSITY-FOCUSED RESEARCH

Most international feminist media scholarship available in either the United States or in English remains centered on Britain and Australia. A little more is included about Canada and South Africa, but English language research on most of the rest of the world is in an emergent stage, although we have noted its presence at various points above in our discussion of different specific media. Research on global media is a crucial area for growth in feminist media study. This research, however, does have specific dangers, as Hegde discusses in her chapter in this volume. For example, Shohat (1998) warns that a "flavor of the month" approach often reduces third world feminists to temporary native informants or to a set of static stereotypes, a danger in all types of scholarship. Global feminist media research has been carefully documented by Gallagher (1981, 2001, 2003). Shohat and Stam's (1994) *Unthinking Eurocentrism* and Shohat's (1998) *Talking Visions* collection remain models of careful and thorough gender and media analysis treating issues of globalism. Both Gallagher and Shohat stand out in that their reference lists actually include a significant number of sources not published in English. Roach (1993) is yet another scholar who assiduously documents gendered issues of international scope.

Feminist media scholarship is increasing globally, such as the recent research on

Latin American *telenovelas* (Acosta-Alzuru, 2003a, 2003b; La Pastina, 2004). Literature on Indian media and gender issues is also growing, ranging from fashion (Moorti, 2003) to romance novels and their readers (Parameswaran 1999, 2003). Shome and Hegde (2002) and Ganguly (1992) focus on contemporary theories of globalization and postcoloniality, and their contributions, together with others we have mentioned, set the stage for further development in this area. With the emphasis on issues of globalization increasing in media research generally, research focusing on gender/feminism within this area is one of the newest and most important growth areas for feminist media scholarship.

◆ Conclusion

This chapter offers one way of organizing the vast literature of feminist approaches in media studies. There are many other ways to organize and discuss these issues, and there are many emphases, such as popular music, that we did not touch on in this chapter. We have made choices to fit our discussion within the space allotted, but we wish to emphasize that feminist media studies is a huge area within communications studies, one that also contributes to English, sociology, political science, psychology, history, anthropology, and linguistics and to the newer interdisciplines of gender and women's studies, ethnic studies, global studies, American studies and so on.

This attempt to map out feminist media studies seeks to include global concerns often missing from U.S. research. We want to reiterate that the missing global material, which is quite likely available in a range of other languages, is by no means inferior; rather, our inability to access it speaks to the parochial aspects of our culture in general and our academic culture in particular. We would like to see much more research from the understudied regions of the world, especially Africa, Latin America, and certain regions of Asia. Once we have a broader understanding of the greater range of issues, we can proceed to understand commonalities and differences in a relational manner that does not ignore unequal power and access to resources. We suspect that media vary across regions yet we also know that homogenizing global trends will generate many similarities.

We hope we have communicated how intellectually rich feminist media studies are. A wealth of scholars working with a variety of theories and methodologies continually extend the parameters of our area of study. Thus we can already sketch a history of this field as well as a set of discernible stages. What has not changed is the contested character of feminist media studies. Whether we look at production, content/ text, audience/reception or effects, major issues are still being debated that have yet to be resolved. Postfeminism notwithstanding, issues of symbolic annihilation and the glass ceiling have not disappeared, and research must continue to document the ways mass media offer both constraints and possibilities for efforts toward gender justice around the globe.

◆ References

Acosta-Alzuru, C. (2003a). "I'm not a feminist . . . I only defend women as human beings": The production, representation, and consumption of feminism in a *telenovela*. *Critical Studies in Media Communication, 20*(3), 269–294.

Acosta-Alzuru, C. (2003b). Tackling the issues: Meaning making in a *telenovela*. *Popular Communication, 1*(4), 193–216.

Acosta-Alzuru, C. (2005). Home is where my heart is: Reflections on doing research in my native country. *Popular Communication, 3*(3), 181–194.

Acosta-Alzuru, C., & Kreshel, P. J. (2002). "I'm an American girl . . . whatever that means": Girls consuming Pleasant Company's American girl identity. *Journal of Communication, 52*(1), 139–161.

Acosta-Alzuru, C., & Lester Roushanzamir, E. P. (2003). "Everything we do is a celebration of you!" Pleasant Company constructs American girlhood. *Communication Review,* 6(1), 45–69.

Ang, I. (1985). *Watching* Dallas: *Soap opera and the melodramatic imagination* (D. Couling, Trans.). London: Methuen.

Attille, M., & Blackwood, M. (1986). Black women and representation. In C. Brunsdon (Ed.), *Films for women* (pp. 202–208). London: British Film Institute. (Reprinted from *Undercut, 14/15,* 60–61, 1984)

Badley, L. (2000). Scully hits the glass ceiling: Postmodernism, postfeminism, posthumanism, and *The X-Files.* In E. R. Helford (Ed.), *Fantasy girls: Gender in the new universe of science fiction and fantasy television* (pp. 61–90). Lanham, MD: Rowman & Littlefield.

Baehr, H., & Gray, A. (1996). *Turning it on: A reader on women and the media.* New York: Arnold.

Barker-Plummer, B. (1995). News as a political resource: Media strategies and political identity in the U.S. women's movement. *Critical Studies in Mass Communication,* 12(3), 306–324.

Barker-Plummer, B. (2002). Producing public voice: Resource mobilization and media access in the National Organization for Women. *Journalism and Mass Communication Quarterly,* 79(1), 188–205.

Barthel, D. L. (1988). *Putting on appearances: Gender and advertising.* Philadelphia: Temple University Press.

Bathrick, S. (1984). *The Mary Tyler Moore Show* . . . Women at home and at work. In J. Feuer, P. Keer, & T. Vahimagi (Eds.), *MTM: "Quality television"* (pp. 99–131). London: British Film Institute.

Bean, J. M., & Negra, D. (Eds.). (2002). *A feminist reader in early cinema.* Durham, NC: Duke University Press.

Beasley, M. H., & Gibbons, S. J. (1993). *Taking their place: A documentary history of women and journalism.* Washington, DC: American University Press.

Beasley, M. H., & Silver, S. (1977). *Women in media: A documentary source book.* Washington, DC: Women's Institute for Freedom in the Press.

Berger, J. (1973). *Ways of seeing.* London: British Film Institute.

Bobo, J. (1988). *The Color Purple:* Black women's responses. *Jump Cut, 33,* 43–51.

Bobo, J. (1995). *Black women as cultural readers.* New York: Columbia University Press.

Bodroghkozy, A. (1992). "Is this what you mean by color TV?": Race, gender, and contested meanings in NBC's *Julia.* In L. Spigel & D. Mann (Eds.), *Private screenings: Television and the female consumer* (pp. 143–167). Minneapolis: University of Minnesota Press.

Bolotin, S. (1982, Oct. 17). Voices from the post-feminist generation. *New York Times Magazine,* pp. 28–31, 103, 106–7, 114, 116–117.

Bradley, P. (2003). *Mass media and the shaping of American feminism, 1963–1975.* Jackson: University of Mississippi Press.

Brown, M. E. (1994). *Soap opera and women's talk: The pleasure of resistance.* Thousand Oaks, CA: Sage.

Bruno, G., & Nadotti, M. (Eds.). (1988). *Off screen: Women and film in Italy.* London: Methuen.

Brunsdon, C. E. (1982). *Crossroads:* Notes on soap opera. *Screen, 22*(4), 32–37.

Busby, L. (1975). Sex role research in the mass media. *Journal of Communication, 25*(2), 107–131.

Byerly, C. M. (1999). News, feminism and the dialectics of gender relations. In M. Meyers (Ed.), *Mediated women: Representations in popular culture* (pp. 383–404). Cresskill, NJ: Hampton Press.

Byers, M. (1998). Gender/sexuality/desire: Subversion of difference and construction of loss in the adolescent drama of *My So-Called Life. Signs: Journal of Women in Cultural and Society, 23*(3), 711–734.

Carter, C., Branston, G., & Allan, S. (Eds.). (1998). *News, gender, and power.* New York: Routledge.

Carter, C., & Steiner, L. (Eds.). (2004). *Critical readings: Media and gender.* New York: McGraw-Hill.

Cere, R. (2005). Review of women and media: International perspectives in feminist media studies. *Feminist Media Studies, 5*(2), 261–264.

Cloud, D. (1992). The limits of interpretation: Ambivalence and the stereotype in *Spencer for Hire. Critical Studies in Mass Communication, 9*(4), 311–324.

Cohan, S., & Hark, I. R. (Eds.). (1993). *Screening the male: Exploring masculinities in Hollywood cinema.* New York: Routledge.

Condit, C. M. (1989). The rhetorical limits of polysemy. *Critical Studies in Mass Communication, 6*(2), 103–122.

Cook, P. (1988). Approaching the work of Dorothy Arzner. In C. Penley (Ed.), *Feminism and film theory* (pp. 46–56). New York: Routledge. (Reprinted from *The works of Dorothy Arzner*, pp. 9–18, by C. Johnston, Ed. 1975, London: British Film Institute)

Cook, P., & Johnston, C. (1988). The place of woman in the cinema of Raoul Walsh. In C. Penley (Ed.), *Feminism and film theory* (pp. 25–35). New York: Routledge. (Reprinted from *Raoul Walsh,* by P. Hardy, Ed., 1974, Colchester: Edinburgh Film Festival)

Courtney, A. E. (1983). *Sex stereotyping in advertising.* Lexington, MA: Lexington Books.

Courtney, A. E., & Whipple, T. W. (1974). Women in TV commercials. *Journal of Communication, 24*(2), 110–118.

Coward, R. (1985). *Female desires: How they are sought, bought, and packaged.* New York: Grove Press.

Cowie, E. (2000). Woman as sign. In E. A. Kaplan (Ed.), *Feminism and film* (pp. 48–65). Oxford, UK: Oxford University Press (Reprinted from *m / f, 1,* 49–63, 1978)

Cronin, A. M. (2000). *Advertising and consumer citizenship: Gender, images, and rights.* New York: Routledge.

Crowther, B. (1995). Towards a feminist critique of television natural history programs. In P. Florence & D. Reynolds (Eds.), *Feminist subjects, multi-media: Cultural methodologies* (pp. 127–146). Manchester, UK: Manchester University Press.

Cuklanz, L. M. (2000). *Rape on prime-time: Television, masculinity, and sexual violence.* Philadelphia: University of Pennsylvania Press.

D'Acci, J. (1994). *Defining women: Television and the case of* Cagney & Lacey. Chapel Hill: University of North Carolina Press.

De Lauretis, T. (1984). *Alice doesn't: Feminism, semiotics, cinema.* Bloomington: Indiana University Press.

Deming, R. H. (1992). *Kate and Allie:* "New" women and the audience's televisual archives. In L. Spigel & D. Mann (Eds.), *Private screenings: Television and the female consumer* (pp. 203–216). Minneapolis: University of Minnesota Press.

Desjardins, M. (1999). Lucy and Desi: Sexuality, ethnicity, and TV's first family. In M. B. Haralovich & L. Rabinovitz (Eds.), *Television, history and American culture: Feminist critical essays* (pp. 56–74). Durham, NC: Duke University Press.

Doane, M. A. (1982). Film and the masquerade: Theorizing the female spectator. *Screen, 23*(3/4), 74–87.

Doane, M. A. (1987). *The desire to desire: The woman's film in the 1940s.* Bloomington: Indiana University Press.

Doty, A. (1993). *Making things perfectly queer: Interpreting mass culture.* Minneapolis: University of Minnesota Press.

Douglas, S. J. (1994). *Where the girls are: Growing up female with the mass media.* New York: Random House.

Douglas, S. J. (2004). *Listening in: Radio and the American imagination.* Minneapolis: University of Minnesota Press.

Dow, B. J. (1996). *Prime time feminism: Television, media culture, and the women's movement since 1970.* Philadelphia: University of Pennsylvania Press.

Dow, B. J. (1999). Spectacle, spectatorship, and gender anxiety in television news coverage of the 1970 Women's Strike for Equality. *Communication Studies, 50*(2), 143–157.

Dow, B. J. (2003). Feminism, Miss America, and media mythology. *Rhetoric and Public Affairs, 6*(1), 127–160.

Dow, B. J. (2004). Fixing feminism: Women's liberation and the rhetoric of television documentary. *Quarterly Journal of Speech, 90*(1), 55–80.

Dow, B. J., & Condit, C. M. (2005). The state of the art in feminist scholarship in communication. *Journal of Communication, 55*(3), 448–478.

Downing, J. D. (2001). *Radical media: Rebellious communication and social movements.* Thousand Oaks, CA: Sage.

Driscoll, C. (2002). *Girls: Feminine adolescence in popular culture and cultural theory.* New York: Columbia University Press.

Dubrofsky, R. (2002). Ally McBeal as postfeminist icon: The aestheticizing and fetishizing of the independent working woman. *Communication Review, 5*(4), 265–284.

Dubrofsky, R. (in press). *The Bachelor: Whiteness in the harem. Critical Studies in Media Communication.*

Early, F. H. (2001). Staking her claim: Buffy the Vampire Slayer as transgressive woman warrior. *Journal of Popular Culture, 35*(3), 11–27.

Farrell, A. E. (1995). Feminism and the media: Introduction. *Signs: Journal of Women in Culture and Society, 20*(3), 643–645.

Farrell, A. E. (1998). *Yours in sisterhood: Ms. magazine and the promise of popular feminism.* Chapel Hill: University of North Carolina Press.

Feng, P. X. (2000). Recuperating Suzie Wong: A fan's Nancy Kwan-dary. In D. Y. Hamamoto & S. Liu (Eds.), *Countervisions: Asian American film criticism* (pp. 40–56). Philadelphia: Temple University Press.

Ferguson, M. (1983). *Forever feminine: Women's magazines and the cult of femininity.* London: Hienemann.

Ferguson, M. (1990). Images of power and the feminist fallacy. *Critical Studies in Mass Communication, 7*(3), 215–230.

Feuer, J. (1984). Melodrama, serial form, and television today. *Screen, 25*(1), 4–16.

Feuer, J. (1989). Reading *Dynasty*: Television and reception theory. *South Atlantic Quarterly, 88*(2), 443–460.

Fiske, J. (1987). *Television culture.* London: Methuen.

Flitterman-Lewis, S. (1990). *To desire differently: Feminism and the French cinema.* Urbana: University of Illinois Press.

Florence, P., & Reynolds, D. (Eds.). (1995). *Feminist subjects, multi-media: Cultural methodologies.* New York: Manchester University Press.

Foster, G. A. (1997). *Women filmmakers of the African and Asian Diaspora: Decolonizing the gaze, locating subjectivity.* Carbondale: Southern Illinois University Press.

Fregoso, R. L. (1993). *The bronze screen: Chicana and Chicano film culture.* Minneapolis: University of Minnesota Press.

Fregoso, R. L. (2003). *Mexicana encounters: The making of social identities on the borderlands.* Berkeley: University of California Press.

Friedan, B. (1963). *The feminine mystique.* New York: Norton.

Gaines, J. (1986). White privilege and looking relations: Race and gender in feminist film theory. *Cultural Critique, 4,* 59–79.

Gaines, J. (1990). From elephants to Lux soap: The programming and "flow" of early motion picture exploitation. *Velvet Light Trap, 25,* 29–43.

Gallagher, M. (1981). *Unequal opportunities: The case of women and the media.* Paris: UNESCO.

Gallagher, M. (2001). The push and pull of action and research in feminist media studies. *Feminist Media Studies, 1*(1), 11–15.

Gallagher, M. (2003). Feminist media perspectives. In A. N. Valdivia (Ed.), *A companion to media studies* (pp. 19–39). Oxford, UK: Blackwell.

Ganguly, K. (1992). Accounting for others: Feminism and representation. In L. F. Rakow (Ed.), *Women making meaning* (pp. 60–79). New York: Routledge.

Gibson-Hudson, G. (1994). Aspects of black feminist cultural ideology in films by black women independent artists. In D. Carson, L. Dittmar, & J. R. Welsch (Eds.), *Multiple voices in feminist film criticism* (pp. 365–379). Minneapolis: University of Minnesota Press.

Gill, R. (2003). From sexual objectification to sexual subjectification: The resexualisation of women's bodies in the media. *Feminist Media Studies, 3*(1), 100–106.

Gledhill, C. (1984). Developments in feminist film criticism. In M. A. Doane, P. Mellencamp, & L. Williams (Eds.), *Re-Vision: Essays in feminist film criticism* (pp. 18–48). Frederick, MD: American Film Institute.

Goffman, E. (1976). *Gender advertisements.* New York: Harper and Row.

Gray, H. (1995). *Watching race: Television and the struggle for "blackness."* Minneapolis: University of Minnesota Press.

Gunn Allen, P. (2004). Who is your mother? Red roots of white feminism. In L. F. Rakow & L. A. Wackwitz (Eds.), *Feminist communication theory: Selections in context* (pp. 29–37). Thousand Oaks, CA: Sage.

Hamamoto, D. Y., & Liu, S. (Eds.). (2000). *Countervisions: Asian American film criticism*. Philadelphia: Temple University Press.

Hansen, M. (1986). Pleasure, ambivalence, identification: Valentino and female spectatorship. *Cinema Journal, 25*(4), 6–32.

Haralovich, M. B. (1989). Sitcoms and suburbs: Positioning the 1950s homemaker. *Quarterly Review of Film and Video, 11,* 61–83.

Harris, A. (Ed.). (2004a). *All about the girl: Culture, power, and identity.* New York: Routledge.

Harris, A. (2004b). *Future girl: Young women in the twenty-first century.* New York: Routledge.

Harrison, T., Projansky, S., Ono, K.A., & Helford, E. R. (Eds.). (1996). *Enterprise zones: Critical positions on* Star Trek. Boulder, CO: Westview Press.

Haskell, M. (1974). *From reverence to rape: The treatment of women in the movies.* New York: Penguin.

Hegde, R. (1998). A view from elsewhere: Locating difference and the politics of representation from a transnational feminist perspective. *Communication Theory, 8*(3), 271–297.

Heide, M. J. (1995). *Television culture and women's lives:* thirtysomething *and the contradictions of gender.* Philadelphia: University of Pennsylvania Press.

Helford, E. R. (2000). Feminism, queer studies, and the sexual politics of *Xena: Warrior Princess.* In E. R. Helford (Ed.), *Fantasy girls: Gender in the new universe of science fiction and fantasy television* (pp. 135–162). Lanham, MD: Rowman & Littlefield.

Hermes, J. (2003). Practicing embodiment: Reality, respect, and issues of gender in media reception. In A. N. Valdivia (Ed.), *A companion to media studies* (pp. 382–398). Oxford, UK: Blackwell.

Hermes, J. (2005). *Re-reading popular culture.* Oxford, UK: Blackwell.

Hershfield, J. (1996). *Mexican cinema/Mexican woman, 1940–1950.* Tucson: University of Arizona Press.

Heung, M. (1995). Representing ourselves: Films and videos by Asian American/Canadian women. In A. N. Valdivia (Ed.), *Feminism, multiculturalism, and the media:*

Global diversities (pp. 82–104). Thousand Oaks, CA: Sage.

Higashi, S. (1978). *Virgins, vamps, and flappers: The American silent movie heroine.* St. Albans, VT: Eden Press Women's Publications.

Hilmes, M. (1999). Desired and feared: Women's voices in radio history. In M. B. Haralovich & L. Rabinovitz (Eds.), *Television, history, and American culture: Feminist critical essays* (pp. 17–35). Durham, NC: Duke University Press.

Holmlund, C. (2005). Postfeminism from A to G. *Cinema Journal, 44*(2), 116–121.

Holmlund, C., & Fuchs, C. (Eds.). (1997). *Between the sheets, in the streets: Queer, lesbian, and gay documentary.* Minneapolis: University of Minnesota Press.

hooks, b. (1989). "Whose pussy is this?" A feminist comment. In *Talking back: Thinking feminist, thinking black* (pp. 134–141). Boston: South End Press.

hooks, b. (1992). The oppositional gaze: Black female spectators. In *Black looks: Race and representation* (pp. 115–131). Boston: South End Press.

hooks, b., & Dash, J. (1992). Dialogue between bell hooks and Julie Dash. In J. Dash with T. C. Bambara & b. hooks (Eds.), Daughters of the Dust: *The making of an African American woman's film* (pp. 27–67). New York: New Press.

Jayamanne, L. (2004). Pursuing micromovements in *Room 222. Signs: Journal of Women in Culture and Society, 30*(1), 1248–1256.

Jeffords, S. (1994). *Hard bodies: Hollywood masculinity in the Reagan era.* New Brunswick, NJ: Rutgers University Press.

Jenkins, H. (1992). *Textual poachers: Television fans and participatory culture.* New York: Routledge.

Johnson, L. A. (1995). Forum in feminism and the media: Afterword. *Signs: Journal of Women in Culture and Society, 20*(3), 711–719.

Johnson, M. A. (2003). Constructing a new model of ethnic media. In A. N. Valdivia (Ed.), *A companion to media studies* (pp. 272–292). Oxford, UK: Blackwell.

Johnson, M.A., David, P., & Huey, D. (2004). Looks like me? Body image in Hispanic women's magazines. In A. Tait & G. Meiss (Eds.), *AHANA and media*. Westport, CT: Greenwood.

Johnston, C. (2000). Women's cinema as counter-cinema. In E. A. Kaplan (Ed.), *Feminism and film* (pp. 22–33). Oxford, UK: Oxford University Press. (Reprinted from *Notes on women's cinema*, C. Johnston, Ed., 1973, London: British Film Institute)

Johnston, C. (1988). Dorothy Arzner: Critical strategies. In C. Penley (Ed.), *Feminism and film theory* (pp. 36–45). New York: Routledge. (Reprinted from *The works of Dorothy Arzner*, C. Johnston, Ed., 1975 London: British Film Institute)

Jones, A. (1992). Feminism, incorporated: Reading "postfeminism" in an anti-feminist age. *Afterimage, 20*(5), 10–15.

Jones, S. G. (2000). Histories, fictions and *Xena: Warrior Princess*. *Television and New Media, 1*(4), 403–418.

Joyrich, L. (1996). Feminist enterprise? *Star Trek: The Next Generation* and the occupation of femininity. *Cinema Journal, 35*(2), 61–84.

Kaplan, E. A. (1983). *Women and film: Both sides of the camera*. New York: Methuen.

Kaplan, E. A. (1986). Feminist film criticism: Current issues and problems. *Studies in Literary Imagination, 19*(1), 7–20.

Kaplan, E. A. (1987). *Rocking around the clock: Music television, postmodernism, and consumer culture*. New York: Methuen.

Kaplan, E. A. (1990). The case of the missing mother: Maternal issues in Vidor's *Stella Dallas*. In P. Erens (Ed.), *Issues in feminist film criticism* (pp. 126–136). Bloomington: Indiana University Press. (Reprinted from *Heresies, 16,* 81–85, 1983)

Kaplan, E. A. (2004). Global feminisms and the state of feminist film theory. *Signs: Journal of Women in Culture and Society, 30*(1), 1236–1248.

Kennedy, L. (1992). The body in question. In G. Dent (Ed.), *Black popular culture* (pp. 106–111). Seattle, WA: Bay Press.

Kilbourne, J. (1979). *Killing us softly: Advertising's image of women* [Film]. Cambridge, MA: Cambridge Documentary Films.

Kitch, C. (2001). *The girl on the magazine cover: The origins of visual stereotypes in American mass media*. Chapel Hill: University of North Carolina Press.

Knight, J. (1992). *Women and the new German cinema*. London: Verso.

Kuhn, A. (1982). *Women's pictures: Feminism and cinema*. London: Routledge.

Kuhn, A. (1984). Women's genres: Melodrama, soap opera, and theory. *Screen, 25*(1), 18–28.

Kuhn, A. (2004). The state of film and media feminism. *Signs: Journal of Women in Culture and Society, 30*(1), 1221–1228.

Lafky, S. (1999). Gender, power, and culture in the televisual world of *Twin Peaks*: A feminist critique. *Journal of Film and Video, 51*(3–4), 5–19.

Lane, C. (2000). *Feminist Hollywood: From Born in Flames to Point Break*. Detroit, MI: Wayne State University Press.

La Pastina, A. (2004). *Telenovela* reception in rural Brazil: Gendered readings and sexual mores. *Critical Studies in Media Communications, 21*(2), 162–181.

Leibman, N. C. (1995). *Living room lectures: The fifties family in film and television*. Austin: University of Texas Press.

Lesage, J. (1981). *Broken Blossoms*: Artful racism, artful rape. *Jump Cut, 26,* 51–55.

Lesage, J. (1990). The political aesthetics of the feminist documentary film. In P. Erens (Ed.), *Issues in feminist film criticism* (pp. 222–237). Bloomington: Indiana University Press. (Reprinted from *Quarterly Review of Film Studies, 3,* 507–523, 1978)

Lewis, L. A. (1990). *Gender politics and MTV: Voicing the difference*. Philadelphia: Temple University Press.

Liu, C. W. (2000). When dragon ladies die, do they come back as butterflies? Re-imagining Anna May Wong. In D. Y. Hamamoto & S. Liu (Eds.), *Countervisions: Asian American film criticism* (pp. 23–39). Philadelphia: Temple University Press.

López, A. M. (1994). Tears and desire: Women and melodrama in the "old" Mexican cinema. In D. Carson, L. Dittmar, & J. R. Welsch (Eds.), *Multiple voices in feminist film criticism* (pp. 254–270). Minneapolis: University of Minnesota Press.

Lotz, A. D. (2001). Postfeminist television criticism: Rehabilitating critical terms and identifying postfeminist attributes. *Feminist Media Studies 1*(1), 105–121.

Lubiano, W. (1992). Black ladies, welfare queens, and state minstrels: Ideological war by narrative means. In T. Morrison (Ed.), *Race-ing justice, en-gendering power: Essays on Anita Hill, Clarence Thomas, and the construction of social reality* (pp. 323–363). New York: Pantheon Books.

Martin-Márquez, S. (1999). *Feminist discourse and Spanish cinema: Sight unseen.* Oxford, UK: Oxford University Press.

Martinez, K. (2004). Latina magazine and the invocation of a panethnic family: Latino identity as it is informed by celebrities and Papis Chulos. *Communication Review, 7*(2), 155–174.

Masciarotte, G-J. (1991). C'mon girl: Oprah Winfrey and the discourse of feminine talk. *Genders, 11,* 81–110.

Mastronardi, M. (in press). *After Ophelia: Feminism, popular culture, and female adolescence in crisis.* Urbana: University of Illinois Press.

Mattelart, M. (1977). *La cultura de la opresión femenina.* Mexico: Ediciones Era.

Mattelart, M. (1986). *Women, media, crisis: Femininity and disorder.* London: Comedia.

Mayne, J. (1985). Feminist film theory and criticism. *Signs: Journal of Women in Culture and Society, 11*(1), 81–100.

Mayne, J. (1988). "L.A. Law" and prime-time feminism. *Discourse, 10*(2), 30–47.

Mayne, J. (1990). *The woman at the keyhole: Feminism and women's cinema.* Bloomington: Indiana University Press.

Mayne, J. (1994). *Directed by Dorothy Arzner.* Bloomington: Indiana University Press.

Mayne, J. (2004). Marlene, dolls and fetishism. *Signs: Journal of Women in Culture and Society, 30*(1), 1257–1264.

Mazzarella, S. R. (Ed.). (2005). *Girl wide web: Girls, the Internet, and the negotiation of identity.* New York: Peter Lang.

Mazzarella, S. R., & Pecora, N. O. (Eds.). (1999). *Growing up girls: Popular culture and the construction of identity.* New York: Peter Lang.

McCarthy, A. (2001). *Ambient television: Visual culture and public space.* Durham, NC: Duke University Press.

McCracken, E. (1993). *Decoding women's magazines: From* Mademoiselle *to* Ms. New York: St. Martin's Press.

McKinley, M. A., & Jensen, L. O. (2003). In our own voices: Reproduction health radio programming in the Peruvian Amazon. *Critical Studies in Media Communication, 20*(2), 180–203.

McKinnon, L. M. (1995). *Ms.*ing the free press: The advertising and editorial content of *Ms.* magazine, 1972–1992. In D. Abrahamson (Ed.), *The American magazine: Research perspective and prospects* (pp. 98–107). Ames: Iowa State University Press.

McRobbie, A. (1991). *Feminism and youth culture: From* Jackie *to* Just Seventeen. Boston: Unwin Hyman.

McRobbie, A. (2000). *Feminism and youth culture.* New York: Routledge.

McRobbie, A. (2004). Post-feminism and popular culture. *Feminist Media Studies, 4*(3), 255–264.

Means Coleman, R. R. (Ed.). (2002). *Say it loud! African American audiences, media, and identity.* New York: Routledge.

Meehan, E. R. (2001). Gendering the commodity audience. In E. R. Meehan & E. Riordan (Eds.), *Sex and money: Feminism, political economy, and media studies* (pp. 209–222). Minneapolis: University of Minnesota Press.

Meehan, E. R., & Byars, J. (2000). Telefeminism: How Lifetime got its groove 1984–1997. *Television and New Media 1*(1), 33–51.

Mellencamp, P. (1986). Situation comedy, feminism, and Freud: Discourses of Gracie and Lucy. In T. Modleski (Ed.), *Studies in entertainment: Critical approaches to mass culture* (pp. 80–95). Bloomington: Indiana University Press.

Mellencamp, P. (1995). *A fine romance: Five ages of film feminism*. Philadelphia: Temple University Press.

Metz, C. (2000). The imaginary signifier (B. Brewster, Trans.). In R. Stam & T. Miller (Eds.), *Film and theory: An anthology* (pp. 408–436). Oxford, UK: Blackwell. (Reprinted from *Screen, 16*[2], 1975)

Meyers, M. (2004). African American women and violence: Gender, race, and class in the news. *Critical Studies in Media Communication, 21*(2), 95–118.

Millium, T. (1975). *Images of women: Advertising in women's magazines*. London: Chatto & Windus.

Mills, K. (1988). *A place in the news: From the women's pages to the front page*. New York: Dodd, Mead.

Mitchell, C. (2004). "Dangerously feminine?" Theory and praxis of women's alternative radio. In K. Ross & C. Byerly (Eds.), *Women and media: International perspectives*. Oxford, UK: Blackwell.

Modleski, T. (1984). *Loving with a vengeance: Mass-produced fantasies for women*. New York: Methuen.

Modleski, T. (1991). *Feminism without women: Culture and criticism in a "postfeminist" age*. New York: Routledge.

Molina Guzmán, I. (2005). Gendering Latinidad through the Elián news discourse about Cuban women. *Latino Studies, 3*, 179–204.

Moorti, S. (2003). Out of India: Fashion culture and the marketing of ethnic style. In A. N. Valdivia (Ed.), *A companion to media studies* (pp. 293–308). Oxford, UK: Blackwell.

Morse, M. (1990). An ontology of everyday distraction: The freeway, the mall, and television. In P. Mellencamp (Ed.), *Logics of television: Essays in cultural criticism* (pp. 193–221). Bloomington: Indiana University Press.

Mulvey, L. (1975). Visual pleasure and narrative cinema. *Screen, 16*(3), 6–18.

Mumford, L. S. (1994–95). Stripping on the girl channel: Lifetime, *thirtysomething*, and television form. *Camera Obscura, 33–34*, 167–190.

Nakamura, L. (2002). *Cybertypes: Race, ethnicity, and identity on the Internet*. New York: Routledge.

Negra, D. (2001). *Off-white Hollywood: American culture and ethnic female stardom*. London: Routledge.

Negra, D., & Tasker, Y. (in press). *Interrogating postfeminism: Gender and the politics of popular culture*. Durham, NC: Duke University Press.

Nightingale, V. (1996). *Studying audiences: The shock of the real*. New York: Routledge.

Nochimson, M. (1992). *No end to her: Soap opera and the female subject*. Berkeley: University of California Press.

Oishi, E. (2000). Bad Asians: New film and video by queer Asian American artists. In D. Y. Hamamoto & S. Liu (Eds.), *Countervisions: Asian American film criticism* (pp. 221–241). Philadelphia: Temple University Press.

Ono, K. A. (2000). To be a vampire on *Buffy the Vampire Slayer*: Race and ("other") socially marginalizing positions on horror TV. In E. R. Helford (Ed.), *Fantasy girls: Gender in the new universe of science fiction and fantasy television* (pp. 163–186). Lanham, MD: Rowman & Littlefield.

Parameswaran, R. (1999). Western romance fiction as English-language media in postcolonial India. *Journal of Communication, 49*(2), 84–105.

Parameswaran, R. (2003). Resuscitating feminist audience studies: Revisiting the politics of representation and resistance. In A. N. Valdivia (Ed.), *A companion to media studies* (pp. 311–336). Oxford, UK: Blackwell.

Parameswaran, R. (2005). Journalism and feminist cultural studies: Retrieving the missing citizen lost in the female audience. *Popular Communication, 3*(3), 195–208.

Parry-Giles, S. J. (2000). Mediating Hillary Rodham Clinton: Television news practices and image-making in the postmodern age. *Critical Studies in Media Communications, 17*(2), 205–226.

Pearson, K. (1999). Mapping rhetorical interventions in "national" feminist histories: Second wave feminism and "Ain't I a Woman." *Communication Studies, 50*(2), 158–173.

Penley, C. (1989). "A certain refusal of difference": Feminism and film theory. In *The future of an illusion: Film, feminism and psychoanalysis* (pp. 41–54). Minneapolis: University of Minnesota Press.

Penley, C., & Willis, S. (Eds.). (1993). *Male trouble*. Minneapolis: University of Minnesota Press.

Poirot, K. (2004). Mediating a movement, authorizing discourse: Kate Millett, sexual politics, and feminism's second wave. *Women's Studies in Communication, 27*(2), 204–235.

Press, A. L. (1991). *Women watching television: Gender, class, and generation in the American television experience*. Philadelphia: University of Pennsylvania Press.

Probyn, E. (1990). New traditionalism and post-feminism: TV does the home. *Screen, 31*(2), 147–159.

Probyn, E. (1993). Choosing choice: Images of sexuality and "choiceoisie" in popular culture. In S. Fisher & K. Davis (Eds.), *Negotiating at the margins: The gendered discourses of power and resistance* (pp. 278–294). New Brunswick, NJ: Rutgers University Press.

Projansky, S. (2001). *Watching rape: Film and television in postfeminist culture*. New York: New York University Press.

Rabinovitz, L. (1989). Sitcoms and single moms: Representations of feminism on American TV. *Cinema Journal, 29*(1), 3–19.

Rabinovitz, L. (1992). Soap opera bridal fantasies. *Screen, 33*(3), 274–283.

Rabinovitz, L. (1998). *For the love of pleasure: Women, movies, and culture in turn-of-the-century Chicago*. New Brunswick, NJ: Rutgers University Press.

Rabinovitz, L. (1999). Ms.-Representation: The politics of feminist sitcoms. In M. B. Haralovich & L. Rabinovitz (Eds.), *Television, history, and American culture: Feminist critical essays* (pp. 144–167). Durham, NC: Duke University Press.

Radway, J. A. (1984). *Reading the romance: Women, patriarchy, and popular literature*. Chapel Hill: University of North Carolina Press.

Rakow, L. F. (1986). Feminist approaches to popular culture: Giving patriarchy its due. *Communication, 9*(1), 19–24.

Rakow, L. F., & Kranich, K. (1991). Woman as sign in television news. *Journal of Communication, 41*(1), 8–23.

Rakow, L. F., & Wackwitz, L. A. (Eds.). (2004). *Feminist communication theory: Selections in context*. London: Sage.

Riaño, P. (1994). *Women in grassroots communications: Furthering social change*. Thousand Oaks, CA: Sage.

Roach, C. (1993). *Communication and culture in war and peace*. Newbury Park, CA: Sage.

Roberts, R. A. (2000). Science, race, and gender in *Star Trek: Voyager*. In E. R. Helford (Ed.), *Fantasy girls: Gender in the new universe of science fiction and fantasy television* (pp. 203–221). Lanham, MD: Rowman & Littlefield.

Robertson, N. (1992). *The girls in the balcony: Women, men and the New York Times*. New York: Random House.

Rojas, V. (2004). The gender of Latinidad: Latinas speak about Hispanic television. *Communication Review, 7*, 125–153.

Rony, F. T. (1996). *The third eye: Race, cinema, and the ethnographic spectacle*. Durham, NC: Duke University Press.

Rosen, M. (1973). *Popcorn Venus: Women, movies, and the American dream*. New York: Avon.

Ross, K., & Byerly, C. (Eds.). (2004). *Women and media: International perspectives*. Oxford, UK: Blackwell.

Roth, L., Nelson, B., & Davis, M. (1995). Three women, a mouse, a microphone, and a telephone: Information (mis)management during the Mohawk/Canadian governments' conflict of 1990. In A. N. Valdivia (Ed.), *Feminism, multiculturalism, and the media: Global diversities* (pp. 48–81). Thousand Oaks, CA: Sage.

Rowe, K. (1990). Roseanne: Unruly woman as domestic goddess. *Screen, 31*(4), 408–419.

Santa Cruz, A., & Erazo, V. (1980). *Compropolitan: El orden transnacional y su modelo femenino: Un estudio de las revistas femeninas en América Latina*. México City: ILET, Nueva Imagen.

Scanlon, J. (1995). *Inarticulate longings: The Ladies' Home Journal, gender, and the promises of consumer culture*. New York: Routledge.

Scanlon, J. (Ed.). (2002). *The gender and consumer culture reader.* New York: New York University Press.

Seiter, E. (1995). Mothers watching children watching television. In B. Skeegs (Ed.), *Feminist cultural theory: Process and production* (pp. 137–151). Manchester, UK: Manchester University Press.

Shattuc, J. (1997). *The talking cure: Women and TV talk shows.* New York: Routledge.

Shields, V. R. (1996). Selling the sex that sells: Mapping the evolution of gender advertising research across three decades. In B. Burleson (Ed.), *Communication yearbook* (Vol. 20, pp. 71–109). Thousand Oaks, CA: Sage.

Shields, V. R. (2002). *Measuring up: How advertising affects self-image.* Philadelphia: University of Pennsylvania Press.

Shields, V. R. (2003). The less space we take, the more powerful we'll be: How advertising uses gender to invert signs of empowerment. In A. N. Valdivia (Ed.), *A companion to media studies* (pp. 247–271). Oxford, UK: Blackwell.

Shohat, E. (Ed.). (1998). *Talking visions: Multicultural feminism in a transnational age.* New York: New Museum of Contemporary Art.

Shohat, E., & Stam, R. (1994). *Unthinking Eurocentrism: Multiculturalism and the media.* New York: Routledge.

Shome, R. (1996). Postcolonial interventions in the rhetorical canon: An "other" view. *Communication Theory, 6*(1), 40–59.

Shome, R. (2000). Outing whiteness. *Critical Studies in Mass Communication, 17*(3), 365–371.

Shome, R., & Hegde, R. S. (2002). Postcolonial approaches to communication: Charting the terrain, engaging the intersections. *Communication Theory, 12*(3), 249–270.

Smith, V. (1992). The documentary impulse in contemporary U.S. African-American film. In G. Dent (Ed.), *Black popular culture* (pp. 56–64). Seattle, WA: Bay Press.

Smith-Shomade, B. E. (2002). *Shaded lives: African-American women and television.* New Brunswick, NJ: Rutgers University Press.

Spigel, L. (1992). *Make room for TV: Television and the family ideal in postwar America.* Chicago: University of Chicago Press.

Spigel, L. (1995). From the dark ages to the golden age: Women's memories and television reruns. *Screen 36*(1), 16–33.

Spigel, L. (2004). Theorizing *The Bachelorette*: "Waves" of feminist media studies. *Signs: Journal of Women in Culture and Society, 30*(1), 1209–1221.

Staiger, J. (1995). *Bad women: Regulating sexuality in early American cinema.* Minneapolis: University of Minnesota Press.

Stamp, S. (2000). *Movie-struck girls: Women and motion picture culture after the nickelodeon.* Princeton, NJ: Princeton University Press.

Steinem, G. (1990). Sex, lies, and advertising. *Ms., 1*(1), 1–20.

Steiner, L. (1998). Stories of quitting: Why did women journalists leave the newsroom? *American Journalism, 15,* 89–116.

Steiner, L. (1999). *New York Times* coverage of Anita Hill as a female cipher. In M. Meyers (Ed.), *Mediated women: Representations in popular culture* (pp. 225–252). Cresskill, NJ: Hampton Press.

Straayer, C. (1996). *Deviant eyes, deviant bodies: Sexual re-orientations in film and video.* New York: Columbia University Press.

Studlar, G. (1996). *This mad masquerade: Stardom and masculinity in the Jazz Age.* New York: Columbia University Press.

Suárez Soto, M. (2000). *Women's voices on FIRE: Feminist international radio endeavour.* Austin, TX: Anomaly Press.

Tajima, R. E. (1989). Lotus blossoms don't bleed: Images of Asian women. In Asian Women United of California (Eds.), *Making waves: An anthology of writings by and about Asian American women* (pp. 308–317). Boston: Beacon Press.

Tasker, Y. (1993). *Spectacular bodies: Gender, genre and the action cinema.* London: Routledge.

Tasker, Y., & Negra, D. (2005). In focus: Postfeminism and contemporary media studies. *Cinema Journal, 44*(2), 107–110.

Tedesco, N. S. (1974). Patterns in prime time. *Journal of Communication, 24,* 119–124.

Thom, M. (1997). *Inside Ms.: 25 years of the magazine and the feminist movement.* New York: H. Holt.

Thompson, M. E., Anfossi Gómez, K., & Suárez Soto, M. (2005). Women's alternative radio and feminist interactive communications: Audience perceptions of feminist international radio endeavor (FIRE). *Feminist Media Studies, 5*(2), 215–136.

Torres, S. (1989). Melodrama, masculinity and the family: *thirtysomething* as therapy. *Camera Obscura, 19*, 86–106.

Trinh, T. M-H. (1989). *Woman, native, other: Writing postcoloniality and feminism.* Bloomington: Indiana University Press.

Tuchman, G. (1978). *Making news: A study in the construction of reality.* New York: Free Press.

Tuchman, G., Daniels, A., & Benét, J. (Eds.). (1978). *Hearth and home: Images of women in the mass media.* New York: Oxford University Press.

Valdivia, A. N. (1995). (Ed.). *Feminism, multiculturalism, and the media: Global diversities.* Thousand Oaks, CA: Sage.

Valdivia, A. N. (1996). Rosie goes to Hollywood: The politics of representation. *Review of Education/Pedagogy/Cultural Studies, 18*(2), 129–141.

Valdivia, A. N. (2000). *A Latina in the land of Hollywood and other essays on media culture.* Tucson: University of Arizona Press.

Valdivia, A. N. (2005). The location of the Spanish in Latinidad: Examples from Contemporary U.S. popular culture. *Letras Femeninas, 31*(1), 60–78.

Van Zoonen, L. (1991). Feminist perspectives on the media. In J. Curran & M. Gurevitch (Eds.), *Mass media and society* (pp. 33–54). London: Edward Arnold.

Van Zoonen, L. (1994). *Feminist media studies.* Thousand Oaks, CA: Sage.

Vargas, L. (2000). Genderizing Latino news: An analysis of a local newspaper's coverage of Latino current affairs. *Critical Studies in Media Communication, 17*(3), 261–293.

Vavrus, M. D. (1998). Working the Senate from the outside in: The mediated construction of a feminist political campaign. *Critical Studies in Mass Communication, 15*(3), 213–235.

Vavrus, M. D. (2000). Putting Ally on trial: Contesting postfeminism in popular culture. *Women's Studies in Communication, 23*(3), 413–428.

Vavrus, M. D. (2002). *Postfeminist news: Political women in media culture.* Albany: State University of New York Press.

Walkowitz, R. L. (1993). Reproducing reality: Murphy and illegitimate politics. In M. Garber, J. Matlock, & R. L. Walkowitz (Eds.), *Media spectacles* (pp. 40–56). New York: Routledge.

Wallace, M. (1988, June 4). Spike Lee and black women. *The Nation,* pp. 800–803.

Walters, S. D. (1995). *Material girls: Making sense of feminist cultural theory.* Berkeley: University of California Press.

Weiss, A. (1992). "A queer feeling when I look at you": Hollywood stars and lesbian spectatorship in the 1930s. In *Vampires and violets: Lesbians in the cinema* (pp. 30–50). London: Jonathan Cape.

White, M. (1992). *Tele-advising: Therapeutic discourse in American television.* Chapel Hill: University of North Carolina Press.

White, P. (1999). *Uninvited: Classical Hollywood cinema and lesbian representability.* Bloomington: Indiana University Press.

Wilcox, R. V. (1999). "There will never be a 'very special' *Buffy*": *Buffy* and the monsters of teen life. *Journal of Popular Film and Television, 27*(2), 16–23.

Williams, L. (1990). "Something else besides a mother": *Stella Dallas* and the maternal melodrama. In P. Erens (Ed.), *Issues in feminist film criticism* (pp. 137–162). Bloomington: Indiana University Press. (Reprinted from *Cinema Journal, 24*[1], 2–27, 1984)

Williamson, J. (1978). *Decoding advertisements: Ideology and meaning in advertisements.* London: Marion Boyars.

Winship, J. (1987). *Inside women's magazines.* London: Pandora.

Wolf, N. (1991). *The beauty myth: How images of beauty are used against women.* New York: Morrow.

Zhang, Y. (1996). *The city in modern Chinese literature and film: Configurations of space, time, and gender.* Stanford, CA: Stanford University Press.

16

GENDER, RACE, AND
MEDIA REPRESENTATION

◆ Dwight E. Brooks and Lisa P. Hébert

I n our consumption-oriented, mediated society, much of what comes to pass as important is based often on the stories produced and disseminated by media institutions. Much of what audiences know and care about is based on the images, symbols, and narratives in radio, television, film, music, and other media. How individuals construct their social identities, how they come to understand what it means to be male, female, black, white, Asian, Latino, Native American—even rural or urban—is shaped by commodified texts produced by media for audiences that are increasingly segmented by the social constructions of race and gender. Media, in short, are central to what ultimately come to represent our social realities.

While sex differences are rooted in biology, how we come to understand and perform gender is based on culture.[1] We view culture "as a process through which people circulate and struggle over the meanings of our social experiences, social relations, and therefore, our *selves*" (Byers & Dell, 1992, p. 191). Just as gender is a social construct through which a society defines what it means to be masculine or feminine, race also is a social construction. Race can no longer be seen as a biological category, and it has little basis in science or genetics. Identifiers such as hair and skin color serve as imperfect indicators of race. The racial categories we use to differentiate human difference have been created and changed to meet the dynamic social, political, and economic needs of our society. The premise that race and gender are social constructions underscores their centrality to the processes of human reality. Working from it compels us to understand the complex roles played by social institutions such as the media in shaping our increasingly gendered and racialized media culture. This chapter explores some of the ways mediated communication in the United States represents the social constructions of race and gender and ultimately contributes to our understanding of both, especially race.[2]

Although research on race, gender, and media traditionally has focused on underrepresented, subordinate groups such as women and minorities, this chapter discusses scholarship on media representations of both genders and various racial groups. Therefore, we examine media constructions of masculinity, femininity, so-called people of color, and even white people.[3] On the other hand, given the limitations of this chapter and the fact that media research on race has focused on African Americans, we devote greater attention to blacks but not at the exclusion of the emerging saliency of whiteness studies, which acknowledge whiteness as a social category and seek to expose and explain white privilege.[4]

Our theoretical and conceptual orientation encompasses research that is commonly referred to as "critical/cultural studies." Numerous theoretical approaches have been used to examine issues of race, gender, and media, but we contend that critical/cultural studies represent the most salient contemporary thinking on media and culture. More important, unlike most social and behavioral scientific research, most critical and cultural approaches to media studies work from the premise that Western industrialized societies are stratified by hierarchies of race, gender, and class that structure our social experience. Moreover, cultural studies utilizes interdisciplinary approaches necessary for understanding both the media's role in the production and reproduction of inequity and for the development of more equitable

and democratic societies. Cultural studies scholars have devoted considerable attention to studies of media audiences, institutions, technologies, and texts. This chapter privileges textual analyses of media that explicate power relationships and the construction of meaning about gender and race and their intersections (Byers & Dell, 1992). In addition, we draw considerably from research employing various feminist frameworks. Generally, our critical review of literature from the past two decades demonstrates the disruption of essentialist constructions of gender, race, and sexual identities.

◆ Black Feminist Perspectives and Media Representations of Black Women

A feminist critique is rooted in the struggle to end sexist oppression. We employ feminism as a multidisciplinary approach to social analysis that emphasizes gender as a major structuring component of power relations in society. We believe media are crucial in the construction and dissemination of gender ideologies and, thus, in gender socialization. We acknowledge feminism and feminist media studies' tendency to privilege gender and white women, in particular, over other social categories of experience, such as race and class (hooks, 1990; Dines, 1995; Dines & Humez, 2003). Black feminist scholars have acknowledged the neglect which women of color, specifically black women, have experienced through their selective inclusion in the writings of feminist cultural analysis (hooks, 1990; Bobo & Seiter, 1991; Valdivia, 1995). Black feminism positions itself as critical social theory (Hill Collins, 2004) and is not a set of abstract principles but of ideas that come directly from the historical and contemporary experience of black women. It is from this perspective that we begin our discussion of black female representation in the media.

Much contemporary academic writing has criticized mainstream media for their negative depictions of African American women (Bobo, 1995; Hill Collins, 2000, 2004; hooks, 1992; Lubiano, 1992; Manatu, 2003; McPhail, 1996; Perry, 2003). Challenging media portrayals of black women as mammies, matriarchs, jezebels, welfare mothers, and tragic mulattoes is a core theme in black feminist thought. Author bell hooks (1992) contends that black female representation in the media "determines how blackness and people are seen and how other groups will respond to us based on their relation to these constructed images" (p. 5). Hudson (1998) and Hill Collins (2000, 2004) both advance the notion that media images of black women result from dominant racial, gender, and class ideologies. Furthering hooks's discussion of representation, Hudson (1998) argues that "these stereotypes simultaneously reflect and distort both the ways in which black women view themselves (individually and collectively) and the ways in which they are viewed by others" (p. 249). The study of black female representation is informed by whiteness studies and, according to Dyer (1997), "the only way to see the structures, tropes, and perceptual habits of whiteness, is when nonwhite (and above all, black) people are also represented" (p. 13).

Scholars have studied black female representation in a variety of media contexts. Meyers (2004) used discourse analysis to examine the representation of violence against African American women in local TV news coverage during "Freaknik," a spring break ritual held in Atlanta, Georgia, throughout the 1990s. Her study concluded that the news "portrayed most of its victims as stereotypic Jezebels whose lewd behavior provoked assault" (p. 95). Orbe and Strother's (1996) semiotic analysis of the biracial title character in *Queen,* Alex Haley's miniseries, demonstrated how

Queen fell in line with "traditional stereotyping of other bi-ethnic characters as beautiful, yet threatening, inherently problematic, and destined for insanity" (p. 117). Larson's (1994) study of black women on the soap opera *All My Children* found the show consistently embraced the matriarch stereotype. In fact, the image of the black woman as oversexed fantasy object, dominating matriarch, and nonthreatening, desexualized mammy figure remains the most persistent in the media (Edwards, 1993).

Black feminist thought also challenges the way some media outlets run by black men engage in misogynistic depictions of black women. Burks (1996) notices the saliency of hooks's phrase, "white supremacist capitalist patriarchy," in many black independent films. She explains that "black independent cinema is not necessarily free of the dominant white, male, heterosexual hegemony that has succeeded, at one point or another, in colonizing us all" (p. 26). Several cultural critics have focused their studies of black female representation on majority-produced and directed Hollywood films (Bobo, 1995; Bogle, 2001; Holtzman, 2000; hooks, 1992, 1994). Many other media scholars have focused their analyses on the way black filmmakers depict black femininity, as part of a trend that Burks (1996) argues leaves mainstream (white) Hollywood producers free to construct the black female image in any way they like and to reach a larger viewing audience in the process.

Black female scholars Wallace (1990) and hooks (1993) both have written extensively on the work of black writer/director Spike Lee's portrayal of black women. Hooks contends that while Lee is

uncompromising in his commitment to create images of black males that challenge perceptions and bring issues of racism to the screen, he conforms to the status quo when it comes to images of females. Sexism is the familiar construction that links his films to all the other Hollywood dramas folks see. (p. 14)

McPhail (1996) continues hooks's argument and argues that Lee's films "subscribe to essentialist conceptions of race and gender that reify the same ideological and epistemological assumptions that undermine both the representation of race and gender in mainstream media" (p. 127). According to our (Brooks & Hébert, 2004) study of Lee's *Bamboozled*, he creates female characters who become defined by the men in their lives. We claim that although his films fight to challenge racist frameworks within the mass media and society, they simultaneously perpetuate sexist norms as they relate to black womanhood. Although Spike Lee is not the only black male filmmaker who perpetuates negative representations of women, he has garnered the most attention by cultural critics. This is an area of study that requires additional work, as African American filmmakers are moving from the margins of independent films to the center of multibillion dollar studios and networks that are run by heterosexual white males, thus potentially contributing to black women's oppression.

Prime time television has tended to confine black female roles to white models of "good wives" and to black matriarchal stereotypes. Byers and Dell's (1992) analysis of characterization in the CBS workplace ensemble *Frank's Place* demonstrates that it was no exception to this trend. Their study provides an excellent example of a feminist textual analysis of the intersection of race and gender from a cultural studies perspective. Despite drawing inspiration from the situation comedy's association with the feminine, the series worked from a distinctly masculine perspective. Although *Frank's Place* presented a fairly wide range of representations of African American men, it provided a much narrower range of representations of African American women. The attention it gave to inequities in skin color and class was rarely afforded to its female characters. Instead, feminine beauty was related to light skin, straight hair, thinness, relative youthfulness, and middle-class status. Despite the show's conscious attempt to illustrate the social ramifications of the

representation of racial difference, it was oblivious to the ways gender and class inflect race (Byers & Dell, 1992).

Much academic writing has focused on historically situated negative portrayals of black women, and the most recent theoretical trend in black feminist media scholarship is the representation of black female sexuality in the media (Hill Collins, 2004; Manatu, 2003; Perry, 2003). Sexuality is not discussed in reference to sexual orientation but to how popular culture has commodified the black female body as hypersexed. Some theorists (Guerrero, 1993; Iverem, 1997; Manatu, 2003) contend that black women are portrayed only as sexual beings and not as romantic characters, as indicated by Halle Berry's Oscar-winning performance in *Monster's Ball*. It has been argued that she played an oversexed jezebel and tragic mulatto at the same time (Hill Collins). Others assert that the habitual construction of a subversive woman's sexual image may come to define women culturally (Kennedy, 1992; Nelson, 1997).

While the black jezebel mythos is not new to film and television studies, it has found a home in music videos. Much as black music of the 1950s was repurposed by the industry as a new category called rock and roll, and made its way into suburban white homes, popular culture today "draws heavily from the cultural production and styles of urban Black youth" (Hill Collins, 2004, p. 122). It is within this black cultural production, reworked through the prism of social class, "that the sexualized Black woman has become an icon in hip-hop culture" (p. 126). A theory of the body and of how black women are objectified as sexual commodities fuels this debate that has become popular in academic circles. Within this context three primary research interests have emerged: the objectification of black women's bodies for the voyeuristic pleasure of men (Hill Collins, 2004; hooks, 1994; Jones, 1994); the impact of sexual representation and ideal Westernized body images on young black females (Perry, 2003); and black female sexuality as a symbol of agency (Gaunt, 1995; Hill Collins, 2004; Rose, 1994).

The objectification of black women's bodies in hip-hop music videos, according to Jones (1994), is particularly disturbing because these videos are produced primarily by black men. Edwards (1993) argues that music videos play into male sexual fantasies and that the notion of the black woman as a sex object or whore is always placed in opposition to the image of black woman as mammy. Hooks (1994) warns that while feminist critiques of the misogyny in rap music must continue and that black males should be held accountable for their sexism, the critique must be contextualized. She continues:

> Without a doubt black males, young and old, must be held politically accountable for their sexism. Yet this critique must always be contextualized or we risk making it appear that the problems of misogyny, sexism, and all the behaviors this thinking supports and condones, including rape, male violence against women, is a black male thing. (p. 116)

Most academic writing on this subject focuses on black men's portrayals of black women, but we argue that the music videos of hip-hop artists who are not black follow a similar misogynist formula in which scantily clad women surround the artist in a poolside, hot tub, or nightclub setting. Latino artists Fat Joe and Geraldo (otherwise known as Rico Suave), and white artists Justin Timberlake and Vanilla Ice all fall into this category, substituting Latina and white women's bodies for black ones. This discussion becomes more salient as white-centered visual music outlets such as MTV and VH-1 dedicate more programming time to hip-hop culture and create late night programs designed to show so-called uncut and uncensored videos that make clear references to the culture of strip clubs and pornography. As Fiske (1996) contends, "Whiteness is particularly adept at

sexualizing racial difference, and thus constructing its others as sites of savage sexuality" (p. 45).

In line with theories of the body that say the mass media promotes images of "an ideal body type," Perry (2003) explains that the messages these videos send to young women about their bodies are harmful. She argues that "the beauty ideal for black women presented in these videos is as impossible to achieve as the waif-thin models in *Vogue* magazine are for White women" (p. 138). In addition to the black body ideal of large breasts, thin waist and round buttocks presented in videos, many of the black women featured depict a Westernized beauty ideal of lighter skin, long hair, and blue or green eyes. Edwards (1993) takes the concept of a beauty ideal one step further and contends that the black women featured in music videos exemplify physical characteristics of the tragic mulatto. According to hooks (1994), racist and sexist thinking informs the way color-caste hierarchies affect black females. She contends:

> Light skin and long, straight hair continue to be traits that define a female as beautiful and desirable in the racist white imagination and in the colonized black mindset. . . . Stereotypically portrayed as embodying a passionate, sensual eroticism, as well as a subordinate feminine nature, the biracial woman has been and remains the standard other black females are measured against." (p. 179)

The other side of this discussion about negative sexual imagery concerns black female sexual agency. Hill Collins (2004) notes that many African American women rappers "identify female sexuality as part of women's freedom and independence" (p. 127), maintaining that being sexually open does not make a woman a tramp or a "ho," which is a common term placed upon women in hip-hop. Rose (1994) demands a more multifaceted analysis of black women's identity and sexuality within rap music, while Perry (2003) asserts that any power granted to female rappers based upon their being labeled attractive in conventional ways limits the feminist potential of their music.

MULTICULTURAL FEMINIST PERSPECTIVES AND MEDIA REPRESENTATIONS OF ASIAN, LATINA, AND NATIVE AMERICAN WOMEN

Acknowledging Valdivia's (1995) assertion that feminist work has focused on white women as ethnic and race studies have focused primarily on African Americans, we seek to include other "women of color" in our analysis of stereotypic female representation. As we stated in the beginning of this chapter, our analysis relies primarily on black women, as that is where the majority of scholarship on race, gender, and the media focuses. However, we agree with Hill Collins (2004) that many of the arguments made previously about black women also apply to women from India, Latin America, Puerto Rico, and Asia, "albeit through the historical specificity of their distinctive group histories" (p. 12).

Asian women and Latinas are often portrayed in the media as the exotic, sexualized "other as well. According to Tajima (1989), "Asian women in film are either passive figures who exist to serve men as love interests for White men (lotus blossom) or as a partner in crime of men of their own kind (dragon ladies)" (p. 309). Pursuing this lotus blossom/dragon lady dichotomy, Hagedorn (1997) argues that most Hollywood movies either trivialize or exoticize Asian women: "If we are 'good,' we are childlike, submissive, silent and eager for sex. And if we are not silent, suffering doormats, we are demonized . . . cunning, deceitful, sexual provocateurs" (pp. 33–34).

Much academic writing surrounding Asian female representation in the media is steeped in postcolonial theory and Orientalist discourse, both of which are concerned with otherness. The global other, in media terms, is always paired with the West as its binary companion (Furguson, 1998). Shome (1996) explains that when whiteness is comfortable in its hegemony, it constructs the other as strange or different and itself as the norm. Drawing from Said's study of Orientalism, Heung (1995) says, "The power of the colonizer is fundamentally constituted by the power to speak for and to represent" (p. 83). Furthering the discussion of an East/West binary, the West is portrayed in the media as active and masculine while the East is passive and feminine (Wilkinson, 1990).

Though the number of female Asian characters represented in the media, especially television, is miniscule, the way they are portrayed in the media is crucial because stereotypes of underrepresented people produce socialization in audiences that unconsciously take this misinformation as truth (Heung, 1995; Holtzman, 2000). Thus, the portrayal of Ling Woo, Lucy Liu's character in the television series *Ally McBeal*, garnered much scholarly attention. Although Woo breaks the submissive china doll stereotype, she is the epitome of the stereotypical dragon lady when she growls like an animal or enters a scene to music associated with the Wicked Witch of the West in *The Wizard of Oz* (Sun, 2003). She is knowledgeable in the art of sexual pleasure, which is unknown to her Westernized law firm colleagues, with the exception of Richard Fish, her white boyfriend who experiences it first hand. Patton (2001) explains that the Woo character is particularly detrimental to Asian and Asian American women not because the oversexed seductress reifies existing stereotypes, but because "she is the only representative of Asian women on television (besides news anchors and reporters), leaving no one else to counteract this prominent mediated stereotype" (p. 252).

While it is difficult to propose more work on Asian female representation when the number of females in the media are sparse, an obvious place to begin would be to look into production studies to find out what producers are looking for in casting an Asian female. Can she not play a detective or attorney on one of the three *Law and Order* series? Can she be a strong and funny mom on an Asian American sitcom? And is she just as discontented with her suburban life as white women such that she could be considered for *Desperate Housewives?* That popular program has a Latina and has added an African American character for the fall 2006 season, but it features no Asian women as of this writing.

Although most of the academic literature regarding black and Asian media representation focuses on historically situated stereotypes, this does not hold true for Latinas. While there has been some reference to Latinas being portrayed as exotic seductresses (Holtzman, 2000), as tacky and overly emotional (Valdivia, 1995), and as the hypersexualized spitfire (Molina Guzmán & Valdivia, 2004), the majority of literature on Latino/a representation has focused on men. Jennifer Lopez has made her mark in Hollywood, but her films have both reified stereotypes of Latinas as domestic workers (*Maid in America*, 2003) and broken them when she has played roles that are not ethnically marked (*The Wedding Planner*, 2001; *Gigli*, 2003; *Monster in Law*, 2005). In these roles, however, Lopez is always paired with a white male love interest and, because she rarely plays characters true to her ethnicity (except of course when she played a maid, a role that emphasized it), she becomes an assimilated character who does nothing to negate Latina stereotypes. Molina Guzmán and Valdivia assert that Lopez is most often allowed to perform whiteness, which renders her seemingly raceless and cultureless.

García Canclini (1995) contends that "the contemporary experience of Latinas, which also holds true of other populations shaped by colonialism, globalization, and transnationalism, is informed by the complex dynamics of hybridity as a cultural practice and expression" (as cited in Molina Guzmán & Valdivia, 2004, p. 214).

Hill Collins (2004) calls this color-blind racism and explains that the significance attached to skin color, especially for women, is changing. She argues that "in response to the growing visibility of biracial, multiracial, Latino, Asian, and racially ambiguous Americans, skin color no longer serves as a definitive mark of racial categorization" (p. 194). This notion of hybridity or Latinidad, defined as the state and process of being, becoming, or appearing Latino/a (Martinez, 2004; Molina Guzmán & Valdivia, 2004; Rojas, 2004), is gaining scholarly attention. However, as a social construct it lends itself to an essentialist group identity, instead of acknowledging difference between Dominicans, Mexicans, Cubans, and Puerto Ricans, all of whom epitomize Latinidad (Estill, 2000).

Latinas are also finding a place within the music world and, as with black women, their sex appeal is played up heavily in their music videos. Shakira and Jennifer Lopez are some of the most visible who have enjoyed music/acting crossover fame. One of the most common tropes surrounding these and other mediated Latina hypersexualized bodies within popular culture is tropicalism (Aparicio & Chavez-Silverman, 1997; Martinez, 2004). According to Molina Guzmán & Valdivia (2004), bright colors, rhythmic music, and olive skin fall under the trope of tropicalism, and sexuality plays a central role. Dominant representations of Latinas in music videos place emphasis on the breasts, hips, and buttocks (Gilman, 1985; Molina Guzmán & Valdivia, 2004; Negrón-Muntaner, 1991). Desmond (1997) calls the Latina body "an urbane corporeal site with sexualized overdetermination" (as cited in Molina Guzmán & Valdivia, 2004, p. 211).

While not enough academic research is conducted on Native American media representation, we would be remiss if we did not mention two studies that examine how Native American women are portrayed. Portman and Herring (2001) discuss the "Pocahontas paradox," a historical movement that persists in romanticizing and vilifying Native American women. They argue that Native American women are viewed in the media as either strong and powerful or beautiful, exotic, and lustful and that both images have merged together into one representation through the stereotype of Pocahontas. While Ono and Buescher's (2001) study on Pocahontas examines the commodification of products and cultural discourses surrounding the popular Disney film, they also assert that new meanings have been ascribed to the animated figure, thus recasting the Native American woman in a Western, capitalist frame (p. 25). Ultimately, Pocahantas is no more than a sexualized Native American Barbie. Both Portman and Herring (2001) and Ono and Buescher (2001) agree that the Pocahontas mythos is particularly harmful to Native women because of the way this historical figure has been exoticized by media discourses that emphasize her relationship with her white lover, John Smith.

MEDIA REPRESENTATIONS OF RACIALIZED MASCULINITIES

Research on gender and media traditionally has focused on questions about women (and has been conducted primarily by women). In fact, as noted above, the focus on gender in media studies has come mainly from feminists. However, in recent decades the study of gender has expanded to include studies on men and masculinities (Connell, Hearn, & Kimmel, 2005). Feminist scholarship also has produced a proliferation of whiteness studies that include increased research on white masculinity and, to a lesser extent, white womanhood. This work interrogates gender identities and performances while exploring how masculine forms relate to patriarchal systems. Masculinity is defined broadly as "the set of images, values, interests, and activities held important to a successful achievement of male adulthood" (Jeffords, 1989, quoted in Ashcraft & Flores, 2000, p. 3). We agree with calls to refer to these gender roles as

"masculinities" to reinforce the notion that ideals of manhood vary by race and class across time and cultural contexts (Dines & Humez, 2003, p. 733). Cultural studies' focus on white masculinity as the invisible norm, and (to a lesser extent) on black men and black masculinity as deviant, works to reinforce the conception that black is the trope for race (Nakayama, 1994). Yet another intellectual movement inadvertently may have contributed to this notion.

CRITICAL RACE THEORY AND MEDIA REPRESENTATIONS OF BLACK MEN AND BLACK MASCULINITIES

Critical Race Theory (CRT) emerged from critical legal studies in the 1970s as an intellectual response to the slow pace of racial reform in the United States. CRT places race at the center of critical analysis and traces its origins to the legal scholarship of Derrick Bell, Richard Delgado, and Kimberlé Crenshaw, who challenged the philosophical tradition of the liberal civil rights color-blind approach to social justice. A central premise of CRT is that racism is an ordinary fact of American life. Although CRT occasionally probes beyond the black-white binary of race, it privileges African American experiences. Much of the critical edge in critical race studies is provided by a combination of legal, feminist, multicultural, social, political, economic, and philosophical perspectives (Delgado & Stefancic, 1999). Despite CRT's focus on legal studies and policy, we would expect that the field's search for new ways of thinking about race, the nation's most enduring social problem, eventually would include media. Unfortunately, media studies scholars have not consciously employed CRT and few critical race theorists have devoted detailed attention to media institutions and their representations.[5]

Herman Gray's (1995, 1989) work shares many of the assumptions of CRT. His ideological analysis (1986) of black male representations in prime time situation comedies argues that television's idealization of racial harmony, affluence, and individual mobility is not within the grasp of millions of African Americans. In the 1983–84 television season, four programs— *Benson, Webster, Different Strokes* and *The Jeffersons,* provided an assimilationist view of racial interaction that emphasized individualism, racial invisibility, and perhaps most important, middle-class success. The ideological function of these representations worked to support the contention that in the context of current political, economic and cultural arrangements, all individuals— regardless of color (and gender)—can achieve the American dream. On the other hand, such representations subsist in the absence of significant change in the overall status of African Americans in the United States (Gray, 1986).

In an article on another genre of prime time television, the so-called real life crime series (formerly labeled as "reality" crime shows), Hogrobrooks (1993) argues that this type of programming contributed to the "denigration and dehumanization" of African American males (p. 165). Hogrobrooks quotes a news director who acknowledged that "young black men—the unwitting 'media darlings' of the explosion of America's 'real-life, prime time crime' programs—are, in reality, victims of character assassination by a greedy television industry, hungry for higher and higher ratings" (p. 167).

MacDonald's (2004) analysis of depictions of homicide detectives in television and film represents the more recent focus in media studies on masculinity and race. Specifically, she illustrates the ways in which both the police drama *Homicide: Life on the Street* and Spike Lee's film *Clockers* highlight the struggle of various men to come to terms with their own masculinities. MacDonald argues that these texts offer "new potential" for men of different races to reject traditional stereotypes of masculinity (p. 221). She commends *Homicide*'s two black male detectives for offering a cultural construction of black masculinity that is neither "tokenistic nor predictable" (p. 223). Conversely, *Clockers* demonstrates the failure of the white male homicide detective (Rocco Klein) to develop an in-depth understanding of African American life mainly because of his insistence on performing as a tough cop who resorts to "a desperate use of physical violence, racism, and tough talk in order to reassure himself of his unshakable masculinity" (p. 225). Nevertheless, MacDonald claims that collectively these texts teach viewers that masculinity is a complex idea that coexists with various other complex ideas such as class and race and that these complexities are increasing being portrayed in media culture.

Byers and Dell (1992), in their study of representations of masculinity and femininity across numerous characters in *Frank's Place,* argue that its most important contribution to television programming in particular and American culture in general was the construction of new ways of representing African Americans. Byers and Dell contextualize these constructions of masculinity of race in *Frank's Place* in the historical representations of African American males, where racial and gender hierarchies function to reinforce each other. Such imagery can be traced to slavery when black manhood could not be realized or maintained because of the slave's inability to protect black women in the same fashion that "convention dictated that inviolability of the body of the White woman" (Carby, 1987, quoted in Byers & Dell, p. 196). Further, the historical images of the shuffling Uncle Tom, the animalistic savage (positioned as a threat to white women), and the childlike Sambo function to exclude black men from the category of "true men."

Unlike the "new black male" constructed in Gray's analysis of 1980s sitcoms, *Frank's Place* made the struggle over race and gender highly visible. The lead character, Frank Parish, propelled the series to simultaneously confront African American male stereotypes and to participate in the construction of the "new man" (Byers & Dell,

1992, p. 196). Despite the absence of the Uncle Tom stereotype, Frank reinforces the caricature of the ignorant, ineffectual Sambo, while his education and drive challenge this stereotype. Frank's character also invoked the image of the sexually aggressive black male without representing a threat to white women. Perhaps most important, by displaying "feminine" attributes such as nonaggressive behavior and sensitivity, Frank—like many white male characters— challenged essentialist, macho notions of masculinity. Ultimately, Frank functioned as a site for the interplay of characteristics traditionally defined as masculine and feminine and offered a way to envision a new black masculinity. In this sense, *Frank's Place*— and to a lesser extent, *Homicide: Life on the Street*—appears to be exceptions to most media portrayals of black masculinity.

Dines (2003) focuses on the image of the black man as a sexual spoiler of white womanhood in cartoons in *Hustler*—a hard-core porn magazine. She locates such depictions within "a much larger regime of racial representation, beginning with *The Birth of a Nation* and continuing with Willie Horton, which makes the black man's supposed sexual misconduct a metaphor for the inferior nature of the black 'race' as a whole" (Dines, p. 456). This racist ideology claims that failure to contain black masculinity will result in a collapse of the economic and social fabric of white society. Specifically, Dines draws on the work of Kobena Mercer in analyzing how the depiction of black men as being obsessed with the size of their penises is one example of how the dominant regime of racial representation constructs blacks as "having bodies but not minds" (Mercer, 1994; quoted in Dines, p. 456). *Hustler* cartoons construct a world populated by white working-class hustlers and losers, where black men possess two status symbols that white men lack, big penises and money.

However, Dines maintains that it is not white men as a group who are being ridiculed, just lower-working-class white men—a class few whites see themselves as belonging to, regardless of their income:

The lower-class, sexually impotent White man in *Hustler* cartoons is, thus, not an object of identification, but rather of ridicule, and serves as a pitiful reminder of what could happen if White men fail to assert their masculinity and allow the black man to roam the streets and bedrooms of White society. (Dines, 2003, p. 459)

Dines points out that although racial codings of masculinity may shift depending on socioeconomic conditions, black masculinity continues to be constructed as deviant.

Orbe's (1998) semiotic analysis of black masculinity on MTV's *The Real World* focuses on the imagery and signification processes surrounding three black males featured throughout the six seasons in the so-called reality (unscripted) series. The images of the three black men work to signify all black men as inherently angry, potentially violent, and sexually aggressive. Orbe argues that when such images are presented as real life they function to reinforce the justification of a general societal fear of black men (p. 35). He also argues that what is notably absent from the six seasons are any considerable representations that "signify Black masculinity in a positive, healthy, or productive manner" (p. 45). Equally important, the mediated images of black masculinity on *The Real World* represent a powerful source of influence because they are not presented as mediated but as real life images captured on camera.

Martin and Yep (2004) demonstrate that black masculine performances in the media are not restricted to black males. Drawing on the work of Orbe and others that locate black masculine identities in angry, physically threatening, and sexually aggressive behaviors and discourses, Martin and Yep utilize a whiteness framework to examine how the white rap artist Eminem has been presented in the media. Whiteness refers to the "everyday invisible, subtle cultural, and social practices, ideas, and codes that discursively secure the power and privilege of White people, but that strategically remain unmarked, unnamed, and untapped in contemporary society" (Shome, 1996, quoted in Martin & Yep, p. 230). One prominent feature of whiteness is that it is universal, which makes it seemingly devoid of race and culture. Therefore, whiteness studies also pursue strategies for both marking and naming whiteness and exposing white privilege (Martin & Yep, 2004, p. 230). Eminem exploits one privilege of whiteness—the ability to appropriate aspects of other cultures—in this case, black masculinity. And as Martin and Yep note, although black masculinity is not an essential, unified, or monolithic category, in hip-hop culture (which includes rap music) it represents anger, violence, and sexual aggressiveness. Eminem manifests these features in both his lyrics and mainstream media representations.

MEDIA REPRESENTATIONS OF ASIAN AND NATIVE AMERICAN MEN

Research on media constructions of race, men, and masculinity exemplify the black-white binary of racial discourse prevalent in contemporary discourse in the United States. Unfortunately, few studies examine Latino or Native American males in the media. Thus, we know considerably less about constructions of masculine identities within groups of men who are not white or African American. One exception to this trend comes from research on Asian American masculinity. Historically, portrayals of Asian and Asian American men (seldom is any distinction made) in mainstream American media have been restricted to motion pictures. These films represented men of Asian descent as threatening foreigners (Fu Manchu), Americanized detectives (Charlie Chan), laborers and laundry men, and most recently, as (corrupt) businessmen and martial artists. Most often these men are not seen as possessing traditionally dominant masculine characteristics—most notably sexual prowess. Sexuality, like race and gender, is a socially

constructed category of power, and the desexualized or effeminate Asian male stereotype works in conjunction with depictions of Asian women as ultrafeminine sexual objects used by white men to emasculate Asian men. Consequently, Asian American men are redefined as an angry threat to American culture (Feng, 1996). However, the ideological and power relations embedded in the intersections of race, gender, and sexuality warrant greater attention in cultural studies.

Nakayama (1994) addresses this void by examining Asian and white masculinity in the Hollywood film *Showdown in Little Tokyo*. He identifies ways that white heterosexual masculinity is recentered and argues for the importance of spatial relations in constructing identities. The vulnerability of white heterosexual masculinity is apparent in the wake of the emasculating of the United States in Vietnam and its inevitable multicultural future. Nakayama demonstrates how racial and homoerotic tensions are used to "fuel the fire that breathes life into the cultural fiction of white heterosexual masculinity" (p. 165).

One additional study, Locke's (1998) analysis of comedic representations of Judge Lance Ito from episodes of *The Tonight Show,* disrupts the black-white duality of race so common to critical media/cultural studies. Locke uses John Fiske's notion of racial recoding to read Ito's inscrutability as a racial signifier consistent with the legacy of coding Asians in popular culture as people who pose a threat and who keep their motives and means hidden. Locke reads another skit on *The Tonight Show* that ridiculed Ito's child as exposing "the threat of a racially compromised future: the daughter as the freakish miscegenated offspring of Ito and his white American wife" (p. 252). Even as Locke's analysis points to the show's stereotypical visual coding of blackness as an explanation of how the show "desires race" (p. 246), he compels scholars to consider such important issues as how binary racial discourses contribute to what constitutes the racial, how media texts code a variety of racial groups, and ultimately, how these codes work together within a larger sphere of racial discourse.

Scholarship on representations of Native American males is scarce, but the novel *The Indian in the Cupboard* and the film of the same name have received some scholarly attention about Native American masculinity and paternalism. Taylor (2000) argues that "the image of the Indian as the savage, a paternalistic role for the White protagonist, and an auxiliary role for the Indian as the faithful sidekick" all reify existing stereotypes about Native American males. While Sanchez and Stuckey (2000) agree that the movie was an improvement over the book, they disagree with Taylor and assert that *The Indian in the Cupboard* challenges hegemonic codes and demeaning stereotypes. In line with Hall's encoding/decoding model, Sanchez and Stuckey provide a negotiated reading of the film and argue that the casting of Native American actors and consultants both lends authenticity and provides a resolution to "the tension between paternalism and interdependence" (p. 87).

MEDIA REPRESENTATIONS OF WHITE MASCULINITY

As the previous discussion illustrates, the fundamental delineation in media research is between the dominant, normative, white, heterosexual, and middle-class masculinity and subordinated masculinities. The crisis in white masculinity is perhaps the most overriding feature of constructions of dominant masculinity, and the most common response to this crisis is violent behavior by white men (Katz, 2003).

Shome (2000) uncovers the way in which the crisis of white masculinity is marked and negotiated in contemporary film. One dominant theme—that of the presidency or the U.S. government in crisis—evident in such films as *Air Force One, Murder at 1600, Independence Day, Dave,* and *The Pelican*

Brief, all focus on an "ultimate site" of white masculinity where whiteness, masculinity, and nationhood converge (Shome, p. 369). In these films, the subtheme is that of "one bad white guy" who is outed by a "good white guy" who "saves, salvages, and restores the Presidency and the 'people'" (p. 369). Another inflection of this theme occurs when whiteness is conflated with nationhood and is marked as being threatened and tortured by aliens (e.g., *Air Force One* and *Independence Day*). The common Hollywood strategy of depicting others (as "aliens") is significant in this context because "White nationalized masculinity, as symbolized by the Presidency is first represented as being 'oppressed' and weakened (by aliens) and through great [violent] struggles—that tend to constitute the major plot action of these films—it recuperates and salvages itself" (p. 370).

Ashcraft and Flores (2000) also examine Hollywood film for ways in which masculine performances offer identity to middle-class heterosexual white men. Specifically, they analyze discursive performances in two films—*Fight Club* and *In the Company of Men*—that provide identity politics to "white/collar men" (p. 1). Each film's discourse laments the imminent breakdown of the corporate man, "over-civilized and emasculated by allied obligations to work and women" (p. 2). To restore the beleaguered corporate man, the films (re)turn to "civilized/primitive" masculinity wherein the hardened white man finds healing in wounds (p. 2). Ultimately, this tough guy obscures the race and class hierarchy in which it resides by overtly appealing to gender division.

As much of the research discussed above indicates, both whiteness and hegemonic (white) masculinity do not appear to be cultural/historical categories, thus rendering invisible the privileged position from which (white) men in general are able to articulate their interests to the exclusion of interests of women, men and women of color, and children (Hanke, 1992, p. 186). Masculinity—whether black or white—must be uprooted from essentialist thinking that understands gender—as well as race, class and many other constructs of personal and collective identity—not as biologically determined or subject to universal laws of science or nature, but as products of discourse, performance, and power.

The research discussed above utilizes a variety of methodological and theoretical frameworks to examine intersections of race, gender, and media. This chapter has focused on one of the more prominent perspectives, social constructivism, in which media texts, images, and narratives are seen as intimately connected with broader social relations of domination and subordination. Although studies of representation fuel the majority of this chapter, we would be remiss if we did not include a brief discussion on audience reception studies.

◆ Audience Studies

The 1980s saw an emerging interest in reader/audience studies especially relating to women's genres such as romance, melodrama, and soap opera. Some of the works were Ang's (1985) *Watching Dallas,* Radway's (1984) *Reading the Romance,* and Hobson's (1982) *Crossroads: The Drama of a Soap Opera.* In fact, McRobbie (1991) was one of the first scholars to look at how young girls negotiate meaning through magazines. While they did not specifically look at gender, cultural critics John Fiske (1987) and David Morley (1980) have conducted several studies on audiences and television. On a similar note, Rockler's (2002) study of both African American and European American interpretations of the comic strips *Jump Start* and *The Boondocks* revealed blacks' oppositional readings of the comics through the terministic screen of race cognizance. In contrast to African American readings that underscored the relevance of racial politics and oppression, white's interpretations were produced through the terministic screen of whiteness that deflected attention

from racial power structures that privilege white people (Rockler, 2002, p. 416).

Many cultural critics (Bobo, 1995; Clifford, 1983; hooks, 1990) have called attention to the "unequal power relations inherent in the ethnographic enterprise and to the 'objectification' of the subject in ethnographic discourse" (Bobo & Seiter, 1991, p. 290). Thus they argue "the notions of gender difference deriving from ethnographic work with all-white samples in current circulation are reified and ethnocentric," leaving voices of women of color "unheard, unstudied, untheorized" (p. 291). While some authors did devote some time to studies of ethnic media audiences (Katz & Liebes, 1985) leading this call to include women of color in audience research was Jackie Bobo (1988, 1995) and her central work, *The Color Purple: Black Women as Cultural Readers,* which first appeared as a single study and later became a book. In this book, Bobo (1995) studied how black women negotiate meaning in two film texts, *The Color Purple* by white male filmmaker Steven Spielberg, and *Daughters of the Dust* by female filmmaker Julie Dash. Bobo discovered that despite *The Color Purple's* patriarchal nature, black women found ways to empower themselves through negotiated readings of its text.

Lee and Cho (2003) looked at Korean soap opera fans in the United States and examined why they preferred the Korean to the American variety. The authors concluded that, despite arguments of cultural imperialism, third world audiences like to watch their own cultural products (Lee & Cho). Two recent audience studies on women of color may indicate a resurging interest in this line of scholarship. Oppenheimer, Adams-Price, Goodman, Codling, and Coker (2003) studied how men and women perceived strong female characters on television, noting that women were more accepting than men of the powerful female characters and that African Americans related better to the strong characters than did whites. Rojas (2004) argues there is a lack of information on how Latinas consume popular culture and how they interact and respond to Spanish-language media (p. 125). She addresses the point echoed by Latino/a scholars (Desipio, 1998; Rodriguez, 1999) that little or no attention has been paid to Latino audiences as subjects of academic research. She examined how immigrant and nonimmigrant Latinas from Austin, Texas "evaluate and negotiate the content and representations presented in Univision and Telemundo, the two largest Hispanic networks in the United States" (Rojas, 2004, p. 125). As the U.S. population includes more native Spanish speakers, this type of bilingual/bicultural research becomes more significant to communication studies. Although these studies vary considerably by topic, collectively they point to some of the important ways race and gender identities influence struggles over meaning. Further, while the audience studies cited above have provided a strong foundation for future research, women—and especially men—from nonwhite races still remain sorely underrepresented in ethnographic audience studies.

◆ Directions for Research

With the world becoming more multicultural/racial, there must be further study regarding the malleability of ethnicity depending upon the role being played. As Hill Collins (2004) points out in her discussion of Halle Berry, blackness can be worked in many ways. As noted in the case of Jennifer Lopez, skin color or ethnicity is not a marker of racial categorization. Actresses like Jennifer Beals, who is black, usually play characters that lack racial marking, although she currently portrays a black woman in the Showtime series, *The L Word*. This trend has continued into movies like the remake of *Guess Who's Coming to Dinner* (1967), titled *Guess Who* (2005), which starred Zoe Saldana, a Latina who plays a black woman. Lumping together

races and ethnicities into one homogenized group ignores the cultural diversity that characterizes human difference.

The multitude of studies on African American representations far outnumbers those on Asians, Latinos, and Native Americans. The dearth of representations of these races/ethnicities represented in "mainstream" media makes it even more difficult to examine constructions of these cultures. Studies of media institutions and their production and encoding processes could provide invaluable insights into our understanding of the ways the intersections of race, gender, and sexuality structure media content. We must continue to dismantle the black-white binary that persists in shaping our understanding of race.

One avenue toward this end is Critical Race Theory, which we briefly discuss above, but which deserves additional attention from media scholars. Beyond changing the way we look at and study race, Critical Race Theory's more complete understanding of human difference offers enormous potential for understanding our multicultural world. Media scholars must join scholars from education and political science and sociology who have broadened this fast-growing field from its roots in legal studies. Critical race scholars have made an important step in this direction by embracing critical race feminism and critical white studies. And critical race theory's critiques of essentialism and challenges to social science orthodoxies are compatible with the premises of critical/cultural studies.

Another stream of scholarship that we discuss above also deserves more critical work. Hip-hop culture is a central contemporary arena through which to examine mediated intersections of race and gender. While cultural studies have a tradition of examining the cultural engagement with various forms of music, hip-hop culture as constructed in the media and popular culture epitomizes many of the contemporary tensions within U.S. media culture along the lines of race, gender, class, sexuality, regionalism, and age. Beyond the misogyny and heterosexism prevalent in hip-hop culture, scholars must remain vigilant in resisting hip-hop's repeated allusions to certain racial and gender authenticities. As an international movement, hip-hop culture can shed light on postcolonial struggles and a so-called global economy that relegates more than a third of its citizens to poverty and economic despair.

Critical/cultural scholarship on the intersections of race and gender in advertising also deserves further development. The images, narratives, types of products promoted, and stereotypical portrayals (i.e. black families advertising Popeye's chicken, or Asian men shown as the office computer whiz) in both print and electronic advertisements are in need of critical study. In addition, audience interpretations of ads remain understudied. One notable exception is Watts and Orbe's (2002) analysis of Budweiser's successful "Whassup?!" ad campaign. They examine how spectacular consumption by the (African American) Budweiser guys is constitutive of white American ambivalence toward "authentic" blackness (p. 1). Spectacular consumption describes an important "process whereby the material and symbolic relations among the culture industry, the life worlds of persons, and the ontological status of cultural forms are transformed in terms generated by public consumption" (p. 5). Their textual analysis of the Budweiser "True" commercial focuses on a site where gender and cultural performances are conditioned by sports and spectatorship, with masculinity and blackness emerging as key themes in this setting. Watts and Orbe argue that the campaign constitutes and administers cultural authenticity as a market value (p. 3). In terms of spectacular consumption, the force of the pleasure of consuming the other is both directly and paradoxically tied to the replication and amplification of so-called authentic difference (p. 3).

In a related vein, Merskin's (2001) semiotic study of Native American brand names and trademarks explains how advertising uses "pictorial metaphors" to reinforce ideologies about Native Americans started by whites (p. 159). She argues that companies that use these images are trying "to build an association with an idealized and romanticized notion of the past through the process of branding" (p. 160).

Finally, mediated representations of sports constitute a particularly fruitful arena for scholarly study of the intersections of race and gender. Some work has incorporated the study of sport within broader cultural studies themes such as media and consumption (McKay & Rowe, 1997) and cultural critiques of race relations (Boyd, 1997). Other scholars have drawn from critical/cultural studies to analyze the meanings of race, gender, and sports in specific media texts. For example, Cole and King (1998) analyze the ways the film *Hoop Dreams* reveals cultural tensions about race and gender in a postindustrial, post-Fordist, and postfeminist America. Pronger's (2000) examination of the suppression of the erotic and the narrowing of the concept of masculinity in mainstream gay sports asks who wins when gay men embrace the very cultural forms that have been central to their historical oppression. The most relevant stream in this research is the work that analyzes the variations in media coverage of women's and men's sports as well as constructions of race and gender in sports. Before concluding, we turn briefly to this literature.

Not only do female athletes receive a fraction of the coverage afforded to male athletes, but the traditional trappings of femininity—fashion, motherhood, beauty, morality, and heterosexuality—characterize their constructions (Messner, Dunbar, & Hunt, 2000; Messner, Duncan, & Wachs, 1996). Banet-Weiser's (1999) study of the development of the Women's National Basketball Association (WNBA) examined the gendered and racialized meanings that surround both male and female professional basketball players. She finds that the WNBA

has strategically represented itself in such a way as to counteract the American public's fears about the players—and thus, by association, the sport—being homosexual. Fans and sponsors are encouraged to see basketball as a sport to be played not only by those women labeled as deviant by dominant ideology but also by those who follow the normative conventions of heterosexual femininity. (p. 404)

Conversely, male basketball players, and especially black men, have been constructed as fetish objects, so much so that personality, glamour, and so-called bad boy behavior have become the central features of the sport. Media portrayals of the NBA represent black players as potentially dangerous and menacing, which in turn allows the WNBA to market itself in positive opposition to these racial politics (Banet-Weiser, 1999).

Finally, two studies can be cited for their illumination of the intersections of gender with race and sexual orientation. McKay (1993) documented the ways the media responded to basketball player Earvin "Magic" Johnson's revelation that he was HIV-positive by inserting Johnson's sexual promiscuity onto "wanton women." Dworkin and Wachs's (1998, 2000) comparison of media treatment of three stories of HIV-positive male athletes illustrated the manner in which social class, race, and sexual orientation came into play in the very distinct media framings of the three stories.

◆ Conclusion

Although the research this chapter describes is quite diverse, it is clear that it has enhanced our knowledge of the social constructions of race and gender in important ways. Collectively, this literature has made another contribution that is less transparent: it has dismantled essentialist ways of thinking about and representing race and gender. As a term used to describe the notion that humans, objects, or texts possess underlying essences that define

their true nature or identity, essentialist arguments have little credibility in academic circles. However, essentialist thinking is common in the public sphere as popular notions of what is natural in men and women, or in stereotypes of racial and ethnic groups (Brooker, 2003). The research described in this chapter has exposed the various ways the media construct monolithic notions of race and gender. Several studies have demonstrated how layered representations challenge static constructions, leaving, in turn, ambivalent space for alternative definitions of gender, race, and even sexuality. Our scholarship must continue along these antiessentialist paths, especially in the face of backlash and conservative ideals that seek to promote and implement a regressive politics of difference. Media will continue to play a prominent role in these struggles, making the work of media scholars all the more important.

◆ Notes

1. For an alternative perspective that argues that biology itself must be viewed as a cultural construction, see Sloop, this volume.

2. Issues of gender, race, and media from a global perspective are discussed in Section 5 of the *Handbook* on intercultural communication.

3. Borrowing from Dyer (1997), we contend the well-intentioned term *people of color* functions to reinforce the erroneous notion that white people do not constitute a race of people.

4. We use African American and black interchangeably in referring to the multiple identities, experiences, and cultures of Americans of African descent. We use white to refer to those of European/Anglo descent.

5. Another feature of CRT is the use of storytelling or narrative style. In this vein, although not deliberately employing CRT, Brooks and Jacobs (1996) analyzed HBO's televisual adaptation of Derrick Bell's narrative on race (*The Space Traders*). The analysis focused on the main character, a black man who employed multiracial identities in combating racism.

◆ References

Ang, I. (1985). *Watching* Dallas: *Soap opera and the melodramatic imagination*. London: Methuen.

Aparicio, F. R., & Chavez-Silverman, S. (1997). *Tropicalizations: Transcultural representations of Latinidad*. Hanover, NH: University Press of New England.

Ashcraft, K. L., & Flores, L. A. (2000). "Slaves with white collars": Persistent performances of masculinity in crisis. *Text and Performance Quarterly, 23*(1), 1–29.

Banet-Weiser, S. (1999). Hoop dreams: Professional basketball and the politics of race and gender. *Journal of Sport and Social Issues, 23*(4), 403–420.

Bird, E. (1999). Gendered construction of the American Indian in popular media. *Journal of Communication, 49*(3), 61–84.

Bobo, J. (1988). *The Color Purple*: Black women as cultural readers. In E. D. Pribram (Ed.), *Female spectators: Looking at film and television* (pp. 90–109). London: Verso.

Bobo, J. (1995). *Black women as cultural readers*. New York: Columbia University Press.

Bobo, J., & Seiter, E. (1991). Black feminism and media criticism: *The Women of Brewster Place. Screen, 32*(3), 286–302.

Bogle, D. (2001). *Toms, coons, mulattoes, mammies and bucks: An interpretive history of Blacks in American films* (4th ed.). New York: Continuum.

Boyd, T. (1997). *Am I black enough for you? Popular culture from the 'hood and beyond*. Bloomington: Indiana University Press.

Brooker, P. (2003). *A glossary of cultural theory* (2nd ed.). New York: Oxford University Press.

Brooks, D. E., & Jacobs, W. R. (1996). Black men in the margins: Space traders and the interpositional strategy against backlash. *Communication Studies, 47*, 289–302.

Brooks, D. E., & Hébert, L. P. (2004). *Lessons learned or bamboozled? Gender in a Spike Lee film*. Unpublished manuscript.

Burks, R. (1996). Imitations of invisibility: Women and contemporary Hollywood cinema. In V. Berry & C. Manning-Miller (Eds.), *Mediated messages and African-American culture: Contemporary issues* (pp. 24–39). Thousand Oaks, CA: Sage.

Byers, J., & Dell, C. (1992). Big differences on the small screen: Race, class, gender, feminine beauty, and the characters at "Frank's Place." In Lana F. Rakow (Ed.), *Women making meaning: New feminist directions in communication* (pp. 191–209). New York: Routledge.

Carby, H. (1987). *Reconstructing womanhood: The emergence of the Afro-American woman novelist*. New York: Oxford University Press.

Clifford, J. (1983). On ethnographic authority. *Representations, 1*(2), 118–146.

Cole, C. L., & King, S. (1998). Representing black masculinity and urban possibilities: Racism, realism, and hoop dreams. In G. Rail (Ed.), *Sport and postmodern times* (pp. 49–86). Albany: State University Press of New York Press.

Connell, R. W., Hearn, J., & Kimmel, M. S. (2005). Introduction. In R. W. Connell, J. Hearn, & M. S. Kimmel (Eds.), *Handbook of studies on men and masculinities* (pp. 1–12). Thousand Oaks, CA: Sage.

Delgado, R., & Stefancic, J. (Eds.). (1999). *Critical race theory: The cutting edge* (2nd Ed.). Philadelphia: Temple University Press.

Desipio, L. (1998). *Talking back to television: Latinos discuss how television portrays them and the quality of programming options*. Claremont, CA: Tomas Rivera Policy Institute.

Desmond, J. C. (1997). *Meaning in motion: New cultural studies of dance*. Durham, NC: Duke University Press.

Dines, G. (1995). Class, gender and race in North American media studies. *Race, Gender & Class, 3*(1), 97–112.

Dines, G. (2003). King Kong and the white woman: Hustler magazine and the demonization of masculinity. In G. Dines & J. M. Humez (Eds.), *Gender, race, and class in media: A text-reader* (2nd ed., pp. 451–461). Thousand Oaks: Sage.

Dines, G., & Humez, J. M. (2003). *Gender, race, and class in media: A text-reader* (2nd ed.). Thousand Oaks, CA: Sage.

Dworkin, S. L., & Wachs, F. L. (1998). Disciplining the body: HIV-positive athletes, media surveillance, and the policing of sexuality. *Sociology of Sport Journal, 15,* 1–20.

Dworkin, S. L., & Wachs, F. L. (2000). The morality/manhood paradox: Masculinity, sport, and the media. In J. McKay, M. A. Messner, & D. F. Sabo (Eds.), *Masculinities, gender relations, and sport* (pp. 47–66). Thousand Oaks, CA: Sage.

Dyer, R. (1997). *White.* London: Routledge.

Edwards, A. (1993, Winter/Spring). From Aunt Jemima to Anita Hill: Media's split image of Black women. *Media Studies Journal,* pp. 214–222.

Estill, A. (2000). Mapping the minefield: The state of Chicano and Latino literary and cultural studies. *Latin American Research Review, 35*(3), 241–250.

Feng, P. (1996). Redefining Asian American masculinity: Steven Okazaki's American Sons. *Cineaste, 22*(3), 27–30.

Fiske, J. (1987). *Television culture: Popular pleasures and politics.* London: Methuen.

Fiske, J. (1996). *Media matters: Race and gender in U.S. politics.* Minneapolis: University of Minnesota Press.

Fiske, J., &, Hartley, J. (1978). *Reading television.* London: Methuen.

Furguson, R. (1998). *Representing race: Ideology, identity and the media.* London: Arnold.

García Canclini, N. (1995). *Hybrid cultures: Strategies for entering and leaving modernity.* Minneapolis: University of Minnesota press.

Gaunt, K. (1995). African American women between hopscotch and hip-hop: Must be the music (that's turning me on). In A. Valdivia (Ed.), *Feminism, multiculturalism, and the media: Global diversities* (pp. 277–308). Thousand Oaks: Sage.

Gilman, S. (1985). *Difference and pathology: Stereotypes of sexuality, race, and madness.* Ithaca, NY: Cornell University Press.

Gray, H. (1986). Television and the new Black man: male images in prime-time situation comedy. *Media, Culture and Society, 8,* 223–242.

Gray, H. (1989). Television, Black Americans, and the American dream. *Critical Studies in Mass Communication, 6,* 376–386.

Gray, H. (1995). *Watching race: Television and struggle over blackness.* Minneapolis: University of Minnesota Press.

Guerrero, E. (1993). The black image in protective custody: Hollywood's biracial buddy films of the eighties. In M. Diawara (Ed.), *Black American Cinema* (pp. 237–246). New York: Routledge.

Hagedorn, J. (1997). Asian women in film: No joy, no luck. In S. Biagi & M. Kern-Foxworth (Eds.), *Facing difference: Race, gender, and mass media* (pp. 32–37). Thousands Oaks, CA: Pine Forge Press.

Hall, S. (1973/1993). Encoding/decoding. In S. During (Ed.), *The cultural studies reader* (pp. 90–103). New York: Routledge.

Hanke, R. (1992). Redesigning men: Hegemonic masculinity in transition. In S. Craig (Ed.), *Men, masculinity and the media* (pp. 185–198). Newbury Park, CA: Sage.

Heung, M. (1995). Representing ourselves: Films and videos by Asian American/ Canadian women. In A. Valdivia (Ed.), *Feminism, multiculturalism, and the media: Global diversities* (pp. 82–104). Thousand Oaks, CA: Sage.

Hill Collins, P. (2000). *Black feminist thought: Knowledge, consciousness, and the politics of empowerment* (2nd ed.). New York: Routledge.

Hill Collins, P. (2004). *Black sexual politics: African Americans, gender, and the new racism.* New York: Routledge.

Hobson, D. (1982). *Crossroads: The drama of a soap opera.* London: Methuen.

Hogrobrooks, H. A. (1993). Prime time crime: The role of television in the denigration and dehumanization of the African-American male. In J. W. Ward (Ed.), *African American communications: An anthology in traditional and contemporary studies* (pp. 165–172). Dubuque, IA: Kendall/ Hunt.

Holtzman, L. (2000). *Media messages: What film, television, and popular music teach us about race, class, gender, and sexual orientation.* Armonk, NY: M. E. Sharpe.

hooks, b. (1990). *Yearning: Race, gender and cultural politics*. Boston: South End Press.

hooks, b. (1992). *Black looks: Race and representation*. Boston: South End Press.

hooks, b. (1993). Male heroes and female sex objects: Sexism in Spike Lee's *Malcolm X*. *Cineaste, 19*(4), 13–15.

hooks, b. (1994). *Outlaw culture: Resisting representations*. New York: Routledge.

Hudson, S. (1998). Re-creational television: The paradox of change and continuity within stereotypical iconography. *Sociological Inquiry, 68*(2), 242–257.

Iverem, E. (1997, May 25). What about black romance? *Washington Post*, pp. G1, G4-G5.

Jeffords, S. (1989). *The remasculinization of America: Gender and the Vietnam War*. Bloomington: Indiana University Press.

Jones, L. (1994). *Bulletproof diva: Tales of race, sex, and hair*. New York: Doubleday.

Katz, E., & Liebes, T. (1985). Mutual aid in the decoding of *Dallas*: Preliminary notes from a cross-cultural study. In P. Drummond & R. Paterson (Eds.), *Television in transition* (pp. 187–198). London: British Film Institute.

Katz, J. (2003). Advertising and the construction of a violent white masculinity: From Eminem to Clinique for men. In G. Dines & J. M. Humez (Eds.), *Gender, race, and class in media: A text-reader* (2nd ed., pp. 349–358). Thousand Oaks, CA: Sage.

Kennedy, L. (1992). The body in question. In G. Dent (Ed.), *Black popular culture* (pp. 106–111). Seattle: Bay Press.

Larson, S. G. (1994). Black women on *All My Children*. *Journal of Popular Film and Television, 22*(1), 44–48.

Lee, M., & Cho, C. H. (2003). Women watching together: An ethnographic study of Korean soap opera fans in the United States. In G. Dines & J. Humez (Eds.), *Gender, race, and class in media: A text-reader* (2nd ed., pp. 482–487). Thousand Oaks, CA: Sage.

Locke, D. (1998). Here comes the judge: The dancing Itos and the televisual construction of the enemy Asian male. In S. Torres (Ed.), *Living color: Race and television in the United States* (pp. 239–253). Durham, NC: Duke University Press.

Lubiano, W. (1992). Black ladies, welfare queens, and state minstrels: Ideological war by narrative means. In T. Morrison (Ed.), *Race-ing justice, engendering power: Essays on Anita Hill Clarence Thomas and the construction of social reality* (pp. 323–363). New York: Pantheon.

MacDonald, E. (2004). Masculinity and race in media: The case of the homicide detective. In R. A. Lind (Ed.), *Race/gender/media: Considering diversity across audiences, content, and producers* (pp. 221–227). Boston: Pearson.

Manatu, N. (2003). *African American women and sexuality in the cinema*. Jefferson, NC: McFarland.

Martin, J. B., & Yep, G. Y. (2004). Eminem in mainstream public discourse: Whiteness and the appropriation of Black masculinity. In R. A. Lind (Ed.), *Race/gender/media: Considering diversity across audiences, content, and producers* (pp. 228–235). Boston: Pearson.

Martinez, K. (2004). *Latina* magazine and the invocation of a panethnic family: Latino identity as it is informed by celebrities and Papis Chulos. *Communication Review, 7*, 155–174.

McKay, J. (1993). "Marked" men" and "wanton women": The politics of naming sexual deviance in sport. *Journal of Men's Studies, 2*, 69–87.

McKay, J., & Rowe, D. (1997). Field of soaps: Rupert vs. Kerry as masculine melodrama. *Social Text, 50*, 69–86.

McPhail, M. (1996). Race and sex in black and white: Essence and ideology in the Spike Lee discourse. *Howard Journal of Communications, 7*, 127–138.

McRobbie, A. (1991). *Feminism and youth culture: From "Jackie" to "Just Seventeen."* Boston: Unwin Hyman.

Mercer, K. (1994). *Welcome to the jungle: New positions in Black cultural studies*. New York: Routledge.

Merskin, D. (2001). Winnebagos, Cherokees, Apaches, and Dakotas: The persistence of stereotyping of American Indians in American advertising brands. *Howard Journal of Communications, 12*, 159–169.

Messner, M. A., Dunbar, M., & Hunt, D. (2000). The televised sports manhood formula. *Journal of Sport and Social Issues, 24,* 380–394.

Messner, M. A., Duncan, M. C., & Wachs, F. L. (1996). The gender of audience building: Televised coverage of men's and women's NCAA basketball. *Sociological Inquiry, 66,* 422–439.

Meyers, M. (2004). African American women and violence: Gender, race and class in the news. *Critical Studies in Media Communication, 21,* 95–118.

Molina Guzmán, I., & Valdivia, A. (2004). Brain, brow, and booty: Latina iconicity in U.S. popular culture. *Communication Review, 7,* 205–221.

Morley, D. (1980). *The nationwide audience: Structure and decoding.* London: British Film Institute.

Nakayama, T. (1994). Show/down time: "Race," gender, sexuality, and popular culture. *Critical Studies in Mass Communication, 11,* 162–179.

Negrón-Muntaner, F. (1991). "Jennifer's Butt." *Aztlán, 22,* 182–195.

Nelson, J. (1997). *Straight, no chaser: How I became a grown-up black woman.* New York: Putnam.

Ono, K. A., & Buescher, D. T. (2001). Deciphering Pocahontas: Unpackaging the commodification of a Native American woman. *Critical Studies in Media Communication, 18,* 23–43.

Oppenheimer, B., Adams-Price, C., Goodman, M., Codling, J., & Coker, J. D. (2003). Audience perceptions of strong female characters on television. *Communication Research Reports, 20(2),* 161–173.

Orbe, M. P. (1998). Constructions of reality on MTV's *The Real World*: An analysis of the restrictive coding of black masculinity. *Southern Communication Journal, 64,* 32–47.

Orbe, M., & Strother, K. (1996). Signifying the tragic mulatto: A semiotic analysis of Alex Haley's *Queen*. *Howard Journal of Communications, 7,* 113–126.

Patton, T. (2001). Ally McBeal and her homies: The reification of white stereotypes of the other. *Journal of Black Studies, 32(2),* 229–260.

Perry, I. (2003). Who(se) am I? The identity and image of women in hip-hop. In G. Dines & J. Humez (Eds.), *Gender, race, and class in media: A text-reader* (2nd ed., pp. 136–148). Thousand Oaks, CA: Sage.

Portman, T. A., & Herring, R. (2001). Debunking the Pocahontas paradox: The need for a humanistic perspective. *Journal of Humanistic Counseling, Education and Development, 40,* 185–200.

Pronger, B. (2000). Homosexuality and sport: Who's winning? In J. McKay, M. A. Messner, & D. F. Sabo (Eds.), *Masculinities, gender relations, and sport* (pp. 222–244). Thousand Oaks, CA: Sage.

Radway, J. (1984). *Reading the romance: Women, patriarchy, and popular literature.* Chapel Hill: University of North Carolina Press.

Rockler, N. R. (2002). Race, whiteness, "lightness," and relevance: African American and European American interpretations of *Jump Start* and *The Boondocks*. *Critical Studies in Media Communication, 19,* 398–418.

Rodriguez, A. (1999). *Making Latino news: Race, language, class.* Thousand Oaks, CA: Sage.

Rojas, V. (2004). The gender of Latinidad: Latinas speak about Hispanic television. *Communication Review, 7,* 125–153.

Rose, T. (1994). *Black noise: Rap music and black culture in contemporary America.* Hanover, NH: University Press of New England.

Sanchez, V. E., & Stuckey, M. E. (2000). Coming of age as a culture? Emancipatory and hegemonic readings of *The Indian in the Cupboard*. *Western Journal of Communications, 64(4),* 78–89.

Shome, R. (1996). Race and popular cinema: Rhetorical strategies of whiteness in *City of Joy*. *Communication Quarterly, 44,* 502–519.

Shome, R. (2000). Outing whiteness. *Critical Studies in Media Communication, 17,* 366–371.

Sun, C. F. (2003). Ling Woo in historical context: The new face of Asian American stereotypes on television. In G. Dines & J. Humez (Eds.), *Gender, race, and class in media: A text-reader* (2nd ed., pp. 656–664). Thousand Oaks, CA: Sage.

Tajima, R. (1989). Lotus blossoms don't bleed: Images of Asian women. In Asian Women

United of California (Ed.), *Making waves: An anthology of writings by and about Asian American women* (pp. 308–317). Boston: Beacon.

Taylor, R. H. (2000). *Indian in the Cupboard*: A case study in perspective. *International Journal of Qualitative Studies in Education, 13*(4), 371–384.

Valdivia, A. (1995). Feminist media studies in a global setting: Beyond binary contradictions and into multicultural spectrums. In A. Valdivia (Ed.), *Feminism, multiculturalism, and the media: Global diversities* (pp. 7–29). Thousand Oaks: Sage.

Wallace, M. (1990). *Invisibility blues: From pop to theory*. New York: Verso.

Watts, E. K., & Orbe, M. P. (2002). The spectacular consumption of "true" African American culture: "Whassup" with the Budweiser guys? *Critical Studies in Media Communication, 21*, 1–20.

Wilkinson, E. (1990). *Japan versus the west: Image and reality*. London: Penguin.

17

CRITICAL STUDIES IN GENDER/SEXUALITY AND MEDIA

◆ John M. Sloop

I f I had been asked a decade and a half ago to provide an overview of the state of critical studies of gender/sexuality and media—especially as engaged by communication scholars—I could have written a very short essay focusing on a very small number of readings of representations of (homo)sexuality in mass mediated texts. Moreover, I would have discovered that rarely did these readings interrogate gender/sexuality theoretically or critically. Indeed, as Yep (2004) has recently observed, the field of communication studies in general has long operated under an assumed heteronormativity, given that the first essay focusing on sexuality was published in the *Quarterly Journal of Speech* as late as 1976. While the number of published essays increased throughout the following decade, each unquestioningly assumed a stable and essential notion of gay and lesbian identity and subjectivity. The dominant political purpose of each was to argue for social acceptance of members of an imagined and unified gay community.

It was not until the 1990s that communication scholars, largely following the theoretical grounding supplied in founding texts by theorists such as Foucault (1978), Butler (1990), and Sedgwick (1990), produced a body of queer scholarship that looked not only at the ways sexuality was represented in mass mediated texts but also how mass mediated discourses were *productive* of—that is, worked to create or constitute— gendered/sexualized subjectivities. The political purpose of such work moved from assimilation or acceptance to a broadening of sex/gender possibilities as well as an understanding of the ways sex/gender is performed and constrained. I should note here that while there are numerous scholarly works that quantitatively track the appearance of gays, lesbians, and queers in mass mediated texts, I will maintain my focus on those that criticize and problematize dominant representations of queered gender/sexuality as well as the norms of, and constraints on, gender/sexual subjectivity.[1]

Although Yep (2004) argues that the critical condition of the study of gender/sexuality in communication studies continues to be relatively poor, I want to suggest that the intersection of media and gender/sexuality studies has been enriched primarily because gay and lesbian characters have become staples of prime-time television just as queer theories have become prominent. I take "queer scholarship" to refer in its broadest sense to work that, as Warner (1993) puts it, "rejects a minoritizing logic of toleration or simple political interest-representation in favor of a more thorough resistance to regimes of the normal" (p. xxvi). Such work "has the effect of pointing out a wide field of normalization, rather than simple intolerance, as the site of violence" and serves as "a way of cutting against mandatory gender divisions" (p. xxvi). Simply put, assuming the performativity of gender/sexuality, queer scholarship works against the ways in which gender/sexuality is disciplined ideologically and institutionally and works toward a culture in which a wider variety of genders/sexualities might be performed.

As I discuss in the conclusion, there clearly are a number of limitations to recent work in critical communication studies inspired by queer theory, yet the work has become more complex and nuanced, offering insights into cultural meanings and into the production and reproduction of those meanings. In this chapter, I describe some of the theoretical assumptions that guide contemporary studies of gender, sexuality, and media. Second,

I divide recent critical scholarship into three broad areas of research—studies focusing on ideological clawback (i.e., constraint and confinement), studies dealing with the political ambivalence of mediated texts, and studies focusing on politically progressive readings of mass mediated texts. Finally, I will outline some of the limitations of work in media/gender/sexuality studies and will suggest potential critical pursuits in this area.

◆ Theoretical Assumptions

Since the early 1990s, studies of gender/sexuality within the field of communication largely have been influenced and shaped by the turn to theories of discourse and gender performativity. Indeed, if one were to look at critical work in the area of gender/sexuality studies from the 1980s, the dominant paradigm would begin with the common grounding assumption of a fairly nonproblematic distinction between gender and sex in which *sex* refers to the body's male or female genitalia and *gender* refers to the socially constructed meanings applied to the body within a given culture. Within such a framework, sexuality is simply tied to the types of bodies toward which one is attracted relative to one's own body. When two people of the same sex engage in sexual activities, the act is homosexual (and one who prefers such sex is a homosexual) and, of course, pursuing sex with those of the opposite sex is heterosexual behavior between heterosexuals.

In 1990, the publication of Butler's *Gender Trouble* in effect brought about a paradigm shift that made it impossible not only to separate the categories and questions of gender/sex and sexuality clearly but also to identify sexuality in terms of distinct categories. Arguing that gender must be seen as "performative," as always already emerging as a recitation of cultural norms, Butler in some sense deconstructed the sex-gender binary, arguing in effect that sex is always already gendered. That is, not only does the material, physical body have meaning and matter only as it is understood through cultural discourses and sanctions, but the individual's understanding of self and acts of self-discipline are largely influenced by the preexisting discursive structure of gender that acts through the behavior of others working with similar understandings. To be sure, Butler was not denying that the body is material nor that an individual body's organic structure/networks influence and/or limit behaviors (i.e., she is not a "social constructionist" properly speaking). She was arguing that each body—irrespective of its constraints and limits—is always understood, influenced, and encouraged to operate within the parameters of a given temporal-geographic-discursive culture.

As a result, research and criticism concerning sexuality over the last decade and a half is not easily—if at all—separable from research focusing on gender because the very meaning of gender implies an assumption about sexuality. For example, given that we live in a heteronormative culture, to say that one is performing capably as a man assumes that one is sexually attracted to those who are performing properly as women. A man who is not sexually attracted to women is suspect as a man precisely because he is not properly performing his gender. Or, to make the point differently, if one decides to alter one's gender surgically, it makes little heteronormative sense to do so unless the ultimate sexual orientation one will transition into is a heterosexual one. To be clear, this is not to say, first, that people do not make vernacular distinctions between gender and sexuality—of course they do. Second, it is also not to say that a critical study cannot separate gender and sexuality—focus can be, and has been, placed on either (e.g., one could study representations of men and women without *explicit* reference to sexuality or one could study masculinity and femininity as concepts removed from men and women and instead performed differently by either). It is to say that if one accepts the assumptions

of gender performativity—and this is certainly the case of the largest portion of the critical landscape in contemporary communication studies—one finds that claims about representations of the performance of sexuality necessarily have implications for the cultural meanings of gender (and vice versa). These implications are not always manifest within a given essay, but often they are.

◆ Major Critical Perspectives on Gender/Sexuality and Media

With these theoretical assumptions in mind, critics interested in gender/sexuality and mass mediated texts have approached their task from different angles. The ultimate purpose of gender/sexuality studies seems to be similar among these projects (i.e., an expansion of accepted ways to perform gender/sexuality, an erosion of patriarchal heteronormativity), but critics vary their focus on a continuum stretching from an emphasis binding ideological constraints to an emphasis on progressive and liberatory parodic performances. In the following sections, I group essays in three categories—from essays that emphasize the way gender/sexuality are ideologically contained, to work emphasizing the way audiences can read some texts as both/either liberatory or constraining, to those emphasizing progressive or fluid understandings of gender/sexuality, as the scholarship discussed below indicates.

◆ Gender/Sexuality and Ideological Clawback

Far and away the dominant focus media critics have taken when it comes to studies of gender/sexuality has been on the ways in which contemporary representations have been constrained or "held in place" rather than on the ways in which texts offer progressive representations or facilitate liberatory readings. While there are a variety of ways of discussing constraint, my tendency has been to draw upon Fiske and Hartley's (1978) notion of "ideological clawback" (pp. 86–87). They suggest that mass mediated texts, for a variety of reasons, function to "claw back," or discipline, meanings that fall outside of dominant ideology: first, in the simple terms of discursive intelligibility, any message must fit within the parameters of the audience's understanding of the world. Hence, in their example, when one watches a "nature" show, the host of the show often anthropomorphizes animals, giving their actions "human" meanings and human motives (pp. 86–87). Similarly, and directly related to questions of gender/sexuality, anthropologist Zuk (2002) has criticized numerous "public scientists" for the ways they provide human sexual desires and human subject positions to the behavior of animals—often for political purposes—irrespective of the incommensurability of the meanings of human and animal behaviors. Fiske and Hartley (1978) also argue that mass mediated texts in a capitalist economy clawback transgressive or oppositional meanings because it is in the financial interests of producers to gain the largest possible audience. As Condit (1989) observes, mass media outlets do "regressive" or conservative ideological work simply "by addressing the dominant audience that also constitutes the public" (p. 112).

In general, those critics focusing on constraint are not operating from the assumption that constraint works to maintain stereotypes that keep gays and lesbians from presenting their "true selves." Rather, having taken the "performative turn," their readings understand constraint to be the very possibility of meaning. That is, mass mediated texts hold in place representations that provide relatively stable—yet problematic—subject positions for gays and lesbians. These are part of the material from which they are understood and come to

understand themselves. Further, this focus on constraint is meant to be progressive and enabling. By explaining or underlining the ways in which—and the needs for which—representations/identities are stabilized, such work simultaneously makes their ultimate instability visible or transparent and thereby illustrates "new possibilities for gender that contest the rigid codes of hierarchical binarisms" (Butler, 1990, p. 185). Critics outline the ways in which ideological constraint operates precisely to encourage the creation of other possibilities, other imaginary spaces of identity.

In communication studies, media criticism of this type has covered a wide range of mass media and mediated texts. For example, among a number of critical studies of film, three serve as strong examples of the ways in which potentially progressive representations of gays and lesbians are drawn back, constrained in ways that reflect heteronormative grids of intelligibility. Evans (1998), for example, argues—countering many liberatory readings given to Butler's work—that drag operates in both *The Crying Game* and *The Birdcage* to rearticulate male gay sexuality in very traditional ways and femininity in regressive ways, rather than in the progressive/nontraditional ways seen by other critics. For Evans, because we have—post-Butler—come to think of drag as necessarily progressive, consumers are taking in very conservative images in the name of liberation. Second, Nakayama's (1994) analysis of *Showdown in Little Tokyo* investigates the intersection of race, gender, and sexuality in a text that could have been and was read by some as being progressive on all grounds. Instead, Nakayama suggests that the film recenters white heterosexual masculinity and reconstructs Asian masculinity along conservative or traditional lines. Finally, in an essay combining traditional textual criticism and readings of tertiary texts, Brookey and Westerfelhaus (2002) argue that the "extratext" included on the DVD of the film *Fight Club* worked purposefully to constrain or discipline homoerotic and homosocial readings which the film encouraged. That is, while the original film was clearly open to ambiguous readings of the two male lead characters, the DVD included both reviewers and commentary by actors and the director that explicitly argued against queered readings. In each of these readings, critics detail the ways in which texts that potentially allowed for queered or homoerotic readings were disciplined back into a heteronormative frame. In explaining the disciplinary process, the critic encourages readers to undermine that very process and re-queer the text.

This process of ideological clawback takes place in gay media outlets as well as mainstream ones. In her important analysis of representations of the gay male habitus constructed in *The Advocate*—a magazine oriented toward gay consumers—Sender (2001) suggests that heteronormative under-standings of gay males are reified even within the pages of a so-called gay maga-zine. By focusing on a site created/designed for and by gay consumers, Sender highlights the processes through which economic pres-sures and ideological interpellation function to encourage gay consumers to write them-selves into confined understandings of their own lives.

Prime-time television has been an espe-cially rich area of study through which critics have examined and explained the process of ideological discipline and con-straint. This is especially important critical work if only because mass media producers have patted themselves on the back repeat-edly as a result of the increasing number of gay characters on prime time television. That is, while earlier criticism could often simply point to the "invisibility" of gay characters on television and the homopho-bic representations of those that did exist, more recent work has to grapple with read-ings of gay and lesbian characters in a con-text in which "visibility" alone is being celebrated as liberatory.[2]

Two gay/lesbian prime-time markers on mainstream television most often cited dur-ing this period were the coming-out episode of the situation comedy *Ellen* and the long-running success of *Will and Grace*.[3] Using a Foucauldian framework, Dow (2001) provided a particularly insightful read not only of *Ellen* as text but also of the discourse that surrounded the show and the event. Dow argues that while the public "confessions" of Ellen worked overtly through a discourse in which she was able to express "truth" about her sexuality (as if it were essential to be uncovered and dis-closed), the discourse itself implicitly pro-duced mainstream and safe meanings for lesbianism. In part, then, the discourse sur-rounding the show was productive of a safely assimilated meaning for lesbianism, but it also—and importantly—personalized Ellen's coming out, curtailing the political meaning of the event to the personal.

In similar fashion, Battles and Hilton-Morrow (2002) argued that *Will and Grace* ultimately reaffirmed heteronormative cul-ture through its employment of conservative situation comedy norms—norms that were necessary because of television's need for repetition and predictability. Not only do Battles and Hilton-Morrow argue that the program equates gayness with a lack of mas-culinity, but they suggest that by infantilizing the most potentially subversive characters and emphasizing the characters' interper-sonal relationships over their connection to the larger social world (paralleling Dow's, 2001, argument), the show ultimately under-stands these individual characters according to the preexisting assumptions of heteronor-mative culture, undermining their potential liberatory influence.

Shugart (2003) provided a more detailed explanation of the heteronormative framing of *Will and Grace* by arguing that while the gay male/heterosexual female friendship has become a stock coupling in contemporary mass mediated texts, the political valence of this coupling is mixed at best. On the one hand, it has provided mainstream visibility for gay men; on the other, this dynamic is popular precisely because it fits snugly within existing ideological understandings of male-female relations familiar from situation comedies. Shugart suggests that this particular dynamic largely undermines its progressive potential because it reproduces traditional patriarchal privilege for the male. Shugart details the commonalities of these texts and the way in which the relationship between the two characters consistently recenters the male, blunting the representation of homosexuality and gay male identity.

Although I realize the importance of all mediated representation, I hold news reports (regardless of the medium) to be an especially vital arena of study because news outlets claim, and are often granted, the mantle of objectivity in their accounts of people and events. While little of the work discussed here relies explicitly on Warner's (2002) work on public and counterpublic spheres, much of it shares the idea that there is a variety of so-called counterpublics that resist or operate differently than a dominant public. Moreover, as Warner notes, a vernacular or queer counterpublic is only able to "circulate up to a point, at which it is certain to meet intense resistance," being clawed back into dominant understandings of sexuality (p. 424). I will discuss work focusing on counterpublic resistance; the research here is interested in the ways the "intense resistance—both intentional and implicit" (p. 424) of mass mediated discussions of gender/sexuality issues contains those meanings.

Criticism focusing on news coverage of gender/sexuality issues ranges from discussions of particular policy/scientific debates to coverage concerning particular individuals. On the most general level, Smith and Windes (1997) argued that when progay and antigay political positions are covered in news programs, both positions—albeit it in different ways—ultimately work to reaffirm static representations of gays and lesbians. Gross (2001) argues in *Up From Invisibility* that both entertainment and news media maintain conventional understandings of the lives of gay men and lesbians and have proven unable to represent the complex richness of gay identity. Thompson (2002) in *Mommy Queerest* argued that lesbian mothers either met invisibility and erasure from mainstream news coverage or were represented within

traditional and constrained understandings of lesbian behavior and lesbian appearance. In an investigation of news discourse surrounding Rosie O'Donnell's coming out and her simultaneous emergence as an advocate for gay parenting and gay adoption, Shugart (2005) suggests that O'Donnell's political agenda was largely silenced and contained because she was situated within conventional discourses of motherhood and childhood. More recently, Vavrus (2002), in a particularly insightful essay, argued that news coverage of stay-at-home dads consistently framed both the story about the impetus for the fathers' decisions to stay home and the work they performed in the domestic sphere through a heterosexual frame, reinscribing patriarchal privilege. Again, a story and behavior that could potentially challenge both gender and sexuality worked to reinscribe notions of femininity, masculinity, and the proper accompanying gender/sexuality.

News reports and narratives concerning individuals also have repeatedly worked to reify dominant understandings of sexuality and its link with proper gender performance. For example, Morris (2002) argues that, while suspending the question on J. Edgar Hoover's lived sexual practice, a public moral panic concerning sex crimes and sexuality during Hoover's rise to power functioned to make everyone's sexual behavior suspect. As a result, regardless of his actual sexuality, suspicions of Hoover's being homosexual forced him to pass as straight, ultimately reifying the gay/straight understandings of behavior and the accompanying valences. Both the news coverage of Hoover and his own reported behaviors provide evidence of the strength of heteronormative expectations in shaping bodily performance and public discourse.

My own work has focused directly on the ways news coverage of individual cases ideologically reinscribes both gender and sexual expectations. In a variety of case studies, I (Sloop, 2004) criticized the ways transgendered individuals (e.g., Brandon Teena, Calpernia Addams), surgically altered individuals (e.g., David Reimer), lesbians (k.d. lang) and masculine females (i.e., Janet Reno) have been represented in news coverage. Again, in each case, I look at the ways both gender and sexuality are met with the strong gaze of heteronormative assumptions, shaping public understandings of each case and of proper behavior at large. In a metalevel essay exploring similar grounds, Squires and Brouwer (2002) argue that news analysis fixes "the identities of passers" (both race and gender passers) along heteronormative and class lines. They argue in great detail that gender passers (i.e., transgender individuals) find themselves understood through a news lens which understands their "true" gender as proven or supported by their (hetero)sexual practices.

Finally, media scholars also have focused on the multiple ways in which scientists and scientific organizations have covered gender and sexuality. Most notably, Patton has written several books that have shown in part how news media spokespersons describe and discuss the science of the AIDS epidemic and the victims of AIDS. Not surprisingly perhaps, such news coverage, Patton (1990) argues, represents AIDS as linked to promiscuous and unhygienic behaviors by homosexual men.

Debates about the gay gene and the history of gay science also have been fertile ground for critical queer work. A number of scholars outside of communication studies have talked about the ways public science—in debates on animal behavior or the gendered brain—produce and reproduce a bigendered, heteronormative culture by understanding or framing all nonheterosexual, bigendered behavior as an aberration. Brookey (2001, 2002) has taken a strong rhetorical focus to the ways in which the "gay gene" controversy has played out publicly by investigating the ways such debates frame homosexuality as genetic and as an "either heterosexual or homosexual" issue. He suggests that this misguided coverage creates a rhetorical situation in which debates over sexuality avoid the grounds on which one might argue that antigay discrimination could be seen as a choice regardless of the meaning of the behavior itself. Hence, a scientific logic that might have been meant to help gays and lesbians is reframed as an argument which crystallizes the basis of homosexuality as a genetic structure and public argument into a no-win situation.

A number of examples of criticism illustrate the ways mass media coverage works, in a seemingly natural way, to reinforce dominant understandings of gender/sexuality and the links between gender and sexuality. While ideological movement does indeed take place, it is necessarily slow because commercial discourses function most effectively when they reflect the logic of common sense. If we take seriously the idea that the discourses about gender/sexuality help reaffirm the standards of performativity under which we all live, shaping our understandings of our own behaviors and identity, then the task of outlining the relentlessness of ideological constraint is a vital one.

◆ Ambivalence and Gender/Sexuality

A second body of scholarship focuses on the ways representations of gays, lesbians, and queers have functioned in politically ambivalent ways—both stabilizing and destabilizing dominant meanings. This section on ambivalent meanings is not intended to point to scholarship on bodies or identities which are ambiguous (unrecognizable gender or puzzling sexuality), although we could certainly profit from more scholarship of this type. Rather, the critical work in this section suggests that while representations of gays and lesbians may indeed be constrained by the demands of performative recognition and capitalist appeal, these texts and representations encourage a politically progressive transformation of dominant meanings of gays, lesbians, and queers in other ways.

A particularly strong example of criticism that deals with political ambivalence is Asen's (1998) reading of Robert Mapplethorpe's photography. Focusing on the framing of these models and the genre in which these photographs most reasonably fit, Asen argues that because these photographs of male nudes are framed with techniques of the classical genre of the nude and are simultaneously framed as erotic, the photographs themselves are open to being read both through a lens of artistic appreciation and through a lens of male sexual desire (both male and female desire of male bodies). As Asen suggests, the intersection of the classical style with erotic content provides an overall interpretive frame that allows readers to easily understand the text in either politically progressive or artistically constrained ways.

In a similar vein, although more closely connected with economic rather than aesthetic concerns, Sender (1999) provides a rich critical look at "gay window dressing." She focuses on print advertisements that she argues are designed to be read (and in fact are read) ambivalently. On the one hand, the models can be read through a heteronormative frame in which they are assumed to be heterosexual (and engaging in heterosexual behavior); on another, they are read through a gay/lesbian/queer frame with the models understood as gay or lesbian. Relying on focus group readings of a variety of ads by both heterosexual and gay/lesbian consumers, Sender argues that advertisers respond to the economic incentive of multiple consumers by encouraging products to be read differently by different groups. The advertisements are designed to be read differently by individual readers rather than ambiguously by everyone so that homophobic consumers do not associate the product with gay values. In effect, the advertisements function as heteronormative for some consumers while they may be read transgressively by others.

Gross's (1993) discussion of the ethics and politics of outing in *Contested Closets* was, at least implicitly, both a challenge to stabilizing understandings of identity and a critique of the ways in which identity gets stabilized through outing. In the book Gross notes that "an ethic of honesty" (and standards of journalism) suggest that individuals should represent their "authentic selves" to the world. Simultaneously, however, gay individuals are often targets of discrimination when they are outed as homosexual. As Gross works through the ethics of outing and the ways it works as a challenge to journalistic practices, individual privacy, and community accountability, he simultaneously offers a problematization of the assumptions that underlie outing. In short, if we read identity as queer rather than as gay/lesbian, then outing's assumption of an authentic self is a constricted view of identity rather than a view of the self as transitional. Hence, while the politics of outing is controversial regardless of how we understand identity, the assumptions that undergird most discussions of it are themselves somewhat constraining, as outing reinforces gay identity.

This same dynamic regarding queered vs. stabilized identities (and the turn toward queered readings) is paralleled in Erni's (1998) critique of the television coverage of Michael Jackson's first pedophilia case. Using the essay as a way to open up "queer media studies" and relying on Rubin's "Thinking Sex" (1993), Erni (1998) is interested in understanding both the politically progressive possibilities offered by news coverage of individuals like Jackson and the politically regressive ways that news coverage continues to work. In effect, Erni (1998) argues that while the pre-charge coverage of Jackson was politically progressive in that Jackson's behavior was un-recognizable through standard heteronormative frames (i.e., he was neither traditionally heterosexual nor homosexual; his desires seemed to have no particular age framing), once charges of pedophilia were raised, the queered Jackson was then easily moved back into traditional and disciplined frames of understanding. What was once queered became disciplined through a heteronormative lens. While noting the heteronormative frame employed in mass mediated texts, Erni (1998) goes on to consider ways in which queer media criticism can work to persistently challenge heteronormative readings.

Another strong example of work that underlines both the constraining and progressive possibilities of mediated texts is Brookey's (1996) "A Community like *Philadelphia*." Brookey reads the film *Philadelphia* in a way that allows him to simultaneously critique the assimilationist representations of gays and to provide an example of a queered reading that undermines the basis of the assimilationist critique. Although Brookey agrees with numerous past readers of *Philadelphia* who argued that the film attempted to show the gay characters as "just like" the heterosexual characters (hence, promoting a politics of assimilation by not providing "authentic" homosexual experience or individuals), he goes to on provide a second critique by assuming—in performative fashion—that homosexuality (gays, lesbians) is itself a constructed identity. Like Erni, Brookey suggests that queer media critics need not only to understand how gender/sexuality is tied into heteronormative expectations but to create and disseminate messier ways of reading and, therefore, of being.

In her broad critique of gay visibility in the contemporary mediascape (from television shows to advertisements to film), Walters (2001) provides a textured reading of both the constricted (stereotypical) meanings associated with such visibility as well as the more complicated and progressive representations. In short, Walters argues that gay visibility is not necessarily progressive but neither is it necessarily contained by heteronormative meanings (see also Mayne, 2000). Walters illustrates the ways in which gay visibility offers openings for necessarily slow, semiotic changes. Similarly, investigating the growing visibility of male-male public kissing, Morris and I (Morris & Sloop, in press)—drawing in part on Walters—have discussed the ambivalent ways in which such visibility currently functions and have encouraged critics to take up the task of complicating the meaning of these images.

◆ Progressive Possibilities and Gender/Sexuality

The final group of essays—and by far the smallest group—includes those that provide a celebration of dominant or mainstream representations of gender/sexuality to the degree that these representations are politically progressive or challenging to dominant ideology. What I find especially interesting about these essays is that, unlike the embrace by cultural studies in the late 1980s and early 1990s of liberatory readings of regressive texts by consumers, these critical readings understand the texts themselves as corrective, as encouraging counter-hegemonic possibilities. Meyer (2003), for example, reads the construction and outing of gay character Jack McPhee on *Dawson's Creek* as offering a useful and beneficial representation of a gay man for adolescent sexual identity formation. After praising the program for constructing Jack's sexual identity as acceptable socially rather than in terms of political or legal rights, Meyer suggests that the show provides a strong template through which gay adolescents can learn to enact their own relationships and to develop their own sense of identity. Meyer relies on previous ethnographic work on gay men's use of mediated texts, and the argument itself relies on the liberatory potential of the text rather than of the readings of it.

Offering a similar reading, Herman (2003) criticizes the thesis that dominant media outlets provide only images of assimilated gays and lesbians (or the gay habitus discussed by Sender, 2001) by looking at *Bad Girls*, a British drama set in a women's prison. In part because of its prison setting, the show does not offer the expected read of lesbianism through the male gaze or within a heteronormative context; rather, *Bad Girls* offers a "gay market" semiotics of lesbianism, presenting it as normal, desirable, and possible. Herman notes that the show offers one model by which the meanings of gender and sexuality can be contested in public. While acknowledging that the show is ideologically constrained in other ways (e.g., in terms of race, especially, the show presents expected/stereotypical images), Herman celebrates the show for its counter-hegemonic representations of sexuality.

One critic who has consistently offered celebratory readings of nonheteronormative texts is Cooper. With coauthor Pease, Cooper (2002) analyzes an episode of *Ally McBeal* as providing a progressive and liberatory interpretation of a transgendered character. After first acknowledging that transgendered characters historically have been presented through a comic frame which ensures that they ultimately reaffirm U.S. culture's dominant heterosexism, assumption of biologically based gender, and a general intolerance of difference, Cooper and Pease investigate an episode of *Ally McBeal* in which a presurgical MTF (i.e., person transitioning from male to female) was murdered. The episode, by also featuring a (comic) funeral of a man who was bigoted toward short people, provides a narrative structure which ultimately indicts bigotry and intolerance and thus "resists heteronormative culture by exposing the inevitable limitations and consequences of the dominant discourse of heterosexual ideology" (p. 325).

Similarly, Cooper (2002) turned her focus to the Brandon Teena narrative found in the film *Boys Don't Cry* and argues that the film works in multiple ways to challenge and disrupt heteronormativity, despite the fact that news articles about the case interpreted Brandon Teena through a traditional heteronormative lens. In short, Cooper argues that the text offers itself as a problematization of heteromasculinity, centers female masculinity, and blurs the boundaries of gender and sexuality. Countering multiple other readings of the film which investigated its ultimate folding into heteronormative expectations, Cooper notes that the film not only privileges gender diversity but also exposes sexual bigotry by highlighting the deadly consequences of prejudice.

Shugart (2001) reads the employment of gender parody on *Ellen* as challenging heteronormative gender roles. Shugart focuses on episodes in which Ellen parodies female performance (that is, each episode features a parody of femininity by a woman) and the ways straight and gay audiences read the show in order to suggest that the show worked to challenge both heteronormative understandings of females and the link between females and traditional femininity. In short, Ellen's ability to parody femininity (and her inability to perform it properly) not only illustrates that femininity in general is a performance (hence, denaturalizing gender) but that it also renders the traditional male gaze arbitrary and ludicrous. In that way, the show undermines the erotic potential of Ellen's feminine performance for heterosexual male viewers. For Shugart, when the audience sees this as emanating not only from a female subjectivity but also from a lesbian, it undermines the male gaze and implicitly deconstructs heterosexual desire and heterosexual vision.

While my own reading of each of these televisual/film texts would probably challenge the claims that each should be celebrated for antiheteronormative narratives, these critical readings at the very least function to offer "ideal" readings of texts, opening up the political imaginary to rethink what texts might mean and how culture might understand gender and sexuality differently. In each case, the critic suggests ways that texts can be constructed (e.g., through the juxtaposition of narratives, through parody) in ways that undermine heteronormativity and heterosexual expectation. As such, these critics move us to consider the creation of progressive readings and progressive texts.

◆ Conclusion: Assessments and Future Directions

In *Prime-Time Feminism*, Dow (1996) argues that, regardless of the multiple meanings a text might provide to consumers, "criticism is not about discovering or reporting the meaning in a text. Rather, it becomes a performative activity that is, in some sense, dedicated to creating meaning" (pp. 3–4). While the critical works I have reviewed here may have a variety of different particular purposes and a variety of different starting assumptions, each loosely shares some underlying assumptions and political goals. In general, each would argue for an expansive definition of sexuality and sexual acts in which a larger variety of behaviors and identities (providing they are noncoercive) would be acceptable, marked, and rendered intelligible. Hence, and again in general, the underlying purpose of each criticism is to expand the variety of representations of sexuality that are acceptable. Given this loosely shared project, we, as a critical community (rather than as individual critics), need to reflect on a number of points.

BALANCING CONSTRAINT AND LIBERATION

First, in many early readings of Judith Butler's *Gender Trouble* (1990), scholars were fascinated by her brief argument that gender norms (hence, sexuality norms) could be challenged through parody and subversion. The ensuing arguments concerning drag and liberation reached such a peak (and so quickly) that Butler almost immediately toned down and clarified her claims in *Bodies That Matter* (1993), suggesting that critics needed to keep a strong focus on constraint because constraint offers the very possibility for meaning and because the cultural sanctions against nonheteronormative genders/sexualities were more powerful than she had initially argued. In communication and media studies, however, we rarely find the move to liberatory or celebratory readings. While critical readings of constraint can indeed function to loosen the bindings of sexuality, as scholars trained in the art of persuasion and change we may want to provide more focus not only on sites of liberation but on more expansive ways by which such arguments can be made. I would argue that we, as a community, need a stronger sense of balance in readings we provide.

THE POLITICS OF VISIBILITY

Second, media critics—at least within communication studies—should give more careful consideration to the politics of visibility. While those interested in the relationship between mass mediated representations and gender/sexuality are of course interested in the question of visibility and the problematics of particular types of visibility, most of this work simply assumes—implicitly—that visibility is the first step toward progressive visibility. That is, when we do employ discussions of visibility, there is rarely a consideration that perhaps invisibility might be the better option. For example, although Dow (2001) discusses the politics and problematics of lesbian visibility in the case of Ellen DeGeneres's coming out, she does not discuss the possibility of a politics of invisibility. As another example, in a review of critical work on media and gender/sexuality, Fejes and Petrich (1993) assume that invisibility is something to be worked against. However, as Butler (2004) recently reminds us, we should remain aware that at times, "there are advantages to remaining less than intelligible," less than visible (p. 3). While it may seem contradictory for someone interested in mediated images to focus on the advantages of invisibility, there are moments and conditions under which invisibility and unintelligibility may be a progressive space for gays, lesbians, queers, and transgendered individuals. Although such a focus need not be the work of every individual critic, it should be more fully represented in the critical community as a whole.

INTERSECTIONALITY STUDIES AND GLOBAL STUDIES

Third, while most work on sexuality and mass mediated representations of sexuality also (and perhaps necessarily) discusses its links with gender, we remain a group that could work harder to highlight other intersections (e.g., to race, class, age, region). While this is perhaps a predictable critique, it is nonetheless a necessary one. While intersectional critiques are becoming more common in a wide range of work, they are not a strength of gender/sexuality studies. This issue is magnified in my mind not simply because of the relative absence of intersectionality but because quite often authors allow mainstream studies of white, middle-class characters to stand in universally for all comments about gender/sexuality. That is, while we clearly need understandings of gender/sexuality and its links with white middle-class U.S. identity, this is neither the totality of what is needed nor should it stand in as commentary for all representations of gender/sexuality. The best example of the richness of intersectionality in communication studies is Johnson's (2003) *Appropriating Blackness,* but other notable exceptions include Ashcraft and Flores's (2003) discussion of gender, class and sexuality in contemporary film, Erni's (1998) read of the queering of Michael Jackson, Sender's (2001) arguments concerning gay representation and class, Vavrus's (2002) discussion of masculinity and domesticity, and Nakayama's (1994) take on race and sexuality through an analysis of film.

Similarly, commitment to the notion that gender/sexuality has meaning only within culture necessitates greater effort to investigate their function beyond a U.S. context, where the majority of the studies discussed here are confined (for an exception, see Herman, 2003).

By including discussions of gender/sexuality and media studies in other national contexts (or across national boundaries), we will broaden our understandings of both the types of constraints that hold gender/sexuality in place as well as the ways in which other possibilities might be imagined.

QUESTIONING THE STABILITY OF IDENTITY

Fourth, one of the aspects of studies of gender/sexuality and media studies that most surprised me as I was reflecting for the purposes of this chapter is that, even in a critical context in which theories of performativity are assumed, there remains slippage between the understanding of identity assumed by performativity and the way it is often discussed in critical studies. That is, a theory of performativity necessarily queers any stable understanding of identity, but one gets the sense that, as a whole, we remain tied to stability. Often, a critical focus on constraint seems to implicitly suggest that it holds one back from the expression of a "true" identity (e.g., one passes as a straight man rather than expressing a true and essential homosexuality). But the discourses which constrain also set up the frames through which one performs an identity. Identity is always expressed through the frame of performativity. Focusing on constraint does not solely or simply serve the purpose of helping individuals express their "true" selves because we alter constraints to change the conditions of possibility through which identities may emerge. While I certainly understand the calls for what Prosser (1998) calls a politics of "home identities" (i.e., stable identity categories for those who desire them), we should productively interrogate the construction of those categories before endorsing the theory as a whole (pp. 13–15).

QUEER STUDIES AND FEMINISM

Finally, one of the ongoing struggles faced by critics and theorists of gender/sexuality and the media (for that matter, of anyone interested in questions of gender/sexuality)—especially as such studies have become more queered and more engaged with issues of transgenderism and intersexuality—is the relationship between a queer project and particular brands of feminism. In Butler's recent *Undoing Gender* (2004), she once again tackles the meanings and import of both gender and sexuality under the loose umbrellas of "feminism" and gender or queer studies. Most notably, Butler is interested in the tensions between queer criticism and those feminist projects that require or rely upon relatively clear gender/sexuality divisions (i.e., man/woman, hetero/bi/homosexual). Ultimately, Butler (2004) notes that the struggles that take place under these broad categories, as well as the meanings of the shared terms employed under them (sex, gender, sexuality), are ones that should be productively kept alive, "so that we might work theoretically and politically in broad coalitions. The lines we draw are invitations to cross over" (p. 203). Her point here, to my mind, is a powerful one: the tensions between feminism and queer studies are neither to be solved nor ignored. Rather, these tensions, and the questions they raise, are productive when used to continually focus and interrogate our terms. This lesson is one that needs to be learned by all, even those who are not necessarily inclined to think within both domains. Regardless of where one publishes or with whom one talks, consistently interrogating the terms and thinking about the challenges brought about by these tensions helps create strong work both theoretically and politically, opening new possibilities.

◆ Notes

1. In the same way, I should also note that this chapter focuses on intersections of gender and sexuality, thus bracketing out studies critiquing gender primarily, such as those of mass mediated representations of women or of media constructions of masculinity which are not crosscut with discussions of sexuality.

2. Fejes and Petrich (1993) provide a very nice summary of work on the invisibility of gays in mass mediated texts in the early 1990s that is worth a read in light of the larger number of gay representations now on prime-time television.

3. Certainly, *Queer Eye for the Straight Guy* will join this list. Already a special section of the journal *GLQ* titled "Queer TV Style" (2005) as well as a portion of the Commentary and Criticism section of *Feminist Media Studies* are dedicated to it.

◆ References

Asen, R. (1998). Appreciation and desire: The male nude in the photography of Robert Mapplethorpe. *Text & Performance Quarterly, 18,* 50–62.

Ashcraft, K. L, & Flores. L. A. (2003). "Slaves with white collars": Persistent performances of masculinity in crises. *Text & Performance Quarterly, 23,* 1–29.

Battles, K., & Hilton-Morrow, W. (2002). Gay characters in conventional spaces: *Will and Grace* and the situation comedy genre. *Critical Studies in Media Communication, 19,* 87–105.

Brookey, R. A. (1996). A community like *Philadelphia. Western Journal of Communication, 60,* 40–46.

Brookey, R. A. (2001). Bio-rhetoric, background beliefs and the biology of homosexuality. *Argumentation and Advocacy, 4,* 171–183.

Brookey, R. A. (2002). *Reinventing the male homosexual: The rhetoric and power of the gay gene.* Bloomington: Indiana University Press.

Brookey, R. A., & Westerfelhaus, R. (2002). Hiding homoeroticism in plain view: The *Fight Club* DVD as digital closet. *Critical Studies in Media Communication, 19,* 21–43.

Butler, J. (1990). *Gender trouble: Feminism and the subversion of identity.* New York: Routledge.

Butler, J. (1993). *Bodies that matter: On the discursive limits of "sex."* New York: Routledge.

Butler, J. (2004). *Undoing gender.* New York: Routledge.

Commentary and criticism. (2004). *Feminist Media Studies, 4,* 347–355.

Condit, C. (1989). The rhetorical limits of polysemy. *Critical Studies in Mass Communication, 6,* 103–122.

Cooper, B. (2002). *Boys Don't Cry* and female masculinity: Reclaiming a life & dismantling the politics of normative heterosexuality. *Critical Studies in Media Communication, 19,* 44–63.

Cooper, B., & E. C. Pease. (2002). "Don't want no short people 'round here": Confronting heterosexism's intolerance through comic and disruptive narratives in *Ally McBeal*. *Western Journal of Communication, 66,* 300–318.

Dow, B. J. (1996). *Prime-time feminism: Television, media culture, and the women's movement since 1970.* Philadelphia: University of Pennsylvania Press.

Dow, B. J. (2001). Ellen, television, and the politics of gay and lesbian visibility. *Critical Studies in Media Communication, 18,* 123–140.

Erni, J. N. (1998). Queer figurations in the media: Critical reflections on the Michael Jackson sex scandal. *Critical Studies in Media Communication, 15,* 158–180.

Evans, N. (1998). Games of hide and seek: Race, gender and drag in *The Crying Game* and *The Birdcage. Text & Performance Quarterly, 18,* 199–216.

Fejes, F., & Petrich, K. (1993). Invisibility, homophobia and heterosexism: Lesbians, gays, and the media. *Critical Studies in Media Communication, 10,* 396–404.

Fiske, J., & Hartley, J. (1978). *Reading television.* New York: Methuen.

Foucault, M. (1978). *The history of sexuality, volume one: An introduction.* (Trans., R. Hurley) New York: Vintage Books.

Gross, L. (1993). *Contested closets: The politics and ethics of outing.* Minneapolis: University of Minnesota Press.

Gross, L. (2001). *Up from invisibility: Lesbians, gay men, and the media in America.* New York: Columbia University Press.

Herman, D. (2003). "*Bad Girls* changed my life": Homonormativity in a women's prison drama. *Critical Studies in Media Communication, 20,* 141–159.

Johnson, E. P. (2003). *Appropriating blackness: Performance and the politics of authenticity.* Durham, NC: Duke University Press.

Mayne, J. (2000). *Framed: Lesbians, feminists, and media culture.* Minneapolis: University of Minnesota Press.

Meyer, M. D. E. (2003). "It's me. I'm it.": Defining adolescent sexual identity through relational dialectics in *Dawson's Creek. Communication Quarterly, 51,* 262–276.

Morris, C. E. (2002). Pink herring & the fourth persona: J. Edgar Hoover's sex crime panic. *Quarterly Journal of Speech, 88,* 228–244.

Morris, C. E., & Sloop, J. M. (in press). "What lips these lips have kissed": Refiguring the politics of queer public kissing. *Communication and Critical/Cultural Studies, 3.*

Nakayama, T. (1994). Show/down time: "Race," gender, sexuality, and popular culture. *Critical Studies in Media Communication, 11,* 162–179.

Patton, Cindy. (1990). *Inventing AIDS.* New York: Routledge.

Prosser, J. (1998). *Second skins: The body narratives of transsexuality.* New York: Columbia University Press.

Queer TV style. (2005). *GLQ: A Journal of Lesbian and Gay Studies, 11,* 95–117.

Rubin, G. (1993). Thinking sex: Notes for a radical theory of the politics of sexuality. In L. S. Kaufman (Ed.), *American feminist thought at century's end: A reader* (pp. 3–63). Cambridge, UK: Blackwell.

Sedgwick, E. (1990). *Epistemology of the closet.* Berkeley: University of California Press.

Sender, K. (1999). Selling sexual subjectivities: Audiences respond to gay window dressing. *Critical Studies in Mass Communication, 16,* 172–196.

Sender, K. (2001). Gay readers, consumers, and a dominant gay habitus. *Journal of Communication, 51,* 73–95.

Shugart, H. A. (2001). Parody as subversive performance: Denaturalizing gender and reconstituting desire in *Ellen. Text & Performance Quarterly, 21,* 95–113.

Shugart, H. A. (2003). Reinventing privilege: The new (gay) man in contemporary popular media. *Critical Studies in Media Communication, 20,* 67–91.

Shugart, H. A. (2005). On misfits and margins: Narrative, resistance, and the poster child. *Communication and Critical/Cultural Studies, 2,* 52–76.

Sloop, J. M. (2000). Disciplining the transgendered: Brandon Teena, public representation, and normativity. *Western Journal of Communication, 64,* 165–189.

Sloop, J. M. (2000). "A van with a bar and a bed": Ritualized gender norms in the John/Joan case. *Text & Performance Quarterly, 20,* 130–149.

Sloop, J. M. (2004). *Disciplining gender: Rhetorics of sex identity in contemporary culture.* Amherst: University of Massachusetts Press.

Smith, R. R., & R. R. Windes. (1997). The pro-gay and antigay issue culture: Interpretation, influence, and dissent. *Quarterly Journal of Speech, 83,* 28–48.

Squires, C. R., & Brouwer, D.C. (2002). In/discernible bodies: The politics of passing in dominant and marginal media. *Critical Studies in Media Communication, 19,* 283–310.

Thompson, J. M. (2002). *Mommy queerest: Contemporary rhetorics of lesbian maternal identity.* Amherst: University of Massachusetts Press.

Vavrus, M. D. (2002). Domesticating patriarchy: Hegemonic masculinity and television's "Mr. Mom." *Critical Studies in Media Communication, 19,* 352–375.

Walters, S. D. (2001). *All the rage: The story of gay visibility in America.* Chicago: University of Chicago.

Warner, M. (1993). Introduction. In M. Warner (Ed.), *Fear of a queer planet: Queer politics and social theory* (pp. vii-xxxi). Minneapolis: University of Minnesota Press.

Warner, M. (2002). Publics and counter-publics. *Quarterly Journal of Speech, 4,* 413–325.

Yep, G. A. (2004). The violence of heteronormativity in communication studies: Note on injury, healing, and queer world-making. In G. A. Yep, K. E. Lovass, & J. P. Elia (Eds.), *Queer theory and communication* (pp. 11–60). Binghamton, NY: Haworth Press.

Zuk, M. (2002). *Sexual selections: What we can and can't learn about sex from animals.* Berkeley: University of California Press.

18

GENDERED VIOLENCE AND MASS MEDIA REPRESENTATION

◆ Lisa M. Cuklanz

erhaps the single greatest challenge in considering gendered violence in media is to create a framework for limiting this subject to a category of texts. Many scholars of mass media and sex crime have observed that gendered violence is so commonplace and so normalized that it is hard to conceive of a category of mass mediated text that would be devoid of it. In her groundbreaking work, "The Symbolic Annihilation of Women," Tuchman (1978) observes that across several mass media, including magazines and television, women were depicted far less frequently than men. Female characters tended to be victims of violence or to have subordinate roles. In her analysis of the history of rape in U.S. film, Projansky (2001) asserts that rape functions "as the narrative motor for individual films . . . forming genres, shaping expectations, and naturalizing the cultural pervasiveness of sexual violence against women" (p. 63). Caputi (1987) asserts that "clearly, it is not only the content of the patriarchal media (the stereotyping, erasure, subordinations, and victimizations) which further the world view of sex crime, but also something about the forms and properties of the media themselves" (p. 169). In the United States, the overwhelming majority (often over 90%) of gendered crimes of violence (those against a person of a different gender) are committed by men against women and girls.[1] Representations by mass media in the United States of gendered violence reflect this pattern. Violence against women by men is a central theme in

◆ 335

genres including news, Hollywood film, popular music videos, and video and computer games. Less mainstream genres such as pornography exaggerate this tendency. This is the meaning of gendered violence and the premise for most scholarship on gendered violence in mass media, and my analysis starts with it. However, violence here is understood in its broader sense, as physical acts and other forms including sexual objectification and voyeurism.

Another important and productive way to understand gendered violence is to examine the role of media representations in constructing notions of gender itself. A significant strand of scholarship currently examines how media constructions of masculinity emphasize and even glorify violence. Conversely, media often link victimization through violence to definitions of what it means to be female. A relatively new strand of scholarship examines the emergence of violent femininity in media products.

Tuchman's (1978) definition of "symbolic annihilation" includes absence, trivialization, denigration, victimization, or condemnation. She argues that these characteristics dominate mass media's representation of women. Tuchman notes that women were more likely to be depicted as the victims of violence, and that "the pattern of women's involvement with television violence reveals approval of married women and condemnation of single and working women" (p. 13). Previous work to establish gender differences was largely empirical. Tedesco ("Patterns in Prime Time," 1974) found that female characters were victims of murder three times as often as they committed it, whereas male characters murdered twice as often as they were murdered. Tuchman's essay and the collection entitled *Hearth and Home* in which it appeared began to define a field of enterprise around analysis of gender representation and mass media that has since developed to encompass many disparate areas of inquiry.

Because the depiction of gendered violence in mass media is such an extensive subject, I narrow the purview of this discussion according to methodology, categories and genres. This chapter examines the central, best-developed strands of scholarship on gendered violence in news discourses, prime time television, mainstream Hollywood film, rap/hip-hop music and music video, and video/computer games. These broad forms of media are familiar to most readers. Many other strands of scholarship in the general area of gendered violence in mass media are productive, including analyses of independent and alternative films (Projansky, 2001), talk shows (Moorti, 1998), the World Wrestling Federation (Heinecken, 2004), westerns (Osgerby & Gough-Yates, 2001), and soap operas (Brown, 1990; Modleski, 1984). This chapter also does not cover the important and much-researched subject of pornography (see Cornell, 2000). Most research on pornography is undertaken from a psychological perspective, and/or it focuses on effects rather than patterns of representation. I am focusing on mainstream media representations, which reach a larger and broader audience. Pornography traverses media and is common in Internet, film, video, and magazine forms. Indeed, it could consume its own chapter.

A significant stream of scholarship on gendered violence (including pornography) examines the effects of viewing violence. Because this chapter focuses on representation (rather than on effects or reception), I will not discuss this scholarship at length. It is important to note, however, that many studies have shown how media representations of rape, domestic violence and sexual assault potentially influence human attitudes and behavior (see Donnerstein & Linz, 1986; Linz, Donnerstein, & Adams, 1989; Linz, Donnerstein, & Penrod, 1984; Wilson, Linz, Donnerstein, & Stipp, 1992; Zillmann & Bryant, 1982). Linz, Donnerstein, and Penrod's (1984) study is representative of studies utilizing experimental methodology. After viewing five films depicting violence against women, subjects "came to have fewer negative emotional reactions" to them and "to consider them significantly less degrading to women" (p. 130). Allen, Emmers, Gebhart, and Biery (1995) summarize a vast body of scholarly work investigating exposure to pornography and acceptance of rape myths. They conclude that "nonexperimental methodology shows almost no effect . . . while experimental studies show positive effect" (p. 5). Although some research confirms effects, such as desensitization and influence on beliefs, empirical studies have not conclusively demonstrated a causal connection between exposure to sexually violent media and real-world violence in general. Brief reviews of the methodological approaches discussed below are included in each section of the chapter. These approaches share a focus on representation and emphasize elements of symbolism and meaning.

◆ Representations of Gendered Violence in News Discourse

Scholarship on news coverage of rape, sexual assault, and battering takes part in a larger stream examining the "social construction of news" (see Bennett, 2001; Nimmo & Combs, 1990). Studies in this area question the values and definitions of news that result in flawed and often superficial coverage. They trace the ways ideologies and stereotypes are transmitted through news that purports to be objective. Traditionally, coverage of rape, sexual assault, and battering has focused on cases of extreme violence and has been characterized by sensationalism and voyeurism. Since the start of rape law reform in 1974 and the concomitant development of interest in and public information about these crimes, the effect of these practices has been mitigated by the occasional inclusion of feminist discourses or voices and by changes in how the crimes were reported. However, because of the ways in which news is defined and structured, coverage of gendered violence has remained skewed in many ways.

Scholarship on news coverage of gendered violence reflects the fact that news focuses primarily on rape and sexual assault, rarely on battering. Coverage of rape, sexual assault, and battery, like other news, tends to select single events, to favor incidents of extreme violence or other markers that supposedly make the event unique, to focus on drama and conflict, to seek what is regarded as balance in the two sides of an issue, to eschew discussions of background and historical/social issues, and to include elements of sensationalism, such as titillating or bizarre details. Each of these "news biases" (to use Bennett's, 2001, term) has a detrimental effect on the ability of media to provide fair and accurate coverage of gendered violence. Numerous scholars (Benedict, 1992; Cuklanz, 1996; Kitzinger, 2004; Moorti, 2002) have found that, because of the biases that define news, most of it about rape focuses on particular trials. Trials and legal proceedings that involve celebrities receive many times more coverage than those with previously unknown litigants (see Lule, 1995; Maxwell, Huxford, Borum, & Hornik, 2000; Moorti, 2002). Maxwell et al. (2002) found that even after the unprecedented coverage of the O. J. Simpson case, there was no lasting "shift from incident focused to socially focused reporting" (p. 258) of domestic violence. Because trial news is the most common format for news of gendered violence, there is a coherent body of scholarship in this area. These studies tend to examine the mythic frameworks (both feminist and traditional) for understanding rape that structure the reporting on it and on sexual assault.

Much of this work has focused on or included significant discussion of coverage of the victim. Benedict (1992) shows accusers being treated either as innocent, sweet, virginal, and undeserving victims of violent crime or as deceitful, manipulative, sexually experienced women of questionable motive. In attacks by strangers, particularly when extreme violence was used, the accuser is likely to be framed as a virgin. In cases of date or acquaintance rape, where guilt hinges more clearly on consent, accusers are usually framed as vamps who either deserved or brought about their own attacks. My work (Cuklanz, 1993, 1995b, 1996) focuses on high-profile cases and illustrates how the framing of the victim depends on the facts of the case. Projansky's (2001) more recent work is important in its examination of popular press stories that "[step] back from the focus on actual rape cases" (p. 91) and discuss issues related to sexual assault in general. She illustrates the centrality of postfeminist discourses within this coverage. They range from assumptions that violence against women is motivated by hate to an emphasis on the supposedly dangerous or threatening aspects of feminist perspectives on rape. Projansky shows that discussions of the constructions of "murkiness" or "confusion" surrounding rape in the writings of authors, including Ellen Goodman, Naomi Wolf, and Katie Roiphe, cast doubt on victim claims and suggest that guilt is difficult to assess. In many of these discussions, such confusions are explicitly blamed on feminism. Horeck (2004) argues that because the 1984 Big Dan's tavern gang rape case was the first nationally televised trial on CNN, it (and rape in general) "played a pivotal role in establishing the technology of a new genre of reality programming" (p. 90). Horeck finds troubling the idea that "we may be participating in a rape by 'just looking,' be it in Big Dan's tavern or in the comfort of our living rooms" (p. 90).

Several studies cover the intersection of race and gendered violence in news (Benedict, 1992; Meyers, 1997; Moorti, 2002), and the most thorough of these is Moorti's *Color of Rape* (2002). Moorti's analysis of news coverage of highly publicized assault cases concludes that, in general, "news coverage shifts attention from sexual assault to a discussion of masculinity" (p. 71) and that mainstream news discourses in the United States are "enunciated from a white, normative standpoint" (p. 71). Studies have found that coverage of cases involving victims of color is rare, that race and ethnicity are highlighted in troubling ways, and that many cases involving obvious guilt and/or conviction involve nonwhite perpetrators (see Consalvo, 1998; Cuklanz, 1995a; Horeck, 2004). Moorti (2002) notes that when such cases are covered "the news tends to foreground race-based assumptions of sexuality" (p. 73), such as the belief in the hypersexuality of African American women and the comparative rapaciousness of African American men. Meyers (1997) notes that stories with African American perpetrators or victims are frequently framed in terms of drug abuse, violence, and prostitution. She says that "details surrounding the act of violence, such as the woman's use of drugs or alcohol or her engagement in prostitution or other illegal or dangerous activities, serve to blame the victim" (p. 120). Meyers's (2004) more recent work on news coverage of black victims of sexual assault illustrates how racial stereotypes shape constructions of guilt and innocence. Like Moorti, she argues for the importance of considering the intersectionality of race, class, and gender.

Studies on news coverage of wife battering are less numerous. Carter's (Carter, Branston, & Allen, 1998) analysis of British news argues that emphasis on violent stranger attacks may encourage "readers to accept certain ideological justifications for male sexual violence as a typical, even inevitable feature of everyday life" (p. 221). Meyers (1994, 1997) provides the most in-depth analysis of this issue in her examination of several cases of wife battering as well as rape. She faults the coverage for failing to provide social or historical context for violence against women, for locating explanations of violence only within the psyche of the abuser or the victim's behavior, for treating counselors and victim advocates as biased sources rather than as experts, and for providing unnecessary details that are often damaging or shameful to victims. News about battering is especially problematic in its common failure to understand spousal murders as (often) the culmination of a husband's efforts to control, humiliate, and harm his wife. Consalvo's (1998) work on coverage of mail-order brides and domestic violence stemming from the Blackwell murders in Seattle is important for its discussion of mainstream representations of victims' guilt as related to their being foreigners and for its comparison of mainstream and minority press coverage. Consalvo's study affirms that mainstream news appears ill equipped to examine wife battering as a long-term relational pattern and widespread social problem, and she finds that alternative news sources can provide a clearer understanding. Her study of two minority newspapers in Seattle found that they provided more balance and better development of the idea that domestic violence is a public health problem as well as an open critique of the limitations of mainstream news coverage (p. 207).

Most of the studies reviewed here include some discussion of how coverage of gendered violence could be improved (see Kitzinger, 2004). Scholars agree that reporters need to be educated about the realities of rape and about the syndromes of rape trauma and wife battering. They could do more to treat victims with empathy and dignity by eliminating unnecessary details that might identify the victim or cause shame and humiliation. They could move away from stories that follow traditional myths about rape and wife battering, such as the idea that victims provoke their own attacks through dress or behavior or that assaults occur when psychically abnormal men suddenly snap. Byerly's (1994) essay on teaching about news coverage of these issues covers many of the same points.

While the work reviewed has provided important insights into the ideological functions of news on rape and battering, it tends to focus on individual cases and thus has done less to establish the breadth and quantity of such news generally. Although some studies, such as Benedict's (1992), do discuss the question of how trials are chosen to be covered, the mechanisms for case and topic selection are not well understood. Intersections of international and global discourses with these topics also have remained largely unexamined, although Stables's (2003) shows how coverage of gendered violence in Kosovo followed the general pattern of focus on

extreme cases and fragmentation of feminist ideas. Studies should also examine broader issues, such as the characteristics of highly publicized rape trials over time, coverage of cases in which the perpetrator is not male and the victim not female, the incidence and location of news stories that do not focus on trials, or the differential coverage of celebrity versus noncelebrity cases. Research might also focus on wife battering to raise questions about which cases receive coverage and whether it has improved or changed its framework, and document trends in coverage. Comparisons between the mainstream and alternative/ minority press, such as Consalvo's (1998), should be pursued about a range of cases and issues. Finally, as the definition of news continues to shift and expand, efforts, such as Rapping's (2003), can be made to examine discourses of wife battering wherever they exist, such as in nonfiction, so-called real crime programs such as *Unsolved Mysteries* or *Cops*.

◆ Representations of Gendered Violence in Prime-Time Entertainment Television

Text-based analyses of gendered violence on prime time television fit mostly under the cultural studies rubric. Cultural studies approaches set out to examine the role of media texts within a cultural context and how meanings are circulated and controlled within them, as well as how such meanings are related to issues of power. This research tends to focus on the construction of masculinity and femininity in mass media texts; the relationship among constructed gender, violence, and victimization; gaps or absences in representation of violence (such as the nearly total lack of images depicting women prevailing over or against male violence); and the relationships between prime time representation and ideologies that are external to television. In this section, I review scholarship on gendered violence on prime time television from a cultural/critical studies perspective. Since the publication of *Hearth and Home* in 1978, examinations of the relationships among stereotypes, violence, and representation have expanded and become more sophisticated. However, specific studies of gendered violence in television have emerged only very recently (Cuklanz, 2000; Moorti, 2002; Projansky, 2001). Scholarship on gendered violence and television is best developed in relation to the genres of crime/detective fiction and the made-for-TV movies.[2]

REPRESENTATIONS OF GENDERED VIOLENCE IN CRIME/DETECTIVE FICTION

Media scholars and cultural critics have observed common links between popular definitions of masculinity and violence in the world and within textual constructions of gendered violence (see Craig, 1992; Fiske, 1987; Holmlund, 2002; Jeffords, 1994; Kirkham & Thumin, 1993; Miedzian, 1991; Scharrer, 2001). This linkage is particularly pronounced in specific genres of film and television related to detective and police work, westerns, military and war genres. Of these, detective and police genres have received the most scholarly attention. Work on them also points to developments in the construction of alternative masculinities in relation to violence against women. Fiske (1987) and others have written about uses of the signs of masculinity found within such genres (such as guns, vehicles and other machines, and bulky muscles) as displays of idealized masculinity (see also Jeffords, 1994). Scharrer (2001) refers to extreme displays of these elements as "hypermasculinity," a form of representation of exaggerated masculine traits accompanied by the use of violence. Scholars have frequently noted that, like many other representational forms under discussion here (including the rape-revenge formula and the slasher film),

hypermasculinity represents a generalized insecurity about male roles in the wake of feminist activism.

My work (Cuklanz, 1998) documents the disproportionate representation of rape narratives within the cop/detective genres on prime time. Approximately 80% of prime time rapes were shown in these genres during the late 1970s. In these narratives, the perpetrators are most often male. However, as Moorti (2002), Projansky (2001), and I (Cuklanz, 1998; 2000) have all noted, the version of masculinity associated with these criminal activities is often marginalized and certainly not valorized. Rapists in stranger-rape narratives studied by all three scholars since the mid-1970s have most often been depicted as abnormal, horrific, extreme, psychotic, sociopathic, or otherwise far beyond the realm of normal or admirable masculinity. Narrative elements, such as extreme brutality, emphasis on victims' injuries and suffering, multiple attackers, and serial crimes, tend to emphasize the extremity of evil characterized by rapists. In narratives centering on date or acquaintance rape (more common since the mid-1980s), the perpetrator's attitudes and language set him apart from the normal or ideal male. Often he is known by the use of sexist language, callous attitudes toward women, and defensive denials of guilt. My work (Cuklanz, 2000) illustrates how negative masculine characters use violence against women and positive masculine characters protect and avenge women, using violence only against perpetrators. Violence is thus retained as an integral part of both masculine types.

Hanke (1992) employs the term "hegemonic masculinity" as a label for the dominant construction of masculinity in mass mediated texts. His work as well as my own delineates some ways in which this hegemonic masculinity has the ability to shift in response to social and cultural trends, such as attacks from feminists who have denounced the association of masculinity and the harming of women and children (in ways that include objectification, pornography, and rape). I argue, for example, that protagonist detectives in recent decades are often depicted as emotional, expressive, thoughtful, empathetic and caring toward victims (Cuklanz, 2000). They work well with female colleagues and can even express feminist points of view. Projansky (2001) provides a more nuanced account of the ideological functions of what she calls "male feminists" in rape narratives. She notes that the sympathetic friend/witness of rape who often comes forward to provide needed testimony is nearly always male, in effect a "hero . . . who articulates the truth about rape" (p. 113). The projection of the rape scene from the point of view of the noncomplicit male onlooker can be seen as both a redemptive discourse for hegemonic masculinity and as a construction of males as those with the correct "moral voice of the narrative" (p. 113). Projansky asserts that when men teach women about errors in law and about feminist views on rape, "men emerge as 'better' feminists than women, taking over the voice of feminism in the text, and thus depicting feminism without women" (p. 112). Moorti (2002) makes a similar observation about *L.A. Law*. To Projanksy (2001), some texts represent "the rape as a vehicle for understanding men" (p. 113). She notes that men's perspectives are also central in narratives that include African American characters. This phenomenon creates a recuperative, alternative form of masculinity that ideologically counteracts associations of normal masculinity with violence against women.

Accompanying these tendencies to place male characters at the center of rape narratives is an obvious correlative: the marginalization of women within these same stories. My book (Cuklanz, 2000) documents the many ways in which female victims are rendered mute in rape stories within the detective fiction genre through the 1980s. Victims are murdered, severely injured and rendered comatose, or go into shock and remain silent for days. When they have not been physically eliminated from the script, victims become frightened

and needy. Peripheral female characters (i.e., any other than the victim) are quite rare. Female detectives in prime time police series prior to 1990 were often used as decoys for rapists or other violent criminals, or they went undercover as sex workers (Buxton, 1990; Cuklanz, 2000). This trope placed the female officer in a vulnerable position from which she could be rescued by male colleagues. And, as Buxton notes in a discussion of *Miami Vice*, it also enabled "them to be portrayed in the crudest sex-symbol terms" (p. 159) and to legitimize "rough justice" on the part of the police/victim later in the story.

Findings on intersections of race and representations of rape in detective fiction are well established, with Moorti's (2002) work providing the most detailed examination. Moorti concludes that rape and race are usually kept separate, such that complex experiences of victims of color are very seldom explored. Certainly, the programs Moorti and others have analyzed have carefully avoided any echo of the myth of the black rapist. In fictionalized rape stories based on actual cases, racial identities other than white are usually altered (Moorti, p. 127). Moorti summarizes that "[t]he only subject position offered to nonwhite characters [in these inverted story lines] is as victims; nonwhite men are falsely charged with rape while nonwhite women suffer violation by white men" (p. 129). These episodes sometimes include racist characters and dialogue but "fail to present how a black woman's experience of rape is shaped by these myths of black female sexuality" (p. 131). Projansky's (2001) analysis emphasizes the way in which black victims of sexual violence are often depicted as the recipients of extreme violence that is visually explicit. These graphic depictions of sexualized violence play into myths of African American sexuality (see Crenshaw, 1995) and work against myths about race, violence, and victimization. Moorti (2002) and Projansky (2001) conclude that contemporary detective fiction narratives (as well as other forms and genres) cannot, in

Projansky's words "address the intersections of gender, race, and rape" (p. 194). Both believe that rape is often used to refer to or lead to discussion of other social problems. Rape or sexual violence becomes what Moorti calls an "absent presence" in the narratives, enabling or setting off the story's action, but receding quickly from view.

REPRESENTATIONS OF GENDERED VIOLENCE IN MADE-FOR-TV MOVIES

The made-for-television movie is known for its often sentimental or sensationalized treatment of "women's issues." As Rapping (2003) points out, these issues are usually construed as those related to gendered violence, particularly rape and battering, because other issues do not provide the excitement and sexual dimension so easily exploited by television programming. Rapping argues that contemporary programs on these issues have lost most of the feminist political edge that she documented in her earlier (1992) book. Her 2003 work documents the move away from issues as sociopolitical terrain and toward their treatment in exclusively legal terms. Rapping considers this move a conservative one that enables a shift away from feminist discourses. Themes of victim voice and empowerment, the constructed nature of gender and personality, and the potential for social change have been largely removed from the genre's more recent treatments of rape and battering.

Rapping's earlier work (1992) examined TV movies such as *The Burning Bed* (1984) (based on the Francine Hughes case) and *Silent Witness* (1985) (loosely based on the Big Dan's rape case) as "social issue" movies that dealt (with varying degrees of subtlety and success) with issues such as the intersection of class and victimization, female empowerment, personal growth and change, and even feminist politics. My own earlier work (Cuklanz, 1996) also noted that made-for-TV movies of the previous decades could sometimes do a better job than news discourses of articulating feminist or victim perspectives about rape and spouse abuse.

Although Rapping (1992) often deals with rape representation at the same time, her work is unique among studies of gendered violence on prime time television in its lengthy treatment of wife battering. Rapping asserts that in the early 1980s "network television was apt to present what . . . were highly progressive, feminist-informed portrayals of [battering], its root causes, and its potential cures" (p. 139). She also documents the era (early to mid-1980s) of the social issue TV movie as well as its demise in the late 1980s. Although she finds much worth praise in these movies, such as their general tendency to contradict obvious racial stereotypes concerning violence, she is critical of their limitations in focusing on individual solutions to social problems, in their lack of context, in depicting graphic violence mainly against working-class women, and in offering seamless narrative closure (Rapping, 1992, chap. 3). While Rapping's work discusses the contradiction of central racial stereotypes, Bobo and Seiter (1997) argue that a TV movie such as *The Women of Brewster Place* (1989) is different from similar "white" texts in its "emphasis on the process and survival of grief," among other things (p. 182).

DIRECTIONS FOR RESEARCH

Analyses of televisual representations of rape, like studies of news, are more developed than those of battering and other forms of violence. What is largely missing are studies of incidental violence in genres or episodes not especially focused on gendered violence but which nonetheless include such violence as part of another plot line. Hollywood film production could serve as a model for this type of television study. Studies of violence in cable programs, especially HBO series such as *The Sopranos*, *Oz*, or *The Wire*, are also rare. There is little work examining racial categories other than the typical black-white dichotomy, and themes of globalization are generally ignored.

◆ *Representations of Gendered Violence in Hollywood Film*

Haskell's (1987) book, *From Reverence to Rape: The Treatment of Women in the Movies,* provided the first book-length examination of women's roles in Hollywood film from the 1920s through 1960s. Although not focusing on gendered violence, Haskell asserts that the Hollywood film industry perpetuated "the idea of women's inferiority" (p. 1) "through the myths of subjection and sacrifice that were its fictional currency" (p. 3). Projansky (2001) provides an essential history of the subject in U.S. film from 1903 through 1979, documenting the significance of rape narratives. After illustrating their centrality in genres as disparate as westerns and screwball comedies, Projansky argues that rape has been so pervasive and so central to such a large corpus of films in this country that "violence against women . . . seems to be necessary to the film itself, but it concomitantly naturalizes the policing and negotiation of gendered, classed, racialized, and national boundaries these films engage" (p. 63). Projansky's work is the first to document this cross-genre significance of the subject of rape to the development of Hollywood film history.

The best-developed area of scholarship on Hollywood representation of gendered violence utilizes psychoanalytic theory to interrogate the film text. Such approaches start with the idea that film viewing, taking place within a darkened theater and projected in dreamlike fashion before a passive and psychologically isolated viewer, can productively be understood as related to subconscious mental processes which can be interrogated through close textual analysis. This general approach was initially linked to feminist analysis by Laura Mulvey

(1975) in her landmark essay, "Visual Pleasure in Narrative Cinema," in which she argues that many Hollywood films address an implicitly male viewer primarily through their framing of sexuality and violence toward the female body. Mulvey noted the links in many violent films between male heterosexual desire (of the female body) and the enactment of violence upon it. Since the publication of her essay, many theorists have challenged and refined this basic premise. Beginning with the concept of the male gaze, a psychoanalytic approach is interested in interrogating the inherent violence (and masculinized desire) within the film-viewing relationship. While subsequent works, such as those of Gaines (1988), hooks (1992), and Gamman and Marshment (1988), have examined the possibilities of film viewing from other points of view (especially those of black, lesbian, and female spectators), the basic validity of Mulvey's insights remains intact in much contemporary scholarship on gender, violence, and Hollywood film. Doane (1991), Mayne (1990), Silverman (1988), Gaines (1988), and Clover (1992a; 1992b) have made important contributions to feminist psychoanalytic film theory, and cultural studies approaches also have been used to examine gendered violence in film (see Boyle, 2005).

In her discussion of early Hollywood film, Kaplan (1983) identifies three representational mechanisms used in "the attempt of patriarchy to eliminate woman's threat" (p. 73). These include "dominating her through the controlling power of the gaze . . . fetishizing her" (p. 73), and murder. Kaplan notes that films from the late 1960s were first dominated by buddy films and female-victim films that "showed women being raped and subjected to violence," (p. 73) such as *Last Tango in Paris* (1972), *A Clockwork Orange* (1972), *Klute* (1971), *Straw Dogs* (1971), and *Lipstick* (1976). These films portray prostitution, rape, physical and verbal abuse, and "rage" against women. Rape revenge narratives are also prominent as well as the representation of sexual contact that begins as forcible rape but results in arousal of the victim followed by consensual sex. Haskell (1987) notes that two new trends started in the early 1980s: films geared to female audiences, "dealing explicitly with issues that the women's movement ha[d] raised" (p. 74), and films depicting explicit rape-murder-torture that were "relegated to the 'B' film and to the horror genre" (p. 74). As a result, much scholarship on gendered violence in post-1980s Hollywood film has focused on this somewhat marginal genre.

REPRESENTATIONS OF GENDERED VIOLENCE IN HORROR/SLASHER FILMS

On the surface, horror films depict acts of violence against victims of both sexes, with female victims often receiving the most brutal, and sexually symbolic, treatment at the hands of male monster-perpetrators. Scholars commenting on the overt messages of these films note that murders often follow sexual activity. The one female survivor is often "the girl who does not give in to sexual temptation" with the clear message that "sex does not pay" (Kottack, 1990, p. 98).[3] More recent scholarship is concerned with the symbolic work involved in the excessive and apparent sadism of horror films and the potential impact on the psychology of their viewers. In horror films, perhaps even more obviously than in other genres of Hollywood film, the rape, torture, humiliation, and degradation of women are understood as symbolic means of containing or eliminating threats to male power. As Creed (1999) puts it, "Woman's body is slashed and mutilated. . . . In the guise of 'madman' [the male] enacts on her body the one act he most fears himself, transforming her entire body into a bleeding wound" (p. 257). Although there are subtle differences in analysis among scholars, this basic link between male psychological fears and anxieties and the filmic violence against women in the horror genre is a point of agreement.

Much of the work on horror films focuses on audience psychology. Modleski (1986) focuses on the "feminization" of the audience as a whole through their identification with the (often female) victims of the horror genre monster. She also maintains that there is a difference between male and female viewers because these films project "the experience of submission and defenseless onto the female body." They "enable the male spectator to distance himself somewhat from the terror" while "as usual, it is the female spectator who is *truly* deprived of 'solace and pleasure'" (p. 163). Clover (1992b) argues that horror film audiences (including males) have the ability to identify with characters across gender lines. Clover maintains that film themes such as masochism and victimization are feminized in mainstream film, whereas aggression, dominance, and violence are markers of masculinity.

REPRESENTATIONS OF VIOLENT WOMEN IN HOLLYWOOD FILMS

Inness (1999, 2004) examines recent developments of the violent female action hero in Hollywood cinema.[4] Although aggressive and violent women were important in the film noir genre of the 1940s and 1950s (see Kaplan, 1978), contemporary histories of violent action heroines, including that of Inness (1999), usually trace the type to Sigourney Weaver's Ripley in the *Alien* trilogy (1979–1992; see Vaughn, 1995) and Linda Hamilton's Sarah Conner in *Terminator II: Judgment Day* (1991). More recent contributions to the genre include *Lara Croft: Tomb Raider* (2001; see Herbst, 2004) and *Barb Wire* (1996; Brown, 2004), although other films in the action heroine genre have also been examined (see Williams, 1996, 1999). In these films, female characters perform masculinity, undertaking acts of violence, usually in the cause of justice or world salvation. The female protagonist is either hypermasculinized as a figurative male (with enormous muscles and total lack of emotional connection to other people) or hypersexualized as a male fantasy (with exaggerated breasts, hips, lips, and so forth), or both. The linkages between exaggerated feminine physical traits and the use of violence in action heroines has been the subject of much discussion (see Brown, 2004; Herbst, 2004; Neroni, 2005; Tasker, 1993).[5] While Herbst (2004) argues that Lara Croft represents a linkage between sex and death (2004), Brown (2004) shows how the action heroine is transgressive because she "personifies a unity of disparate traits in a single figure" and "refutes any assumed belief in appropriate gender roles via an exaggerated use of those very roles" (p. 49). Action heroines offer tough and effective "masculine" heroines, but have also made scenes of violence against women engaged in physical combat more common.

Violent women also are featured in rape-revenge films, another significant focus of scholarship (see Clover, 1992a; Franco, 2004; Projansky, 2001; Read, 2000; Wilson, 2001). Clover discusses the development of this formula in slasher-type films that feature both prolonged graphic brutalization of women and systematic, effective murderous revenge on male perpetrators. Clover reads *The Accused* (1988) as a better produced and funded version of the same plot. What the various versions of the rape-revenge film have in common are strong, highly motivated rape victims intent on retribution. These films take on the victim's point of view and are sympathetic to her feelings and actions. However, they feature some of the most graphic and difficult scenes of gendered violence. Projansky is critical of the formula for its use of rape as an empowering event for protagonist women characters, impelling them toward action on their own behalf (see also Horeck, 2004; Wilson, 2001). She notes that in many films rape is the only impetus that can move women toward independent physical action. Several authors have discussed the film *Thelma and Louise* (1991) (see Boozer, 1995; Dargis, 1992; Hollinger, 1998; Projansky, 2001) as a unique Hollywood offering that depicts violence by "normal" women. Most analysts believe that the film

became very controversial because of its relatively realistic depiction of violence by average women against men (including a rapist).

A number of books examine Hollywood film narratives that construe lesbians as menacing, threatening, mentally deranged, and/or violent, which is also a pattern in representation of gay men (see Russo, 1987). Hart (1994) examines films such as *Single White Female* (1992) and *Basic Instinct* (1992) that feature violent lesbian protagonists. She (Hart, 1994) notes that "lesbians in mainstream representations have almost always been depicted as predatory, dangerous, and pathological" (p. x) and argues that lesbian violence has led the way for depictions of violent women in general. Hart (1994) asserts that because of the imperatives of presumptive heterosexuality and the maleness of desire, and the resulting need to marginalize both female desire and lesbian sexuality, mainstream culture "has made the lesbian and the female criminal synonomous [sic] by displacing women's aggression onto the sexual deviant" (p. xii). Violence and lesbianism are also linked in B-list women's prison films. Mayne (2000) argues for the ability of this somewhat marginal genre to offer "much more than the standard feminist account of women in the traditional cinema would suggest" (p. 143) precisely because of their marginal nature. She observes that "scenes of rape and torture are staples of the genre" and that they "play on the helplessness and victimization of women" (p. 115). However, this genre often is able to combine race and sexuality in ways that are both stereotypical and complex.

DIRECTIONS FOR RESEARCH ON REPRESENTATIONS OF GENDERED VIOLENCE IN HOLLYWOOD FILM

Scholars have given a great deal of attention to representations of gendered violence in Hollywood films. With a few exceptions, the well-developed lines of research on rape revenge narratives and lesbian criminal characterizations have been undertaken from a psychoanalytic perspective. Future work could productively utilize a cultural studies approach to mainstream film to examine violence in more realist genres and in genres less clearly defined by violence.

REPRESENTATIONS OF GENDERED VIOLENCE IN RAP MUSIC, MUSIC VIDEO, AND VIDEO/COMPUTER GAMES

In addition to the significant scholarship on representations of gendered violence in news, television, and Hollywood film outlined above, important work is emerging on newer forms of media, including rap music, music video, and video/computer games. Because other chapters in this section, including the chapter on new media and the chapter on race, gender, and media examine these forms in detail, this section presents only a brief overview of some of the central issues and debates involving gendered violence within them.

MTV specifically and music video more generally have been criticized by many researchers for their symbolic annihilation of women. Some researchers have studied potential links between music videos and attitudes or violent behavior (Johnson, Adams, Ashburn, & Reed, 1995; Miranda & Claes, 2004). A number of studies have documented sexism and stereotyping of women in music videos (see Seidman, 1992; Sherman & Dominick, 1986; White, 2001). Gow (1996) notes that early music video was widely critiqued for its underrepresentation of women and the depiction of women as scantily clad "targets of men's condescending actions" (p. 2). After protests from various groups, broadcast networks created the Broadcast Standards Network that prohibited nudity and portrayals of violence against women. Gow's (1996) study finds that "the regulations regarding video content may have contributed to a decrease in overt acts of violence against women," but that "women continued to be underrepresented and portrayed in a manner that stressed their physical appearance" (p. 6). Signorelli and McLeod (1994) found that MTV commercials were similarly stereotypical, portraying women in relation to their physical appearance (in scanty clothing, as the object of other's gaze, as physically attractive) and less frequently overall compared with male characters.

The sexually objectifying and violent content of hip-hop/rap music has received more media and scholarly attention than gendered violence in any other genre of popular music. According to Cole and Guy-Sheftall (2003), "Rap music videos are notorious for featuring half-clothed young Black women gyrating obscenely and functioning as backdrops, props, and objects of lust for rap artists who sometimes behave as predators" (p. 186). While noting that not all forms of rap are misogynistic, Cole and Guy-Sheftall believe that in general "hip-hop is more misogynistic" than other popular music genres and that "casual references to rape and other forms of violence" (p. 186) are especially damaging to their target audience of black male youth. They believe in part that rap lyrics reflect lived experience as well as a displacement of rage against civil and political institutions, including police, onto the black woman. Smith-Shomade (2002) labels the excessively angry, violent, and misogynistic lyrics of the 1980s as "anger-for-profit" produced by Reaganomics (see also Ro, 1996). Other analysts question both the assertion that rap music is more misogynist than other forms of popular music and the means through which rap's use of violence against women is critiqued. Crenshaw's (1997) subtle analysis of the controversy over 2 Live Crew lyrics observes the disproportionate attention given to rap lyrics compared with other similarly sexist music genres. She concludes that of the two main defenses of 2 Live Crew lyrics by black analysts, "Neither presents sufficient justification for requiring Black women to tolerate such misogyny" (p. 261). However,

Crenshaw also identifies racism in the legal process against 2 Live Crew's lyrics, thus finding harm to black women in both the lyrics and the legal prosecution of them.[6] Other authors have examined the empowering representational strategies of feminist rappers such as Queen Latifah (Morgan, 1999; Roberts, 1994; Savage, 2001).

Scholarship examining gendered violence in video and computer games also is well established. Much scholarly discussion focuses on the link between the target audience of adolescent boys and the gendered violence in video and computer games. Herbst (2004) maintains that "on the virtual terrain of war-inspired computer games, the female, biologically inescapably tied to the processes of reproduction, is represented in an unprecedented display of eroticism and violence" (p. 23). Herbst argues that computer game character Lara Croft, for example, links reproduction and destruction, sex and death. She argues that since Croft's body is designed such that it could not possibly be capable of reproduction, she presents less threat to male identity and its need for exclusive control over the powers of destruction (p. 33). Her analysis also emphasizes the intertextual and intergeneric aspect of the Lara Croft character, which has moved from computer game to Hollywood film. Cassell and Jenkins's (2000) volume focuses on the challenges of creating interesting games without violent content while convincing producers to consider girls as a serious market. In addition, Subrahmanyam and Greenfield (2000) investigate the question of the appeal of video games to children of each gender. They note that "research suggests that girls do not find . . . violence appealing" (p. 51). Several researchers have examined the gendered nature of video games' appeal with similar findings (Goldstein, 1994; Lin & Lepper, 1987). Flanagan (2002) notes that most games are still created by and for males. She argues that a gamer, unlike a user of traditional media, enjoys "double embodiment" or "double consciousness," the simultaneous experience of "the class, race, and gender identity of the user's physical body, as well as the virtual body (or bodies) of the character he or she 'becomes'" (p. 438).

◆ Conclusion

Gendered violence in mass media covers an apparently infinite range of texts and examples. Scholarship on this subject is vast, even if a narrow definition of gendered violence is employed. This chapter has narrowed the range of genres and media to those around which coherent bodies of text-based scholarship on representation have emerged—mainstream news, prime-time television, Hollywood film, music video, rap/hip-hop, and video/computer games. It has traced a partial history of mass mediated representations of gendered violence through the period when feminist discourses were gaining acceptance and creating disturbances in traditional representational codes and into the postfeminist era of gender role experimentation and female empowerment. While essay- and book-length studies of discourses surrounding rape and other forms of gendered violence are now numerous, much ground has yet to be covered. With the passing of the era of educational mass media texts informing citizens about so-called new feminist issues such as wife battering and rape, scholars are currently grappling with how stories about rape and other physical abuses are currently being rendered as entertaining narratives in a postfeminist cultural context. Others are working to keep pace with the rapid transformation and invention of new genres of mass media that take up gendered violence in unexpected ways. Work should continue to examine the ways in which gender, race, class, sexuality, and cultural politics intersect to form new themes and codes of mass media representation of gendered violence.

◆ Notes

1. In its examination of persons who committed murder in 2003, the FBI Uniform Crime Report (2003, Table 2.5) cited approximately 8.5 times (10,218) as many male murderers as female (1,213). According to Bureau of Justice statistics (Rennison & Welchans, 2002), 94% victims of completed rape are female, and 91% of victims of attempted rape are female (p. 1).

2. As noted later in this chapter, the relatively new fantasy genre that includes programs such as *Buffy the Vampire Slayer* and *Dark Angel* has received a great deal of recent attention. This section focuses on made-for-TV movies rather than the somewhat redundant genre of action heroine fantasy.

3. A significant stream of empirical scholarship examines the physiological responses or arousal of subjects upon viewing filmed violence (see Frost & Stauffer). Oliver (1994) found that, within the graphic horror genre, portrayals of sexuality increased enjoyment of male viewers and viewers who rated high on "measures of sexual permissiveness" (p. 1). For further studies of horror films and sexuality, see Molitor and Sapolsky (1993) and Weaver (1991). For experimental studies of the effects of filmed violence see also Donnerstein and Berkowitz (1981) and Cantor, Zillman, and Einseidel (1978). For examinations of connections between sex/sexuality and violence/aggression in media, see Hansen and Hansen (1990) and Linz, Donnerstein, and Penrod (1987).

4. Several recent analyses examine the allied trend of violent/masculine girls and women in televisual portrayals, particularly in the fantasy genre that includes *Buffy the Vampire Slayer, Dark Angel,* and *Xena: Warrior Princess.* Crosby (2004) argues that (contrary to action heroes) all three televisual action heroines are alienated and guilty because of their power and wish to disown it. For additional analyses of "masculine" female heroines on television, see Ross (2004), Wilcox and Lavery (2002), Osgerby and Gough-Yates (2001).

5. For examinations of gender and violence in science fiction genres see Flanagan and Booth (2002) *Reload: Rethinking Women &* *Cyberculture* and Roberts (1999) *Sexual generations: "Star Trek: The Next Generation" and gender.*

6. For a concurring opinion on the politics of mainstream critiques of rap's misogyny, see Potter (1995) and Rose (1996). Potter argues that "the criticism of 'violence' and misogyny in rap lyrics is a tactical move characteristic of what critics . . . describe as 'moral panics'" and that it relies on familiar racist stereotypes (p. 90). Rose argues that "the way rap and rap-related violence are discussed in the popular media is fundamentally linked to the larger social discourse on the special control of black people" (p. 237).

◆ References

Allen, M., Emmers, T., Gebhart, L, & Biery, M. A. (1995). Exposure to pornography and acceptance of rape myths. *Journal of Communication, 45*(1), 5–26.

Benedict, H. (1992). *Virgin or vamp: How the press covers sex crimes.* New York: Oxford University Press.

Bennett, W. L. (2001). *News: The politics of illusion* (4th ed.). White Plains, NY: Longman.

Bobo, J., & Seiter, E. (1997). Black feminism and media criticism: *The Women of Brewster Place.* In C. Brunsdon, J. D'Acci, & L. Spigel (Eds.), *Feminist television criticism: A reader* (pp. 167–183). Oxford, UK: Clarendon Press.

Boozer, J. (1995). Seduction and betrayal in the heartland: *Thelma & Louise. Literature & Film Quarterly, 23*(3), 188–196.

Boyle, K. (2005). *Media and violence: Gendering the debates.* London: Sage.

Brown, J. (2004). Gender, sexuality, and toughness: The bad girls of action film and comic books. In S. Inness (Ed.), *Action chicks: New images of tough women in popular culture* (pp. 47–74). New York: Palgrave Macmillan.

Brown, M. E. (1990). *Television and women's culture: The politics of the popular.* Newbury Park, CA: Sage.

Buxton, D. (1990). *From* The Avengers *to* Miami Vice: *Form and ideology in television series*. Manchester, UK: Manchester University Press.

Byerly, C. (1994). An agenda for teaching news coverage of rape. *Journalism Education,* Spring, 59–69.

Cantor, J. R., Zillman, D., & Einseidel, E. F. (1978). Female response to provocation after exposure to aggressive and erotic films. *Communication Research, 5,* 395–411.

Caputi, J. (1987). *The age of sex crime.* Bowling Green, OH: Bowling Green University Popular Press.

Carter, C., Branston, G., & Allen, S. (Eds.). (1998). *News, gender and power.* New York: Routledge.

Cassell, J., & Jenkins, H. (Eds.). (2000). *From* Barbie *to* Mortal Kombat: *Gender and computer games.* Cambridge: MIT Press.

Clover, C. (1992a). High and low: The transformation of the rape-revenge movie. In P. Cook & P. Dodd (Eds.), *Women and film: A* Sight and Sound *reader* (pp. 76–85). Philadelphia: Temple University Press.

Clover, C. (1992b). *Men, women, and chain saws: Gender in the modern horror film.* Princeton, NJ: Princeton University Press.

Cole, J., & Guy-Sheftall, B. (2003). *Gender talk: The struggle for women's equality in African American communities.* New York: Ballantine Books.

Consalvo, M. (1998). 3 shot dead in courthouse: Examining news coverage of domestic violence and mail-order brides. *Women's Studies in Communication, 21,* 188–211.

Cornell, D. (2000). *Feminism and pornography.* New York: Oxford University Press.

Craig, S. (Ed.). (1992). *Men, masculinity, and the media: Research on men and masculinities.* Thousand Oaks, CA: Sage.

Creed, B. (1999). Horror and the monstrous-feminine: An imaginary abjection. In S. Thornham (Ed.), *Feminist film theory: A reader* (pp. 251–266). New York: New York University Press.

Crenshaw, K. W. (1995). Mapping the margins: Intersectionality, identity politics, and violence against women of color. In C. Crenshaw,

N. Gotanda, G. Peller, & K. Thomas (Eds.), *Critical race theory: The key writings that formed the movement* (pp. 357–383). New York: The New Press.

Crenshaw, K. W. (1997). Beyond racism and misogyny: Black feminism and 2 Live Crew. In D. Meyers (Ed.), *Feminist social thought* (pp. 245–263). New York: Routledge.

Crosby, S. (2004). The cruelest season: Female heroes snapped into sacrificial heroines. In S. Inness (Ed.), *Action chicks: New images of tough women in popular culture* (pp. 153–180). New York: Palgrave MacMillan.

Cuklanz, L. M. (1993). Truth in transition: Discursive constructions of character in the Rideout rape in marriage case. *Women's Studies in Communication, 16*(1), 74–101.

Cuklanz, L. M. (1995a). News coverage of ethnic and gender issues in the Big Dan's rape case. In A. N. Valdivia (Ed.), *Feminism, multiculturalism, and the media* (pp. 145–162). London: Sage.

Cuklanz, L. M. (1995b). Opposing verdicts in the Webb-Dotson rape case: Legal versus news constructions. *Communication Studies, 46,* 45–56.

Cuklanz, L. M. (1996). *Rape on trial: How the mass media construct legal reform and social change.* Philadelphia: University of Pennsylvania Press.

Cuklanz, L. M. (1998). The masculine ideal: Prime time representations of rape, 1976–1978. *Critical Studies in Mass Communication, 15,* 423–448.

Cuklanz, L. M. (2000). *Rape on prime time: Television, masculinity, and sexual violence.* Philadelphia: University of Pennsylvania Press.

Dargis, M. (1992). *Thelma and Louise* and the tradition of the male road movie. In P. Cook (Ed.), *Women and film: A* Sight and Sound *reader* (pp. 86–92). Philadelphia: Temple University Press.

Doane, M. A. (1991). *Femmes fatales: Feminism, film theory, and psychoanalysis.* New York: Routledge.

Donnerstein, E., & Berkowitz, L. (1981). Victim reactions in aggressive erotic films as a factor in violence against women. *Journal of Personality and Social Psychology, 41,* 710–724.

Donnerstein, E., & Linz, D. (1986). Mass media sexual violence and male viewers: Current theory and research. *American Behavioral Scientist, 29,* 601–618.

Federal Bureau of Investigation. (2003). *Uniform Crime Report.* Retrieved October 15, 2004, from www.fbi.gov/ucr/03cius .htm

Fiske, J. (1987). *Television culture.* New York: Methuen.

Flanagan, M. (2002). Hyperbodies, hyperknowledge: Women in games, women in cyberpunk, and strategies of resistance. In M. Flanagan & A. Booth (Eds.), *Reload: Rethinking women & cyberculture* (pp. 425–455). Cambridge: MIT Press.

Flanagan, M., & Booth, A. (Eds.). (2002). *Reload: Rethinking women & cyberculture.* Cambridge: MIT Press.

Franco, J. (2004). Gender, genre and female pleasure in the contemporary revenge narrative: *Baise Moi* and *What It Feels Like for a Girl. Quarterly Review of Film and Video, 21*(1), 1–10.

Frost, R., & Stauffer, J. (1987). The effects of social class, gender, and personality on physiological responses to filmed violence. *Journal of Communication, 37*(2), 1–17. Retrieved April 10, 2005 from PCI Full Text database.

Gaines, J. (1988). White privilege and looking relations: Race and gender in feminist film theory, *Screen, 29*(4), 12–27.

Gamman, L., & Marshment, M. (Eds.). (1988). *The female gaze: Women as viewers of popular culture.* London: Women's Press.

Goldstein, J. H. (1994). Sex differences in toy play use and use of video games. In Goldstein, J. H. (Ed.), *Toys, play, and child development* (pp. 110–129). New York: Cambridge University Press.

Gow, J. (1996). Reconsidering gender roles on MTV: Depictions in the most popular music videos of the early 1990s. *Communication Reports, 9*(2), 1–9. Retrieved April 10, 2005, from Ebsco Host database.

Hanke, R. (1992). Redesigning men: Hegemonic masculinity in transition. In Craig, S. (Ed.), *Men, masculinity, and media.* Newbury Park: Sage.

Hansen, C. H., & Hansen, R. D. (1990). The influence of sex and violence on the appeal of rock music videos. *Communication Research, 17,* 212–234.

Hart, L. (1994). *Fatal women: Lesbian sexuality and the mark of aggression.* Princeton, NJ: Princeton University Press.

Haskell, M. (1987). *From reverence to rape: The treatment of women in the movies.* London: Routledge.

Heinecken, D. (2004). No cage can hold her rage? Gender, transgression, and the World Wrestling Federation's Chyna. In S. Inness (Ed.), *Action chicks: New images of tough women in popular culture* (pp. 181–206). New York: Palgrave Macmillan.

Herbst, C. (2004). Lara's lethal and loaded mission: Transposing reproduction and destruction. In S. Inness (Ed.), *Action chicks: New images of tough women in popular culture* (pp. 21–46). New York: Palgrave Macmillan.

Hollinger, K. (1998). *In the company of women: The contemporary female friendship film.* Minneapolis: University of Minnesota Press.

Holmlund, C. (2002). *Impossible bodies: Masculinity and femininity at the movies.* New York: Routledge.

hooks, b. (1992). *Black looks: Race and representation.* Boston: South End Press.

Horeck, T. (2004). *Public rape: representing violation in fiction and film.* New York: Routledge.

Inness, S.A. (1999). *Tough girls: Women warriors and wonder women in popular culture.* Philadelphia: University of Pennsylvania Press.

Inness, S.A. (2004). *Action chicks: New images of tough women in popular culture.* New York: Palgrave Macmillan.

Jeffords, S. (1994). *Hard bodies: Hollywood masculinity in the Reagan era.* New Brunswick, NJ: Rutgers University Press.

Johnson, J. D., & Adams, M. S., Ashburn, L., & Reed, W. (1995). Differential gender effects of exposure to rap music on African American adolescents' acceptance of teen dating violence. *Sex Roles: A Journal of Research, 33*(7–8), 597–605.

Kaplan, E. A. (1978). Women in film noir. London: British Film Institute.

Kaplan, E. A. (1983). *Women and film: Both sides of the camera.* New York: Methuen.

Kirkham, P., & Thumin, J. (1993). *You Tarzan: Masculinity, movies and men.* New York: St. Martins.

Kitzinger, J. (2004). Media coverage of sexual violence against women and children. In K. Ross & C. Byerly (Eds.), *Women and Media: International Perspectives* (pp. 13–37). Malden, MA: Blackwell.

Lin, S., & Lepper, M. (1987). Correlates of children's use of video games and computers. *Journal of Applied Psychology, 17,* 72–93.

Linz, D., Donnerstein, E., & Adams, S. (1989). Physiological desensitization and judgments about female victims of violence. *Human Communication Research, 15,* 509–522.

Linz, D., Donnerstein, E., & Penrod, S. (1984). The effects of multiple exposures to filmed violence against women. *Journal of Communication, 34,* 130–147.

Linz, D., Donnerstein, E., & Penrod, S. (1987). Sexual violence in the mass media: Social psychological implications. In P. Shaver & C. Hendrick (Eds.), *Review of personality and social psychology* (pp. 95–123). Newbury Park, CA: Sage.

Lule, J. (1995). The rape of Mike Tyson: Race, the press and symbolic types. *Critical Studies in Mass Communication, 12*(2), 176–195.

Mayne, J. (1990). *Woman at the keyhole: Feminism and women's cinema.* Bloomington: Indiana University Press.

Mayne, J. (2000). *Framed: Lesbians, feminists, and media culture.* Minneapolis: University of Minnesota Press.

Maxwell, K. A., Huxford, J., Borum, C., & Hornik, R. (2000). Covering domestic violence: How the O. J. Simpson case shaped reporting of domestic violence in the news media. *Journalism and Mass Communication Quarterly, 77*(2), 258–272.

Meyers, M. (1994). News of battering. *Journal of Communication, 44*(2), 47–63.

Meyers, M. (1997). *News coverage of violence against women: Engendering blame.* Thousand Oaks, CA: Sage.

Meyers, M. (2004). African American women and violence: Gender, race, and class in the news.

Critical Studies in Media Communication, 21(2), 95–118.

Miedzian, M. (1991). *Boys will be boys: Breaking the link between masculinity and violence.* New York: Anchor Doubleday.

Miranda, D., & Claes, M. (2004). Rap music genres and deviant behaviors in French-Canadian adolescents. *Journal of Youth and Adolescence, 33*(2), 113–122.

Modleski, T. (1984). *Loving with a vengeance: Mass produced fantasies for women.* New York: Methuen.

Modleski, T. (1986). The terror of pleasure: The contemporary horror film and postmodern theory. In T. Modleski (Ed.), *Studies in entertainment: Critical approaches to mass culture* (pp. 155–166). Bloomington: Indiana University Press.

Molitor, F., & Sapolsky, B. S. (1993). Sex, violence, and victimization in slasher films. *Journal of Broadcasting and Electronic Media, 37,* 233–242.

Moorti, S. (1998). Cathartic confessions or emancipatory texts? Rape narratives on *Oprah Winfrey Show. Social Text, 16*(4), 83–102.

Moorti, S. (2002). *Color of rape: Gender and race in television's public spheres.* Albany: State University of New York Press.

Morgan, J. (1999). *When chickenheads come home to roost: My life as a hip-hop feminist.* New York: Simon & Schuster.

Mulvey, L. (1975). Visual pleasure and narrative cinema. *Screen, 16*(3), 6–18.

Neroni, H. (2005). *The violent woman: Femininity, narrative, and violence in contemporary American cinema.* Albany: State University of New York Press.

Nimmo, D., & Combs, J. E. (1990). *Mediated political realities.* New York: Longman.

Osgerby, B., & Gough-Yates, A. (Eds.). (2001). *Action TV: Tough guys, smooth operators, and foxy chicks.* New York: Routledge.

Oliver, M. B. (1994). Contributions of sexual portrayals to viewers' responses to graphic horror. *Journal of Broadcasting and Electronic Media, 38*(1), 1–14. Retrieved April 10, 2005, from Ebsco Host database.

Potter, R. (1995). *Spectacular vernaculars: Hip-hop and the politics of postmodernism.* Albany: State University of New York Press.

Projansky, S. (2001). *Watching rape: Film and television in postfeminist culture*. New York: New York University Press.

Rapping, E. (1992). *The movie of the week: Private stories/public events*. Minneapolis: University of Minnesota Press.

Rapping, E. (2003). *Law and justice as seen on TV*. New York: New York University Press.

Read, J. (2000). *The new avengers: Feminism, femininity, and the rape-revenge cycle*. New York: Manchester University Press.

Rennison, C. M., & Welchans, S. (2002). *Rape and sexual assault: Reporting to police and media attention, 1992–2000*. Bureau of Justice Statistics. Retrieved May 1, 2005, from www.ojp.usdoj.gov/bjs/pub/pdf/ rsarp00.pdf

Ro, R. (1996). *Gangsta: Merchandising the rhymes of violence*. New York: St. Martins Press.

Roberts, R. (1994). "Ladies first": Queen Latifah's Afrocentric feminist music video. *African American Review, 28*(2), 245–251.

Roberts, R. (1999). *Sexual generations: "Star Trek: The Next Generation" and gender*. Urbana: University of Illinois Press.

Rose, T. (1996). Hidden politics: Discursive and institutional policing of rap music. In W. E. Perkinds (Ed.), *Droppin' science: Critical essays on rap music and hip hop culture* (pp. 236–257). Philadelphia: Temple University Press.

Ross, S. (2004). "Tough enough": Female friendship and heroism in *Xena* and *Buffy*. In S. Inness (Ed.), *Action chicks: New images of tough women in popular culture* (pp. 231–256). New York: Palgrave Macmillan.

Russo, V. (1987). *The celluloid closet: Homosexuality in the movies*. New York: Harper & Row.

Savage, A. (2001). Music, womankind, and patriarchy: Women break music industry ideological myths. *Women & Language, 24*(1), 45.

Scharrer, E. (2001). Tough guys: The portrayal of hypermasculinity and aggression in televised police dramas. *Journal of Broadcasting and Electronic Media, 45*, 615–634.

Seidman, S. A. (1992). An investigation of sex-role stereotype in music videos. *Journal of Broadcasting & Electronic Media, 36*, 209–216.

Sherman, B. L., & Dominick, J. R. (1986). Violence and sex in music videos: TV and rock n' roll. *Journal of Communication, 36*, 79–93.

Signorelli, N., & McLeod, D. (1994). Gender stereotypes in MTV commercials: The beat goes on. *Journal of Broadcasting & Electronic Media, 38*(1), 91–101.

Silverman, K. (1988). *The acoustic mirror: The female voice in psychoanalysis and cinema*. Bloomington: Indiana University Press.

Smith-Shomade, B. E. (2002). *Shaded lives: African-American women and television*. New Brunswick, NJ: Rutgers University Press.

Stables, G. (2003). Justifying Kosovo: Representations of gendered violence and U.S. military intervention. *Critical Studies in Media Communication, 20*(1), 92–115.

Subrahmanyam, K., & Greenfield, P. M. (2000). Computer games for girls: What makes them play? In J. Cassell & H. Jenkins (Eds.), *From* Barbie *to* Mortal Kombat*: Gender and computer games* (pp. 46–71). Cambridge: MIT Press.

Tasker, Y. (1993). *Spectacular bodies: Gender, genre, and action cinema*. New York: Routledge.

Tedesco, N. (1974). Patterns in prime time. *Journal of Communication, 24*, 119–24.

Tuchman, G. (1978). The symbolic annihilation of women in the mass media. In Tuchman, G., Daniels, A. K., & Benet, J. (Eds.), *Hearth and home: Images of women in the mass media* (pp. 3–38). New York: Oxford University Press.

Vaughn, T. (1995). Voices of sexual distortion: Rape, birth, and self-annihilation metaphors in the "Alien Trilogy." *Quarterly Journal of Speech, 81*(4), 423–435.

Weaver III, J. B. (1991). Are "slasher" horror films sexually violent? A content analysis. *Journal of Broadcasting and Electronic Media, 35*, 385–392.

White, L. A. (2001). A re-investigation of sex-role stereotyping in MTV music videos. *Women & Language, 24*(1), 45.

Wilcox, R.V., & Lavery, D. (2002). *Fighting the forces: What's at stake in* Buffy the Vampire Slayer. New York: Rowman & Littlefield.

Williams, L. (1996). Demi Moore takes it like a man: Body talk. *Sight & Sound, 7*(1), 18–21.

Williams, L. (1999). Film bodies: Gender, genre and excess. In S. Thornham (Ed.), *Feminist film theory: A reader* (pp. 267–281). New York: New York University Press.

Wilson, A. (2001). *Persuasive fictions: Feminist narrative and critical myth*. Lewisburg, OH: Bucknell University Press.

Wilson, B. J., Linz, D., Donnerstein, E., & Stipp, H. (1992). The impact of social issue television programming on attitudes toward rape. *Human Communication Research, 19*(2), 179–208.

Zillmann, D., & Bryant, J. (1982). Pornography, sexual callousness, and the trivialization of rape. *Journal of Communication, 32,* 10–21.

GENDER AND NEW MEDIA

◆ Mia Consalvo

The term *new media* is ambiguous and relative—what was new in the early 1990s (World Wide Web pages, for example) became mundane and accepted within a decade and was quickly replaced by newer new media such as digital video recorders and Weblogs. Moreover, many new technologies (or media) fail to take the path predicted for them in their use or future development (Marvin, 1988). They may not even be thought of as media or communication technologies at all—as was the case with electricity. Such problems can also make researchers working in this area feel that they are pursuing a moving target and struggling to keep up with the latest trends.

What remains constant across those developments are the theoretically informed questions that researchers ask about them through the lens of what we already know. This can lead to newer theories and the refinement of existing ones, but in any case it leads to a more contextualized understanding. In this chapter, I focus on the role of gender in the production, texts, and use of new media. I focus on studies that examine the Internet and uses of it (Web sites, home pages, Weblogs, newsgroups, and other applications), digital games, and cell phones. While there are certainly other forms of new media that warrant discussion, these are the major research areas. I also examine theories that relate to new media/new technology and gender such as cybertheory, cyborg theory, and the social shaping/construction of technology.

Studying the intersections of gender and new media research is critical to the advancement of the field of gender and communication generally.

In popular media, new technologies are often promoted with wild optimism. For example, early hype about the Internet promised a virtual world with a frictionless economy that could revolutionize democracy, education, politics, communication, and entertainment. Alternatively, new media can evoke panic and fear, as video game arcades did in the early 1980s. More recently, violent games such as *Manhunt* and *Grand Theft Auto: San Andreas,* have inspired calls for regulation and censorship. Yet, informed questions and critiques based on gender are missing from much of this public discourse. How does gender shape these new media products? How is it represented within them? What role does gender play in who has access and who does not? Does it even make a difference? Research in this area answers such urgent questions while new media researchers often pursue similar sounding yet quite distinct areas of investigation. For example, some studies examine differences between men and women in their uses of new media, while others investigate the construction of masculine and feminine activities and artifacts in online environments. Although sometimes these approaches overlap, we should keep in mind that there is an important difference between the two foci.

In my own research I have been concerned with several things: how women have used new media technologies in particular instances; how popular media have portrayed such technologies in relation to gender and gendered uses; and how the structure of media industries has formed workplaces that are gendered. My research has been mainly qualitative and informed by feminist theory, theories of the social shaping/construction of technology, and of political economy of media. Quantitative as well as humanistic/critical research, however, figure importantly in the study of new media as well. Other researchers have explored these areas from different disciplinary perspectives—psychology, sociology, political science, rhetoric, and anthropology, to name a few.

Most researchers working in this area are open to varying theoretical and methodological perspectives and approaches, but one of their most important concerns is how to adequately survey or sample the vast quantities of information that appear and disappear daily. Developing reliable methodological techniques to sample or gather data is a challenge. Given the rapid development and innovative uses of new media, researchers must also struggle to find the most current research on a topic. Increasingly, much of that information is found online, in Web-based journals, conference proceedings, and published private research, as citations in this chapter indicate. Many researchers have raised concerns about the privacy of individuals when online. Should posts to a message board about breast cancer, for example, be treated as public or private? Should the researcher ask permission to gather data and thus potentially alter the data that are gathered? How will the researcher know when enough data have been sampled or that the topic of interest is not some small anomaly in a wider pool? While I will not be exploring methods explicitly in this chapter, I will point out problems with methods in some research.

Boiling down the central research questions in this area is difficult, as the field is constantly evolving. One crucial question concerns how gender matters or comes to matter in new media. Perhaps one of the largest achievements of early gender researchers studying new media was to assert that gender did matter, thus challenging the early rhetoric that new media such as the Internet created a space where bodies (including their relative genders, races, classes, sexual identities, and so on) could be easily left behind. Early Internet researchers such as Herring (1992, 1996) made convincing arguments that this was not the case, and much more complicated work needed to be done to determine the many ways that gender did matter for the Internet and new media generally. This chapter explores that research, critiquing and contextualizing it, summing up what we have learned in the past 15 years, and pointing to the urgent questions that we should begin asking in the next decade.

◆ Major Theories of Gender and New Media

The theories covered here include the social shaping/construction of technology, identity theory, and embodiment and related body theory, which constitute the dominant approaches of researchers in this area. After a detailed examination of theories, I highlight another, feminist political economy, which I argue should be more widely used to better understand certain processes, such as the makeup, regulation, and competition of new media companies and the information economy generally. Finally, I conclude the section with an assessment of the current state of theory development. In the following discussion, note that many researchers in this area use the terms *new technology* and *new media* somewhat interchangeably when referencing the Internet, computers, computer games, cell phones, and similar devices and software. Although the terms do not always overlap, here they are used in tandem to discuss any type of digital communications/entertainment device or software.

SOCIAL SHAPING/CONSTRUCTION OF TECHNOLOGY

Wajcman (1991) and Cockburn and Ormrod (1993) have provided major conceptual advances in understanding how technology is constantly shaped and reshaped by societies and cultures. Rather than seeing technology as a neutral tool to be given value through use, Wajcman has argued that technologies have particular biases, with certain uses and users preferred above others. Those uses can be reconfigured, given enough user time and demand. And those technologies typically are gendered in some way, with information technologies traditionally being masculine.

Wajcman argues that the creation of new technologies (or new media) is usually considered to be a masculine job, while consumption can vary based on early design considerations. For example, the microwave was originally developed by men, targeted as a masculine device (marketed to men), and sold in electronics aisles alongside stereos and other electronic components. When that market failed to materialize, the gender of the microwave was switched, and it was sold next to kitchen appliances, becoming feminized.

Researchers have examined the construction, representation, and use of new media to see how gender plays a part in shaping them. For example, Springer (1996) argues that even though cyborgs have been conceptualized in some arenas as human-machine hybrids that may confuse traditional boundaries (an argument I'll expand on shortly in relation to Haraway and cyborgs), many popular representations have instead tended to portray a violent masculinity for cyborg identity (p. 99). Springer believes that this is because of "contemporary discourses that cling to nineteenth-century notions about technology, sexual difference, and gender roles in order to resist the transformations brought about by the new postmodern social order" (p. 100). Balsamo (1996) echoes those concerns:

> Contemporary discourses of technology rely on a logic of binary gender identity as an underlying organizational framework. This underlying structure both enables and constrains our engagement with new technologies. In many cases, the *primary* effect of this technological engagement is the reproduction of a traditional logic of binary gender-identity which significantly limits the revisionary potential of new technologies. (pp. 9–10)

Balsamo concludes that while new technologies (and by extension new media) may offer the opportunity for transformation and rising above current bodily limitations, such possibilities are often illusory, and these technologies usually reinscribe typically gendered norms of appearance and behavior.

As I discuss in the section on current research, such theorization about the social construction of technology has been adopted and integrated by new media researchers as they have examined how the Internet and video games have been gendered and how that process is negotiated and shaped over time (Consalvo, 2002; Kendall, 2002; Paasonen, 2002; Spender, 1995).

THEORIES OF ONLINE IDENTITY

Theorization about identity formation and maintenance in relation to new media exploded in the mid-1990s in response to early theorizing about the Internet which suggested it was a place where identity could be unfixed from bodily limitations (Rheingold, 1993). Feminists and gender theorists quickly refuted such claims both through empirical research and alternative theorization about the Internet and new media technologies (Herring, 1992; Stone, 1996).

They argued that gender was present in newsgroups, Listservs, Web pages, and computer games, sometimes in disturbing and sexist ways (Brail, 1996; Clerc, 1996; Miller, 1995). Some scholars argued that gender performance was present online (as well as involved in the construction of new media) and needed to be further studied (Turkle, 1995), while others believed that behaviors gendered feminine were ideally suited to and would soon take control of new media (Plant, 1997). Many of those arguing from the natural empowerment of women approach were labeled part of the cyberfeminist movement, but that movement also had members who took the more liberal feminist view that women and girls needed to be taught about new media in order to take control of powerful new technologies (Spender, 1995). After the collapse of the Internet economy in the late 1990s, cyberfeminism faded from view as a major theoretical and practical movement.

Other theorists such as Turkle (1995) and Stone (1996) believed that new media could be a site for identity play and exploration, with the construction (and reconstruction) of gender to be worked out and experimented with both online and in places such as computer games. Scholars later challenged that carefree approach to identity play, arguing that gender (and race) experimentation online often resulted in the reiteration of stereotypes common in other places (Nakamura, 2000; Paasonen, 2002). Paasonen (2002), for example, explored women's construction of personal Web sites and questioned their use of feminized images as at odds with the alleged freedom to be bodiless online. She concluded that while individuals may play with aspects of gender when using new media, doing so is not about creating new or alternate identities but is a more limited form of play that is more akin to trying on different masks or personas. Likewise, others researchers have determined that gender is persistently tied to identity online through linguistic cues (Herring, 1992), construction of Web pages and Weblogs (Herring, Kouper, Scheidt, & Wright, 2004; Stern, 2004), and personal interests (Oksman, 2002; Tiernan, 2002). While researchers do not believe that individuals are permanently and indelibly stuck with a particular identity, the consensus that gender performances in new media are difficult to radically change echoes Butler's (1993) belief that gender may be a performance but that it is not easy to change or to take on and off at will.

Most researchers would agree that gender cannot be completely set aside or ignored through new media use, but scholars in this field have had less to say about other axes of identity. Important work has been done on sexual identity construction (Bryson, 2004; Case, 1996; Poster, 2002) in relation to the Internet, the role of racial stereotypes online and in computer games (Kolko, 2000; Nakamura, 2000; Ow, 2000), and some work has been dedicated to class (Bird & Jorgenson, 2002). However, there is little that ties these areas together to create a larger theory about gender and identity formation. Although some valuable work comes out of research about the digital divide (Clark, 2003), much of the rest is tied to access and skills, rather than more deeply related to identity formation or expression. Theory in this area is developing and robust, yet more could be done to integrate research about gender and new media use to other axes of identity.

EMBODIMENT AND BODY THEORY

Early work dealing with embodiment, gender, and new media revolved around virtual reality and the figure of the cyborg, while more recent theory has focused on computer game use and notions of place and space. As a form of new media, virtual reality (VR) has not fulfilled the promises of proponents from the early 1990s (Lanier & Biocca, 1992; Rheingold, 1993). Rhetoric about VR sounded an optimistic note about the future uses of the technology, including the creation of virtual worlds for play, work, education, and general living. However, the reality never really surmounted problems involved with the technology, including the bulkiness of interface devices (and the inability to miniaturize or surpass those devices), the huge expenses involved, and the lack of a profitable application for the medium. While VR has had some success in medicine and in specialized arcade machines, the commercial mass market potential has either faded or remains in the future.

Regardless, early attention to VR promised it to be a disembodied space (much like the Internet) with greater capabilities for motion, sensation, and experiences. Early gender theorists, however, critiqued that simplified view on the grounds that VR did not actually eliminate the body, privileged sight over other senses, encouraged a masculine view of the world, and perpetuated a Cartesian-like mind/body split that falsely believed gender could become irrelevant (Balsamo, 1996; Kramarae, 1995). These critiques can be easily transferred to the Internet and online digital games. These technologies have also been hyped as allowing for a disembodied user that can easily inhabit any position desired.

As scholars have demonstrated, however, the body is not so easily left behind. Balsamo (1996), for example, questions whether new media technologies, while seemingly liberating in their rhetoric, actually mask regressive ideas about gender and its proper expression. Theorists have tied new media use firmly to bodily relations through the metaphor of the cyborg made famous by Haraway (1985). She argued that the rapid developments of technoscience demand that feminists acknowledge the potential power of technology and claim it for their own use. They must become cyborgs, which resist dualisms such as male/female and machine/human. Haraway's manifesto also critiqued the Cartesian dualism found in new media hype, and sought a ground that did not view the construction and use of new technologies as solely about masculine pleasures and opportunities. Haraway's vision has resulted in an avalanche of related theorization exploring the possibilities and limits of the cyborg for its impact on gender among other things (Consalvo, 2004c; Hicks, 2002; Springer, 1996; Wajcman, 2004). More recently, theorists interested in embodiment have begun exploring women's and men's uses of new media more empirically, trying to see how practice fits with (or alters) theory.

For example, researchers interested in young adult creations of Web home pages (Stern, 2002, 2004) and Weblogs (Herring et al., 2004) have found that the body is often inscribed in online spaces—talked about and discussed—and made real through discourse rather than elided or glossed over. This process also has been explored in studies of computer game use as well as in the design of digital games. Taylor (2003) has done extensive studies of online game players and has found that gender is a significant factor in understanding their approaches to in-game characters or avatars. For women in particular, the hypersexualization of avatars in the game *Everquest* can cause a disconnection between player and avatar. Identification of player with in-game character is then made more difficult, and for some potential players the leap is sometimes too great to make (Royse, Lee,

Baasanjav, Hopson, & Consalvo, in press). In such spaces, embodiment is still key, even if the body being considered is imaginary.

Last, the role of space and place has attracted attention by gender scholars as they study gendered spaces to determine their benefits and/or drawbacks. Although not a project focused particularly on gender, Baym's (2000) examination of the newsgroup rec.arts.tv.soaps (rats) has been used as a model for understanding how various groups sustain community online, particularly with regard to differences in gender, race, age, or other identity markers. More recently, Gustafson (2002) examined the terms of service for three online sites geared toward women—iVillage, Oxygen, and women.com. She found that the sites constructed gender in similar ways, with generic stereotypical assumptions about women's interests and the appropriate design strategies. The failure of those sites in the past several years validates gender scholars' arguments that women's experiences cannot be captured by such watered-down offerings. Clerc (1996), Cumberland (2002), Poster (2002), and Tiernan (2002) have studied gendered spaces online, either those created in response to a particular interest, such as that of women Vietnam veterans (Tiernan, 2002), or as places where gender differences contributed to a breakdown in communication (Clerc, 1996). Such research reaffirms the belief that gender does matter online as well as in more narrow spaces such as digital games and cannot be shrugged off or simplistically designed in or out.

GAPS IN THEORETICAL APPROACHES

The majority of work done about gender and new media has drawn on theories of the social shaping/construction of technology and on theories of identity. Researchers working outside communication fields also draw on their own disciplinary paradigms, although many do come back to these central approaches. My work has also fallen into line with these approaches. I have studied

(Consalvo, 2002) how women were discursively constructed in early media representations about the Internet as well as how identity is related in particular ways to enjoyment of digital games (Royse et al., in press). However, these are not the only ways to approach the topic, and they cannot get at every aspect of new media that relates to gender.

One theoretical tradition that needs to be brought into the study of gender and new media is feminist political economy. As researchers working in that area have argued, scholars in the West (in particular) have been reluctant to go beyond representations and uses to consider ownership structures and how these shape the future of the information economy (Riordan, 2002). McChesney (2000) has provided a much-needed critique of mass media and new media ownership, but little to no scholarship explores how those structures relate to gender.

One area ripe for study is the digital games industry. With growing economic power and increasing numbers of women playing games (Entertainment Software Association (ESA), 2006), there are now louder calls for a greater representation of women in the industry's workforce. Yet, the gender ratio in the industry hovers around 90/10 male/female workers. An analysis of the gendered roots of the industry—the rise of genres, the increasing pressure for visual realism, rising costs and the related fear of risks—all mask gendered decisions and assumptions about players, the projected market, and the interests of producers themselves (Consalvo, 2004a, 2004b). Political economy theory with gender as a central component must be applied to new media if we are to expand our understandings of these phenomena beyond representation and use.

◆ Emphases in Gender and New Media Research

In addition to the broader theoretical advancements in gender and new media, certain themes have dominated research over the past decade. I have broken these down into categories that serve to tie together bodies of work addressing the same conceptual issues. They include studies of virtual community, exploration of the split (or lack thereof) between online and offline activity, the design of new media, differential use patterns, and the gendering of new technologies. I address each in turn.

GENDER AND VIRTUAL COMMUNITY

Much of the earliest work concerned the possible creation of virtual communities or virtual cultures. Baym's (2000) study of a newsgroup (mentioned above) was among these. Orgad (2004) and Lennie, Grace, Daws, and Simpson (1999) have studied how online spaces can serve the particular gendered needs and interests of individuals and how gender can be invoked to demand access as needed. For example, Orgad (2004) explored the formation of online support groups for victims and survivors of breast cancer. She found that women were the predominant users of such sites, and gendered forms of use occurred, such as a tendency to favor cooperative, supportive forms of communication.

Scholars also have investigated the gendered structure of the community metaphor for the Internet. For example, Millar (1998) critically analyzed the rhetoric of *Wired* magazine for its attempts to create a new digital ideology that was distinctively "hypermacho." Through the use of profiles of great men in Internet history and the marshalling of the cowboy and new frontier mythos in describing the future of Internet use, *Wired,* she argues, is gendering the structure of the Internet to be masculine in tone and appearance and hypermacho at that—not the technogeek of days past. Miller (1995) argues that although the Internet was made popular with masculine metaphors of a lawless society where only the brave would care to go, the coming of women and children to cyberspace meant

that it must be cleaned up for those perceived as too weak to defend themselves. Warnick (1999) echoes those assertions, arguing that persuasive appeals to get women online ironically may have served to marginalize or exclude them because of the types of rhetoric used. I argue (2002) that the claim for women and children to be protected online was merely a secondary strategy in order to establish a safe space for commerce. Women are still the primary purchasers, and they must be made to feel safe online; otherwise, businesses would set up shop and just as quickly go out of business. Although more macro- than micro-oriented, such studies of the Internet at large are important to understanding how the Internet has been defined and redefined as embodying or giving rise to particular types of community in different times for various strategic reasons.

More recently, attention has shifted to tracing connections between online activity and life offline to determine which activities online are unique and which are extensions. Likewise, the role of the Internet in allowing communities to form online and then have real world influence and organization has gained attention, such as queer sites that allow gays and lesbians more information and support (Nip, 2004).

GENDER AND ONLINE/ OFFLINE CROSSOVERS

Although many studies begin by examining media use in isolation, more researchers are widening the scope of analysis to gain a better understanding of how new media use is contextualized/integrated in a person's daily life. Although not focusing on gender, Wellman and Hampton (1999) and Leander and McKim (2003) argue that Internet use is not an isolated activity, and should be studied in tandem with the real-life concerns and interests of users. Likewise, early research by Gould and Lerman (1998) found that on the AOL site NetGirl, participants were constantly negotiating aspects of offline and online activity, particularly as they related to ideas about bodies and identities.

More recently, Bird and Jorgenson (2002) studied the introduction of computers into working-class family life in rural Florida as part of a grant project to give at-risk children access. According to the terms of the grant, children receiving the computers were to use them for a set period daily for math and reading exercises, and a parent was required to upload test scores to the child's teacher. Rather than focus exclusively on the children's use, Bird and Jorgenson examined how the computer affected family life—who took responsibility for seeing that children used it (almost always mothers); who used it otherwise; and how those uses often were at odds with the expected (middle-class) uses of computers and the Internet. Such studies give us a much better picture of how gender operates in specific situations, here related to class and computer use, and how new media are not isolated technology but can become welcome, hostile, or ambivalent additions to a family household.

Nip (2004) sought to determine exactly how much online and offline activity crossed over in her study of the bulletin board and women's group Queer Sisters, located in Hong Kong.

> The bulletin board community pursued goals and held norms very different from those of the Queer Sisters. Participation on the bulletin board increased sense of belonging to and participation in the Queer Sisters, but the increase is affected by differences in goals and norms between the two communities and differences in logic of action between the two realms. (p. 421)

Nip concludes that although there is some overlap in the two groups online and offline, there does not need to be complete coherence for the groups to function successfully (p. 424). Studies such as this give us a better idea of how communities function online, and how online/offline migrations can shift the focus of groups, or create entirely new forms of them.

GENDER AND PRODUCTION/DESIGN

One area receiving increasing attention is how gender is a factor in the production and design of new media. It is not to be confused with a political economic approach to new media, however, because scholars working on production/design analysis are interested in the gendering of work and the workforce, as well as the gendering of design decisions affecting computer games and Web sites.

Turkle (1995) conducted some of the earliest and most influential work done in this area in the 1980s and early 1990s. She determined that there were two predominant approaches to working with and programming computers—a hard and a soft approach. Although not explicitly tying those styles to gender, she believed the hard style was more top-down, rule-based, and usually appealed more often to men (p. 51). The soft style, which drew more women, was a more bottom-up approach that attempted to solve problems "on the fly" rather than plan everything in advance with rigid structures (pp. 51–54). That explanation helped researchers understand how computer science and related fields were often gendered masculine (American Association of University Women, 2000).

That concern for how production processes are gendered led to studies that have investigated why women working in IT fields define their work as less technical than men's (Dorer, 2002) and how hacker culture has come to be seen as masculine and overwhelmingly male (Håpnes & Sørensen, 1995). In addition, researchers concerned with the production process have studied how various elements of design help construct or deemphasize gendered spaces.

Not all of the interesting work being done in this area comes from scholarly sources. Blogs by industry professionals often provide valuable insights and careful analyses of how gender gets inscribed—sometimes unintentionally—in new media design. The Red

Polka Dot blog (RedPolka.org, 2004) contains a perceptive critique of the rise of prefabricated design templates for Web site/blog/new media use that are sold as embodying a feminine style. The blog writer carefully examines that claim and the templates being offered, pointing to how gender is being made visible in stereotypical ways (feminine styles often include pastel colors, flowing shapes, and certain font styles) and being devalued as well.

The process of gendering other new media in the design phase is also under study. The use of cell phones is becoming heavily gendered, much as the original telephone was (Frissen, 2000; Rakow, 1992). The careful marketing of those devices to girls and women and the development of cell phone jewelry also make clear how gendering can be seized upon by corporations to help sell a product. Likewise, the gendering of computer games as masculine products created by a masculine industry also is gaining attention (Consalvo, 2004a; Davies, 2002).

In summary, researchers are actively investigating new media forms to see how gender is both willfully as well as unconsciously being worked into the design of products and services with results that can restrict, open, value, or devalue various types of access and use.

GENDER AND DIFFERENTIAL USE PATTERNS

Perhaps overlooked in more detailed analyses of production, consumption, and texts is a more basic concern—that of use. Because new media are constantly evolving, with fluctuations in types of services, price points, rising technology standards, and many other factors, even simple use or nonuse can be difficult to measure. However, researchers have managed to track some figures over time to determine how new media diffuse across populations as well as how types of use can and do change over time.

The use of cell phones has typically been tied to gender, with early research showing that men and boys were more likely to own a cell phone and be more proficient in using them (Ling, 1999). More recently, researchers have found there are more mobile phone connections than landline phone subscriptions worldwide and that the numbers of male and female subscribers have evened out (Rice & Katz, 2003).

During the early 1990s, when Internet use was beginning to diffuse into the general population in the West, estimates showed that only 5% to 10% of users were women (Consalvo, 2002). That situation changed rapidly however, and women have now surpassed men as the dominant percentage of users (Herring et al., 2004). The Pew project has found that both genders use the Internet for many daily activities of life, although men are "more likely than women to use the Internet more for information gathering and entertainment," while women are "more likely than men to use the Internet to communicate" (Fallows, 2004). Seniors comprise one of the fastest growing groups of Internet users according to Riggs (2004), and racial barriers are shrinking as well (Rice & Katz, 2003). One of the last remaining differences is in urban and suburban versus rural users—there are still fewer rural users, and they are far more likely to have a slower connection, such as dialup rather than broadband (Bell, Reddy, & Rainie, 2004).

Gender differences can be pronounced in the use of digital games but can also be unstable. Over the past several years, the Entertainment Software Association has claimed that the proportion of women and girls playing games has been rising—to currently about 39% (ESA, 2004). Gender differences are more pronounced when more detailed data are considered. For example, estimates are that only 15% of console players are women, but more women play computer games (Vance, 2004). Great attention has recently been paid to the rising number of adult women (including those 40+) who play online games—particularly in the "casual games" markets developed by AOLGames, Pogo, MSN, and YahooGames

(Goodale, 2004). Adult women online spend considerable amounts of time playing, but more young adult men than young adult women report more time spent gaming overall (Jones, 2003). In relation to gender, then, use of digital games is not precise, and is likely to keep fluctuating.

THE GENDERING OF NEW TECHNOLOGIES

Along with the social shaping approach, researchers are investigating how new technologies become gendered through use, production, and other avenues. They are also interested in how such media become identified with a particular gender or how gendering can change over time through various innovations or shifts in use. In this section, I focus on the gendering of blogs, and the uses and popular representations of PCs and the Internet.

Weblogs, or blogs, are a relatively new form of Internet site that has become popular due in part to politically themed blogs that have received extensive news attention. As Herring et al. (2004) report, most of the sites reported on in popular media, and those generally cited as the most well-known, are news filter blogs that are updated frequently, have many links to articles and other information, and offer some commentary on the links or topics of interest. Those sites also are typically run by men. To determine if they are representative of the blog universe, Herring and colleagues conducted a random sample and studied them for gender and age of owner and type of blog. Their results indicate that an equal number are written by males and by females, although females tend to write more of the journal-style blog that resembles a diary. They conclude:

> Public commentators on Weblogs, including many bloggers themselves, collude in reproducing gender and age-based hierarchy in the blogosphere, demonstrating once again that even an open access technology—and high hopes for its use—cannot

guarantee equitable outcomes in a society that continues to embrace hierarchical values. (n. p.)

Cassidy (2001) examines marketing discourses of the 1990s and how sellers addressed women in order to sell more computers for home use. Cassidy found that the discourse "undermines the computer's utopian promises for women . . . . Material placement of the machine cannot surmount the home's gendered spatial divisions" (p. 60). Although Cassidy does suggest that home use can destabilize traditional work divisions in the home, ultimately the discourse returns women's work almost exclusively to the private sphere.

Although popular media can attempt to gender the use of new media, individuals must also either accept that characterization or attempt to find their own definition of acceptable and appropriate use. To determine how new media are gendered through domestic use, van Zoonen and Aalberts (2002) studied how young Dutch couples prioritized their differential uses of the home computer and Internet with their television use. They found that couples fell into several categories, including nontraditional, traditional, and negotiated uses. Overall, they discovered "many households in which the computer and Internet were used in deliberation and were made part of the common culture of the couple" (p. 307). Those research findings indicate that individuals take an active role in negotiating new media use and that use is still being deliberated as traditionally and nontraditionally gendered.

◆ Conclusion

This chapter has reviewed the major theoretical approaches taken and some of the more recent research done studying gender as it is expressed, constructed, and deconstructed in new media. What it indicates is that just as gender is a difficult concept to contain, so too is new media. I have generally conflated the research into two main areas of new media: the Internet and digital games. These are the dominant strands of current research, although some additional work mentioned here studies cell phones and computer use generally. In this conclusion, I comment briefly on how cultural factors might have influenced which theory and research foci do (and do not) receive attention from scholars, and I then indicate useful directions for research.

INFLUENCE OF CULTURAL FACTORS

As with many other types of gender research and theory, much of it on new media is concerned with women and girls and then generalized to gender as a conceptual term. Some work is upfront about studying the experiences of women and/or girls, but gender is often code for female. Part of the reason for that may be the strong traditions in gender theory of such conflation and the continual mixing of feminist and gender theories as ways to approach studying men and women as sexed beings. That slippage, however, can still be problematic, as it means we continue to associate gender with female or feminine without much critical reflection.

Gender research, however, has been quite influential in new media studies partly because it was an early focus. Books and articles exploring the construction of gender online and exposing the numbers of women using or not using the Internet began appearing in the mid-1990s, just as popular attention was exploding. And because many new media are targeted initially to men, created by men, or both, the inclusion of women and girls becomes a catalyzing agent. Thus, scholars have quickly taken up the study of why women and girls undersubscribe and how or where they are making contributions.

Yet why do we see this kind of gender and new media research? In part, the answer is related to the standpoint of academic researchers, who by and large are middle class, highly educated, and often white. Early research was quite celebratory, it then became more cautionary, and now it is more attentive to the context of daily life. We are seeing more attention to working-class and poor users of new media, and researchers taking alternate perspectives into account. But as with early feminist research, class, race, and age biases all can play a part in who is privileged to speak and who is not.

The research has been dominated by the Western world. The successful penetration of mobile phones in Asia and the spread of high-speed Internet connections in South Korea and Japan mean that more global accounts of new media use and production will take place, but that is just getting under way. As with the Internet itself, the dominant language of research has become English, so researchers limited to knowing another language will be shut out of contributing to and learning from most theory and research in the field.

DIRECTIONS

More investigation into the ways in which masculinity is part of new media use is critical to gain a better understanding of how masculinity is negotiated around digital game play, blog authoring, and cell phone use. Currently we know little about such areas. Additionally, how identity markers such as class, age, and race intersect with masculinity has been largely ignored, except when in surface analyses of phenomena such as the digital divide.

Additionally, we need more global study and more resulting comparative analyses of gendered uses worldwide. Western uses are often regarded as the de facto standards, with researchers measuring other uses as either meeting or more often failing to meet uses that are always contextual, culturally based, and changing over time. Related to that, more sharing of research across language boundaries is a necessity if we are to gain from the knowledge work that has already been done.

There have been many analyses of popular representations and individual uses, and they are certainly important to understanding new media. However, more sustained attention to the political and economic structures of new media is critical, especially if we can determine how those structures are gendered or how they come to define gender in particular ways. More policy analysis is crucial for moving research in this area beyond understanding and explanation to engagement with public policy and toward changing some of the uses, structures and systems we see and recognize as flawed. Those omissions are partly a result of academic biases in America, where communication and new media studies do not have political economy as a strong component, as they do in Canada and Europe.

Research in this area is exciting and conceptually challenging. As currently new media such as the Internet become commonplace and better understood, we will always have newer media to draw from—new practices found on the Internet, new technological devices, or new combinations of such forms. As this discussion indicates, such new developments always have implications for gender and thus deserve the continued scrutiny of researchers.

◆ References

American Association of University Women. (2000). *Tech-savvy: Educating girls in the new computer age*. Retrieved February 2, 2006, from www.aauw.org/research/girls_education/techsavvy.cfm

Balsamo, A. (1996). *Technologies of the gendered body: Reading cyborg women*. Durham, NC: Duke University Press.

Baym, N. K. (2000). *Tune in, log on: Soaps, fandom and online community*. Thousand Oaks, CA: Sage.

Bell, P., Reddy, P., & Rainie, L. (2004). Rural areas and the Internet. *Pew Internet & American Life Project*. Retrieved February 2, 2006, from www.pewinternet.org/PPF/r/112/report_display.asp

Bird, S. E., & Jorgenson, J. (2002). Extending the school day: Gender, class and the incorporation of technology in everyday life. In M. Consalvo & S. Paasonen (Eds.), *Women and everyday uses of the Internet: Agency and identity* (pp. 255–274). New York: Peter Lang.

Brail, S. (1996). The price of admission: Harassment and free speech in the wild, wild west. In L. Cherny & E. R. Weise (Eds.), *Wired_ women: Gender and new realities in cyberspace* (pp. 141–157). Seattle, WA: Seal Press.

Bryson, M. (2004). When Jill jacks in: Queer women and the net. *Feminist Media Studies, 4*(3), 239–254.

Butler, J. (1993). *Bodies that matter: On the discursive limits of "sex."* New York: Routledge.

Case, S. E. (1996). *The domain-matrix: Performing lesbian at the end of print culture*. Bloomington: Indiana University Press.

Cassidy, M. (2001). Cyberspace meets domestic space: Personal computers, women's work, and the gendered territories of the family home. *Critical Studies in Media Communication, 18*(1), 44–65.

Clark, L. S. (2003). Challenges of social good in the world of "Grand Theft Auto" and Barbie: A case study of a community computer center for youth. *New Media & Society, 5*(1), 95–116.

Clerc, S. (1996). Estrogen brigades and "Big Tits" threads: Media fandom online and off. In L. Cherny & E. R. Weise (Eds.), *Wired_ women: Gender and new realities in cyberspace* (pp. 73–97). Seattle, WA: Seal Press.

Cockburn, C., & Ormrod, S. (1993). *Gender and technology in the making*. Thousand Oaks, CA: Sage.

Consalvo, M. (2002). Selling the Internet to women: The early years. In M. Consalvo & S. Paasonen (Eds.), *Women and everyday uses of the Internet: Agency and identity* (pp. 111–138). New York: Peter Lang.

Consalvo, M. (2004a, May). *The digital games industry: The changing role of women in and behind games*. Paper presented at the Console-ing Passions annual meeting in New Orleans.

Consalvo, M. (2004b, September). *Quality of life: Male and female perspectives*. Paper presented at the Women's Game Conference annual meeting in Austin, TX.

Consalvo, M. (2004c). Borg babes, drones, and the collective: Reading gender and the body in *Star Trek. Women's Studies in Communication, 27*(2), 177–203.

Cumberland, S. (2002). *The five wives of Ibn Fadlan*: Women's collaborative fiction on Antonia Banderas Web sites. In M. Flanagan & A. Booth (Eds.), *Reload: Rethinking women and cyberculture* (pp. 175–194). Cambridge: MIT Press.

Davies, J. (2002). Male dominance of videogame production and consumption: Understanding the social and cultural processes. *Gamasutra*. Retrieved February 2, 2006, from www.gamasutra.com/education/theses/20020708/davies_01.shtml

Dorer, J. (2002). Internet and the construction of gender: Female professionals and the process of doing gender. In M. Consalvo & S. Paasonen (Eds.), *Women and everyday uses of the Internet: Agency and identity* (pp. 62–89). New York: Peter Lang.

Entertainment Software Association. (2006). *Facts & research*. Retrieved February 12, 2006, from www.theesa.com/facts/gamer_ data.php

Fallows, D. (2004). The Internet and daily life. *Pew Internet & American Life Project*. Retrieved February 2, 2006, from www .pewinternet.org/pdfs/PIP_Internet_and_Daily_Life.pdf

Frissen, V. (2000). ICTs in the rush hour of life. *The Information Society, 16*(1), 65–75.

Goodale, G. (2004, June 11). Games women play. *Christian Science Monitor*. Retrieved February 2, 2006, from www.csmonitor .com/2004/0611/p13s01-stin.html

Gould, S., & Lerman, D. (1998). "Postmodern" versus "long-standing" cultural narratives in consumer behavior: An empirical study of NetGirl online. *European Journal of Marketing, 7*(8), 644–654.

Gustafson, K. (2002). Join now, membership is free: Women's Web sites and the coding of community. In M. Consalvo & S. Paasonen (Eds.), *Women and everyday uses of the Internet: Agency and identity* (pp. 168–190). New York: Peter Lang.

Håpnes, T., & Sørensen, K. H. (1995). Competition and collaboration in male shaping of computing: A study of a Norwegian hacker culture. In K. Grint & R. Gill (Eds.), *The gender-technology relation: Contemporary theory and research* (pp. 174–191). London: Taylor & Francis.

Haraway, D. (1985). A manifesto for cyborgs: Science, technology, and socialist feminism in the 1980s. *Socialist Review, 80*, 65–108.

Herring, S. C. (1992). *Gender and participation in computer-mediated linguistic discourse*. Washington, DC: ERIC Clearinghouse on Languages and Linguistics. (ERIC Document Reproduction Services No. ED345552)

Herring, S. C. (1996). Gender and democracy in computer-mediated communication. In R. Kling (Ed.), *Computerization and controversy* (2nd ed., pp. 476–489). San Diego, CA: Academic Press.

Herring, S. C., Kouper, I., Scheidt, L. A., & Wright, E. (2004). Women and children last: The discursive construction of Weblogs. In L. Gurak, S. Antonijevic, L. Johnson, C. Ratliff, & J. Reyman (Eds.), *Into the blogosphere: Rhetoric, community, and culture of Weblogs*. Retrieved February 2, 2006, from http://blog.lib.umn.edu/ blogosphere/women_and_children.html

Hicks, H. (2002). Striking cyborgs: Reworking the "human" in Marge Piercy's *He, She and It*. In M. Flanagan & A. Booth (Eds.), *Reload: Rethinking women and cyberculture* (pp. 85–106). Cambridge: MIT Press.

Jones, S. (2003). Let the games begin: Gaming technology and entertainment among college students. *Pew Internet & American Life Project*. Retrieved February 2, 2006, from http://207.21.232.103/PPF/r/93/report_display.asp

Kendall, L. (2002). *Hanging out in the virtual pub: Masculinities and relationships online*. Berkeley: University of California Press.

Kolko, B. (2000). Erasing @race: Going white in the (inter)face. In B. Kolko, L. Nakamura, & G. Rodman (Eds.), *Race in cyberspace* (pp. 213–232). New York: Routledge.

Kramarae, C. (1995). A backstage critique of virtual reality. In S. Jones (Ed.), *Cybersociety: Computer-mediated communication and community* (pp. 36–56). Thousand Oaks, CA: Sage.

Lanier, J., & Biocca, F. (1992). An insider's view of the future of virtual reality. *Journal of Communication, 42*(4), 150–172.

Leander, K., & McKim, K. (2003). Tracing the everyday "sitings" of adolescents on the Internet: A strategic adaptation of ethnography across online and offline spaces. *Education, Communication & Information, 3*(2), 211–240.

Lennie, J., Grace, M., Daws, L., & Simpson, L. (1999). Empowering on-line conversations: A pioneering Australian project to link rural and urban women. In W. Harcourt (Ed.), *Women@Internet: Creating new cultures in cyberspace* (pp. 184–196). London: Zed Books.

Ling, R. (1999, July). *We release them little by little: Maturation and gender identity as seen in the use of mobile telephones.* Paper presented at the International Symposium on Technology and Society: Women and Technology: Historical, Societal and Professional Perspectives. New Brunswick, NJ.

Marvin, C. (1988). *When old technologies were new: Thinking about electric communication in the late nineteenth century.* New York: Oxford University Press.

McChesney, R. (2000). So much for the magic of technology and the free market: The World Wide Web and the corporate media system. In A. Herman & T. Swiss (Eds.), *The World Wide Web and contemporary cultural theory* (pp. 5–36). New York: Routledge.

Millar, M. S. (1998). *Cracking the gender code: Who rules the wired world?* Toronto: Second Story Press.

Miller, L. (1995). Women and children first: Gender and the settling of the electronic frontier. In J. Brook & I. Boal (Eds.), *Resisting the virtual life: The culture and politics of information* (pp. 49–58). San Francisco: City Lights.

Nakamura, L. (2000). Where do you want to go today? Cybernetic tourism, the Internet, and transnationality. In B. Kolko, L. Nakamura, & G. Rodman (Eds.), *Race in cyberspace* (pp. 15–26). New York: Routledge.

Nip, J. (2004). The relationship between online and offline communities: The case of the Queer Sisters. *Media, Culture & Society, 26*(3), 409–428.

Oksman, V. (2002). "So I got it into my head that I should set up my own stable": Creating virtual stables on the Internet as girls' own computer culture. In M. Consalvo & S. Paasonen (Eds.), *Women and everyday uses of the Internet: Agency and identity* (pp. 191–210). New York: Peter Lang.

Orgad, S. (2004). Just do it! The online communication of breast cancer as a practice of empowerment. In M. Consalvo, N. Baym, J. Hunsinger, K. B. Jensen, J. Logie, M. Murero, & L. Shade (Eds.), *Internet research annual volume 1: Selected papers from the Association of Internet Researchers Conferences 2000–2002* (pp. 231–240). New York: Peter Lang.

Ow, J. (2000). The revenge of the yellowfaced cyborg: The rape of digital geishas and the colonization of cyber-coolies in 3D Realms' *Shadow Warrior.* In B. Kolko, L. Nakamura, & G. Rodman (Eds.), *Race in cyberspace* (pp. 51–68). New York: Routledge.

Paasonen, S. (2002). Gender, identity, and (the limits of) play on the Internet. In M. Consalvo & S. Paasonen (Eds.), *Women and everyday uses of the Internet: Agency and identity* (pp. 21–43). New York: Peter Lang.

Plant, S. (1997). *Zeros + ones: Digital women + the new technoculture.* London: Fourth Estate.

Poster, J. (2002). Trouble, pleasure and tactics: Anonymity and identity in a lesbian chat room. In M. Consalvo & S. Paasonen (Eds.), *Women and everyday uses of the Internet: Agency and identity* (pp. 230–254). New York: Peter Lang.

Rakow, L. (1992). *Gender on the line: Women, the telephone and community life.* Urbana: University of Illinois Press.

Redpolka.org. (2004). [Weblog]. Accessed at http://redpolka.org/blog

Rheingold, H. (1993). *The virtual community: Homesteading on the electronic frontier.* Reading, MA: Addison-Wesley.

Rice, R., & Katz, J. (2003). Comparing Internet and mobile phone usage: Digital divides of usage, adoption, and dropouts. *Telecommunications Policy, 27,* 597–623.

Riggs, K. E. (2004). *Granny @ work: Aging and new technology on the job in America.* New York: Routledge.

Riordan, E. (2002). Intersections and new directions: Of feminism and political economy. In E. Meehan & E. Riordan (Eds.), *Sex and money: Feminism and political economy in the media* (pp. 3–15). Minneapolis: University of Minnesota Press.

Royse, P., Lee, J., Baasanjav, U., Hopson, M., & Consalvo, M. (in press). Women and games: Technologies of the gendered self. *New Media & Society.*

Spender, D. (1995). *Nattering on the Net: Women, power and cyberspace.* North Melbourne, Victoria, Australia: Spinifex Press.

Springer, C. (1996). *Electronic eros: Bodies and desire in the postindustrial age.* Austin: University of Texas Press.

Stern, S. (2002). Virtually speaking: Girls' self-disclosure on the WWW. *Women's Studies in Communication, 25*(2), 223–253.

Stern, S. (2004). Expressions of identity online: Prominent features and gender differences in adolescents' World Wide Web home pages. *Journal of Broadcasting & Electronic Media, 48*(2), 218–243.

Stone, A. R. (1996). *The war of desire and technology at the close of the mechanical age.* Cambridge: MIT Press.

Taylor, T. L. (2003). Multiple pleasures: Women and online gaming. *Convergence, 9*(1), 21–46.

Tiernan, J. (2002). Women veterans and the Net: Using Internet technology to network and reconnect. In M. Consalvo & S. Paasonen (Eds.), *Women and everyday uses of the Internet: Agency and identity* (pp. 211–229). New York: Peter Lang.

Turkle, S. (1995). *Life on the screen: Identity in the age of the Internet.* New York: Touchstone.

Vance, P. (2004, September). [Keynote speech]. Presented at the annual meeting of the Women's Game Conference, Austin, TX.

Van Zoonen, L., & Aalberts, C. (2002). Interactive television in the everyday lives of young couples. In M. Consalvo & S. Paasonen (Eds.), *Women and everyday uses of the Internet: Agency and identity* (pp. 292–310). New York: Peter Lang.

Wajcman, J. (1991). *Feminism confronts technology.* University Park: Pennsylvania State University Press.

Wajcman, J. (2004). *Technofeminism.* Cambridge, UK: Polity Press.

Warnick, B. (1999). Masculinizing the feminine: Inviting women on line ca. 1997. *Critical Studies in Mass Communication, 16*(1), 1–19.

Wellman, B., & Hampton, K. (1999). Living networked on and offline. *Contemporary Sociology, 28*(6), 648–654.

PART V

GENDER AND COMMUNICATION IN INTERCULTURAL AND GLOBAL CONTEXTS

Introduction

◆ Fern L. Johnson

The final section of the *Handbook* focuses on the increasingly prominent cultural approach to scholarship on gender and communication. The central proposition of cultural analysis is that culture is *con*-text—it must be read *against* any and every text—pushing against it, changing it, shaping it, making it more than may appear on the surface. Culture and cultural diversity categories are neither variables nor unified containers. Culture makes texts, and texts make culture. We are at a point in gender theory and scholarship where cultural analyses are on the rise because contact, hybridity, fusion, and translation are all gathering steam at the same time that cultural clashes, assertions of identity, and racial profiling are part of everyday life. Connell (2002) observes that "whatever new issues emerge, the problems of institutionalization, reaction, deconstruction, diversity and globalization are issues that must be incorporated into our understanding of gender" (p. 135).

Explorations of culture as con-text for gender first appeared in U.S. scholarship in women's studies as calls for greater race and class inclusiveness. A hallmark in the maturity of second-wave feminism was the recognition—most often by women of color—of the limited sociocultural focus in the vast majority of work. This maturity was prompted by harsh criticism across a range of academic disciplines; the criticism indicted particular interests motivating research and the tendency to study the communication of only some people—those who were white, middle class, heterosexual, Western, able-bodied, and so forth. I have vivid memories of participating in a yearlong interdisciplinary seminar involving faculty from five colleges in the 1980s that was devoted to studying the intersections of race and gender.[1] The goal was to introduce new courses that would bridge the gender-and-race chasm that was widening between women's studies and black studies and to address existing tensions that resulted from the attack on women's studies as racist and black studies as sexist. The hot topic in women's studies was racism—implicit and institutional—and this topic both divided feminists and became the energizing force for new thinking.

Read across disciplines, *This Bridge Called My Back: Writings by Radical Women of Color* was first published in 1981 (see Moraga & Anzaldúa, 1983). This volume gave voice to a broad range of women of color—scholars, creative writers, activists. Emblematic of the debates about racism, Audre Lorde in "An Open Letter to Mary Daly" (dated May 6, 1979, and published in Moraga & Anzaldúa, 1983) sent harsh words to Daly about her book titled *Gyn/Ecology* (1978). Daly had written about men's mutilation of women through the practice of suttee in India, footbinding in China, genital mutilation in Africa, witch burning in Europe, and gynecology in the United States. She challenged women to understand and to exorcise these practices and to capture the inspiration of rediscovered goddesses. Lorde noted that only those goddess images familiar to Western-European women were included and that Daly had overgeneralized the condition of women under patriarchy: "Where was Afrekete, Yemanje, Oyo and Mawulisa? Where are the warrior-goddesses of the Vodum, the Dohomeian Amazons and the warrior-women of Dan? . . . What you excluded from *Gyn/Ecology* dismissed my heritage and the heritage of all other non-european women" (pp. 94, 95). The rift between Lorde and Daly catapulted cultural diversity and global culture to the center of feminist inquiry.

Inspired by the heat of this debate, Elizabeth Spellman (1988), a Eurowhite philosopher, would later focus on the inadequacy of simply seeing race and class as additive to gender; she termed this "the ampersand problem." Working from Spellman's analysis, Candace West and Sarah Fenstermaker (1995) cautioned against trying to mathematically account for that by the addition or multiplication of gender, race, and class "with results dependent on the valence . . . of those multiplied variables" (p. 12).

During the same period of time, Marsha Houston (Houston Stanback, 1985) challenged the adequacy of scholarship on women's language, boldly pointing out that "neither . . . research on language and gender nor that on black communication coherently describes black women's communicative experiences" (p. 177). Houston's work would become a beacon for scholars attempting to rectify this inadequacy.

Also building steam in the 1980s were interdisciplinary and transdisciplinary social research and, more specifically, research on gender and communication. Within the interdisciplinary field of discourse studies, one of the first reference works for scholars of gender appeared in 1983 with the publication of *Language, Gender and Society,* which was edited by Barrie Thorne (sociology), Cheris Kramarae (communication), and Nancy Henley (psychology). This volume contained essays plus a large annotated bibliography of works; unlike the earlier version (Thorne & Henley, 1975), many sections in it included a subsection for work focused on what the editors termed "Other Languages." This was at least a beginning in the project to destabilize white, U.S., and largely middle-class voices as the metonym for women's expression.

None of this is to suggest that the 1980s produced a flood of published scholarship in communication that centered on diversity or culture, let alone gender, diversity, and culture. Within the subfield of intercultural communication, feminist study was marginalized just as much as it was elsewhere in academia. And intercultural communication still tended to neglect cultural diversity within the United States in favor of the area studies view described by Hegde in Chapter 23 and the quest to understand domestic-foreign encounters.

As we entered the 1990s, Lana Rakow (1992) would characterize the growing feminist inquiry in the field as an important challenge to traditional categories of analysis in communication studies: "The general disregard of feminist scholars for the sanctity of the field's boundaries and categories flies in the face of the efforts of many in the field who feel they must continually retrace the lines that have been, however faintly,

marked off as the territory of communication scholars" (p. 13). Rakow boldly asserted that feminist scholars needed to challenge the dominant paradigm, which she described as "racist patriarchy (or patriarchal racism" (p. 15). In a 1995 volume sponsored by the National Communication Association on the future of communication studies, I called explicitly for "bring[ing] culture to the center of the discipline and not leav[ing] it in the margins or among optional areas to be included or excluded" (Johnson, p. 163).

The foregoing description of trends in scholarship does not apply only to the past. Even today, a considerable amount of U.S. literature on gender and communication— and communication studies in general—is silent about the role that culture and its many contexts play in all codes of gendered discourse. In some cases, *cultural* can be taken to mean mainstream U.S. culture simply because no other inference fits the research or the theories and concepts involved, and the scholarship usually focuses on gender and communicative practices in the United States (e.g., gender issues in organizational communication, gender roles in broadcast news, gender differences in persuasibility). In other cases, the ubiquity of culture is silenced because culture is treated as an attribute of the other—a particular ethnic group or zone, a country, and sometimes even a continent or broad region of the world. In these cases, culture surfaces as relevant only to those locales that are out of the mainstream or far away (in, for example, textbooks on subfields that include chapters on cultural diversity). Yet over the past 20 years some scholars have increasingly recognized cultural multiplicity as important to the analysis of gender and communication—not just as a consideration of place but as a consideration of the foundation for all human communication and for the analysis of the political, ideological implications of discourse. It is the turn to cultural analysis of gendered discourse that provides the center for the chapters to follow.

The chapters in this section were not guided by a uniform definition of culture or of intercultural communication. Yet every author addresses the fruits and challenges of the "cultural turn" in the study of gender, of the fundamental tenet of cultural studies that culture must be treated as "emergent, as dynamic and as continual renewal," that culture implies "conflict rather than order" (Jenks, 1993, p. 159). Indeed, these essays are motivated in different ways by a view of gender that grows from cultural studies as an opening up of the political implications of discourse. Broadly speaking, culture is a way of life and, more specifically, interrelated systems of abstractions (values, beliefs, percepts, and so on), material artifacts (architecture, clothing, personal adornments, and the like), and language and broader communicative expression (Johnson, 2000). "Culture makes the world meaningful," writes David Chaney (1994), "but is itself an articulation of ideology" (p. 23). Where the borders and boundaries are drawn between and among the cultures will always be a matter of analytical viewpoint, of judging which practices are worthy of a frame. Border theory itself explores the meeting of cultural experiences and systems of meaning.

The authors in this section highlight in various ways how cultural actors and their practices are positioned vis-à-vis other cultural actors and their practices. Dominant cultural groups and their practices displace, marginalize, and sometimes silence groups and practices at the margins; yet, cultural studies (and especially critical discourse analysis) has taught us that cultural resistance from below or to the side happens regularly. We can also take it as axiomatic that dominant cultural groups through their cultural practices often fail to recognize or understand the integrity of quite distinctive cultural systems operating within the "same" space. The view from nondominant groups is sharper in explicitly recognizing the nature of cultural practices that are imposed and hegemonic versus those that are lived: this is the transparency of culture from below or from the side and the opacity of culture from the top. The chapters in this section of the *Handbook* include discussion of a wealth of research that provides evidence for the clarity of insight into cultural life that often characterizes members of nondominant groups.

Within the field of communication, scholars interested in the complexities of gender in cultural context have drawn from and contributed to both the wider discourses of cultural studies and the growing body of work within the communication field. Although a number of journals and textbooks give some attention to issues related to gender, the coverage is slim even for scholarly analysis of decontextualized gender. Scholarship that treats gender as implicated in multiple cultural locations is even slimmer in volume. *Critical Studies in Media Communication* and the newer *Communication and Critical/Cultural Studies* (launched in 2004) are more hospitable to bold work on the dimensions of gender and culture in communicative practices. Outside of sponsorship by the major communication associations, two journals have offered greater opportunities for scholarship addressed to gender and culture. *Women & Language,* edited by Anita Taylor, was a pioneer in including work focused on women and communication outside the United States; in 2003, a special issue of this journal was devoted to "Global Issues in Feminism: Challenges, Opportunities, Insights." The *Howard Journal of Communications* has been another home since 1988 to inquiry "from a cultural perspective" (editorial statement from volume 1). On yet another front, a major contribution to enriching the discourse about culture and communication entered the scene in 1994 with the publication of a collection of essays titled *Our Voices: Essays in Culture, Ethnicity, and Communication* (2004) and edited by Alberto González, Marsha Houston, and Victoria Chen (also referred to in Chapter 20). Now in its fourth edition this book engages the complexities of gender intersections with race, ethnicity, religion, sexuality, and other cultural positionings and doings. It remains true, however, that the work identified in this section of the *Handbook* appears most frequently in a broad array of journals outside the field of communication and in edited collections that are often of an interdisciplinary nature. This is certainly not a sign of weakness in the work but rather makes a statement about the community likely to read this work. Those already engaged in work on gender, culture, and communication have learned how to navigate the scholarly terrain and to locate work by other scholars. Those new to this trajectory may find it more difficult, and we hope this section helps them.

Certain themes run through all of the chapters in this section— intersectionality, center-margin relations, language and power relations, the limitations of domestic (U.S. or American) analysis, and the significance of particular situational contexts (what Houston and Scott call "community cognizant" scholarship and Hegde refers to as "layered construction of context"). Other threads relate to resistance as a force against dominant gender discourses and the hegemonic ideologies they encode. The authors use terms in somewhat different ways, but each essay draws important distinctions between essentializing categories and cultural multiplicity, and each author consistently exercises control over the terms that she or he uses. The inadequacy of everyday language in the United States for rendering accounts of complexity places a special burden on scholars of gender and culture to use terms more precisely than might ordinarily be the case. Race in the U.S. too often is calcified into the familiar labels of *Black, White, Asian,* and *American Indian* that suppress differences within and among the indexical relations of persons to language categories. The authors of the chapters that follow have carefully chosen the terms *black* and *African American, white* and *Eurowhite, global* and *postcolonial.* Even the choice of capitalization is critical in *black-white* versus *Black-White.* Terms like *ancestry, heritage,* and *national culture* all carry the burden of intragroup differences and distinctions. Gender labeling of women and men/feminine and masculine operates similarly to force polarized thinking, but it is difficult to find a linguistic scheme that gets around this deeply rooted semantic proposition of polarization.

Scholars of gender and culture must continuously come to terms with the political force of language to essentialize cultural locations and create isomorphic relations between cultural identities and particular communication practices. Much of this research explicitly distinguishes where the beam of scholarship is aimed from the too often tacitly assumed European origin U.S./Anglo horizon. In any case, scholarship always points to moments of cultural practice, either as the rationale for theoretical inquiry or as the focus for analysis. Lilie Chouliaraki and Norman Fairclough's (1999) discussion of practices is instructive for both conducting projects and reading the literature on culture as the context for gender and communication. Practices, they propose, (a) produce social life, (b) are "located within a network of relationships to other practices," and (c) function reflexively because "people always generate representations of what they do as part of what they do" (p. 22).

The organization of the chapters in this volume reflects my own assessment of the relatedness of the topics covered. Lisa Flores's focus in Chapter 20, "Gender With/out Borders: Discursive Dynamics of Gender, Race, and Culture," is the broadest and it serves as a useful, resource-packed overview for reading the other chapters. Flores undertakes an analysis of two different orientations to the study of culture, communication, gender and race: gender and race as identities associated with cultural differences and as contested ideologies. She marks out the main intellectual questions posed by scholars of gender and culture in communication. Flores provides a sophisticated understanding of the debates entailed in these broad perspectives and offers a constructive, integrative perspective that transcends the debates. Readers will see the distinctions highlighted by Flores in the ways the other authors in the section approach their subject matter.

The next two chapters are more specific in their focus, their intent being to provide review essays that also delve more deeply into particular current topics in cultural analysis of gender and communication. Marsha Houston and Karla Scott ("Negotiating Boundaries, Crossing Borders: The Language of Black Women's Intercultural Encounters") focus on Black women's cross-cultural talk by posing two questions: Does the history of unequal social status still permeate Black women's intercultural encounters? and What are Black women's communicative practices in intercultural encounters? This chapter offers especially compelling first-person research accounts from both Houston and Scott, whose ethnographic projects with middle-class Black women are the basis of a grounded critical discourse analysis of Black women's cross-cultural talk. Of special interest in this chapter is the treatment of Black women's communication as conceptualized negatively by dominant discourse and also as oppositional and resistant—as an affirmative cultural practice of Black women's experience and values. Taking up the theme of resistance, my chapter, "Transgressing Gender in Discourses Across Cultures," addresses scholarship that explores several different manifestations of resistance to dominant conceptions of gender through transgressive processes of "doing gender" and "doing difference" in cultural con-text. The chapter focuses on several theoretical approaches for understanding resistance, with application to three areas of gender transgression in discourse: sociolinguistic analyses of women's resistance in cultures quite different from those in the United States, third-wave gender expressions, and gender refusal and refusers (lesbians, gays, bisexuals,

transgenders). The essay advances ideas of gender as performative and engages scholarship from several different disciplines as well from transdisciplinary gender studies.

The last chapter in the section, like the first, is more general in scope. In "Globalizing Gender Studies in Communication," Radha Hegde addresses one of the most significant newer advances in the study of cultural contextualization of gender and communication. Hegde is concerned with the analytical stance and methodologies brought to bear in feminism's global reach. The goal of research in this area must, she asserts, be "ultimately about building an innovative feminist intellectual space that is both vibrant and responsive to global and local forces and that . . . does not fetishize the transnational over the national and the popular over the everyday." Hegde considers the transnational transformation of feminism, assesses the limitations of the area studies approach to scholarship on international communication, and discusses the productive possibilities of scholarship that conjoins feminist, cultural studies, and postcolonial approaches.

Together, the chapters in this section draw upon literatures and perspectives from different disciplinary axes to lead the way to a more comprehensive understanding of gender and communication as a complex, culturally and contextually layered focus of inquiry. These chapters are a starting point, and while they do not include all possible approaches to cultural studies of gender and communication, they do capture the main issues and trends in this line of scholarly inquiry. Some years ago, Rose Brewer (1993) urged that "feminism must reflect in its theory and practice the race and class terrain upon which hierarchy and inequality are built globally and within the USA" (p. 27). The authors in this section hope that our discussions of the con-text of culture for gender studies of communication will fruitfully guide further inquiry, bringing culture as a framing principle from margins to center and from optional to mandatory.

◆ Note

1. The seminar was funded by a grant from the Fund for Improvement of Post-secondary Education to Five Colleges Inc. The seminar drew from faculty at Amherst, Mount Holyoke, Smith, and Hampshire colleges and the University of Massachusetts–Amherst. Participation was based on applications, with some faculty participating as individuals and some in pairs.

◆ References

Brewer, R. (1993). Theorizing race, class and gender: The new scholarship of Black feminist intellectuals and Black women's labor. In S. M. James & A. P. A. Busia (Eds.), *Theorizing black feminisms: The visionary pragmatism of black women* (pp. 13–30). London: Routledge.

Chaney, D. (1994). *The cultural turn: Scene setting essays on contemporary cultural history*. London: Routledge.

Chouliaraki, L., & Fairclough, N. (1999). *Discourses in late modernity: Rethinking critical discourse analysis*. Edinburgh: Edinburgh University Press.

Connell, R. W. (2002). *Gender*. Cambridge: Polity Press.

Daly, M. (1978). *Gyn/ecology: The metaethics of radical feminism*. Boston: Beacon Press.

González, A., Houston, M., & Chen, V. (2004). *Our voices: Essays in culture, ethnicity, and communication* (4th ed.). Los Angeles: Roxbury.

Houston Stanback, M. (1985). Language and woman's place: Evidence from the Black middle class. In P. Treichler, C. Kramarae, & B. Stafford (Eds.), *For Alma Mater: Theory and practice in feminist scholarship* (pp. 177–193). Urbana: University of Illinois Press.

Jenks, C. (1993). *Culture: Key ideas*. New York: Routledge.

Johnson, F. L. (1995). Centering culture in the discipline of communication. In J. T. Wood & R. B. Gregg (Eds.), *Toward the 21st century: The future of speech communication* (pp. 151–167). Cresskill, NJ: Hampton Press, 1995.

Johnson, F. L. (2000). *Speaking culturally: Language diversity in the United States*. Thousand Oaks, CA: Sage.

Lorde, A. (1983). An open letter to Mary Daly. In C. Moraga & G. Anzaldúa (Eds.), *This bridge called my back: Writings by radical women of color* (pp. 94–97). New York: Kitchen Table/Women of Color Press.

Moraga, C., & Anzaldúa, G. (Eds.). (1983). *This bridge called my back: Writings by radical women of color*. New York: Kitchen Table/Women of Color Press.

Rakow, L. (1992). The field reconsidered. In L. Rakow (Ed.), *Women making meaning: New feminist directions in communication* (pp. 3–17). New York: Routledge.

Spellman, E. V. (1988). *Inessential women: Problems of exclusion in feminist thought*. Boston: Beacon Press.

Thorne, B. & Henley, N. (Eds.). (1975). *Language and sex: Difference and dominance*. Rowley, MA: Newbury House.

Thorne, B., Kramarae, C., & Henley, N. (Eds.). (1983). *Language, gender and society*. Rowley, MA: Newbury House.

West, C., & Fenstermaker, S. (1995). Doing difference. *Gender & Society, 9*, 8–37.

20

GENDER WITH/OUT BORDERS

Discursive Dynamics of Gender, Race, and Culture

◆ Lisa A. Flores

Invested in both the study of distinct cultures and the concept of culture, scholars have sought to complicate intercultural communication by identifying and examining various cultural enactments and communicative facets. As the discipline has evolved, those interested in the intricacies of culture have increasingly infused the literature with attention to differences, not just between different cultures, but within them. That attention to understanding and explicating intercultural and intracultural communication has generated diverse bodies of work investigating and exploring gender and race. Perhaps not surprisingly, culture and communication scholars "discovered" the theoretical insights of race/ethnicity before they gave sustained attention to gender and sexuality. After all, the study of intercultural communication initially was heavily influenced by questions of national difference, as its origins were largely practical (Leeds-Hurwitz, 1990). And in its evolution, the discipline remains committed to the practical, though it has been and is theoretically motivated as well. The practical concerns that impel scholarly analysis, however, shift and move with time, history, and context. And over the last few decades, as national cultures have fragmented and trans/national communities have developed, the terrain of culture and the need for various kinds of cultural knowledge have expanded such that gender and racial difference not only have become more visible, but the study of them is more imperative.

This chapter reviews scholarship on culture, communication, gender, and race as it explores the emerging relationships at play among them. More specifically, I emphasize a recent and evolving approach to culture and communication (critical intercultural communication) and attend to two bodies of literature within critical intercultural communication which manifest varying degrees of convergence and divergence. For instance, scholars from both approaches study the simultaneity of gender and race: One group attends to individual identity; the second examines ideologies. Presenting them as distinct, my categorization is necessarily problematic. That is, seen through different eyes, these studies may well be divided and discussed differently. That caveat aside, I detail varying conceptions of culture, gender, and race and offer examples of key research themes and questions that recur. I begin with literature that takes a micro approach to gender and race, situating them as aspects of individual identity and emphasizing marginalized individuals and their communicative and cultural practices. I then review studies that assume a more macro focus, defining gender and race as ideologies while conceptualizing culture as contested and negotiated. This perspective promotes discursive study of gender and race as it expands its focus to include dominant populations.

◆ Gender and Race as Cultural Difference

A first perspective on gender, race, and culture, which I refer to as a cultural difference perspective, conceives of gender and race as aspects of identity and positions culture as social communities inhabited by diverse populations whose gendered and racial differences result in a diverse range of communicative behaviors. Seen as relatively stable aspects of an individual's overall identity, both gender and race are pieces of a culture's larger picture. Cultural boundaries are not necessarily limited by physical borders, such as those that delimit nation space. Instead, cultures are described in terms of populations, which may or may not share a physical space. While gender, race, and culture here are dynamic and shifting, they also appear relatively stable and recognizable. The relationships among them are multifaceted, with each providing insights into the other. For instance, examinations of ethnic minority communities become more complex when gender differences are uncovered.

STUDIES OF DIFFERENCE

A significant body of work in this perspective is devoted to the exploration of "difference." For some, gender and race are differences to be unpacked (Spellers, 1998; Uchida, 1997). For instance, Philipsen (1975) traces a particular manifestation of urban, White working-class masculine speech. Others emphasize culture as composed of differences (Collier, 2003; Dolphin, 1994; Hegde, 1998a). Consider Folb's (1994) depiction of the United States as encompassing various communities distinguished by gender, race, geography, and ability. Across both emphases, gender, race, and culture are givens. That is, little time is spent defining and/or theorizing gender, race, and culture as abstract concepts. Instead, beginning with assumptions that particular gendered and racial cultures exist (e.g., African American women), scholars attend to the enactments and features of particular cultures and communities as well as to the individuals within them.

For those scholars for whom culture is the primary intellectual focus, race and gender are markers of identity and difference whose exploration enhances and complicates the study. Culture is the site or space in which individuals, marked by gender and racial identity, interact. The communicative patterns of cultural groups can be identified, as they are thought to exhibit identifiable and perhaps predictable behaviors that reflect distinct gender and racial as well as other identities. Gender and race are important cultural differences, and the distinctions that result from them reflect the overall dynamic of culture and demonstrate the many micro dimensions of it that deserve scholarly attention. A limited body of work explores culture by examining intercultural communication concepts and theories through the lens of such differences. For instance, elaborating a theory of cultural identity, Collier (1998b) describes gender and race as two of many factors that make up an individual's identity. In such work, the emphasis is on theorizing cultural difference rather than on gender and/or race. Studies are devoted to communicative practices, including nonverbal communication (Borisoff & Merrill, 2003; Dolphin, 1994) and discourse (Johnson, 2003; Rakow & Wackwitz, 1998), as well as to particular sites of communicative interaction, including the classroom (Gay, 2003; Le Roux, 2006) and the neighborhood (Philipsen, 1975). Other work elaborates theories of identity (Collier, 2003) and relationships (Collier, 1998a; Stringer, 2006).

STUDIES OF RACE AND GENDER

A second emphasis in this perspective comes from those whose primary intellectual focus is race and gender. Beginning with these differences, this work positions culture as a product of communication and interaction and argues that excessive attention to national culture can overlook the variations—such as race and gender—that exist within nations. A key early work reflecting this argument was *Our Voices: Essays in Culture, Ethnicity, and Communication.* Edited by Gonzalez, Houston, and Chen (1994) and now in its fourth edition (2004), this anthology of mostly narrative and personal essays chronicles the experiences and

perspectives of ethnic and gender minorities. Situated as a disciplinary intervention, the book, and related publications, sought to extend the purview of intercultural communication by highlighting and centering voices and stories that mostly had been ignored. As Asante (1994), in the foreword to the book's first edition, explained, "The appearance of the book . . . is a remarkable achievement. . . . It reflects the evolution of a field that has too long marginalized the voices of African, Asian, Latino, Native, Jewish, and Arab Americans" (p. vii). Authors contributed work designed to increase the visibility, experiences, and perspectives of subordinated populations. Given this goal, gender generally referred to women, while race mostly referred to people of color.

The explicit attention to race and gender, as well as to marginalized racial and gender identities, generated a conceptual link between race, gender, and politics. In many ways aligned with feminist and antiracist perspectives that emphasize what has come to be known as "identity politics," authors writing in this group situate gender and race identities as significant facets of personal identity and community membership. Moreover, gender and racial identities signal political identity and affiliation. That is, gender and ethnic minorities construct identities and perspectives that emerge out of and reflect personal and historic experiences of discrimination and oppression. Much of this work emphasizes the political solidarity that comes from shared membership in groups and communities defined by gender and race. Generally situated in a broader, social constructionist paradigm, theorists position gender and race as socially and communicatively produced and evolving (James, 2004). Simultaneously, however, because one's politics reflect one's identity, gender and race—though broadly conceived as dynamic—are specific, concrete, and relatively stable. A seeming contradiction, this tension is best explained by the argument that individuals develop their gender and racial identities in and through their social and cultural experiences, which differ, often dramatically, both across and within groups. At the same time, members of traditionally disadvantaged gender and racial groups (e.g., White women, African Americans, Latinas/os) have some similar experiences, particularly discrimination. Such similarities foster connections and shape cultural identities that bind people together and come to constitute culture. For instance, Houston (2004) describes the shared experiences that Black women have in their friendships with White women and vice versa. She notes that while they may be engaged in one conversation they often hear two different cultural messages.

As scholars increasingly studied co-cultures and their racial and gender differences, they also reconceptualized culture. That is, the cultures that emerge from politically oriented communities are not just ones of racial and gender difference; they are also about political difference. González and Tanno (1997) argue that when we study race and gender from politically motivated perspectives such as feminism and antiracism, we begin to see culture at work: "'Culture' becomes visible only as interests collide and struggle" (p. 4). The study of culture then also becomes the study of marginalization, power relations, and social justice. Moon (2002), for instance, calls for an expanded vision of culture, one that "allows us to come to hear and perhaps appreciate the varieties of cultural experiences and views that make up what we understand as 'America' and gives us a way of thinking about cultural politics that can point us in the direction of social change" (p. 14).

An important move in these studies on politicized cultures occurs in discussions of identity. Advocating pluralism, those writing here explicitly and implicitly theorize identity—notably gender and racial identity—and argue that the simultaneous study of gender and race means that the experiences, identities, and cultures of several groups are explored. Pluralism emerges as writings detail the differences within and among groups, and studies shift from discussions

of women's experiences or Latino communication to Black women's experiences and White women's communication. Unlike dominant populations, particularly White men, marginalized communities are described in this work as communicating in ways that reflect their historic and social marginalization. Long excluded from dominant public spaces and their respective communication styles, women of color, both within the academy and without, communicate and theorize through narrative and personal experience, emphasizing the mundane and everyday rather than more traditionally elite forms of knowledge. Significant research (James, 2004; Leland & Martinez, 1998; Tanno, 2004) details the stories of women of color and reflects varying experiences of identity, self, and marginalization. For some, identities are clearly marked by the simultaneity of gender and race (Davis, 1998; Spellers, 1998) and the particular insights that emerge from experiences of multiple forms of oppression. For instance, women of color describe the double consciousness they develop as they see the world through various lenses (Chen, 2004) and occupy particular standpoints (Harris & Donmoyer, 2000). Others note stages in their awareness of identity and the ways in which various experiences, for instance of class (Martinez, 2000) and history (Tanno, 2004) enabled them to delay social consciousness of their racial identity.

REFLEXIVITY

With the emphasis on personal and cultural identity comes a discussion of reflexivity. Authors address reflexivity in terms of the research process, examining both methods and author positionality. Exploring knowledge production, scholars engage in explicit questioning of traditional assumptions—of what counts as evidence, experience, authenticity, and legitimacy. Considerable work centers narrative as a valid and valuable epistemological tool. One's personal stories are not simply descriptions of varying experiences that provide insight into cultural differences. They are situated as the "stuff out of which theory gets made" (Leland & Martinez, 1998, p.86). Madison (1993) notes that stories of gender and race serve resistive functions, as they "privilege agency and interrogate notions of . . . 'voiceless victims'" (p. 214). Making visible and prominent the lives and experiences of women of color, narratives and counternarratives become tools through which women of color write themselves into existence and offer strategies for survival (Flores, 2000; Halualani, 1998; James, 2004). Elaborating on the theoretical importance of this work, authors ask for scholarly skepticism about traditional forms of evidence, arguing that everyday experiences—cooking, kitchen table gossip—have epistemological value (Davis, 1999; Flores, 1996). Reflexivity is also turned inward as writers ask, even demand, that authors implicate themselves into their work. Delineating the politics of positionality, or the ways in which authors' identities are implicated in the work they do, those writing in this perspective argue that scholars gain insight into the workings of gender and race when they reflect upon the gendered and racial ways of thinking they bring to their own work (Cooks, 2003).

Extending the reflexivity debate further, many argue that work on race and gender should be seen as opportunities to expand the province of both. In other words, women of color writing about race *and* gender identify the limitations of work that addresses either gender *or* race. Dobris (1996) argues, for instance, that Black feminism extends feminist theory by challenging assumptions of sisterhood. By accounting for the differences among women, she argues, possibilities for solidarity become greater. Similarly, Dace (1998) calls upon African American studies to attend to the ways in which analyses of blackness negate and/or ignore underlying sexism.

These studies make inroads into what will later emerge as an emphasis on intersectionality, or what K. Crenshaw (1991) identifies

as "the need to account for multiple grounds of identity when considering how the social world is constructed" (p. 1245). That is, authors begin to unpack the multiplicity of gender and race, noting the ways in which women of color simultaneously experience them. Elaborating on what Spelman (1988) labeled the "ampersand" problem (p. 115), attention is given to the struggle to talk about women and people of color in complex ways that account for race and gender. Houston (1992) clarifies: "the parts of nondominant women's identities, their experiences of oppression cannot accurately be conceived as separable, summative, or 'piled on.' For example, women of color do not experience sexism *in addition* to racism, but sexism *in the context of* racism" (p. 49, emphasis in original). Demonstrating Houston's point, Patton (2004) identifies the particular face of racism and sexism as experienced by a Black female professor.

In an explicit, early account of intersectionality in communication, C. Crenshaw (1997b) argues that intersectionality, as both theoretical and methodological lens, shifts the analysis, providing a means of rethinking gender as an analytic frame and category. As illustration, Lee (1998) identifies the contextual nature of race and gender as she examines how meanings surrounding Chinese women's identities constantly change as these women move in and out of different communities and contexts. Further, intersectionality provides one means of recognizing the political importance of identity politics while it enables critics to move toward coalitional practices (Allen, 2004; Harris & Donmoyer, 2000). The turn to intersectionality also enabled a shift in the configuring of gender and race, for as scholars explicitly expressed commitment to intersectionality, they engaged more directly in theorizing race and gender. One clear manifestation of this shift is in the small, but growing body of literature on marginalized masculinities. Masculinity studies examine the experiences (Jackson & Dangerfield, 2003; Orbe, 1997) and common representations (Orbe & Hopson,

2002) of Black men as they begin to question how men and masculinity relate to existing research on gender, women, and femininity.

REFLECTIONS AND CONCLUSIONS ON THE CULTURE AS DIFFERENCE PERSPECTIVE

Without question, literature written from the culture as difference perspective has broad significance. Complicating limited notions of gender, race, and culture, authors writing in this paradigm provoke conversation between gender(s) and race(s). Their work challenges the idea that there is a "woman's" experience that is shared widely, if not universally, and identifies instead the many women's experiences and the connections and distinctions among them. By attending to gender and racial identities, scholars uncover the complex ways women of color make sense of their lives, their histories, and their stories. The "double vision" (Chen, 2004) that many women of color develop gives them access to a wide range of ways to understand and live in the world. Martinez (2000), for instance, emphasizes personal experience and narrative and explores the various degrees through which she came to understand gender and race. Through such narratives of identity and struggle, authors writing in this perspective describe how marginalized communities face and resist oppression, often "making the best with what [they] got" (González & Flores, 1994, p. 37). Such details on both oppression and resistance are vital. As Ono and Sloop (1995) explain, "without an examination of the rhetoric of those struggling to survive, no significant social statements can be made about political, social, and cultural liberation" (p. 40). Moreover, the emphasis on personal experience highlights the everyday aspects of cultural knowledge and exposes the very cultural constructed-ness of unquestioned and unexplored patterns of daily life. This perspective turns to individual experiences of gender and race so as to trace and make culture visible. Much of this work challenges, at least implicitly, arguments dominating postmodern conversations proclaiming the "death of the subject." In response, these scholars loudly pronounce the existence of the gendered and racial subject. They argue that postmodern and poststructuralist critiques of identity and essentialism fail to account for the political significance of cultural groups. Social change emerges when communities, often united because of gender and racial identities, act together.

Although the move to localized knowledges and experiences serves to identify the many differences that comprise cultures and to challenge essentialist ideas of gender and race, that emphasis has limitations. By demonstrating how individuals experience race and gender in their everyday lives and through their bodies, scholars rely on fixed concepts of gender and race. Theoretically, the move is from singular conceptions of gender and race to multiple ones. Studies now describe the many ways women experience gender but provide little critical reflection on gender as a concept. Instead, gender and racial identities are presumed to be outcomes of biology, even as they are culturally informed. In other words, while we may not be able to describe women's experiences, we can describe White women's, Black women's, and Latinas' experiences. This work adopts intersectionality, but it does so in limited ways.

The privileging of marginalized identities and experiences also has potential limitations for theories of power, oppression, and resistance. By locating gender and race identity at the individual level, these studies offer limited views of larger contexts and power dynamics. The individual voice of marginalization takes precedence, and subordinated identities, as they are added to the larger population of voices, are less likely to be directly challenged. Instead, there is a tendency to celebrate those stories unreflexively and to presume that the very experience of marginalization means that one's voice is politically informed and productively resistive to dominant culture. Noting the dangers of such assumptions, Delgado (1998) reminds us that even those who speak from the "margins" may perpetuate existing hierarchies of race and/or gender; their voices, like those of dominant populations, should be subject to careful analysis.

In sum, the cultural difference perspective draws attention to the complexities within cultures, notably as those differences emerge out of gender and racial identities. Privileging the voices, perspectives, and experiences of gender and ethnic minorities, authors expand the theoretical and conceptual boundaries of culture as they challenge and extend traditional and elite standards for assessing culture, knowledge, and theory. Culture, both the space in which individuals and communities come together and the outcome of that communication, is made up of difference. And that difference is productive, both in its ability to generate culture and in its tendency to provoke contestation. Rejecting essentialist perspectives on gender and race that fail to account for the many ways in which individuals and communities experience and understand themselves, this work situates gender and race as aspects of individual identity and argues that attention to different gender and racial identities renders political and personal experiences more visible.

◆ Gender, Race, and Culture as Contested Ideologies

A second perspective on gender, race, and culture shifts toward a discursive and ideological frame. Culture, gender, and race are configured as performances, circulating in and among social narratives. While the first perspective centered bodies and populations by, for example, examining the communicative dynamics of Latinas as a means of uncovering cultural patterns, bodies in this other perspective are only part of the focus, as attention is also directed to larger ideologies invoked and evoked by

those bodies as well as by discourse about them. In this sense, then, culture becomes what Martin and Nakayama (1999) identify as a "contested site" where meanings converge and diverge in constant dynamic flux. Gender and race are as likely to be constituted as ideologies, discourse, and performance as they are to be captured in marked bodies. Cultures emerge more as a result of conflicting and complementary narratives than through a population of particular people, and their boundaries and borders "are increasingly murky and overlapping" (Collier, 2000, p. 3). Collier identifies a shift in theoretical interest away from an identification of cultural differences and toward a politics of difference that seeks not just to give voice to marginalized communities but also to identify the political, discursive, and cultural contestations in play. This turn in emphasis provokes a macro approach to the study of gender, race, and culture.

PERFORMATIVITY AND IDEOLOGY

Work in this perspective takes a performative and ideological approach to gender, race, and other aspects of identity, emphasizing the study of ideologies of gender and race. As noted in the introduction to the *Handbook* and in chapters by Bell and Blauer, Sloop, and others, a performative view begins with the assumption that identities of gender and race, for instance, emerge and are (re)produced discursively. To study gender this way is to study historic and contemporary enactments and performances of masculinity and femininity. Also reflecting a social constructionist frame, this work disrupts the connection between bodies and ideologies that informs much of the difference perspective. In other words, although performances are often embodied and individuals perform masculinity and femininity, such embodied acts are not necessarily linked to the biological/sexual bodies. Whereas those who are labeled "women" because of biology may be more likely to perform femininity than masculinity, they do not do so necessarily. Indeed, much of this work investigates the tensions and dilemmas that come from mediating "the materiality of the body" and the argument that bodies are "constructed through a ritualized repetition of norms" (Butler, 1993, p. ix–x). As ideologies and discourses, gender and race are sets of images, circulating narratives, and embodied performances (Butler). Neither stable nor unified, they may simultaneously conjure images and conceptions of physical bodies—of men, women, African Americans, Whites—while also remaining theoretically almost distinct. Shome (2001) notes that "*White femininity* . . . is not meant to suggest a physical body or a property with some ontological origin. Rather, I use it to mean an ideological construction through which meanings about White women and their place in the social order are naturalized" (p. 323). Theories of intersectionality are extended so that gender and race are partial, contradictory, and incomplete, and references to men and women become references to, for instance, White masculinity and Latinidad. In other words, gender is enmeshed with race, class, and sexuality (Ashcraft & Flores, 2003).

As in the first perspective, this work examines identity. Rather than emphasizing identity and voice, however, the ideological perspective seeks to subvert the idea of individual gender and race identity and to emphasize the instability and fluidity of performances. Shome and Hegde (2002b), for instance, argue that identity is "above all a performative expression of transnational change" (p. 266). In other words, attention shifts from the fact of identity, gender, and race, to its invocations, uses, and expressions; "the issue is how they matter, how they are evoked, how they are produced, where they are produced, and how they are reconstituted" (Shome & Hegde, 2002a, p. 176). Gender and race, along with culture, sexuality, nation, class, and so on, are constantly being negotiated, and these negotiations illustrate both the possibilities of identity and the limitations of traditional identity categories, such as male/female, Black/White. Zimmerman and Geist-Martin (2006) describe the queer body as one that exceeds gender categories, for it is never fully masculine nor feminine, man nor woman: "A queer gender body, then, disrupts this binary of all male or all female, creating a dialectical tension" (p. 79). Exploring identity, authors examine authenticity (Liera-Schwichtenberg, 2000), hybridity (Kraidy, 1999), and passing (Squires & Brouwer, 2002) as they highlight doing over being and situate gender and race as two of many facets.

The performative take on gender, race, and culture leads to considerable study of "the problem of ideology," as scholars in this perspective seek to "give an account . . . of how social ideas arise" (Hall, 1996, p. 26). Studies emphasize the circulation of social ideas and trace the dominant stories surrounding gender and race to uncover the meanings at work. Assessing larger cultural discourses, scholars turn somewhat away from individual bodies and toward mediated ones, examining what Valdivia (1998) identifies as the "politics of representation," or the need to reflect critically on the production, circulation, reception, and mediation of images (p. 247). This work details representations of gender and race, noting the circulation of reductive stereotypes of Latinas (Molina Guzmán & Valdivia, 2004) and Latinos (Calafell & Delgado, 2004), of Asian American women (Halualani, 1995) and men (Nakayama, 1994), and of African American women (McPhail, 1996) and men (Watts & Orbe, 2002). Across this work, scholars trace not just these representations but also the ideologies in play. One interesting conclusion reached by several authors is that, for all the diversity among mediated representations, gender and race are commonly linked to sexuality such that women and men of color are often depicted as highly sexualized, generally in ways that align non-White racial identities with deviant, hyper, and "primitive" sexualities (Ashcraft & Flores, 2003; Molina Guzmán & Valdivia, 2004), while White femininity and White women emerge as pure but endangered through exposure to non-White masculinities (Shome, 2000).

The theoretical shift in this perspective toward ideologies of gender and race has considerable implications for the conceptualization of culture. Not just a composite of people or a manifestation of patterns and behaviors, culture is an ideological production infused with assumptions of gender and race. Scholars influenced by interdisciplinary work in cultural studies, feminist theory, and critical race studies argue that cultures and nations are gendered and raced (Berlant, 1997; Young, 1995). In her key account of the cultural shaping of citizenship through politics, social institutions, and practices, Bederman (1995) identifies historic patterns in masculinity, race, and nation that enable a conflation of White masculinity as civilized masculinity and thus "truly" American, and a linking of Black masculinity with primitive, savage, Other. Centering the discursive construction of gender, race, and nation, she argues that if competing ideologies come to constitute bodies and cultures, studying those ideologies provides insight into the assumptions that guide social perception and practice. Likewise, Shome (2001), examining media spectacle surrounding Princess Diana, traces discourses of gender, race, and nation and argues that the abstract concepts are infused with overlapping ideologies such that the ideal nation is embodied by White femininity and its aura of purity, domesticity, heterosexuality, and motherhood. Gender, race, and culture function as (in)distinct ideologies. Their intersections, while not necessarily intentionally and strategically designed, are rarely innocent or insignificant. Instead, affiliations among them sustain larger hegemonic narratives. Buescher and Ono (1996) identify similar dynamics in Disney's *Pocahontas;* here, a story of colonization and control becomes a romantic tale of love across cultures that legitimates civilized White masculine protection of savagery, associated in this case with Native

Americans. Femininity, mostly captured in Pocahontas, is earthy, spiritual, "natural," an identity that can only be enhanced by its affiliation with civilized whiteness.

Gendered and racialized bodies in these discourses—whether of Princess Di or Pocahontas—are repositories for meanings. As represented in discourse, these bodies legitimize existing hegemonic relations, justifying capitalism (Cloud, 1996) as well as war and violence (Stables, 2003). They also invest culture and nation with gender and race such that the study of cultural and national identity is almost simultaneously the study of femininity, masculinity, and whiteness (Owen, 2002). As this work investigates nation it also disrupts that category, revealing the permeability of national boundaries—both geopolitical and ideological. Adopting postcolonial and global perspectives that theorize gender, race, and nation as hybrid sites, authors explore the implications of transnationalism and its invocations of gender and race (Lee, 1998; Supriya, 2001). They identify the ways in which ideologies of consumerism, desire, whiteness, and femininity are mobilized globally to reinscribe the ideal body as that of White femininity (Zacharias, 2003).

STUDIES OF DOMINANCE

As the study of gender and race becomes the study of ideologies, the scope of it expands to include analysis of dominance. Here we see a marked conceptual shift away from the race and gender as cultural difference perspective that almost exclusively highlights traditionally subordinated groups (women, people of color). Scholars interested in dominance have begun to examine masculinity (Ashcraft & Flores, 2003; Carillo Rowe & Lindsey, 2003; Nakayama, 1994), whiteness (C. Crenshaw, 1997a; Ehlers, 2004; Moon, 1999; Shome, 1999), and heteronormativity (Squires & Brouwer, 2002; Zimmerman & Geist-Martin, 2006). Several core questions drive studies of dominance. For some, depicting the landscape is key: What do masculinity, whiteness, and heteronormativity look like (Moon, 1999)? Others inquire into operations: How does dominance work (Warren, 2001)? What strategies secure its privilege (Carillo Rowe, 2000; Zacharias, 2003)? What communicative dynamics disrupt its hold (Flores & Moon, 2002)?

Across these studies is an examination of ideologies of dominance. Centrally, dominance is problematized such that static relations of oppressor/oppressed are challenged as the complexities of identities, voices, and locations emerge. Condit (1993) explains: "It is no longer so easy to identify single categories of victim and victor. Who is the villain? the Black female lawyer? the White unemployed male construction worker? the Norwegian homosexual college professor? the happy homemaker?" (p. 187). Studies that detail the complexities and disjunctions replace analyses that identify clear boundaries between the haves and the have-nots. For instance, representations of "exotic" Others are often managed through ambivalence, which allows simultaneous and competing senses of desire and disgust to circulate through those representations (Cloud, 1996; Durham, 2001). That ambivalence seemingly mediates racist and hetero/sexist representations as it fosters the appearance of appreciation for nondominant populations while masking the commodification and consumption of difference (Lalvani, 1995; Watts & Orbe, 2002).

In the literature on dominance are studies of how discourses of gender and race operate and secure culture, even if only momentarily. Ideologies of gender and race, particularly in their interimplication, become significant for what they reveal about larger power dynamics, notably privilege and hegemony. A major impetus behind this shift is the theoretical goal of visibility, which was also a theme in the first perspective. Visibility functions differently for scholars writing in this vein. Whereas in the first perspective it highlights giving voice and raising the profile of

marginalized communities who had traditionally been ignored, in this camp visibility is focused on a different absence—the invisibility of the norm. Arguing that dominance operates through invisibility—that it gives whiteness, masculinity, and heteronormativity their persistent power—scholars seek to make dominance visible and disrupt its presumed universality (Nakayama & Krizek, 1995; Projansky & Ono, 1999). The examination of privilege has also generated research examining its seductive pull—how and why individuals, even from subordinated communities, participate in power structures, including those that foster their own oppression. Here, scholars address what Lipsitz (1998) identifies as the "possessive investment" in privilege. While Lipsitz focused on whiteness, detailing the ways in which people of color participate in whiteness even while relegated to its margins, others have directed similar attention to gender and sexuality. Carillo Rowe (2000) identifies White women's contradictory position at the intersection of whiteness and femininity, as they "negotiate between gender oppression, on one hand, and racial privilege, on the other" (p. 68). Following others interested in power and oppression, Carillo Rowe argues that the examination of tensions in White femininity uncovers the complexities of power, privilege and domination, pushing scholars to trace how individuals are simultaneously implicated in privilege as they also experience oppression. Brookey (1996) identifies similar contradictory tensions in queer representations, in which gay male culture is made palatable and mainstream through its affiliations with whiteness, class privilege, and family values. Finally, McPhail (1996) brings a critical eye to contemporary representations of Black masculinity that conflate blackness and masculinity in ostensibly productive ways, offering new visions of Black culture while reinscribing hetero/sexist ideologies that relegate Black femininity to tired scripts emphasizing Black women's alleged hypersexuality. Exposing the pleasures of privilege, this work complicates ideas of power, its maneuverability and its appeal, suggesting perhaps that there is no, or at least little, avoiding complicity.

REFLECTIONS AND CONCLUSIONS ON THE IDEOLOGICAL PERSPECTIVE

In sum, in its turn to performativity, the ideological perspective expands the scope of the study of gender, race, and culture in productive and provocative ways. Disrupting the assumption that to study gender and/or race means to study women and/or ethnic minorities, scholars trace gender and race ideologies and examine assumptions and enactments of femininity, masculinity, and whiteness. Moreover, they look at the manifestations of these ideologies in social discourses and so advance the argument that institutions themselves—nation, media, family—are gendered and racialized. This work begins to uncover the complex ways in which these ideologies are woven into the very fabric of culture. Masculinity, whiteness, and heteronormativity emerge as foundational assumptions that constitute what we experience as culture. Yet, while such patterns of domination are described as pervasive, scholars also trace the connections between dominant and subordinated discourses. Relations of power emerge as negotiations between seemingly contradictory positions. Neither individuals nor institutions appear guilty or guiltless, oppressor or oppressed. This work contests arguments that conclude, for example, that it is men who promote hetero/sexism and Whites who practice racism. White women and people of color also participate in ideologies of dominance. Further, individuals are just one small part of the larger culture. In their attention to the discourses of cultural contestation, authors expand the terrain of culture and offer a holistic and intertextual account of tensions and contradictions, acknowledging

that those contradictions may well be at the core of culture. Extending the intersections of gender and race, this work positions them as just two of the major ideologies in play and looks to the connections among gender, race, class, hetero/sexuality, and nation.

The turn to the institutional and ideological has not gone unchallenged. Authors who assess dominant discourses sometimes neglect those produced by subordinated communities. If the argument advanced by the race and gender as cultural difference perspective is correct and marginalized communities develop strategies for resistance in their everyday lives, the emphasis on dominant discourses may well miss the lessons of that resistance. What's more, the separation of gendered and racialized bodies from ideologies of gender and race can lead to what K. Crenshaw (1991) calls "vulgar constructionism." She argues that when scholars shift too dramatically toward ideologies and away from the material bodies at play, they potentially reduce everything to discourse, as if there are no actual populations experiencing material social struggles. If the goal of critical scholarship is to promote social change, it must retain its grounding in the materiality of everyday life (Cloud, 1994). As Ono and Sloop (2002) note, while the deconstruction of dominant discourses is necessary, that alone is insufficient. Critical scholars of gender and race must be willing to take a stand, to judge, and to delineate possibilities.

Viewing race and gender as cultural ideologies offers an accounting of them as they interact with and permeate social structures and institutions. Writers expand the terrain to include masculinity, whiteness, and heteronormativity, trace the strategies of dominance, and reveal the complex workings of power. Conceding the perpetual struggle of culture, this perspective advances what might be considered a multicultural feminism which, as Shohat (1998) describes it, is "not an easy Muzak-like harmony but rather a polyrhythmic staging of a full-throated counterpoint where tensions are left unresolved. It does not offer . . . a single ideological position" (p. 3).

◆ Conclusion

In this chapter, I have reviewed literature broadly conceived of as contributing to the study of critical intercultural communication with an eye toward that which assesses and theorizes race and gender. As I noted earlier, the boundaries I impose may well be as permeable or murky as those examined in this literature. Still, I identify two primary perspectives that frame gender and race, and I argue that scholars tend toward either a micro perspective, which emphasizes difference, or a macro approach, which concentrates on ideologies. I conclude by considering these two bodies of work in conversation with each other, both noting their overlapping and distinct arguments and contributions and proposing productive tensions resulting from that conversation.

Scholars working in both perspectives begin with an interest in race and gender. The studies reviewed here contest, implicitly and explicitly, universal assumptions about gender and race by making both particular. In other words, whether studying individual bodies or abstract discourses, authors expose the many faces of gender and race. In the *cultural difference perspective,* authors position race and gender as identifiable and relatively stable aspects of identity; culture is both the site in which differences play out and a primary constitutive space that generates difference. In the *cultural ideologies perspective,* authors define gender and race as fluid, dynamic, and constantly negotiated, their negotiations being the very stuff of culture, which is itself an ideological enactment infused with gender and race. Scholars using either perspective look to the intersections of gender and race. The first is a micro approach

that centers individuals; the second is more macro and turns to discourse and ideology.

Regardless of their emphasis, authors situate scholarship within the larger realm of politics and social change. The study of gender and race is not a neutral intellectual inquiry. It is motivated by a larger, sometimes peripheral, sometimes central, commitment to social justice. This often explicit agenda emerges in the careful attention to power that pervades this work. Though relevant across the literature, power is defined differently in the two perspectives. The *cultural difference perspective* illustrates the juridical dimensions of power, noting how dominant populations oppress subordinated ones who develop creative tactics for resistance. The *cultural ideology perspective* frames power as pervasive and seductive, such that individuals and communities participate in it in varied ways. The *cultural ideology perspective* looks to the institutional dimensions of power and seeks to expose its subtle manifestations. Scholars in both perspectives assess representations. While authors in the *cultural difference perspective* work to increase representations of marginalized communities, those writing in the *cultural ideologies perspective* critique those representations as well as dominant ones. The political emphasis extends to include a general critique of scholarly activity, as scholars in both perspectives implore others to reflect upon the research paradigm and account for our implication, as writers, in the critical work that we do.

Both perspectives extend the boundaries and borders of ways of thinking about and doing gender and race. Shohat (1998) describes this work as "a polyphonic space where many critical voices engage in a dialogue in which no one voice hopefully muffles the others" and which envisions "dissonant polyphony" rather than harmony (p. 2). If she is correct, critical intercultural scholars might be best served by exploring the productive tensions in play across these perspectives. Authors writing from either the micro or macro perspectives yield knowledge as they simultaneously obscure vision. Despite considerable criticism of the essentialism of identity politics, social movement scholars illustrate the power for social change that comes from a group of like-minded or like-bodied individuals working together. The material changes that emerged from U.S. women's rights and civil rights groups are significant examples of that power. At the same time, gender and race scholars chronicle the dissolution of social groups when the foundation of their presumed unity of identity is exposed as shaky (Spelman, 1988). A second productive tension may well be the attention to voice and resistance of the *cultural difference* scholars versus that paid to power and dominance by the *cultural ideology* authors. Where writers in the first perspective may overemphasize the possibilities of resistance, those writing from the second perspective tend toward a paralyzing power-is-inescapable argument. Each group offers useful correction to the other by pointing out possibilities.

As research continues to examine gender and race in critical intercultural communication, new perspectives may yield insights. The study of identity and difference has begun to push beyond assessment of women of color to include study of masculinity and race. So far, attention to the intersections of queer identities with racial identity is limited. It is crucial that gender be expanded to include the range of gender identities. Calls for reflexivity must be met with sharply critical assessments of the ways in which marginalized communities marshal what limited privilege may be available to them, sometimes in ways that perpetuate logics of domination. Meanwhile, analysis of social discourses must continue to push national borders and examine the global implications of domestic relations. A growing body of literature has argued that ideologies of gender and race exceed national boundaries in ways that have profound implications, particularly for third world cultures. That literature challenges U.S. scholars to extend definitions and conceptions of race and gender to at least recognize the limitations of domestic analyses (Hegde, 1998b; Supriya, 2002). Undoubtedly, work along the lines suggested here, as well as other work, will continue. And as it does it will likely reconfigure what it means to study gender, race, and culture.

◆ References

Allen, B. J. (2004). Sapphire and Sappho: Allies in authenticity. In A. González, M. Houston, & V. Chen (Eds.), *Our voices: Essays in culture, ethnicity, and communication* (4th ed., pp. 198–203). Los Angeles: Roxbury.

Asante, M. K. (1994). Foreword. In A. González, M. Houston, & V. Chen (Eds.), *Our voices: Essays in culture, ethnicity, and communication* (4th ed., p. vii). Los Angeles: Roxbury.

Ashcraft, K. L., & Flores, L. A. (2003). "Slaves with white collars": Persistent performances of masculinity in crisis. *Text and Performance Quarterly, 23*, 1–29.

Bederman, G. (1995). *Manliness & civilization: A cultural history of gender and race in the United States, 1880–1917.* Chicago: University of Chicago Press.

Berlant, L. (1997). *The queen of America goes to Washington city: Essays on sex and citizenship.* Durham, NC: Duke University Press.

Borisoff, D., & Merrill, L. (2003). Gender and nonverbal communication. In L. A. Samovar & R. E. Porter (Eds.), *Intercultural communication: A reader* (10th ed., pp. 269–278). Los Angeles: Belmont.

Brookey, R. A. (1996). A community like "Philadelphia." *Western Journal of Communication, 60*, 40–56.

Buescher, D. T., & Ono, K. A. (1996). Civilized colonialism: *Pocahontas* as neocolonial rhetoric. *Women's Studies in Communication, 19*, 127–153.

Butler, J. (1993). *Bodies that matter: On the discursive limits of "sex."* New York: Routledge.

Calafell, B. M., & Delgado, F. P. (2004). Reading Latina/o images: Interrogating *Americanos. Critical Studies in Media Communication, 21,* 1–21.

Carillo Rowe, A. M. (2000). Locating feminism's subject: The paradox of White femininity and the struggle to forge feminist alliances. *Communication Theory, 10,* 64–80.

Carillo Rowe, A. M., & Lindsey, S. (2003). Reckoning loyalties: White femininity as "crisis." *Feminist Media Studies, 3,* 173–191.

Chen, V. (2004). (De)hyphenated identity: The double voice in *The Woman Warrior.* In A. González, M. Houston, & V. Chen (Eds.), *Our voices: Essays in culture, ethnicity, and communication* (4th ed., pp. 16–25). Los Angeles: Roxbury.

Cloud, D. L. (1994). The materiality of discourse as oxymoron: A challenge to critical rhetoric. *Western Journal of Communication, 58,* 141–163.

Cloud, D. L. (1996). Hegemony or concordance? The rhetoric of tokenism in "Oprah" Winfrey's rags-to-riches biography. *Critical Studies in Mass Communication, 13,* 115–137.

Collier, M. J. (1998a). Intercultural friendships as interpersonal alliances. In J. N. Martin, T. K. Nakayama, & L. A. Flores (Eds.), *Readings in cultural context* (pp. 370–379). Mountain View, CA: Mayfield.

Collier, M. J. (1998b). Researching cultural identity: Reconciling interpretative and postcolonial perspectives. In D. V. Tanno & A. González (Eds.), *Communication and identity across cultures* (Vol. 21, pp. 122–147). Thousand Oaks, CA: Sage.

Collier, M. J. (2000). Constituting cultural difference through discourse: Current research themes of politics, perspectives, and problematics. In M. J. Collier (Ed.), *Constituting cultural difference through discourse* (Vol. 23, pp. 1–25). Thousand Oaks, CA: Sage.

Collier, M. J. (2003). Understanding cultural identities in intercultural communication: A ten-step inventory. In L. A. Samovar & R. E. Porter (Eds.), *Intercultural communication: A reader* (10th ed., pp. 412–429). Los Angeles: Belmont.

Condit, C. M. (1993). The critic as empath: Moving away from totalizing theory. *Western Journal of Communication, 57,* 178–190.

Cooks, L. (2003). Pedagogy, performance, and positionality: Teaching about Whiteness in interracial communication. *Communication Education, 52,* 245–257.

Crenshaw, C. (1997a). Resisting Whiteness' rhetorical silence. *Western Journal of Communication, 61,* 253–278.

Crenshaw, C. (1997b). Women in the Gulf War: Toward an intersectional feminist rhetorical criticism. *Howard Journal of Communications, 8,* 219–235.

Crenshaw, K. (1991). Mapping the margins: Intersectionality, identity politics, and violence against women of color. *Stanford Law Review, 43,* 1241–1299.

Dace, K. L. (1998). "Had Judas been a Black man." Politics, race, and gender in African America. In J. M. Sloop & J. P. McDaniel (Eds.), *Judgment calls: Rhetoric, politics, and indeterminacy* (pp. 163–181). Boulder, CO: Westview.

Davis, O. I. (1998). A Black woman as rhetorical critic: Validating self and violating the space of otherness. *Women's Studies in Communication, 21,* 77–89.

Davis, O. I. (1999). In the kitchen: Transforming the academy through safe spaces of resistance. *Western Journal of Communication, 63,* 364–381.

Delgado, F. P. (1998). When the silenced speak: The textualization and complications of Latina/o identity. *Western Journal of Communication, 62,* 420–438.

Dobris, C. A. (1996). Maya Angelou: Writing the "Black voice" for the multicultural community. *Howard Journal of Communications, 7,* 1–12.

Dolphin, C. Z. (1994). Variables in the use of personal space in intercultural transactions. In L. A. Samovar & R. E. Porter (Eds.), *Intercultural communication: A reader* (7th ed., pp. 252–263). Belmont, CA: Wadsworth.

Durham, M. G. (2001). Displaced persons: Symbols of South Asian femininity and the returned gaze in U.S. media culture. *Communication Theory, 11,* 201–217.

Ehlers, N. (2004). Hidden in plain sight: Defying juridical racialization in *Rhinelander v. Rhinelander. Communication and Critical/Cultural Studies, 1,* 313–334.

Flores, L. A. (1996). Creating discursive space through a rhetoric of difference: Chicana feminists craft a homeland. *Quarterly Journal of Speech, 82,* 142–156.

Flores, L. A. (2000). Challenging the myth of assimilation: A Chicana feminist response. In M. J. Collier (Ed.), *Constituting cultural difference through discourse* (Vol. 23, pp. 26–46). Thousand Oaks, CA: Sage.

Flores, L. A., & Moon, D. G. (2002). Rethinking race, revealing dilemmas: Imagining a new racial subject in *Race Traitor. Western Journal of Communication, 66,* 181–207.

Folb, E. A. (1994). Who's got the room at the top? Issues of dominance and nondominance in intracultural communication. In L. A. Samovar & R. E. Porter (Eds.), *Intercultural communication: A reader* (7th ed., pp. 131–139). Belmont, CA: Wadsworth.

Gay, G. (2003). Culture and communication in the classroom. In L. A. Samovar & R. E. Porter (Eds.), *Intercultural communication: A reader* (10th ed., pp. 320–337). Los Angeles: Belmont.

González, A., & Flores, G. (1994). Tejana music and cultural identification. In A. González, M. Houston, & V. Chen (Eds.), *Our voices: Essays in culture, ethnicity, and communication* (pp. 37–42). Los Angeles: Roxbury.

González, A., Houston, M., & Chen, V. (2004). *Our voices: Essays in culture, ethnicity, and communication* (4th ed.). Los Angeles: Roxbury.

González, A., & Tanno, D. V. (1997). Imaginative frames for politics, communication, and culture. In A. González & D. V. Tanno (Eds.), *Politics, communication, and culture* (Vol. 20, pp. 3–8). Thousand Oaks, CA: Sage.

Hall, S. (1996). The problem of ideology: Marxism without guarantees. In D. Morley & K.-H. Chen (Eds.), *Stuart Hall: Critical dialogues in cultural studies* (pp. 25–46). New York: Routledge.

Halualani, R. T. (1995). The intersecting hegemonic discourses of an Asian mail-order bride catalog: Pilipina "Oriental butterfly" dolls for sale. *Women's Studies in Communication, 18,* 45–64.

Halualani, R. T. (1998). Seeing through the screen: A struggle of "culture." In J. N. Martin, T. K. Nakayama, & L. A. Flores (Eds.), *Readings in cultural context* (pp. 264–275). Mountain View, CA: Mayfield.

Harris, T. M., & Donmoyer, D. (2000). Is art imitating life? Communicating gender and racial identity in *Imitation of Life. Women's Studies in Communication, 23,* 91–110.

Hegde, R. S. (1998a). Translated enactments: The relational configurations of the Asian Indian immigrant experience. In J. N. Martin, T. K. Nakayama, & L. A. Flores (Eds.), *Readings in cultural context* (pp. 315–322). Mountain View, CA: Mayfield.

Hegde, R. S. (1998b). A view from elsewhere: Locating difference and the politics of representation from a transnational perspective. *Communication Theory, 8,* 271–297.

Houston, M. (1992). The politics of difference: Race, class, and women's communication. In L. F. Rakow (Ed.), *Women making meaning: New feminist directions in communication* (pp. 45–59). New York: Routledge.

Houston, M. (2004). When Black women talk with White women: Why dialogues are difficult. In A. González, M. Houston, & V. Chen (Eds.), *Our voices: Essays in culture, ethnicity, and communication* (4th ed., pp. 119–125). Los Angeles: Roxbury.

Jackson III, R. L., & Dangerfield, C. L. (2003). Defining Black masculinity as cultural property: Toward an identity negotiation paradigm. In L. A. Samovar & R. E. Porter (Eds.), *Intercultural communication: A reader* (10th ed., pp. 120–131). Los Angeles: Belmont.

James, N. C. (2004). When Miss America was always White. In A. González, M. Houston, & V. Chen (Eds.), *Our voices: Essays in culture, ethnicity, and communication* (4th ed., pp. 61–65). Los Angeles: Roxbury.

Johnson, F. L. (2003). Cultural dimensions of discourse. In L. A. Samovar & R. E. Porter (Eds.), *Intercultural communication: A reader* (10th ed., pp. 184–197). Los Angeles: Belmont.

Kraidy, M. M. (1999). The global, the local, and the hybrid: A native ethnography of globalization. *Critical Studies in Mass Communication, 16,* 456–476.

Lalvani, S. (1995). Consuming the exotic other. *Critical Studies in Mass Communication, 12,* 263–286.

Le Roux, J. (2006). Social dynamics of the multicultural classroom. In L. A. Samovar, R. E. Porter, & E. R. McDaniel (Eds.), *Intercultural communication: A reader* (11th ed., pp. 343–353). Belmont: Wadsworth.

Lee, W. S. (1998). Patriotic breeders or colonized converts: A postcolonial feminist approach to antifootbinding discourse in China. In D. V. Tanno & A. González (Eds.), *Communication and identity across cultures* (Vol. 21, pp. 11–33). Thousand Oaks, CA: Sage.

Leeds-Hurwitz, W. (1990). Notes in the history of intercultural communication: The Foreign Service Institute and the mandate for intercultural training. *Quarterly Journal of Speech, 76,* 262–281.

Leland, D., & Martinez, J. M. (1998). Chicana y Chicana: Dialogue on race, class, and Chicana identity. In J. N. Martin, T. K. Nakayama, & L. A. Flores (Eds.), *Readings in cultural context* (pp. 85–92). Mountain View, CA: Mayfield.

Liera-Schwichtenberg, R. (2000). Passing or Whiteness on the edge of town. *Critical Studies in Mass Communication, 17,* 371–374.

Lipsitz, G. (1998). *The possessive investment in Whiteness: How White people profit from identity politics.* Philadelphia: Temple University Press.

Madison, D. S. (1993). "That was my occupation": Oral narrative, performance, and Black feminist thought. *Text and Performance Quarterly, 13,* 213–232.

Martin, J. N., & Nakayama, T. K. (1999). Thinking dialectically about culture and communication. *Communication Theory, 9,* 1–25.

Martinez, J. M. (2000). *Phenomenology of Chicana experience and identity: Communication and transformation in praxis.* Lanham, MD: Rowman & Littlefield.

McPhail, M. L. (1996). Race and sex in Black and White: Essence and ideology in the Spike Lee discourse. *Howard Journal of Communications, 7,* 127–138.

Molina Guzmán, I., & Valdivia, A. N. (2004). Brain, brow, and booty: Latina iconicity in U.S. popular culture. *The Communication Review, 7,* 205–221.

Moon, D. G. (1999). White enculturation and bourgeois ideology: The discursive production of "good (White) girls." In T. K. Nakayama & J. N. Martin (Eds.), *Whiteness: The communication of social identity* (pp. 177–197). Thousand Oaks: CA: Sage.

Moon, D. G. (2002). Thinking about "culture" in intercultural communication. In J. N. Martin, T. K. Nakayama, & L. A. Flores (Eds.), *Readings in intercultural communication: Experiences and contexts* (2nd ed., pp. 13–21). Boston: McGraw Hill.

Nakayama, T. K. (1994). Show/down time: "Race," gender, sexuality, and popular culture. *Critical Studies in Mass Communication, 11,* 162–179.

Nakayama, T. K., & Krizek, R. L. (1995). Whiteness: A strategic rhetoric. *Quarterly Journal of Speech, 81,* 291–309.

Ono, K. A., & Sloop, J. M. (1995). The critique of vernacular discourse. *Communication Monographs, 62,* 19–46.

Ono, K. A., & Sloop, J. M. (2002). *Shifting borders: Rhetoric, immigration, and California's Proposition 187.* Philadelphia: Temple University Press.

Orbe, M. P. (1997). Utilizing an inductive approach to studying African American male communications. In L. A. Samovar & R. E. Porter (Eds.), *Intercultural communication: A reader* (8th ed., pp. 227–234). Belmont, CA: Wadsworth.

Orbe, M. P., & Hopson, M. C. (2002). Looking at the front door: Exploring images of the Black male on MTV's *The Real World.* In J. N. Martin, T. K. Nakayama, & L. A. Flores (Eds.), *Readings in intercultural communication: Experiences and contexts* (2nd ed., pp. 219–226). Boston: McGraw Hill.

Owen, A. S. (2002). Memory, war and American identity: *Saving Private Ryan* as cinematic jeremiad. *Critical Studies in Media Communication, 19,* 249–282.

Patton, T. O. (2004). Reflections of a Black woman professor: Racism and sexism in academia. *Howard Journal of Communications, 15,* 185–200.

Philipsen, G. (1975). Speaking "like a man" in Teamsterville: Culture patterns of role enactment in an urban neighborhood. *Quarterly Journal of Speech, 61,* 13–22.

Projansky, S., & Ono, K. A. (1999). Strategic Whiteness as cinematic racial politics. In T. K. Nakayama & J. N. Martin (Eds.), *Whiteness: The communication of social identity* (pp. 149–174). Thousand Oaks, CA: Sage.

Rakow, L. F., & Wackwitz, L. A. (1998). Communication of sexism. In M. L. Hecht (Ed.), *Communicating prejudice* (pp. 99–111). Thousand Oaks, CA: Sage.

Shohat, E. (1998). Introduction. In E. Shohat (Ed.), *Talking visions: Multicultural feminism in a transnational age* (pp. 1–62). London: The MIT Press.

Shome, R. (1999). Whiteness and the politics of location. In T. K. Nakayama & J. N. Martin (Eds.), *Whiteness: The communication of social identity* (pp. 107–128). Thousand Oaks, CA: Sage.

Shome, R. (2000). Media and colonialism: Race, rape, and "Englishness" in *The Jewel in the Crown.* In M. J. Collier (Ed.), *Constituting cultural difference through discourse* (Vol. 23, pp. 135–157). Thousand Oaks, CA: Sage.

Shome, R. (2001). White femininity and the discourse of the nation: Re/membering Princess Diana. *Feminist Media Studies, 1,* 323–342.

Shome, R., & Hegde, R. S. (2002a). Culture, communication, and the challenge of globalization. *Critical Studies in Media Communication, 19,* 172–189.

Shome, R., & Hegde, R. S. (2002b). Postcolonial approaches to communication: Charting the terrain, engaging the intersections. *Communication Theory, 12,* 249–270.

Spellers, R. E. (1998). Happy to be nappy! Embracing an Afrocentric aesthetic for beauty. In J. N. Martin, T. K. Nakayama, & L. A. Flores (Eds.), *Readings in cultural context* (pp. 70–78). Mountain View, CA: Mayfield.

Spelman, E. V. (1988). *Inessential woman: Problems of exclusion in feminist thought.* Boston: Beacon Press.

Squires, C. R., & Brouwer, D. C. (2002). In/discernible bodies: The politics of passing in dominant and marginal media. *Critical Studies in Media Communication, 19,* 283–310.

Stables, G. (2003). Justifying Kosovo: Representations of gendered violence and U.S. military intervention. *Critical Studies in Media Communication, 20,* 92–115.

Stringer, D. M. (2006). Let me count the ways: African-American/European-American marriages. In L. A. Samovar, R. E. Porter, & E. R. McDaniel (Eds.), *Intercultural communication: A reader* (11th ed., pp. 170–177). Belmont, CA: Wadsworth.

Supriya, K. E. (2001). Evocation of and enactment in *Apna Ghar:* Performing ethnographic self-reflexivity. *Text and Performance Quarterly, 21,* 225–246.

Supriya, K. E. (2002). *Shame and recovery: Mapping identity in an Asian women's shelter.* New York: Peter Lang.

Tanno, D. V. (2004). Names, narratives, and the evolution of ethnic identity. In A. González, M. Houston, & V. Chen (Eds.), *Our voices: Essays in culture, ethnicity, and communication* (4th ed., pp. 38–41). Los Angeles: Roxbury.

Uchida, A. (1997). Doing gender and building culture: Toward a model of women's intercultural communication. *Howard Journal of Communications, 8,* 41–76.

Valdivia, A. N. (1998). Big hair and bigger hoops: Rosie Perez goes to Hollywood. In J. N. Martin, T. K. Nakayama, & L. A. Flores (Eds.), *Readings in cultural context* (pp. 243–249). Mountain View, CA: Mayfield.

Warren, J. T. (2001). Doing Whiteness: On the performative dimensions of race in the classroom. *Communication Education, 50,* 91–108.

Watts, E. K., & Orbe, M. P. (2002). The spectacular consumption of "true" African American culture: "Whassup" with the Budweiser guys? *Critical Studies in Media Communication, 19,* 1–20.

Young, R. J. C. (1995). *Colonial desire: Hybridity in theory, culture and race.* New York: Routledge.

Zacharias, U. (2003). The smile of Mona Lisa: Postcolonial desires, nationalist families, and the birth of consumer television in India. *Critical Studies in Media Communication, 20,* 388–406.

Zimmerman, A. L., & Geist-Martin, P. (2006). The hybrid identities of gender queer: Claiming neither/nor, both/and. In L. A. Samovar, R. E. Porter, & E. R. McDaniel (Eds.), *Intercultural communication: A reader* (11th ed., pp. 76–82). Belmont, CA: Wadsworth.

21

NEGOTIATING BOUNDARIES, CROSSING BORDERS

The Language of Black Women's Intercultural Encounters

◆ Marsha Houston and Karla D. Scott

To be able to use the range of one's voice, to attempt to express the totality of self, is a recurring struggle.

Barbara Christian (1985, p. 234)

To speak freely within a discourse different from the expectations for speaking in mainstream American institutions and public life is to speak with constraint, to have less voice, to have less chance in the marketplace of ideas.

Fern Johnson (2000, p. 248)

In the wake of the nationwide controversy which was precipitated by the decision of the school board in Oakland, California to adopt Ebonics readers and which erupted in the national press in 1996–97,[1] Marsha was asked to moderate an open forum on Black language and speaking styles. At first she refused, unequivocally. The level of misinformation, defensiveness, and outright language bashing in nearly every

◆ 397

discussion of Ebonics in the press—primarily by Black reporters—and in the streets, especially among the Black students and professional people whom she knew, told her that any attempt to shed the light of communication scholarship on the subject would be met with resistance, even by the members of the Black student group that was co-sponsoring the forum. But she relented, and the forum was held with approximately the results she had predicted. After the discussion, a Black woman student approached her with tears in her eyes. She acknowledged what Marsha had said about the roots of Ebonics in African languages, its use by the majority of Black Americans as an informal, in-group speaking style, and its relationship to the language of rap and hip-hop culture. Then she expressed the concern that had brought her to tears: "I just don't want people to think *all* of us talk like that!" Marsha knew what the student meant when she said she didn't want *people* to think all of *us* talk like *that*: the student was Black, female, middle class, and she had achieved what the Oakland students were struggling to achieve, including the proper voice for success in the American mainstream. And she wanted *White* people to hear and respect that voice, yet not judge her as an exceptional Black who was disconnected from her cultural group because she used it. At the same time, she did not want *Black* people to hear that voice and judge her as a sellout or race traitor.

The student's tearful statement speaks volumes about the complex connections between speaking style, self-concept, and the enduring politics of race in the United States. Racial and gender politics are inextricably intertwined for an aspiring middle-class Black professional woman, whose gendered cultural role entails linguistic propriety (Houston (Stanback), 1985). Black men are allowed greater latitude than Black women in using Black English (i.e., Ebonics) without having their respectability questioned (Folb, 1980). As Rosina Lippi-Green (1997) explains, the Oakland controversy forced many college-educated Black people to confront the tension between Black and dominant cultural language practices: "To make two statements: *I acknowledge that my home language is viable and adequate, and I acknowledge that my home language will never be accepted,* is to set up an unresolvable conflict" (p. 9).

The same point is made by Johnson (2000) when she notes that "in the context of mainstream, especially White, devaluation of African American linguistic and discourse forms, it is not surprising that African Americans themselves possess complex and often contradictory feelings and attitudes about their language" (pp. 157–158). The student's tearful statement and the insights from Lippi-Green and Johnson also underscore the precariousness of doing scholarship on the language and communication of Black women in the United States; that is, the challenge of writing about our[2] talk without essentializing, pathologizing, romanticizing, or otherwise distorting our ways of speaking. Certainly, most U.S. Americans are well aware of the distorted views of Black women's talk that pervade the culture. As sociolinguist Barbara Hill Hudson (2001) notes:

> The speech of African American females is often imitated, parodied, or stereotyped. Generally these stereotypes allow for only a limited range of expressions, familiar to most who have seen or read material that contained images of strong mothers, chastising and advising; sassy young females, using popular slang; and no nonsense older women making salty comments on life. (p. 1)

As with most stereotypes, these images capture *some* of the truth about the communication of *some* Black women in *some* situations, but represent a limited view of the speaking repertoire of any individual, real-life Black woman.

The task that feminist sociolinguists and communication scholars have set for themselves over the past 30 years has been to illumine Black women's speaking perceptions and practices without reproducing the stereotypes. As we review their work on Black women's cross-cultural talk, we do so with the understanding that Black women communicators are not monolithic. Not only are Black women a heterogeneous social group, but every subset of Black women, as defined by socioeconomic class, sexual orientation, region, generation, profession, or any other demographic category, is a chorus of diverse and often divergent voices. Sometimes, or in some ways, we are linguistically indistinguishable from other groups of speakers (e.g., similarly situated Black men, other women of color, or White women), and sometimes and in other ways we are quite distinct from similarly situated groups. Yet, in spite of the diversity among Black women, and the similarities between us and other social groups, it is undeniable that the vast majority of us share a unique social history and present-day social situation in the United States. African provenance, U.S. enslavement, collaboration in the protracted struggle for civil rights and social justice, and persistent, simultaneous racial and sexual oppression are key elements of Black women's history and contemporary life (Collins, 2000; Guy-Sheftall, 1995). Anyone who listens to the talk among Black women at any contemporary gathering, from a few friends at lunch to the vast crowds at the empowerment seminars at the *ESSENCE FEST* in New Orleans,[3] cannot escape being struck by the common themes and outlooks underlying our individual experiences and the common communication practices characterizing our talk.

◆ Chapter Focus

In this chapter, we explore two central questions suggested by scholarship on Black women's talk in encounters with members of other (non-Black) cultural or racial/ethnic groups: *(a) Does Black women's history of unequal social status—from enslavement through segregation—still permeate the communicative here and now of our intercultural*

encounters? (b) What repertoire of communicative practices is employed by Black women in intercultural encounters? The first question concerns the overarching speaking context or discourse environment for Black women's talk (van Dijk, 1987). We suggest that the micropolitics of interindividual interactions are often influenced by macropolitical definitions of Black women as a social group, the origins of which can sometimes be traced back hundreds of years. The second question concerns Black women's ways of negotiating the discourse environment through culturally learned communication practices, including their competence in shifting language codes and speaking styles.

THE COMPETING DISCOURSE ENVIRONMENTS OF BLACK WOMEN'S TALK

We examine the context of Black women's intercultural communication by addressing the question: Does Black women's history of unequal social status—from enslavement through segregation—still permeate the communicative here and now of our intercultural encounters? We suggest that there are two competing discourses about Black womanhood—one constructed and disseminated by the dominant, Euro–White culture, and an alternate one constructed and expressed by Black women themselves.

DOMINANT DISCOURSE

Consider the following entry from the diary of 17-year-old Charlotte Forten, a well-to-do, free Black woman who grew up among Philadelphia's Black elite when America practiced slavery:

Wednesday, September 12 (1855) . . . I have met [white] girls in the schoolroom—they have been thoroughly kind and cordial to me—perhaps the next day [I] met them on the street—they feared to recognize me; these I can but regard now with scorn and contempt.... Others give the most distant recognition possible—I, of course, acknowledge no such recognition.... These are but trifles, certainly, to the great public wrongs which we [Black people] ... are obliged to endure. But to those who experience them ... they reveal volumes of deceit and heartlessness, and early teach a lesson of suspicion and distrust. (Billington, 1953, p. 10)

Charlotte Forten was born to both freedom and wealth during a time when most African Americans were enslaved. She was given an education and encouraged by her Abolitionist family to be politically aware when most women were denied both schooling and political consciousness. Yet she was constantly reminded, through the ordinary intercultural encounters of her everyday life, that she belonged to a despised social group. The excerpt from her diary presents many of the exigencies that historically have defined Black women's intercultural encounters: the uncertainty and inconsistency of White interlocutors, the persistent small indignities that are psychologically "wearing and discouraging," the developing mindset of "suspicion and distrust" of intercultural contact. The excerpt also reveals Forten's communicative goals and strategies, such as maintaining her identity and self-esteem through her own silence, "scorn and contempt."

In the "trifles" of ordinary intercultural encounters, the ways her White schoolmates used talk and silence to construct their personal relationships with her, Forten saw connections to the "great public wrongs" of racism and chattel slavery that defined the political relationship of the majority of Black Americans to the U.S. social order of her time. Feminist sociolinguists and communication scholars also perceive the micropolitics of everyday talk to be connected to larger social power relationships (Coates, 1996; Crawford, 1995; Johnson, 2000). They suggest that the politics of

everyday talk are more than mere reflections of power differences among social groups: they are one means by which those differences are constituted—sustained, reinforced, re-created, and justified. They have demonstrated reciprocal relationships among ideology, communication, and social power by documenting the manner in which dominant social groups define their ways of speaking as prestigious, powerful, or correct, while demeaning and diminishing that of less powerful groups.

The excerpt from Forten's diary illumines elements of the discourse environment of Black women's intercultural encounters. Van Dijk (1987) defines discourse environment as including the speaking demands created by the material circumstances of a speaker's life; for example, the situational contexts in which she routinely speaks as determined by her education, work, leisure, and family roles, as well as the demands created by the ideological circumstances of her life; for example, the ways in which her social group is represented in the dominant public discourse of the society. In their discussions of the origins, transformation, and reproduction of the derogatory stereotypes that continue to dominate social definitions of Black women in the United States, Black feminist scholars (e.g., Collins, 2000, 2004; Giddings, 1984; hooks, 1984; James, 1999), similarly emphasize the central role of public discourse, including news media, magazines, educational materials, novels, comics, movies, advertising, political speeches, laws, regulations, and other institutional documentation. Because public discourse provides the overarching environment in which everyday conversations are embedded, long-standing definitions of a social group, reproduced in public discourse, may permeate the here and now of everyday intercultural conversations, without conversational participants being fully aware of them (Giles & Coupland, 1991).

Key to the discourse environment experienced by contemporary Black women speakers is an evolving set of derogatory stereotypes that expresses the interdependent ideologies of racism and sexism that are integral to dominant cultural definitions of Black women. Such longstanding, derogatory stereotypes as the super-strong, asexual "mammy" and the hypersexual, amoral Jezebel function as controlling images intended to limit and direct not only how others define and behave toward Black women but also how we define ourselves and participate in the social order (Collins 2000, 2004). Black feminist scholars trace the origins of racist and sexist stereotypes of Black women to the centuries of U.S. enslavement and cite their popularization in the minstrel shows, silent films, and other mass entertainment of the later 19th and early 20th centuries (Anderson, 1997). Collins (2004) also documents their transformation into more complex, class-related controlling images reproduced in the mass media and other public discourse of the ostensibly color-blind United States in the late 20th and early 21st centuries. She argues that contemporary working-class Black women are represented as loud, aggressive, oversexed so-called bitches or bad mothers. For example, the seemingly endless parade of unwed, working class "baby mamas" (i.e., never-married Black mothers) who become obstreperous on the *Maury* and *Jerry Springer* television talk shows as they await the results of DNA tests on the men who allegedly fathered their children, reinscribe stereotypes of Black working-class women as sexually promiscuous in the ideology of the dominant culture. On the other hand, Collins argues that Black middle-class women are represented in contemporary public discourse as either asexual "modern mammies" (as exemplified by Oprah Winfrey), as proper, uptight "Black ladies" (such as Clair Huxtable of the 1980s situation comedy *The Cosby Show*), or as "educated bitches" (educationally credentialed Black women whom others define by their bodies rather than by their minds). Among the discourses that support the educated bitch image are those opposing affirmative action programs on the basis that those benefiting from the programs are, by definition,

unqualified and will lower the standards of business and academic organizations.

As factors that contextualize and can permeate contemporary intercultural communication encounters, culturally shared negative controlling images of Black women may automatically or unconsciously activate cognitive models that a speaker has developed over time for interpreting communication from or about Black women or trigger scripts for communicating with Black women that are part of the speaking repertoire of the speaker's group (Giles & Coupland, 1991). In whatever way they invade the conversational here and now, these longstanding, evolving stereotypes significantly contribute to the creation of exigent discourse environments for Black women's intercultural encounters.

In her studies of Black[4] women in the United States and The Netherlands, sociolinguist Philomema Essed (1990, 1991) documented some of the ways that negative controlling images invade intercultural encounters. One of her research participants made the following observation about communication with customers in the bookstore where she worked:

> If I'm standing next to one of my White coworkers, customers will say to me, "Where's such and such a book?" . . . and they say to my White co-worker, "Well, have you read the book, and what do you think . . . ?" To *me* it's . . . service kind of things. To talk about the intellectual aspects of the books, the information—it's as if I'm illiterate. (1990, p. 207)

Essed (1991) coined the term *underestimation* to describe Euro-White people's frequently expressed presumptions of Black women's incompetence (as exemplified by the bookstore customers), and *gendered racism* to describe the underlying intersections of racism and sexism that inform such presumptions (see pp. 48–51).

In their discussion of communication in Black women's everyday encounters, Mark

Orbe, Darlene Drummond, and Sakile Camara (2002) offer an example of how underestimation is expressed by White students in academic settings. A Black woman student describes what happened when she prepared to challenge a comment made in class:

> When I raised my hand, a couple of White girls behind me were like, "GET 'EM GIRL!" and I just turned around and looked . . . it was like they expected me to roll my head and snap my fingers and tell someone off . . . I'm trying to be intellectual and join in a conversation or discussion in class and they are like, "GET 'EM GIRL." I really wanted to turn around and say, "I'M NOT *YOUR* GIRL." (p. 131)

As Orbe, Drummond, and Camara point out, the White students attempted to express an inappropriate level of familiarity with the Black student by using *girl*, a word that has a very different meaning when used in ingroup conversations *among* Black women (Scott, 1995) than when *applied to* a Black woman by a member of an outgroup (e.g., a White person), particularly one who is not a close friend. The Black and White students are mere classmates, not close friends, who might choose to blur or even erase the usual boundaries between ingroup and outgroup speech. In addition, the comment by the White women ("Get 'em . . .") invokes the stereotype of Black women as super-tough and aggressive and has the effect of transforming a situation in which the Black woman sought to emphasize her intellect into one in which a stereotype of her physicality is foregrounded. Thus, the encounter also suggests something of the complexity of the oxymoronic controlling image of the educated bitch, the perception of Black women as educationally credentialed but not intellectually equal to Whites, as defined primarily by our embodiment as Black and female.

Like the slights the young Charlotte Forten experienced from her classmates, underestimation and other everyday gendered racist behaviors seem trivial on their own, although they are nerve-racking and can engender wariness and suspicion in intercultural encounters. But as Essed (1991) explains, "Everyday [gendered] racism cannot be reduced to incidents or specific events. . . . It is the process of the system working through multiple relations and situations" (p. 51). In summary, one of the more disturbing findings in research on Black women's intercultural encounters is that our history of unequal social status invades the communicative here and now at unexpected moments. Despite our individual efforts to resist particular oppressive situations, lingering, longstanding, gendered racist stereotypes continue to contextualize our intercultural encounters. We now turn to an exploration of scholarship that reveals how Black women challenge and resist dominant cultural controlling images.

◆ Oppositional Discourse

Although scholarship on Black women's language and communication was not conducted and published until the late 20th century, that is not an indication that Black women did not engage in strategic use of language prior to that time. Feminist communication scholarship on Black women's public rhetoric from the 18th century to the present reveals oppositional definitions of Black womanhood that consciously resist the controlling images promulgated by the dominant culture. In an examination of the narratives of enslaved Black women, Olga Davis (1999) notes:

> The narrative genre afforded Black women, for the first time in American history, a chance to declare their presence by rhetorically stating, "I am here" . . . creating an oppositional discourse that identified black women as thinkers, creators, and namers of themselves. (p. 154)

Examined in the context of the times, Black women's language use in slave narratives is understood as a "rhetorical act of survival and a discursive struggle for change" (O. Davis, 2002, p. 39). The struggle for change was a theme of Black women's communication in the public sphere from the moment in 1832 when Maria Miller Stewart, a free Black woman in Boston and the first American woman to speak in public, questioned our confinement to servitude in the domestic sphere (Guy-Sheftall, 1995). Scores of noted Black women orators, from abolitionists and feminist political activists such as Sojourner Truth and Fannie Barrier Williams to Ida B. Wells, Shirley Chisholm (Williamson-Ige, 1988), Fannie Lou Hamer (Hamlet, 1996), and Audre Lorde embraced public discourse not only as a means for collective resistance to politically oppressive systems, but also as a means to create and sustain affirming definitions of Black womanhood (White & Dobris, 2002).

Discourses resisting negative controlling images not only are found in Black women's oratory, but also in fine and folk art and popular culture created and/or performed by Black women. Through plays, films, fiction, poetry, painting, sculpture, quilts, and music, Black women consistently have constructed alternative definitions of self and community. In the early 20th century, blues music was "a space for Black women of the poor and working class communities to locate their voice in the public sphere while illuminating the private sphere of love and sexuality as everyday experience" (O. Davis, 2002, p. 44).

Popular music continues to be a space in which the masses of Black women challenge negative controlling images (J. L. Davis, 2002). Some women hip-hop performers have challenged demeaning, hypersexual, patriarchal representations of women by their male counterparts (Watts, 2002); and more recently, rhythm and blues singer Fantasia, the first Black woman to win the "American Idol" competition on television, valorized the struggles of never-married, young, single mothers like herself in the song, "Baby Mama":

I see ya payin' ya bills,

I see ya workin' ya job

I see ya goin' to school

And girl I know it's hard.

And even though ya fed up

With makin' beds up,

Girl, keep ya head up.[5]

(Acklin, Dinkins, & Colapietro, 2004)

In the tradition of her abolitionist, civil rights, and blues foremothers, and in contrast to those of her contemporaries who choose to collude in their own oppression by appearances on the *Maury* and *Jerry Springer* shows, Fantasia offers public discourse that resists the "bitch" and "bad mother" stereotypes of working-class, never-married Black mothers.

As Black women entered the professorate, politics, and media in larger numbers in the latter half of the 20th century, our oppositional discourses became more audible in U.S. American culture, enhancing the discursive resources that ordinary Black women speakers could deploy in resisting, confronting, and challenging everyday gendered racism. The majority of the Black women respondents to Marsha's open-ended questionnaire about perspectives on "talking like a black woman" (Houston, 2000a) expressed what she termed a "celebratory perspective." From this perspective, respondents focused on the social and interpersonal functions of talk and emphasized the ways in which Black women communicate wisdom, fortitude, and care in everyday interactions.

In summary, we suggest that Black women negotiate intercultural encounters in the context of competing public discourses. There is an inescapable, dominant discourse that continues to reproduce negative controlling images of Black womanhood, but also there is our own, evolving tradition of oppositional discourse that valorizes Black women's ways of being in the world. In the next section, we discuss scholarship on Black women's intercultural communication practices in the context of this discourse environment.

◆ Black Women's Intercultural Communication Practices

We explore the ways Black women cross the borders of intercultural encounters by addressing the question: *What repertoire of communicative practices is employed by Black women in intercultural encounters?* One hundred and forty years after Charlotte Forten wrote of her encounters in her journal, Karla Scott conducted research on the language use of young Black women at a predominantly White, Midwestern university (Scott, 1995, 2000). These young women, accustomed to such populations, talked of being very careful not to speak in their Black woman's voice, or rather the language of home, in classrooms and other settings where they were the minority. This was a strategy enacted to be perceived as intelligent and worthy of attendance at the prestigious university and not just mere tokens. But they also reported a use of their voice in instances when they needed to mark racial identity as distinct from their classmates. Such instances included refuting White classmates' misperceptions about the experiences of Blacks in America or in the Black community. The women discussed a shared response of "going into my Blackness" or changing to vernacular Black English in order to explain to White classmates how race can and does make a difference in one's experiences. In the context of this university, the young women felt such intercultural encounters were an opportunity to refute long held misconceptions of Blacks and challenge White classmates' thinking on race. They used language to mark their intelligence and academic credibility as on par with White classmates ("I'm just as worthy of being here as you.") and, when required, to mark identity as Black ("I am different from you and can speak about lived experiences of Blacks in this country.").

Though proficient at this form of cultural border crossing, the women still expressed frustration at the perceptions held by classmates and the constant need to prove themselves through language use. And like Charlotte Forten, the women found "these apparent trifles . . . most wearing and discouraging," teaching them in early young adulthood "a lesson of suspicion and distrust."

As the students in Karla's study demonstrate, Black women set their own goals for intercultural encounters and engage in language and communication practices designed for both impression management and positive identity maintenance. In this section, we discuss the following five language and communication practices: code- and style-switching, positive self-talk, evasion, culture specific framing, and strategic use of culture specific language features.

CODE- AND STYLE-SWITCHING

The college women in Karla's (1995) study, summarized at the outset of this section, reported being very careful not to speak in their "Black woman's voice" in order to establish their intellectual credibility and "going into [their] Blackness" or changing to a more Black English (BE) speaking style in order to explain to White classmates how race can and does make a difference in one's experiences. Their communication practices underscore the value Black women place on communicative flexibility. The language development of most Black children includes some degree of learning to switch between language codes and/or styles. Code-switching is defined as "the juxtaposition of passages of speech belonging to two grammatical systems" (Gumperz, 1982, p. 59). For many speakers socialized in Black communities, code-switching is the selective use of two related dialects, Black English (BE) and U.S. Standard English (USSE), depending on the topic, conversational participants, and/or situation (Giles, Bourhis, & Taylor, 1977; Houston (Stanback), 1983). Style-switching, also a common language practice in Black communities, is more general than code-switching, and may only include changes in prosody, paralanguage, narrative structure and interaction strategies (Hecht, Jackson, & Ribeau, 2002). Code- and style-switching are not mutually exclusive language practices; speakers may engage in one or both in a single utterance. The following example, from Marsha's corpus of conversations (Houston, 1980–86), is spoken by a Black professional woman, proficient in both BE and USSE, during a conversation among Black women friends about childhood memories:

> And then my sister, my oldest sister, came out and beat the socks off that child, y'know. "You don't be hurtin' MY sister!" Because we'd fight among each other, but gi-ir-l, kill everybody if they START botherin' one of us.

The speaker switches from USSE to BE grammar in the second sentence, when she uses the verb *to be* in the perpetual tense (be hurtin') to express what she imagines were her older sister's thoughts. This tense, common in West African languages but not present in English, signifies events that always occur, or in this case, should never occur; the older sister asserts that no one should ever physically attack her sister. Note also the speaker's shift to a more dynamic, emphatic speaking style characterized by elongating vowels (gi-ir-l) and hyperemphasizing selected words (MY; START).

Scholars have pointed out that BE speech consists of a range of styles. Sociolinguist John Baugh (1983) reminds us that

> all speakers, regardless of language, have their personal range of formal to informal styles of talking. The reason that this phenomenon is more complicated for black Americans has to do with the *breadth* [italics added] of speaking styles that are actively used. Speakers with different backgrounds will possess ranges of styles that reflect their personal

history and social aspirations. . . . Think of black American dialects as dynamic entities which, as does the chameleon, adapt to and blend with the immediate setting. (p. 4)

Marsha has argued that the typical Black woman may have a more complex communicative repertoire than the typical White woman due to our cultural tradition of participating in both the domestic and public spheres (Houston (Stanback), 1985). Developing communication competencies for the multicultural social order of the contemporary United States may have further complexified the repertoires of those Black women whose identities and parameters of contact still include working-class Black communities.

Both code- and style-switching function as cultural identity markers in Black speaking communities (Scott, 2002). The literature on these language practices offers compelling examples of how Black women negotiate intercultural encounters. For example, Linda Nelson (1990) describes her study of code-switching in Black women's narratives as motivated by "pleasure in listening to the meandering rhythms, the hyperbole and the novel metaphors of the casual kitchen table discourse of my women friends and family members" (p. 142). The narratives, generated during interviews with 30 Black women all over age 30 included women from diverse socioeconomic groups. Nelson noted that during the interviews speakers often began narratives in what could be identified as USSE but later switched to some level of BE depending on the speaker's perception of the relationship between the two women. Switching to a form of language used more in Black speech communities illustrates an aspect of identity for the speaker:

> An identity that says I am speaking to you out of my experience and if it sounds rough, please don't judge me because it sounds rough. Try to look at me and judge me for what I have come

through. . . . I am a Black woman struggling for that identity, finding that identity, liking that identity and being proud of where it comes from. (p. 147)

Nelson (1990) further connects language and identity in a reference to one of the participants who points out "that in order to talk about Black cultural experience" she needs the language created out of that experience as opposed to the "power code." Nelson concludes that switches from USSE to BE also indicate the narrator's solidarity with the elicitor and that such switches should be interpreted as a "challenge to hegemony" (p. 152).

Michelle Foster (1995) also found in her study of Black women teachers who were fluent in both USSE and BE that linguistic forms and discourse features were used to invoke solidarity, power and community. Stylistic devices employed by women in the classroom included manipulation of grammatical structures, repetition, use of symbolism and figurative language, intonational contours, vowel elongation and changes in meter, tempo and cadence. The most common form of code-switching was the use of multiple negations to report the speech of others as found in the following example:

And do you know we have only one white teacher that will teach Black history? Only one, only one, she doesn't mind teaching the Black History but the rest of them say "*I don't know nothing about it!*" You see I don't know enough about it to teach it. I leave that to Miss Ruthie. (pp. 342–343)

Like Nelson, Foster (1995) maintains that switches in language style index social identity and communicate a particular stance or point of view that is best expressed in Black English. Both studies reveal that the use of BE in certain contexts by women who also are competent speakers of USSE is an indication of language competency.

The young Black women who participated in one-on-one and group interviews for Karla's work on Black women's language (Scott, 1995, 2000, 2002) described "talking like a Black woman" and the specific contexts of language use in predominantly White environments. Their responses indicate that in one world, the world shared with other Black women, identified by participants as "my girls," "talking like a Black woman" means employing many of the stylistic and grammatical features of BE to mark solidarity with others who not only share an identity but also understand the experiences of that identity. Similarly, Karla's study of the use of "girl" and "look" reveals that lexical choice not only marks identity but also solidarity and an ideological stance on identity (Scott, 2000).

Karla also found that young Black women's language use in identity negotiation was often a response to stereotype threat (Scott, 2004). Black women participants between the ages of 18 and 28 all spoke with familiarity about the derogatory stereotypes of Black women that they believe accompany them on the campuses of predominantly White universities, including underestimation and the Jezebel myth. The participants described both verbal and nonverbal strategies for resisting and dispelling the stereotypes, including code-switching to a form of USSE during classes, paying careful attention to dressing in a way that was not sexually suggestive or provocative, and constantly monitoring nonverbal behaviors, such as neck movements or eye rolling, associated with the stereotype of the "angry Black woman." One participant also explained, "Sometimes I will leave my paper out in the open to say, 'Yeah, I got the only A in the class.'" For these young Black women, such strategies are just as important as studying to ensure academic success. Their descriptions suggest that competence in code- and style-switching is viewed as a necessary skill for the success of the post-Civil Rights, post-women's movement generation.

Although many Black women are proficient at code- or style-switching, they interpret such practices as *strategic language perfor-mances* intended to establish credibility, to manage impressions, to create a degree of sol-idarity with White interlocutors who are unable or unwilling to accommodate to them, or to accomplish other interaction goals. None of the Black women participants in our own studies and in those we reviewed regarded shifting to a prestige language code or more mainstream communication style as an identity altering act or as an indication that they had assimilated to; that is, uncritically accepted, the values, beliefs, and social prac-tices of the dominant Euro-White culture of their university, neighborhood, or workplace.

◆ *Specific Strategies for Intercultural Communication Encounters*

In addition to code- and style-switching, feminist scholars have explored a variety of other communicative practices through which Black women endeavor to negotiate intercultural communication encounters. We briefly discuss four of these specific strategies below: positive self-talk; evasion; culture-specific framing; and strategic use of culture-specific language features and interaction styles.

Positive Self-Talk. As the narrative at the outset of this section indicates, Karla's work demonstrates the sort of self-reflexive, posi-tive self-talk that enables Black women to maintain affirming self-definitions in exigent discourse environments. In the following excerpt from Marsha's corpus of conversa-tions (Houston, 1980–86), a Black middle-class, professional woman uses positive self-talk to resist her White coworkers' con-struction of her as an atypical Black person:

> I was kinda puzzled for a long time until I sat down and said, "Now what IS THIS, y'know, why am I feelin' strange like this?" . . . And it's almost like they look at you like, "Wow, you're human, too" . . . like they were awed or some-thin' . . . that I could talk or think. And the same for other black people . . . It was like they were surprised we knew what we were talkin' about. . . . It was really weird.

By analyzing her White coworkers' behavior toward her and other Black col-leagues, and characterizing that behavior as really weird, the speaker resists those who would "Whiten" her identity by labeling her an exceptional or atypical Black woman because she is a competent employee.

Evasion. Brenda Allen (1998) offers a clear case of evasion as a resistance strategy. Allen explores the challenges of being a member of two historically oppressed groups (Blacks and women) and working in the predominantly White world of the academy. Using feminist standpoint theory, Allen interrogates her standpoint as a Black woman and the only Black person in her academic department in order to under-stand Black women's socialization to the academy and other complex organizations. She identifies the stereotypical roles Black women are expected to fulfill in organiza-tions, such as beneficiary, token, mammy, and matriarch. Allen suggests that these roles are a function of White coworkers' inexperience in interacting with Black women. She explains that part of the chal-lenge in being perceived and used as a token is that, "People seem to expect that I can or should provide insight as a representative of women, people of color, Black people, or Black women . . . I sometimes feel more like a symbol or representative than an indi-vidual" (p. 580). One way that Allen nego-tiates the stereotypic roles ascribed to her is by evading or refusing to perform them. When a Black student on her campus was accused of rape, she felt that she was asked to choose between her identity as a woman and a Black person. Allen reports that she "sidestepped the situation by not doing anything" (p. 580). Marsha found that some respondents to her study of Black women's speaking perspectives (2000a) also used evasion as a way of resolving conflicts between their identities as individual Black women and social definitions of Black women's talk to which they did not subscribe. She suggests that while evasion may appear to be a denial of one's Black womanhood, it can more usefully be understood as a strategy for resisting racist stereotypes.

Culture-Specific Framing. In her analysis of Black women executives in predominantly White organizations, Patricia Parker (2003) reveals how participants used culture specific frames to define their communicative practices. One of Parker's interviewees explains:

> First of all, I think you have to always remember that you were Black, you're Black, and you're going to always be Black.... Why is that important? It is because ... you are always mindful of being true to what your sincere beliefs are. You don't sway to fit the mold. (p. 14)

Similarly, Patricia Hill (2003) explains that some roles Black women choose to perform in intercultural contexts are versions of those we choose to perform in Black cultural contexts. For example, the participants in her study of Black women's communication in a culturally diverse neighborhood often discursively assumed the role of other mothers, or fictive kin who nurture other people's children, by speaking out about situations affecting the entire community.

Culture-Specific Language Practices. Mary Bucholtz (1996) uses Collins's (2000) conception of Black feminist epistemology to illumine the culture-specific linguistic practices used by two Black women to subvert the institutional relationship between themselves and the moderator of a radio program in which they participated and to build political alliances with other panelists. She argues that the women used "questions and assessments, deixis, vernacular features, and

backchanneling to effectively restructure the speech situation, offering an alternative to the dominant institutional conventions" (p. 284). In the following example, EH, a Black woman community organizer, first raises a question that conforms to the norms of the panel format, but her subsequent questions challenge these norms and force answers from the moderator [LF] that "require him to authorize a restructuring of the discussion, one in which every participant can select any other to speak" (pp. 276– 277):

EH: Can I [ask a question?]

LF: [Yeah.] Mmh?

EH: Do we have to be so dry in [here?]

LF: [Nuh.](.) Please.

EH: Can we talk across the-

LF: =Jump in.

EH: =I mean can we be real?

LF: =Yes. (h::)

EH: =Its gettin' on my nerves. Okay. Th(h)ank y(h)ou.

In summary, the literature on Black women's intercultural communication reveals a variety of language and communication practices through which Black women negotiate intercultural encounters. We accommodate to other cultural conversation partners through code- or style-switching, and/or they may use positive self-talk, evasion, culture-specific framing and Black language and interaction styles to resist, demystify or gain a measure of control over intercultural encounters.

◆ Conclusion: Directions for Research

As we wrote this chapter, we were struck by our greater confidence in describing the overarching discourse environment in which

Black women speak than in delineating the communication practices with which Black women negotiate that environment. We suggest that this is because there remains a paucity of communication scholarship on our cross-cultural talk. In addition, most intercultural communication research involving Black women (or men) analyzes encounters with White people. We could discover no studies of communication between Black women and other people of color. In light of the increasing social diversity of U.S. culture, we hope that scholars will begin to study Black women communicators with greater cultural inclusiveness, frequency, and depth.

As we encourage more communication research on Black women, we also caution that increasing the number of studies of less powerful social groups does not necessarily provide the sort of emancipatory scholarship that feminist scholars desire. As Houston and Davis (2002) note, "Studies that uncritically apply masculinist or Whitecentric concepts and methods to Black women's communicative lives may actually have the effect of deepening gendered racism and other oppressive communication practices" (p. 3). Thus, we encourage more research that, like the studies discussed in this chapter, employs feminist methodology and Black feminist theories. Feminist methodology centers gender politics and gender relationships in the exploration of women's lived experiences, primarily through qualitative and interpretive methods that capture lived experiences, such as interviewing, narrative analysis, critical discourse analysis, ethnography, and autoethnography (Carter & Spitzack, 1989; Fonow & Cook, 1991). Black feminist theories take account of the material and ideological contexts of Black women's lived experiences, honor their interpretations of those experiences, and facilitate scholarship that is emancipatory for the masses of Black women (Collins, 2000; hooks, 1984; James, 1999). For example, Black feminist sociolinguistic and communication scholarship resists essentializing Black women's talk by illuminating the variety of language and communication choices, styles, and strategies that inform our everyday interaction. Marsha has termed this approach to communication scholarship on Black women "community-cognizant" for its attention to both Black women scholars and the masses of other Black women as "voices of authority" on their own communicative lives (Houston, 2000b, p. 684).

With this approach to scholarship in mind, we suggest two directions for future research on Black women's intercultural communication: (a) studies of how womanhood is performed by particular demographic groups of Black women in particular intercultural contexts and (b) studies of the material, social, and psychological costs and consequences of Black women's language and communication choices in intercultural encounters.

A performative approach to studying gender, language and communication presumes that gender identities and relationships are constructed, reinforced, and transformed by the verbal and nonverbal choices speakers make in particular situational contexts (Coates, 1996; Wodak, 1997). For example, we found not a single study of how Black lesbians negotiate border crossings between what they perceive as their home community (in-group) and the other cultural contexts of their communicative lives. Mary McCullough's (1996) work suggests that an interracial or multicultural lesbian cohort can feel more like home to a Black lesbian than a group of straight Black women friends, but we know nothing of the language practices that distinguish the performance of Black womanhood in either situation (see also Clarke, 2002).

Scholars have only begun to explore how Black women perform the gendered, cultural, self, and group images we valorize. Cherise Jones and Kumea Shorter-Gooden (2003) note that many Black women embrace "the myth that Black women are invulnerable and indefatigable, that they always persevere and endure against all odds without being negatively affected (p. 3)." They argue that there is "peer pressure among Black women to keep the myth alive, to keep juggling [multiple roles and myriad tasks], to keep accommodating" (p. 3). Fantasia's "Baby Mama," illustrates the valorization of this myth in its second stanza: " 'Cuz we the backbone (of the hood)/I always knew that (that we could)/We can go anywhere, we can do anything/I know we can make it if we dream" (Acklin, Dinkins, & Colapietro, 2004). Respondents to Marsha's study of Black women's speaking perspectives also valorized this myth by including communicating "fortitude" among the perspectives they celebrate (Houston 2000a). Through what communicative practices is the myth of super strength and other positive constructions of Black womanhood (e.g., sisterhood, forthrightness, the "other mother" role) performed by Black women in intercultural situations? How do the performances differ across women of varying generations and social classes? How does the level of intimacy of the intercultural relationship influence the performance?

We must also ask about the material, social, and psychological costs and consequences of the communicative practices through which Black women choose to perform their gender identities. Jones and Shorter-Godden's (2003) study offers compelling evidence that negotiating boundaries and crossing borders in the everyday contexts of contemporary Black women's lives (e.g., work, romantic relationships, mothering, the church) places us at a higher risk for depression (see also Allen, 1998). Intercultural communication scholars might inquire into whether and/or how communicative choices figure into this risk. Is the psychological and emotional labor that Black women expend in negotiating encounters with members of the dominant culture greater than that expended by members of the dominant cultural group? If so, do Black women evidence depression and lowered self-esteem, as Jones and Shorter-Gooden contend, or is there evidence of feelings of empowerment and enhanced self-esteem as we develop superior competencies for

communicating in an increasingly diverse social order? Might there be evidence of both?

Scholars might situate their inquiries in predominantly White academic and professional contexts. Thanks to the Civil Rights and women's movements, the current generations of Black women have greater access to such contexts. Yet they often confront the same derogatory, oppressive stereotypes as their foremothers (Hill, 2003; Parker, 2003). For example, although on the surface it may appear that access to a job or admission to a university is granted on the premise that one *does not* conform to the pejorative stereotypes of Black womanhood, all too often the expectation—albeit implicit—is that one *will* conform. Black women often realize this implicit expectation only after accepting a professional or academic opportunity. Does a decision to communicatively resist stereotypical images of Black womanhood threaten job security, good grades, social interaction, or professional growth? Does conforming assure them? For what reasons, under what circumstances, and through what language practices might a Black woman choose to resist or conform? Are certain strategies employed for the purpose of accommodating others in the name of success or submission? Or are they enacted as tactics of empowerment?

Intercultural communication scholars might also enlarge the scope of encounters considered intercultural by examining the increasing demographic diversity among Blacks in the United States. When a Black woman who grew up in a predominantly White speech community where she was socialized to speak USSE exclusively, enters a university in which the majority of Black students learned to code-switch between BE and USSE as they grew up in predominantly Black communities, she may face accusations of being a sellout by virtue of her language style and find herself isolated from her Black peers. To what extent do such experiences with linguistic prejudice challenge Black women's gendered cultural identities and emotional well-being (see e.g., Miles, 1995)?

Scholarship that examines the costs and consequences of Black women's linguistic and communicative choices in specific contexts will deepen our understanding of how the politics of gender and race continue to permeate present day intercultural encounters, despite the progress engendered by the Civil Rights and women's movements. As we learn more about how Black women struggle to express our full range of identities, to speak freely across cultural borders in a discourse environment intent on limiting and constraining our voices, we also deepen knowledge of the role of gender in all human communication in the 21st century.

◆ Notes

1. In 1996, the school board in Oakland, California, concluded that the majority of their mostly Black working class students were not learning to read soon enough and well enough to keep them from failing. On the advice of reading and language arts specialists, the board mandated the adoption of a set of first readers for the primary grades designed to help students comprehend the differences between the language variety they already knew and spoke in their homes and neighborhoods, Black English, and the variety they had to learn to read in order to be successful in school, U.S. Standard English. The readers consisted primarily of stories written in Black English or what the authors called Ebonics. The story of the Oakland school board's decision to adopt Ebonics readers became national news in December 1996 and sparked a nationwide controversy about the value and validity of Black speaking styles. (For a collection of scholarship on the Oakland Ebonics controversy, see *The Black Scholar*, Vol. 27, #2, 1997).

2. As Black women who are feminist/womanist scholars, we have chosen to use first-person references to Black women in an effort to avoid objectifying ourselves and artificially separating us from the women about whom we write.

3. The *Essence* Music Festival (*ESSENCE FEST*) is an annual event sponsored by the Black women's magazine *Essence* and held in New Orleans. A prominent feature of the event is a "Sister to Sister" empowerment seminar in which Black women celebrities and feature writers for the magazine offer brief motivational speeches on subjects related to contemporary Black women's lives to a mostly Black, mostly female audience.

4. Essed's participants in the Netherlands were Dutch citizens who were natives of the former Dutch colony of Surinam or their descendents living in the Netherlands.

5. We note the features of Black English grammar and lexicon in the title and in several lyrics. In the title, the possessive is unmarked (i.e., "baby mama" not "baby's mama") and the meaning of the two words has been expanded beyond the U.S. Standard English meaning ("a child's mother") to signify a never-married, single mother. Expansion of the meanings of ordinary English words is a common feature of Black English. ("Cuz": gloss = "because.")

◆ References

Acklin, B., Dinkins, N., & Colapietro, V. (2004). Baby mama [Recorded by Fantasia]. On *Free Yourself* [CD]. Los Angeles: J-Records. Lyrics retrieved April 7, 2005, from www .sing365.com/lyric.nsf

Allen, B. J. (1998). Black womanhood and feminist standpoints. *Management Communication Quarterly, 12,* 575–586.

Anderson, L. M. (1997). *Mammies no more: The changing image of Black women on stage and screen.* Lanham, MD: Rowman & Littlefield.

Baugh, J. (1983). *Black street speech.* Austin: University of Texas Press.

Billington, R. A. (Ed.). (1953). *The journal of Charlotte L. Forten: A young Black woman's reactions to the White world of the Civil War era.* New York: Norton.

Bucholtz, M. (1996). Black feminist theory and African American women's linguistic practice. In V. L. Bergvall, J. M. Bing, & A. F. Freed (Eds.), *Rethinking language and gender research: Theory and practice* (pp. 268–290). London: Longman.

Carter, K., & Spitzack, C. (Eds.). (1989). *Doing research on women's communication: Perspectives on theory and method*. Norwood, NJ: Ablex

Christian, B. (1985). Trajectories of self-definition: Placing contemporary Afro-American women's fiction. In M. Pryse & H. J. Spillers (Eds.), *Conjuring: Black women, fiction, and literary tradition* (pp. 233–248). Bloomington: Indiana University Press.

Clarke, C. (2002). Lesbianism 2000. In G. L. Anzaldua & A. Keating (Eds.), *This bridge we call home: Radical visions for transformation* (pp. 232–239). New York: Routledge.

Coates, J. (1996). *Women talk*. Oxford, UK: Blackwell.

Collins, P. H. (2000). *Black feminist thought: Knowledge, consciousness and the politics of empowerment* (2nd ed.). New York: HarperCollins.

Collins, P. H. (2004). *Black sexual politics: African Americans, gender, and the new racism*. New York: Routledge.

Crawford, M. (1995). *Talking difference*. London: Sage.

Davis, J. L. (2002). Sweet Honey in the Rock: Building communities through resistant voices. In M. Houston & O. I. Davis (Eds.), *Centering ourselves: African American feminist and womanist studies of discourse* (pp. 215–239). Cresskill, NJ: Hampton Press.

Davis, O. I. (1999). Life ain't been no crystal stair: The rhetoric of autobiography in Black female slave narratives. In J. L. Conyers, Jr. (Ed.), *Black lives: Essays in African American biography* (pp. 151–159). Armonk, NY: M. E. Sharpe.

Davis, O. I. (2002). Theorizing African American women's discourse: The public and private spheres of experience. In M. Houston & O. I. Davis (Eds.), *Centering ourselves: African American feminist and womanist studies of discourse* (pp. 35–51). Cresskill, NJ: Hampton Press.

Essed, P. (1990). *Everyday racism: Reports from women of two cultures*. (C. Jaffe, Trans).

Claremont, CA: Hunter House. (Original work published 1984)

Essed, P. (1991). *Understanding everyday racism: An interdisciplinary theory*. Newbury Park, CA: Sage.

Folb, E. (1980). *Runnin' down some lines: The language and culture of Black teenagers*. Cambridge, MA: Harvard University Press.

Fonow, M. M., & Cook, J. A. (Eds.). (1991). *Beyond methodology: Feminist scholarship as lived research*. Bloomington: Indiana University Press.

Foster, M. (1995). Are you with me? Power and solidarity in the discourse of African American women. In K. Hall & M. Bucholtz (Eds.), *Gender articulated: Language and the socially constructed self* (pp. 330–350). New York: Routledge.

Giddings, P. (1984). *When and where I enter: The impact of Black women on race and sex in America*. New York: Bantam.

Giles, H., Bourhis, R. Y., & Taylor, D. (1977). Towards a theory of language in ethnic group relations. In H. Giles & R. St. Clair (Eds.), *Language, ethnicity and intergroup relations* (pp. 307–348). London: Academic Press.

Giles, H., & Coupland, N. (1991). *Language: Contexts and consequences*. Pacific Grove, CA: Brooks/Cole.

Gumperz, J. J. (1982). *Discourse strategies*. Cambridge, UK: Cambridge University Press.

Guy-Sheftall, B. (Ed.). (1995). *Words of fire: An anthology of African-American feminist thought*. New York: New Press.

Hamlet, J. (1996). Fannie Lou Hamer: The unquenchable spirit of the civil rights movement. *Journal of Black Studies, 12*(5), 560–576.

Hecht, M. L., Jackson, R. L., & Ribeau, S. A. (2002). *African American communication: Exploring identity and culture*. Mahwah, NJ: Lawrence Erlbaum.

Hill, P. S. (2003). And still I rise: Communicative resistance of African American women in a culturally diverse community. *Electronic Journal of Communication, 13*. Retrieved

February 3, 2005, from www.cios.org/www/tocs/EJC.htm

hooks, b. (1984). *Feminist theory: From margin to center*. Boston: South End Press.

Houston, M. (1980–86). [Conversations among Black and White women friends]. Unpublished raw data.

Houston (Stanback), M. (1983). *Code-switching in Black women's speech*. Unpublished doctoral dissertation, University of Massachusetts.

Houston (Stanback), M. (1985). Language and Black woman's place: Lessons from the Black middle class. In P. Treichler, C. Kramarae, & B. Stafford (Eds.), *For Alma Mater: Theory and practice in feminist scholarship* (pp. 177–193). Urbana: University of Illinois Press.

Houston, M. (2000a). Multiple perspectives: African American women conceive their talk. *Women and Language, 23*, 11–17.

Houston, M. (2000b). Writing for my life: Intercultural communication methodology and the study of African American women. J. N. Martin & O. I. Davis (Eds.), Ethnicity and methodology [Special issue]. *International Journal of Intercultural Relations, 24*, 673–686.

Houston, M., & Davis, O. I. (Eds.). (2002). *Centering ourselves: African American feminist and womanist studies of discourse*. Cresskill, NJ: Hampton Press.

Hudson, B. H. (2001). *African American female speech communities: Varieties of talk*. Westport, CT: Bergin & Garvey.

James, J. (1999). *Shadowboxing: Representations of Black feminist politics*. New York: Mayfield.

Johnson, F. L. (2000). *Speaking culturally: Language diversity in the United States*. Thousand Oaks, CA: Sage.

Jones, C., & Shorter-Gooden, K. (2003). *Shifting: The double lives of Black women in America*. New York: HarperCollins.

Lippi-Green, R. (1997). What we talk about when we talk about Ebonics: Why definitions matter. *The Black Scholar, 27*, 7–11.

McCullough, M. W. (1996). *Black and White women as friends: Building cross-race friendships*. Cresskill, NJ: Hampton Press.

Miles, T. (1995). Murky waters. *Women & Language, 23(1)*, 21–22.

Nelson, L. W. (1990). Code-switching in the oral life narratives of African American women: Challenges to linguistic hegemony. *Journal of Education, 173(3)*, 142–155.

Orbe, M., Drummond, D., & Camara, S. (2002). Phenomenology and Black feminist thought: Exploring African American women's everyday encounters as points of contention. In M. Houston & O. I. Davis (Eds.), *Centering ourselves: African American feminist and womanist studies of discourse* (pp. 123–144). Cresskill, NJ: Hampton Press.

Parker, P. S. (2003). Learning leadership: Communication, resistance and African American women's executive leadership development. *Electronic Journal of Communication, 13*. Retrieved February 3, 2005, from www.cios.org/www/tocs/EJC.htm

Scott, K. D. (1995). *"When I'm with my girls": Identity and ideology in Black women's talk about language and cultural borders*. Doctoral dissertation, University of Illinois, Urbana-Champagne.

Scott, K. D. (2000). Crossing cultural borders: "Girl" and "look" as markers of identity in Black women's language use. *Discourse and Society, 11*, 237–248.

Scott, K. D. (2002). Conceiving the language of Black women's everyday talk. In M. Houston & O. I. Davis (Eds.), *Centering ourselves: African American feminist and womanist studies of discourse* (pp. 53–73). Cresskill, NJ: Hampton Press.

Scott, K. D. (2004, November). *Young, shifting and Black: Identity negotiation in the communication strategies of Black women*. Paper presented at the 90th annual meeting of the National Communication Association, Chicago.

Van Dijk, T. (1987). *Communicating racism: Ethnic prejudice in thought and talk*. Newbury Park, CA: Sage.

Watts, E. K. (2002). The female voice in hip-hop: An exploration into the potential of the erotic appeal. In M. Houston & O. I.

Davis (Eds.), *Centering ourselves: African American feminist and womanist studies of discourse* (pp. 187–213). Cresskill, NJ: Hampton Press.

White, C., & Dobris, C. (2002). The nobility of womanhood: "Womanhood" in the rhetoric of 19th century Black club women. In M. Houston & O. I. Davis (Eds.), *Centering ourselves: African American*

feminist and womanist studies of discourse (pp. 215–239). Cresskill, NJ: Hampton Press.

Williamson-Ige, D. (1988). Shirley Chisholm with Black and White women's audiences. In B. Bate & A. Taylor (Eds.), *Women communicating: Studies of women's talk* (pp. 91–106). Norwood, NJ: Ablex.

Wodak, R. (Ed.). (1997). *Gender and discourse.* London: Sage.

22

TRANSGRESSING GENDER IN DISCOURSES ACROSS CULTURES

◆ Fern L. Johnson

I recently attended an informal presentation at my university by Kathy Davis (Utrecht University), who has chronicled the travels of *Our Bodies, Ourselves* (*OBOS*) (Boston Women's Health Book Collective, 1971) into translations, adaptations, and "inspired versions" in 29 countries (Davis, 2002; in press). As Davis talked about the changes that authors around the world had made to the U.S. version of this now-classic feminist self-help health guidebook, I was struck by how compactly *OBOS*'s travels tell the story of multiple feminisms around the world—often in contrast to the United States.

> OBOS is a distinctively North American product. . . . It draws upon a long populist tradition of self-help . . . and empowerment through knowledge. . . . The critique of medicine found in OBOS is informed by the specific problems which women face in a highly medicalized culture where health is a consumer good and the health care system puts profit above the equitable distribution of care. (Davis, 2002, p. 225)

Several examples identified by Davis demonstrate how cultural context shaped the ways in which *OBOS* changed with location. The Dutch translators rejected the division between lesbianism and heterosexuality. The Spanish adaptation for Latin America removed the self-help orientation and replaced it with a family and community focus emphasizing mutual help. The South African version was intended to be read aloud as part of the oral tradition. The authors of the Egyptian version opposed genital excision, but they

> routinely took along an imam [a Muslim male spiritual leader who is considered divinely appointed to guide believers in prayer and religious practice] who . . . would stand up and announce that there was nothing in the Q'uran which required female genital excision, thereby lending the book legitimacy among religious women. (p. 240)

Two themes stood out in Davis's recounting of the travels of *OBOS*. First, all versions challenged dominant ideologies, but each version ultimately reflected choices about content made within a specific cultural context. Second, behind each version there was a story about women's communication that led to the adaptations and changes. Davis (2002) remarked that, "Women collectively sharing knowledge about their embodied experiences seems to be what fired the imagination of women in different parts of the world" (p. 240). In short, *OBOS*'s travels revealed multiple feminisms at work to speak to and with women, often in ways and about topics that violated the cultural norms of specific groups. These themes led me to probe more deeply into how communication in multiple places asserts women's voices and asserts challenges to hegemonic gender normativities.

Every act against cultural normativity of gender—whatever the culture and its codes—is an act of transgression. Such acts, both small and large, disrupt the social order and the codes of communication that are taught in the process of what psychologist Sandra Bem (1993) calls "the making of a gendered native"—that part of the cultural process that produces gender and its appropriate coordinates. In the United States, most of the scholarship on gender and communication continues to be about white women, notwithstanding significant contributions that have grown from the challenge of broadening scholarship to encompass diversity—ethnic and racial, affectional, class, and cultural (see the introduction to this section).

◆ Chapter Focus

In this chapter, I provide a glimpse into the work focused on transgressions of gendered discourse in a range of cultural contexts. The scholars whose work I review take as their subject the spaces, places, and voices of girls and women in a range of contexts— all different from any of the spaces, places, and voices of the large middle ground of white women in the United States. Many of the studies enter the domain of gender and power relations, and as such they represent "the emerging work on resistance to gender domination—especially the important work on linguistic resistance—[that] is a powerful critique of social theory" (Gal, 1995, p. 175).

My purpose is to open up the cultural context of how we think about the expression of gender and the voice of "woman" communicating to challenge, disrupt, or simply speak contrary to gender normativity. As much as it would be desirable to avoid grounding this overview in an ideology of binary organizations of both sex and gender, the work to be discussed is in some way always about "women" and "men" communicating in cultural contexts infused by ideology that supports these binaries. Spivak's (1985/1996) point about the definition of *woman* is germane: "I construct my definition as a woman not in terms of a woman's putative essence but in terms of words currently in use. 'Man' is such a word. . . . Not *a* word, but *the* word" (p. 54). The scholarship reviewed in this chapter discusses and documents communication that challenges the cultural codes associated with gender—codes in the service of the binary of man and woman. For the most part, the work addresses how women—at any ages and in specific cultural locations— discursively counter-construct and reconstruct sex/gender against both sides of the male-female/man-woman binary.

The chapter has four sections. The first includes a selection of theories and concepts that directly deal with the cultural construction of gender through discourse (broadly defined). The theories and conceptualizations reviewed originate in various disciplines but share the growing transdisciplinary space of gender studies. In the second section, examples are provided of research that demonstrates the cultural specificity of women's gendered voices that resist gender normativity. Much of this research is linguistic in nature and based in analysis of language varieties. The third section highlights discursive disruptions in the generational enactments of gender. In this section, the central questions probe what it means to be and to communicate as a girl or woman. The fourth section focuses on gender refusal and refusers (lesbians, gays, transgenders, and so on). The purpose of this section is to highlight the debates about gender categories and how they have been characterized in communication scholarship and to provide a sampling of work conducted to illuminate the discursive construction of gender refusals.

The body of work reviewed here is not exhaustive. Rather, it points to representative approaches to questions regarding gender transgressions through discourse within the specificity of cultural context. Neither is this overview concerned with capturing the totality of women's discourse in any given cultural context. Some of the relevant literature appears in communication journals, but the range of sources discussed below reveals the transdisciplinary character of gender studies.

◆ Theorizing Gender as Cultural Discourse

Theoretical thinking about gender and communication over the past three decades has taken many twists and turns, largely moving with broader discourses in feminist and gender studies. A review of developments in theory would more than fill a separate chapter. Here I highlight approaches that seem the richest for illuminating how discourse works to create and challenge gender in multiple cultural locations: (a) the performativity approach, (b) community of practice as an organizing concept for understanding discourse and identity, and (c) queer linguistics.

GENDER PERFORMATIVITY

This approach has various roots, but in the study of gender and discourse, Candace West and Don Zimmerman's (1987) article on "doing gender" was foundational. They argued that "gender is not a set of traits, nor a variable, nor a role, but the product of social doings of some sort" (p. 129). In discussing the distinctions often made between *sex* and *gender,* these authors observed that this very distinction serves to naturalize gender because it "links the institutional and interactional levels ... [and] legitimates social arrangements based on sex category [such that] doing gender furnishes the interactional scaffolding of social structure" (p. 147). It follows that failure to "do gender" as expected in cultural context can lead to negative sanctions but can also signify purposeful resistance. West and Fenstermaker (1995) expand this conceptualization to "doing difference" by incorporating race and class into the analysis. They do not deal explicitly with culture, but the analysis they offer can easily be extrapolated to the workings of culture in framing communication.

The performativity approach gained hold with Judith Butler's publication in 1990 of *Gender Trouble* (see Butler, 1999). Against the backdrop of prevailing conceptualizations of sex as a biological category and gender as a social and cultural category, Butler presented an elaborate, post-structuralist analysis that brought new thinking to the study of gender and discourse. Butler's perspective posits both gender and sex as products of discursive construction. Butler contends that gender, when it is cast as the cultural elaboration of sex, functions as "the discursive/cultural means by which 'sexed nature' or 'a natural sex' is produced and established as 'prediscursive,' prior to culture, a politically neutral surface *on which* culture acts" (Butler, 1999, p. 7). Key to this conceptualization is the idea of *performativity:* "gender proves to be performative, that is, constituting the identity it is purported to be" (p. 25). More specifically, "gender is the repeated stylization of the body, a set of repeated acts within a highly rigid regulatory frame that congeal over time to produce the appearance of substance, of a natural sort of being" (p. 33). This process, in Butler's analysis, sets up a binary opposition that enforces compulsory heterosexuality. Critical study and awareness of this process make gender transgression possible. Although Butler was mainly concerned with destabilizing the binary of male and female sex and questioning the "stability of gender as a category of analysis" (p. xi) to open up the potential of queer parody "of the very notion of the original" (p. 138), the perspective is broadly useful for an understanding of discursive disruptions of the ideological systems that uphold sex and gender categorizations in a broad range of cultural contexts. Butler's (2004) recent book turns the analysis inside out to consider the "undoing" of gender, which is more specifically grounded in particular challenges to gender normativity and the interplay of agency and social control.

COMMUNITY OF PRACTICE

Many scholars of gender and discourse have found the concept of a community of practice (CofP) useful for understanding how, on what terms, and with what effects on identity people join together in shared discourse practices (see Wenger, 1998, who developed the approach). Penelope Eckert and Sally McConnell-Ginet (1999) define the CofP as "an aggregate of people who, united by a common enterprise, develop and share ways of doing things, ways of talking, beliefs, and values—in short, practices" (p. 186). The conceptual apparatus of CofP guides gender researchers to consider "people's active engagement in the reproduction of or resistance to gender arrangements in their communities" and to look at gender practices in relation to other aspects of identity in context (Eckert & McConnell-Ginet, 1992, p. 472).

CofP complements the more traditional sociolinguistic concept of *speech community* because of the explicit focus on practices rather than aggregates of people *per se.* The practices of individuals jointly engaged with one another construct the identity of the community and of its participants. A body of research that draws on CofP highlights how masculinities and femininities are accomplished in context (Paechter, 2003a, 2003b).

QUEER LINGUISTICS

The relatively new field of queer linguistics (QL) offers another approach that questions the foundations and cultural normativity of sex and gender. Mary Bucholtz and Kira Hall (2004) define QL as "the study of sexuality as a relational and contextual sociopolitical phenomenon" incorporating both sexuality and gender and focused on both identity and desire; sexuality refers to "the systems of mutually constituted ideologies, practices, and identities that give sociopolitical meaning to the body as an eroticized and/or reproductive site" (p. 470). Their presentation of QL parts with the "desire paradigm" (see Cameron & Kulick, 2003; Kulick, 2000), which features sexuality as rooted in desire alone. QL deals with the production of sexuality in language—not only in relation to those labeling themselves as "queer" but also for any sexually marginalized practice or group; for example, Bucholtz and Hall (2004) cite Cohen's (1997) example of the prohibition of marriage for African American women and men during slavery.

Drawing on a number of sociolinguistic concepts, Bucholtz and Hall (2004) call for an approach that recognizes identity as integral to sexuality, that conceptually accounts for the various ways in which language establishes power relations (not only between dominant and marginalized groups but also within the discourses of marginalized groups), and that maps the possibilities for forming social subjectivity and intersubjectivity (identity) through social practice. These scholars outline various analytical tools (which they label "tactics") for creating a broad range of intersubjectivities through language use in specific contexts. They also point out that QL reaches beyond queer discourses and sexuality to offer a vantage point for understanding the creation of identities designed to be or functioning in resistance to dominant ideology.

◆ The Cultural Specificity of Gender Transgressions in Discourse

I use the term *transgression* to describe instances of language-in-use that in some way counter the conventional expectations for gender enactments. The research examples in this chapter demonstrate transgressions whereby girls, women, and gender refusers assert their voices to disrupt normativity. Some of the research points specifically to the linguistic code (syntax, phonology, and so on), while other research examines broader patterns of discourse (for example, style and narrative).

TRANSGRESSIONS IN THE LINGUISTIC CODE

Women Speaking Japanese. The most well developed non-English line of research on changes in the linguistic structure of women's language comes from scholars working on the variety of Japanese spoken by women. Japanese women's speech (*onna-rashii* or "womanly" speech) is traditionally considered powerless in relation to the speech of men. Sachiko Ide (cited in Furo, 1996) describes the characteristics of Japanese women's language as "more polite than that of men, especially in their (1) use of different personal pronouns, (2) avoidance of vulgar expressions, (3) use of beautification/hypercorrect honorifics, and (4) use of feminine sentence-final particles" (p. 247). Janet Shibamoto Smith (1992) notes that "the 'polite' nature of Japanese women's speech—held to be expressed in part by women's frequent use of honorific and humiliative forms—is linked to their social powerlessness, at least in the public domain" (p. 59). Okamoto (1995) cites research supporting the conclusion that the speech of Japanese women is "polite, gentle, soft-spoken, nonassertive, and empathetic . . . characteristics . . . often interpreted as reflecting women's lower social status or powerlessness" (p. 298). Katsue Akiba Reynolds (1998) contrasts women's and men's speech on the dimension of assertiveness, with the most masculine speech using assertive and forceful variants; even though there is some overlap in variants that may be used, "the risk of stepping into the overlapping area . . . is greater for females than for males" (p. 301).

Against the traditional role of women in Japanese society and the forms of Japanese women's speech related to and constitutive of their relative powerlessness, younger generations of Japanese women have introduced innovations. A leading scholar in this area, Shigeko Okamoto (1995) studied women's use of "men's language" by examining the use of masculine, neutral, and feminine sentence-final forms in conversations between pairs of college-age women friends in Tokyo. For example, the particle *wa* with rising intonation at the end of a sentence is strongly feminine and gives mild emphasis, whereas the particles *ze* and *zo* for assertion are strongly masculine. Okamoto found that the women in her study used neutral forms most frequently (65%), and when using feminine forms (only 12%), used those classified as mildly feminine. These women also used more masculine sentence-final forms (19%) than feminine forms. Earlier research by Okamoto and Sato (1992) and by Takasaki (published in Japanese in 1993 and cited in Okamoto, 1995) shows that younger Japanese women use less traditionally feminine speech forms than older women, but that occupational status (homemaker, office worker, professional) also correlates with speech style. These results suggest that social role, age cohort, and language variety are intertwined, and that not only do young women counter the norm for feminine speech but older women also do so in certain situations.

If there is a social perception that women are challenging language conventions, that perception might be evident in media representations. Okamoto (1996) analyzed the scripting of women's speech in comics, films, and television dramas by focusing on three speech varieties: *otoko kotoba* (men's language), *Shitamachi kotoba* (Shitamachi, which is the language variety of downtown Tokyo and shares many features of *otoko kotaba*), and *Osaka-ben* (Osaka dialect). These varieties all carry gendered meanings. The first two are associated with traditional Japanese forms of masculine speech, while *Osaka-ben* is an urban variety said to carry rough and abusive expressions and to also be associated with humor. Okamoto found a number of complexities in the scripting of women's speech in popular culture genres, demonstrating that masculine forms signify not only younger women but women of varying ages who are tough or working class. Taking a somewhat different approach, Yoshiko Matsumoto (1996) compared the language used in fashion magazines that targeted young women with the language in magazines directed to older women. She found "abundant use of sentence final expressions that are conventionally considered masculine" (p. 456) in magazines directed to high school and college age students but almost none of these in magazines directed to older women. Yet, her textual analysis reveals that the use of conventional masculine forms does not

always convey a masculine image but, rather, is part of an emerging "cute culture" (which is also evident in young men's discourse). Matsumoto views young women's language choices as resisting adult ideology "by strategically ignoring the conventional (and normative) differentiation of women's language from men's and by avoiding the honorifics that are sensitive to the traditional power structure" (pp. 464–465).

Several additional studies focus on stylistic devices used by women speaking Japanese to reject traditional codes for women's language. Smith (1992) explored new strategies used by women in uttering directives. She compared the speech used by a woman hosting a cooking program on television with the speech used by a man hosting a home carpentry program. The woman employed a hybrid power form for directives that preserved politeness but did not replicate men's language. These strategies she labeled "Motherese," because they take the form of those between mother and child, and "Passive Power Strategy," in which directives are given with either no verb or a verb that is followed by an auxiliary verb with a "positive assertive form"— what Smith calls "passive but assured waiting" (p. 78). She provides this example:

Yakusoku o mamotte moraitai (desu).

(polite) a

I'd like [to receive the favor of] you keep[ing] your promise. (p. 81)

The male expert on the carpentry program did not use these forms. Furo (1996) focused on a comparison of the form of directives for instruction and for discipline given by female and male teachers in a Japanese school in Washington, DC. The female teachers in this study "issue instruction directives as if they were making requests but discipline directives as if they were giving orders" (p. 257). They also depart from the phonological norms for women related to high pitch and "fade-out" at the ends of sentences.

Scholars who study Japanese women's language have dealt as much with the overall complexity of language use based on age, class, social role, and situation as they have with the more general trend for younger women to reject traditional expectations for women's passive language forms. The vitality of inquiry regarding gender and Japanese is highlighted by the appearance in 2004 of an edited volume titled *Japanese language, gender, and ideology* (Okamoto & Shibamoto-Smith) and by research on how Kogals (teenage girls in Japan) use slang (Miller, 2004).

The Case of Lakota. Several interesting studies have been undertaken regarding the ways in which various groups of Native American women use language. Bea Medicine (1987) noted that in all three dialects of Lakota Sioux (Lakota, Dakota, and Nakota), women reinforce the obligatory structural markers in the language that distinguish first-person women's speech from first-person men's speech (linguists refer to this as the gender particle system). She also reported, however, that Lakota women serve the role for their community as the "language power brokers" and mediators in relations with whites because of their greater control of Standard English, and that they exercise considerable language control through their role in decisions about language learning by their children.

Sara Trechter (1996) studied the gender particle system more specifically in her linguistic ethnography of Lakota on the Ridge and Rosebud reservations in South Dakota. Linguists have typically described the particle system as consisting of several binary features associated with gender. Trechter lists six complementary gender particles recorded by linguists based on native informants: for example, the male imperative *yo* contrasts with the female imperative *ye*, and the male expression of surprise *wã* contrasts with the female expression of surprise *ma*. Of particular interest is the *yo/ye* distinction; in this case, Trechter's position is that the gender binary is overstated in linguistic

descriptions and representations by native speakers (also see Trechter, 1995) because the *ye* particle is used by men as well as women, making only *yo* gender restricted. One interesting part of Trechter's analysis from the perspective of linguistic transgression has to do with her report that younger male speakers are shunning the "use [of] *ye* as an assertion or even the morphologically distinct *ye*, as an entreaty" because of its association with female "bossiness" (p. 751). In this case, female transgression may be leading to regenderizing by males.

DISCOURSE CLAIMS BY WOMEN

Several interesting projects document women's performance of discourse styles that are counternormative, and in some cases purposefully disruptive, to the gender ideology in force within a specific culture. Marcelle Williams (1989), who has studied immigrant Punjabi-speaking women working in canneries in California, found that they manipulated their language use in ways that gave them greater control in the workplace. These Sikh women did have limited English proficiency, but they also frequently feigned more extensive lack of understanding of their English-speaking supervisors as a way of resisting certain types of communication.

Writing about gender and language in Ukraine, Laada Bilaniuk (2003) presents findings showing that even though many women tend to reject feminism in preference for more traditional feminine roles, high school and college women who participated in a matched guise study demonstrated attitudes toward language that counter broadly held beliefs in the country. Ukrainian became the official language in 1989 as an official rebuke to Soviet-imposed Russian. In a context where Russian remains a lingua franca and English is on the rise, women are considered protectors of the Ukrainian language. Young women in the study, however, valued the use of English more highly than the use of Ukrainian. Bilaniuk suggests that the myth that women are protectors of the Ukrainian language is one of the beliefs that upholds patriarchy.

Fatima Sadiqi (2003) offers a fascinating analysis of Moroccan women's code-switching between Moroccan Arabic and French and between Berber and French.[1] Four languages are prominent in Morocco: Berber and Moroccan Arabic, mother tongues which are spoken languages only, Standard Arabic, and French. "Moroccan women," Sadiqi says, "make appropriate usage of code-switching with the aim of exploiting the position of the marginalized for strategic purposes" (p. 41). Code-switching is empowering in several ways: (a) by attracting and maintaining attention in conversation in both women's and mixed groups; (b) by imposing the speaker in a conversation through "snatching turns" (p. 40); (c) by asserting linguistic power in mixed settings where the men who dominate are less educated; (d) by offering a linguistic recourse for adolescent girls to distinguish themselves from adolescent boys; and (e) by conveying a "new style" that indexes "modernity" (p. 41). Writing about a different national site, Esther Kuntjara (2005), in a recent article about women selling their goods in two urban East Java markets (Malany and Surabaya), counters the prevailing social belief that women are passive and submissive with ethnographic accounts of the assertive language strategies used by women in the market as both buyers and sellers. Her point is that totalizing generalizations about women's roles miss the complexity of situational factors that influence discourse.

The Yapima village in the Brazilian Amazon is the site of Janet Chernela's research on women's language-in-use contrasted to traditional discourse roles for women (see Chernela's 2004 discussion of patrilineal community and language ideology among the Amerindian speakers she studied). Chernela (1997) documents the telling of an ancestral Wanano tale by an elder Wanano woman who violates community rules for doing gender in discourse. The woman tells the tale to a group of women in a public setting and changes the tale to switch blame from a wife's betrayal of her husband to a husband's betrayal of his wife. Her countertale and her taking public space for women is "a moment that ruptures the gender hierarchy characterizing everyday life" (p. 74) and which "provides us with an unusual opportunity to hear from an otherwise muted segment of the population" (p. 89). In a later study, Chernela (2003) uses the concept of community of practice (CofP) to frame her understanding of the function of the rituals used by women when they are welcoming women from other villages. Here she demonstrates how otherness created by women's position in patrilineal communities is used as a basis for solidarity through "wept texts"—the greeting rituals in which "the singer's own living death, her social isolation and separation" (p. 795) from her native language and birth community invite the participation of the other women and the creation of a CofP. These greetings, called *kaya basa* ("sad songs"), resist the social isolation of women that is part of the ideology operating in the Tukanoan society. In related research, Charles Briggs (1992) discussed the weeping rituals as recontextualizations of men's discourse as a challenge to their power.

The discourse of women in each of the locations documented in the foregoing examples shows gender in motion in ways either explicitly counter to conventional cultural practices or at odds with the ideological gender codes that are assumed to exist within the particular social context. Together, the examples show essentializing to be invalid; for each case, the ways in which language constructs gender are understandable only in the specific cultural context.

◆ Discursive Disruptions in Generational Gendering

In the past 15 years, considerable attention has been directed to what has been dubbed the third-wave of feminism and its varieties— "power feminism," "grrrl power," "DIY— Do-It-Yourself feminism." It is appropriate to discuss these more recent trends under the rubric of gendered communication in cultural context because they represent a cultural shift in gender ideologies in the United States and elsewhere. These emerging feminisms have created the conditions for the kind of generation gap that characterizes cultural tensions in core values, beliefs, and modes of expression.

STRANDS OF NEW FEMINIST EXPRESSION

In a useful review essay, Anita Harris (2001) outlines three ways in which the feminism of younger women tends to be classified.[2] The first is *power feminism*—the term taken from Naomi Wolf's *Fire with Fire* (1993). Power feminism focuses on women's power rather than their subordination, emphasizing gains that have been made and issues yet to face. "It makes a clear distinction between the personal and the political, and tends to display commitment to either individual empowerment or single issue groups rather than a women's 'movement'" (Harris, 2001, ¶ 6). The second variety includes *DIY* and *grrrlpower,* which are associated with music and new media such as Web pages and zines. Harris characterizes grrrlpower as aimed at issues still facing young women, "especially regarding the body and sexuality. . . . [I]t emphasizes autonomy, sassiness, and is sometimes depicted as sexy and aggressive" (¶ 8). Harris names the third variety Third Wave to designate those young feminists who "actively embrace the term 'third Wave' to mark their place as the next 'wave' in the tradition of the previous two women's movements" (¶ 11). Self-proclaimed third wavers emphasize ethnic, sexual, and economic diversity. According to Harris, this variety is "associated with either the problems faced by women as they attempt to put second wave gains into action . . . or with obstacles that are less obvious but just as

real" (¶ 13). (The term *Third Wave* is sometimes used to include all of the newer forms of grrrlpower expression.) Chilla Bulbeck (2001) observes that in all the debates and different emphases among younger feminists, "no-one wants to be labelled a victim feminist" (¶ 20). Jennifer Drake (1997) emphasizes the centrality of pleasure in all the forms of the third wave "because we're young or because we're such well-trained consumers or because we're into some kind of playful postmodern aesthetic or because we watched too much TV growing up" (p. 106).

A recent collection of essays (Gillis, Howie, & Munford, 2004) includes selections on sexuality and gender, popular culture expressions of third wave, and cultural multiplicity and postcolonial perspectives. Lotz (2003) and Fixmer and Wood (2005) also offer useful analyses of varieties of third wave.

Music, zines, and conventions became expressive venues for the 1990s new generation of feminism. Grrrl power bands emerged, notably Bikini Kill and Bratmobile, and there was soon a "Riot Grrrls" movement. Riot Grrrls had its beginning on August 20, 1991, in Olympia, Washington, at the International Pop Underground convention (Riot grrrl, n.d.). What began with music, spread to other forms of expression about gender and society. The zines (e.g., *Girl Germs*) became especially important for dealing with "a variety of feminist topics, frequently attempting to draw out the political implications of intensely personal experiences with sexism, mental illness, body image, sexual abuse, and homosexuality" (Riot grrrl, n.d.). One of my students produced a zine in 2003 on body issues for middle school girls; she showed me numerous examples of zines on a range of issues— some seriously political, others purely hedonistic. One riot grrrl Web site (Newitz) posted the following greeting:

> You've come to the right place. A shrine to all girls who wish their gender started

with a grrrrwl! And a tribute to all women who are too pissed off, unhappy, tough, geeky, or brainy to do and think what they're told. As Bikini Kill says, "We want a REVOLUTION!" Here you can find everything for the person who says FUCK YOU when the world says BE QUIET AND OBEY.

Web sites such as these and various zines proclaim freedom for girls by celebrating the body and eschewing images about ideal body images. From these 1990s forms came a vast array of current Web sites and blogs addressed to a broad range of specific issues. This is polyvocal feminist expression directed to anyone who might be interested and have access—much of this expression is ephemeral.

Michelle Fine and Pat Macpherson (1994) published an essay ripe with insights into younger generational thinking. These two seasoned feminist scholars invited four teenage women to talk with them over two separate dinners about gender. These evenings were critical, collaborative group interviews. The four included two African Americans who were living in "relatively impoverished circumstances" (p. 225), one "WASP," and one Korean American—the latter two "living in relatively comfortable circumstances" (p. 226). The African American young women expressed their enmeshment in community through fluid connections with women of all ages and their comfort in "using public talk as a place to 'work out' concerns, constraints and choices" (p. 225). The white and Korean American women expressed much greater distance from family (especially mothers), reported that privacy was foremost for working out issues and basic survival, and set their goal as becoming independent women. What these four young women shared was resistance to male dominance and their embrace of "the benign version of masculinity that allowed them to be 'one of the guys'" (p. 220)—to take risks, have fun, and be honest and accepting. Fine and Macpherson summarized this attitude:

Girls can be good, bad or—best of all—they can be boys. This version of individualized resistance, or feminism, reflects a retreat from the collective politics of gender, and from other women, and an advance into the embattled scene of gender politics—alone, and against boys, in order to become one of them. (p. 241)

This portrayal, although not standing for young women in general, offers keys to the links of identity and discourse that separate many younger women from older women in their views of doing gender. They embrace those aspects of masculinity that appeal to a grounded identity where expression and risk-taking are important. Also revealed in the talk of these four young women is a cultural split, with the two African Americans more grounded in women's community and the other two more interior and personal.

CRITIQUE

Among the dissections of the politics and priorities of younger generation women and their notions of gender are several analyses and critiques from communication scholars. Helene Shugart (2001) argues that what has been identified as third wave is a broader Generation X subculture. She characterizes Gen X (and third wave) as an *aesthetic* rather than a *generation*: its qualities are "camp, satire, cynicism, irony, and outrageousness, in very heavy doses" (p. 136). Shugart mapped these qualities in the fame of four Gen X poster girls (Alanis Morissette, Courtney Love, Winona Ryder, and Janeane Garofalo). Although Shugart recognizes the distinctiveness of third wave from Gen X in its inclusion of diversity, she concludes by critiquing it as an "'anything goes' feminism [that] may ultimately compromise the fundamental tenet of feminism: to expose and rectify the oppression of women" (p. 164). Shugart, Waggoner, and

Hallstein (2001) offer a harsh assessment of new feminism in the hands of mass media. Their project analyzes media commodification of third-wave feminism through case studies of Alanis Morissette, Kate Moss, and Ally McBeal. These scholars argue that mass media deflect the resistance of third-wave feminism by appropriating its characteristics into commodities. The result, these scholars conclude, is that "messages of resistance are co-opted, commodified, and sold to audiences as a 'genuine imitation'—something whose code appears strikingly similar to the resistant discourse but . . . is devoid of challenge" (p. 198).

Another angle of criticism on the third-wave agenda comes from postcolonial Filipino scholar Angeli Diaz (2003). Grounded in Radha Hegde's (1998, see also her essay in this volume) entreaty that feminist theory take into account the power relations established through colonialism, Diaz faults the third wave for its absorption in the self and individual circumstances and priorities. Diaz sees no connection between the third-wave agenda and her lived experiences: "The omission of any reference to the global political, economic, and cultural scenario in the writings of third-wave feminists predisposes their celebration of diversity and inclusiveness to be paradoxically an exclusive one" (p. 15). This is a powerful critique that opens interesting questions about the politics of inclusiveness.

From the perspective of (mainly white) U.S. feminists, some strands of the third-wave agenda appear apolitical because of both the de-emphasis on collective action and the reclaiming/refashioning of many codes that have upheld hegemonic sexism. At the same time, much of third-wave thinking and expression celebrates diversity more fully and less self-consciously than earlier feminisms.[3] In the global context, the critique is somewhat reversed. Third wave explicitly rejects the earlier second-wave notion of global sisterhood, we-are-all-in-the-same-situation thinking related to integrating diversity through collective action.

But in the global political context, third wave can also be critiqued for insufficient political valence because it lacks a mandate for a postcolonial agenda. In any case, younger women have ushered in important cultural shifts in the doing of gender and the meanings for gender encoded and expressed through those doings.

◆ Gender Refusal/Refusers and Cultural Transformation

Like third-wave priorities and practices, the assault on normative gender relations and especially heteronormativity by those who refuse to do gender through conventional codes represents powerful cultural shifts. I am using the term *gender refusal* to designate any pattern of purposeful communication designed to reject conventional male and female assignment in its heteronormative context, with its corresponding actors being *gender refusers* (most often designated as lesbian, gay, bisexual, transgendered, and queer—LGBTQ). In this short section, my purpose is to characterize the types of scholarship focused on gender refusal, but not to review the literature in its entirety.

THE LANGUAGE OF GENDER REFUSAL

A number of scholars ask, Are there distinctive gay and lesbian voices? In the United States at least, the stereotype of the exaggerated, overly femme vocal stylization often stands as the quintessential sign of the gay male voice. Less firm is the stereotype of the deep-voiced "butch" side of the lesbian relationship. These styles certainly exist, often as identity codes and sometimes as parodic enactments of gender polarities. Yet, no research has established a consistent pattern in the voice (Jacobs, 1996; Smyth, Jacobs, & Rogers, 2003). Approaching the question differently, William Leap (1995) put together a collection of studies under the rubric of "lavender linguistics" that demonstrates the textual complexity of lesbian and gay male language. What emerges from the range of studies in specific settings collected in this volume are *"distinctively constructed* lesbian and gay *languages"* (p. x). Leap was interested in documenting how the language practices of specific lesbians and gays both create an authentic identity and appropriate and remake heterosexual discourse. The essays in the volume show the usefulness of the CofP perspective and also broaden the cultural analysis of gay and lesbian discourse by including studies centered in a number of different locales.

Drawing from the emerging field of queer studies, Anna Livia and Kira Hall (1997) put together a collection of essays in a book titled *Queerly Phrased: Language, Gender and Sexuality*. The three sections of the book serve as a typology for the direction scholarship and practice on gender refusal were moving by the mid-1990s: "Lavender Lexicality," "Queerspeak," and "Linguistic Gender-Bending." The collection includes a range of chapters on gay, lesbian, bisexual, and transsexual language; together, these chapters map what is now called "queer linguistics." Writing about developments in the study of language and gender identities, Hall (2003) frames the purpose of QL: "Like queer theory, queer linguistics is necessarily concerned with how heterosexual normativity is produced, perpetuated, and resisted, but it seeks to localize these productions within specific communities of practice" (p. 375). From a cultural perspective, focusing on specific communities of practice is especially significant. *Queerly Phrased* includes case studies of a number of different cultural groups from around the world.

NEWER DIRECTIONS IN QUEER STUDIES OF DISCOURSE

Within what has come to be identified as "global queer studies," increasing attention

is being given to the place of language in constructing resistive identities and, more specifically, LGBTQ performativity in ethnic and racial perspective. In 2003, *GLQ: A Journal of Lesbian and Gay Studies* published a series of papers titled "New Directions in Multiethnic, Racial, and Global Queer Studies." Authors in that series speak to the central issue in the development of global queer studies: bringing particular circumstances of ethnicity and race to the center of queer analysis. This issue mirrors that found in other areas of gender scholarship—the need to bring diversity into visibility from a theoretical discourse that disappears it. Work of this nature has become more visible in recent years: for example, Besnier's (2003) project on *fakaleiti* (transgenders) in Tongan society, Sullivan and Jackson's (2001) collection focused on identity and culture among gays and lesbians in Asian countries, and Leap and Boellstorff's (2004) edited collection on globalization and gay language.

Black queer studies is another area of important development in understanding the cultural complexity of gender transgressions in the discourse of gender refusal. Rusty Barrett (1999), for example, draws on Judith Butler's analysis of drag in his project on the speech of African American drag queens (AADQs). Barrett uses discourse analysis to demonstrate how AADQs use a "white woman style" and how they confront gender ideology by indexing their "polyphonous" identity as African Americans, gay men, and drag queens. Based on his interview study with black gay men in various parts of the United States, E. Patrick Johnson (2004) unfolds a rich description of a transgressive discourse of domesticity that "simultaneously celebrates black and gay culture as it critiques and resists the oppression found in both" (p. 274)." As a subfield, then, black queer studies theorizes and analyzes race and sexuality together. Elisa Glick (2003) sees the crucial task as "how to make legible not simply the bifurcation of race and sexuality but their interrelation, and second, how to theorize the emergence of gay and lesbian identity in relation to capitalism's increasing investment in producing and regulating desire" (p. 124).

As technology and access to it have grown, so too has the role of the Internet as a medium of communication for gender refusal and refusers. Issues of performativity are especially provocative in Internet communication because of the ostensible openness of the medium to creative identity construction, as Consalvo discusses in her chapter on gender and new media in this volume. Scholars have studied the representation of queer identities on Web sites and personal pages (Alexander, 2002) and the use of the electronic bulletin board to mobilize social movement participation (Nip, 2004). Several interesting studies detail the use of the Internet as a vehicle of communication for marginalized gender groups. Joyce Nip (2004) reports on The Queer Sisters, a women's group in Hong Kong, and John Erni (2003) provides an analysis of how the Internet is being used in many Asian countries both for queer contacts and for exploration of sexual politics.

CRITIQUE

The literatures on GLBTQ as a movement with associated discourses have broadened our understanding of the processes of gender refusal that were previously restricted to considerations such as gay lexicon and speech patterns. Queer studies and the more specific QL referenced in the theory section in this chapter bring into play the complexity of gender, sexuality, and identity. One of the limitations within the domain of study reviewed here is, like others, a limited engagement with broader cultural complexity. QL as articulated by Bucholtz and Hall (2004) conceptually addresses this issue by emphasizing the significance of specific sociocultural contexts. A second critique concerns the category of transgendered individuals and claims to the rights of the category of women. Belinda Sweeney (2004), in a critique of the international movement by transactivists to press for

access to women's organizations and the rights they represent, faults this type of activist for their interest in status quo constructions of gender that are oblique to the reality of women's oppression. "Trans-inclusion in women's events, organizations, and service provisions," Sweeney says, "runs counter to the interests of those for and by whom women-only spaces were established to protect" (p. 86). Finally, the very categories of interest in the literature on gender transgressions also raise concerns. David Valentine (2004), a participant in *GLQ*'s forum on sex and sexuality, expresses concern "that the recent tendency to claim, as empirical fact, that gender and sexuality are separate and separable experiences results in a substitution of an analytic distinction for actual lived experience" (p. 217) and focuses too heavily on Western identities.

◆ Conclusion

The literatures reviewed in this chapter all address resistance to gender normativity in its cultural context. Although distinctive in focus, studies of women's communicative resistance in different cultures, scholarship on third-wave expressions, and examinations of the discourses of gender refusers all point to dynamic processes through which language, identity, and cultural ideology mix in the contesting of "doing gender" and "doing difference." The voice of gender transgression is, indeed, polyphonic, and no one model neatly connects local practices far distant from one another. As scholars of gender and communication; of masculinities and femininities; and of the many expressions of lesbian, gay, bisexual, transgender, and queer identities, we need to resist both common threading and endless particularization. A decade ago, Sally McConnell-Ginet (1996) commended the new generation of linguists working on gender issues for their commitment to "look . . . beyond 'typical' women and men in a community to examine points where gender norms and expectations are being disrupted, resisted, and reshaped" (p. 792). That move is the one taken up in this chapter. Scholarship on disruption, resistance, and reshaping of gender normativity has come from several fields—communication, linguistics, and anthropology among them. Finding the literatures that deserve connection is often difficult, but we are well served by the various edited collections and by publications such as *Women & Language* where editor Anita Taylor has skillfully foregrounded diverse scholars working with diverse methodologies in a broad array of cultural settings.

As specific and local as resistance to gender normativity is, understanding resistance demands a principled view of its function in grounded, cultural circumstances. We are long past the quest for what women have in common the world over, but that should not dull our understanding that gender transgression in its many voices and multiple discourses ruptures the taken-for-granted gender order to create, in Butler's terms, "gender trouble" and the "undoing of gender."

◆ Notes

1. Sadiqi's article appears in a special issue of *Women & Language* called "Global Issues in Feminism: Challenges, Opportunities, Insights." Edited by Deborah Ballard-Reisch, the issue is one of few publications where one can find a sustained focus on women's discourse in cultural contexts around the world.

2. This article was part of a special issue on the theme of feminism and generation published in *Outskirts,* an Australian online journal.

3. Hogeland (2001) argues differently in proposing that generation is not the important characteristic of difference and that focusing on generation masks political issues of importance. She notes, for instance, that indicting the second wave for racism wipes out the contributions of many women of color during the 1970s.

◆ References

Alexander, J. (2002). Homo-pages and queer sites: Studying the construction and representation of queer identities on the World Wide Web. *International Journal of Sexuality & Gender Studies, 7*(2–3), 85–106.

Ballard-Reisch, D. (Ed.). (2003). Global issues in feminism: Challenges, opportunities, insights [Special issue]. *Women & Language, 26*(1).

Barrett, R. (1999). Indexing polyphonous identity in the speech of African American drag queens. In M. Bucholtz, A. C. Liang, & L. A. Sutton (Eds.), *Reinventing identities: The gendered self in discourse* (pp. 313–331). New York: Oxford University Press.

Bem, S. L. (1993). *The lenses of gender.* New Haven, CT: Yale University Press.

Besnier, N. (2003). Crossing genders, mixing languages: The linguistic construction of transgenderism in Tonga. In J. Holmes & M. Meyerhoff (Eds.), *The handbook of language and gender* (pp. 279–301). Malden, MA: Blackwell.

Bilaniuk, L. (2003). Gender, language attitudes, and language status in Ukraine. *Language in Society, 32,* 47–78.

Boston Women's Health Book Collective. (1971). *Our bodies, ourselves* (1st ed.). New York: Simon and Schuster.

Briggs, C. (1992). "Since I am a woman, I will chastise my relatives": Gender, reported speech, and the (re)production of social relations in Warao ritual wailing. *American Ethnologist, 19,* 337–361.

Bucholtz, M., & Hall, K. (2004). Theorizing identity in language and sexuality research. *Language in Society, 33,* 469–515.

Bulbeck, C. (2001). Feminism by any other name? Skirting the generation debate. *Outskirts—Feminisms Along the Edge, 8.* Retrieved March 18, 2005, from www.chloe.uwa.edu.au/outskirts/archive/volume8/bulbeck

Butler, J. (1999). *Gender trouble: Feminism and the subversion of identity* (10th anniversary ed.). New York: Routledge.

Butler, J. (2004). *Undoing gender.* New York: Routledge.

Cameron, D., & Kulick, D. (2003). *Language and sexuality.* Cambridge, UK: Cambridge University Press.

Chernela, J. M. (1997). The "ideal speech moment": Women and narrative performance in the Brazilian Amazon. *Feminist Studies, 23,* 73–96.

Chernela, J. M. (2003). Language ideology and women's speech: Talking community in the Northwest Amazon. *American Anthropologist, 105,* 794–806.

Chernela, J. M. (2004). The politics of language acquisition: Language learnings as social modeling in the Northwest Amazon. *Women & Language, 27*(1), 13–21.

Cohen, C. (1997). Punks, bulldaggers, and welfare queens: The radical potential of queer politics? *Gay and Lesbian Quarterly, 3,* 437–465.

Davis, K. (2002). Feminist body/politics as world traveler: Translating *Our Bodies, Ourselves. European Journal of Women's Studies, 9,* 223–247.

Davis, K. (in press). *The making of* Our Bodies, Ourselves: *How feminist knowledge travels across borders.* Durham, NC: Duke University Press.

Diaz, A. R. (2003). Postcolonial theory and the third wave agenda. *Women & Language, 26(1),* 10–17.

Drake, J. (1997). Third wave feminisms. *Feminist Studies, 23,* 97–108.

Eckert, P., & McConnell-Ginet, S. (1992). Think practically and look locally: Language and gender as community-based practice. *Annual Review of Anthropology, 21,* 461–490.

Eckert, P., & McConnell-Ginet, S. (1999). New generalizations and explanations in language and gender research. *Language in Society, 28,* 185–201.

Erni, J. N. (2003). Run queer Asia run. *Journal of Homosexuality, 45,* 381–384.

Fine, M., & Macpherson, P. (1994). Over dinner: Feminism and adolescent female bodies. In H. L. Radtke & H. J. Stam (Eds.), *Power/gender: Social relations in theory and practice* (pp. 219–246). London: Sage.

Fixmer, N., & Wood, J. T. (2005).The personal is *still* political: Difference, solidarity and embodied politics in third wave feminism. *Women's Studies in Communication, 28,* 235–257.

Furo, H. (1996). Linguistic conflict of Japanese women: Is that a request or an order? In N. Warner, J. Ahlers, L. Bilmes, M. Oliver, S. Wertheim, & M. Chen (Eds.), *Gender and belief systems: Proceedings of the Fourth Berkeley Women and Language Conference* (pp. 247–259). Berkeley: University of California Press.

Gal, S. (1995). Language, gender, and power: An anthropological review. In K. Hall & M. Bucholtz (Eds.), *Gender articulated: Language and the socially constructed self* (pp. 169–182). New York: Oxford University Press.

Gillis, S., Howie, G., & Munford, R. (Eds.). (2004). *Third wave feminism: A critical exploration.* New York: Palgrave Macmillan.

Glick, E. (2003). Introduction: Defining queer ethnicities. *GLQ, 10,* 127–137.

Hall, K. (2003). Exceptional speakers: Contested and problematized gender identities. In J. Holmes & M. Meyerhoff (Eds.), *The handbook of language and gender* (pp. 353–380). Malden, MA: Blackwell.

Harris, A. (2001). Not waving or drowning: Young women, feminism, and the limits of the next wave. *Outskirts—Feminisms Along the Edge, 8.* Retrieved March 18, 2005, from www.chloe.edu.au/outskirts/archive/VOL8/harris

Hegde, R. S. (1998). A view from elsewhere: Locating difference and the politics of representation from a transnational feminist perspective. *Communication Theory, 8,* 271–297.

Hogeland, L. M. (2001). Against generational thinking, or some things that "Third Wave" feminism isn't. *Women's Studies in Communication, 24,* 107–121.

Jacobs, G. (1996). Lesbian and gay male language use: A critical review of the literature. *American Speech, 71,* 49–71.

Johnson, E. P. (2004). Mother knows best: Black gay vernacular and transgressive domestic space. In W. Leap & T. Boellstorff (Eds.). *Speaking in queer tongues: Globalization and gay language* (pp. 251–278). Urbana: University of Illinois Press.

Kulick, D. (2000). Gay and lesbian language. *Annual Review of Anthropology, 29,* 243–285.

Kuntjara, E. (2005). Gender and assertiveness: Bargaining in the traditional market in East Java. *Women & Language, 28*(1), 54–61.

Leap, W. (Ed.). (1995). *Beyond the lavender lexicon.* Amsterdam: Gordon & Breach.

Leap, W., & Boellstorff, T. (Eds.). (2004). *Speaking in queer tongues: Globalization and gay language.* Urbana: University of Illinois Press.

Livia, A., & Hall, K. (Eds.). (1997). *Queerly phrased: Language, gender and sexuality.* New York: Oxford University Press.

Lotz, A. D. (2003). Communicating third-wave feminism and new social movements: Challenges for the next century of feminist endeavor. *Women & Language, 26(1),* 2–9.

Matsumoto, Y. (1996). Does less feminine speech in Japanese mean less femininity? In N. Warner, J. Ahlers, L. Bilmes, M. Oliver, S. Wertheim, & M. Chen (Eds.), *Gender and belief systems: Proceedings of the Fourth Berkeley Women and Language Conference* (pp. 455–467). Berkeley: University of California Press.

McConnell-Ginet, S. (1996). *Language, gender and society:* Personal reflections on its ancestry and offspring. In N. Warner, J. Ahlers, L. Bilmes, M. Oliver, S. Wertheim, & M. Chen (Eds.), *Gender and belief systems: Proceedings of the Fourth Berkeley Women and Language Conference* (pp. 789–795). Berkeley: University of California Press.

Medicine, B. (1987). The role of American Indian women in cultural continuity and transition. In J. Penfield (Ed.), *Women and language in transition* (pp. 159–166). Albany: State University of New York Press.

Miller, L. (2004). Those naughty teenage girls: Japanese Kogals, slang and media assessments. *Journal of Linguistic Anthropology, 14,* 225–247.

Newitz, A. (n.d.). *Riot Grrrls.* Retrieved April 16, 2005, from www.techsploitation.com/Socrates/riot.grrls.html

Nip, J. Y. M. (2004). The Queer Sisters and its electronic bulletin board: A study of the internet for social movement mobilization. *Information, Communication & Society, 7,* 23–49.

Okamoto, S. (1995). "Tasteless" Japanese: Less "feminine" speech among young Japanese women. In K. Hall & M. Bucholtz (Eds.), *Gender articulated: Language and the socially constructed self* (pp. 297–325). New York: Oxford University Press.

Okamoto, S. (1996). Representations of diverse female speech styles in Japanese popular culture. In N. Warner, J. Ahlers, L. Bilmes, M. Oliver, S. Wertheim, & M. Chen (Eds.), *Gender and belief systems: Proceedings of the Fourth Berkeley Women and Language Conference* (pp. 575–587). Berkeley: University of California Press.

Okamoto, S., & Sato, S. (1992). Less feminine speech among young Japanese females. In K. Hall, M. Bucholtz, & B. Moonwomon (Eds.), *Locating power: Proceedings of the Second Berkeley Women and Language Conference* (pp. 478–488). Berkeley, CA: Berkeley Women and Language Group.

Okamoto, S., & Shibamoto-Smith, J. S. (Eds.). (2004). *Japanese language, gender, and ideology.* New York: Oxford University Press.

Paechter, C. (2003a). Learning masculinities and femininities: Power/knowledge and legitimate peripheral participation. *Women's Studies International Forum, 26,* 541–552.

Paechter, C. (2003b). Masculinities and femininities as communities of practice. *Women's Studies International Forum, 26,* 69–77.

Reynolds, K. A. (1998). Female speakers of Japanese in transition. In J. Coates (Ed.), *Language and gender: A reader* (pp. 299–308). Oxford, UK: Blackwell.

Riot grrrl. (n.d.). Retrieved February 18, 2005, from http://en.wikipedia.org/wiki/Riot_grrl

Sadiqi, F. (2003). Women and linguistic space in Morocco. *Women & Language, 26(1),* 35–43.

Shugart, H. A. (2001). Isn't it ironic? The intersection of third-wave feminism and

Generation X. *Women's Studies in Communication, 24,* 131–168.

Shugart, H. A., Waggoner, C. E., & Hallstein, D. L. O. (2001). Mediating third-wave feminism: Appropriation as postmodern media practice. *Critical Studies in Media Communication, 18,* 194–210.

Smith, J. S. (1992). Women in charge: Politeness and directives in the speech of Japanese women. *Language in Society, 21,* 59–82.

Smyth, R., Jacobs, G., & Rogers, H. (2003). Male voices and perceived sexual orientation: An experimental and theoretical approach. *Language in Society, 32,* 329–350.

Spivak, G. (1996). Feminism and critical theory. In D. Landry & G. MacLean (Eds.), *The Spivak reader: Selected works of Gayatri Chakravorty Spivak* (pp. 53–74). New York: Routledge. (Original work published 1985)

Sullivan, G., & Jackson, P. A. (Eds.). (2001). *Gay and lesbian Asia: Culture, identity, community.* New York: Haworth Press.

Sweeney, B. (2004). Trans-ending women's rights: The politics of trans-inclusion in the age of gender. *Women's Studies International Forum, 27,* 75–88.

Trechter, S. (1995). Categorical gender myths in Native America: Gender deictics in Lakhota. *Applied Linguistics, 6,* 5–22.

Trechter, S. (1996). The intersection of grammar, metalinguistic knowledge and ideology in Lakota gendered speech. In N. Warner, J. Ahlers, L. Bilmes, M. Oliver, S. Wertheim, & M. Chen (Eds.), *Gender and belief systems: Proceedings of the Fourth Berkeley Women and Language Conference* (pp. 743–754). Berkeley: University of California Press.

Valentine, D. (2004). The categories themselves. *GLQ, 10,* 215–220.

Wenger, E. (1998). *Communities of practice.* New York: Cambridge University Press.

West, C., & Fenstermaker, S. (1995). Doing difference. *Gender & Society, 9,* 8–37.

West, C., & Zimmerman, D. (1987). Doing gender. *Gender & Society, 1,* 125–151.

Williams, M. (1989). Ladies on the line: Punjabi cannery workers in central California. In Asian Women United of California (Ed.), *Making waves: An anthology of writings by and about Asian American women* (pp. 148–159). Boston: Beacon Press.

Wolf, N. (1993). *Fire with fire.* New York: Random House.

23

GLOBALIZING GENDER STUDIES IN COMMUNICATION

◆ Radha S. Hegde

> *The point of feminist inquiry—and for me its continuing appeal—has always been in its refusal to accommodate the status quo.*
>
> Joan Scott (1999, p. xii)

If feminism has taught us anything, it is the importance of scholarship that is driven by a vision of democratic transformation—a vision that should serve as impetus for our intellectual endeavors at this global juncture. The emergent issues and complex repercussions of the globalizing process require sustained attention to both the layered construction of context in our scholarship and the logics that constitute the gendered subject of our inquiry. In this essay, I reflect on the challenges of extending the global reach and scope of communication scholarship on gender and sexuality.

To think globally about globalization requires a critical engagement with its complex contradictions and also with the disciplinary structures that frame our mappings of the world. The serious, gendered consequences of globality require intervention and scholarly attention. How and why do we refine and direct a feminist analytical gaze to engage with the realities and consequences of colliding global processes?

Producing feminist knowledge about the global order is not just about supplementing new information. It is also about recasting the geographies of knowledge and radically revising the ways in which we formulate our questions. To do this we need to ask questions about the unquestioned and often unquestionable premises on which the seemingly transparent logics of globalization rest. As Hardt and Negri (2000) argue, the forces of globalization are neither univocal nor neutral, and the political task is to reorganize and redirect these multiple processes to new ends. A commitment to democratic ends and a refusal to perpetuate the status quo provide cogency of purpose for feminist scholarship.

Engaging with the implications of the global swell requires first of all that we resist insular conceptualization of issues and pay attention to dominant discursive structures within which we conceptualize our research terrain. As problems in a global world get progressively multilayered, we in the academy, by extension, cannot force our analyses into disciplinary straitjackets. This ability to connect our research initiatives to macrostructures sharpens methodological choices and shapes the significance of our contributions. These are trying times to do global feminist work because at every turn and level there is either a direct or indirect dismissal of gender issues. For example, despite the fact that reality as experienced on the ground is clearly both gendered and racialized, the subject of gender is visibly absent in most discussions of globalization (e.g., Bergeron 2001; Freeman, 2001; Gibson-Graham, 1996). Under the global sway of neoliberalism, with its celebration of consumerism and privatization, social issues are recoded as private challenges, and this compromises the very idea of political agency. As Comaroff and Comaroff (2000) write, "It is not just that the personal is political. The personal is the only politics there is, the only politics with a tangible referent or emotional valence" (p. 305). To feminists, this twist has a palpable irony. Media's celebration of so-called

postfeminist freedoms displaces feminism, making it seem "decisively aged and redundant" (McRobbie, 2004). As the strains of neoliberalism and postfeminism reverberate globally, feminism experiences another international wrenching.

Globalization, militarization, and the rise of new patriarchal formations pose complex challenges for women's democratic futures. Women's issues, particularly from the global South, are being visibly drafted into the public sphere in troubling ways by varying constituencies—local, national, and global. In a 2001 radio address, Laura Bush gathered support to "kick off a worldwide effort to focus on the brutality against women." She appealed "to our common humanity" and reminded her listeners that "all of us have an obligation to speak out" against the Taliban's brutality against Afghan women. Feminists need to pause and pay critical attention to the renewed entrance of the benevolent gaze of the West as well as to the retelling of the liberation myth that has been triggered by current geopolitical events. In actuality, this form of hypervisible acknowledgment of the victim status of women distracts attention from the everyday struggles of third world women. The dichotomous classification of cultures in simple, clashing binaries restages in stark terms the static, stereotypical coding of difference. As Scott (2002) writes, "Lines are being drawn, categories produced, to give schematic coherence to the messy entanglements of local, national, regional and international politics" (p. 5). The deployment of these racial and gendered categories of difference have serious consequences for knowledge production in the academy. For feminists, the recent turn of events has served as a wake-up call to respond to global imperatives. The challenges are grounded in thinking simultaneously about intellectual work and its relationship to building a truly democratic transnational feminism.

Across the social sciences, the intellectual momentum to address issues of globalization is closely accompanied by disciplinary boundary debates and dilemmas. Scholars who are driven by the study of emergent global questions gravitate intellectually to others across disciplinary lines who share a common political horizon and a scholarly outlook that is critical of "departmental business-as-usual" (see Rosaldo, 2001), providing productive disruptions to disciplines that otherwise tend to be sedentary. It is true that feminist scholarship has traditionally entertained an ambiguous affiliation to disciplines since the political project itself provided a provocative alternative space from which feminist scholars could advance a radical critique of dominant epistemological structures. The current world situation has posed an opening to reimagine feminist theory and praxis against the shifting configurations of globalization.

Disciplinary locations both limit and influence the nature of feminist investigation, especially due to the rampant protectionism practiced by disciplines (Appadurai, 1996). To add to this policing, the historical paths of particular intellectual fields also shape the formations through which international issues are introduced (see Calhoun, 2001). In the field of communication, feminist scholars who wish to pursue global questions have to critically engage with canonical intellectual structures and the forms of knowledge that have been historically valorized. In this chapter, I discuss why this is a necessary step as global feminist scholarship develops its theoretical edge and incisive methodological bases to understand, represent, and analyze the multiple types and levels of global intersections.

Our work as feminist scholars is intricately tied up with that of other cultural workers striving for the same democratic ends. Activist work, particularly work done by feminist NGOs in the third world at the grassroots level, has contributed substantially to a global awareness and informational base about women's exploitation. This, in turn, has significantly influenced both academic inquiry on transnational issues and

the project to deconstruct the assumptions that drive dominant versions of academic feminism in the West. How do we represent and integrate this decolonizing move into our theoretical perspectives? Wrestling with the provocative question raised by Spivak (1988), "What is the constituency of an international feminism?"(p. 135), is an extremely important reminder as we think through the relation between feminist inquiry and global politics. From our various academic locations, we need to pay close attention to how feminism is articulated both in its global and local inflections within the conceptualization and circulation of our research. Internationalizing is not merely the comparative assemblage of difference or the hierarchical ordering of gendered oppression from various parts of the world. The goal is ultimately about building an innovative feminist intellectual space that is responsive to global and local forces and that, at the same time, does not fetishize the transnational over the national and the popular over the everyday.

This chapter deals with feminist engagement with gender in global contexts and examines how the shape of this practice is influenced by intellectual boundaries within disciplines. In the context of corporatized demands for utility-based education, feminist research, particularly on the global South, is beset with obstacles. Scholarship concerning third world cultures and gender is embedded in a fraught colonial and Orientalist history which one must learn to negotiate from within and across disciplines. What are the limits and opportunities posed by disciplinary affiliations and boundaries for feminist scholarship and its political project? I outline how the formation of intellectual spaces in the academy, and more specifically within departments of communication and media studies, has influenced feminist representation and circulation of research on transnational gender issues. To do this, I consider three topics: (a) the larger terrain of feminism and its transnational transformations, (b) the influence of the model of area studies on communication studies, and (c) the space for transnational feminist inquiry within cultural studies in communication. I conclude by outlining how and why global feminist perspectives can revitalize the theoretical and methodological reach of communication research and contribute to alternative understandings of globalization.

◆ Feminism and Global Transformations

Theorizing the transnational collision of cultural, economic, and political forces is a central concern of feminist thought today. Feminist scholars concur that our scholarship must go beyond facile cultural relativism to provide strategic and differentiated understanding of the ways in which gendered categories are being calibrated in the current global context (Shohat, 1998, 2001; Young, 2003). They agree that new global forms of cultural production, consumption and sites of oppression need interdisciplinary investigation and attention (Basu, Grewal, Kaplan, & Malkki, 2001). The reconfigured global landscape has led to the diversification of the feminist project in the academy and hence to a renewed problematization of what constitutes the subject of feminism. The driving question is, How do we complicate the analytical understanding of the constitution and mobilization of gender inequality and its impact on the experiential realities of women's lives in a global context?

SHIFTING REGISTERS OF FEMINISM

Collective academic memory casts early academic feminism as "a romance in which the impulse of social activism, committed

pedagogy and scholarly aspiration were integrated by the intense energy of a women-centered consciousness that was both personal and experienced as collective" (Moglen, 1997, p. 182). The appeal of feminist organizing around a singular identity was soon disrupted with resistance from the margins, but the passion for social change still singularly defines the community of feminist scholars. For scholars who take their feminist politics seriously, there is always a persistent questioning of what distinguishes feminist research and makes it stand apart from other types of inquiry. As Dow and Condit (2005) assert, the "moniker of feminist" is reserved for research that is oriented toward the achievement of gender justice (p. 449). The very concept of gender justice and equity is, however, being subject to transnational feminist critique, as critical feminist scholars forge an alternative internationalism prompted by a heightened level of intellectual self-consciousness.

The synchrony of the theoretical-cum-political project of feminism has enabled scholars to address issues of social justice and concurrently to produce a stringent critique of the practices of knowledge production. As de Lauretis (1987) notes, no boundary separates or insulates feminism from other social practices or makes it impervious to the institutions of civil society. The mapping of feminism as originating from multiple points of departure served both to explode the myth of the unified category of woman and to pave the way for more nuanced, historicized readings of the particularities of women's locations. We are at a stage when feminist engagement must transcend mere acknowledgement of difference but include, as Friedman (1998) notes, "a commitment to difference as a (if not the) major explanatory paradigm mediating all analyses of gender" (p. 69). The feminist challenge is to find innovative, intellectual approaches by which to realize this integrative paradigmatic view in our research pursuits.

The emphasis on pluralism and multivocality resulted in extending the reach of feminist inquiry not only to pay attention to issues of race but also to take seriously the impact of colonialism and imperialism on gender (Hegde, 1998; Shome & Hegde, 2002a, 2002b). This changing focus of feminist scholarship has been precipitated by the global scenario and also in part by the changing demographics of the academy. The increasing presence of diasporic, third world scholars in the West with very different personal and political relationships to geographical locations in the global South has contributed to the emergence of postcolonial research directions in the field of communication. In light of the new questions that are being crafted and examined, it is inevitable that canonical frameworks are being questioned. Feminist scholars recognize that anticolonial struggles and gender issues of the global South cannot be ignored and are in fact critical to the overall advancement of feminist theorizing and understanding of gender subordination and resistance (see Bhavnani, 2001). In a globalized world, Friedman (1998) argues, the register with which we need to think about feminism has shifted from the temporal to the spatial:

A locational approach to feminism incorporates diverse formations because its positional analysis requires a kind of geopolitical literacy built out of a recognition of how different times and places produce different and changing gender systems as these intersect with other different and changing societal stratifications and movements for social justice. (p. 5)

The new global configurations of power that produce gendered absences, erasures, and silences demand strategic forms of theorizing in order to explain gendered encounters with modernity and its global variants. Racialized and gendered regimes of the nation combine with the mobility of transnational structures of capitalism to re-narrate patriarchal power. In the complex meeting ground of these intersecting forces, it is the gendered subaltern body that slips through the unaccounted and undocumented spaces between the local and the global or the national and the transnational. In response to the ways in which gender tends to be appropriated or redefined in the context of globalization, feminist scholars are arguing for a more inclusive, relational, and contextual understanding of gender in the context of race, class, sexuality, national boundaries, and shifting patterns of power (see Kaplan & Grewal, 2002; Shohat, 2001).

These global crossroads present stumbling blocks as well as opportunities to pursue interdisciplinary and oppositional epistemological practices. Ideally, the subject of feminist inquiry is driven by a commitment to social justice and not by the mandates of what constitutes the naturalized object of disciplinary interest. Realistically, reconciling academic expectations and political conviction is complicated and often results in disillusionment with traditional disciplinary divisions and academic structures. Given the territorialism of disciplines, Nelson and Gaonkar (1996) remark that the advice to intellectuals to pursue what matters whatever the consequences is far from harmless. Doing revisionary work requires disciplinary and institutional maneuvers on the part of scholars who study transnational questions of gender, especially when they are situated outside of departments or programs of women's studies. In order to address the mosaic of issues that constitute the crisis of gender in globality, an incisive feminism has to bridge the national/transnational divide on multiple levels.

Consider some examples of global issues that envelope women's lives—sex trafficking, the global trail of domestic workers, violence against women in all its varied forms, the gendered backlash of immigration policies worldwide, and the gendered implications of new forms of empire. Clearly, the manipulation of the presence and absence of the female body by the collision of discourses and regimes of power requires both theoretical and methodological breadth in order to bring into focus what de Lauretis (1987) calls "the space-off," or the space to be inferred from the frame. Mobilizing around these transnational issues has added political momentum to feminist scholarship and enabled more intellectual- and praxis-oriented alliances between first and third world locations. Organizing around a global sisterhood platform is becoming less meaningful in the contemporary context: neither gender nor feminism is singular or homogeneous. Gender struggles are increasingly located and made visible in conjunction with other types of oppression. The World Social Forum (WSF) held in Mumbai, India in 2004 provides a striking example of the new conditions for feminist internationalism. This mobilization for alternative democratic futures was shaped by the oppositional energies of various social justice movements committed to resist the consequences of neoliberal globalization. The Mumbai Forum is hailed as a landmark because record numbers of women participated and drew worldwide attention to the urgent and continuing issues of violence (see Sen & Saini, 2005; Vargas 2003). It is the convergence of multiple social issues and the dramatic nature of their interrelationship that sets the stage for a changing international feminist agenda.

THE GLOBAL SUBJECT OF FEMINIST INQUIRY

How does academic feminism reflect the global and local interweaving that is taking place in the articulation of the feminist movement? How does the subject of feminist academic inquiry come into focus against the backdrop of globality? These questions motivate scholars to redefine the scope of feminist scholarship and seek theoretical frameworks and vocabularies both within and across disciplinary boundaries. Cross-national issues have forced academic feminist thinking to go beyond culturalist explanations and strive to provide more strategic accounts of transnational formations of power as they suppress, control, and exclude women's participation in the economic and social spheres. We need to reread the social and economic terrain with the intent of recovering those evicted from the centers of globality. As Sassen (1999) writes, devalorized components of the economy are "articulated with sectors considered central but are articulated in ways that present them as marginal, backward, unnecessary" (p. 356). The feminist subject of transnationality offers a strategic site for rendering more dynamic conceptualizations of gender and globalization.

Let me briefly examine the situation of domestic violence when it is compounded by the global mobility of capital and first/third world split—the backdrop against which feminist theorizing is being reimagined. I was asked a few years ago by a lawyer to provide testimony to immigration authorities for a young woman who was severely abused by her husband, a software engineer recruited from India to work in a major U.S. corporation. I was requested to write a letter to support a petition filed by the woman to the U.S. Immigration and Naturalization Service for a visa extension allowing her to stay in the country and to work. The attorney suggested that I explain why the United States is a much better place for a woman *in her situation*, as the social system in India would not allow her the *freedom* or ability to flourish in any way. As a feminist, I resented the logic in this mission and of course the structured West/rest argument which, the lawyer told me, was the only way that this woman could be granted an extension to stay in the country and negotiate child visitation rights. This scenario revealed an interesting twist on Spivak's (1990) notion of *strategic essentialism*:

essentialize the barbarism of the country left behind to differentiate it adequately from the civilized, progressive structures of the United States. The highly male-dominated information technology world plays right into the racialized, gendered hierarchies coded into the immigration policies of the United States. If a highly skilled worker on what is known as an H-1 visa divorces a spouse, she is immediately deportable. A gender and class bias is built into the structures of immigration through laws that favor productive contributors to the economy and give low (if any) priority to the wives of the largely male, skilled foreign worker cohort.

I cite this case to demonstrate what the coming together, the collision, of categories entails in terms of the study of gender and the complexities of women's lives and identities. This is a case where citizenship, nation, ethnicity, class, political economy, and the law are all imbricated—where categories clash, logics are defined and identities are caught within large discourses of self, other, and nation. This case also demonstrates that issues such as domestic violence in the transnational realm require analytical approaches that disrupt traditional models that focus on the dysfunctional immigrant family, patriarchal home, or individual subject as units of analysis. There is nothing essentially Indian about spousal abuse, nor is there a badge of victimhood that distinguishes Indian women. Yet, in the retelling of cultural narratives in this example, a coherence is secured though the deployment of rigid binaries. The case also demonstrates how the categories of private and public are disrupted in this borderless economy. As Bhattacharjee (1997) argues, if we attend to the global parameters of immigrant women's experiences, "there are no unambiguous spaces to be labeled 'public' or 'private'" (p. 323). A similar dichotomous bind secures Orientalist images such as the reductive interpretation of veiling as the ultimate marker of Islamic women's subordination (see Abu-Lughod

2002). Culturalist explanations often reinforce the colonial prototype of the third world woman as a victim in need of saving (see Hegde, 1999; Khan, 2001).

The illustrations described above demonstrate the need for locally nuanced, transnationally situated, relational understandings of gender politics. The situations in which these illustrations occur have to be located against the intricate web of economic, social, and political forces, both contemporary and historical, against which these practices gain meaning and significance. Refusing this analytic move is to perpetuate the idea of a third world woman as always brought into focus in contradiction to the West and its modernity—a subject denied contemporaneity with the West (Ong, 1988; Shih, 2005). Although subject to extensive critique, the image of the third world woman as passive victim continues to persist and demands further examination of its formation. Ultimately, feminist focus on the global rearticulations of patriarchy and the contradictory positioning of women vis-à-vis modernity should be able to advance, as Lowe and Lloyd (1997) write, a "new conception of the political subject" (p. 19).

As many critical scholars have pointed out, the challenge for feminism today is not only to globalize its reach but to be able to read globalization oppositionally or from below. This foregrounding becomes especially important in accounting for the new formations of invisibility where, as Spivak (2002) states, the subaltern is both made to unspeak herself and converted into the production of data. Ultimately, it is the commitment to the centrality of gender that sustains the momentum of feminist inquiry. Feminist scholars have made provocative arguments and continue to offer pragmatic suggestions about how to rethink the intellectual pursuit without compromising feminist politics. Sangari and Vaid (1990) make a compelling argument that feminist historiography is about rethinking historiography as a whole:

Such a historiography acknowledges that each aspect of reality is gendered and it is thus involved in questioning all that we think we know in a sustained examination of analytical and epistemological apparatus and in dismantling of the ideological presupposition of so-called gender neutral methodologies. (p. 2)

This is a choice, they write persuasively, offered not in a tokenist spirit but as one open to all historians. This transformative choice is, as Radhakrishnan (1996) notes, a form of historical and political inevitability that cannot but be made. In a more recent formulation, Sangari and Chakravarti (2001) write that all historical shifts in social formation and modes of production have to be reexamined against changes in patriarchal structures (p. iv)—a point to be taken seriously in the landscape of global transformations.

To summarize, the dynamics of globalization have created new forms of control and exacerbated older forms of exploitation with regard to women. With the shifting axes of power, the very fabric of everyday life has been redefined, throwing static views of culture, communication, and identity into crisis. To broaden the theoretical scope of feminist thought, we need to problematize cultural practices and performative routines that write and overwrite the female body in multiple sites across the globe. As feminists, the goal is to explain and expose the workings of a complex network of power that colonizes women's lives worldwide. The enterprise of globalizing the reach of feminist inquiry is complicated by disciplinary locations and equally by the relational politics of the first and third world dynamic in terms of the production, circulation, and reception of knowledge (see John, 1996; Narayan, 1997). It is through interdisciplinary exchange that global feminist scholarship can sustain itself and contribute significantly to the transformation of knowledge production. In the next section, I turn to the field of communication and address the genealogy of spaces made available for studying the international and the impact of the field's history on feminist research on global issues.

◆ The Globe, Gender, and Communication Studies

How does the world beyond the nation enter the academy and its disciplinary quarters? This is a complex, institutional narrative with significant epistemological and curricular overtones that overflow into individual, intellectual trajectories.

ENCLAVES OF INTERNATIONAL STUDY

If one looks at the development of the communication discipline, as with most other social sciences, the spaces to consider world regions have been few (see Lee, 1995; Vitalis, 2001). The communication discipline in its infancy naturalized the domain of public reason and dialogue, straight from the fountainhead of Greek rhetorical tradition. In spite of its humanist base and predisposition to the study of culture, there has been considerable pressure, especially in the late 1950s and 1960s, to gain status and legitimacy as a social science. Communication, particularly mass communication, evolved largely into social science influenced by behaviorist psychology favoring experimental methodologies and quantitative analysis. Within this evolution was also a clear separation of the domestic and the international, complete with a fundamental assumption about the autonomous, masculinist agent and an undisputed emphasis on a homogeneous nationalism. My goal is to demonstrate how the study of race and gender in the non-West have been situated in the discipline and how this positioning is now being challenged in light of global conditions.

Classical Orientalist scholarship and its representation of the non-Western world helped justify the colonial enterprise and its civilizing mission. As Said (1979) argued, "Orientalism is more particularly valuable as a sign of European-Atlantic power over the Orient than it is as a veridic discourse about the Orient" (p. 6). This early scholarship and its later transformations via area studies have left an enduring epistemological legacy across the social sciences, such as the Orientalist images of racial and gendered bodies, the colonial hierarchy of cultures, and the failure to recognize the violence of colonialism in the third world. The logic of area studies that developed during the Cold War years was articulated to provide policy recommendations and support the work of the U.S. government. Through language training and fieldwork, social science disciplines provided pragmatic and instrumental knowledge about world regions (see Burton, Ibryamova, Khanna, Mazurana, & Mendoza, 2002). This orientation, together with its associated assumption of liberal modernization, has played an important role in the organizational structure of cross-cultural knowledge. Secluding geographical areas of study carried over to disciplines like communication, a field conceptualized in post-World War II years (at least in its avatar as social science). The domains of intercultural and international communication rose as the area enclaves within communication, and their canonical modes of inquiry are now being put to the test.

In a detailed critique, Rafael (1994) makes the point that area studies are positioned as integral, yet subordinate, to the epistemological authority of the disciplines. This model institutionalized the separation of world regions from disciplinary boundaries and kept the unquestioned centrality of national interest as the organizing principle. The consequences have been far-reaching:

> For within the interdisciplinary optic of the liberal notion of area studies, the area and presumably its populations remained at a safe remove, managed by the operations of the social sciences into stages of comparable development,

cultural groupings of discrete ethnolinguistic realms. (p. 97)

Hall's 1947 report on wartime academic developments states that area instruction was devised to train people quickly to do specific and limited jobs and was of necessity largely makeshift (see also Wallerstein, 1997). Simpson (1994) chronicles the influence of government programs on the early development of communication research in the 1940s and 1950s: "In truth, the primary object of U.S. psychological operations during this period was to frustrate the ambitions of radical movements in resource-rich developing countries" (p. 7). Within intercultural communication research, the instrumental orientation contributed to essentialized portraits of nationality groups, static representations of culture, and an overall gender blindness.

Today the demand for skills to survive in multicultural environments has become a justification for internationalization of academic initiatives (Holzner, 2002). Instrumentalist knowledge about managing cultural differences circulates in a social context where the value of a subject of study is directly related to its market demand (Rutherford, 2005). Over time this management of international consensus translated into the management of difference rhetoric spurred by apolitical versions of corporate multiculturalism. These developments are all centered on the assumption that culture is insular and contained within geographical boundaries. In this globe-trotting vision, there is no mention made of the violence of colonialism, patriarchy, racism, whiteness, or for that matter, history (see Collier, Hegde, Lee, Nakayama, & Yep, 2002; Nakayama & Martin, 1999).

IMPACTS ON FEMINIST KNOWLEDGE

The significant issue here is how this academic itinerary of the area studies model and its epistemological consequences for communication have in turn impacted the production of feminist knowledge. In a field that has been so fiercely instrumental from its inception, the incorporation of feminist perspectives—particularly global, postcolonial ones—has been slow (see Carillo Rowe, 2000). If we wish to promote what Spivak (1993) characterizes as a transnational literacy about global feminism and not a facile touristic view of cross-cultural difference, then our mode of engagement should begin with the fact that gender and globalization are ineluctably political processes. Feminist scholars have offered trenchant critiques of the exclusion of gender in the research on development and communication, with its strong emphasis on theories of modernization (see Bhavnani, Foran, & Kurian, 2003; Steeves, 1993; Valdivia, 1996). Promoting the value of Westernization, this line of inquiry implicitly endorsed concepts of the intrinsic backwardness of third world societies and of women ensconced in a state of antiquity waiting to be saved from unmentionable third world contagions. Feminism gets equated with Western women, thereby infantilizing the gendered subaltern from the third world and rendering her, as postcolonial feminists have theorized, both speechless and objectified.

To study globalization through a feminist optics is to place subaltern lives at the center in order to examine and theorize power and inequalities. The feminist goal is, after all, to make visible the multiple ways in which the female body disappears within the overarching influence of universalizing discourse. Neither the autonomous subject of Western liberalism nor the pastiche personality of postmodernism begins to address the realities faced by third world women (see Hegde, 1999). Pursuing area-specific feminist scholarship often requires a justification of its disciplinary fit and relevance. In a disciplinary context where sound-bite information about cultures predominates in reserved curricular spaces, the process of addressing the politics of subalternity is a fraught process, particularly in terms of seeking disciplinary validity.

Recovering silenced voices registered only as numbers or statistics is often a very personal quest for feminist scholars. Participating in global feminist work motivates researchers to engage in projects that seek to restore dignity and voice to the overlooked female body. A burgeoning of critical research on questions of race, nation, and gender has raised global antennas. Ethnographic work on diasporic groups, transcultural communities, and global media flows utilizing interdisciplinary frameworks are also is making a visible impact on the theoretical contours of the discipline. No longer concentrated within one domain, this increasingly interdisciplinary critical research is appearing with a commitment to issues rather than to disciplinary divisions. Scholarship, particularly over the last decade, has problematized the notion of disciplinary enclaves set aside for the study of global regions formed in a dated colonial mode of knowledge production.

Rafael (1994), speculating on how an immigrant imaginary would complicate the integrationist logic behind the cultures of area studies, writes:

> For indeed, the category of the immigrant—in transit, caught between nation-states, unsettled and potentially uncanny—gives one pause, forcing one to ask about the possibility of a scholarship that is neither colonial nor liberal nor indigenous, yet constantly enmeshed in all these states. (p. 107)

Feminist scholarship on third world areas is similarly complicated by globalization and productively unsettled by an emerging nomadic sensibility permeating the academy.

TRANSNATIONAL FEMINISM AND CULTURAL STUDIES

A renewed awareness of an intertwined global history has become very apparent in the post-September-11th environment when local and remote experiences have been connected in personally and politically explosive ways. The assertions of American exceptionalism have rearticulated a moral calculus demarcating the incommensurablity of the West and its Others. It is within this space that we see a renewal of essentialist discourses and representational logics in the portrayal of race, gender, and culture. This in turn has led scholars within cultural studies to engage with the production of the civilized subject of the West and with how this very construction is predicated on the quarantining of the racial and sexual other (see Puar & Rai, 2002).

The primary concern for political engagement is what brings feminism and cultural studies together or, in more material terms, what makes global feminist scholars in communication gravitate towards cultural studies. According to Hall (1992), for cultural studies, the intervention of feminism was "specific and decisive," as it reorganized the field in concrete ways (p. 282). The relationship between feminism and cultural studies has a history of difficult and productive moments (see Franklin, Lury, & Stacey, 1996). But today both intellectual projects find themselves at a global moment, confronted by new types of questions that need innovative analytical turns. In his 1996 interview, Hall repeatedly emphasizes the need for cultural studies to be open-ended, to be reinvented by new international influences. In addition, both projects overlap in the engagement with the problematics of Western modernity and the politics of knowledge formation. Hall's articulation of cultural studies as a diasporic narrative redirects attention to the historical structures of colonialism and the impact of the West on the politics of race (see Morley & Chen, 1996). Gendering this historical narrative in multiple local domains constitutes the current transnational feminist preoccupation.

Presenting these connections and points of overlap between cultural studies and feminism is not to overstate the closed boundaries of either. The appeal of both to progressive scholars is the fluidity of the two fields and their hybridic ability to absorb, transform, and recharge their political critique. Regarding the internationalist spirit of cultural studies, Chen (1998) writes that although the specificities of oppression vary, gender, sexuality, race, ethnicity, and class have been coordinating categories across geographical, national, and regional boundaries. Dominant versions of academic feminism grounded in assumptions of whiteness and liberal individualism have been slow in integrating global perspectives but are now beginning to emphasize both the importance and need to do so (see Gedalof, 1999). It is clear that feminism and cultural studies can mutually complicate or "interrupt" each other, to echo Spivak's famous words (1990, p. 44). Both share an oppositional view of knowledge and a commitment to what Grossberg (1997) calls "politicizing theory and theorizing politics" (p. 4).

To scholars who engage in feminist scholarship on third world issues, institutional locations play a significant role in how their research circulates and is received. When situated in disciplines like communication where the sites to pursue international questions have traditionally been limited (as discussed earlier), the "conjunctural" quality of cultural studies is intellectually seductive. Pedagogical issues also play into this scenario. According to Rooney (1996), women's studies has an enormous advantage over cultural studies in that its students are a politically conscious constituency before they enter the field of women's studies. This connection to so-called real-world politics serves as a reminder that the field is not ideologically neutral or merely disciplinary.

This is a serious issue when discussing topics related to oppression, women, and the third world in classes where one does not have a politically engaged student body. There is a sense of experiential and political disconnect that makes the feminist project outside of women's studies very vulnerable to what Rooney (1996) calls political neutralization. For many feminist scholars in communication, there is a disjuncture between their teaching experience and their global research interest because of the traditional cordoning of disciplinary areas. But as the national and transnational scripts intertwine in the real world, these disciplinary structures are beginning to yield. The days when we did a week or a chapter on the global are formally over. How, for instance, do we teach a class in communication today and talk about culture without referring to the gendered and racialized fall out of global discourses of immigration, war, and nationalism? Or how do we address any topic in communication without referencing globalization? How do we decide what vocabularies and disciplinary division best represent the exploration of these issues? The examination of these issues and reconceptualization of gender, culture, and communication are central to critical inquiry. This persistent energy to combine our intellectual and interventionist work captures the pedagogical purpose of both feminist scholarship and cultural studies.

Cultural studies scholarship is entering new ground as globalization and new technologies reorganize our economic, cultural, and social life. The concerns of cultural studies have gone beyond the textual to a much broader understanding of media practices, the politics of representational practices, and identity productions (see Couldry, 2000). An impressive body of interdisciplinary cultural studies knowledge in the international arena presents an enabling moment for global feminist scholarship (see Abbas & Erni, 2005; Valdivia, 2003).

The extraordinary popularity of cultural studies today in the academy worldwide is linked to its refusal to adopt a language of universalization, to a resolute insistence on local specificity, and to a self-conscious problematization of speaking positions. Cultural studies provide an academic rubric to bring together a network of progressive intellectual practices. In its internationalist turn, cultural studies calls into question both the modern assumption of a natural isomorphism between the national and the cultural and the hierarchical ordering of national entities (see Stratton & Ang, 1996). The arrival of postcolonial work within cultural studies has furthered the international agenda by introducing the need to historicize cultural practices. Grossberg (2002) argues that postcolonial studies have contributed to an enriched understanding of contexts:

> If contexts have to be understood in geographical and historical terms, then at least part of the understanding of any contemporary social context involves its location within the history and geography of colonialism as a crucial and deep structure of North Atlantic modernity. (p. 369)

Postcolonial studies have revitalized the space of cultural studies by placing issues of race, gender, nation, citizenship, and sexuality at theoretical center stage. It is this coming together of various critical intellectual strands that gives cultural studies both its rigor and vibrancy. If cultural studies tends to overemphasize the popular, then a feminist optics serves as a reminder that we need to return to the subaltern, to concerns about class that were the original emphasis of the Birmingham tradition. We need to think about media in ways other than just popular culture and to resuscitate an analytical interest in the constitution of everyday life. Transnational feminist disruptions of the boundaries between private and public, national and transnational, center and periphery resonate with the worldliness of cultural studies. The spirit of Hall's (1992) comment about cultural studies—"It can't be just any old thing which chooses to march under a particular banner" (p. 278)—is just as true for transnational feminist scholarship.

◆ Conclusion

In this essay, I have tried to map the disciplinary and societal landscape that feminist communication scholarship faces as it globalizes.

My sketch of this terrain rests on the premise that knowledge is situated and that we have to be responsive to the material circumstances that frame our intellectual pursuit. Foregrounding the complex construction of gender in the global moment poses methodological challenges that involve, as I have shown, navigating disciplinary structures and boundaries. As I emphasize throughout, there is a critical need to examine genealogies of disciplinary spaces and the ways in which they influence and shape the very object of inquiry. This is an important and necessary metatheoretical exercise for feminist scholars who are trying to construct alternate narratives of globalization—narratives that focus on gender as produced within the economic, social, and political layers of contemporary life.

The current context presents feminists with an opportunity to produce complex representations of the contradictions and inequalities folded into the globalizing process. Feminist and other critical scholars concur that globalization has to be examined as an inherently contradictory process and, hence, has to be studied from below—paying attention to local specificity. Kellner (2002) argues that globalization, as a theoretical construct, varies according to the assumptions and commitments of the theory in question. It is no surprise that, as feminist scholars point out, many accounts of globalization are masculinist and completely overlook women. Alternatively, they render women as passive and unproductive and naturalize their subordination (see Ong, 2000). Global processes are sustained by the reproduction of inequities. Reading the global dynamic through a feminist perspective should render visible the selective and unequal promotion of identities in the new configurations of social and economic life.

In closing, I would like to return to the body of the global subaltern whose entry into the global circuit is manipulated by the racialized, sexualized regimes of transnational capital. A woman in a call center in India with an assumed name conducts a faceless masquerade with a customer half way across the world. Here is a global worker whose presence and insertion in the virtual limbo needs to be contextualized. Her story has to be situated as part of a global postcolonial narrative. She is certainly not what popular discourse would have us believe—the cause of the "fear and loathing" of "pissed-off programmers" in the U.S. who are losing their jobs to global outsourcing (Pink, 2004, p. 96). Friedman (2004), in his paean to a flattened world, sees Indian call center employees as "liberated" by a job with a global corporation. He writes that "many have credit cards and have become real consumers, including of U.S. goods, for the first time. All of them seem to have gained self-confidence and self-worth" (p. 413). These facile conclusions completely bypass the fact that transnational formations, while they enable women to escape some social regulations, also subject them to other types and patterns of global subordination.

Where do we begin the narrative of an overworked larynx and how it enters the global circuit? What registers do we use to document the experiences of women whose invisible labor holds up global cities? What critical lenses do we employ to understand the representational modalities within which gendered lives in the global economy are cast? How do we read the images in popular discourse and their impact on social experiences? We need more ethnographically grounded work where global questions of gender and sexuality are considered within the political economies in which everyday experiences are defined. Communication and media cultures provide points of access to examine the complex intersections of the local and global, individual and community, homogeneous and hybrid. It is within the communication terrain that we can examine how the narratives of race, class, gender, citizenship, and the globe merge into the experiential and the quotidian. Complex social issues are exceeding the scope and reach of epistemological frameworks, and it is important to pay attention to these interstitial positions in order to reveal the limits and normative centers of our theories.

Feminist emphasis on epistemological self-reflexivity and openness to interdisciplinary perspectives can energize our efforts to produce alternative understandings of globalization. The feminist commitment to progressive politics reminds us to ask questions that expose contemporary formations of power, focus on sites of agency and resistance, and thereby challenge hegemonic accounts of globalization. In short, feminist questioning enables us to step outside the discipline only to revitalize it. With Friedman (1998), I believe that our intellectual pursuits as feminists in the academy do matter. They matter in terms of how we represent, circulate, and above all keep gendered experiences visible in the global public sphere.

◆ Note

Author Note: Earlier versions of this essay were presented at conferences in Goldsmiths College, University of London (May 2004) and at the University of Illinois (December 2004). I thank Sujata Moorti, Arvind Rajagopal, and Anjali Ram for their comments on earlier drafts. I am grateful to feminist scholars in the communication discipline who have built the infrastructure for our work to continue.

◆ References

Abbas. A., & Erni, J. N. (2005). *Internationalizing cultural studies.* Malden, MA: Blackwell.

Abu-Lughod, L. (2002). Do Muslim women really need saving? Anthropological reflections on cultural relativism and its others. *American Anthropologist, 104,* 783–790.

Appadurai, A. (1996). Diversity and disciplinarity as cultural artifacts. In C. Nelson & D. Gaonkar (Eds.), *Disciplinarity and dissent in cultural studies* (pp. 23–36). New York: Routledge.

Basu, A., Grewal, I., Kaplan, C., & Malkki, L. (Eds.). (2001). Globalization and gender [Special issue]. *Signs, 26*(4).

Bergeron, S. (2001). Political economy discourses of globalization and feminist politics. *Signs, 26*(4), 983–1006.

Bhattacharjee, A. (1997). The public/private mirage: Mapping homes and undomesticating violence work in the South Asian Immigrant community. In M. J. Alexander & C. T. Mohanty (Eds.), *Feminist genealogies, colonial legacies, democratic futures* (pp. 308–329). New York: Routledge.

Bhavnani, K. (2001) Introduction. In K. Bhavnani (Ed.), *Feminism and race* (pp. 1–13). Oxford, UK: Oxford University Press.

Bhavnani, K. K., Foran, J., & Kurian, P. (2003). An introduction to women, culture and development. In K. Bhavnani, J. Foran, & P. Kurian (Eds.), *Feminist futures: Re-imagining women, culture and development* (pp. 22–40). London: Zed Books.

Burton, B., Ibryamova, N., Khanna, R., Mazurana, D., & Mendoza, L. (2002). Cartographies of scholarship: The end of nation-states, international studies, and the cold war. In M. Lay, J. Monk, & D. Rosenfelt (Eds.), *Encompassing gender: Integrating international studies and women's studies* (pp. 21–45). New York: Feminist Press CUNY.

Bush, L. (2001, November). *Radio address by Mrs. Bush.* Retrieved Oct. 24, 2005, from www.whitehouse.gov/news/releases/2001/11/20011117.html

Calhoun, C. (2001). Opening remarks. Roundtable on rethinking international studies in a changing global context. *Items: Social Science Research Council, 3*(3–4), 1–3.

Carillo Rowe, A. (2000). Locating feminism's subject: The paradox of white femininity and the struggle to forge feminist alliances. *Communication Theory, 10*(1), 64–80.

Chen, K. (1998). The decolonization question. In K. Chen (Ed.), *Trajectories: Inter-Asia cultural studies* (pp. 1–53). New York: Routledge.

Collier, M. J., Hegde, R. S., Lee, W, Nakayama, T. K., & Yep, G. (2002). Dialogue on the edges: Ferment in communication and culture. In M. J. Collier (Ed.), *Transforming communication about culture* (pp. 219–280). Thousand Oaks, CA: Sage.

Comaroff, J., & Comaroff, J. L. (2000). Millenial capitalism: First thoughts on a second coming. *Public Culture, 12*(2), 291–343.

Couldry, N. (2000). *Inside culture: Re-Imagining the method of cultural studies.* Thousand Oaks, CA: Sage.

De Lauretis, T. (1987). *Technologies of gender: Essays on theory, film and fiction.* Bloomington: Indiana University Press.

Dow, B. J., & Condit, C. M. (2005). The state of the art in feminist scholarship in communication. *Journal of Communication, 55*(3), 448–478.

Franklin, S., Lury, C., & Stacey, J. (1996). Feminism and cultural studies: Pasts, presents, futures. In J. Storey (Ed.), *What is cultural studies?* (pp. 255–272). London: Arnold.

Freeman, C. (2001). Is local:global as feminine:masculine? Rethinking the gender of globalization. *Signs, 26*(4), 1007–1037.

Friedman, S. S. (1998). *Mappings: Feminism and the cultural geographies of encounter.* Princeton, NJ: Princeton University Press.

Friedman, T. L. (2004, February 29). 30 little turtles. *New York Times,* Sec. 4, p. 13.

Gedalof, I. (1999). *Against purity: Rethinking identity with Indian and western feminism.* London: Routledge.

Gibson-Graham, J. K. (1996). *The end of capitalism (as we knew it): A feminist critique of political economy.* Oxford, UK: Blackwell.

Grossberg, L. (1997). Introduction: 'Birmingham' in America. In *Bringing it all back home: Essays on cultural studies* (pp. 1–32). Durham, NC: Duke University Press.

Grossberg, L. (2002). Postscript (special issue on postcolonial approaches to communication). *Communication Theory, 12*(3), 367–370.

Hall, R. (1947). *Area studies: With special reference to their implications for research in the social sciences.* New York: Social Science Research Council.

Hall, S. (1992). Cultural studies and its theoretical legacies. In L. Grossberg, C. Nelson, &

P. Treichler (Eds.), *Cultural studies* (pp. 277–294). New York: Routledge.

Hall, S. (1996). Cultural studies and the politics of internationalization: An interview with Stuart Hall by K. Chen. In D. Morley & K. Chen (Eds.), *Stuart Hall: Critical dialogues in cultural studies* (pp. 392–408). New York: Routledge.

Hardt, M., & Negri, A (2000). *Empire.* Cambridge, MA: Harvard University Press.

Hegde, R. S. (1998). View from elsewhere: Locating difference and the politics of representation from a transnational feminist perspective. *Communication Theory, 8*(3), 271–297.

Hegde, R. S. (1999). Marking bodies, reproducing violence: A feminist reading of female infanticide in south India. *Violence Against Women, 5*(5), 507–524.

Holzner, B. (2002). Global change and the organizational and intellectual challenges for international studies in the United States. *Items: Social Science Research Council, 3*(3–4), 5–8.

John, M. E. (1996). *Discrepant dislocations: Feminism, theory and postcolonial histories.* Berkeley: University of California Press.

Kaplan, C., & Grewal, I. (2002). Transnational practices and interdisciplinary feminist scholarship: Reconfiguring women's and gender studies. In R. Wiegman (Ed.), *Women's studies on its own* (pp. 66–81). Durham, NC: Duke University Press.

Kellner, D. (2002). Theorizing globalization. *Sociological Theory, 20*(3), 285–305.

Khan, S. (2001). Performing the native informant: Doing ethnography from the margins. *Canadian Journal of Women and the Law, 13*(2), 266–283.

Lee, B. (1995). Critical internationalism. *Public Culture, 7,* 559–592.

Lowe, L., & Lloyd, D. (1997). Introduction. In L. Lowe & D. Lloyd (Eds.), *The politics of culture in the shadow of capital* (pp. 1–32). Durham, NC: Duke University Press.

McRobbie, A. (2004). Post-feminism and popular culture. *Feminist Media Studies 4*(3), 255–264.

Moglen, H. (1997). Losing their edge: Radical studies from the seventies to the nineties. In E. A. Kaplan & G. Levine (Eds.), *The politics of research* (pp. 181–192). New Brunswick, NJ: Rutgers University.

Morley, D., & K. Chen (Eds.). (1996). *Stuart Hall: Critical dialogues in cultural studies* (pp. 392–408). New York: Routledge.

Nakayama, T. K., & Martin, J. M. (Eds.). (1999). *Whiteness: The communication of social identity*. Thousand Oaks, CA: Sage.

Narayan, U. (1997). *Dislocating cultures: Identities, traditions and third world feminisms*. New York: Routledge.

Nelson, C., & Gaonkar, D. P. (1996). Cultural studies and the politics of disciplinarity. In C. Nelson & D. Gaonkar (Eds.), *Disciplinarity and dissent in cultural studies* (pp. 1–29). New York: Routledge.

Ong, A. (1988). Colonialism and modernity: Feminist re-presentations of women in non-Western societies. *Inscriptions 3*, 79–93.

Ong, A. (2000). The gender and labor politics of postmodernity. In P. O'Meara, H. D. Mehlinger, & M. Krain (Eds.), *Globalization and the challenges of a new century* (pp. 253–281). Bloomington: Indiana University Press.

Pink, D. (2004, February). Meet the new face of the silicon age. *Wired*, pp. 94–138.

Puar, J. K., & Rai, A. (2002). Monster, terrorist, fag: The war on terrorism and the production of docile patriots. *Social Text, 20*(3), 117–148.

Radhakrishnan, R. (1996). *Diasporic mediations*. Minneapolis: University of Minnesota Press.

Rafael, V. L. (1994). The cultures of area studies in the United States. *Social Text, 41*, 91–111.

Rooney, E. (1996). Discipline and vanish: Feminism, the resistance to theory and the politics of cultural studies. In J. Storey (Ed.), *What is cultural studies?* (pp. 208–220). London: Arnold.

Rosaldo, R. (2001). Reflections on interdisciplinarity. In J. Scott & D. Keates (Eds.), *Schools of thought: Twenty-five years of Interpretive Social Science* (pp. 67–82). Princeton, NJ: Princeton University Press.

Rutherford, J. (2005). Cultural studies in the corporate university. *Cultural Studies, 19*(3), 297–317.

Said, E. (1979). *Orientalism*. New York: Vintage.

Sangari, K., & Chakravarti, U. (2001). Disparate women: Transitory contexts, persisting structures. In K. Sangari & U. Chakravarti (Eds.), *From myths to markets* (pp. ix–xxx). New Delhi, India: Manohar.

Sangari, K., & Vaid, S. (1990). *Recasting women: Essays in Indian colonial history*. New Brunswick, NJ: Rutgers University.

Sassen, S. (1999). Analytical borderlands: Race, gender and representation in the New City. In Toress, R. T., Miron, L. F., & Inda, J. X. (Eds.), *Race, identity and citizenship* (pp. 355–372). Malden, MA: Blackwell.

Scott, J. W. (1999). *Gender and the politics of history*. New York: Columbia University Press.

Scott, J. W. (2002). Feminist reverberations. *Differences: A Journal of Feminist Cultural Studies, 13*(3), 1–23.

Sen, J., & Saini, M. (2005). *Are other worlds possible? Talking new politics*. New Delhi, India: Zubaan.

Shih, S. (2005). Towards an ethics of transnational encounters, or "When" does a "Chinese" woman become a "Feminist"? In F. Lionnet & S. Shih (Eds.), *Minor transnationalism* (pp. 73–108). Durham, NC: Duke University Press.

Shohat, E. (1998). Introduction. In E. Shohat (Ed.), *Talking visions: Multicultural feminism in a transnational age* (pp. 1–62). Cambridge: MIT Press.

Shohat, E. (2001). Area studies, transnationalism and the feminist production of knowledge. *Signs, 26*, 1269–1272.

Shome, R., & Hegde, R. S. (2002a). Postcolonial approaches to communication: Charting the terrain, engaging the intersections. *Communication Theory, 12*(3), 249–270.

Shome, R., & Hegde, R. S. (2002b). Critical communication studies and the challenge of globalization. *Critical Studies in Media Communication, 19*(2), 172–189.

Simpson, C. (1994). *Science of coercion: Communication research and psychological warfare*. Oxford, UK: Oxford University Press.

Spivak, G. (1988). *In other worlds: Essays in cultural politics*. New York: Routledge.

Spivak, G. (1990). *The postcolonial critique: Interviews, strategies, dialogues*. New York: Routledge.

Spivak, G. (1993). Scattered speculations on the question of cultural studies. In *Outside in the teaching machine* (pp. 255–284). New York: Routledge.

Spivak, G. (2002). Postcolonial scholarship—Productions and directions: An interview with G. Spivak. *Communication Theory, 12*(3), 271–286.

Steeves, H. L. (1993). Creating imagined communities: Development communication and the challenge of feminism. *Journal of Communication, 43*(3), 218–229.

Stratton, J., & Ang, I. (1996). On the impossibility of a global cultural studies. In D. Morley & K. Chen (Eds.), *Stuart Hall: Critical dialogues in cultural studies* (pp. 361–391). New York: Routledge.

Valdivia, A. (1996). Is modern to male as traditional to female? Revisioning gender construction in international communications. *Journal of International Communication, 3*, 5–25.

Valdivia, A. (2003). *A companion to media studies*. Malden, MA: Blackwell.

Vargas, V. (2003). Feminism, globalization and the global justice and solidarity movement. *Cultural Studies, 17*, 905–920.

Vitalis, R. (2001). International studies in America. *Items: Social Science Research Council, 3*, 3–4.

Wallerstein, I. (1997). The unintended consequences of cold war area studies. In N. Chomsky et al. (Eds.), *The cold war and the university* (pp. 195–231). New York: New Press.

Young, I. (2003). The logic of masculinist protection: Reflections on the current security state. *Signs, 29*, 1–25.

AUTHOR INDEX

SUBJECT INDEX

ABOUT THE EDITORS

Bonnie J. Dow (Ph.D., University of Minnesota, 1990) is Associate Professor of Speech Communication at the University of Georgia. She is the author of *Prime-Time Feminism: Television, Media Culture, and the Womens Movement Since 1970* (1996). She is former coeditor (with Celeste Condit) of *Womens Studies in Communication* and former coeditor (with Celeste Condit) of *Critical Studies in Media Communication.*

Julia T. Wood (Ph.D., Pennsylvania State University, 1975) is Professor of Communication Studies and Lineberger Distinguished Professor of Humanities at the University of North Carolina at Chapel Hill. She teaches and conducts research on personal relationships, intimate partner violence, feminist theory, and the intersections of gender, communication, and culture. She has authored or edited 23 books, including *Who Cares? Women, Care and Culture,* and *Gendered Lives,* now in its 7th edition. In addition, she has published more than 70 articles and book chapters. During her career, she has received 12 awards for scholarship and 11 for teaching.

ABOUT THE CONTRIBUTORS

Karen Lee Ashcraft is Associate Professor and Director of Graduate Studies in the Department of Communication at the University of Utah. Her research examines occupational identities and organizational forms, with particular attention to gender, race, and class relations. Her work has appeared in forums such as *Communication Monographs, Administrative Science Quarterly,* and the *Academy of Management Journal.* Her coauthored book with Dennis Mumby, *Reworking Gender,* explores the relationship between feminist and critical organization studies and develops a communicative approach to the study of gendered organizing.

Jacqueline Bacon is the author of the book *The Humblest May Stand Forth: Rhetoric, Empowerment, and Abolition,* as well as articles on a variety of topics, including African American history, media criticism, and the history of rhetoric, with a particular emphasis on African American rhetoric and women's rhetoric. An independent scholar, Bacon lives in San Diego, California.

Vanessa B. Beasley (Ph.D., The University of Texas at Austin, 1996) is Associate Professor of Speech Communication at the University of Georgia. Her research focuses on political communication and the role of rhetoric within a diverse democracy. In addition to numerous scholarly essays and book chapters, she is the author of *You, the People: American National Identity in Presidential Rhetoric* and the editor of *Who Belongs in America? Presidents, Rhetoric, and Immigration.*

Elizabeth Bell (Ph.D., The University of Texas at Austin, 1983) is Associate Professor of Communication at the University of South Florida. Her research and teaching converge at the intersection of performance studies and postmodern feminist theory. She is the coeditor of *From Mouse to Mermaid* (1995) and coauthor of *Theories of Performance* (Sage, in press). She has published over 20 articles, chapters, and book reviews. Bell is the recipient of 10 teaching awards from national, state, and university groups.

Daniel Blaeuer (M.A., University of South Florida, 2005) is a doctorate student in the Department of Communication at the University of South Florida. His academic work focuses on the connections between pedagogy, performance, and environmental activism.

Dwight E. Brooks (Ph.D., University of Iowa, 1991) is Associate Professor in the Department of Telecommunications at the University of Georgia's H. W. Grady College of Journalism and Mass Communication. He teaches and researches in the areas of critical/cultural studies; race, gender, and media; media literacy; and electronic media program management.

Patrice M. Buzzanell is Professor of Communication at Purdue University. She examines gendered workplace processes, especially as they relate to career. She has edited or coedited *Rethinking Organizational and Managerial Communication From Feminist Perspectives* and *Gender in Applied Communication Contexts*. She also has published in journals such as *Communication Monographs, Communication Theory, Human Communication Research,* and *Journal of Applied Communication Research*.

Karlyn Kohrs Campbell is Professor of Communication Studies at the University of Minnesota, Twin Cities. She is a rhetorical theorist and critic who studies the public discourse of women and U.S. presidents. She is the author of *Man Cannot Speak for Her: A Critical Study of Early Feminist Rhetoric* and *Man Cannot Speak for Her: Key Texts of the Early Feminists*.

Rosalyn Collings Eves is a doctoral candidate at Pennsylvania State University. Her interests include the intersections of rhetoric and gender, particularly in 19th-century America, alternative rhetorics, and memory studies. She is currently working on her dissertation on 19th-century American women's rhetorics in the American West and has previously published in *Rhetoric Review*.

Mia Consalvo (Ph.D., University of Iowa, 1999) is Associate Professor in the School of Telecommunications at Ohio University. She is the executive editor of the Association of Internet Researchers' *Research Annual* series, and she has also edited the volume *Women and Everyday Uses of the Internet: Agency and Identity* with Susanna Paasonen. Her current research focuses on women and games, the video game industry, and pedagogical uses of games. She is writing a book on the role of cheating in the digital game industry.

Lisa M. Cuklanz is Associate Professor in the Department of Communication at Boston College. She is the author of *Rape on Trial: How the Mass Media Construct Legal Reform and Social Change* (1996) and *Rape on Prime Time: Television, Masculinity, and Sexual Violence* (2000).

Lisa A. Flores (Ph.D., University of Georgia) is Associate Professor in Communication and Ethnic Studies at the University of Utah, where she also serves as Director of Chicana/o Studies and Coordinator of the Ethnic Studies Program. Her research, exploring cultural discourses of race and gender, has appeared in places such as the *Quarterly Journal of Speech, Critical Studies in Media Communication,* and *Text & Performance Quarterly*. Currently, she is theorizing race and its intersections with gender, nation, sexuality, and class/labor, by tracing the racialization of Mexican/ Americans both into and out of whiteness.

Kathleen M. Galvin is Professor of Communication Studies at Northwestern University. Her research interests are in family communication, specifically the communicative construction of family identity. She is the senior author of *Family*

Communication: Cohesion and Change (6th ed.) and author of family-related handbook chapters, articles, and a PBS video series.

Cheryl Glenn (Ph.D., The Ohio State University) is Professor of English at Pennsylvania State University and Chair of the 2008 Conference on College Composition and Communication. She has three complementary areas of scholarly interests: histories of women's rhetorics and writing practices, delivery systems for the teaching of writing, and inclusionary rhetorical practices and theories. Among her many publications are *Rhetoric Retold: Regendering the Tradition From Antiquity Through the Renaissance; Rhetorical Education in America; Unspoken: A Rhetoric of Silence; The St. Martin's Guide to Teaching Writing; The Writer's Harbrace Handbook;* and *Making Sense: A Real-World Rhetorical Reader.*

Lisa P. Hébert is a doctoral student in the H. W. Grady College of Journalism and Mass Communication at the University of Georgia. She also is a research assistant with the George Foster Peabody Awards. In addition to examining how women of color are represented in the media, her research focuses on beauty ideals in media and their influence on young girls.

Radha S. Hegde (Ph.D., Ohio State University) is Associate Professor of Culture and Communication at New York University. She has published in the areas of feminist theory, South Asian diaspora, violence and reproductive politics, postcolonial feminism, and globalization. Her research in these areas has appeared in numerous journals. She is a former chair of the Feminist and Women's Studies Division of NCA. She serves on numerous editorial boards, including *Feminist Media Studies, Communication and Critical/Cultural Studies* and *Critical Studies in Media Communication.* She is also a founding member of Manavi, the first South Asian feminist group in the United States. Her current research in India examines issues of gender, technology, and the global workplace.

Marsha Houston (Ph.D., University of Massachusetts–Amherst) is Professor of Communication Studies at the University of Alabama. Her scholarship on Black feminist thought, Black women's talk, and U.S. Black culture and communication has appeared in numerous journals and anthologies. She is coeditor of two collections and has chaired both the Feminist and Women Studies and African American Culture and Communication Divisions of the NCA. In 1994, she was the first woman of color to receive the Francine Merritt Award for significant contributions to the lives of women in the discipline from the NCA's Women's Caucus. Her current research is an autoethnographic study of Black festive culture.

Fern L. Johnson (Ph.D., University of Minnesota-Twin Cities) is Professor of English at Clark University. Her research focuses on cultural dimensions of language and communication, with emphasis on gender, race, and multicultural discourse in the United States. Her work appears in numerous articles and book chapters and in *Speaking Culturally: Language Diversity in the United States.* She is the recipient of two NCA awards: the *Robert J. Kibler Memorial Award* (1994) for dedication to excellence and commitment to the profession and the *Francine Merritt Award* (1999) for significant contributions to the lives of women in the discipline. Her current research focuses on the circulation of cultural codes in advertising through discourse imaging.

Michael P. Johnson is Associate Professor Emeritus of Sociology, Women's Studies, and African and African American Studies at the Pennsylvania State University. He received his doctorate in sociology from the University of Michigan, Ann Arbor. His major areas of research are intimate partner violence and commitment to personal relationships. Recent papers are available at his Web site at www.personal.psu.edu/mpj.

Zornitsa Keremidchieva is a doctoral candidate in communication studies at the

University of Minnesota with graduate minors in feminist studies and literacy and rhetorical studies. Her dissertation examines intersections between discourses on women, immigration, and Americanization in the 1920s. She is an instructor in theater arts and communication studies at Hamline University, St. Paul, Minnesota.

Marianne LeGreco is a doctoral candidate in the Hugh Downs School of Human Communication at Arizona State University. Her research interests include organizational and health policy, the intersections of gender and class, and critical/cultural approaches to the study of consumption. Her dissertation illustrates the interplay of health policy, promotion, and practice in the organization of school lunch programs.

Kristen Lucas is a doctoral candidate in the Department of Communication at Purdue University. Her research and teaching interests center on issues of dignity in the workplace, meaningful career development for individuals, and blue-collar organizations. Her dissertation examines the career identities and processes of people who came of age at the time their hometowns experienced rapid deindustrialization.

Sandra Metts (Ph.D., University of Iowa, 1983) is Professor in the School of Communication at Illinois State University. Her research interests include facework and politeness, relationship transgressions and forgiveness, sexual communication, and emotional expression. Her work appears in a variety of journals and edited volumes. She has served as associate editor for the *Journal of Social and Personal Relationships* and is a former president of the Central States Communication Association.

Michael Monsour is Professor of Communication at the University of Colorado and Health Sciences Center in Denver, Colorado. His research interests are in gender issues, cross-sex friendships, and interpersonal perception. He is the author of *Women and Men as Friends: Relationships Across the Life Span in the 21st Century* (2002). He has published articles on cross-sex friendships in *Sex Roles* and the *Journal of Social and Personal Relationships*.

Dennis K. Mumby is Professor and Chair of the Department of Communication Studies at the University of North Carolina at Chapel Hill. His research examines the relationships among discourse, power, gender, and organization. He serves on numerous editorial boards, including those for *Communication Theory, Communication Monographs,* and *Management Communication Quarterly*. He is currently Vice-Chair of the Organizational Communication Division of the International Communication Association. He is the coauthor (with Karen Ashcraft) of *Reworking Gender* (Sage, 2004) and coeditor (with Steve May) of *Engaging Organizational Communication Theory and Research* (Sage, 2005).

Sarah Projansky (Ph.D., University of Iowa, 1995) is Associate Professor of Gender and Women's Studies and of Cinema Studies at the University of Illinois, Urbana–Champaign. She is a coeditor of *Enterprise Zones: Critical Positions on Star Trek* (1996) and author of *Watching Rape: Film, Television, and Postfeminist Culture* (2001). She has published articles in *Cinema Journal, Signs,* and various anthologies. Currently, she is working on a project about girls in U.S. popular culture.

Cliff Scott (Ph.D., Arizona State University, 2005) is Assistant Professor of Communication Studies at the University of North Carolina, Charlotte. His research and teaching are united by overlapping interests in organizational discourse, identity formation, and the everyday assessment of emergent health and safety risks in the workplace. Most recently, he has studied how identity discourse enables and constrains the manner in which firefighters define, appraise, and negotiate a variety of organizational and occupational hazards.

Karla D. Scott (Ph.D., University of Illinois, Urbana–Champaign) is Associate Professor of Communication and Director of African American Studies at Saint Louis University. Her research interest in culture, language, and communication focuses on race, gender, class, and health in the lives of Black women. Her research on Black women's talk has appeared in several journal articles and book chapters. She currently serves as project director for a federally funded AIDS prevention program that provides culturally specific HIV prevention education for African Americans. Her research on HIV prevention strategies for women of color appears in *Health Care for Women International.*

John M. Sloop (Ph.D., University of Iowa, 1992) is Professor of Communication Studies at Vanderbilt University. His research interests include critical media studies of race, gender, and sexuality. In addition to essays, he is author and editor of a number of books, the most recent being *Disciplining Gender: Rhetorics of Sex Identity in Contemporary U.S. Culture* (2004).

Nathan Stormer (Ph.D., University of Minnesota, 1997) is Associate Professor of Communication and Journalism at the University of Maine. He is the author of *Articulating Life's Memory: U.S. Medical Rhetoric About Abortion in the Nineteenth Century.* His research interests include rhetorical theory, cultural memory, and the historiography of rhetoric.

Angela Trethewey (Ph.D., Purdue University, 1994) is Associate Professor in the Hugh Downs School of Human Communication at Arizona State University. Her research explores the intersections between organizing, discourse, and gendered identity and

has been published in outlets including *Management Communication Quarterly, Journal of Applied Communication Research,* and *Communication Monographs.* Her interest in feminist theorizing is informed and complicated by her experiences as a working mother to her daughter, Anna.

Nikki C. Townsley (Ph.D., Purdue University, 2002) is Assistant Professor of Communication at the University of Colorado at Boulder. Her research and teaching examines the nexus of gender; work, employment, and organization; and globalization. She also favors poststructuralist and ethnographic perspectives in her work on power and representation. Her work appears in *Management Communication Quarterly, Organization,* and the *Western Journal of Communication.*

Angharad N. Valdivia (Ph.D., University of Illinois, Urbana–Champaign, 1991) is Research Professor at the Institute of Communications Research at the University of Illinois, Urbana–Champaign, with appointments in Media Studies, Gender and Women Studies, and Latina/o Studies. She is also affiliated with the faculty at the Center for Latin American and Caribbean Studies and the Women and Gender in Global Perspectives Program. Her research, teaching, and publications focus on the intersection of media studies with international and transnational issues, especially in the area of popular culture, foregrounding issues of gender and ethnicity. Trained as an international communications scholar with an emphasis on political economy, in the tradition of Latin American scholarship, she attempts to bridge the divide between political economy and culture, between agency and structure. Her book, *A Latina in the Land of Hollywood* (2000), edited collections, and essays have been attempts to deploy this strategy.